WILTON
DECORATING
IDEAS AND
INSPIRATION

NOW AVAILABLE
WHEREVER YOU ARE
& WHENEVER
YOU WANT THEM!

CREATIVE DIRECTOR
Daniel Masini

SENIOR DIRECTOR OF CAKE & VISUAL DESIGN
Steve Rocco

ASSISTANT CAKE DESIGNERS
Jenny Jurewicz   Kathy Krupa
Valerie Pradhan

DECORATING ROOM SUPERVISOR
Cheryl Brown

SENIOR CAKE DECORATORS
Mary Gavenda   Susan Matusiak

CAKE DECORATORS
Ella Buitrago   Kathy Krupa
Emily Easterly   Mark Malak
Kim Feledy   Andrea Nickels
Jenny Jurewicz   Michele Poto
Diane Knowlton   Valerie Pradhan
Kim Zarobsky

DIRECTOR OF EDITORIAL
Jo-El M. Grossman

EDITOR/WRITER
Jeff Shankman

COPY EDITORS
Janet Stock   Ivan Rioja-Scott

WRITERS
Mary Enochs   Jane Mikis
Barbara McHatton   Marita Seiler
Ann Wilson

PRODUCTION MANAGER
Challis Yeager

ASSOCIATE PRODUCTION MANAGERS
Sandy Peterson   Mary Stahulak

SENIOR GRAPHIC DESIGNER/PRODUCTION
Courtney Porter

GRAPHIC DESIGN/PRODUCTION
Sam Mullineaux   RNB Graphics
Richard Tracy

PREPRESS MANAGER
Dennis Trojan

PREPRESS TECHNICIANS
Brian Block   Greg Boone
Paul Christon

PHOTOGRAPHY MANAGER
Dale DeBolt

PHOTOGRAPHY
Peter Rossi-PDR Productions
Black Box Studios

PHOTO STYLIST
Carey Thornton

CREATIVE SERVICES ASSISTANT
Judi Graf

PRODUCT DEVELOPMENT/PUBLICATIONS
Tina Celeste
Joanne Winston-Spencer

For photography purposes, many cakes in this book were decorated (by right- and left-handed decorators) with royal icing. Printed in U.S.A.

Wilton Industries, Inc.
2240 West 75th Street, Woodridge, IL 60517
www.wilton.com

Retail Customer Orders:
Phone: 800-794-5866 • Fax: 888-824-9520
Online: www.wilton.com

Class Locations:
Phone: 800-942-8881
Online: www.wilton.com/classes/classlocator.cfm

IN CANADA
Wilton Industries Canada Company
98 Carrier Drive, Etobicoke, Ontario M9W5R1 Canada
Phone: 416-679-0790

Class Locations:
Phone: 416-679-0790, ext. 200
E-mail: classprograms@wilton.ca

¡SE HABLA ESPAÑOL!
Para mas informacion, marque 800-436-5778
In Mexico: www.wiltonenespanol.com

How to use this book!

Our 2013 Wilton Yearbook of Cake Decorating has a ton of fantastic ideas for every theme, season and celebration! We want to make it easy for you to create amazing cakes and treats from this year's edition.

Here are a few simple steps that you can follow to ensure success:

1. Pick a Project
Get the kids involved! They will have so much fun browsing through the different sections and giving you their favorites for birthdays, holidays and more!

2. Read the instructions
Before you begin, go over your project as well as read the Decorating Guide (p. 114). This section is a wealth of information from Wilton experts that you can use for any project!

3. Get your supplies
Create a shopping list— you can even use your smartphone with our new feature through the Wilton Cake Ideas & More app. Purchase products needed for projects in this book at your local retailer, through the Yearbook or on wilton.com.

4. Decorate your project
Now you can let the fun really begin! You'll want to continue to reference the Yearbook instructions and the Decorating Guide as you create your cake or treat.

5. Celebrate with family
They will be amazed at what you've created just for them!

2013 WILTON YEARBOOK

p. 6

These cakes aren't shy about celebrating. With streamers, balloons and birthday greetings stamped right on some designs, your guests will get the message! Create a first birthday carriage cake decked out for a princess or a racer. Decorate with a dump truck—our cake pours a payload of sprinkles on your party cupcakes!

Host a meet-and-greet (and eat!) with the kids' favorite characters. *Darth Vader* is a force for fun with a special birthday message from a galaxy far, far away. *Mickey Mouse* sails into the celebration on a candy-filled pirate ship for the birthday boy, while *Minnie Mouse* celebrates the birthday girl with a tower of gifts cake and a zebra-striped mini cake purse.

p. 45

The zombies are coming...and your Halloween party will never be the same! Everyone will love this horde of stand-up cookies, each decorated with different gory details. It's just one of the ways we help you put a new spin on every season. Look for a jewel-paneled gingerbread house, a colossal crown-topped cupcake for Mother's Day, whoopie pie burgers for July 4th, and much more.

Big moments, big excitement! When the family is growing, we have the perfect peas-in-a-pod cake and candies for the shower. For religious occasions, discover cakes that capture the spirit with beautiful color flow plaque toppers. Honor the grad with a cake featuring dazzling details in colorful edible paper.

Bold is beautiful for wedding cakes this season. The focus is on rich textures with great details, such as cornelli lace-look ruffles, gathered fondant belts with dot imprints, clusters of ribbon roses packed over every inch of the cake, and imprinted flowers etched with brush embroidery.

p. 94

Cake is fashion! Define your event with designer flourishes unimaginable until now. Chunky molded fondant buttons and bracelets in silver and jewel-tones. A bold black bow tie with rippling streamers that towers over stacked pink tiers. And our eye-popping cover cake, decked with daisies, waves of curls and a zesty zebra print. Our cake designs step off of the runway and into your party!

It's easy to find the help you need! It's all here—step-by-step instructions, great recipes, construction guides and cutting charts, cookie and candy how-tos.

Everything you need to create the exciting ideas in this Yearbook! From decorating tips to famous Wilton bakeware, character candles to elegant wedding ornaments, find it all here.

p. 100

Let's Party!

At birthdays, it's all about the cake! Jungle animals, dump trucks, pirates and fairies... it tells a lot about the birthday boy's or girl's personality. This section has just the cake and treat projects that fit any theme or style. And whether the party guests are awestruck by a princess castle or taking home a smiling cupcake, your celebration is sure to be the talk of the town.

Party Patchwork Cake

Pans: 11 in. x 15 in. x 2 in. Sheet, p. 161; Cooling Grid, p. 171

Colors: Teal, Sky Blue, Lemon Yellow, Violet, Kelly Green, Leaf Green, Red-Red, Orange, p. 139

Fondant: White Ready-To-Use Rolled Fondant (80 oz.), Gum-Tex, p. 148; Kids Party Designs Gum Paste & Fondant Mold, p. 150; 9 in., 20 in. Fondant Rollers, Roll-N-Cut Mat, Fondant Smoother, p. 152; White Pearl Dust, Pure Lemon Extract, Brush Set, p. 153

Recipe: Buttercream Icing, p. 128

Also: 2013 Pattern Book (cake top patch layout and size guide), p. 143; Fine Tip Neon Colors FoodWriter Edible Color Markers (purple), p. 153; Piping Gel, p. 141; Cake Boards, Fanci-Foil Wrap, p. 186; Spatula, p. 137; 13 in. x 17 in. plywood or foamcore board (½ in. thick)

See p. 114 for a list of commonly used decorating items you may need.

2 days in advance: Prepare base board and card. Tint 40 oz. fondant teal. Roll out ⅛ in. thick. Prepare and cover base board (p. 120). Add 1 teaspoon Gum-Tex to remaining teal fondant. Roll out ⅛ in. thick. Cut a 5½ in. square. Roll out a small amount of white ⅛ in. thick. Cut a 4½ in. square. Let both dry on cornstarch-dusted board.

Bake and cool 1-layer cake. Ice cake smooth in white. Tint fondant: 12 oz. yellow; 6 oz. violet; 4 oz. sky blue; 3 oz. each dark green, lime green, red, orange; 2 oz. pink. Roll out ⅛ in. thick as needed. Use pattern to cut various squares and rectangles in assorted colors. Position on cake top, trimming as needed. For horizontal stripes, use Party Designs mold to make loop border in violet; cut strips to 3¾ in. and attach ½ in. to ⅝ in. apart. For ribbon on presents, cut red strips ¼ in. x 2⅜ in.

Use fondant and mold to make pinwheels, various size stars, small bows, party hats, candles with flames and cupcakes in various colors. Attach using damp brush. For pinwheel sticks, cut two ⅛ in. x 2¼ in. long blue strips; attach. Mold yellow loop border strips and attach around base of cake, trimming as needed. Paint party shapes and border with Pearl Dust/lemon extract mixture (p. 118). Attach prepared white message square to teal square with damp brush. Print message with edible marker. Position on cake. Serves 27.

*Combine Leaf Green with Lemon Yellow for lime green shown. Add a little Red-Red color to white fondant for pink shown.

◄ Big Screen Cupcake!

Pans: Dimensions Large Cupcake, p. 167; Cooling Grid, p. 171

Colors: Orange, Violet, Lemon Yellow, Leaf Green, Sky Blue, p. 139

Fondant: White Ready-To-Use Rolled Fondant (17 oz.), p. 148; Kids Party Designs Gum Paste & Fondant Mold, p. 150; Brush Set, p. 153

Recipes: Buttercream Icing, p. 128; Thinned Fondant Adhesive, p. 127

Also: Spatula, p. 137; Cake Board, Cake Circles, Fanci-Foil Wrap, p. 186; 4 in. Lollipop Sticks, p. 178

See p. 114 for a list of commonly used decorating items you may need.

1 day in advance: Make cupcake pleats. Tint 13 oz. fondant orange. Use loop border cavity of mold to make 25 strips. Cut strips in half. Let dry on cornstarch-dusted board.

Also: Make candles. Tint 1 oz. portions of fondant blue, green, yellow and violet. Use candle cavity of mold to make six or seven candles each in blue, green and violet with yellow flames. Let dry on cornstarch-dusted board. Attach flames and candles to lollipop sticks with thinned fondant adhesive.

Bake and cool 2-part large cupcake. Ice bottom smooth. Attach pleat strips with icing, smooth edges out, in pleated fashion; trim as needed. Position cupcake top; spatula ice.

Insert candles into cake. Serves 12.

*Combine Lemon Yellow with Leaf Green for green shown.

◀ Cupcake Candlepower!

Pan: Dimensions Large Cupcake, p. 167
Tips: 2A, 6, p. 134
Sugar Sheets! **Edible Decorating Paper/Tools:** Mod Dots, White (2 each), Purple, Bright Yellow (1 each), p. 144; Punch Set with Oval Cutting Insert, Spiral Cutting Insert, Slide-N-Cut Edge Cutter, Rotary Cutter, p. 145
Recipe: Buttercream Icing, p. 128
Also: Cake Circles, Fanci-Foil Wrap, p. 186; 8 in. Lollipop Sticks, p. 178; Brush Set, p. 153; Piping Gel, p. 141
See p. 114 for a list of commonly used decorating items you may need.

Bake and cool 2-part large cupcake. Assemble on foil-wrapped cake board. Ice cupcake bottom smooth. Use Slide-N-Cut to cut 3½ in. x 4 in. strips from mod dots edible paper. Gently fold in ⅜ in. pleats; attach to cupcake bottom with piping gel. Ice cupcake top fluffy. Use punch with spiral insert to cut approximately 64 spirals from white edible paper. Twist in various shapes and position on cupcake top.

For candle, use Slide-N-Cut to cut a purple strip 3½ in. x 6 in. Roll up strip to about ⅞ in. diameter, securing edges with piping gel. Use wide end of tip 2A to cut a purple circle for top candle opening. Use narrow end of tip 6 to cut a small opening for stick. Insert lollipop stick into cake top, leaving 5 in. extended. Position candle over stick; slide candle top onto stick and attach to candle with piping gel.

For flame, use rotary cutter to cut two yellow teardrop shapes, ¾ in. x 1¼ in. Stack together, securing shiny sides with piping gel; attach to stick with icing. Serves 12.

▶ Tiered Treat

Candy: White Candy Melts Candy (1 pk. makes 8 treats), Primary (all colors), Garden (green) Candy Color Sets, p. 175; 3-D Cake Large Lollipop Candy Mold, p. 177
Also: Parchment Triangles, p. 136; Kids Party Designs Gum Paste & Fondant Mold, p. 150; Clear Mini Plate Kit, p. 188; Martini Glasses Favor Kit, p. 197; candy-coated chocolates, assorted fruit jelly candies, spice drops
See p. 114 for a list of commonly used decorating items you may need.

In advance: Mold candy cakes. For 8 treats, tint ½ oz. portions of white candy red, blue, green, and 1 oz. yellow and orange. Use piping method (p. 123) to mold red, blue and green garlands and yellow borders; chill until set. Snap mold halves together and fill with melted white candy; tap to settle, chill until firm. **Also:** Mold candy candles. Use piping method to fill candle cavity of party mold with orange and yellow candy; chill until firm. Attach candle to cake with melted candy; let set.

Fill glass with assorted candies. Place mini plate over top of glass. Place bag from kit over glass and turn upside down; gather at stem and tie. Attach candy cake to base of glass with melted candy; let set. Each serves 1.

▲ Fun Under The Big Top Candies

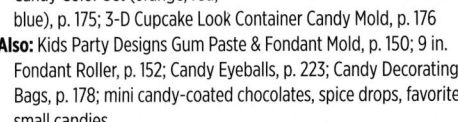

Candy: White Candy Melts candy (1 pk. makes 6 treats), Primary Candy Color Set (orange, red, blue), p. 175; 3-D Cupcake Look Container Candy Mold, p. 176
Also: Kids Party Designs Gum Paste & Fondant Mold, p. 150; 9 in. Fondant Roller, p. 152; Candy Eyeballs, p. 223; Candy Decorating Bags, p. 178; mini candy-coated chocolates, spice drops, favorite small candies
See p. 114 for a list of commonly used decorating items you may need.

In advance: Mold candy cupcakes. For each treat you will need ¾ oz. melted white candy for top and ¾ oz. melted tinted candy in assorted colors for bottom. Make candy cupcakes in 3-D mold. Chill until firm. Smooth edges on warm pan if needed for an even fit. **Also:** Make hats. Use melted tinted candy and party mold to make one hat for each treat. Tap to settle; chill until firm.

Use melted candy to attach trims. Attach candy eyeballs and mini chocolate nose. Roll out spice drops on waxed paper sprinkled with granulated sugar. Use scissors to cut a ¾ in. wide smile; attach smile and hat. Cut a ⅝ in. x ⅞ in. piece for pompom. Cut slits ⅛ in. wide and ⅝ in. deep; roll up piece. Attach to back of hat. Fill bottom with favorite candy; position top. Each serves 1.

▶ Stampin' Celebration Cake

Pans: 6 in., 8 in., 10 in. x 3 in. Round, p. 161; Cooling Grid, p. 171

Tip: 4, p. 134

***Sugar Sheets!* Edible Decorating Paper/Tools:** Light Pink, Light Blue (2 each), Light Green, Light Yellow (1 each), p. 144; Slide-N-Cut Edge Cutter, Star Mini Punch, Rotary Cutter, p. 145; Yellow, Red, Orange, Blue, Green Dab-N-Color Edible Color, 6-Pc. Party Fun Cake Stamp Set, p. 146; Dab-N-Hold Edible Adhesive, p. 145

Recipe: Buttercream Icing, p. 128

Also: 4-Pc. Circles Nesting Metal Cutter Set, p. 172; White Candy Melts Candy, p. 175; Disposable Decorating Bags, p. 136; Spatula, p. 137; Piping Gel, p. 141; 6 in. Lollipop Sticks, p. 178; Brush Set, p. 153; Dowel Rods, p. 194; Cake Circles, Fanci-Foil Wrap, p. 186; Fine Tip Primary Colors FoodWriter Edible Color Markers, p. 153

See p. 114 for a list of commonly used decorating items you may need.

In advance: Make topper. Use black edible marker and largest circle cutter to trace two circles on shiny side of light pink edible paper. Use marker and second largest circle cutter to trace one circle on shiny side of light yellow edible paper. Cut out circles. Use edible colors and birthday cake stamp to stamp design on yellow circle (p. 122). Let dry. Attach pink circles, shiny sides together with melted candy; let set. Attach yellow circle with edible adhesive. Attach lollipop stick to back using melted candy, leaving 3 in. extended at bottom to insert into cake. Let set.

Bake and cool three 1-layer cakes. Ice cakes smooth. Prepare for stacked construction (p. 120). Cut, stamp and attach edible paper panels to cake sides one at a time. Use Slide-N-Cut to cut light green 2⅜ in. wide x 3 in. high; stamp with gift package. Cut light pink 2¼ in. wide x 3 in. high; stamp with cupcake. Cut light blue 2⅜ in. wide x 3 in. high; stamp with streamers. You will need nine panels each of green, pink and blue.

Attach blocks, ¾ in. apart, using piping gel. Use mini punch to make 27 stars in each panel color. Attach three between each block with piping gel. Pipe tip 4 bead bottom borders. Insert topper. Serves 30.

◀ Our Star Shines Cake

Pans: Star, p. 165; Cooling Grid, p. 171

Tip: 18, p. 134

***Sugar Sheets!* Edible Decorating Paper/Tools:** Stars (3), Red (2), p. 144; 25-Pc. Classic Alphabet, 10-Pc. Classic Numbers Cake Stamp Sets, Black Dab-N-Color Edible Color, Dab-N-Hold Edible Adhesive, p. 146; Rotary Cutter, p. 145

Recipe: Buttercream Icing, p. 128

Also: 2013 Pattern Book (center star, diamond), p. 143; Cake Board, Fanci-Foil Wrap, p. 186; Disposable Decorating Bags, p. 136; Spatula, p. 137; Piping Gel, p. 141; Fine Tip Primary Colors FoodWriter Edible Color Markers, Brush Set, p. 153

See p. 114 for a list of commonly used decorating items you may need.

Bake and cool 1-layer cake. Ice cake smooth. Use patterns and yellow edible marker to trace five diamond shapes on shiny side of stars edible paper and using black edible marker trace two star shapes on red edible paper. Cut out using rotary cutter.

Position diamond shapes on cake top. Attach shiny sides of stars together with edible adhesive. Stamp name and number with black edible color. Attach star to cake with edible adhesive. Pipe tip 18 shell bottom border. Serves 12.

▶ Throwing A Curve Cake

Pans: 6 in. x 2 in. Square, p. 161; Cooling Grid, p. 171
Tip: 8, p. 134
Color: Black, p. 139
***Sugar Sheets!* Edible Decorating Paper/Tools:** Wild Stripes (5), Light Blue (2), p. 144; 26-Pc. Classic Alphabet Cake Stamp Set, Black Dab-N-Color Edible Color, p. 146; Rotary Cutter, p. 145
Fondant/Gum Paste: Ready-To-Use Gum Paste (12 oz.), p. 148; 9 in. Fondant Roller, Roll-N-Cut Mat, p. 152; Brush Set, p. 153; Fondant Ribbon Cutter, p. 149; Fine Tip Primary Colors FoodWriter Edible Color Markers (blue), p. 153
Recipe: Buttercream Icing, p. 128
Also: 2013 Pattern Book (starburst), p. 143; Blue Candy Melts Candy, p. 175; 11¾ in. Lollipop Sticks, p. 178; Piping Gel, p. 141; Disposable Decorating Bags, p. 136; Cake Boards, Fanci-Foil Wrap, p. 186
See p. 114 for a list of commonly used decorating items you may need.

2 days in advance: Make scrolls. Tint gum paste black. Roll out ¹⁄₁₆ in. thick. Use cutter/embosser with two straight wheels and 1 in. spacer to cut 24 strips from 6 in. to 9 in. long. Roll up one end for finished scrolls from 1½ in. to 5½ in. long. Let dry on sides for 48 hours on cornstarch-dusted boards. **Also:** Make topper. Use blue edible marker to trace two starburst patterns on shiny side of light blue edible paper; reverse pattern for second cut. Cut two shapes with rotary cutter. Stamp message on front with black edible color. Attach shiny sides together with melted candy. Let set. Attach stick to back using melted candy, leaving 7½ in. extended at bottom.

Bake and cool 3-layer cake (6 in. high). Ice cake smooth. Cut five squares, 6 in. x 6 in., from wild stripes edible paper. Attach to cake top and sides with piping gel, trimming as needed. Attach six scrolls in assorted sizes to each side of cake with tip 8 dots of icing. Insert topper. Serves 12.

▲ We're Talkin' Fun! Cookies

Cookie: 4-Pc. Circles Nesting Metal Cutter Set, p. 172; Cookie Sheet, Cooling Grid, p. 171
***Sugar Sheets!* Edible Decorating Paper/Tools:** White (1 sheet makes 3 treats), Light Blue, Light Green, Light Yellow (1 sheet each makes 15 treats), p. 144; Punch Set with Oval Cutting Insert, Square Caption Cutting Insert, Dab-N-Hold Edible Adhesive, Rotary Cutter, p. 145
Recipes: Buttercream Icing, Roll-Out Cookies, p. 128
Also: Fine Tip Primary Colors FoodWriter Edible Color Markers, Brush Set, p. 153
See p. 114 for a list of commonly used decorating items you may need.

Prepare and roll out dough. Cut cookies using second largest circle cutter. Bake and cool. Use black edible marker to trace second largest cutter on shiny side of white edible paper; cut circles with rotary cutter. Use punch with message insert to cut word balloon; write message with black edible marker. Use various color edible markers to draw stick figure, party hat and gift on white circle. Attach message to white circle with edible adhesive. Ice cookie smooth; position white circle. Each serves 1.

▶ Poppin' Balloons Cookie Pops

Pans: Cookie Sheet, Cooling Grid, p. 171
***Sugar Sheets!* Edible Decorating Paper/Tools:** White (1 sheet makes 12 treats), p. 144; Punch Set with Oval Cutting Insert, Balloon Cutting Insert, p. 145; 4-Pc. Balloons Cake Stamp Set, Yellow, Red, Blue and Green Dab-N-Color Edible Color, p. 146
Recipes: Buttercream Icing, Roll-Out Cookies, p. 128
Also: 6 in. Lollipop Sticks, p. 178; White Candy Melts Candy (1 oz. makes 8 treats), p. 175; Spatula, p. 137; red, green, blue, yellow curling ribbon (13 in. per treat)
See p. 114 for a list of commonly used decorating items you may need.

In advance: Make cookies. Prepare and roll out cookie dough. Use top half of balloon insert to imprint shapes on dough; cut out with knife. Bake and cool cookies.

Make balloons. Use same-size insert to cut balloon shapes from white edible paper. Stamp using edible color and same-size stamp. Let dry.

Attach stick to back of cookie with melted candy; chill until firm. Ice cookie smooth. Immediately, position stamped balloon. Curl ribbon; tie around stick. Each serves 1.

▶ Her Convertible Coach Cake

Pans: Princess Carriage, p. 164; Cooling Grid, p. 171
Tips: 2, 3, 12, 16, 18, p. 134
Colors:* Sky Blue, Rose, Black, Copper (for skin tone shown), Lemon Yellow, Golden Yellow, p. 139
Recipe: Buttercream Icing, p. 128
Also: 2013 Pattern Book (carriage), p. 143; Disposable Decorating Bags, p. 136; Spatula, p. 137; Cake Circle, Fanci-Foil Wrap, p. 186; Heart Cut-Outs Fondant Cutters, p. 151
See p. 114 for a list of commonly used decorating items you may need.

Bake and cool cake. Ice sides and background areas smooth in blue; wheels background in white. Trace carriage pattern on cake top with toothpick. Outline wheels with tip 12; pat smooth with finger dipped in cornstarch. Outline carriage and details with tip 3.

Cover carriage and crown with tip 16 stars. Imprint smallest heart Cut-Out on crown and back of carriage. Pipe in hearts with tip 3; pat smooth. Pipe tip 3 dot door handle. Pipe tip 12 outline steering wheel.

Pipe a tip 12 mound for face; pat smooth to create a 2½ in. circle. Pipe tip 12 outline arm. Pipe tip 3 dot fingers and nose. Pipe tip 2 outline mouth and tooth, pat smooth. Pipe tip 3 sunglass lenses and outline frames. Pipe tip 3 outline hair and hairband. Imprint medium heart Cut-Out on front tire, large on back tire. Pipe in hearts with tip 12; pat smooth. Pipe tip 18 zigzag puff bottom border. Serves 12.

*Combine Lemon Yellow with Golden Yellow for yellow shown.

◀ Gifting Grizzly Cake & Cupcakes

Pans: 14 in. x 2 in. Round, p. 161; Standard Muffin, p. 162; Non-Stick Medium Cookie Sheet, Cooling Grid, p. 169
Tips: 1, 1A, 2, 3, 8, 10, 12, 14, 21, p. 134
Colors:* Royal Blue, Moss Green, Rose, Brown, Red-Red, Garden Tone 4-Icing Color Set (aster mauve), p. 139
Candy: Dessert Dome Candy Mold, p. 176; 10-Pack Candy Mold Set, p. 178; White (2 pks.), Light Cocoa (1 pk.) Candy Melts Candy, Primary (blue), Garden (pink, green, black) Candy Color Sets, p. 175; Candy Dipping Set, Decorator Brush Set, p. 178
Recipe: Buttercream Icing, p. 128
Also: Bubble Stripes Standard Baking Cups, p. 181; 13-Count Standard Cupcakes-N-More Dessert Stand, p. 183; 4-Pc. Circles Nesting Metal Cutter Set, p. 172; Parchment Triangles, Disposable Decorating Bags, p. 136; 8 in. Decorator Preferred Smooth Edge Plate, Dowel Rods, p. 194; 16 in. Round Silver Cake Base, p. 187; Cake Circles, p. 186; small black jelly bean, large marshmallows, ½ in. wide pink satin ribbon (52 in.)
See p. 114 for a list of commonly used decorating items you may need.

In advance: Make candy bear topper. Reserve two light cocoa candy wafers for ears. Make four shells for head and body using melted cocoa candy and large halves of dessert dome, following mold instructions. Run shell edges over warm pan to smooth; attach halves together with melted candy to make two balls. Gently run bottom of top ball (head) and bottom ball (body) over warm pan to flatten slightly. Balls will sit flat at neck and on base. Attach balls with melted candy. **Also:** Make base. Place second smallest circle cutter on cookie sheet. Fill ¼ in. deep with melted cocoa candy. Chill until firm. **And:** Assemble topper. For arms and legs, cut two marshmallows in half; dip in melted cocoa candy. Place on parchment; chill until firm. Attach bear to base and arms and legs to bear with melted candy; chill. Run reserved candy wafers over warm pan to create flat edge; attach for ears with melted candy. Tint portions of melted white candy black and pink with candy color. Using melted candy in a cut parchment bag, pipe eyes, nose and "1"; pipe smile. Using buttercream, pipe tip 1A pull-out party hat with tip 14, pull-out star fringe and pompom. **Also:** Make 12 presents. Tint portions of candy blue, pink and green. Use painting method (p. 123) to fill ribbon areas; chill until firm. Fill remainder of cavity with contrasting color. Tap to settle; chill until firm.

Bake and cool 2-layer cake and 12 cupcakes. Ice smooth. Prepare cake for separator plate construction (p. 120). Position plate in center, feet down. Print tip 8 name. Pipe dots on cake sides in assorted colors using tip 8 (small), tip 10 (medium) and tip 12 (large). Pipe tip 21 shell top and bottom borders. Position candy presents on cupcakes, supporting with icing dots if necessary. Position cupcake stand on plate. Position cupcakes on stand. Position bear on stand, securing with melted candy. Attach ribbon around base with tape. Cake serves 63; each cupcake serves 1.

*Combine Aster Mauve with Rose for rose. Combine Brown with Red-Red for brown shown.

▶ A Great First Impression! Cake

Pans: #1, p. 164; 12 in. x 2 in., 16 in. x 2 in. Square, p. 161; Cooling Grid, p. 171

Tip: 8, p. 134

Color: Lemon Yellow, p. 139

Sugar Sheets! **Edible Decorating Paper/Tools:** Streamers (5), Light Yellow (4), Red (2), Bright Blue, Bright Green, Black Alphabet (1 each), p. 144; Punch Set with Oval Cutting Insert, Layered Circles Cutting Insert Set, Slide-N-Cut Edge Cutter, p. 145

Candy: White (36 oz.), Red (12 oz.) Candy Melts Candy, Primary Candy Color Set (yellow), p. 175; Decorator Brush Set, 6 in. Lollipop Sticks, p. 178

Recipe: Buttercream Icing, p. 128

Also: 2013 Pattern Book (paper tears, flame), p. 143; Wave Flower Former Set, p. 142; Towering Tiers Stand (Cake Corer, 16 in. plate, plate support, center post foot, 5 base feet, 1 tall and 1 short center post), p. 193; Piping Gel, p. 141; Plastic Dowel Rods, p. 194; 13 in. x 19 in. Cake Board, Fanci-Foil Wrap, p. 186; 17 in. x 17 in. square foamcore board (½ in. thick), Disposable Decorating Bags, p. 136

See p. 114 for a list of commonly used decorating items you may need.

In advance: Make #1 candy plaque (p. 123). **Also:** Make paper tears and flame. Tint 4 oz. melted white candy yellow. Place two sheets of yellow edible paper shiny sides together on cake board. Position paper tears pattern and cut out with knife. You will need 16 to 18 2-layer shapes. Carefully peel apart layers. Brush one shiny side with yellow candy; immediately position matching shape on top. Form a curved shape and let set on large flower former. Repeat process for cutting flame; let dry flat. For candle wick, cut a strip, 1½ in. long x 1¼ in. wide, from edge of alphabet edible paper.

Use melted candy to attach wick and flame to lollipop stick; let set. **And:** Prepare boards. For base board, mark center of foamcore. Cut away a 1½ in. circle to allow for center post. Cut a 12 in. square board. Mark center of 12 in. cake board. Cut away a 2⅜ in. circle to allow for center post base. Wrap base board with foil.

Bake and cool two 2-layer cakes. Ice cakes smooth, 12 in. cake in yellow, 16 in. cake in white. Prepare for towering tiers construction (p. 121) and stacked construction (p. 120).

For 16 in. cake, cut eight strips from short end of streamers edible paper, 4 in. high x 8 in. wide, reserving remainder from each sheet for cake top. Attach to cake sides using piping gel. Attach two strips, 8 in. x 2¾ in., side by side on front end of cake top; repeat with two more strips for back end. Cut two strips, 2¾ in. x 10¾ in.; attach on remaining cake top borders, between previously placed strips. For ribbon, cut four strips, 2 in. wide x 6½ in. long, from red edible paper. Attach with piping gel, centering over seams from attached strips.

For 12 in. cake, use punch with layered circle inserts to cut 10 small and eight large circles each from red, bright green and bright blue edible paper. Attach randomly on cake with piping gel, trimming as needed.

Assemble cakes. Position 16 in. cake with short center post. Add tall center post and 12 in. cake. Cut two dowel rods to 4 in. Insert in 12 in. cake top 4 in. apart, where candy plaque will rest. Using full length dowel rod, dip 2 in. of end in melted candy to fit more securely in tall center post. Let set. Use melted candy to attach dowel rod 2 in. inside post extending 9 in. at top. Attach candy plaque to extended rod with melted candy. Attach flame to back of plaque. Position paper tears around plaque, securing with tip 8 dots of icing. Serves 128.

◀ Buggy Racer Cake

Pans: Baby Buggy, p. 164; Cookie Sheet, Cooling Grid, p. 171

Tips: 3, 5, 12, 16, 21, p. 134

Colors:* Christmas Red, Sky Blue, Kelly Green, Lemon Yellow, Golden Yellow, Brown, Red-Red, Black, p. 139

Recipes: Buttercream Icing, Roll-Out Cookies, p. 128

Also: 2013 Pattern Book (exhaust cloud, lightning bolt, number circle), p. 143; 4-Pc. Circles Nesting Metal Cutter Set, p. 172; Cake Circle, Fanci-Foil Wrap, p. 186; Disposable Decorating Bags, p. 136; Spatula, p. 137; large marshmallows

See p. 114 for a list of commonly used decorating items you may need.

1 day in advance: Make cookie trims. Prepare and roll out dough. Use pattern to cut cloud. Use smallest circle cutter to cut head. Bake and cool cookies.

Bake and cool cake. Ice cake sides and background areas smooth in sky blue. Ice background of tires smooth in gray. Lightly ice lightning bolt areas and number circle smooth in yellow. Use toothpick and patterns to mark lightning bolts and number circle. Fill in bolts and circle with tip 16 stars.

Outline buggy and hood with tip 3. Cover with tip 16 stars. Overpipe tip 16 yellow stars on buggy rim. Ice head smooth with skin tone icing. Use tip 5 to outline and pipe in helmet; pat smooth with finger dipped in cornstarch. Pipe tip 5 number. Use tip 3 to outline and pipe in goggles; pat smooth. Pipe tip 3 dot eye, nose and outline smile. Attach head. Pipe tip 12 outline steering wheel and tapered arm; pipe tip 3 dot fingers over wheel. Pipe tip 5 outline spokes and dot axle inside wheels; pipe tip 12 tires. Pipe tip 21 shell bottom border in blue. Ice cloud smooth. Pipe tip 3 message. Position cloud using marshmallows for support. Cake serves 12; each cookie serves 1.

*Combine Lemon Yellow with Golden Yellow for yellow shown. Combine Brown with Red-Red for skin tone shown.

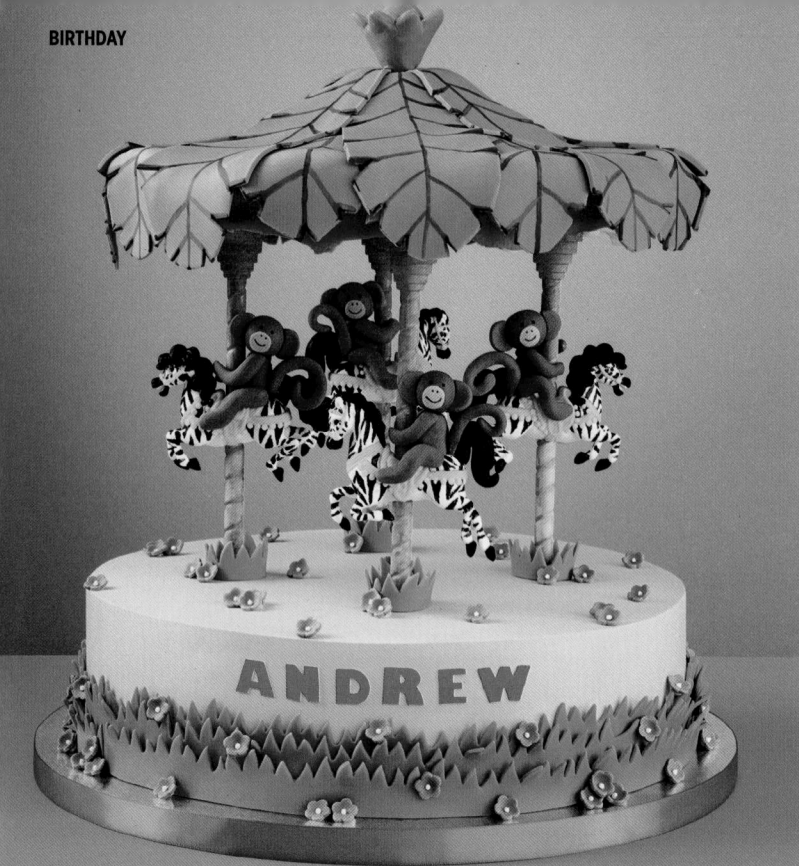

Lunchtime Hangout Cake

Pans: 6 in. x 2 in., 8 in. x 3 in. Round, p. 163; Cooling Grid, p. 171
Tips: 3, 5, 16, 18, 233, 352, p. 134-135
Colors:* Sky Blue, Kelly Green, Brown, Red-Red, Orange, p. 139
Candy: Light Cocoa (8 oz.), White (12 oz.), Peanut Butter (½ oz.) Candy Melts Candy, Primary (blue, yellow), Garden (black, green) Candy Color Sets, p. 175; Monkey Large Lollipop Mold, p. 177; 8 in. Lollipop Sticks, p. 178
Recipe: Buttercream Icing, p. 128
Also: 2013 Pattern Book (tree), p. 143; Parchment Triangles, p. 136; Cake Circles, p. 186; 10 in. Round Silver Cake Base, p. 187; Dowel Rods, p. 194; Spatula, p. 137; Disposable Decorating Bags, p. 136; ½ in. wide green satin ribbon (33 in.)
See p. 114 for a list of commonly used decorating items you may need.

1 day in advance: Make monkey candies. Using candy colors, tint small amounts of melted white candy black, light yellow, dark yellow, green and light blue. Mix 1 oz. white with ½ oz. peanut butter for light brown. Mold two swinging monkeys (one on stick) and one monkey behind plants using piping method (p. 123). Chill until firm. **Also:** Make tree. Cover pattern with waxed paper. Pipe in tree trunk with light cocoa candy; chill until firm. Turn over and pipe a line of candy down center; position lollipop stick, leaving 4 in. extended at bottom. Overpipe entire tree trunk with melted candy; chill until firm.

Bake and cool 2-layer cakes (for 8 in. cake, trim layers to 2½ in. for a 5 in. high cake). Prepare for stacked construction (p. 120). Position on base board and ice cakes smooth. Insert tree and monkey on stick. Cover front of tree with tip 18 lines on trunk and large branches; cover small branches with tip 16 lines.

On bottom cake, attach monkey candies without sticks with icing. Pipe tip 18 tree trunk with tip 16 branches. Pipe tip 352 leaves on trees and for plants on top and bottom cakes. Pipe tip 3 vines. Pipe tip 233 pull-out grass on bottom borders and cake top. Print tip 5 name. Attach ribbon around base with tape. Cake serves 32; each candy serves 1.

*Combine Brown with Red-Red for brown shown.

Monkey-Go-Round Canopy Cake

Pans: 12 in. x 3 in. Round, p. 163; Cooling Grid, p. 171
Tips: 2, 2A, p. 134
Colors:* Black, Lemon Yellow, Ivory, Brown, Red-Red, Kelly Green, Leaf Green, Violet, Rose, p. 139
Sugar Sheets! **Edible Decorating Paper/Tools:** Primary Alphabet, p. 144; Flower Mini Punch, Border Punch Set with Scallop Border Cutting Insert, Grass Border Cutting Insert, p. 145
Fondant: White Ready-To-Use Rolled Fondant (56 oz.), p. 148; 9 in., 20 in. Fondant Rollers, Roll-N-Cut Mat, 10-Pc. Gum Paste/Fondant Tool Set, p. 152; Pure Lemon Extract; Brush Set, Extra Fine Tip FoodWriter Edible Color Markers, p. 153; Shaping Foam, p. 155
Recipes: Buttercream, Royal Icings, p. 128
Also: 2013 Pattern Book (leaf), p. 143; Meringue Powder, p. 141; Carousel Cake Display Set, p. 209; Wave Flower Former Set, p. 142; Disposable Decorating Bags, p. 136; Spatula, p. 137; Cake Circle, p. 186; 14 in. Round Silver Cake Base, p. 187; Piping Gel, p. 141; 10 in. x 2 in. round craft foam block, ½ in. wide green satin ribbon (45 in.)
See p. 114 for a list of commonly used decorating items you may need.

2 days in advance: Prepare zebras, monkeys, carousel canopy and pillar placement pattern. Tint fondant: 48 oz. dark green, 6 oz. brown, ½ oz. light brown, Reserve all excess fondant.
Zebras: Position horses on pillars at various heights, allowing 3 in. at bottom for inserting in cake. Insert in craft block to decorate. Paint details with thinned royal icing: black stripes, yellow saddles and bridles, ivory pillars. Let

dry at least 24 hours. **Make monkeys:** (p. 123).
Canopy: Roll out dark green fondant ⅛ in. thick. Use fondant cutter to cut a 13 in. circle; cover canopy, securing with piping gel. Use pattern and knife to cut 16 leaves; cut triangle slits in various sizes. Paint veins with Leaf Green icing color/lemon extract mixture. Attach leaves to canopy with damp brush. Cover finial top with dark green fondant.

Also: Make flowers. Tint 1½ oz. fondant violet. Roll out ⅛ in. thick. Use mini punch to cut approximately 75 flowers. Cup centers on thick foam using small ball tool. Let dry on cornstarch-dusted small sections of flower former.

Bake and cool 1-layer cake. Ice cake smooth with light green buttercream. Position on cake base. Use 10 in. plate from kit to mark pillar placement on cake top. Roll out reserved dark green fondant ⅛ in. thick. Cut three strips, 2½ in. x 12 in. Use punch to cut grass insert to cut border. Attach around cake with piping gel. Repeat for second layer with three strips, 2¼ in. x 12 in., and third layer with three strips 1¾ in. x 12 in. Cut four strips, 1½ in. x 4 in.; cut grass as above. Attach ends with damp brush and position at pillar markings. Attach flowers and pipe tip 2 dot centers with buttercream. Attach edible paper letters to cake with piping gel.

At party: Insert canopy pillars, zebras and monkeys. Position canopy. Attach ribbon around base with tape. Cake serves 40.

*Combine Kelly Green with Leaf Green for dark green shown.
  Combine Brown with Red-Red for dark brown shown.
  Combine Violet with Rose for violet shown.

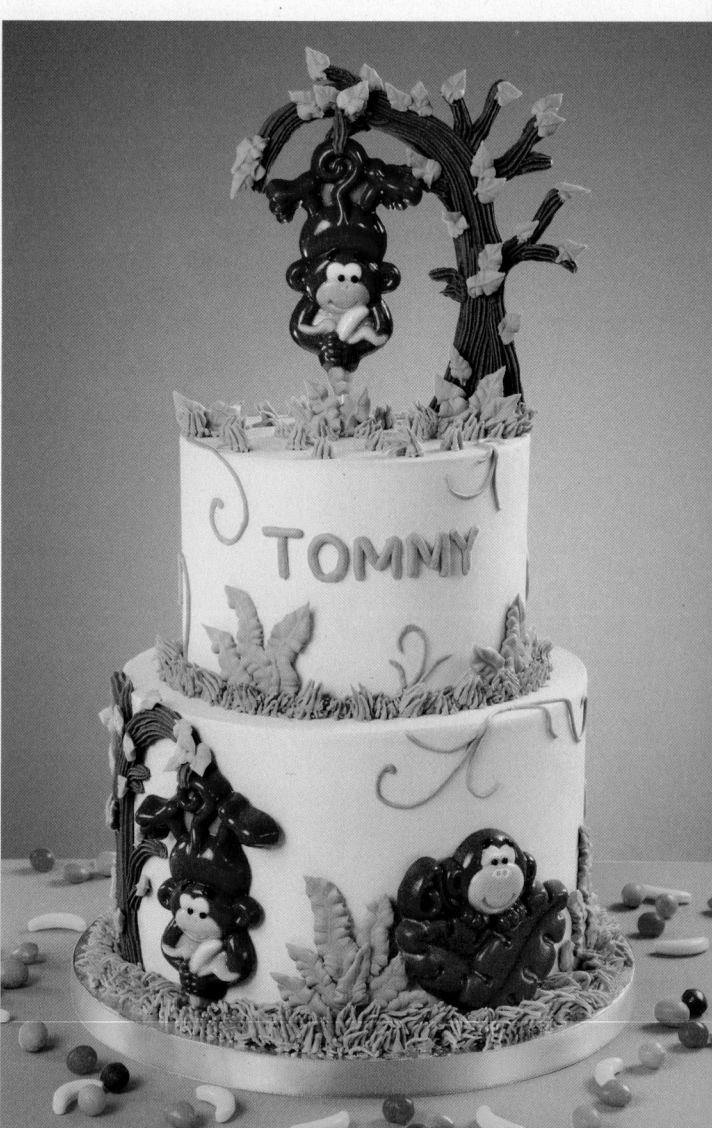

Farm-Raised Cupcakes & Cake

Pans: 14 in. x 2 in. Round, p. 161; Standard Muffin, p. 162; Cooling Grid, p. 171
Tips: 2, 3, 8, 12, 16, 45, 47, 234, 352, p. 134-135
Colors:* Kelly Green, Rose, Lemon Yellow, Brown, Red-Red, Orange, Black, p. 139
Recipe: Buttercream Icing, p. 128
Also: Assorted Pastel Standard Baking Cups, p. 180; 13-Ct. Standard Cupcakes-N-More Dessert Stand, p. 183; Disposable Decorating Bags, p. 136; Dowel Rods, p. 194; Spatula, p. 137; 8 in. Decorator Preferred Smooth Edge Separator Plate, p. 194; 16 in. Round Silver Cake Base, p. 187; ½ in. wide green satin ribbon (52 in.)
See p. 114 for a list of commonly used decorating items you may need.

Bake and cool 2-layer round cake (bake two 1½ in. layers for a 3 in. high cake) and position on base. Ice cake smooth. Prepare for separator plate construction (p. 120). Position plate, feet down, on cake top. Use toothpick to mark cake sides for vertical fence posts 3 in. apart. Pipe tip 47 (smooth side up) overlapping diagonal lines between marks. Pipe tip 45 vertical fence posts. Pipe tip 234 pull-out grass.

Bake and cool cupcakes. Ice tops smooth, forming a rounded shape. For cows, pipe in spots with tip 2; pat smooth with finger dipped in cornstarch. Pipe tip 352 pull-out ears, tip 12 ball snout; flatten with finger dipped in cornstarch. Pipe tip 2 outline mouth, dot eyes and nostrils. For chickens, pipe tip 16 pull-out hair tuft, tip 2 dot eyes and tip 352 pull-out beak. For pigs, pipe tip 12 ball snout; flatten with finger. Imprint nostrils using narrow end of tip 2 dipped in cornstarch. Score smile line using toothpick. Pipe tip 352 pull-out ears, tip 2 dot eyes. For lambs, pipe tip 12 ball muzzle; flatten. Pipe tip 8 pull-out ears, tip 3 outline inner ears. Pipe tip 16 swirl hair. Pipe tip 2 outline mouth, dot eyes and nose.

At party: Position dessert stand on cake top. Position cupcakes in stand and on cake top. Attach ribbon around base with tape. Cake serves 63; each cupcake serves 1.

*Combine Brown with Red-Red for brown shown.

Oinkredible Candies

Pan: Non-Stick Cookie Sheet, p. 169
Candy: White (12 oz. makes 2 treats), Light Cocoa Candy Melts Candy (¼ oz. makes 6 treats), Garden Candy Color Set (pink), p. 175; Animal Nose Fun Face Lollipop Mold, p. 177
Also: 4-Pc. Circles Nesting Metal Cutter Set, p. 172; Leaf Cut-Outs Fondant Cutters, p. 151; Parchment Triangles, p. 136; candy-coated chocolates
See p. 114 for a list of commonly used decorating items you may need.

Place second largest circle cutter and medium leaf Cut-Out on cookie sheet. Using pink-tinted candy, fill circle cutter ⁵⁄₁₆ in. deep for head, leaf Cut-Out ¼ in. deep for ear. Tap to settle; chill until firm. Reverse leaf Cut-Out for second ear; chill until firm. For nose, use piping method (p. 123) to fill pig cavity with pink candy. Chill until firm; unmold. Pipe nostrils using dark pink-tinted candy and mouth using light cocoa. Chill until firm.

Cut curve at bottom of each ear using second largest circle cutter. Attach ears, nose and brown candy-coated chocolate eyes to head with melted candy. Let set. Each serves 1.

Animals in Action Cookies

Pans: Cookie Sheet, Cooling Grid, p. 171
Color: Kelly Green, p. 139
***Sugar Sheets!* Edible Decorating Paper/Tools:** Light Blue (1 sheet makes 6 treats), Bright Green (1 sheet makes 1 treat), p. 144; Border Punch Set with Scallop Cutting Insert, Grass Cutting Insert, Rotary Cutter, p. 145; 6-Pc. Animals Cake Stamp Set, Brown, Black, Yellow, Blue, White, Pink Dab-N-Color Edible Color*, p. 146; Dab-N-Hold Edible Adhesive, p. 145
Recipes: Buttercream Icing, Roll-Out Cookies, p. 128
Also: Brush Set, p. 153
See p. 114 for a list of commonly used decorating items you may need.

In advance: Make cookies. Prepare and roll out dough. For giraffes, use knife to cut rectangles 4½ in. x 5½ in. For monkeys, cut squares 4½ in. x 4½ in. For elephants, cut rectangles 5½ in. x 4¾ in. Bake and cool cookies.

Use rotary cutter to cut bright green backgrounds: 6 in. x 7 in. for giraffes and elephants; 6 in. x 6 in. for monkeys. Use punch and insert to cut grass on each edge. Ice cookies smooth in light green icing; position grass. Cut light blue backgrounds: 3 in. x 4 in. for giraffes; 3 in. x 3 in. for monkeys; 3½ in. x 4 in. for elephants. Use stamps and edible colors to stamp animal designs with various edible colors. Let dry. Paint open areas and details with edible colors. Let dry. Attach stamped designs to grass with edible adhesive. Each serves 1.

*Combine Brown with White edible color and Pink with White edible color to lighten.

▲ Sweetness for Her Highness Cake

Pans: Enchanted Castle, p. 166; 4-Pc. Oval Set (second largest used), p. 160; Cooling Grid, p. 171

Tips: 5, 16, 21, p. 134

Colors:* Leaf Green, Sky Blue, Rose, Violet, Lemon Yellow, Golden Yellow, p. 139

***Sugar Sheets!* Edible Decorating Paper/Tools:** Light Blue, Light Pink, Light Yellow, Light Green (1 each); Cupcake Border (2), p. 144; Punch Set with Oval Cutting Insert, Layered Circles Cutting Insert Set, Dab-N-Hold Edible Adhesive, p. 145

Candy: White (36 oz.), Light Cocoa (4 oz.) Candy Melts Candy, Primary Candy Color Set (yellow), p. 175

Recipe: Buttercream Icing, p. 128

Also: Jumbo Rainbow Nonpareils Sprinkles, Flowerful Medley 6-Cell Sprinkles (confetti), p. 156; Disposable Decorating Bags, p. 136; Plastic Dowel Rods, p. 194; Cake Boards, Fanci-Foil Wrap, p. 186; Piping Gel, p. 141; Brush Set, p. 153; craft foam block, jelly spearmint leaves, large spice drops

See p. 114 for a list of commonly used decorating items you may need.

In advance: Make castle candy plaque. Tint 28 oz. melted white candy light yellow. Pour into castle pan. Tap to settle; chill until firm. Unmold. Use hot knife to level bottom edge. Use melted light cocoa candy to fill in door and windows. Let set. Attach dowel rod to back center using melted candy; leave 4 in. extended at bottom to insert into cake. Let set. Insert in craft block. Tint portions of icing violet, yellow, pink, green and blue. Cover turrets with tip 21 horizontal outlines. Use white icing to pipe tip 16 outlines around windows. Position nonpareils in icing. Pipe tip 5 pull-out drips below windows (match to turret color). Use blue to pipe tip 16 outline around door; attach confetti for doorknob. Use white to pipe tip 16 swirls and zigzag swags across center; attach confetti to each swirl and point.

Bake and cool 2-layer cake. Ice cake smooth (sides white, top green). Attach edible paper scallop border around bottom, dot border around top with edible adhesive. Use punch with largest circle insert to cut four circles from each solid color of edible paper. Attach a cupcake design to each circle using edible adhesive. Attach circles around cake side, ¼ in. apart, with edible adhesive. Cut two dowel rod sections 4 in. long. Insert into cake, 5 in. apart, where plaque will sit. Insert plaque. Cut spearmint leaves in half. Attach to plaque with melted candy. Attach confetti for walkway with icing. Position spice drops around cake. Serves 30.

*Combine Violet with Rose for violet shown. Combine Lemon Yellow with Golden Yellow for yellow shown.

▼ Tricked-Out Truck Cake

Pans: Dump Truck, p. 166; 11 in. x 15 in. x 2 in. Sheet, p. 161; Standard Muffin, p. 162; Cookie Sheet, Cooling Grid, p. 171
Tips: 2, 3, 18, p. 134
Colors:* Leaf Green, Violet, Royal Blue, Orange, Black, Red-Red, Lemon Yellow, Golden Yellow, Copper, Brown, p. 139
Candy: Yellow (24 oz.), Red (12 oz.), White (20 oz.) Candy Melts Candy, Primary (orange), Garden Candy Color Sets (black), p. 175; 6 in. Lollipop Sticks, p. 178
Recipes: Buttercream, Royal Icings, Roll-Out Cookies, p. 128
Also: Jumbo Rainbow Nonpareils Sprinkles, p. 156; Brush Set, p. 153; Gingerbread Boy Metal Cutter, p. 172; Silicone Pastel Round Baking Cups, p. 182; Meringue Powder, Piping Gel, p. 141; Spatula, p. 137; Parchment Triangles, Disposable Decorating Bags, p. 136; Plastic Dowel Rods, p. 194; Happy Birthday Icing Decorations, p. 200
See p. 114 for a list of commonly used decorating items you may need.

In advance: Make dump truck candy plaque (p. 123). **Also:** Make candy shells in baking cups (p. 123), using 1 oz. portions of orange- or red-tinted candy for each. **And:** Make cookies (p. 123).

Bake and cool 1-layer cake and four cupcakes in silicone cups supported by cookie sheet. Unmold cupcakes from cups; place in candy shells. Ice cake and cupcake tops smooth in buttercream icing. Sprinkle cupcakes with jumbo nonpareils. Mark cake sides for drop strings 1⅞ in. apart and 1 in. deep. Pipe tip 3 double drop strings ½ in. and 1 in. deep. Pipe tip 18 shell bottom border.

At Party: Insert candy plaque into cake. Position one cupcake behind dump truck bed on side of cake. Insert end of topping stream and attach other end to plaque with melted candy; let set. Position remaining cupcakes and kid cookies. Position icing decorations on cake top. Cake serves 27; each cupcake serves 1.

*Combine Lemon Yellow with Golden Yellow for yellow shown. Combine Brown with Red-Red for brown shown.

◀ Bon Appétit Candy Treat

Pan: Non-Stick Cookie Sheet, p. 169
***Sugar Sheets!* Edible Decorating Paper/
Tools:** White (1 sheet makes 20 treats), p. 144; Dab-N-Hold Edible Adhesive, p. 145
Candy: White Candy Melts Candy (6 oz. makes 1 treat), Primary (blue, yellow, red, orange), Garden (black) Candy Color Sets, p. 175; 3-D Cupcake Look Container Candy Mold, p. 176
Also: Round Comfort-Grip Cutter, Gingerbread Boy Metal Cutter, p. 172; Parchment Triangles, p. 136; Brush Set, p. 153; Flowerful Medley 6-Cell Sprinkles (confetti), p. 156; candy-coated chocolates
See p. 114 for a list of commonly used decorating items you may need.

For each treat, use candy colors to tint portions of melted candy light orange (for skin tone shown), yellow, blue, black and red. Reserve remainder white.

For base and chef, place cutters on cookie sheet. Fill round cutter ⅜ in. deep with white candy, boy cutter ¼ in. deep with skin tone candy. Tap to settle; chill until firm. Using melted candy in cut bag, pipe black eyes, mouth and shoes, skin tone nose, yellow shirt and blue pants; chill until firm. Mold 3-D cupcake with red bottom, white top; chill until firm.

Make chef's details with white edible paper and scissors. Cut a hat 1 in. high x 2 in. wide; pastry bag 1½ in. high x ½ in. wide; apron ¾ in. high x 1½ in. wide at bottom, tapering to 1 in. high at top. Cut straps ⅛ in. wide x 1 in. long. Attach details to chef with edible adhesive. Attach confetti sprinkles to side of base with melted candy. Attach chef and cupcake bottom to base with melted candy; chill until firm. Fill cupcake bottom with candy-coated chocolates; position cupcake top. Each serves 1.

◀ Miss Monarch Cake

Pans: Butterfly, p. 164; Cookie Sheet, Cooling Grid, p. 121
Tips: 1, 2A, 3, 5, 14, 103, p. 134-135
Colors:* Rose, Copper (for skin tone shown), Lemon Yellow, Golden Yellow, Black, p. 139
***Sugar Sheets!* Edible Decorating Paper/
Tools:** Light Pink (2), Bright Pink (1), Scrolls (2), p. 144; Punch Set with Oval Cutting Insert, Layered Flowers Cutting Insert Set, Dab-N-Hold Edible Adhesive, Rotary Cutter, p. 145
Recipes: Buttercream, Color Flow Icings, Roll-Out Cookies, p. 128
Also: 2013 Pattern Book (dress, crown, wing inserts), p. 143; 101 Cookie Cutters (large circle), p. 173; Oval Cut-Outs Fondant Cutters, p. 151; White Sugar Pearls, p. 157; Color Flow Mix, Piping Gel, p. 141; Spatula, p. 137; Disposable Decorating Bags, p. 136; Parchment Paper, p. 158; Fine Tip Primary Colors FoodWriter Edible Color Markers (black), p. 153; 4 in. Lollipop Sticks, p. 178; Cake Boards, Fanci-Foil Wrap, p. 186; pink striped candy sticks
See p. 114 for a list of commonly used decorating items you may need.

2 days in advance: Make girl cookies. Prepare and roll out dough. Use patterns to cut crown and dress. Use largest circle cutter from set to cut head. Bake and cool cookies. Outline cookies with tip 3 and full-strength Color Flow; pink for crown and dress, skin tone for face (reserve portions of each color and some white). Flow in cookies with thinned icing. Let dry on parchment-covered boards.

1 day in advance: Use reserved icing to attach crown and head cookies to lollipop sticks; let dry. Attach candy stick legs to back of dress, leaving 3 in. of legs extended. Let dry.

Bake and cool cake. Ice cake smooth with white buttercream. Pipe tip 5 bead bottom border. Use pan as a guide to make wing cake top pattern on parchment. Use black edible marker to trace pattern on shiny sides of scrolls edible paper; cut out shapes with rotary cutter (reverse pattern for opposite wing). Position on cake top. Trace large and small wing insert patterns on shiny side of light pink edible paper (reverse large for opposite side). Cut out four of each shape; attach two shiny sides together with edible adhesive.

Pipe tip 103 ruffle on dress in buttercream. Use medium oval Cut-Out to cut two shoes from light pink edible paper. Attach shoes to legs with edible adhesive. Decorate girl with reserved full-strength Color Flow; tint portions of white icing yellow and black. Pipe tip 14 outline and rosette hair. Pipe tip 3 dot eyes, nose and mouth. Pipe tip 1 dot eye highlights. Position dress on cake top, supporting with icing if needed. Position head, overlapping ¼ in. of dress, supporting with icing. Pipe tip 2A outline arms. Use punch with medium flower insert to cut flower from bright pink edible paper. Attach flower and white Sugar Pearl center with dots of icing. Cake serves 12; each cookie serves 1.

*Combine Lemon Yellow with Golden Yellow for yellow shown.

▶ Flower Flyer Cupcakes

Pans: Standard Muffin, p. 162; Cooling Grid, p. 171
Tip: 2A, p. 134
Recipe: Buttercream Icing, p. 128
Also: Pink, Lavender, Yellow Petal Standard Baking Cups, p. 180; Disposable Decorating Bags, p. 136; Warm, Cool Butterfly Picks, p. 190; Gum Paste Wire and Tape, p. 155; plastic champagne glasses, silk leaves (9 per treat)
See p. 114 for a list of commonly used decorating items you may need.

In advance: Make cupcake stands. Turn glass upside down. Wrap stem with florist tape. Tape leaves to glass.

Bake and cool cupcakes. Cover tops with tip 2A swirl. Position butterflies on cupcakes without picks. Position cupcake on stand. Each serves 1.

◀ Frolic in the Flowers Cake

Pans: Ballerina Bear, p. 164, Cooling Grid, p. 171
Tips: 3, 5, 16, 18, p. 134
Colors:* Violet, Rose, Lemon Yellow, Golden Yellow, Orange, Royal Blue, Leaf Green Brown, Red-Red, Christmas Red, Black, p. 139
***Sugar Sheets!* Edible Decorating Paper/ Tools:** Punch Set with Oval Cutting Insert, Layered Flowers Cutting Insert Set, Border Punch Set with Scallop Cutting Insert, Grass Cutting Insert, p. 145
Fondant: White Ready-To-Use Rolled Fondant (80 oz.), Gum-Tex, p. 148; 9 in., 20 in. Fondant Roller, 20 in. Fondant Roller Guide Rings, Roll-N-Cut Mat, p. 152; Flower Forming Cups, p. 155
Recipes: Buttercream Icing, p. 128; Thinned Fondant Adhesive, p. 127
Also: Candy Melting Plate, p. 178; Piping Gel, p. 141; 13 in. x 19 in. Cake Boards (3), Fanci-Foil Wrap, p. 186; Disposable Decorating Bags, p. 136; Spatula, p. 137
See p. 114 for a list of commonly used decorating items you may need.

3 days in advance: Prepare base board. Tint fondant: 36 oz. green, 30 oz. blue, 4 oz. each rose, yellow, orange. Reserve 2 oz. white. Tape together three 13 in. x 19 in. cake boards. Wrap with foil. Roll out green and blue fondant ⅛ in. thick. Cover top 14 in. of board with blue fondant (p. 120). Cover bottom portion of board with green fondant, overlapping blue portion. Use knife to cut a wavy horizontal line, 6½ in. from bottom, through overlapping fondant. Remove excess and smooth seam. Reserve excess green fondant. **Also:** Make fondant flowers and trims (p. 123).

Bake and cool cake; trim off bow and trim down ruffles. Ice sides and background areas smooth in blue. Use tip 3 to outline and pipe in mouth; pat smooth with finger dipped in cornstarch. Pipe tip 5 bead tongue; pat smooth. Use tip 3 to outline girl and clothes. Fill in areas with tip 16 stars. Overpipe nose and cheeks with tip 16 stars. Pipe tip 3 dots on dress. Pipe tip 18 pull-out hair and pigtails. Pipe tip 5 outline hair bands.

Position cake on board, 2 in. from bottom. Pipe tip 5 bead bottom border. Pipe tip 5 name. Attach supports to grass strips with thinned fondant adhesive. Position grass, beginning at girl's legs with sections on ¼ in. supports and reserved scraps from punch. Continue layering grass sections at graduated heights to bottom of board. Attach flowers and clouds with thinned fondant adhesive. Serves 12.

*Combine Violet with Rose for light and dark violet shown. Combine Lemon Yellow with Golden Yellow for yellow shown. Combine Brown with Red-Red for skin tone shown.

▶ Shading Ladybugs Cake

Pans: Dancing Daisy, p. 166; 12 in. x 2 in. Round, p. 161; Mini Ball, p. 165, Cooling Grid, p. 171
Tips: 1D, 2, 3, 12, 16, p. 134
Colors: Kelly Green, Black, Red-Red, p. 139
Candy: Yellow (1 pk.), Orange (2 pks.), Dark Green (1 pk.) Candy Melts Candy, p. 175; Decorator Brush Set, p. 178
Recipe: Buttercream Icing, p. 128
Also: Cake Circles, p. 186; Towering Tiers Cake Stand (14 in. plate, short and tall center posts, center post foot, 4 base feet, Cake Corer), p. 193; Cake Dividing Chart, p. 137; Parchment Triangles, Disposable Decorating Bags, p. 136; Coupler Ring Set, p. 140; Spatula, p. 137; Candy Eyeballs, p. 157; Plastic Dowel Rods, p. 194; lemon leaves, black shoestring licorice
See p. 114 for a list of commonly used decorating items you may need.

1 day in advance: Make candy plaque flower (p. 123). Pipe melted candy into cake pan using cut parchment bags; chill until set after each addition. Use yellow candy for center, orange for petals. Chill until firm. Unmold onto soft cloth. Attach plastic dowel rod to back of flower with melted candy, extending 7½ in. at bottom.

Position coupler ring as a spacer between extended section of dowel rod and flower to create a slight gap; this will enable you to insert dowel rod in center post on cake without dislodging flower. Chill until firm. Remove coupler ring. **Also:** Make flower stem. Brush tall center post from towering tiers set above wide ridge with melted green candy. Refrigerate until firm on waxed paper-covered board. **And:** Make candy leaves (p. 123). Brush back of clean, dry lemon leaves with melted green candy. Refrigerate until firm. Carefully peel off leaves for reuse; you will need 90 candy leaves.

Bake and cool 2-layer round cake and two mini ball cakes. Prepare round cake for towering tiers construction (p. 121); ice cake smooth. Divide cake into 16ths, marking top and bottom. Attach feet, center post foot and short center post to 14 in. plate; position cake. Pipe a tip 1D (serrated side up) stripe at each division mark. For mini ball ladybugs, pipe tip 3 wing line. Cover cakes with tip 16 stars. Pipe tip 12 ball head. Pipe tip 2 outline mouth. Attach candy eyeballs and licorice antennae with icing. Pipe tip 2 dot antenna ends.

Insert flower stem post into short center post. Attach candy leaves to base of cake with icing and to stem with melted candy. Insert flower into center post. Position ladybugs on cake top. Serves 42.

▶ Beak Chic Cake

Pans: 3-D Sports Ball Set, p. 165; Cooling Grid, p. 171
Tips: 2, 2A, 4, 4B, 16, 21, p. 134
Colors:* Violet, Rose, Black, p. 139
Fondant: White Ready-To-Use Rolled Fondant (12 oz.), p. 148; 9 in. Fondant Roller, Roll-N-Cut Mat, p. 152; Baroque Designs Gum Paste & Fondant Mold, p. 150; White Pearl Dust, Brush Set, p. 153
Recipe: Buttercream Icing, p. 128
Also: 2013 Pattern Book (beak, hat, leg, purse, wing, tail), p. 143; Cake Circles, 13 in. x 19 in. Cake Boards, Fanci-Foil Wrap, p. 186; Disposable Decorating Bags, p. 136
See p. 114 for a list of commonly used decorating items you may need.

1 day in advance: Make fondant trims. Roll out white fondant ⅛ in. thick for wing and ½ in. thick for tail. Use patterns and knife to cut out. Tint 6 oz. fondant violet, 3 oz. rose. Roll out fondant as directed and use patterns and knife to cut trims as follows: ½ in. thick hat and purse, ⅜ in. thick beak and leg, ⅛ in. thick purse flap. Attach flap to purse with damp brush. Roll out remaining rose fondant 1/16 in. thick. Use narrow end of tip 2A to cut six polka dots; attach to hat with damp brush, trimming as needed. For purse snap, roll two rose fondant balls 3/16 in. Pinch at one end and flatten to form heart shape. Attach to purse with damp brush. Brush hat and purse with white Pearl Dust. For pompom, cut a 1 in. x 6 in. strip. Cut ¾ in. deep slits for fringe. Brush uncut portion with water and roll up strip. Adjust fringe with fingers for a full look. Attach to hat with damp brush. Let all dry on cornstarch-dusted board.

Bake and cool cake. Cover with tip 16 stars. Position leg, hat and tail.

For strap, use baroque mold and white fondant to make large pearl chain; cut into 5 in. and 2 in. lengths. Brush with Pearl Dust. Position beak, purse and strap on base board. Cover tail with tip 4B shells. Pipe tip 2A ball eye; pat smooth with finger dipped in cornstarch. Pipe tip 4 dot pupil; pat smooth. Pipe tip 2 outline eyelashes. Attach wing with icing; cover with tip 21 pull-out feathers. Serves 12.

*Combine Violet with Rose for violet shown.

◀ Party Present Cookies

Cookie: 4-Pc. Blossoms, 4-Pc. Circles Nesting Metal Cutter Sets, p. 172; Cookie Sheet, Cooling Grid, p. 171
***Sugar Sheets!* Edible Decorating Paper/Tools:** White (1 sheet makes 6 treats), Light Blue, Bright Pink, Light Yellow, Light Green (1 sheet each makes 2 treats; reserve scraps for mini circles), p. 144; Blue, Green, Pink, Yellow Dab-N-Color Edible Color, 6-Pc. Party Fun Cake Stamp Set, p. 146; Round Mini Punch, Dab-N-Hold Edible Adhesive, p. 145
Recipes: Buttercream Icing, Roll-Out Cookies, p. 128
Also: Brush Set, p. 153; Spatula, p. 137

See p. 114 for a list of commonly used decorating items you may need.

Prepare and roll out dough. Cut cookies using largest cutter from blossom set. Bake and cool.

Make stamped circles. Use third largest round cookie cutter to cut circle from white edible paper. Stamp gifts using various combinations of edible colors (p. 122). Let dry. Use mini punch to cut approximately 25-30 circles from light blue, light green or light yellow edible paper for each treat. Attach to white circles with edible adhesive. Use largest blossom cutter to cut flowers from bright pink, light yellow and light blue edible paper. Attach decorated circles to edible paper blossoms with edible adhesive. Ice cookies smooth. Immediately position blossoms on cookies. Each serves 1.

▶ High Fashion Heart Cake

Pans: SweetHeart, p. 165; 14 in. x 2 in. Square, p. 161; Cooling Grid, p. 171
Tip: 5, p. 134
***Sugar Sheets!* Edible Decorating Paper/Tools:** Bright Pink (3), Light Pink (3), White (2), Black (1), p. 144; Border Punch Set with Scallop Cutting Insert, Slide-N-Cut Edge Cutter, Rotary Cutter, Heart, Round Mini Punches, p. 145; 26-Pc. Classic Alphabet Stamp Set, Black Dab-N-Color Edible Color, p. 146
Recipe: Buttercream Icing, p. 128
Also: 2013 Pattern Book (heart swirl), p. 143; Brush Set, p. 153; Piping Gel, p. 141; Bamboo Dowel Rods, p. 194; Cake Boards, Fanci-Foil Wrap, p. 186; Fine Tip Primary Colors FoodWriter Edible Color Markers (black), p. 153; 16 in. x 16 in. square plywood or foamcore board (¼ in. thick)
See p. 114 for a list of commonly used decorating items you may need.

Bake and cool 1-layer cakes. Ice cakes smooth in white. Prepare for stacked construction (p. 120). Use black edible marker to trace heart pan on shiny side of light pink edible paper. Cut shape with rotary cutter. Use alphabet stamps and black edible color to stamp name. Let dry. Attach to cake top using piping gel; trim as needed. Trace heart swirl pattern on shiny side of black edible paper. Cut out with rotary cutter; attach.

For square cake, cut two strips, 7 in. wide, from long edge of bright pink edible paper. Attach to top ¾ of cake with piping gel. Cut two strips, 7 in. wide x 3½ in. long, for bottom ¼ of cake top. Attach with piping gel. Position heart cake; pipe tip 5 bead bottom border.

Use heart mini punch to cut 26 hearts from white edible paper; attach. Use border punch with scallop insert to cut six strips, 1½ in. wide x 10½ in. long, from white edible paper. Attach strips to board, scallop edge out. Trim as needed. Cut six strips, 1½ in. wide x 10½ in. long, from light pink edible paper. Trim to ⅞ in. wide. Use mini punch to cut a circle in each scallop. Attach strips over white with piping gel, leaving ⅛ in. white outer border. Serves 44.

◀ Supersize Surprise Cake

Pans: Dimensions Large Cupcake, p. 167; 10 in. x 2 in. Square, p. 161; Cooling Grid, p. 171
Color: Rose, p. 139
***Sugar Sheets!* Edible Decorating Paper/Tools:** Light Pink (2), White (1), Purple (1), Black (1), Red (1), p. 144; Punch Set with Oval Cutting Insert, Scalloped Heart Cutting Insert, p. 145; 4-Pc. Hearts Cake Stamp Set, Pink, Purple Dab-N-Color Edible Color, p. 146; Slide-N-Cut Edge Cutter, Heart Mini Punch, p. 145
Recipe: Buttercream Icing, p. 128
Also: 6 in. Cake Circle, Cake Boards, Fanci-Foil Wrap, p. 186; White Candy Melts Candy, p. 175; Piping Gel, p. 141; Brush Set, p. 153; Dowel Rods, p. 194; 4 in. Lollipop Sticks, p. 178; Spatula, p. 137
See p. 114 for a list of commonly used decorating items you may need.

Bake and cool 2-piece cupcake cake and 2-layer square cake (trim layers to 1½ in. high for a 3 in. high cake). Ice square cake smooth in rose. Prepare for stacked construction (p. 120).

Use edge cutter to cut four strips, 3 in. x 10 in., from long edge of light pink edible paper. Use various heart stamps and pink or purple edible color to stamp three designs on each strip (p. 122); stamp right and left hearts ¾ in. from strip edge and center heart ¾ in. from other hearts. Attach strips to square cake sides with piping gel. Use edge cutter to cut 16 strips, ¼ in. x 3 in., from black edible paper. Attach between hearts and two at each corner with piping gel. For cake top, cut four strips, ½ in. x 10 in., from long edge of purple edible paper; attach at edges with piping gel, overlapping ends.

Cut 24 strips, 1 in. x 3½ in., from white edible paper. Gently crease each strip in half lengthwise. Ice bottom half of cupcake smooth; attach creased strips. Use mini punch to cut 30 hearts from red edible paper. Ice top of cupcake cake fluffy; position hearts. Stack cakes.

Use punch with scalloped heart insert to cut two shapes from red edible paper. Stamp heart design with purple edible color. Let dry. Attach hearts shiny side together with melted candy; let set. Attach lollipop stick to hearts with melted candy; let set. Insert in cake top. Serves 42.

▼ Video Kid Cake

Pans: 3-D Bear Set, p. 164; 9 in. x 13 in. x 2 in. Sheet, p. 161; 9.25 in. x 5.25 in. x 2.75 in. Non-Stick Large Loaf, p. 169; Cooling Grid, p. 171

Tips: 1A, 2, 3, 5, 8, 16, 18, p. 134

Colors:* Christmas Red, Royal Blue, Copper (for skin tone shown), Brown, Red-Red, Black, p. 139

***Sugar Sheets!* Edible Decorating Paper/Tools:** White (1), p. 144; White, Brown, Orange, Red, Blue, Green, Black Dab-N-Color Edible Colors, p. 146

Candy: Black Candy Melts Candy (7 pks.), p. 175; Decorator Brush Set, 4 in. Lollipop Sticks, Candy Melting Plate, p. 178

Recipe: Buttercream Icing, p. 128

Also: 2013 Pattern Book (baseball, football, monster displays), p. 143; 6-Pc. Classic Metal Cutter Set, p. 172; Piping Gel, p. 141; Extra Fine Tip FoodWriter Edible Color Markers (black), p. 153; "Hidden" Pillars, p. 194; Cake Boards, Cake Circles, Fanci-Foil Wrap, p. 186; Disposable Decorating Bags, p. 136; Pastry Brush, p.159

See p. 114 for a list of commonly used decorating items you may need.

In advance: Make candy television and game controller (p. 124).

Bake and cool bear cake. Trim off ears, muzzle, arms and tail. Outline pants with tip 3; cover with tip 16 stars. Pipe tip 1A tapered arms, leaving a 2 in. gap in the middle. Outline shirt with tip 3; cover with tip 16 stars. Use tip 16 to outline soles of shoes. Pipe in with tip 16 zigzags. Cover shoe tops with tip 16 stars.

Use tip 5 to outline and pipe in mouth; pat smooth. Use tip 3 to outline and pipe in eyes; pat smooth. Use tip 8 to build up dot nose and outline ears. Cover face with tip 16 stars. Pipe tip 5 dot pupils (flatten slightly with fingertip) and tip 2 dot eye highlights. Pipe tip 16 outline eyebrows and tip 18 pull-out hair.

Pipe tip 5 dot buttons on controller; insert into cake. Pipe tip 5 outline fingers over controller; cover with tip 16 stars. Position boy in front of television. Cake serves 12.

*Combine Brown with Red-Red for brown shown.

◀ Crumb Catcher Cookies

Cookies: 4-Pc. Circles Nesting Metal Cutter Set, p. 172; Cookie Sheet, Cooling Grid, p. 171

Tip: 4, p. 134

Colors:* Copper (for light skin tone shown), Brown, Christmas Red, p. 139

Recipes: Royal Icing, Roll-Out Cookies, p. 128

Also: Black Candy Melts Candy, p. 175; Mustache Fun Face Lollipop Molds, p. 177; Spatula, p. 137; Meringue Powder, p. 141; Parchment Triangles, p. 136; white candy wafers, brown candy-covered chocolates, black shoestring licorice

See p. 114 for a list of commonly used decorating items you may need.

In advance: Make mustaches. Use piping method (p. 123) to fill molds with melted black candy. Chill until firm.

Prepare and roll out dough. Cut cookies using second largest circle cutter. Bake and cool cookies. Ice cookies smooth.

For hair, cut licorice to various lengths. Attach hair and mustache with tip 4 dots of icing. For eyes, attach candy wafers and chocolate pupils with dots of icing. Each serves 1.

*Combine Brown with Christmas Red for dark skin tone shown.

▲ Raceway Rush Cake

Pans: Checkerboard Set, p. 169; Non-Stick Cookie Sheet, Cooling Grid, p. 169
Tips: 1D, 3, p. 134
Colors:* Royal Blue, Black, Brown, Red-Red, Copper (for light skin tone shown), p. 139
Fondant: White Ready-To-Use Rolled Fondant (18 oz.), p. 148; 20 in. Fondant Roller, Roll-N-Cut Mat, p. 152

Candy: White (2 pks.), Red (1 pk.) Candy Melts Candy, Garden and Primary Candy Color Sets, p. 175; Decorator Brush Set, p. 178; Race Car Pretzel Mold, p. 176; 6 in. Lollipop Sticks, p. 178
Recipes: Buttercream, Royal Icings, p. 128
Also: 101 Cookie Cutters (flags, letters), p. 173; Meringue Powder, Piping Gel, p. 141; Parchment Triangles, Disposable Decorating Bags, p. 136; Extra Fine Tip FoodWriter Edible Color Markers, p. 153; 12 in. Round Silver Cake Base, p. 187; Cake Boards, Cake Circles, Fanci-Foil Wrap, p. 186
See p. 114 for a list of commonly used decorating items you may need.

1 day in advance: Make heads. Using royal icing tinted in various skin tones, pipe 200 puddle dots (p. 119), ½ in. diameter, on waxed paper-covered boards. Let dry. Use edible marker to draw dot eyes and smiles. **Also:** Prepare and cover cake base with 18 oz. fondant tinted gray (p. 120).

And: Make candy trims. Cars: Tint candy assorted colors. Use painting or piping method (p. 123) to mold eight racecars without pretzels. Chill until firm. Swipe over warm cookie sheet to slightly flatten wheels so cars will stand freely. Name: Use cutters from set placed on non-stick cookie sheet to mold red candy letters, ¼ in. deep. Chill until firm. Attach lollipop sticks to back using melted candy, extending 3 in. at bottom to insert into cake. Flags: Use cutter from set on non-stick cookie sheet to mold two white flags, ¼ in. deep (reverse one cutter). Chill until firm. Use toothpick to score ⅜ in. squares on flag for checkerboard pattern. Outline and fill in black checks and pole with black tinted candy. Chill until firm. Fill in white candy checks. Chill until firm. Attach lollipop stick to back using melted candy, extending 4 in. at bottom to insert into cake.

Bake and cool 3-layer cake following pan directions and using white and chocolate batter tinted black for checkerboard design. Ice cake smooth. Position on prepared base board. Pipe tip 1D (smooth side up), band for bottom border. Attach heads with tip 3 icing dots. Insert flags and letters. Position cars. Cake serves 20; each candy serves 1.

*Combine Brown with Red-Red for darker skin tone shown.

▶ He's Having a Ball! Cake

Pans: 11 in. x 15 in. x 2 in. Sheet, p. 161; Cookie Sheet, Cooling Grid, p. 171
Tips: 2, 4, 21, p. 134
Colors:* Christmas Red, Black, Orange, Brown, Red-Red, p. 139
Sugar Sheets! Edible Decorating Paper/Tools: Light Blue (2), p. 144; Slide-N-Cut Edge Cutter, p. 145
Recipes: Buttercream, Color Flow Icings, Roll-Out Cookies, p. 128
Also: 101 Cookie Cutters (sports balls), p. 173; Color Flow Mix, p. 141; Disposable Decorating Bags, p. 136; 13 in. x 19 in. Cake Boards, Fanci-Foil Wrap, p. 186
See p. 114 for a list of commonly used decorating items you may need.

1 day in advance: Make cookies. Prepare and roll out dough. Cut cookies using cutters from set, including desired letters, nine balls using medium round, and three footballs. Bake and cool cookies. Decorate with Color Flow. Use tip 2 and full-strength icing to outline letters; let dry. Place ball cookies on cooling grid over cookie sheet; cover with thinned icing (p. 123). Let dry. Flow in letter cookies with thinned icing; let dry.

Add details with full-strength icing. Use tip 4 to pipe stripes on footballs; pat smooth with finger dipped in cornstarch. Use tip 2 to pipe stitching on footballs, baseballs, and basketballs and section lines on soccer ball. Pipe in black sections of soccer ball with thinned icing. Let dry.

Bake and cool 1-layer cake. Place cake on foil-wrapped double-thick board, cut to 12½ in. x 16½ in. Ice cake smooth in buttercream. Use edge cutter to cut two rectangles from light blue edible paper, 7½ in. x 9 in. Position 1 in. from cake edge. Pipe tip 21 shell bottom border. Position ball and letter cookies. Cake serves 27; each cookie serves 1.

*Combine Brown with Red-Red for brown shade shown.

▲ Camelot Cake and Cookies

Pans: First and Ten Football, p. 165; Cookie Sheet, Cooling Grid, p. 171
Tips: 1, 2, 3, 4, 12, 16, 17, 104, p. 134-135
Colors:* Kelly Green, Leaf Green, Lemon Yellow, No-Taste Red, Black, Copper (for skin tone shown), p. 139
Recipes: Buttercream, Color Flow Icings, Roll-Out Cookies, p. 128
Also: 2013 Pattern Book (spikes, head, neck, legs, and tail); p. 143; Gingerbread Boy Metal Cutter Set, p. 231; Color Flow Mix, p. 141; White Pearl Dust, Brush Set,

p. 153; Parchment Paper, p. 158; Disposable Decorating Bags, p. 136; Spatula, p. 137; Cake Boards, Fanci-Foil Wrap, p. 186; 17 in. x 28 in. plywood or foamcore board (½ in. thick), mini marshmallows

See p. 114 for a list of commonly used decorating items you may need.

2 days in advance: Make Color Flow spikes. Tape spike patterns to cake board; cover with waxed paper. Outline with tip 3 and full-strength Color Flow; let set. Flow in with thinned Color Flow in cut parchment bag. Let dry 48 hours.

Also: Make cookies. Prepare and roll out dough. For dragon, use patterns and knife to cut out

three tails, three necks and four heads, one each back leg and front leg. For knights, cut cookies with boy cutter. Bake and cool cookies.
And: Prepare base board. Position pan, and one cookie of each shape on board to form dragon shape. Trace shape and cut base board; cover with foil.

Bake and cool football cake. Decorate dragon body cake and cookies with buttercream icing (p. 124). Position leg cookies. Insert spikes for each section, supporting with mini marshmallows as needed. For knight cookies, outline bodies with tip 3 and full-strength gray icing; flow in with thinned icing (p. 120).

Let dry. Use full strength icing for details. Place cookies on parchment-covered boards. Outline and fill in skin tone area using tip 2; pat smooth. Outline and fill in helmet and mask using tip 3; pat smooth. Brush gray areas with Pearl Dust (p. 118). Use tip 2 to pipe dot eyes, outline mouth, eyebrows and waistline. Use tip 1 to pipe outline vents on helmet. Pipe plume feathers with tip 17. Let dry. Position knight cookies. Cake serves 12; each cookie serves 1.

*Combine Kelly Green with Leaf Green for dark green shown. Combine Leaf Green with Lemon Yellow for light green shown. Combine Lemon Yellow with Leaf Green for lime green shown.

▶ Jolly Roger Cookies

Cookie: 101 Cookie Cutters (flag), p. 173; Cookie Sheet, Cooling Grid, p. 171
Tip: 9, p. 134
Sugar Sheets! **Edible Decorating Paper/**
Tools: Black (1 sheet makes 8 treats), p. 144; Border Punch Set with Scallop Border Cutting Insert, Grass Border Cutting Insert, p. 145
Candy: Pirate Candy Pick Mold, p. 145; White Candy Melts Candy (12 oz. makes 40 treats), Garden Candy Color Set (black), p. 175
Recipes: Chocolate Buttercream Icing, Roll-Out Cookies, p. 128
Also: Parchment Triangles, p. 136; Spatula, p. 137; Fine Tip Primary Colors FoodWriter Edible Color Markers (black), p. 174

See p. 114 for a list of commonly used decorating items you may need.

In advance: Make candy skull and crossbones. Pipe black tinted candy into eye and nose areas of mold cavity; chill until firm. Pipe in skull and crossbones areas with white candy, leaving pick area open. Tap to settle; chill until firm.

Prepare and roll out cookie dough. Cut dough using flag cutter; cut off top of flag pole. Bake and cool cookies. Use black edible marker and reversed flag cutter to trace shape on shiny side of edible paper, extending edge opposite flag pole ¾ in. Cut out shape with scissors. Use punch with grass border insert to cut tattered edge. Ice flag area smooth. Position shape on cookie. Pipe tip 9 outline flag pole. Attach candy skull with buttercream. Each serves 1.

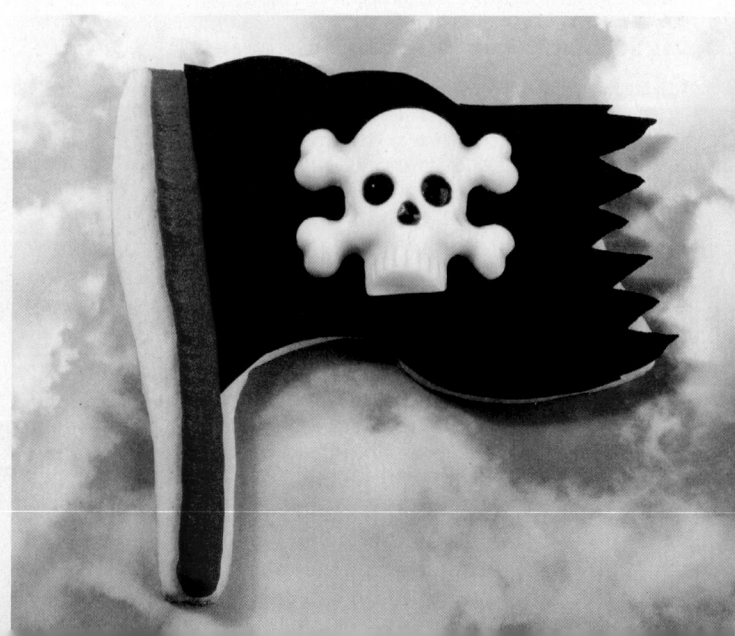

▶ Eyes of Surprise Cake

Pans: Crown, p. 164; Cooling Grid, p. 171
Tips: 1, 2A, 3, 4, 12, 21, p. 134
Colors:* Leaf Green, Lemon Yellow, Violet, Rose, Black, Red-Red, Christmas Red, p. 139
Sugar Sheets! **Edible Decorating Paper/Tools:** Purple, Red (1 each), p. 144; Rotary Cutter, p. 145
Recipe: Buttercream Icing, p. 128
Also: 2013 Pattern Book (nose, mouth, teeth, hand, foot), p. 143; Cake Boards, Fanci-Foil Wrap, p. 186; Spatula, p. 137; Disposable Decorating Bags, p. 136; Piping Gel, p. 141; Fine Tip Primary Colors FoodWriter Edible Color Markers (black), p. 174; pretzel rods, black shoestring licorice
See p. 114 for a list of commonly used decorating items you may need.

Bake and cool cake. Use knife to trim bottom crown detail level. Use pattern and toothpick to mark mouth. Ice area smooth in black; outline with tip 3. Use pattern to mark nose. Cover remainder of cake with tip 21 stars.

Pipe violet nose using tip 2A; pat smooth with finger dipped in cornstarch. Use pattern to mark teeth. Outline and pipe in with tip 4; pat smooth.

Pipe tip 2A mounds for eyes; pat smooth. Pipe tip 12 dot pupils; pat smooth. Pipe tip 1 veins on three eyes. Overpipe tip 21 green stars above eyes for eyelids. Cut 25 licorice strings, 1¾ in. long. Insert five into each eyelid for lashes.

Cut pretzel rods to make 3½ in. long arms and 4½ in. long legs. From purple edible paper, cut 2½ in. wide x 3½ in. long pieces for arms, 2½ in. wide x 4½ in. long pieces for legs with rotary cutter. Wrap around arms and legs, trimming as needed and securing with piping gel. Use black edible marker to trace hand and foot patterns on shiny side of purple and red edible paper; reverse patterns for second cut. Attach hands and feet with tip 3 dots of icing. Insert arms and legs. Serves 10.

* Combine Leaf Green with Lemon Yellow for green shown. Combine Violet with Rose for violet shown. Combine Red-Red with Christmas Red for red shown.

▼ Rattle Me Bones Cake

Pans: Dimensions 3-D Skull, p. 167; Bones Non-Stick Cookie Shapes, p. 220; Cooling Grid, p. 171
Tips: 3, 5, 14, p. 134
Colors:* Black, Christmas Red, Red-Red, Lemon Yellow, Golden Yellow, p. 139
Fondant: White Ready-To-Use Rolled Fondant (8 oz.), Gum-Tex, p. 148; 9 in. Fondant Roller, Roll-N-Cut Mat, p. 152; Round, Leaf Cut-Outs Fondant Cutters, p. 151; Brush Set, p. 153

Recipe: Buttercream Icing, p. 128
Also: 2013 Pattern Book (message scroll), p. 143; White Candy Melts Candy (12 oz. makes 8 treats), p. 175; 4 in. Lollipop Sticks, p. 178; 8 in. Cake Circles, Fanci-Foil Wrap, p. 186; Disposable Decorating Bags, p. 136; black marker, white paper
See p. 114 for a list of commonly used decorating items you may need.

In advance: Make candy bones. Pour melted white candy in cookie pan cavities. Tap to settle; chill until firm. **Also:** Make fondant bandana ties. Tint 6 oz. fondant red. Add ⅛ teaspoon Gum-Tex to ½ oz. of red fondant; reserve remainder. Roll out 1⁄16 in. thick. Cut two leaves with medium Cut-Out. Let dry on cornstarch-dusted board. Attach together with melted candy; let set.

Bake and cool skull cake. Pipe in tip 5 eyes, nose and mouth. Pat smooth with finger dipped in cornstarch. Cover cake with tip 14 stars. Pipe in tip 3 teeth. Pat smooth with finger dipped in cornstarch.

Make fondant trims. Tint 1 oz. fondant each black and yellow. Roll out black ⅛ in. thick. Cut eye patch with largest round Cut-Out; cut ½ in. from top for straight edge. Attach over eye with icing. Reroll black fondant 1⁄16 in. thick; cut a strip for eye patch string ⅛ in. x 8 in. Attach under eye patch with icing and wrap around skull. Roll out reserved red fondant ⅛ in. thick. Using 8 in. cake circle as guide, cut cap area. Attach to top of skull with icing; trim excess from back. Roll out yellow fondant 1⁄16 in. thick. Cut polka dots with medium round Cut-Out. Attach with damp brush. For knot, roll a ½ in. ball of red fondant. Attach bandana ties to knot with melted candy; let set. Attach to lollipop stick with melted candy; let set. Insert in cake.

Cut out scroll pattern from paper. Using marker, write name. Curl paper by loosely rolling up and back. Position message and candy bones around cake. Cake serves 12; each candy serves 1.

* Combine Christmas Red with Red-Red for red shown. Combine Lemon Yellow with Golden Yellow for yellow shown.

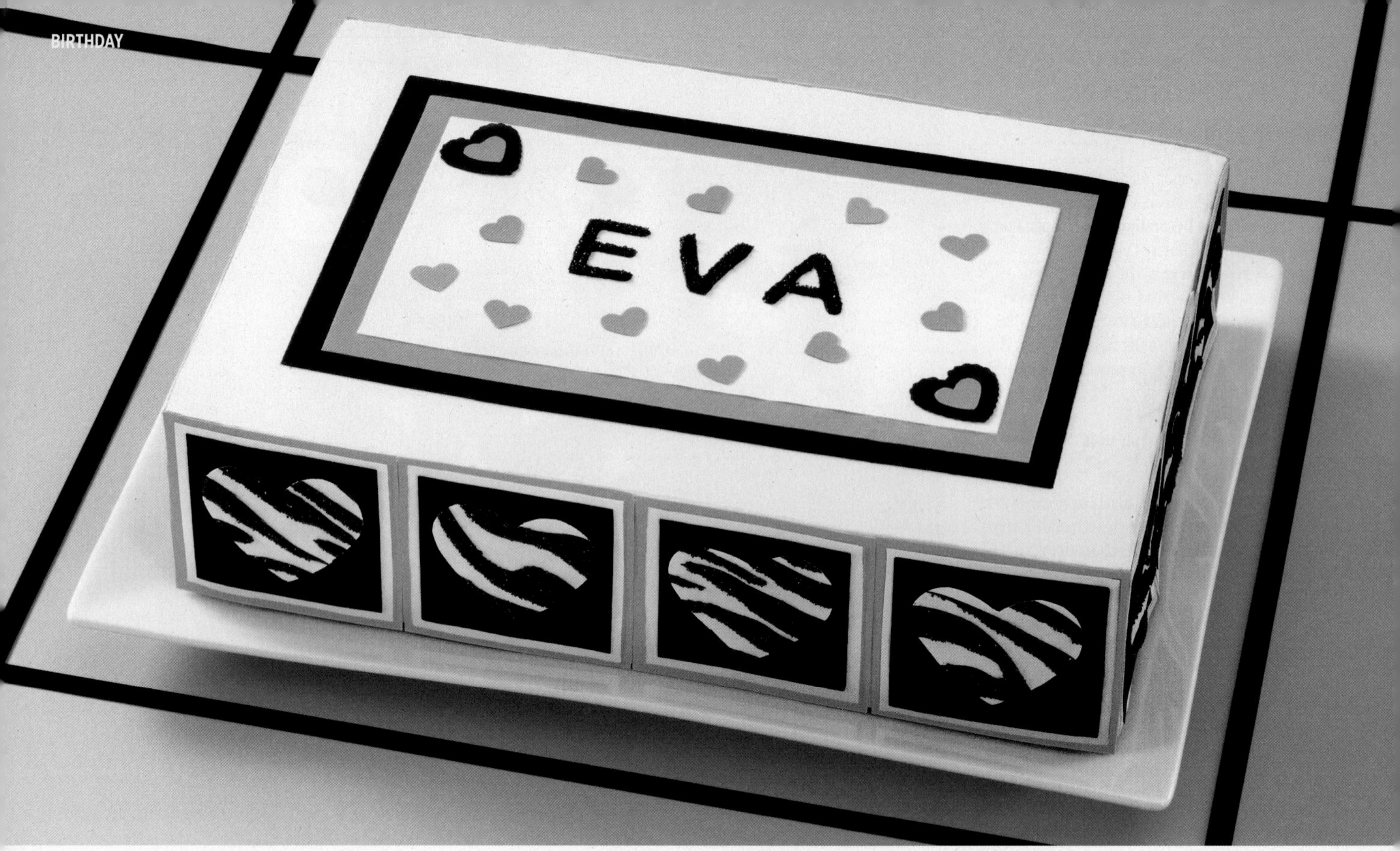

▼ Fancy Footwork Cookies

Cookie: Non-Stick Cookie Sheet, Cooling Grid, p. 169
Tips: 1, 2, p. 134
Colors:* Rose, Violet, Lemon Yellow, Golden Yellow, Ivory, Black, p. 139
Fondant: White Ready-To-Use Rolled Fondant (approximately ¼ oz. per treat), p. 148; 9 in. Fondant Roller, Roll-N-Cut Mat p. 152; Orchid Pink, Lilac Purple, Yellow, Silver, White Pearl Dust, Brush Set, p. 153; Macrame, Jewelry, Nature Designs Gum Paste & Fondant Molds, p. 150
Recipes: Color Flow Icing, Roll-Out Cookies, p. 128
Also: 3-Pc. Princess Metal Cutter Set, p. 202; White Sugar Pearls, p. 157; Color Flow Mix, p. 141; Cake Boards, p. 186; Disposable Decorating Bags, p. 136; Parchment Paper, p. 158
See p. 114 for a list of commonly used decorating items you may need.

1 to 2 days in advance: Make cookies. Prepare and roll out dough. Cut cookies using slipper cutter from set. Bake and cool cookies. Make icing; tint various colors, reserve some white. Outline shoe area and separate oval inset for shoe opening using tip 2 and tinted full-strength icing; flow in shoe area with thinned tinted icing (p. 120). Let dry. Flow in oval inset with thinned icing in a lighter shade. Let dry.

Use tip 2 and full-strength icing to pipe in straps on silver shoe and tip 1 to pipe outline straps on yellow shoe. Tint portions of fondant to match shoe colors. For violet, roll out fondant ⅛ in. thick. Use cutter as a guide to cut triangle bow shapes with knife. Attach with damp brush. Use tinted fondant and silicone molds to mold assorted trims. Attach trims with icing; brush shoe areas with Pearl Dust (use white for black and ivory shoes, silver for white shoe, matching colors for others). Let dry. Each serves 1.

* Combine Lemon Yellow with Golden Yellow for yellow shown.

▲ Passion for Fashion Cake

Pans: 9 in. x 13 in. x 2 in. Sheet, p. 161; Cooling Grid, p. 171
***Sugar Sheets!* Edible Decorating Paper/Tools:** Bright Pink (4), Black (3), White (3), Zebra (2), p. 144; Punch Set with Oval Cutting Insert, Layered Hearts Cutting Insert Set, Slide-N-Cut Edge Cutter, p. 144; 26-Pc. Classic Alphabet Cake Stamp Set, Black Dab-N-Color Edible Color, p. 145
Recipe: Buttercream Icing, p. 128
Also: Black Sugar, p. 156; Piping Gel, p. 141; Disposable Decorating Bags, p. 136; Decorator Brush Set, p. 178; Cake Boards, Fanci-Foil Wrap, p. 186
See p. 114 for a list of commonly used decorating items you may need.

Bake and cool 2-layer cake (bake two 1½ in. layers for a 3 in. high cake). Ice cake smooth. Cut edible paper rectangles for sides using edge cutter as follows: For long front and back, cut eight each, 3¼ in. wide x 3⅛ in. high in bright pink, 3 in. wide x 2¾ in. high in white and 2¾ in. wide x 2½ in. high in black. For shorter sides, cut six each, 3 in. wide x 3⅛ in. high in bright pink, 2¾ in. wide x 2¾ in. high in white and 2½ in. wide x 2½ in. high in black. Use piping gel to attach row of pink, then smaller white panels then smallest black panels (trimming as needed). Cut 14 hearts from zebra edible paper using punch with largest heart insert. Paint black areas with piping gel; sprinkle on black sugar. Attach hearts to panels.

Use edge cutter to cut edible paper rectangles for cake top. Cut and attach in order using piping gel: 10⅝ in. wide x 6¾ in. high in black; 9⅞ in. wide x 5⅞ in. high in bright pink; 9 in. wide x 5 in. high in white.

Use alphabet stamps and black edible color to stamp name; immediately sprinkle with black sugar. Use punch and inserts to cut two medium black hearts and 13 small pink hearts. Attach with piping gel to cake. Serves 36.

▼ Birthday in Bronze Cake

Pans: 4-Pc. Oval Set (smallest and second smallest used) p. 160; Cooling Grid, p. 171
Fondant/Gum Paste: Macrame Designs Gum Paste & Fondant Mold, p. 150; Bronze, White Pearl Dust, Brush Set, p. 153
Recipe: Chocolate Buttercream Icing, p. 128
Also: White (4 oz.), Light Cocoa (15 oz.) Candy Melts Candy, p. 175; Disposable Decorating Bags, p. 136; Cake Boards, Fanci-Foil Wrap, p. 186; Plastic Dowel Rods, p. 194; Spatula, p. 137

See p. 114 for a list of commonly used decorating items you may need.

In advance: Make candy side panels. For ivory panels, add a little melted light cocoa candy to white; use light cocoa for dark panels. Use piping method (p. 123), to fill lattice border cavity of mold. Tap to settle; chill until firm. Make 11 panels in each color. Reserve remaining ivory candy for message. **Also:** Make cake top candy plaque (p. 123). Pour 10 oz. of melted light cocoa candy into smallest oval pan. Tap to settle; chill until firm. Pipe message with reserved ivory candy and bead border with light cocoa candy. Chill until firm. Brush light cocoa panels and bead border with bronze Pearl Dust, ivory panels with white Pearl Dust.

Bake and cool 2-layer cake using second smallest pan. Ice smooth. Trim ivory panels to 4 in. high, light cocoa panels to 4½ in. high. Attach alternating panels to cake sides with icing. Cut two dowel rods to 6 in. long; cut one end at a slight angle. Insert dowel rods, angled ends up. Position candy plaque. Serves 20.

▲ Your Cue To Celebrate! Cake

Pans: 9 in. x 13 in. x 2 in. Sheet, p. 161; Cooling Grid, p. 171
Tips: 2A, 9, p. 134
Colors:* Ivory, Brown, p. 139
Sugar Sheets! **Edible Decorating Paper/ Tools:** Bright Green (2), Black (1), p. 144; Slide-N-Cut Edge Cutter, p. 145
Fondant/Gum Paste: Chocolate (24 oz.), White (5 oz.) Ready-To-Use Rolled Fondant, Gum-Tex, p. 148; 20 in. Fondant Roller, Roll-N-Cut Mat, p. 152; Fine Tip Primary and Neon Colors FoodWriter Edible Color Markers, Decorative Press Set, Brush Set, p. 153
Recipe: Buttercream Icing, p. 128
Also: Cake Boards, Fanci-Foil Wrap, p. 186; Disposable Decorating Bags, p. 136; Spatula, p. 137; Piping Gel, p. 141

See p. 114 for a list of commonly used decorating items you may need.

2 days in advance: Make cue stick and balls. Add 1 teaspoon Gum-Tex to white fondant. Tint 1 oz. ivory; knead in ½ teaspoon of shortening to soften. Use decorative press with circle insert to press a 10 in. rope. Taper one end to ⅛ in. diameter; let dry on cornstarch-dusted board. Roll 14 white balls, ⅞ in. diameter. Let dry. Set one ball aside as cue ball. On remaining balls, trace a circle around narrow end of tip 2A, using edible markers in desired colors. Color in areas outside circle, making striped and solid balls. Draw numbers with black edible marker; color in details on cue stick.

Bake and cool 1-layer cake; ice smooth. Use edge cutter to cut two rectangles, 6½ in. x 9 in. from bright green edible paper. Position on cake top, aligning seams at center. For cushions, roll out chocolate fondant ¼ in. thick; cut two strips, 3 in. x 22 in. Attach to cake sides with piping gel, folding 1 in. over cake top. Use wide end of tip 2A to cut pockets; use same tip to cut six circles from black edible paper. Attach to pockets with piping gel. Use edge cutter to cut 12 bright green strips, ¼ in. x 7 in. Attach to side and top of cushions with piping gel, trimming as needed. Roll out white fondant ⅟₁₆ in. thick. Use narrow end of tip 9 to cut cue ball mark on cake top. Attach with piping gel. Draw dot with black edible marker. Position balls and cue stick. Serves 18.

*Combine Ivory with Brown for ivory shown.

START THE SHOW!

Kids' favorite characters are here, and your birthday treats tell a story they'll love! It's *Elmo*, making your one year old's big day a smash. Or *Thomas*, arriving at the celebration station with a smokestack salute to the birthday boy or girl. Big screen heroes make the scene as well, with *Spider-Man* spanning the skyline and *Darth Vader*™ sending a forceful Happy Birthday greeting! What better birthday party could there be?

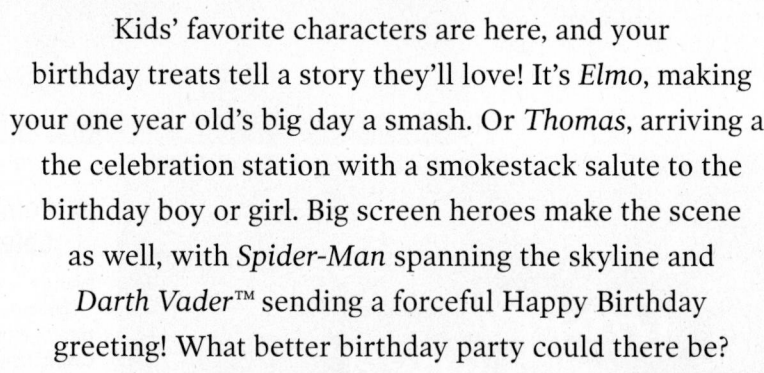

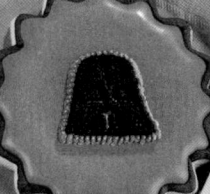

Darth Vader™ Birthday Cake!

Pans: *Darth Vader™*, p. 212; 18 in. x 3 in. Half Round, p. 163
Tips: 2, 3, 4, 6, 13, 16, p. 134
Colors:* Black, Royal Blue, Sky Blue, Christmas Red, Red-Red, p. 139
Fondant: White (140 oz.), Red (16 oz.) Ready-To-Use Rolled Fondant, p. 148; 20 in. Fondant Roller, 20 in. Fondant Roller Guide Rings, Roll-N-Cut Mat, Fondant Smoother, p. 152; Brush Set, p. 153
Recipes: Buttercream Icing, p. 128; Thinned Fondant Adhesive, p. 127
Also: 2013 Pattern Book (*Darth Vader* color guide), p. 143; 101 Cookie Cutters (letters), p. 173; Spatula, p. 137; Disposable Decorating Bags, p. 136; Cake Boards, Fanci-Foil Wrap, p. 186; Dowel Rods, p. 194; 20 in. diameter plywood or foamcore board (½ in. thick)
See p. 114 for a list of commonly used decorating items you may need.

Bake and cool *Darth Vader* and half round cakes (bake four 2 in. high layers, for a 4 in. high round cake). Position round cake on foil-wrapped base board; prepare and cover with 140 oz. fondant tinted navy blue (p. 119). Prepare for stacked construction (p. 120).

Decorate *Darth Vader* cake. Ice inside helmet smooth. Use tip 3 to outline and pipe in eyes, eye details and inside chin. Pat smooth with finger dipped in cornstarch. Use tip 6 to pipe outlines on mouth in black, overpipe with tip 6 outlines in light blue. Use tip 4 to pipe white helmet details and blue eyebrows. Follow pattern to cover remainder of cake with tip 16 stars and tip 13 stars for tight areas in colors shown. Position on round cake.

For message, roll out red fondant ⅛ in. thick. Cut out message with desired cutters from set. Attach letters to cake with damp brush. For bottom border, roll ¾ in. red fondant balls; position on base board, securing to cake side with thinned fondant adhesive. Pipe tip 2 swirls on balls. Serves 122.

Star Wars™ Icing Cookies

Cookie: 101 Cookie Cutters (crinkle circle), p. 173; Cookie Sheet, Cooling Grid, p. 171
Tip: 4, p. 134
Colors:* Royal Blue, Black, Christmas Red, Red-Red, p. 139
Recipes: Color Flow Icing, Roll-Out Cookies, p. 128
Also: *Star Wars™* Icing Decorations, p. 212; Color Flow Mix, p. 141; Parchment Triangles, p. 139
See p. 114 for a list of commonly used decorating items you may need.

Prepare and roll out dough. Cut cookies using crinkle circle cutter. Bake and cool cookies.

Use tip 4 and full-strength Color Flow to outline cookies; let set. Flow in with thinned icing (p. 120). Let dry. Attach icing decorations with full-strength icing. Each serves 1.

▲ Star Wars™ Cupcake Display

Pans: Standard Muffin, p. 158; Cooling Grid, p. 171
Colors:* Royal Blue, Black, p. 139
Recipe: Buttercream Icing, p. 128
Also: 13-Count Standard Cupcakes-N-More Dessert Stand, p. 183; Spatula, p. 137; White Nonpareils, p. 156; *Star Wars™* Candle, Toppers (2 pkgs.), Standard Baking Cups, p. 212
See p. 114 for a list of commonly used decorating items you may need.

Bake and cool cupcakes. Ice tops smooth. Sprinkle with nonpareils. Insert toppers and candle. Position cupcakes on stand. Each serves 1.

▶ Buzz's Blastoff Cake

Pans: Disney • *Pixar Toy Story*, p. 217; Cooling Grid, p. 171
Tips: 1, 1A, 3, 13, 16, p. 134
Colors:* Leaf Green, Violet, Royal Blue, Black, Brown, Juniper Green, Christmas Red, Red-Red, Copper, Lemon Yellow, Orange, Golden Yellow, p. 139
Fondant: White Ready-To-Use Rolled Fondant (72 oz.), Gum-Tex, p. 148; 9 in., 20 in. Fondant Rollers, Roll-N-Cut Mat, Fondant Smoother, p. 152; Brush Set, p. 153
Recipes: Buttercream Icing, p. 128; favorite crisped rice cereal treats
Also: 2013 Pattern Book (rocket, *BUZZ* letters), p. 143; Parchment Paper, p. 136; Cake Board, Fanci-Foil Wrap, p. 186; Piping Gel, p. 141; 17 in. x 19 in. plywood or foamcore board (½ in. thick)
See p. 114 for a list of commonly used decorating items you may need.

In advance: Make clouds (p. 124).

Also: Prepare base board. Tint 51 oz. fondant blue. Prepare and cover base board with 48 oz. blue fondant (p. 120); reserve remainder. **And:** Make rocket. Tint reserved blue darker; roll out dark blue and 3 oz. white fondant ⅛ in. thick. Use pattern to cut out rocket. Use pattern and toothpick to mark window area on rocket and white fondant. Cut out window area from rocket; inlay with white window area. For window panes, cut ¼ in. wide strips from blue fondant. Attach to windows with damp brush. Tint a ½ in. ball of fondant red. Roll out ⅛ in. thick. Cut two dot lights with narrow end of tip 1A. Attach to rocket with damp brush. Let dry on cornstarch-dusted surface. **And:** Make letters. Tint 3 oz. fondant yellow; knead in ⅛ teaspoon Gum-Tex. Roll out ⅛ in. thick. Use pattern to cut out letters. Let dry on cornstarch-dusted surface.

Bake and cool cake. Ice sides smooth. Pipe in eyes and teeth with tip 3; smooth with finger dipped in cornstarch. Pipe in irises and pipe dot pupils with tip 1; pat smooth. Outline remaining details with tip 3. Use tip 3 to pipe in buttons, patches and bolts; pat smooth. Cover suit, headpiece, face and eyebrows with tip 16 stars, fill in smaller areas with tip 13 stars. Position cake and rocket on base board. Insert base of cake into clouds. Attach letters with icing. Cake serves 12; treats serve 8.

©Disney · Pixar

▼ *Lightning's* **Victory Lap Cake**

Pans: *Disney • Pixar Cars*, p. 216; Cooling Grid, p. 171
Tips: 3, 5, 16, p. 134
Colors:* Black, Golden Yellow, Royal Blue, No-Taste Red, Brown, Orange, p. 139
Fondant: White Ready-To-Use Rolled Fondant (80 oz.), p. 148; 9 in., 20 in. Fondant Rollers, 20 in. Fondant Roller Guide Rings, Roll-N-Cut Mat, p. 152; Fine Tip Primary Colors FoodWriter Edible Color Markers (black), Brush Set, p. 153
Recipe: Buttercream Icing, p. 128
Also: 2013 Pattern Book (racing flag), p. 143; 101 Cookie Cutters (letters), p. 173; Black Dab-N-Color Edible Color, p. 146; 13 in. x 19 in. Cake Boards, Fanci-Foil Wrap, p. 186; 24 in. x 15 in. plywood or foamcore board (½ in. thick)
See p. 114 for a list of commonly used decorating items you may need.

1 day in advance: Make checkered flags. Roll out 32 oz. white fondant 1/16 in. thick. Cut flags with poles using pattern; mark open flagpole areas with toothpick. Reserve remaining fondant. Let flags dry overnight on cornstarch-dusted board. When flags are dry, use ruler and black edible marker to mark ¾ in. squares. Paint alternating squares with black edible color. Let dry. To add dimension to flagpoles, roll out white fondant ⅛ in. thick. Cut flagpoles using pattern; attach to flagpole area with damp brush. Reserve remaining fondant.

Also: Make letters. Tint 2 oz reserved fondant yellow (or additional if more letters are needed). Roll out ⅛ in. thick. Cut desired letters using cutters from set. Let dry overnight on cornstarch-dusted board. **And:** Prepare and cover base board with 48 oz. fondant tinted light blue (p. 120).

Bake and cool cake. Ice cake sides, background areas, front windshield, mouth, side windows, small lightning bolts, headlights and wheel wells smooth. Pipe tip 3 outlines on car, windows, mouth, headlights, hood, lightning bolts, number and tires. Pipe tip 3 dot eyes and rivets on hood; smooth with finger dipped in cornstarch. Pipe tip 16 lines on tires. Pipe tip 3 dot pupils; smooth. Cover car, lightning bolt and number with tip 16 stars. Pipe tip 3 outline muffler. Pipe tip 5 bead bottom border.

Position flags on base board. Position cake and letters. Serves 12.

*Combine Brown with No-Taste Red for dark red shown.

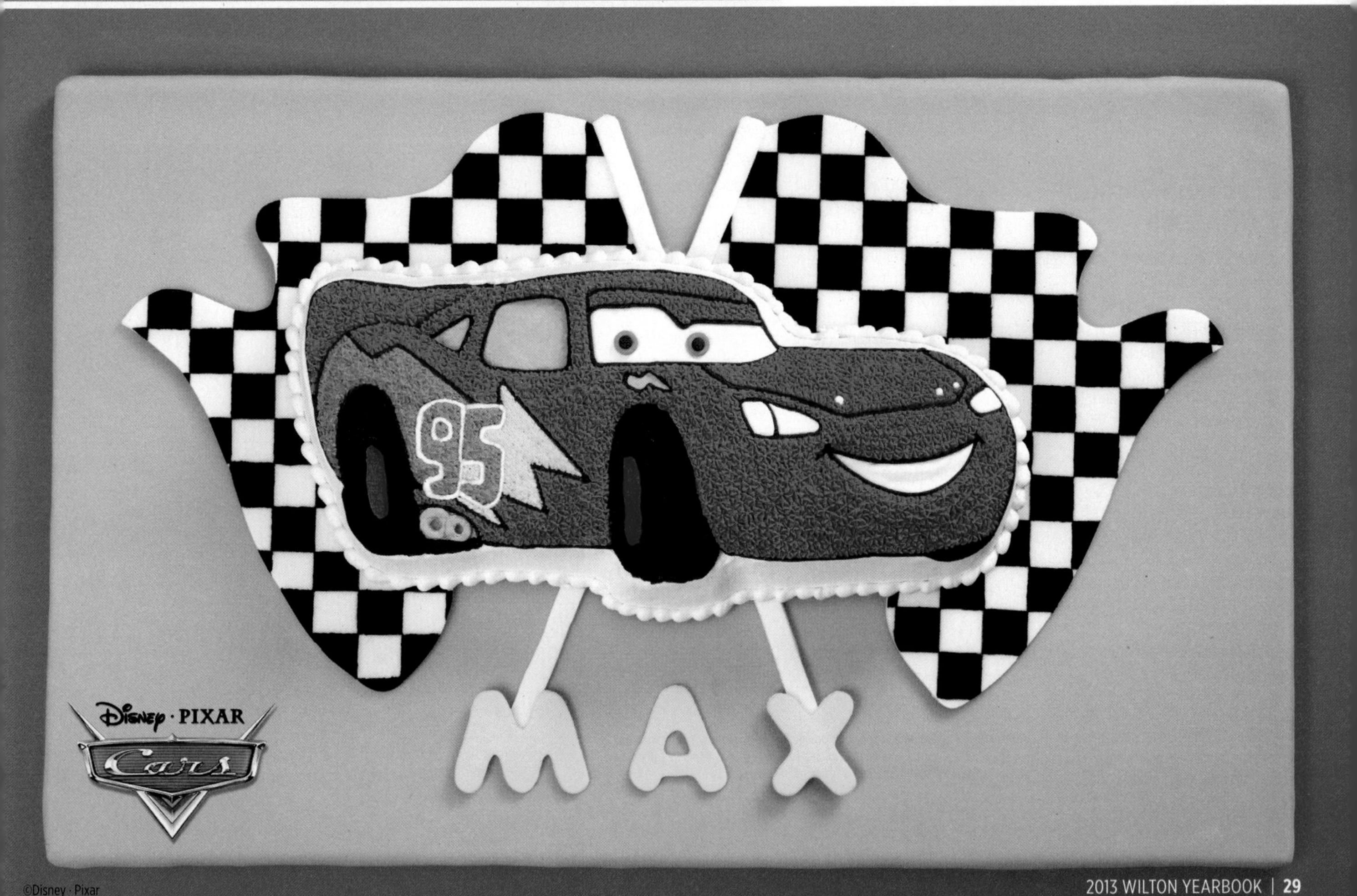

©Disney · Pixar

▼ **Glam Big Night Cookies**

▼ Glam Big Night Cookies

Cookie: From The Heart Nesting Metal Cutter Set, p. 236; Heart Nesting Plastic Cutter Set, p. 235; Cookie Sheet, Cooling Grid, p. 171

Tip: 5, p. 134

Color: Rose, p. 139

Recipes: Royal Icing, Roll-Out Cookies, p. 128

Also: Disposable Decorating Bags, p. 136; *Barbie* Icing Decorations, p. 213; Pink Sugar Pearls, p. 157; Pink Colored Sugar, p. 156; Piping Gel, Meringue Powder, p. 141; Brush Set, p. 153

See p. 114 for a list of commonly used decorating items you may need.

Prepare and roll out dough. Cut cookies using second smallest cutter from metal set and third smallest cutter from plastic set. Bake and cool cookies.

Ice cookie smooth with dark rose icing. Outline cookie with tip 5 using light rose icing; use heavy pressure for large heart. Pat smooth with finger dipped in cornstarch. Immediately attach pink Sugar Pearls. Let dry. Brush dark pink section with piping gel; sprinkle with pink sugar. Attach icing decoration with tip 5 dots of icing. Each serves 1.

▲ Fabulous Birthday Wish Cake

Pans: *Barbie* (with facemaker), p. 213; 18 in. x 3 in. Half Round, p. 163

Tips: 3, 16, 17, 22, 127D, p. 134-135

Colors:* Rose, Burgundy, Lemon Yellow, Golden Yellow, Copper, Orange, p. 139

Fondant: White Ready-To-Use Rolled Fondant (140 oz.), p. 148; 20 in. Fondant Roller, 20 in. Fondant Roller Guide Rings, Roll-N-Cut Mat, Fondant Smoother, p. 152; Heart Cut-Outs Fondant Cutters, p. 151; Brush Set, p. 153

Recipe: Buttercream Icing, p. 128

Also: 101 Cookie Cutters (letters), p. 173; Pink Sparkling Sugar, Lavender Colored Sugar, p. 156; Cake Boards, Fanci-Foil Wrap, p. 186; Dowel Rods, p. 194; Piping Gel, p. 141; Disposable Decorating Bags, p. 136; 22 in. diameter plywood or foamcore board (½ in. thick)

See p. 114 for a list of commonly used decorating items you may need.

Bake and cool *Barbie* cake and half round cakes (bake four 2 in. high layers for a 4 in. high cake). Tint 140 oz. fondant light rose; prepare and cover round cake (p. 119); reserve any remaining fondant. Prepare for stacked construction (p. 120).

Position *Barbie* cake on foil-wrapped board. Use tip 3 to outline v-neck on shirt. Fill in shirt with tip 16 stars; sprinkle with pink sparkling sugar, then lightly with lavender colored sugar. Fill in head and neck with tip 16 stars. Position facemaker. Pipe tip 17 hair. Stack cakes.

Make hearts and letters. Tint remaining fondant darker rose. Roll out ¼ in. thick. Cut desired letters with cookie cutters. Cut hearts with small, medium and large Cut-Outs. Brush with piping gel; sprinkle with sparkling and colored sugar. Attach to cake top with damp brush. For earrings, shape two white fondant logs, ⅛ in. x ⅝ in. long. For each earring, shape one large teardrop ½ in. long and four small teardrops from dark rose fondant. Attach large teardrop to end of white log and small teardrops to sides with damp brush. Attach earrings to cake with dots of icing.

On round cake, pipe tip 22 shell bottom border. Cover shells with a row of tip 127D ruffles. Add two more rows of ruffles above the first, ½ in. apart. Pipe tip 3 dots on cake side. Serves 122.

*Combine Copper with Orange for skin tone shown. Combine Rose with Burgundy for dark and light rose shown. Combine Lemon Yellow with Golden Yellow for yellow shown.

barbie.com®
©2012 Mattel, Inc.
All Rights Reserved.

◄ *Hello Kitty*
Balloon Birthday Cake

Pans: *Hello Kitty*, p. 218; Cookie Sheet, Cooling Grid, p. 171
Tips: 3, 13, 16, p. 134
Colors:* Rose, Royal Blue, No-Taste Red, Lemon Yellow, Golden Yellow, Black, p. 139
Fondant: White Ready-To-Use Rolled Fondant (86 oz.), p. 148; 20 in. Fondant Roller, 20 in. Fondant Roller Guide Rings, Roll-N-Cut Mat, Fondant Smoother, p. 152; Brush Set, p. 153
Recipes: Buttercream, Royal Icings, Roll-Out Cookies, p. 128
Also: 2013 Pattern Book (Body/Dress, Balloon, Arm), p. 143; 101 Cookie Cutters (letters), p. 173; Meringue Powder, Piping Gel, p. 141; Cake Boards, Circles, Fanci-Foil Wrap, p. 186; 18 in. x 24 in. foamcore board (½ in. thick), black shoestring licorice
See p. 114 for a list of commonly used decorating items you may need.

In advance: Make cookies. Prepare and roll out dough. Use patterns to cut one balloon, one arm and two body shapes as follows: Cut one full-size body shape. Cut a second shape following dotted dress line. Bake and cool cookies. Cover balloon with thinned royal icing tinted rose (p. 123). Let dry overnight. **Also:** Prepare and cover base board with 80 oz. fondant tinted blue (p. 120). Reserve 6 oz. white fondant for name.

Bake and cool Hello Kitty cake. Use tip 3 to outline bow and pipe whiskers. Use tip 3 to outline and fill in eyes, nose and center of bow loops; pat smooth with finger dipped in cornstarch. Cover head and bow with tip 16 stars.

Position cake on prepared board. Stack body cookies with buttercream icing, position on board. Decorate body with tip 3 outline and tip 13 stars. Position arm cookie. Mark stripes and shirt details with toothpick. Outline using tip 3. Cover arm with tip 13 stars.

Position balloon cookie. Position licorice string between balloon and hand. Tint reserved white fondant rose; roll out ⅛ in. thick. Cut name using letters from set. Attach using damp brush. Cake serves 12; each cookie serves 1.

*Combine Lemon Yellow with Golden Yellow for yellow shown.

▶ *Hello Kitty* **Cute Combo Cupcakes**

Pans: Standard Muffin, p. 162; Cookie Sheet, Cooling Grid, p. 171
Tip: 7, p. 134
Colors: No-Taste Red, Rose, p. 139
Recipes: Buttercream, Royal Icings, Roll-Out Cookies, p. 128
Also: *Hello Kitty* Standard Baking Cups, Icing Decorations, p. 218; 6-Pc. Star Nesting Plastic Cutter Set, p. 173; Disposable Decorating Bags, p. 136; Meringue Powder, p. 141
See p. 114 for a list of commonly used decorating items you may need.

1 day in advance: Make cookies. Prepare and roll out dough. Cut cookies using third smallest star cutter. Bake and cool cookies. Outline cookie with tip 7 and full-strength royal icing; let set. Flow in with thinned royal icing; let dry overnight. Attach icing decorations with full-strength royal icing.

Bake and cool cupcakes. Ice smooth with buttercream. Position cookie on cupcake, supporting with dots of buttercream as needed. Each serves 1.

©Disney

▼ Jolly *Mickey Mouse* Candy Ship

Candy: Light Cocoa Candy Melts Candy (1 pk. makes 6 treats), p. 175; Dessert Shells Candy Mold, p. 176; 6 in. Lollipop Sticks, p. 178

Recipe: Favorite crisped rice cereal treats

Also: 2013 Pattern Book (pirate flag), p. 128; *Mickey Mouse* Fun Pix, p. 215; candy-coated chocolates, pretzel sticks, hole punch

See p. 114 for a list of commonly used decorating items you may need.

Follow mold instructions to make candy shell boat. Chill until firm.

Prepare cereal treat mixture; press treats into top half of mold. Unmold and let cool. Position treats in candy shell and seal top with melted candy. Let set.

Copy pattern and cut out flag; punch holes at top and bottom center, ⅛ in. from edge. Cut lollipop stick to 5 in. Insert stick through holes in flag. Insert flag, pretzel stick and *Mickey* pick into treat. Cover top with candy-covered chocolates. Each serves 1.

▲ Matey *Mickey Mouse* Cake

Pans: *Mickey Mouse*, p. 215; Cooling Grid, p. 171

Tips: 1A, 3, 5, 16, p. 134

Colors:* Lemon Yellow, Golden Yellow, Copper, Ivory, Creamy Peach, Red-Red, Christmas Red, Black, p. 139

Fondant: White (48 oz.), Chocolate (24 oz.) Ready-To-Use Rolled Fondant, Gum-Tex, p. 148; 10-Pc. Gum Paste/Fondant Tool Set, 9 in. Fondant Roller, Roll-N-Cut Mat, Fondant Smoother, p. 152; Leaf Cut-Outs Fondant Cutters, p. 151; Brown Color Dust, Pure Lemon Extract, Brush Set, p. 153

Also: 101 Cookie Cutters (letters), p. 173; Spatula, p. 137; Disposable Decorating Bags, p. 136; Fanci-Foil Wrap, p. 186; Piping Gel, p. 141; 20 in. x 16 in. plywood or foamcore board (¼ in. thick)

See p. 114 for a list of commonly used decorating items you may need.

In advance: Make base board. Wrap board with foil. Knead 24 oz. chocolate fondant into 36 oz. white fondant for light brown shade shown. Roll out ¼ in. thick. Cut and decorate planks one at a time. Cut three strips, 5⅜ in. x 20 in. Cut waves, notches and slits in edges to create a worn look. Use thin veining tool to score woodgrain lines and knots. Use ball tool to indent knots and soften edges. Paint edges and details with brown Color Dust/lemon extract mixture (p. 118). Attach planks to base board using piping gel.

Bake and cool *Mickey* cake. Position on board. Use tip 3 to outline facial features and pipe in eyes, mouth, pupils and tongue; pat smooth with finger dipped in cornstarch. Cover head with tip 16 stars. Pipe tip 3 dot eye and nose highlights.

For bandana, tint 5 oz. fondant each red and yellow. Roll out ⅛ in. thick. Use pan as a guide to cut bandana; attach to cake with damp brush. Roll a ¾ in. red ball for knot; cut two leaves using medium Cut-Out for tails. Cut and attach polka dots using wide end of tip 1A. Attach to bandana, knot and tails with damp brush, trimming as needed. Attach knot and tails to bandana with damp brush. Cut desired letters using cutters from set. For exclamation point, cut an "L"; trim off bottom and taper end. Cut dot using wide end of tip 3. Attach letters to board with damp brush. Serves 12.

*Combine Copper with Ivory for skin tone shown. Combine Lemon Yellow with Golden Yellow for yellow fondant shown. Combine Christmas Red with Red-Red for red fondant shown.

©Disney

Minnie Mouse Bow-tique

©Disney

◀ Minnie Mouse Clutch Mini Cakes

Pans: 9 in. x 13 in. x 2 in. Sheet, p. 161; Cooling Grid, p. 171
Color: Rose, p. 139
***Sugar Sheets!* Edible Decorating Paper/Tools:** Zebra (1 sheet makes 2 treats), p. 144; Dab-N-Hold Edible Adhesive, p. 145
Fondant: White Ready-to-Use Rolled Fondant (3½ oz. per treat), Gum-Tex, p. 148; Baroque Designs Gum Paste and Fondant Mold, p. 150; 9 in. Fondant Roller, Roll-N-Cut Mat, Fondant Smoother, p. 152; Brush Set, p. 153
Recipe: Thinned Fondant Adhesive, p. 127
Also: 4-Pc. Circles Nesting Metal Cutter Set, p. 172; Spatula, p. 137; Piping Gel, p. 141; Cake Boards, Fanci-Foil Wrap, p. 186; *Minnie* Icing Decorations, p. 215; Cake Leveler, p. 158
See p. 114 for a list of commonly used decorating items you may need.

In advance: Make handle. Knead ¼ teaspoon Gum-Tex into ½ oz. white fondant. Use baroque mold and fondant to make two large pearl chains for each treat. Cut a group of six pearls from each string; attach back to back using damp brush. Shape handle using smallest circle cutter as a guide. Let dry on cornstarch-dusted board.

Bake and cool sheet cake; level to 1½ in. high. Cut purse using second largest circle cutter; trim off 1½ in. from bottom for straight edge. Ice smooth. Use same cutter as a guide to cut two circles for each treat from zebra edible paper. Trim off 1½ in. at bottom and attach to front and back of treat using edible adhesive.

Tint 3½ oz. fondant rose. Roll out ⅛ in. thick. Cut strip, 1½ in. x 7½ in. Attach to top of purse using piping gel. Use small circle cutter to cut two flaps; use second largest circle cutter to trim off ⅝ in. from flaps for a curved top edge. Attach to front and back using piping gel. Attach icing decoration and handle with thinned fondant adhesive. Each serves 1.

▶ Minnie Mouse's Tower of Gifts Cake

Pans: *Mickey Mouse,* p. 215; Cooling Grid, p. 171
Tips: 1A, 2A, 3, 12, 16, p. 134
Colors: * Rose, Black, Creamy Peach, Copper, Ivory, Violet, p. 139
***Sugar Sheets!* Edible Decorating Paper**
Tools: Zebra (1), p. 144
Fondant: White Ready-To-Use Rolled Fondant (165 oz.), Ready-To-Use Gum Paste (6 oz.) p. 148; 9 in. Fondant Roller, Roll-N-Cut Mat, Fondant Smoother, 10-Pc. Gum Paste/Fondant Tool Set, Fondant Trimmer, p. 152; Heart Cut-Outs Fondant Cutters, p. 151; Brush Set, Fine Tip Primary Colors FoodWriter Edible Color Markers (black), p. 153
Recipe: Buttercream Icing, p. 128
Also: 2013 Pattern Book (*Minnie's* bow, gift tag, gifts, package bow, hands, sleeve), p. 128; Cake Board, Fanci-Foil Wrap, p. 186; Pink Color Mist Food Color Spray, p. 139; Piping Gel, p. 141; 20 in. x 28 in. plywood or foamcore board (½ in. thick)
See p. 114 for a list of commonly used decorating items you may need.

3 days in advance: Make *Minnie's* bow. Tint 6 oz. gum paste rose; roll out ⅛ in. thick. Using pattern and knife, cut out one bottom and two top sections. Use veining tool to score lines. Let dry on cornstarch-dusted board overnight. Attach top sections to bottom with damp brush. Roll out white gum paste 1/16 in. thick. Use wide end of tip 2A to cut eight circles; attach to bow with damp brush, trimming as needed. For knot, roll a ½ in. x 2 in. rose log. Taper ends and attach with damp brush. Let dry.

Also: Prepare base board. Tint 120 oz. fondant violet; cover base board (p. 120).

Bake and cool cake. Use tip 3 to outline facial features and pipe in eyes, mouth, pupils and tongue; pat smooth with finger dipped in cornstarch. Cover head with tip 16 stars. Pipe tip 3 dot eye and nose highlights, outline eyelashes.

Tint 5 oz. fondant light rose, 7 oz. medium rose and 3 oz. dark rose. Roll out white and rose fondant ⅛ in. thick. Use patterns to cut gifts, gift tag, top and bottom lids, and gift bow. For middle lid, cut a strip, 2 in. x 8 in. from zebra edible paper. Spray strip with pink food color spray; let dry. For stripes, cut fondant strips, ½ in. x 5 in. or 6 in. For bottom gift, cut polka dots from white fondant using wide end of tips 1A, 2A and 12. For top gift, cut a ribbon strip 1 in. x 5 in. in dark pink fondant. Attach gifts, fondant lids and details to base board with damp brush. Attach middle lid with piping gel. Reserve remaining medium rose fondant.

Position cake. Use pattern to shape top hand from 5½ oz. of white fondant. Cut slits for fingers and shape. Position on base board. Cover with tip 16 stars. Use pattern to shape arm from 10 oz. white fondant and bottom hand from 7 oz. white fondant. Cut and shape fingers as above. Position on base board. Outline cuff with tip 3. Cover arm and hand with tip 16 stars. Roll out reserved medium rose fondant ⅛ in. thick. Cut hearts using large and medium Cut-Outs. Attach to base board with damp brush.

Write name on tag with black edible marker. Cut hole with narrow end of tip 12. For string, cut a strip, ¼ in. x 1¾ in., from dark pink fondant. Attach string and tag with damp brush. Serves 12.

*Combine Copper with Ivory for skin tone shown. Combine Violet with Rose for violet shown.

©Disney

▼ Little Ones Love *Elmo!* Cupcakes

Pans: Standard Muffin, p. 162; Cooling Grid, p. 171
Colors:* No-Taste Red, Lemon Yellow, Leaf Green, p. 139
Fondant: White Ready-To-Use Rolled Fondant (¾ oz. per treat), p. 148; Brush Set, p. 153
Recipe: Buttercream Icing, p. 128
Also: *Elmo* Standard Baking Cups, Icing Decorations, p. 219; 10-Pack Candy Mold Set (Numbers), p. 178; Spatula, p. 137

See p. 114 for a list of commonly used decorating items you may need.

In advance: Make number. Tint ¼ oz. fondant green per treat. Use candy mold to make number, ⁵⁄₁₆ in. deep, for each treat.

Bake and cool cupcakes. Spatula ice tops. Tint ½ oz. fondant red per treat. For arms, roll two ⅜ in. x 2 in. long tapered logs. Flatten end for hand; cut slits for fingers. Position icing decoration head, arms and number on cupcake. Wrap arm around number; support head with icing if necessary. Each serves 1.

*Combine Leaf Green with Lemon Yellow for green shown.

▲ One Big *Elmo* Celebration! Cake

Pans: *Elmo*, p. 219; #1, p. 164; Cooling Grid, p. 171
Tips: 3, 12, 16, p. 134
Colors:* No-Taste Red, Orange, Lemon Yellow, Leaf Green, Violet, Rose, Black, p. 139
Fondant: White Ready-To-Use Rolled Fondant (140 oz.), p. 148; 20 in. Fondant Roller, 20 in. Fondant Roller Guide Rings, Roll-N-Cut Mat, Fondant Smoother, p. 152; Brush Set, p. 153; Round Cut-Outs Fondant Cutters, p. 151
Recipes: Buttercream Icing, p. 128; Thinned Fondant Adhesive, p. 127
Also: 101 Cookie Cutters (letters), p. 173; Piping Gel, p. 141; Cake Boards, Fanci-Foil Wrap, p. 186; Spatula, p. 137; 18 in. x 20½ in. foamcore board (½ in. thick), scissors, tape, ruler, knife

See p. 114 for a list of commonly used decorating items you may need.

In advance: Prepare and cover base board with 60 oz. rolled fondant (p. 120).

Bake and cool #1 cake and *Elmo* cake. Tint 36 oz. white fondant green, 12 oz. yellow, 6 oz. orange.

Roll out ⅛ in. thick as needed. Prepare and cover cake with green fondant (p. 119). Roll out yellow and lightly press inside pan to imprint recessed #1. Remove and cut out. Attach to cake top with damp brush. Roll out orange; cut letters using cutters from set. Attach letters. Reserve excess fondant.

For *Elmo* cake, use #1 pan as a guide to trim area under chin where #1 cake will go. Ice nose, eyes, mouth and cut area under chin smooth. Outline smile with tip 3. Pipe tip 12 dot pupils; flatten with fingertip dipped in cornstarch. Position cakes on prepared base board. Cover *Elmo* with tip 16 stars. For hands, shape two fondant ovals 4 in. x 3 in. x 1 in. thick; cut 1¾ in. deep slits; shape fingers. Position on cake side, wrapping fingers over #1 cake and securing with thinned fondant adhesive. Cover hands with tip 16 stars.

Tint 3 oz. fondant violet. Roll out violet and reserved orange and green fondant ⅛ in. thick. Use Cut-Outs to cut three or four circles in each color in each size. Attach to base board with damp brush, trimming at edges as needed. Serves 24.

*Combine Leaf Green with Lemon Yellow for green shown. Combine Violet with Rose for violet shown.

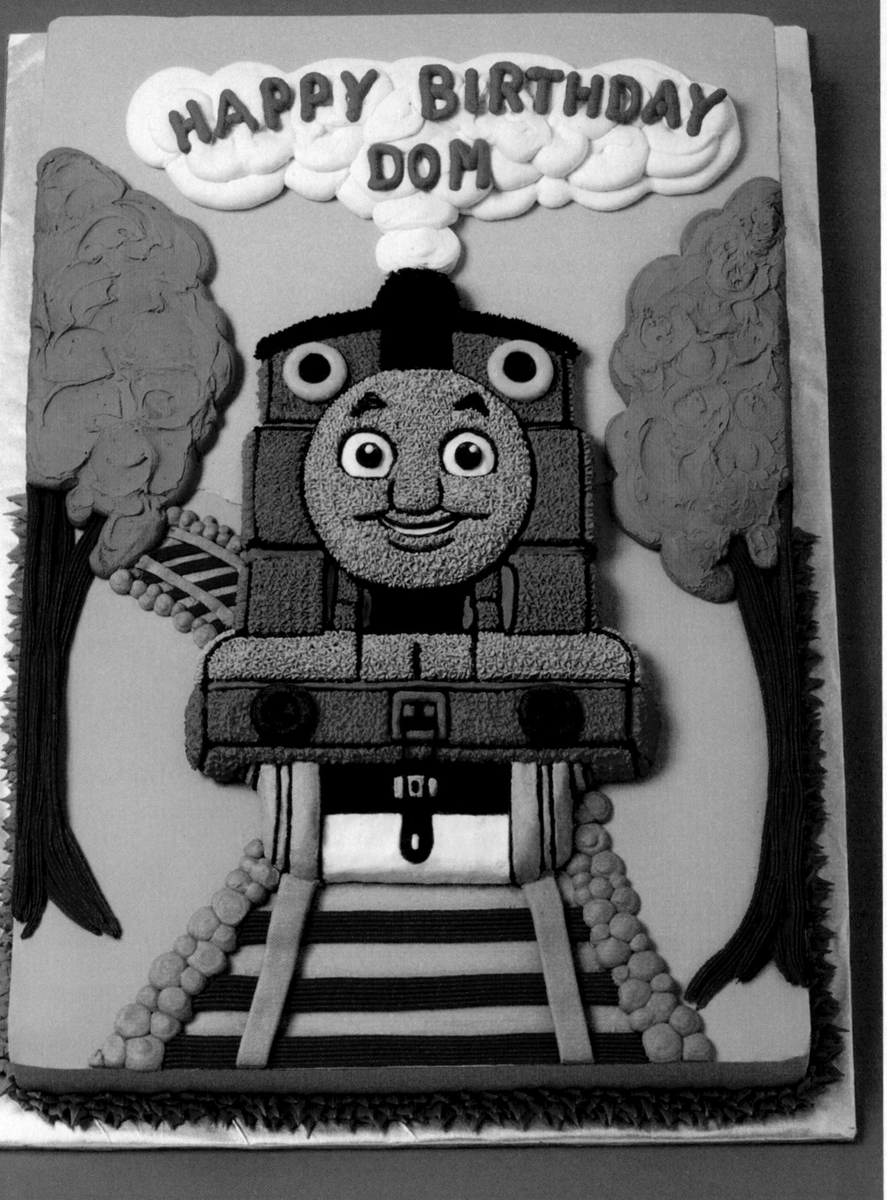

◀ **Thomas Celebration Station Cake**

Pans: *Thomas & Friends*, p. 214; 11 in. x 15 in. x 2 in. Sheet, p. 161; Cooling Grid, p. 171

Tips: 1, 2A, 2B, 3, 5, 8, 12, 16, 18, 47, 352, p. 134-135

Colors:* Kelly Green, Royal Blue, Sky Blue, Brown, Red-Red, Golden Yellow, Lemon Yellow, Black, p. 139

Fondant: White Ready-To-Use Rolled Fondant (96 oz.), p. 148; 20 in. Fondant Roller, 20 in. Fondant Roller Guide Rings, Roll-N-Cut Mat, Fondant Smoother, p. 152; Brush Set, p. 153

Recipe: Snow-White Buttercream Icing, p. 128

Also: 2013 Pattern Book (tree, front and back tracks), p. 143; Meringue Powder, Piping Gel, p. 141; 9 in. Angled Spatula, p. 137; Disposable Decorating Bags, p. 136; Cake Boards, Fanci-Foil Wrap, p. 186; 24 in. x 17 in. foamcore board (¼ in. thick)

See p. 114 for a list of commonly used decorating items you may need.

Bake and cool 1 in. high *Thomas* cake and two 1-layer sheet cakes. Position sheet cakes side by side on foil-wrapped base board. Ice smooth, upper half and sides in light blue, lower half and sides in light green. Use pattern to mark trees on cake top (reverse pattern for tree on right and make trunk slightly longer). Mark front and back tracks. Spatula ice track areas gray. Pipe brown parallel lines, ridged side up, for horizontal tracks: use tip 2B for front tracks, tip 47 for back tracks. Pipe band wheel rails, with tip 2B smooth side up for front tracks, tip 47 for back tracks.

For *Thomas* cake, outline face, facial features, bumper, panels and wheels with tip 3. Pipe in wheels, wheel caps, hitch, eyes, pupils, eyebrows, connector, inside bumper pads and inside of lights with tip 5. Cover cab, roof, bumper and underside of train and cab with tip 16 stars. Overpipe eyebrows with tip 3. Outline edge of lights with tip 12. Pipe tip 1 eye highlight and connector hole.

Position *Thomas* cake on sheet cake about 3½ in. from bottom edge. Pipe tip 18 vertical lines to fill in tree trunks. Pipe tip 2A swirls for tree tops. Smooth edges of cake with spatula. Pipe assorted boulders next to tracks, using tip 12 and tip 8 dots to build out ½ in. to 1 in. wide from track. Pat smooth with finger dipped in cornstarch. Pipe tip 8 message with letters 1 in. tall, on waxed paper-covered board; set in freezer until needed. Pipe tip 5 bead border in blue on upper half of sheet cake. Pipe two rows of tip 352 pull-out leaves in green around bottom half of sheet cake. Pipe tip 2A swirled smoke, starting at *Thomas* cake. Position frozen letters on smoke. Serves 33.

*Combine Royal Blue with Sky Blue for dark blue shown. Combine Brown with Red-Red for brown shown. Combine Golden Yellow with Red-Red for gold shown. Combine Red-Red with Lemon Yellow for red shown.

▶ **Thomas' Tunnel Treats**

Pan: 10.5 in. x 15.5 in. x 1 in. Jelly Roll, p. 162

Tips: 7, 8, 233, p. 134

Colors:* Kelly Green, Brown, Red-Red, Black, p. 139

Recipes: Buttercream, Royal Icings, Roll-Out Cookies, p. 128; favorite crisped rice cereal treats

Also: 2013 Pattern Book (tunnel), p. 143; *Thomas & Friends* Fun Pix, p. 214; 4 in. Lollipop Sticks, p. 178; Disposable Decorating Bags, p. 136; Meringue Powder, p. 141; Spatula, p. 137; Cake Boards, p. 186

See p. 114 for a list of commonly used decorating items you may need.

1 day in advance: Make cookie tunnels. Prepare and roll out dough. Use pattern to cut out tunnels. Bake and cool cookies. Ice smooth with black royal icing. Pipe tip 8 brown dots around curved edge for stones. Pat smooth with finger dipped in cornstarch. Let dry 24 hours on waxed paper-covered boards. Attach lollipop stick to back with icing, allowing 1 in. of stick to extend at bottom. Let dry.

Prepare cereal treat mixture. Press into pan to 1 in. thick. Let set. Cut 3 in. x 3 in. squares. Ice top smooth with buttercream. Insert tunnel cookie and pick, trimming sticks if needed. Pipe tip 233 pull-out grass. Each serves 1.

*Combine Brown with Red-Red for brown shown.

▶ *Dora's* Rainbow Mountain Cupcake Display

Pans: Standard Muffin, p. 162; Cooling Grid, p. 171
Tip: 3, p. 134
Colors:* Leaf Green, Violet, Rose, Sky Blue, Lemon Yellow, Golden Yellow, p. 139
Fondant: White Ready-To-Use Rolled Fondant (8½ oz. makes topper and 20 to 30 treats), Gum-Tex, p. 148; 20 in. Fondant Roller, 20 in. Fondant Roller Guide Rings, Roll-N-Cut Mat, 10-Pc. Gum Paste/Fondant Tool Set, p. 152; Shaping Foam, p. 155; Brush Set, p. 153; Flower Cut-Outs Fondant Cutters, p. 151
Recipes: Buttercream Icing, p. 128; Thinned Fondant Adhesive, p. 127
Also: *Dora the Explorer* Treat Stand, Fun Pix, Baking Cups, p. 219; Disposable Decorating Bags, p. 136; Spatula, p. 137; 8 in. Cake Circle, Cake Boards, p. 186; ruler, cornstarch, knife
See p. 114 for a list of commonly used decorating items you may need.

2 days in advance: Make rainbow topper. Tint 4 oz. fondant royal blue. Roll out ⅛ in. thick. Cut an 8 in. circle using 8 in. cake circle as a pattern. Center and attach *Dora* topper from treat stand over circle using thinned fondant adhesive. Trim fondant straight across bottom, even with topper, leaving a 1½ in. fondant border around topper. Slit fondant to match slits in topper. Tint fondant: sky blue, violet, rose, yellow (1 oz. each); add ⅛ teaspoon Gum-Tex to each. Roll out ⅛ in. thick as needed. Cut and attach ½ in. wide rainbow strips around topper (in order): 14 in. violet; 15 in. sky blue; 16 in. yellow; 17 in. rose. Let dry. Reserve excess fondant. **Also:** Make flowers. Roll out ½ oz. white fondant and reserved violet and rose fondant ¹⁄₁₆ in. thick. Cut 56 flowers in each color using smallest Cut-Out. Place flowers on thick shaping foam and cup centers using small ball tool from set. Let dry on cornstarch-dusted boards.

Bake and cool cupcakes. Spatula ice tops. Insert picks. Pipe tip 3 dot flower centers in yellow; position flowers. Assemble stand; insert rainbow topper. Position cupcakes. Each serves 1.

*Combine Violet with Rose for violet shown. Combine Lemon Yellow with Golden Yellow for yellow shown.

▲ *Dora* Explores the Rainbow Cake

Pans: *Dora the Explorer*, p. 219; 18 in. x 3 in. Half Round, p. 163
Tips: 3, 16, 18, 190, p. 134
Colors:* Royal Blue, Violet, Sky Blue, Lemon Yellow, Golden Yellow, Orange, Rose, Leaf Green, p. 139
Candy: White (3 pks.), Dark Cocoa Candy Melts Candy, Primary and Garden Candy Color Sets, p. 175; Stay Warm Ceramic Melting Cups, Mixing Bowls, Decorator Brush Set, p. 178
Recipes: Buttercream, Royal Icings, p. 128
Also: Meringue Powder, p. 141; Parchment Triangles, Disposable Decorating Bags, p. 136; Cake Leveler, p. 158; Spatula, p. 137; Cake Boards, Fanci-Foil Wrap, p. 186; Plastic Dowel Rods, p. 194; 20 in. x 11 in. plywood or foamcore board (¼ in. thick) cornstarch, knife
See p. 114 for a list of commonly used decorating items you may need.

1 to 2 days in advance: Make candy plaque. Use candy colors to tint candy: 6 oz. skin tone (add orange and a small amount of dark cocoa candy to white candy for skin tone shown); 4 oz. each pink, violet (use violet and a small amount of blue for violet shown); 3 oz. ivory (add small amount of orange to white candy); 1 oz. each black (add black to dark cocoa candy), brown (add white to dark cocoa candy for light brown eyes); ½ oz. each light blue, dark blue, yellow, red. Pipe candy into pan using parchment triangles or disposable decorating bags. Pipe one color at a time, chilling to set each color before piping any touching colors. Add remaining white candy to level back area. Chill completely before unmolding onto soft cloth. Add fine details (pupil highlights, *Map's* eyes and eyebrows and mouth) and overpipe black facial outlines after unmolding. Position candy plaque on foil-wrapped board, cut to fit.

Also: Make flowers. Using royal icing on waxed paper-covered boards, pipe 12 tip 190 drop flowers each in rose, violet and orange. Pipe tip 3 dot flower centers in yellow. Make extras to allow for breakage. Let dry 24 hours.

Bake and cool 1-layer cake; level to 2 in. high. Ice cake smooth with dark blue buttercream. Starting at outside edge, use toothpicks to mark five rainbow stripes ⅞ in. wide. Use various colors to fill in with tip 16 stars. Pipe tip 18 pull-out star grass bottom border. Position flowers. Insert dowel rods where candy plaque will rest. Position candy plaque. Print tip 3 message. Serves 28.

*Combine Violet with Rose for violet shown. Combine Lemon Yellow with Golden Yellow for yellow shown.

▼ *SpongeBob* Rock Star Cookies

Cookie: 6-Pc. Star Plastic Nesting Cutter Set, p. 173; Cookie Sheet, Cooling Grid, p. 171
Tips: 3, 6, p. 134
Colors:* Rose, Burgundy, Sky Blue, Royal Blue, Black, p. 139
Recipes: Color Flow Icing, Roll-Out Cookies, p. 128
Also: *SpongeBob SquarePants* Icing Decorations, p. 214; Color Flow Mix, p. 141; Disposable Decorating Bags, p. 136
See p. 114 for a list of commonly used decorating items you may need.

Prepare and roll out dough. Cut stars using largest cutter from set. Bake and cool cookies. Outline stars with tip 6 and full-strength blue icing. Flow in with thinned black icing (p. 120). Immediately pipe tip 3 dots with thinned rose icing. Let dry.

On icing decoration, outline and fill in sunglasses with tip 3 and full-strength icing. Use tip 3 to pipe highlights on glasses and to print message. Attach icing decoration with icing dots. Let dry. Each serves 1.

*Combine Royal Blue with Sky Blue for blue shown. Combine Rose with Burgundy for rose shown.

▼ Strumming *SpongeBob!* Cake

Pans: *SpongeBob SquarePants*, p. 214; Cookie Sheet, Cooling Grid, p. 171
Tips: 2, 3, 7, 10, 16, p. 134
Colors: Lemon Yellow, Royal Blue, Black, No-Taste Red, Rose, p. 139
Recipes: Buttercream, Color Flow Icings, Roll-Out Cookies, p. 128
Also: 2013 Pattern Book (arm, hands, guitar, musical notes, sunglasses), p. 143; 101 Cookie Cutters (letters), p. 173; Color Flow Mix, p. 141; Cake Boards, Fanci-Foil Wrap, p. 186; Disposable Decorating Bags, p. 136; Spatula, p. 137
See p. 114 for a list of commonly used decorating items you may need.

2 to 3 days in advance: Make cookies. Prepare and roll out dough, ¼ in. thick for guitar and arms, ⅛ in. thick for other cookies. Cut letters using desired cutters; trace patterns for arms, hands, guitar and notes and cut with knife. Bake and cool cookies, baking guitar separately.

Also: Cover guitar, notes and letters with thinned Color Flow icing (p. 123). Tap to settle. Let dry 24 hours. Decorate with full-strength Color Flow icing. Use tip 3 to outline and fill in 1 in. black circles on notes; pat smooth with finger dipped in cornstarch. Use tip 3 to outline body and head of guitar in dark blue. Use tip 2 to outline and fill in bridge, neck, control knobs and tuning pegs in gray; pat smooth. Overpipe outline on control knobs with tip 3 in dark blue. Use tip 2 to pipe strings and overpipe outlines on tuning pegs and bridge in black.

Bake and cool cake. Decorate with buttercream icing. Ice sides and background areas smooth with thinned black icing. Use tip 3 to outline and fill in mouth, tongue, teeth and sponge holes; pat smooth. Use pattern to mark sunglasses. Outline and fill in sunglasses with tip 7 and black icing, building up to about ¼ in. thick. Pipe tip 7 white highlights. Use tip 3 and black icing to outline pants, legs, shoes, nose and smile lines. Cover *SpongeBob* with tip 16 stars. Pipe background dots in light and dark blue and dark rose, using tips 3, 7 and 10. Attach guitar, arms and hands with icing. Outline arm and hands with tip 3 in black; fill in with tip 16 stars in yellow. Surround cake with musical notes and message. Cake serves 12; each cookie serves 1.

▲ Hanging with *Spider-Man* Cake

Pans: *Spider-Sense Spider-Man*, p. 218; 11 in. x 15 in. x 2 in. Sheet, p. 161; Cooling Grid, p. 171
Tips: 2, 21, p. 134
Colors:* Red-Red, Golden Yellow, Lemon Yellow, p. 139
Fondant: White (24 oz.), Black (72 oz.) Ready-To-Use Rolled Fondant, p. 148; 20 in. Fondant Roller, 20 in. Fondant Roller Guide Rings, Roll-N-Cut Mat, Fondant Smoother, p. 152; Orange Color Dust, Brush Set, p. 153
Recipe: Buttercream Icing, p. 128
Also: 2013 Pattern Book (skyline), p. 143; 101 Cookie Cutters (letters), p. 173; Spatula, p. 137; Disposable Decorating Bags, p. 136; Fanci-Foil Wrap, p. 186; Plastic Dowel Rods, p. 194; 16½ in. x 23½ in. foamcore board (½ in. thick)
See p. 114 for a list of commonly used decorating items you may need.

In advance: Make *Spider-Man* candy plaque (p. 124). Combine blue and violet candy colors for blue candy shown. Position candy plaque on foil-wrapped board, cut to fit.

Bake and cool two 1-layer sheet cakes. Position sheet cakes side by side on foil-wrapped base board. Cut two lengths of dowel rod, 2 in. each. Insert in cake where candy plaque will rest. Prepare and cover cakes with black fondant (p. 119). Tint 24 oz. fondant yellow; roll out ⅛ in. thick. Cut a rectangle, 12½ in. x 13½ in. Position pattern on rectangle, lining up edge of tallest building with short top edge of rectangle. Cut out skyline; remove excess fondant. Brush top edge and sides with orange Color Dust. Attach skyline to cake top with damp brush. Cut desired letters using cutters. Brush letters with orange Color Dust; attach to skyline with damp brush.

Pipe tip 21 shell bottom border in red. Position candy plaque on cake. Serves 54.

*Combine Golden Yellow with Lemon Yellow for yellow fondant shown.

Holidays Come Alive!

Every season has its signature symbols, and we're here to show you how to spice them up with color and fun. Create a staggering scene for Halloween, with a horde of cookie zombies stalking your guests. Go mad for plaid this winter with silver-studded snowflakes floating over green and red tartan treats. Spring a surprise for their Easter baskets with cookie chicks inside a candy-coated pretzel nest or cake-filled candy shells topped with a bunny and jelly bean icing decoration. Four seasons of fun start now!

Zombie Zone Cookies

Cookie: Teddy Bear Comfort-Grip Cutter, p. 172; 3-Pc. Haunted Halloween Metal Cutter Set, p. 221; Round Cut-Outs Fondant Cutters, p. 151; Cookie Sheet, Cooling Grid, p. 171

Tips: 1, 2, 3, 4, 5, 7, 12, 16, 46, p. 134-135

Colors:* Black, Moss Green, Brown, Christmas Red, Orange, Copper, Violet, Royal Blue, Lemon Yellow, Ivory, Rose Petal Pink, p. 139

Recipes: Roll-Out Cookies, Royal Icing, p. 128

Also: 2013 Pattern Book (easel back), p. 143; Candy Eyeballs, p. 223; Red, Brown Color Dust, p. 153; Fine Tip Primary and Neon Colors FoodWriter Edible Color Markers, p. 153; Piping Gel, Meringue Powder, p. 141; Brush Set, p. 153; Disposable Decorating Bags, p. 136; Spatula, p. 137

See p. 114 for a list of commonly used decorating items you may need.

In advance: Make cookies. Prepare and roll out dough. Use teddy bear cutter to cut one body for each figure; use knife to trim off ears and arms. Use skull cutter from set or largest round Cut-Out to cut heads. Use pattern to cut two easel backs per figure. Bake and cool cookies.

Use royal icing to decorate heads and bodies separately on waxed paper-covered boards. Ice heads smooth in assorted skin tones, then decorate features as follows.

1. I.M. Rotten: Draw veins on candy eyeball with edible marker; attach with dots of icing. Pipe in tip 5 pants. Pipe tip 46 (smooth side up) band sweater, tip 12 pull-out arms. Pipe tip 3 pull-out fingers, outline eyelids and sockets, build-up bead nose. Pipe tip 2 dot toes, outline sideburns, nostrils, mouth and teeth, pull-out hair.

2. I.C. Brains: Attach candy eyeballs with dots of icing. Pipe in tip 5 pants. Pipe tip 46 (smooth side up) band sweater, tip 12 pull-out arms. Pipe tip 3 pull-out fingers, swirl brains. Pipe tip 2 outline mouth and teeth, pipe-in hair, stitches, dot toes, bead nose and dot nostrils.

3. Barry Deep: Attach candy eyeballs with dots of icing. Pipe in tip 5 pants, outline suspenders and dot buttons. Texturize pants using tip of knife. Pipe tip 12 pull-out arms. Pipe tip 3 pull-out fingers, pipe in eyelids. Pipe tip 2 pull-out hair, outline mouth, pipe in teeth, dot nostrils and toes.

4. Ben Dead: Attach candy eyeballs with dots of icing. Pipe in tip 5 pants and shirt. For tears in pants and shirt insert tip 2 and pipe in areas in blue. Pipe tip 12 pull-out arms. Pipe tip 3 pull-out fingers, outline eyelids and pipe-in hair. Pipe tip 2 outline mouth and nostrils, dot toes. Use knife tip to fringe ends of pants and shirt.

5. Ida B. Dead: Draw veins on candy eyeballs with edible marker; attach with dots of icing. Pipe in tip 5 dress. Pipe tip 12 pull-out arms; pipe in sleeves with tip 5. Pipe tip 4 pull-out hair, pipe in tip 3 bow and dot knot. Pipe tip 2 outline eyebrows, eye sockets, mouth and teeth, dot toes, pull out nose, fingers and fringe.

Create One Zombie... Or An Entire Horde!

6. **Dee Kayed:** Attach candy eyeballs with dots of icing. Pipe in tip 5 dress. Pipe tip 12 pull-out arms; pipe in sleeves with tip 5. Pipe tip 4 pull-out hair. Pipe tip 3 pull-out fingers, outline eyelids, pipe in bow and dot knot. Pipe tip 2 outline mouth and dot toes. Pipe tip 1 pull-out fringe.

7. **Otto B. Alive:** Draw veins on candy eyeballs with edible marker; attach with dots of icing. Pipe in tip 5 pants and sweater. Pipe tip 12 pull-out arms. Pipe tip 3 pull-out fingers. Pipe tip 2 pull-out toes, outline and pipe in mouth, outline teeth, stitches and nose, zigzag intestines.

8. **U.B. Lunch:** Attach one candy eyeball with dots of icing. Pipe in tip 5 pants and shirt; use spatula to pull out bottom for tattered look. Pipe tip 12 pull-out arms. Pipe tip 3 pull-out fingers and ball smaller eye. Pipe tip 2 dot toes and head wounds, pull-out hair, dot pupil outline and pipe in mouth, outline teeth.

9. **Izzy Gone:** Attach candy eyeballs with dots of icing. Spatula ice pants and shirt. Use edge of spatula to texturize shirt. Pipe tip 12 pull-out arms. Pipe tip 3 pull-out fingers and hair, pipe in eyelids and mouth. Pipe tip 2 dot toes and nostrils, outline eye sockets.

10. **Tommy Zombie:** Draw veins on candy eyes with edible marker; attach with dots of icing. Pipe in tip 5 pants and shirt. Use edge of spatula to texturize shirt and fray ends of pant legs. Pipe tip 4 outline belt. Pipe tip 12 pull-out arms. Pipe tip 5 hand. Pipe tip 2 pull-out fingers. Pipe in tip 3 mouth and hair. Pipe tip 2 dot nostrils and toes, pipe in eyelids, sockets, teeth and tongue.

11. **Justin Pieces:** Spatula ice pants and shirt. Pipe tip 12 pull-out arms. Pipe tip 3 pull-out fingers and hair, swirl nerve. Draw veins on candy eyeballs and color in whites with edible markers; attach with dots of icing. Pipe tip 2 outline mouth, pull-out fringe, dot nostrils, toes.

12. **Thurston Flesh:** Color in whites of candy eyeballs with edible marker. Spatula ice pants and shirt, pull-out hair. Pipe tip 12 pull-out arms. Pipe tip 3 pull-out fingers. Pipe tip 2 outline mouth, eye details, nostrils, pull-out teeth, swirl brains, dot toes.

13. **The Newlydeads:** Draw veins on candy eyeballs with edible marker; attach with dots of icing. Pipe in tip 5 wedding dress and tuxedo. Pipe tip 12 pull-out arms; pipe in her sleeves and pull-out hair with tip 5. Pipe tip 3 outline and pipe in mouths, outline eyelids and sockets, pull-out fingers, his pull-out tongue. Pipe tip 1 pull-out dress fringe, dot toes, nostrils and buttons. Pipe tip 7 zigzags for his hair and eyebrows. Pipe tip 16 swirl drop flowers with tip 2 dot centers. Brush flowers with red and brown Color Dust.

For all designs: Attach heads; let dry. Attach easel backs; let dry. Add piping gel tinted red for blood and wounds in cut parchment bag. Each serves 1.

*Skin tones combine Copper, Royal Blue or White with Black. Some clothes/features combine Violet with Christmas Red for violet and Lemon Yellow with Ivory for yellow. Add Brown to various colors as desired for a muted look.

◄ The Departed Has Arrived Cake

Pans: Dimensions 3-D Skull, p. 220; 11 in. x 15 in. x 2 in. Sheet, p. 163; Cooling Grid, p. 171
Tips: 2A, 16, p. 134
Colors:* Ivory, Black, Moss Green, p. 139
Fondant: White Ready-To-Use Rolled Fondant (17 oz.), p. 148; 9 in. Fondant Roller, Roll-N-Cut Mat, p. 152; Red, Brown, White Color Dust, Pure Lemon Extract, Brush Set, p. 153
Recipes: Buttercream Icing, p. 128; favorite chocolate cake
Also: 2013 Pattern Book (eyelids, mouth), p. 143; Disposable Decorating Bags, p. 136; Spatula, p. 137; black shoestring licorice
See p. 114 for a list of commonly used decorating items you may need.

Bake and cool skull cake and 1-layer chocolate sheet cake. Secure skull halves together with icing. Fill in mouth indentation with icing and ice smooth.

Make fondant features (p. 124). Paint pupils with black icing color. Mix black icing color with lemon extract to create a dark gray; paint eyelids. Mix white with a touch of brown Color Dust to make ivory; mix with lemon extract; paint teeth. Mix white, brown, red Color Dust with lemon extract; paint lips. Pipe tip 16 dark gray stars around eyes.

Cover remainder of cake with tip 16 green stars. For hair, cut licorice into 60 pieces, each 1½ in. and 2½ in. long, attach with icing. For hands, roll two 6 in. fondant balls; flatten. Cut slits and shape to make 3 in. long fingers. Roll out reserved black fondant ⅛ in. thick. Use knife to cut ½ in. squares for fingernails. Cover hands with tip 16 green stars to match face. With remaining black fondant make two eyebrows 2¼ in. long x ⅜ in. wide, tapering to ¼ in. wide. **At party:** Crumble chocolate cake and mound around skull cake on board. Position hands.
Serves 12.

*Combine Moss Green with a little Black for green skin tone shown.

▼ Candy Craniums

Candy: Large Skull Candy Mold, p. 223; White Candy Melts Candy (16 oz. per treat), Primary (red, yellow), Garden (black, green) Candy Color Sets, p. 175
Colors: Black, Brown, p. 139
Fondant: White Ready-To-Use Rolled Fondant (1 oz. per treat), p. 148; White, Red, Brown, Periwinkle Blue, Goldenrod Color Dust, Pure Lemon Extract, Brush Set, p. 153; 9 in. Fondant Roller, Roll-N-Cut Mat, p. 152
See p. 114 for a list of commonly used decorating items you may need.

Use small amounts of candy color to tint melted candy in assorted spooky shades (shown: blue with black, green with black and green with yellow). Leave partially mixed for marbleized look. Mold candy skulls (p. 123).

Paint on highlights and shaded areas using Color Dust/lemon extract mixtures (p. 118); combine brown, blue and white for dark gray and black eyebrows, eye sockets, nose and teeth outlines. Combine red and brown for blood. Combine yellow and brown for skin tone on each skull. Let dry 5 to 10 minutes. Add fondant details. Roll ⁵⁄₁₆ in. dia. white eyeballs; attach with damp brush. Paint pupils using black icing, Color Dust/lemon extract mixture. For each skull, tint ½ oz. fondant black and brown for hair. Roll out ⅛ in. thick. Cut assorted strips ⅛ to ¼ in. wide; attach.

▼ Knife of the Party Cupcake Display

Pans: Standard Muffin, p. 162; Cooling Grid, p. 171
Tip: 5, p. 134
Colors:* White-White, Leaf Green, Lemon Yellow, Black, Orange, Red-Red, p. 139
Fondant: White Ready-To-Use Rolled Fondant (8 oz.), Gum-Tex, p. 148; Pure Lemon Extract, Brown, Purple, Spruce Green, Goldenrod Color Dust, Brush Set, p. 153; 9 in. Fondant Roller, Roll-N-Cut Mat, p. 152
Recipes: Buttercream, Royal Icings, p. 128
Also: 2013 Pattern Book (zombie banner), p. 143; Skull and Knife Icing Decorations, (2 pks. each) p. 222; Candy Melting Plate; 4 in. Lollipop Sticks, p. 178, Piping Gel, p. 141; 23-Ct. Cupcakes-N-More Dessert Stand, p. 183; Halloween in 3-D Standard Baking Cups, p. 222; Disposable Decorating Bags, p. 136; Cake Boards, p. 186; thin pretzel sticks, 3¼ in. x 1½ in. craft foam circle, 1½ in. wide green ribbon (11 in. long), spatula

See p. 114 for a list of commonly used decorating items you may need.

2 days in advance: Make 12 right arms and 12 left arms (p. 124). **Also:** Decorate 24 skulls. Use light gray mixture from arms to paint skull icing decorations; let dry at least 4 hours. Add a little more black icing color to mixture for dark gray. Paint inside eyes and nose; let dry. Mix brown, purple, spruce green and goldenrod Color Dust in melting plate cavity; brush on skulls for detail. Paint teeth with white-white icing color; let dry. Roll ⅛ in. fondant balls for eyes; attach to skulls with piping gel. Paint pupils with dark gray mixture. **And:** Make banner. Knead ¼ teaspoon Gum-Tex into 2 oz. fondant; tint orange. Roll out ¼ in. thick. Use pattern and knife to cut banner. Pipe tip 5 message using royal icing. Let dry 48 hours on cornstarch-dusted board. Attach banner to two lollipop sticks with royal icing, leaving 3 in. extending at bottom. Attach skull to lollipop stick with royal icing; let set.

Bake and cool 22 cupcakes; ice fluffy, pulling up tip of spatula for grass effect. Attach skulls to pretzel sticks and knives to hands with royal icing. Let dry. Brush banner lollipop sticks with light gray mixture. Insert arm and skull into each cupcake. For topper, wrap craft foam circle with foil; attach ribbon to side with double stick tape. Ice top to match cupcake tops. Use a clean lollipop stick to make holes for banner, head and arms. Insert banner, skull and arms on sticks in topper; secure with royal icing. Position topper and cupcakes on stand. Each serves 1.

*Combine Leaf Green and Lemon Yellow for green shown. Combine Orange and Red-Red for orange shown.

▲ Horror Hand! Cake and Cupcakes

Pans: 8 in. x 3 in. Round, p. 163; Standard Muffin, p. 162; Cooling Grid, p. 171
Tips: 1, 3, 4, 6, 44, 45, 46, p. 134-135
Colors:* Black, Orange, Leaf Green, Lemon Yellow, Golden Yellow, Teal, Royal Blue, Kelly Green, p. 139
Recipes: Buttercream, Chocolate Buttercream, Color Flow Icings, p. 128
Also: 2013 Pattern Book (hand, words), p. 143; Halloween in 3-D Cupcake Combo, p. 222; 8 in. Cookie Treat Sticks, p. 171; Piping Gel, p. 141, Disposable Decorating Bags, p. 136; Spatula, p. 137; Color Flow Mix, p. 141; Parchment Paper, p. 158; Cake Boards, Cake Circles, p. 186

See p. 114 for a list of commonly used decorating items you may need.

2 days in advance: Make hand topper. Tape pattern to board; cover with parchment paper. Outline hand with tip 3 and full-strength black Color Flow icing. Flow in details, one color at a time, using thinned icing. Let dry 48 hours. Carefully peel off parchment paper and attach cookie stick to back using full-strength icing; let 4 in. of stick extend at bottom to insert into cake. Let dry.

Bake and cool 2-layer cake (trim layers to 2½ in. high for a 5 in. high cake) and cupcakes. Ice all smooth with black-tinted chocolate icing. Use teal icing to pipe tip 46 (smooth side up) horizontal outline around cake 1 in. from bottom. Pipe tip 44 orange and tip 45 green vertical stripes ⅜ in. apart.

In alternating spaces between vertical stripes, pipe a tip 6 teal stripe. Use piping gel and tip 1 to transfer word patterns (p. 119) (two of each) to cake sides. Outline words with tips 3 and 4. Insert hand in cake and picks in cupcakes. Position cupcakes around cake. Cake serves 20; each cupcake serves 1.

*Combine Leaf Green with Lemon Yellow for green shown. Combine Lemon Yellow with Golden Yellow for yellow shown. Combine Teal with Royal Blue and Kelly Green for blue shown.

◄ Crispy Creeps Treats

Pan: Dimensions Multi-Cavity Mini Pumpkin, p. 167
Tip: 5, p. 134
Colors:* Leaf Green, Violet, Lemon Yellow, Rose, p. 139
Recipes: Buttercream Icing, p. 128; favorite crisped rice
    cereal treats
Also: Eyes and Eyebrows Picks, p. 222; spice drops, candy corn
**See p. 114 for a list of commonly used decorating items
you may need.**

Spray pan cavities. Prepare cereal treat mixture; tint melted
marshmallow mixture before adding cereal. Press cereal treat
mixture in bottom cavities only of pumpkin pan to 1½ in. deep.
Let set; unmold.

Using tip 5, pipe line of icing on back edge to attach halves.
Insert picks. Trim yellow bottom off candy corn; attach top for
teeth with icing. Attach spice drop for nose with icing. Each
serves 1.

*Combine Leaf Green with Lemon Yellow for green shown. Combine Violet with
 Rose for violet shown.

▼ Green Meanie Cookies

Cookie: 4-Pc. Pumpkins Nesting Metal Cutter Set, p. 222; Cookie Sheet, Cooling Grid, p. 171
Tips: 2, 3, p. 134
Colors:* Leaf Green, Lemon Yellow, Black, p. 139
Recipes: Color Flow Icing; Roll-Out Cookies, p. 128
Also: Color Flow Mix, p. 141; Cake Board, p. 186; Candy Eyeballs, p. 223; White Candy Melts
    Candy, p. 175; Parchment Triangles, p. 136; black shoestring licorice, spice drops
See p. 114 for a list of commonly used decorating items you may need.

Prepare and roll out dough. Cut pumpkins using third largest cutter from set. Bake and cool
cookies. Make icing; tint portions black, dark green and light green. Reserve white. Use full-
strength icing and tip 3 to outline cookie. Use thinned icing to flow in (p. 120). Immediately
pipe dark green dots using thinned icing in cut parchment bags. Let dry.

Decorate using full-strength Color Flow. Attach candy eyeballs with tip 3 dots. Pipe tip 2
outline mouth and pipe-in teeth. Pipe tip 3 outline hair. Cut a 2 in. licorice piece for each arm
and leg. Flatten two spice drops for hands; cut slits and trim for fingers. Flatten two spice
drops for shoes; trim to shape with knife. Cut a hole in each hand and shoe; insert licorice
arms or legs. Attach arms and legs to cookie with melted candy. Each serves 1.

*Combine Leaf Green with Lemon Yellow for light green shown.

▲ Spritz Having Fits!

Cookie: Cookie Pro Ultra II Cookie Press, p. 170; Cookie Sheet, Cooling Grid, p. 171
Tip: 2, p. 134
Colors:* Orange, Leaf Green, Lemon Yellow, Black, p. 139
Recipes: Buttercream Icing; Spritz Cookies, p. 128
Also: Candy Eyeballs, p. 223
See p. 114 for a list of commonly used decorating items you may need.

Prepare dough and tint portions green and orange. Use bar disk to press 3 in. long green
monster heads; use pumpkin disk to press orange pumpkins. Bake and cool cookies.

Attach eyeballs with icing dots. Pipe tip 2 wavy outline mouths. Outline and fill in hair with tip 2;
pat smooth with fingertip dipped in cornstarch (p. 119). Pipe tip 2 stem. Each serves 1.

*Combine Leaf Green with Lemon Yellow for green shown.

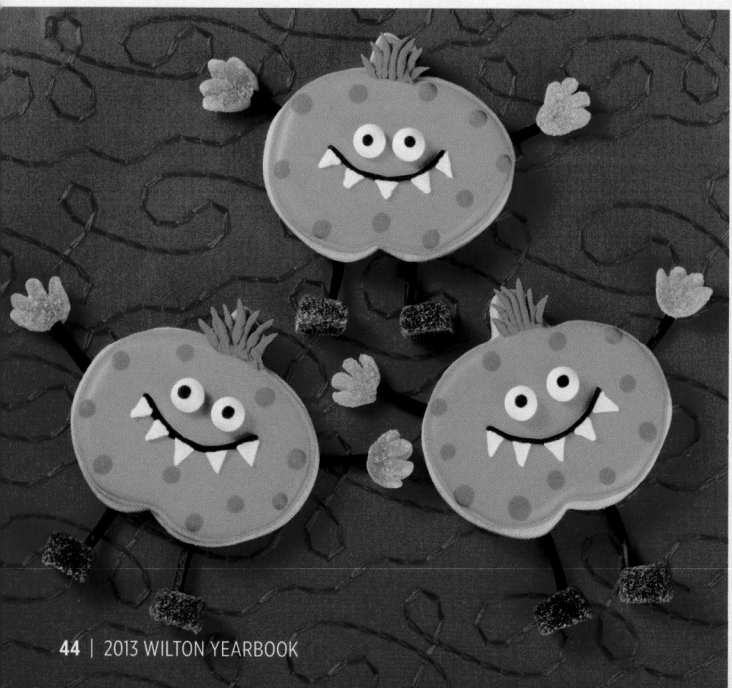

◀ Pumpkin Grins Cookies

Cookie: 4-Pc. Pumpkins Nesting Metal Cutter Set, p. 222; Cooling Grid, p. 171
Tips: 2, 3, p. 134
Colors: Orange, Leaf Green, Black, p. 139
Recipes: Color Flow Icing; Roll-Out Cookies, p. 128
Also: Candy Eyeballs, p. 223; Color Flow Mix, p. 141; Parchment Triangles, p. 136
See p. 114 for a list of commonly used decorating items you may need.

Prepare and roll out dough. Cut cookies using all four cutter sizes; bake and cool. Make icing; tint portions orange, green and black. Reserve some white. Outline pumpkins and mouths using tip 3 and full-strength icing; let set. Flow in areas with thinned icing (p. 120); let dry.

Using full-strength icing and tip 2, attach candy eyes with dots, pipe outline eyebrows, dot nose and fill-in teeth. Pipe in tip 3 stem; pat smooth with finger dipped in cornstarch (p. 119). Let dry. Each serves 1.

▶ Ghost Glee Club Cakes

Cookie: Halloween Non-Stick Cookie Shapes Pan, p. 220; Cookie Sheet, Cooling Grid, p. 171
Candy: White (1 pk. covers 10 to 12 treats), Black Candy Melts Candy, p. 175; Candy Eyeballs, p. 223
Recipe: Sugar Cookies (for pan-shaped cookies), p. 128
Also: Parchment Triangles, p. 136
See p. 114 for a list of commonly used decorating items you may need.

Bake and cool cookies in candy corn cavities of pan. Set on cooling grid over parchment-lined cookie sheet. Cover with melted candy (p. 123). Attach candy eyeballs and pipe assorted mouths with melted candy in cut parchment bag. Each serves 1.

◀ See Them All Crawl! Mini Cakes

Pans: 9 in. x 13 in. x 2 in. Sheet, p. 161, Cooling Grid, p. 171
Candy: Black Candy Melts Candy (1 pk. makes 5 treats), p. 175
Recipe: Favorite Cake Ball Pops, p. 128
Also: 2013 Pattern Book (spider leg), p. 143; Candy Eyeballs, p. 223, Spatula, p. 137; Parchment Paper, p. 158; Cake Board, p. 186
See p. 114 for a list of commonly used decorating items you may need.

In advance: Make candy legs. Cover leg pattern with parchment paper. Add a few drops of water to 2 oz. of black candy to thicken. Place in cut parchment bag and pipe over patterns. Make eight per treat; make extras to allow for breakage. Chill until firm. Turn legs and overpipe backs for strength; chill.

Prepare cake pops mixture. Shape half balls, 2 in. dia. Chill. Ice bottoms with melted candy. Chill. Place on cooling grid over pan; cover with melted candy (p. 123); chill until firm. Attach eyeballs and legs with melted candy. Each serves 1.

▼ Spider's Spooky Celebration

Pans: 8 in. x 2 in. Round, p. 161; Mini Ball, p. 165; Standard Muffin, p. 162; Cooling Grid, p. 171
Tips: 2, 2A, 12, 45, p. 134-135
Colors:* Orange, Red-Red, Black, Violet, Rose, p. 139
Candy: Black (2 pks), White Candy Melts Candy, Garden Candy Color Set (green), p. 175
Recipe: Buttercream Icing, p. 128
Also: 2013 Pattern Book (bone, spider legs), p. 143; Cake Dividing Chart, p. 137; Spooky Pop Cupcake Combo, p. 222; Spatula, p. 137; Parchment Triangles, p. 136; 10 in. cake pedestal
See p. 114 for a list of commonly used decorating items you may need.

In advance: Make spider topper. For body, use mini ball cavities and black candy to make two ¼ in. thick shells (p. 123). Attach halves with melted candy, positioning seam vertically. Slide bottom over warm cookie sheet to flatten slightly.

Copy leg patterns, reversing for four legs per side; tape patterns to board and cover with waxed paper. Add a few drops of water to 4 oz. melted black candy to thicken; place in parchment bag, then tape tip 2 to outside of bag. Pipe legs; let set. Turn over legs and overpipe with black candy. Pipe details on spider's body using melted candy in cut bag: Pipe white and green eyes, black pupils and white zigzag smile. Let set. Attach legs to body with melted candy; let set.

Bake and cool 2-layer cake and 24 cupcakes. Ice cake smooth; divide into 12ths. Pipe tip 45 band top and bottom borders. Use piping gel method (p. 119) to transfer bone pattern at division marks. Pipe in bones with tip 12. Cover cupcake tops with tip 2A swirls. Insert picks from combo pack. Position spider on cake top. Cake serves 20; each cupcake serves 1.

*Combine Orange with Red-Red for orange shown. Combine Violet with Rose for violet shown.

▲ Bracing for Halloween Cake

Pans: Iridescents! Jack-O-Lantern, p. 220; Cooling Grid, p. 171
Tips: 2, 3, 4, 12, 16, p. 134
Colors:* Orange, Red-Red, Violet, Rose, Kelly Green, Black, p. 139
Recipe: Buttercream Icing, p. 128
Also: 2013 Pattern Book (eyes, mouth), p. 143; Disposable Decorating Bags, p. 136; Spatula, p. 137; Cake Circles, p. 186
See p. 114 for a list of commonly used decorating items you may need.

Bake and cool cake; lightly ice face area smooth. Mark eye and mouth patterns with toothpick; pipe in with tip 3, pat smooth with finger dipped in cornstarch (p. 119).

Outline eyes, mouth and section lines with tip 4. Pipe tip 12 ball eyes, tip 3 dot pupils. Fill in sections with tip 16 stars. Pipe tip 2 lines for braces. Pipe in tip 12 stem. Serves 12.

*Combine Orange with Red-Red for orange shown. Combine Violet with Rose for violet shown.

SKATEBOARDERS HOWL

RIBS RULE

SKULLY WAS HERE

◀ Spooky Skateboarder Cookies

Cookie: Gingerbread Boy Metal Cutter, p. 172; Cookie Sheet, Cooling Grid, p. 171

Tips: 2, 3, 6, p. 134

Colors:* Violet, Christmas Red, Black, Kelly Green, p. 139

Recipes: Color Flow Icing, Chocolate Roll-Out Cookies, p. 128

Also: 2013 Pattern Book (head, skateboard), Black Candy Melts Candy, p. 175; Color Flow Mix, p. 141; Disposable Decorating Bags, p. 136; black spice drops

See p. 114 for a list of commonly used decorating items you may need.

Prepare and roll out dough. Use boy cutter to cut body. Use patterns and knife to cut head and skateboard. Bake and cool cookies.

Place skateboard cookie on cooling grid over parchment-lined cookie sheet; cover with thinned black icing (p. 123). Outline head with tip 2 and full-strength icing, 1½ in. face portion with white, hat portion with gray; let set. Flow in with thinned icing. Let dry.

Pipe details with full-strength icing: tip 2 purple facial features, pat smooth with finger dipped in cornstarch (p. 119), tip 3 white skeleton and hat trim; tip 6 black hat band. Let dry. For wheels, use melted candy to attach four spice drops, wide end out, to bottom of skateboard cookie; let set. Pipe tip 3 green dot axle. Attach head to body and two spice drops to back of feet with melted candy; let set. Attach skater to skateboard with melted candy; let set. Each serves 1.

*Combine Violet with Christmas Red for violet shown.

▼ Getting A Tune Up! Mini Cakes

Pans: 9 in. x 13 in. x 2 in. Sheet, p. 161; Cookie Sheets, Cooling Grid, p. 171

Also: Green (1 pk. makes 10 treats), Black, White, Yellow Candy Melts Candy, p. 175; Parchment Paper, p. 158; black spice drops, black shoestring licorice

See p. 114 for a list of commonly used decorating items you may need.

Bake and cool sheet cake using firm-textured batter such as pound cake. Use knife to cut out 2¼ in. wide x 2⅝ in. high heads, rounding corners (one cake makes 15 heads). Place on cooling grid over parchment-lined cookie sheet. Cover with melted green candy (p. 123). Chill until firm; repeat if necessary for smooth finish.

Outline and pipe in hair and mouth using melted black candy in cut parchment bag. Pipe black dot eyes and outline brows. Let set. Overpipe yellow and white teeth. Cut spice drops in half; attach wide bottoms for earphones with melted candy. For earphone band, cut a 5 in. piece of licorice. Attach with melted candy. Each serves 1.

▲ Bitty Brownie Bats

Pans: Silicone Round Pops Mold, p. 185; Non-Stick Cookie Sheet; Cooling Grid, p. 169

Candy: Black, White, Orange Candy Melts Candy, Garden Candy Color Set (violet), p. 175

Recipe: Favorite brownie recipe or mix

Also: Leaf Cut-Outs Fondant Cutters, p. 151; Spatula, p. 137; Parchment Triangles, p. 136; chocolate chips

See p. 114 for a list of commonly used decorating items you may need.

In advance: Make candy wings. Tint portion of melted white candy violet. Position medium leaf Cut-Out on non-stick cookie sheet. Fill to ⅛ in. deep with violet candy; tap to settle. Chill until firm; unmold. Turn over Cut-Out and repeat for second wing. Pipe stripes with orange candy in cut parchment bag. Let set. **Also:** Make candy eyes. Mix small portion of black and white melted candy for gray color. Pipe ¼ in. dia. gray and white dot eyeballs on waxed paper. Let set. Pipe black dot pupils. Let set.

Bake and cool brownie pops in silicone mold supported by cookie sheet. Ice bottom and attach chocolate chip ears with black melted candy. Chill. Place on cooling grid over parchment-lined cookie sheet. Cover pops with black candy (p. 123). Chill until firm. Trim wings to match angle of pop. Attach wings and eyes with black candy. Pipe white outline mouth. Each serves 1.

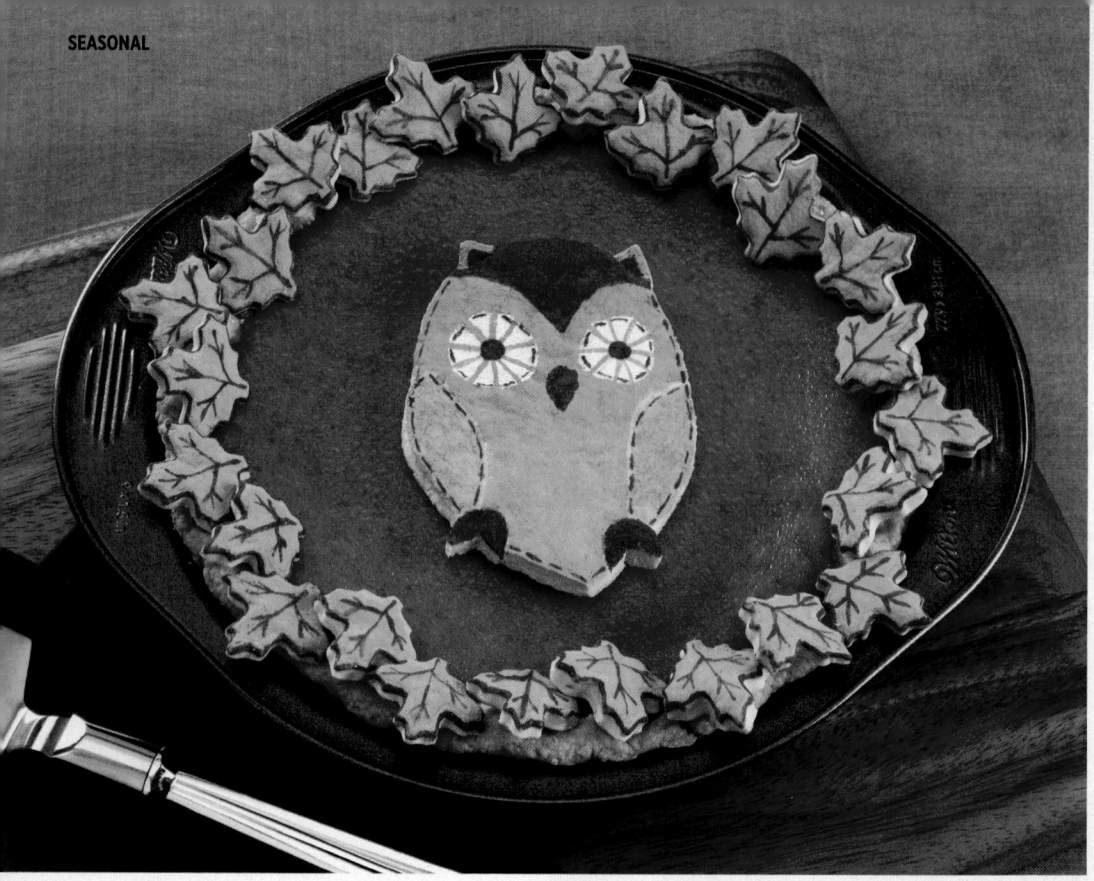

◀ Wise Guy Pie

Pan: 9 in. x 1.5 in. Pie, p. 169
Recipes: Favorite pumpkin pie, additional single pie crust
Also: 2013 Pattern Book (owl), p. 143; 6-Pc. Harvest Mini Metal Cutter Set, p. 225; Orange, Brown, Spruce Green, Periwinkle Blue, White Color Dust, Pure Lemon Extract, Brush Set, p. 153

See p. 114 for a list of commonly used decorating items you may need.

Bake and cool pie. Roll out extra pie crust dough ⅛ in. thick. Use pattern to cut one owl; use mini maple leaf cutter to cut 25 leaves. Bake owl and leaf cookies separately until edges are lightly brown; cool.

Mix orange and white Color Dust for orange shown; mix spruce green and periwinkle blue for green shown. Paint details on owl and leaves using Color Dust/lemon extract mixture (p. 118). Let dry. Arrange on pie. Serves 8.

▶ Fall Off A Log! Cake

Pans: 10.5 in. x 15.5 in. x 1 in. Jelly Roll, p. 162
Tip: 10, p. 134
Colors:* Orange, Brown, Moss Green, Sky Blue, p. 139
Fondant: White Ready-To-Use Rolled Fondant (6 oz.), Gum-Tex, p. 148; 9 in. Fondant Roller, Roll-N-Cut Mat, p. 152; Wave Flower Former Set, p. 142; Orange, Brown, Spruce Green, Periwinkle Blue, White Color Dust, Pure Lemon Extract, Brush Set, p. 153
Recipes: Buttercream, Chocolate Buttercream Icings, p. 128; Jelly Roll Cake, p. 128, Thinned Fondant Adhesive, p. 127
Also: 2013 Pattern Book (owl), p. 143; 9-Pc. Leaves and Acorns Nesting Metal Cutter Set, p. 225; 3-Pc. Icing Comb Set, p. 137; Light Cocoa Candy Melts Candy, p. 175; Disposable Decorating Bags, p. 136; Cake Boards, p. 186; 4 in. Lollipop Sticks, p. 177

See p. 114 for a list of commonly used decorating items you may need.

2 days in advance: Make fondant trims. Tint fondant: 4½ oz. orange, ½ oz. brown, ½ oz. green; reserve ½ oz. white. Add ¼ teaspoon Gum-Tex to orange. Roll out ⅛ in. thick as needed. Use pattern to cut out whole orange owl. Use pattern to cut out brown, white and green details; attach over owl using damp brush. Let dry on cornstarch-dusted board.

Also: Use cutters to cut six small and six medium orange maple leaves; let dry overnight in flower formers. Mix orange and white Color Dust for orange shown; mix spruce green and periwinkle blue for green shown. Paint details on owl and leaves using Color Dust/lemon extract mixture (p. 118). Let dry. Attach lollipop stick to back of owl using thinned fondant adhesive, leaving 2 in. extended at bottom to insert in cake.

Bake cake and roll up to cool following recipe directions. Unroll and fill with chocolate icing; reroll. Ice with chocolate icing; comb lengthwise using wavy side of comb. Lighten some chocolate icing with white icing; cover ends with tip 10 swirl. Insert owl and arrange leaves. Serves 12.

*Combine Orange with Brown for orange fondant shown. Combine Moss Green with Sky Blue for green fondant shown.

▼ Autumn Artistry Cupcakes

Pans: Standard Muffin, p. 162; Cooling Grid, p. 171
Tip: 352, p. 134
Colors:* Ivory, Lemon Yellow, Moss Green, p. 139
Recipe: Buttercream Icing, p. 128
Also: Mystic Autumn Cupcake Combo, p. 225; Micro Leaves Mix Sprinkles, p. 225, pretzel sticks
See p. 114 for a list of commonly used decorating items you may need.

Bake and cool cupcakes; ice cupcakes smooth. For owl, position two pretzel stick branches. Pipe tip 352 leaves. For pumpkin cupcake, position leaf sprinkles. Insert picks. Each serves 1.

*Combine Ivory with Lemon Yellow for ivory shown.

▲ Tri-Tone Pumpkin Cake

Pan: Dimensions Multi-Cavity Mini Pumpkin, p. 167
Colors: Ivory, Orange, Moss Green, p. 139
Fondant: White Ready-To-Use Rolled Fondant (10 oz.), p. 148; 9 in. Fondant Roller, Roll-N-Cut Mat, p. 152; 10-Pc Gum Paste/Fondant Tool Set, p. 152, White Pearl Dust (2), Brush Set, p. 153; Fondant Ribbon Cutter, p. 149
Recipe: Buttercream Icing, p. 128
Also: 6-Pc. Harvest Mini Metal Cutter Set, p. 225; Wave Flower Former Set, p. 142; Piping Gel, p. 141
See p. 114 for a list of commonly used decorating items you may need.

1 day in advance: Make leaves. Tint 2 oz. fondant green per treat. Roll out ⅛ in. thick. Cut leaf using maple leaf mini cutter. Score vein lines with veining tool. Let dry overnight on small flower former. Reserve remaining green fondant.

Bake and cool mini cakes; ice smooth. Tint 2 oz. fondant each dark orange, light orange, and light ivory. Roll out ⅛ in. thick. Use ribbon cutter to cut four strips in each color per treat, 1 in. wide x 5 in. long; taper ends. Attach strips to pumpkins with damp brush, trimming as needed. Using reserved green fondant, roll a ¼ in. x ¾ in. long log stem. Attach to top of pumpkin with piping gel. Attach leaf to stem with piping gel. Each serves 1.

◄ Pumpkin Perfection Cookies

Cookie: 101 Cookie Cutters (large circle), p. 173; 6-Pc. Harvest Mini Metal Cutter Set, p. 225; Cookie Sheet, Cooling Grid, p. 171
Tips: 2, 3, p. 134
Colors:* Brown, Black, Orange, Red-Red, Moss Green, p. 139
Recipes: Color Flow Icing, Roll-Out Cookies, p. 128
Also: Color Flow Mix, p. 141; Parchment Triangles, p. 136
See p. 114 for a list of commonly used decorating items you may need.

Prepare and roll out dough. For each treat, cut one circle using largest round cutter from set and one mini pumpkin. Bake and cool large and mini cookies separately.

Use tip 3 and full-strength icing to outline circle cookie and pumpkin cookie sections; let set. Flow in areas with thinned icing; let dry. Decorate with full-strength icing. Pipe tip 2 e-motion and dots on circle cookie and pipe in stem on pumpkin. Attach pumpkin to circle cookie with icing. Each serves 1.

*Combine Brown with Black for dark brown shown. Combine Orange with Red-Red for orange shown.

Gather your fall cookies and other goodies in Mystic Autumn Shaped Party Bags (p. 225). They capture autumn color with a cornucopia of pumpkins, acorns and leaves!

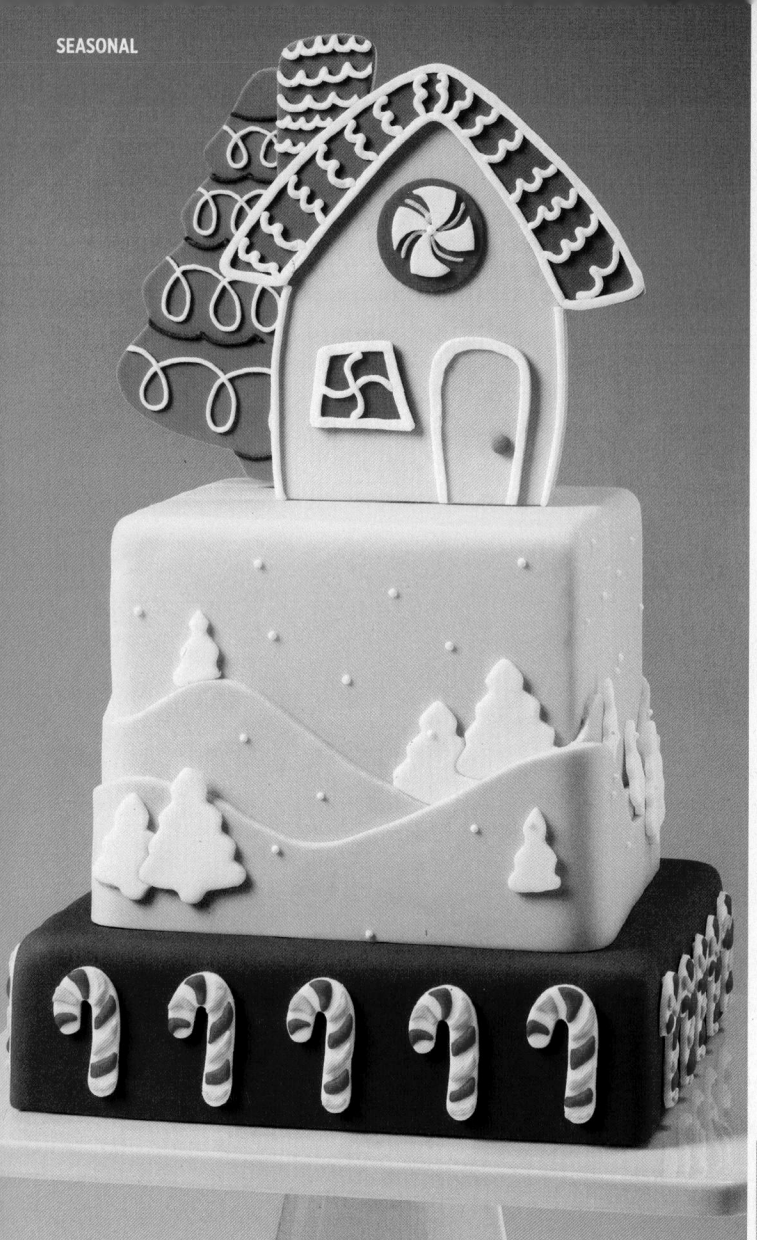

◀ **Hilltop Hideaway Cake**

Pans: 6 in. x 2 in., 8 in. x 2 in. Square, , p. 161; Cooling Grid, p. 171

Tips: 2, 4, p. 134

Colors: Kelly Green, Red-Red, Brown, Rose, Ivory, Creamy Peach, p. 139

Fondant: White (24 oz.), Chocolate (24 oz.), Blue (48 oz.) Ready-To-Use Rolled Fondant, Gum-Tex, p. 148; 20 in. Fondant Roller, Roll-N-Cut Mat, Fondant Smoother, p. 152; Brush Set, p. 153

Recipes: Buttercream, Royal Icings, p. 128

Also: 2013 Pattern Book (house, tree, mountains), p. 143; Meringue Powder, p. 141; White Candy Melts Candy, p. 175; 8 in. Lollipop Sticks, p. 178; 6-Pc. Holiday Mini Metal Cutter Set (candy cane, tree), p. 227; Dowel Rods, p. 194; Cake Boards, Fanci-Foil Wrap, p. 186; Spatula, p. 137; Disposable Decorating Bags, p. 136

See p. 114 for a list of commonly used decorating items you may need.

2 days in advance: Make fondant house. Tint fondant: 5 oz. tan; 3 oz. brown; 2 oz. red; 1 oz. rose. Reserve remaining white fondant. Roll out ⅛ in. thick as needed.

Add ⅔ teaspoon Gum-Tex to tan fondant. Use pattern and knife to cut out house. Use pattern to cut brown roof and chimney, rose door, red square and round windows. Attach to house using damp brush. Use pattern to cut white and rose overlays for round window; attach. Roll a ⅛ in. brown fondant ball for door knob; attach.

Use royal icing and tip 4 to outline roof, door and square window. Pipe tip 2 window pane outlines and scallops over roof and chimney. Let dry 48 hours on cornstarch-dusted board.

Attach two lollipop sticks to back with melted candy, leaving 4 in. extended at bottom to insert into cake.

Also: Make fondant tree. Tint 4 oz. fondant green. Add ½ teaspoon Gum-Tex. Roll out ⅛ in. thick. Use pattern and knife to cut tree. Pipe tip 2 loops and scallops with royal icing. Let dry 48 hours on cornstarch-dusted board. Attach lollipop stick to back with melted candy, leaving 4 in. extended at bottom to insert into cake.

Bake and cool 1-layer 8 in. cake and 3-layer 6 in. cake (trim one layer to 1 in. high for a 5 in. cake). Prepare and cover 6 in. cake with blue fondant, 8 in. cake with chocolate fondant (p. 119). Prepare for stacked construction (p. 120).

8 in. cake: Roll out white fondant ⅛ in. thick. Cut 20 candy canes using mini cutter. Attach five to each side, ⅝ in. apart, using damp brush. Outline and fill in stripes using tip 2 and royal icing in rose and red.

6 in. cake: Roll out blue fondant ⅛ in. thick. Use patterns to cut two each front and back mountains. Attach back mountains around cake using damp brush. Attach front mountains starting where indicated on pattern. Roll out white fondant. Cut 20 trees using mini cutter from set. Trim 12 trees smaller by moving cutter over shape to adjust height and width as needed to fit. Attach trees to cake sides using damp brush. Pipe tip 2 random dots. Insert house and tree. Serves 22.

*Combine Creamy Peach with Ivory for tan shown.
 Combine Brown with Ivory for brown shown.

▶ **Wild About Winter Cupcake Display**

Pans: 6 in. x 2 in. Round, p. 161; Standard Muffin, p. 162; Cooling Grid, p. 171

Tips: 2A, 3, p. 134

***Sugar Sheets!* Edible Decorating Paper/Tools:** White, Red, Light Pink, Brown (1 each), p. 144; Rotary Cutter, Dab-N-Hold Edible Adhesive, p. 145

Recipe: Buttercream Icing, p. 128

Also: Gingerbread Cottage Cupcake Combo, p. 230; 13-Count Standard Cupcakes-N-More Dessert Stand, p. 183; Gingerbread Boy, Circle Metal Cutters, p. 172; 4 in. Lollipop Sticks, p. 178; Light Cocoa Candy Melts Candy, p. 175; Disposable Decorating Bags, p. 136; Cake Board, p. 186; White Sugar Pearls, p. 157

See p. 114 for a list of commonly used decorating items you may need.

Bake and cool 12 cupcakes and a 1-layer round cake. Trim cake to 1 in. high. Use circle metal cutter to cut out cake; ice smooth.

Use rotary cutter to cut edible paper strips as follows; attach to cake with edible adhesive. Cut white strip 1 in. x 9¼ in., attach to side. Cut six strips each ½ in. x 1 in. in red and light pink; attach side by side on white strip, leaving ½ in. between each pair.
Cut two gingerbread boys from brown edible paper using metal cutter. Attach shiny sides together with melted candy; let set. Attach two sticks to back with melted candy, leaving 1 in. extended at bottom to insert in cake. Pipe tip 3 dot and outline details.

Cover cupcakes with tip 2A swirl. Position sugar pearls; insert picks. Position cupcakes and round cake on stand. Insert gingerbread boy. Cake and cupcakes each serve 1.

◀ Ring In The Holidays! Cookies

Cookie: Round Comfort-Grip Cutter, p. 172; 6-Pc. Holiday Mini Metal Cutter Set (gingerbread boy), p. 227; Cookie Sheet, Cooling Grid, p. 171

Tips: 1, 2, 3, p. 134

Colors: Red-Red, Christmas Red, Rose, Brown, p. 139

Recipes: Color Flow Icing, Roll-Out Cookies, p. 128

Also: Color Flow Mix, p. 141; Parchment Triangles, p. 136

See p. 114 for a list of commonly used decorating items you may need.

In advance: Prepare and roll out dough. For each treat, cut one round and one gingerbread boy cookie. Bake and cool round and boy cookies separately. Decorate cookies using full-strength icing for outlines and details, thinned icing for flow-in areas.

For round cookie, outline a 2¼ in. center circle with tip 3 and red icing; let set. Flow in with red; let set. Outline outer edge of cookie with tip 3 in white; let set. Flow in with white; immediately pipe tip 1 lines in thinned red and rose; let set.

For gingerbread boy, outline cookie with tip 3 in white, flow in with brown; let set. Pipe tip 2 dot buttons in white; over pipe with tip 2 red dots. Pipe tip 2 dot eyes and outline mouth in red. Attach boys to round cookies with full-strength icing. Each serves 1.

▶ Munch Merrily Petits Fours

Pans: 17.25 in. x 11.5 in. x 1 in. Large Non-Stick Cookie/Jelly Roll, p. 169; Cookie Sheet, Cooling Grid, p. 171

***Sugar Sheets!* Edible Decorating Paper/ Tools:** Bright Pink, Red (1 each makes 10 to 12 treats), p. 144; Rotary Cutter, p. 145

Also: 6-Pc. Holiday Mini Metal Cutter Set (gingerbread boy), p. 227; 101 Cookie Cutters (smallest round), p. 173; White, Red, Light Cocoa Candy Melts Candy (1 pk. each makes 10 to 12 treats), p. 175; Storage Board, p. 152; Parchment Triangles, p. 136; Piping Gel, p. 141

See p. 114 for a list of commonly used decorating items you may need.

In advance: Make candy gingerbread boys. Place boy cutter from mini set on non-stick pan. Fill ¼ in. deep with melted light cocoa candy. Tap to settle; chill until firm. Use melted white candy in cut parchment bag to pipe outline border and dot buttons. Use melted red candy to pipe dot eyes, outline smile and dots on white buttons. Chill until firm.

Bake and cool cake using firm-textured batter, such as pound cake. Use smallest round cutter from 101 cutter set to mark circles across top (one cake will make 30 petits fours); cut out using a knife.

Place cakes on cooling grid over parchment covered cookie sheet. Cover with melted white candy (p. 123). Tap to settle; chill until firm. Use rotary cutter to cut seven each pink and red edible paper strips for each treat, ¼ in. x 1 in. Use piping gel to attach alternating strips to sides, ¼ in. apart, trimming ends as needed. Attach gingerbread boy to top with melted candy; let set. Each serves 1.

◀ Ginger Guys and Whoopie Pies

Pans: 12-Cavity Whoopie Pie, p. 169; Cooling Grid, p. 171

Tips: 1, 2, 2A, p. 134

Colors:* Red-Red, Christmas Red, Rose, Brown, p. 139

Recipes: Buttercream Icing, Chocolate Whoopie Pies, Whoopie Pie Filling, p. 128

Fondant: White Ready-To-Use Rolled Fondant (6 oz. makes 12 treats), p. 148; 9 in. Fondant Roller, Roll-N-Cut Mat, p. 152; Brush Set, p. 153; Round Cut-Outs Fondant Cutters, p. 151

Also: 6-Pc. Holiday Mini Metal Cutter Set (gingerbread boy), p. 227; Dots Texture Press, p. 147; Red/White Sparkling Sugar, p. 232; Disposable Decorating Bags, p. 136

See p. 114 for a list of commonly used decorating items you may need.

Bake and cool two whoopie pies per treat. Prepare filling. Fill pies using tip 2A. Roll exposed filling edge in sparkling sugar.

For six treats, tint 4 oz. fondant rose, 2 oz. light brown. Roll out ⅛ in. thick as needed. Roll out rose; use knife to cut 3 in. x 6 in. strips. Imprint with texture press. Cut circles using largest Cut-Out. Attach to top of pies with tip 2 icing dots. Cut light brown gingerbread boys. Attach to circle with damp brush. Use white icing and tip 2 to pipe three dot buttons and scalloped outline. Use red icing and tip 1 to pipe dot eyes, button tops and outline smile. Each serves 1.

*Combine Red-Red with Christmas Red for red shown.

▼ Jolly Waddler Treat

Candy: Dessert Dome Candy Mold, p. 176; White (2 oz.), Dark Cocoa (11 oz.) Candy Melts Candy, p. 175; Decorator Brush Set, p. 178

Colors:* Christmas Red, Red-Red, Lemon Yellow, Golden Yellow, Brown, Black, p. 139

Fondant: White Ready-To-Use Rolled Fondant (3 oz.), Gum-Tex, p. 148; 9 in. Fondant Roller, Roll-N-Cut Mat, p. 152; Leaf Cut-Outs Fondant Cutters, p. 151

Also: Parchment Triangles, p. 136; corn syrup

See p. 114 for a list of commonly used decorating items you may need.

Make hat, beak, wings, feet and eyes. Tint ¾ oz. fondant each red and yellow, 1 oz. brown, reserve ½ oz. white. For feet, roll two balls, ⅞ in. diameter; shape into teardrops. Cut slits for toes with knife. For hat, roll a red ball 1¼ in. diameter; shape into a cone, 2 in. high x 1¼ in. wide. Roll out brown and yellow fondant ⅛ in. thick. Cut two brown wings using large leaf Cut-Out (reverse for one). For beak, use knife to cut two yellow triangles, ⅜ in. wide. For eyes, roll two brown balls, ¼ in. diameter; flatten. Roll tiny white balls for eye highlights; attach with damp brush.

For head, paint a heart shape, 2½ in. wide x 2¾ in. high, on inside of large dome mold with melted white candy; let set. Fill remainder of mold with dark cocoa candy; let set. Repeat process for body, painting a teardrop shape, 2 in. wide x 2½ in. high, with white candy before filling with dark cocoa candy. Mold back halves in large dome mold using dark cocoa candy; let set. Slide flat side of halves over warm surface; attach for a 3-D ball. Slide top of body over warm surface; attach head to body. Attach fondant pieces with melted candy; let set. For hat, roll 16 fondant balls, ⅜ in. to ½ in. diameter. Attach for brim and pompom with melted candy. Each serves 1.

*Combine Christmas Red with Red-Red for red shown. Combine Lemon Yellow with Golden Yellow for yellow shown. Combine Brown with Black for brown shown.

▲ Spring In His Step Snowman Cake

Pans: 3-D Soccer Ball, 3-D Sports Ball Set, p. 165; Cookie Sheet, Cooling Grid, p. 171

Tips: 2A, 3, 6, 12, p. 134

Colors:* Christmas Red, Red-Red, Black, Kelly Green, Orange, p. 139

Recipes: Buttercream Icing, Roll-Out Cookies, p. 128

Also: 2013 Pattern Book (hat), p. 143; 18-Pc. Holiday Metal Cutter Set (mittens, boots), p. 227; Heart Cut-Outs Fondant Cutters, p. 151; 6 in. Lollipop Sticks, p. 178; White Candy Melts Candy, p. 175; 13 in. x 19 in. Cake Boards, Fanci-Foil Wrap, p. 186; Disposable Decorating Bags, p. 136; Rolling Pin, p. 159; Spatula, p. 137

See p. 114 for a list of commonly used decorating items you may need.

In advance: Make cookies. Prepare and roll out dough. Cut two mittens and two boots using cutters from set (reverse one of each). Cut two hearts using large Cut-Out and hat using pattern and knife; trim ¾ in. from each heart point. Bake and cool cookies.

Bake and cool cakes in soccer ball and sports ball half. Ice cakes and cookies smooth. Pipe tip 6 zigzag cuffs on boots and mittens. Pipe tip 12 outline hat band, pull-out nose, dot eyes and buttons; pat smooth with finger dipped in cornstarch. Using tip 3, outline and pipe in mouth and tongue; pat smooth. Pipe tip 2A ball cheeks, tip 3 dot eye highlights. Attach two lollipop sticks to back of hat with melted candy, leaving 3 in. extended at bottom; let set. Attach heart cookies for bow tie; pipe tip 2A dot knot. Insert hat cookie; position mittens and boots cookies. Cakes serve 18; each cookie serves 1.

*Combine Christmas Red with Red-Red for red shown.

▼ Joyous Toymaker Cookies

Cookie: Gingerbread Boy Giant Non-Stick Cookie Pan, p. 228; 4-Pc. Gingerbread Boys Nesting Metal Cutter Set, p. 227; 3-Pc. Ice Cream Colored Metal Cutter Set (sugar cone), p. 173; Cookie Sheet, Cooling Grid, p. 171
Tips: 2, 2A, 4, 8, 12, p. 134
Colors:* Leaf Green, Kelly Green, Golden Yellow, Christmas Red, Red-Red, Black, Copper (for light skin tone shown), Brown, p. 139
Recipes: Royal Icing, Giant Sugar Cookies, Roll-Out Cookies, p. 128
Also: Meringue Powder, p. 141; Disposable Decorating Bags, Parchment Triangles, p. 136; Parchment Paper, p. 158
See p. 114 for a list of commonly used decorating items you may need.

For Santa, prepare giant sugar cookie dough; press into pan prepared with vegetable pan spray. Bake and cool cookie. For elves, prepare roll-out dough. Roll out and cut gingerbread boys using second smallest cutter from set. Cut heads/caps using sugar cone cutter. Bake and cool cookies.

Place cookies on cooling grid over parchment-covered cookie sheet. Cover Santa's suit area with thinned red icing (p. 123). Let set. Cover head with thinned skin tone icing. Let set. Cover gingerbread boys and cap area of cone cookies with thinned kelly green icing. Let set. Cover round area of cone cookies with thinned skin tone icing. Let set.

Decorate with full-strength icing. For Santa, pipe tip 2A outline belt. Pipe tip 8 outline buckle, dot eyes and nose, outline hair curl. Pipe tip 4 dot mouth. Pipe tip 12 swirl beard, elongated bead moustache and dot buttons. For elves, pipe tip 8 swirl hat trim, tip 4 zigzag pompom and dot buttons, pull-out nose and ears. Pipe tip 2 dot eyes, outline and pipe in mouth, bead tongue. Attach heads to bodies with icing. Giant cookie serves 12; elf cookies each serve 1.

*Combine Christmas Red with Red-Red for red shown. Combine Brown with Red-Red and Black for dark skin tone shown.

▲ Twosome in Tune Cookies

Cookie: 101 Cookie Cutters (smallest circle), p. 173; Bell Metal Cutter, p. 172; Round Cut-Outs Fondant Cutters, p. 151; Cookie Sheet, Cooling Grid, p. 171
Tips: 2, 3, 5, 12, p. 134
Colors:* Copper (for light skin tone shown), Lemon Yellow, Golden Yellow, Rose, Black, Brown, Red-Red. p. 139
Recipes: Color Flow Icing, Roll-Out Cookies, p. 128
Also: Color Flow Mix, p. 141; Disposable Decorating Bags, p. 136; Gold Pearl Dust, Brush Set, Pure Lemon Extract, p. 153; Parchment Paper, p. 158
See p. 114 for a list of commonly used decorating items you may need.

Prepare and roll out dough. Cut cookies using bell cutter for bodies (trim off clapper), largest round Cut-Out for heads and smallest circle from 101 cutter set for halos. Bake and cool cookies.

Place cookies on cooling grid over parchment-covered cookie sheet. Cover cookies with thinned icing (p. 123) using white for bodies, skin tone for heads, yellow for halos. Decorate and assemble using full-strength icing. Pipe tip 12 outline arms, tip 5 bead hands. Pipe tip 3 outline hair and dot cheeks; flatten and smooth with finger dipped in cornstarch. Pipe tip 2 dot eyes and outline mouth. Brush edges of halos with gold Pearl Dust/lemon extract mixture (p. 118). Let dry. Attach cookies; let set. Each serves 1.

*Combine Lemon Yellow with Golden Yellow for yellow shown. Combine Brown with Red-Red for dark skin tone shown.

▶ Deer Days Cookies

Cookie: 3-Pc. Snowflake Wishes Colored Metal Cutter Set (reindeer head), 18-Pc. Holiday Metal Cutter Set (reindeer), p. 227; Cookie Sheet, Cooling Grid, p. 171
Tips: 2, 3, p. 134
Colors:* Black, Brown, p. 139
Recipes: Color Flow Icing, Roll-Out Cookies, p. 128
Also: Color Flow Mix, p. 141; Parchment Triangles, p. 136
See p. 114 for a list of commonly used decorating items you may need.

Prepare and roll out dough. Use reindeer cutters from sets to cut one each for each cookie. Bake and cool cookies.

Outline cookies with tip 3 and full-strength icing; flow in with thinned icing (p. 120). Let dry. Decorate with tip 2 and full-strength icing. Pipe in tail detail, hooves and inside ears. Pipe outline antler detail and mouth, dot eyes and nose. Attach heads to bodies with full-strength icing. Each serves 1.

*Combine Brown with Black for dark brown shown.

▶ Treats and Sweets Cupcake Tower

Pans: 6 in. x 2 in. Round, p. 161; Standard Muffin, p. 162; Cooling Grid, p. 171
Tip: 2A, p. 134
Sugar Sheets! **Edible Decorating Paper/Tools:**
White (1 sheet makes 8 treats), Red (1 sheet makes 4 treats), p. 144; Rotary Cutter, Dab-N-Hold Edible Adhesive, p. 145
Recipe: Buttercream Icing, p. 128
Also: Sweets & Treats Cupcake Combo, p. 230; 13-Count Standard Cupcakes-N-More Dessert Stand, p. 183; 4-Pc. Snowflakes Nesting Metal Cutter Set, p. 227; Circle Metal Cutter, p. 172; Fine Tip Primary Colors (red, green) FoodWriter Edible Color Markers, Brush Set, p. 153; Parchment Triangles, p. 136; White Candy Melts Candy, p. 175; 4 in. Lollipop Sticks, p. 178
See p. 114 for a list of commonly used decorating items you may need.

In advance: Make snowflake cake topper. Use second smallest cutter from set and red edible marker to mark two snowflakes on shiny side of red edible paper. Cut out using scissors. Brush one shiny side with melted candy; attach second on top. Use melted candy in cut parchment bag to pipe outline and diamond detail on front; let set. Attach lollipop stick to back with melted candy, leaving 1½ in. extended at bottom to insert into cake.

Bake and cool 12 cupcakes and a 1-layer round cake. Trim cake to 1 in. high. Use circle metal cutter to cut out cake; ice smooth. Use rotary cutter to cut one strip, 1 in. x 9 in., from white edible paper. Use red and green edible markers to draw plaid design with lines in various widths, ¼ to ½ in. apart. Let dry. Attach strip around base using edible adhesive. Cover cupcake tops with tip 2A swirl. Insert picks. Position cupcakes and round cake on stand. Insert snowflake topper. Cake and cupcakes each serve 1.

◀ Plaid Tidings Cake

Pans: 6 in., 8 in. x 2 in. Square, p. 161; Cooling Grid, p. 171
Tips: 1, 2, 3, p. 134
Colors:* Moss Green, Brown, Black, p. 139
Fondant: White (48 oz.), Red (24 oz.) Ready-To-Use Rolled Fondant, Gum-Tex, p. 148; 20 in. Fondant Roller, 20 in. Fondant Roller Guide Rings, Roll-N-Cut Mat, Fondant Smoother, Fondant Trimmer, p. 152; Silver Pearl Dust, Brush Set, Pure Lemon Extract, p. 153
Recipes: Buttercream, Royal Icings, p. 128; Thinned Fondant Adhesive, p. 127
Also: 4-Pc. Snowflakes Nesting Metal Cutter Set, p. 227; Meringue Powder, p. 141; 8 in. Lollipop Sticks, p. 178; Dowel Rods, p. 194; Cake Boards, Fanci-Foil Wrap, p. 186; Parchment Paper, p. 158
See p. 114 for a list of commonly used decorating items you may need.

2 to 3 days in advance: Make fondant snowflakes. Add ¾ teaspoon Gum-Tex to 6 oz. white fondant. Roll out ⅛ in. thick. Cut snowflakes: one using largest cutter from set, 12 using smallest cutter from set. Let dry 24 hours on cornstarch-dusted, parchment-covered boards.

Also: Decorate snowflakes with gray royal icing. For large snowflake, pipe tip 3 straight and angled lines; use tip 2 to outline and fill in diamond accents; pat smooth with finger dipped in cornstarch. For small snowflakes, pipe tip 2 straight lines; use tip 1 for angled lines and to outline and fill in diamonds; pat smooth. Let dry 24 hours. Use fine tip brush to paint snowflake details with silver Pearl Dust/lemon extract mixture. Let dry. Use fondant adhesive to attach lollipop stick to back of large snowflake; leave 5 in. extended at bottom to insert into cake.

Bake and cool 3-layer 6 in. square (trim one layer to 1 in. for a 5 in. high cake) and 1-layer 8 in. square. Tint 3 oz. each light green and dark green. Prepare and cover cakes with red or white fondant (p. 119); reserve excess red fondant. Prepare for stacked construction (p. 120).

For plaid lines, roll out fondant colors ¹⁄₁₆ in. thick. Cut approximately 16 strips of each: ⅛ in. wide and ½ in. wide x 10 in. long red; ⁵⁄₁₆ in. wide x 10 in. long light green; ¼ in. wide x 10 in. long dark green. Use damp brush to attach strips to cake sides at a 45° angle, varying spacing from ⁵⁄₁₆ in. to ¾ in. apart. Trim ends as needed. Attach small snowflakes to cake sides using thinned fondant adhesive. Insert large snowflake. Serves 22.

*Combine Moss Green with Brown for lighter green shown. Use a small amount of Black for gray.

◀ Polar Plaid Cookies

Cookie: 4-Pc. Snowflakes Nesting Metal Cutter Set, p. 227; 4-Pc. Circles Nesting Metal Cutter Set, p. 172; Cookie Sheet, Cooling Grid, p. 171

Tips: 1, 2, 3, p. 134

Colors:* Red-Red, Christmas Red, Moss Green, Brown, Black, p. 139

Recipes: Color Flow Icing, Roll-Out Cookies, p. 128

Also: Color Flow Mix, p. 141; Silver Pearl Dust, Pure Lemon Extract, Brush Set, p. 153

See p. 114 for a list of commonly used decorating items you may need.

Prepare and roll out dough. For each treat, cut one round using second largest cutter from set and one snowflake using second smallest cutter from set. Bake and cool round and snowflake cookies separately.

Outline round cookies with tip 3 and full-strength icing; flow in using thinned icing (p. 120). Immediately pipe on plaid lines using tip 1 and thinned, tinted icings (pipe one color at a time). Let dry. Outline snowflake cookies with tip 3 and full-strength white icing; flow in using thinned icing. Let dry. Pipe outline snowflake arms and diamond details using tip 1 and full-strength gray icing. Let dry.

Use fine tip brush to paint snowflake details with silver Pearl Dust/lemon extract mixture (p. 118). Let dry. Attach snowflake to round cookie using full-strength icing. Let set. Each serves 1.

*Combine Red-Red with Christmas Red for red shown. Combine Moss Green with Brown for lighter green shown. Use a small amount of Black for gray.

▶ Snow Shower Petit Fours

Pans: 9 in. x 13 in. x 2 in. Sheet, p. 161; Non-Stick Cookie Sheet, Cooling Grid, p. 169

Colors: Burgundy, No-Taste Red, Rose, p. 139

Fondant: White Ready-To-Use Rolled Fondant (2 oz. makes eight treats), p. 148; 9 in. Fondant Roller, Roll-N-Cut Mat, p. 152; Brush Set, p. 153

Recipe: Buttercream Icing, p. 128

Also: White Candy Melts Candy (1 oz. makes 4 treats), p. 175; Snowflake Large Lollipop Mold, p. 231; 101 Cookie Cutters (smallest circle), p. 173; White Sugar Pearls, p. 157; Piping Gel, p. 141; Parchment Triangles, p. 136; Cake Boards, p. 186; Parchment Paper, p. 158

See p. 114 for a list of commonly used decorating items you may need.

In advance: Make candy snowflakes. Use melted white candy in cut parchment bag to fill snowflake portion of candy mold. Tap to settle; chill until firm. Make one snowflake per treat. Use melted candy to attach sugar pearl to center. Let set.

Bake and cool 1 in. high sheet cake using firm-textured batter, such as pound cake. Use smallest cutter from set to mark circles on cake top (one cake will yield 24 to 26). Use a knife to cut out petits fours. Place on cooling grid over a parchment-covered cookie sheet. Cover with melted candy (p. 123). Chill until firm.

Tint ½ oz. portions fondant each burgundy, red and rose; reserve one portion white. Roll out 1/16 in. thick. Cut into strips, ½ in. wide x 1 in. long. Attach to petits fours sides using piping gel. Attach candy snowflake to top using melted candy dot. Each serves 1.

◀ Winterized Whoopie Pies

Pans: 12-Cavity Whoopie Pie, p. 169; Cooling Grid, p. 171

Tips: 1, 2A, p. 134

Color:* Black, p. 139

Fondant: White Ready-To-Use Rolled Fondant (2 oz. makes 6 treats), p. 148; 9 in. Fondant Roller, Roll-N-Cut Mat, p. 152; Silver Pearl Dust, Brush Set, Pure Lemon Extract, p. 153

Recipes: Royal Icing, Chocolate Whoopie Pies, Whoopie Pie Filling, p. 128

Also: 4-Pc. Snowflakes Nesting Metal Cutter Set, p. 227; White Nonpareils Sprinkles, p. 156; Meringue Powder, Piping Gel, p. 141; Parchment Triangles, p. 136

See p. 114 for a list of commonly used decorating items you may need.

Bake and cool two whoopie pies per treat. Prepare filling. Fill pies using tip 2A. Roll exposed filling edge in nonpareils.

Roll out fondant 1/16 in. thick. Use smallest cutter to cut snowflakes. Pipe tip 1 outline and diamond details in gray. Attach snowflake to pie with piping gel. Paint snowflake details with silver Pearl Dust/lemon extract mixture (p. 118). Each serves 1.

*Use a small amount of Black to make gray.

▼ Yule Jewel Gingerbread House

Cookie: Pre-Baked Gingerbread House Kit (2104-1903), p. 229; 3-Pc. Trees Colored Metal Cutter Set (triangle tree), p. 227
Fondant: White Ready-To-Use Rolled Fondant (46 oz.), Gum-Tex, p. 148; 9 in. Fondant Roller, Roll-N-Cut Mat, p. 152; Jewelry Designs Gum Paste & Fondant Mold, p. 150; Leaf Green, Lilac Purple, Orchid Pink, Silver, White Pearl Dust, Brush Set, Pure Lemon Extract, p. 153
Recipe: Thinned Fondant Adhesive, p. 127
Also: Meringue Powder, Piping Gel, p. 141; Green Sugar Pearls, p. 157; Cake Board, Fanci-Foil Wrap, p. 186
See p. 114 for a list of commonly used decorating items you may need.

2 days in advance: Make fondant trees. Add ¼ teaspoon Gum-Tex to 4 oz. fondant. Roll out ¹⁄₁₆ in. thick. Use triangle tree cutter from set to cut four trees. For easel backs, use same cutter to cut two trees; trim with knife to 2½ in. high from top of tree. Cut lengthwise in half to create four easels. Let all dry 48 hours on cornstarch-dusted boards. Attach easel backs with thinned fondant adhesive. Paint trees with Leaf Green Pearl Dust/lemon extract mixture.

1 day in advance: Use jewelry mold to make fondant trims (p. 124).

Also: Build house. Prepare and cover all gingerbread pieces from kit with fondant rolled out ⅛ in. thick. Attach with damp brush. Assemble house following kit instructions. Let dry 24 hours. Paint front, back and side walls with white Pearl Dust/lemon extract mixture. Let dry.

For front, use piping gel to attach brooch for top window. Attach eight green gems for door. For door frame, attach one 2 in. and two 2¾ in. silver chain link sections. Attach four pink faceted gems for window, two 2 in. silver square chain border sections for window frame and 1½ in. silver chain link section for window sill. Attach white round gems to fill in remaining areas.

For back, decorate same as front, replacing door with a second bottom window. For sides, use piping gel to attach six pink faceted gems for window. Attach two 1¾ in. silver chain link sections for window shutters. Attach white round gems to fill in remaining areas.

For roof, use mold and fondant to make seven mesh borders. Attach to peaks and eaves with piping gel. Attach square gems on top peak. Attach rows of green, rose and violet square gems starting at bottom edge, alternating rows with 6½ in. chain border sections.

Attach sugar pearls to trees with piping gel. Let dry. Position trees.

▲ Fudgy Fir Tree Cake

Pans: Iridescents! Tree, p. 226; Cooling Grid, p. 171
Fondant: Chocolate (24 oz.), White (6 oz.) Ready-To-Use Rolled Fondant, p. 148; 20 in. Fondant Roller, 20 in. Fondant Roller Guide Rings, Roll-N-Cut Mat, p. 152; Brush Set, Decorative Press Set, p. 153
Recipe: Buttercream Icing, p. 128
Also: White Sparkling Sugar, p. 156; Gold, Silver Pearlized Sugar, p. 157; Piping Gel, p. 141; Cake Boards, Fanci-Foil Wrap, p. 186
See p. 114 for a list of commonly used decorating items you may need.

Bake and cool cake. Prepare and cover with chocolate fondant (p. 119). For tree branches, soften white fondant with shortening. Use decorative press with single circle insert to make main branches, trimming from 5 in. to 14 in. long. Make shorter side branches, trimming from ¾ in. to 3 in. Brush with piping gel, sprinkle with white sparkling sugar, then attach. Begin with center trunk, then add shorter branches.

For ornaments, roll 18 white fondant balls, ½ in. diameter. Brush with piping gel and roll in pearlized sugar to coat. Attach to tree with piping gel. Serves 12.

▶ Noël Nester Mini Cakes

Pans: Silicone 3-D Tree Mold, p. 226; 17.25 in. x 11.5 in. x 1 in. Non-Stick Large Cookie/Jelly Roll, p. 169; Cooling Grid, p. 171
Fondant: Red Ready-To-Use Rolled Fondant (½ oz. makes three treats), p. 148; Nature Designs Gum Paste & Fondant Mold, p. 150; Brush Set, White Pearl Dust p. 153
Candy: White (1 pk. makes 5 treats), Light Cocoa (1 pk. makes 12 treats) Candy Melts Candy, Garden (green) Candy Color Set, p. 175
Also: Round Comfort-Grip Cutter, p. 172; Green Sugar Pearls, p. 157; Parchment Paper, p. 136; Cake Boards, p. 186
See p. 114 for a list of commonly used decorating items you may need.

In advance: Make fondant birds in silicone mold. Let dry on cornstarch-dusted board.

Also: Make candy bases. Set round cutter on non-stick pan. Fill ¼ in. deep with melted light cocoa candy. Tap to settle; chill until firm. Make one base per treat.

Bake and cool mini trees. Place on cooling grid over parchment-covered pan. Cover with melted candy tinted green (p. 123). Chill until firm. Brush Pearl Dust over all trees. Use melted, tinted candy in cut parchment bag to pipe scallop garland; immediately position sugar pearl trims. Let set. Use melted candy to attach tree to round base and bird to tree top. Each serves 1.

▼ Poinsettia Pinwheel Cookies

Cookie: 4-Pc. Circles Nesting Metal Cutter Set, p. 172; Cookie Sheet, Cooling Grids, p. 171
Tip: 1A, p. 134
Colors: Red-Red, Kelly Green, p. 139
Fondant: White Ready-To-Use Rolled Fondant (6½ oz. makes 2 cookies), p. 148; 9 in. Fondant Roller, Roll-N-Cut Mat, p. 152; Brush Set, p. 153;
Recipes: Buttercream Icing, Roll-Out Cookies, p. 128
Also: Punch Set with Oval Cutting Insert, Leaf Cutting Insert, p. 145; Red Colored Sugar, p. 156; Yellow Sugar Pearls, p. 157; Piping Gel, p. 141; 12 in. Rolling Pin, p. 159; Cake Boards, p. 186; Spatula, p. 137

See p. 114 for a list of commonly used decorating items you may need.

In advance: Make fondant leaves and flower center. Tint 3 oz. fondant red, ¼ oz. green for each treat. Roll out fondant ⅛ in. thick. Cut red into 2¾ in. x 8 in. strips. Use punch with leaf cutting insert to cut 12 petals per treat. Brush with piping gel; sprinkle with red sugar. Let dry on cornstarch covered board. Use wide end of tip 1A to cut out a green flower center for each treat. Let set.

Prepare and roll out dough. Cut cookies using largest round cutter. Bake and cool cookies. Ice cookies smooth. Position six petals around center of cookie; attach six petals between first petal group with piping gel. Position flower center. Attach sugar pearls with piping gel. Each serves 1.

▲ Shiny Pine Cookies

Cookie: 3-Pc. Trees Colored Metal Cutter Set (triangle tree), p. 227; Cookie Sheet, Cooling Grid, p. 171
Tips: 2, 8, p. 134
Colors:* Christmas Red, Red-Red, Leaf Green, Violet, Rose, Black, p. 139
Fondant: White Ready-To-Use Rolled Fondant (1 oz. per treat), p. 148; 12 in. Rolling Pin, p. 159; Roll-N-Cut Mat, p. 152; Jewelry Designs Gum Paste & Fondant Mold, p. 150; Silver, Leaf Green, Lilac Purple Pearl Dust, Brush Set, p. 153
Recipes: Royal Icing, Roll-Out Cookies, p. 128
Also: Red Sugar, p. 156; Silver Pearlized Sugar, p. 157; Disposable Decorating Bags, p. 136; Meringue Powder, Piping Gel, p. 141
See p. 114 for a list of commonly used decorating items you may need.

Prepare and roll out dough. For each treat cut one square, 4 in. x 4 in., and one tree using

triangle tree cutter from set. Trim off tree trunk. Bake and cool cookies.

Outline square cookie using tip 8 and full-strength gray icing; flow in using thinned red icing (p. 120). Let icing set for 10 to 15 minutes; sprinkle with red sugar. Let dry. Outline tree with tip 2 and full-strength gray icing; flow in with thinned icing. Let icing set for 10 to 15 minutes; sprinkle heavily with silver sugar. Let dry. Brush grey outlines with silver Pearl Dust.

Tint half of fondant green, half violet. Use jewelry mold to make 10 small round gems for each treat. Let dry. Brush with matching Pearl Dust. Attach tree to square and gems to tree with tip 2 icing dots. Let set. Each serves 1.

*Combine Christmas Red with Red-Red for red shown. Combine Violet with Rose for violet shown. Use a small amount of black to make gray icing.

▼ Lovin' Linzer Cookies

Cookie: 7-Pc. Heart Linzer Cutter Set, p. 236; Cookie Sheet, Cooling Grid, p. 171; Pink Cookie Icing, p. 237
Recipe: Linzer Cookies, p. 128
Also: Pink Colored Sugar, p. 237; Red Candy Melts Candy (1 oz. makes 6 treats), p. 235; Parchment Triangles, p. 136; Pink Sugar Pearls, p. 157
See p. 114 for a list of commonly used decorating items you may need.

Prepare and roll out dough. Cut two heart shapes for each treat. Cut heart insert on top cookie. Bake and cool.

Sandwich top and bottom cookies with pink icing. Fill center heart with icing; sprinkle with pink sugar. Using melted red candy in cut parchment bag, pipe a heart on cookie; position Sugar Pearls. Each serves 1.

▲ Solemates Cookies

Cookie: 3-Pc. Princess Colored Metal Cutter Set (shoe), p. 202; 6-Pc. Heart Nesting Plastic Cutter Set, p. 173; Cookie Sheet, Cooling Grid, p. 171
Tips: 2, 3, p. 134
Colors: Rose, No-Taste Red, Black, p. 139
Fondant: White Ready-To-Use Rolled Fondant (¼ oz. per treat.), p. 148; 9 in. Fondant Roller, Roll-N-Cut Mat, p. 152
Recipes: Color Flow Icing, Roll-Out Cookies, p. 128
Also: Color Flow Mix, Piping Gel, p. 141; Disposable Decorating Bags, p. 136; Brush Set, p. 153; Pink, Red, Black Colored Sugar, p. 156
See p. 114 for a list of commonly used decorating items you may need.

In advance: Make fondant hearts. Tint portions of fondant rose, red and black. Roll out ⅟₁₆ in. thick. Cut hearts using smallest cutter. Brush tops with piping gel; sprinkle with colored sugar. Let dry.

Prepare and roll out dough. Cut shoe cookies using metal cutter. Bake and cool.

Tint portions of icing rose, red and black. Outline shoes and openings with tip 3 and full-strength icing. Flow in with thinned icing (p. 120). Let dry. Pipe tip 2 scrolls with full-strength icing. Let dry. Attach hearts to cookies with full-strength icing. Each serves 1.

◄ Sultry Stripes Petits Fours

Pans: 9 in. x 13 in. x 2 in. Sheet, p. 161; Cooling Grid, p. 171
***Sugar Sheets!* Edible Decorating Paper/Tools:** Zebra (1 sheet makes 12 treats), Black (1 sheet makes 22 treats), Red (1 sheet makes 30 treats), p. 144; Rotary Cutter, Dab-N-Hold Edible Adhesive, p. 145
Candy: White Candy Melts Candy (24 oz. makes 12 treats), Garden Candy Color Set (pink), p. 175
Also: 6-Pc. Hearts Nesting Plastic Cutter Set, p. 173; 7-Pc. Hearts Metal Cutter Set, p. 235; Spatula, p. 137; Parchment Paper, p. 158; Fine Tip Primary Colors FoodWriter Edible Color Markers, Brush Set, p. 153; Red Colored Sugar, p. 156; Cake Leveler, p. 158
See p. 114 for a list of commonly used decorating items you may need.

Bake and cool one-layer cake using firm-textured batter like pound cake. Level to 1¼ in. high. Use third smallest plastic cutter to imprint heart shapes; cut out cakes with knife.

Tint half of melted white candy pink. Place cakes on cooling grid over parchment-lined cookie sheet. Cover half of cakes with pink, half with white candy (p. 123). Tap to settle; chill until firm.

For bottom borders, use rotary cutter to cut strips, ⅜ in. wide x 8½ in. long from black edible paper. Attach strips with edible adhesive. Use black edible marker and third smallest plastic cutter to trace shapes on shiny side of zebra edible paper; cut out. Attach to cake tops with edible adhesive. Use black edible marker and smallest metal cutter to trace heart shapes on shiny side of red edible paper; cut out. Brush tops with edible adhesive; sprinkle with red sugar. Attach to cake top with edible adhesive. Each serves 1.

◀ Heart Strings Cookie Pops

Cookie: Heart Cookie Treat Pan, p. 171; 6-Pc. Hearts Nesting Plastic Cutter Set, p. 173; Cooling Grid, 8 in. Cookie Treat Sticks, p. 171

Tip: 7, p. 134

Colors: Red-Red, Rose, p. 139

Fondant: White Ready-To-Use Rolled Fondant (2¼ oz. per treat), p. 148; 9 in. Fondant Roller, Roll-N-Cut Mat, p. 152; Round Cut-Outs Fondant Cutters, p. 151; Fabric Designs Gum Paste & Fondant Mold, p. 150; Dots Texture Press, p. 147; Silver Pearl Dust, Pure Lemon Extract, Brush Set, p. 153

Recipes: Color Flow Icing, Vanilla Sugar Cookies on a Stick, p. 128

Also: Parchment Paper, p. 158; Color Flow Mix, p. 141; Disposable Decorating Bags, p. 136; ⅛ in. wide red ribbon (7 in. per treat)

See p. 114 for a list of commonly used decorating items you may need.

In advance: Make fondant heart pendant. Roll out fondant ⅛ in. thick. Cut heart shape using second smallest cutter. Cut out hole using narrow end of tip 7. Roll a 1⁄16 in. diameter fondant rope. Shape lengths into LOVE letters; attach with damp brush. Paint pendant with silver Pearl Dust/lemon extract mixture (p. 118). Let dry.

Prepare cookie dough and press into pan. Insert cookie stick and bake following pan directions. Cool in pan 3 minutes after baking; unmold and cut hole in cookies using smallest round Cut-Out. Let cool completely. Cover cookies with thinned white icing (p. 123). Let dry.

For each treat, tint 1 oz. fondant red. Use fabric mold to make one bow for each treat; set aside. Roll out remaining red ⅛ in. thick. Cut heart using second largest cutter from set. Center fondant heart on cookie; cut hole with smallest round Cut-Out. Attach to cookie with damp brush. Tint 1 oz. rose; roll out ⅛ in. thick. Imprint with texture press. Cut heart using third largest cutter from set. Center on cookie and cut hole as above. Attach rose heart and bow to cookie with damp brush. Thread ribbon through pendant and tie onto cookie. Each serves 1.

▼ Sweet Scallops Cookies

Cookie: 4-Pc. Blossoms Nesting Metal Cutter Set, Round Comfort-Grip Cutter, p. 173; Cookie Sheet, Cooling Grid, p. 171

***Sugar Sheets!* Edible Decorating Paper/ Tools:** Bright Pink, Light Pink, Black, Red, Pink Hearts (1 sheet each makes 2 treats), p. 144; Punch Set with Oval Cutting Insert, Layered Hearts Cutting Insert Set, Dab-N-Hold Edible Adhesive, Heart Mini Punch, p. 145; 4-Pc. Hearts Cake Stamp Set, Black, Pink, Red Dab-N-Color Edible Color, p. 146

Recipes: Buttercream Icing, Roll-Out Cookies, p. 128

Also: Brush Set, p. 137; Piping Gel, p. 141; Spatula, p. 137; Black, Pink, Red Cake Sparkles, p. 157

See p. 114 for a list of commonly used decorating items you may need.

Prepare and roll out dough. Use largest blossom cutter from set to cut cookies. Bake and cool. Ice smooth.

Use largest blossom cutter to cut one shape for each treat from bright pink, black and red edible paper. Attach blossoms to cookies with piping gel. Use round cutter to cut circles from pink hearts edible paper. Attach to cookies with edible adhesive.

Use punch with largest heart insert to cut one heart for each treat from light pink edible paper. Use heart stamps and edible colors to stamp designs; let dry. Brush stamped areas with piping gel; sprinkle with Cake Sparkles. Attach hearts to cookies with edible adhesive. Use heart mini punch to cut eight hearts for each treat from black, bright pink or light pink edible paper. Attach to scallops with edible adhesive. Each serves 1.

▲ Heart Full of Love Candy Box

Cookie: 12-Cavity Valentine Cookie Shapes Non-Stick Pan, p. 234; 6-Pc. Hearts Nesting Plastic Cutter Set, p. 173; Non-Stick Cookie Sheet, p. 169

Candy: Pink (2 oz. per treat), Light Cocoa (1½ oz. per treat), Candy Melts Candy, Garden Candy Color Set (pink), p. 175

Recipe: Candy Clay, p. 123

Also: Disposable Decorating Bags, p. 136; Jewelry Designs Gum Paste & Fondant Mold, p. 150; 9 in. Fondant Roller, Roll-N-Cut Mat, p. 152; Hearts Favor Candy (1 pk. fills 15 treats), p. 198, corn syrup

See p. 114 for a list of commonly used decorating items you may need.

In advance: Prepare candy clay using light cocoa candy. Let set overnight.

For bright pink base, add pink candy color to melted pink candy. Position third largest heart cutter on cookie sheet; fill ¼ in. deep with pink candy. Tap to settle; chill until firm.

For lid, use quilted heart cavity of cookie shapes pan. Fill center heart area with bright pink candy. Tap to settle, chill until firm. Fill cavity with light cocoa candy. Chill until firm.

For box sides, knead candy clay and press in mesh border cavity of jewelry mold. Trim away excess and unmold. Shape and position strip upright on base. Use lid as a guide to shape strip into a heart. Attach strip to base and seal end seam with melted candy. Let dry. Fill with favor candies. Position lid. Each serves 1.

◀ Cottontail Close-Up Cake

Pans: 8 in. x 2 in. Round, p. 161; 3-Pc. Paisley Set (smallest used), p. 160
Tips: 7, 8, 16, p. 134
Colors: Rose, Black, p. 139
Recipe: Buttercream Icing, p. 128
Also: 2013 Pattern Book (inner ears, nose, mouth and eyes), p. 143; Cake Board, Fanci-Foil Wrap, p. 186; Disposable Decorating Bags, p. 136; Spatula, p. 137

See p. 114 for a list of commonly used decorating items you may need.

Bake and cool 1-layer cakes: one round and two small paisley.

Use toothpick to mark inner ear, nose, mouth and eye patterns on cake tops. Ice inner ears smooth in rose. Pipe tip 7 dot eyes; flatten and smooth with finger dipped in cornstarch. Pipe in tip 8 nose; smooth. Pipe tip 7 outline mouth. Cover cakes with tip 16 stars. Overpipe mouth and nose for dimension. Serves 12.

▶ Festive Flock Nested Cookies

Pans: Mini Wonder Mold, p. 161; Cookie Sheet, Cooling Grid, p. 171
Tip: 2, p. 134
Colors:* Lemon Yellow, Golden Yellow, Orange, Black, p. 139
Recipes: Royal Icing, Roll-Out Cookies, p. 128; favorite crisped rice cereal treats
Also: 9-Pc. Easter Cutter Collection, Chick Comfort-Grip Cutter, p. 239; 6 in. Cookie Treat Sticks, p. 171; Light Cocoa Candy Melts Candy (one bag makes 1 nest), p. 175; Bake Easy! Non-Stick Spray, p. 158; 12 in. Rolling Pin, p. 159; Meringue Powder, p. 141; thin pretzel sticks, waxed paper, cornstarch

See p. 114 for a list of commonly used decorating items you may need.

In advance: Prepare nest. For base, line pan cavities with waxed paper and spray with Bake Easy! non-stick spray. Prepare cereal treats mixture. Press in mixture to fill cavities halfway; let cool then unmold. Cover flat top with melted candy; chill until set. Place flat-side down on waxed paper-covered board. Cover remainder with melted candy; chill until firm. Hand dip pretzel sticks in melted candy. Let set on waxed paper-covered boards. Make about 70 sticks per nest.

Prepare and roll out dough. For each family, cut one large chick using Comfort-Grip cutter and five small chicks using duck cutter from set. Bake and cool cookies.

Outline with tip 2 and full-strength yellow icing; flow in with thinned icing (p. 123). Let dry. Use tip 2 and full-strength icing to outline and fill in orange beak; pat smooth. Pipe tip 2 dot eye and outline wing details. Let dry. Attach cookie stick to backs using melted candy. Let set.

Insert cookies in base, trimming sticks as needed. Attach coated pretzels around base and between cookies using melted candy. Each treat serves 6.

*Combine Lemon Yellow with Golden Yellow for yellow shown.

◀ Nesting Instincts Cupcakes

Pan: Standard Muffin, p. 162
Color: Leaf Green, p. 139
Candy: Fuzzy Bunny Lollipop Mold, p. 241; White Candy Melts Candy (1 pk. makes 6-7 treats), Primary (yellow, orange), Garden (green, black) Candy Color Sets, p. 175; Decorator Brush Set, 4 in. Lollipop Sticks, p. 178
Recipe: Buttercream Icing, p. 128
Also: White Pearl Fence Cupcake Wraps, p. 182; White Standard Baking Cups, p. 181; Royal Icing Nests with Jelly Beans, p. 240; Parchment Triangles, p. 136

See p. 114 for a list of commonly used decorating items you may need.

In advance: Make candy chicks. Melt and tint portions of candy yellow, green, orange and black. Use painting or piping method (p. 123) to mold chick lollipops. Tap to settle; chill until firm.

Bake and cool cupcakes. Spatula ice tops. Position inside cupcake wraps. Insert lollipop, trimming stick as needed. Position nests. Each serves 1.

▼ Bunny's Candy Baskets

Pan: Non-Stick Cookie Sheet, p. 169
Color: Leaf Green, p. 139
Candy: Dessert Dome Candy Mold, p. 176; White, Light Cocoa Candy Melts Candy (1 pk. each makes 3 treats; you will need additional for candy clay recipe), Garden (green) Candy Color Set, p. 175; Decorator Brush Set, p. 178
Recipes: Candy Clay, Basic Truffles, p. 123
Also: 2013 Pattern Book (Basket Handle), p. 143; Macrame Designs Gum Paste & Fondant Mold, p. 150; Circle Metal Cutter, p. 172; Pastel Jordan Almonds, p. 198; Cake Boards, p. 186; shredded coconut

See p. 114 for a list of commonly used decorating items you may need.

2 to 3 days in advance: Make candy bases and shells. For base, tint portion of white candy green using candy color. Place circle cutter on cookie sheet. Fill ¼ in. deep with melted, tinted candy. Tap to settle; chill until firm. For basket bottom, follow mold instructions to make shells in large cavity.

Also: Make ropes and handles. Copy handle pattern and tape to boards; cover with waxed paper. Prepare candy clay (recipe will make 24 handles and trims). Use macrame mold to make three ropes for each treat. Attach one rope over top edge of shell with melted candy; trim ends as needed. Position one rope, flat side up, over handle pattern. Attach second rope, flat side down, with melted candy. Trim ends as needed. Let dry 24 hours. **And:** Tint coconut green (p. 119).

Prepare truffle recipe. Fill shells to ½ in. from top. Seal top with thin layer of melted candy; let set. Attach shell to base and handle to shell with melted candy; let set. Cover top with coconut. Position almonds. Each serves 1.

▲ Bunny's Bounty Treat Shells

Pans: Mini Muffin, p. 162; 9 in. x 13 in. x 2 in. Sheet, p. 161; Cooling Grid, p. 171
Tip: 233, p. 134
Color: Kelly Green, p. 139
Candy: White Candy Melts Candy (24 oz. makes 18 to 20 treats), Primary (blue, yellow), Garden (pink, green) Candy Color Sets, p. 175; Decorator Brush Set, p. 178
Recipes: Buttercream Icing, Favorite Cake Ball Pops, p. 128
Also: White Mini Baking Cups, p. 181; Royal Icing Bunnies with Jelly Beans, p. 240
See p. 114 for a list of commonly used decorating items you may need.

In advance: Make candy shells in baking cups (p. 123). Tint portions of melted white candy yellow, blue, pink and green using candy colors. Follow instructions to make a ⅛ in. thick shell. Chill until firm; remove paper.

Bake and cool 1-layer cake. Prepare cake pops mixture and fill candy shells. Seal tops with a thin layer of melted candy. Chill until firm. Cover tops of treats with tip 233 pull-out grass. Insert bunnies in grass. Each serves 1.

◀ Petal Elation Cake

Pans: Dancing Daisy, p. 166; Cooling Grid, p. 171
Tip: 7, p. 134
***Sugar Sheets!* Edible Decorating Paper/**
Tools: Floral (2), Light Pink, Bright Pink, Light Yellow (1 each), p. 144; Lines Texture Press, p. 147; Dab-N-Hold Edible Adhesive, p. 145; Brush Set, p. 146
Recipe: Buttercream Icing, p. 128
Also: 2013 Pattern Book (large, medium, small petals), p. 143; Cake Circle, Fanci-Foil Wrap, p. 186; Disposable Decorating Bags, p. 136; Fine Tip Neon Colors FoodWriter Edible Color Markers (pink), p. 153; Round Cut-Outs Fondant Cutters, p. 151
See p. 114 for a list of commonly used decorating items you may need.

Bake and cool 1-layer cake. Ice cake smooth. Pipe tip 7 bead bottom border.

Use pink edible marker and pattern to trace six large petals on shiny side of floral edible paper. Cut out with scissors. Position on cake top.

Use pink edible marker and pattern to trace six medium petals each on shiny side of bright pink and light pink edible paper. Cut out. Stack two same-color petals, shiny sides together, to make three petals in each color. Imprint lines with texture press.

Use pink edible marker and pattern to trace six small petals on shiny side of light yellow edible paper. Cut out with scissors. Attach to medium petals with edible adhesive, positioning to left side of each petal. Position petals on cake top in overlapping fashion, securing with edible adhesive. Use medium Cut-Out to cut circle from bright pink edible paper. Attach for flower center with edible adhesive. Serves 12.

▶ Color Spun Strawberries

Pan: Cookie Sheet, p. 171
Candy: White Candy Melts Candy (1 pk. makes 12 to 15 treats), Primary (blue, yellow), Garden (pink, green, violet) Candy Color Sets, p. 175
Also: Parchment Triangles, p. 136; Parchment Paper, p. 158; fresh strawberries
See p. 114 for a list of commonly used decorating items you may need.

Wash and dry strawberries. Dip strawberries into melted white candy; tap to remove excess. Place on parchment-covered cookie sheet. Chill until firm.

Tint portions of candy using candy colors. Drizzle strawberries with lines of melted candy. Chill until firm. Each serves 1.

◀ Mom Rules Cake

Pans: Dimensions Large Cupcake, p. 167; Cooling Grid, p. 171
Tips: 1M, 2A, 3, 12, p. 134
Colors: Rose, Lemon Yellow, Black, p. 139
Fondant: White Ready-To-Use Rolled Fondant (12 oz.), Gum-Tex, p. 148; Jewelry Designs Gum Paste & Fondant Mold, p. 150; 20 in. Fondant Roller, 20 in. Fondant Roller Guide Rings, Roll-N-Cut Mat, Fondant Smoother, p. 152; White, Gold, Ruby Red, Leaf Green, Lilac Purple Pearl Dust, Pure Lemon Extract, Brush Set, p. 153
Recipe: Buttercream Icing, p. 128
Also: 2013 Pattern Book (crown), p. 143; Candy Melting Plate, p. 178; Disposable Decorating Bags, p. 136; Piping Gel, p. 141; Cake Boards, Fanci-Foil Wrap, p. 186
See p. 114 for a list of commonly used decorating items you may need.

2 days in advance: Make crown. Add 1 teaspoon Gum-Tex to 8 oz. white fondant. Roll out ⅛ in. thick. Use pattern and knife to cut crown. Position upright; shape around a 3½ in. diameter can to form crown. Attach ends with piping gel. Let dry 24 hours.

Also: Make fondant crown trims and necklace. Use jewelry mold to make two square chain borders. Attach around base of crown with piping gel, trimming to fit. Use mold to make four each round gems and bases, five each faceted gems and bases and two brooches. Use Pearl Dust/lemon extract mixture to paint (p. 118) bases in gold, round gems in ruby red, faceted gems in lilac purple, one brooch edge in gold and center in leaf green. For necklace, use mold and white fondant to make 40 to 45 round gems. Paint with white Pearl Dust/lemon extract mixture. Let dry overnight.

And: Complete crown. Use mold and fondant to make five chain link borders. Attach for crown top border with piping gel, trimming to fit and cutting mitred ends as needed. Paint crown with gold Pearl Dust/lemon extract mixture. Let dry. Attach gems to bases with piping gel. Attach green brooch and gems to crown with piping gel. Roll a thin fondant rope; shape into initial for necklace brooch; attach with piping gel. Paint necklace brooch with gold Pearl Dust/lemon extract mixture. Let dry.

Bake and cool 2-part giant cupcake. Cover cupcake bottom with tip 2A lines, piping recessed areas first, then raised sections. Pipe tip 12 ball eyes; flatten and smooth with finger dipped in cornstarch. Pipe in tip 3 pupils and mouth; smooth. Pipe tip 3 outline eyelashes. Pipe tip 12 ball cheeks and nose.

Position cupcake top. Cover top with tip 1M rosettes. Position crown. Position white gems for necklace and gold brooch with dots of icing. Serves 12.

▶ Heart of the Family Candy Box

Pans: 6 in. x 2 in. Heart, p. 161; Cookie Sheet, p. 171
***Sugar Sheets!* Edible Decorating Paper/**
Tools: Damask (1), p. 144; Slide-N-Cut Edge Cutter, p. 145
Fondant: Baroque Designs Gum Paste/Fondant Mold, p. 150; Letters & Numbers Gum Paste & Fondant Mold Set, p. 151; White, Bronze, Silver, Orchid Pink Pearl Dust, Brush Set, p. 153
Candy: White (3 pks.), Light Cocoa (4 oz.) Candy Melts Candy, Garden (pink) Candy Color Set, p. 175; Faceted Candy Mold, p. 176
Recipes: Candy Clay, Basic Truffles, p. 123
Also: 4-Pc. From The Heart Nesting Metal Cutter Set, p. 235; Pink Color Mist Food Color Spray, p. 237; Piping Gel, p. 141, Disposable Decorating Bags, p. 136
See p. 114 for a list of commonly used decorating items you may need.

In advance: Prepare ½ candy clay recipe using white candy. Let set overnight.

For box lid, mold candy plaque (p. 123) in heart pan using 6 oz. melted white candy. Tap to settle; chill until firm. For box base, mold a ¼ in. thick candy shell (p. 123) in heart pan using melted white candy. Glide top edges of lid and base over warm pan to level. Box base should be 1¾ in. high.

Use edge cutter to cut two strips, 1¾ in. x 9½ in. from damask edible paper. Use largest cutter from set to cut heart from damask edible paper. Spray strips and heart with pink food color spray; let dry. Attach strips to sides and heart to top of candy box with piping gel; trim excess as needed.

Knead candy clay. Use baroque mold to make small pearl chain. Attach to edge of lid with piping gel, trimming excess as needed. Use letter mold to make candy clay letters. Brush letters with white Pearl Dust; attach to lid with piping gel.

Prepare truffles recipe. Tint ⅓ of melted white candy with pink candy color. Mold eight faceted candy shells each in melted white, pink and cocoa candy (p. 123). Chill until firm; fill with truffle mixture. Attach truffle halves together with melted candy. Brush with Pearl Dust: white with silver, pink with orchid pink and light cocoa with bronze. Position truffles and lid on base. Each truffle serves 1.

◀ USA's Birthday Cupcake!

Pans: Dimensions Large Cupcake, p. 167; Cooling Grid, p. 171

Colors:* Royal Blue, Christmas Red, Red-Red, p. 139

Fondant: White Ready-To-Use Rolled Fondant (18 oz.), p. 148; 9 in., 20 in. Fondant Roller, 20 in. Fondant Roller Guide Rings, Roll-N-Cut Mat, p. 152; Star Cut-Outs Fondant Cutters, p. 151; Fondant Ribbon Cutter, p. 149; Brush Set, p. 153

Recipe: Buttercream Icing, p. 128

Also: Piping Gel, p. 141; White Sparkling Sugar, p. 156; Spatula, p. 137

See p. 114 for a list of commonly used decorating items you may need.

1 day in advance: Make fondant stars. Roll out fondant ¹⁄₁₆ in. thick. Cut approximately 24 stars using medium Cut-Out. Brush tops with piping gel; sprinkle with white sparkling sugar. Let dry overnight.

Bake and cool 2-part large cupcake. Prepare cupcake bottom for rolled fondant (p. 119). Roll out white fondant ⅛ in. thick; use knife to cut a strip, 4 in. x 18 in. Wrap strip around bottom. Smooth in recessed areas of cake; trim off excess. Tint 2 oz. fondant red; roll out ¹⁄₁₆ in. thick. Using ribbon cutter with two straight-edge wheels and ¼ in. spacer, cut 25 strips, 4 in. long. Attach in recessed areas with piping gel.

Position cake top; ice fluffy in blue. Position stars on cake top. Serves 12.

*Combine Christmas Red with Red-Red for red shown.

▼ Ameri-Cupcakes

Pans: Standard Muffin, p. 162; Cooling Grid, p. 171

Color: Royal Blue, p. 139

Fondant: White Ready-To-Use Rolled Fondant (2 oz. makes 6 to 8 treats), p. 148; Kids Party Designs Gum Paste & Fondant Mold, p. 150; Fine Tip Primary Colors FoodWriter Edible Color Markers, p. 153

Recipe: Buttercream Icing, p. 128

Also: Assorted Primary Standard Baking Cups, p. 180; Spatula, p. 137

See p. 114 for a list of commonly used decorating items you may need.

1 day in advance: Make fondant stars. Use kids party mold and fondant to make one each large, medium and small star for each treat. Let dry. Use red and blue edible markers to color in detail areas.

Bake and cool cupcakes. Ice cupcakes smooth in blue. Position stars. Each serves 1.

▲ Patriotic Rockets Mini Cakes

Pans: 9 in. x 13 in. x 2 in. Sheet, p. 161; Cookie Sheet, Cooling Grid, p. 171

Sugar Sheets! Edible Decorating Paper/
Tools: Red (1), Bright Blue (1), p. 144; Punch Set with Oval Cutting Insert, Layered Stars Cutting Insert Set, p. 145

Candy: White (24 oz. makes 12 to 14 treats) Candy Melts Candy, Primary (blue) Candy Color Set, p. 175; Decorator Brush Set, p. 178

Also: 2013 Pattern Book (motion lines), p. 143; 101 Cookie Cutters (smallest circle), p. 173; Piping Gel, p. 141; Parchment Triangles, p. 136; Cake Leveler, p. 158

See p. 114 for a list of commonly used decorating items you may need.

in advance: Make motion lines. Cover patterns with parchment. Tint 2 oz. of candy blue. Add a few drops of water to thicken. Immediately pipe in patterns ⅛ in. thick using blue-tinted melted candy in cut parchment bag. For each treat, you will need two or three motion lines in each curved shape and one straight. Make extras to allow for breakage and chill until firm.

Bake and cool 1-layer sheet cake using firm-textured batter, such as pound cake; level to 1½ in. high. Imprint cake with smallest circle cutter; cut out cakes with knife. Place cakes on cooling grid over parchment-lined cookie sheet and cover with white melted candy (p. 123). Chill until firm. Use toothpick to poke one center hole and eight surrounding holes ⅜ in. from center. Insert straight motion line in center hole and curls in surrounding holes. Use punch with small star insert to cut edible paper star chains, five each in red and blue for each treat. Trim off large center star from chains; attach large stars to cake sides with piping gel and straight motion line with melted candy. Each serves 1.

▶ Sparkling Stars Cheesecake

Pans: 8 in. x 3 in. Springform, 10.5 in. x 15.5 in. x 1 in. Jelly Roll/Cookie, p. 161

Recipe: Favorite no-bake cheesecake mix (three 11.1 oz. pks.) or no-bake recipe for an 8 in. cheesecake

Also: 6-Pc. Stars Nesting Plastic Cutter Set, p. 173; White Nonpareils Sprinkles, p. 156; White Sugar Pearls, p. 157; Cake Boards, Cake Circles, Fanci-Foil Wrap, p. 186; 9 in. Angled Spatula, p. 137; three (3 oz.) packages red gelatin, three (3 oz.) packages blue gelatin, 4 envelopes unflavored gelatin, vegetable oil pan spray

See p. 114 for a list of commonly used decorating items you may need.

In advance: Make stars. Mix 3 packages red gelatin with 2 envelopes unflavored gelatin in heat-proof bowl. Add 3 cups boiling water. Stir until dissolved. Set jelly roll pan flat on refrigerator shelf. Pour in gelatin mixture to ⅜ in. deep. Chill until completely set. Cut one star using largest cutter from set and six stars using smallest cutter from set. Place on waxed paper-covered cake board sprayed with vegetable oil pan spray. Refrigerate until needed. Repeat using blue gelatin. Cut one star using second smallest cutter from set and six stars using smallest cutter from set. Reserve as above.

Lightly spray bottom and sides of springform pan. Prepare crust recipe and press into bottom. Press smallest red and blue stars onto pan sides, about ½ in. to ¾ in. apart. Prepare cheesecake filling. Pour into prepared pan. Level top with small angled spatula. Chill until completely set. Unmold. Position large red star on top; use second smallest cutter to cut out center; insert same size blue star. Sprinkle top with nonpareils and Sugar Pearls. Serves 12.

◀ Patriotic Personal Pizzas

Cookie: Cookie Sheet, Cooling Grid, p. 171; 6-Pc. Stars Nesting Plastic Cutter Set, p. 173

Also: Star Cut-Outs Fondant Cutters, p. 151; Disposable Decorating Bags, p. 136; bulk Italian sausage, refrigerated pizza dough, pizza sauce, mozzarella slices

See p. 114 for a list of commonly used decorating items you may need.

In advance: Prepare sausage. Flatten sausage to ⅛ in. thick. Cook thoroughly in skillet; let cool. Cut stars using medium Cut-Out. **Also:** Prepare crust. Preheat oven to 400°F. Roll out dough. Place on cookie pan lightly sprayed with vegetable oil pan spray. Bake 5 minutes; remove from oven. Use largest star cutter from nesting set to cut individual pizza crusts.

Using cut decorating bag, pipe pizza sauce onto pizza crust stars, leaving space around edge. Cut mozzarella slices into ¼ in. wide strips. Space strips ¼ in. apart on top for striped design. Or, use third largest cutter from nesting set to cut cheese stars. Position on crust. Position sausage star. Bake for 5 minutes or until cheese is melted and crust edges are golden brown. Each serves 1.

◄ Dog Days Candy Pretzels

Candy: Peanut Butter (2 pks. make 9 to 12 treats), White (1 pk. makes 9 to 12 treats) Candy Melts Candy, Primary (yellow, red) Candy Color Set, p. 175
Color: Leaf Green, p. 139
Recipe: Candy Clay, p. 123
Also: White Sparkling Sugar, p. 156; Piping Gel, p. 141; Parchment Triangles, p. 136; pretzel rods, maraschino cherries
See p. 114 for a list of commonly used decorating items you may need.

For hot dog, add a little red color to melted peanut butter candy. Dip pretzel rod halfway; chill until firm. Repeat two more times to reach a ⅛ in. thick coating.

For bun, prepare candy clay using 3 oz. peanut butter candy and 9 oz. white candy. Add a little yellow candy color to mixture. For each bun, shape 1¼ oz. mixture into a flat oval, 2 in. x 4 in. Position hot dog in center. Wrap bun around, shaping with fingers. Tint a small portion of melted white candy yellow. Use melted candy in cut parchment bag to pipe zigzag for mustard; chill. For relish, tint piping gel green; mix in sparkling sugar and small pieces of cherry. Position relish on hot dog. Each serves 1.

▼ Whoopie Pie Cheeseburgers

Pans: 12-Cavity Whoopie Pie, p. 169; Cooling Grid, p. 171
Tip: 2A, p. 134
Colors:* Red-Red, Leaf Green, Lemon Yellow, p. 139
Fondant: White Ready-To-Use Rolled Fondant (2 oz. per treat), p. 148; 9 in. Fondant Roller, Roll-N-Cut Mat, 10-Pc. Gum Paste/Fondant Tool Set, p. 152; Leaf Cut-Outs Fondant Cutters, p. 151; Fondant Shaping Foam, p. 155
Recipe: Favorite yellow cake recipe or mix
Also: Chocolate Ready-To-Use Decorator Icing, p. 141; Red Candy Melts Candy, p. 175; Disposable Decorating Bags, p. 136
See p. 114 for a list of commonly used decorating items you may need.

Bake and cool two cakes for each treat, filling pan cavities ⅔ full.

For each treat, tint 1 oz. fondant green, 1 oz. yellow. Roll out green ¹⁄₁₆ in. thick. Use medium leaf Cut-Out to cut six or seven lettuce leaves for each treat. Place leaves on thin foam with wide end up for top of leaf. Use large veining tool to score vein lines in each leaf. Position leaves on bottom bun cake. Pipe tip 2A burger in chocolate icing. Roll out yellow fondant ⅛ in. thick. Use knife to cut a 2¼ in. square for cheese. Position cheese on burger.

Using melted red candy in cut disposable bag, pipe ketchup. Position top bun cake. Each serves 1.

*Add a little Red-Red to chocolate icing for burger shade shown.

◄ Fruit Picking Picnickers! Cupcakes

Pans: Standard Muffin, p. 162; Cookie Sheets (2), Cooling Grid, p. 161
Colors: Christmas Red, Leaf Green, Black, White-White, p. 139
Fondant: Black Ready-To-Use Rolled Fondant (½ oz. per cupcake),
p. 148; 9 in. Fondant Roller, Roll-N-Cut Mat, p. 152; Heart, Leaf Cut-
Outs Fondant Cutters, p. 151; Brush Set, p. 153
Recipes: Buttercream Icing, Roll-Out Cookies, p. 128
Also: 6-Mix Nonpareils Sprinkles Assortment, p. 156; Red Gingham
Standard Baking Cups, p. 245; Red Candy Melts Candy, p. 175; 8 in.
Cake Circle, p. 186; 4 in. Lollipop Sticks, p. 178; Piping Gel, p. 141;
Spatula, p. 137

**See p. 114 for a list of commonly used decorating items you
may need.**

In advance: Make cookies. Prepare dough; for each watermelon and
strawberry cookie, tint dough 3 oz. light red, ½ oz. dark red, 2 oz.
green, ¼ oz. black, 1 oz. white-white. Roll out all colors ³⁄₁₆ in. thick. Use
knife and 8 in. cake circle as a guide to cut light red watermelon, 3 in.
deep. Taper ends in ¼ in. to shape. For rind, cut a ½ x 10 in. white
strip and a ½ x 12 in. green strip. Use smallest heart Cut-Out to cut
black dough for seeds; cut in half. On cookie sheet, position rind strips
around curve of red strip; position seeds. For strawberry, use largest
heart Cut-Out to cut dark red berry. Use smallest leaf Cut-Out to cut six
green leaves; roll a ¾ in. green log for stem. On a separate cookie sheet
position leaves and stem on berry. Separately bake and cool cookies.
Attach yellow nonpareils for strawberry seeds with piping gel. Attach
lollipop stick to each strawberry cookie and two sticks to watermelon
cookie 3 in. apart with melted candy, leaving 2 in. extended at bottom
to insert in cupcakes. Let set.

Bake and cool cupcakes. Ice smooth. Roll three black fondant balls for
each ant, ½ in. diameter. shaping one into an oval for center and one
into a teardrop for back; attach sections with piping gel. Roll three logs
for legs, ¹⁄₁₆ in. x 1 in. Attach. Position ant on cupcake. Insert cookies to
meet top of ants, trimming sticks as needed. Each serves 1.

► A Slice of Summer Cheesecake

Pan: 9 in. x 2.75 in. Non-Stick Round
Springform, p. 169
Colors:* Christmas Red, Red-Red,
Leaf Green, Kelly Green, p. 139
Recipe: Favorite no-bake
cheesecake mix (three 11.1 oz.
pks.) or no-bake recipe for a 9 in.
cheesecake
Also: 9 in. Angled Spatula, p. 137;
mini chocolate-flavored chips
(1 cup)

**See p. 114 for a list of commonly
used decorating items you may
need.**

Prepare graham cracker crust recipe,
tinting green using Leaf Green
and Kelly Green icing colors. Press
into lightly greased pan, covering
bottom and sides ⅛ to ¼ in. thick.
Prepare no-bake cheesecake filling.
Tint red. Stir in chocolate chips. Pour
into crust. Smooth top with spatula.
Chill until firm. Serves 12.

*Combine Christmas Red with Red-Red for red
shown. Combine Leaf Green with Kelly Green
for green shown.

Seize the Day!

For your proudest moments, choose cakes that make a bold statement. Each design here has a signature element that stands apart. We've placed 3-D babies in delightful settings for the shower—a boy flying through the clouds, a girl playing in the garden and wee little peas in a pod. For communions, you'll see cross cakes with wonderful dimensional fondant detail; for the Quinceañera, discover mega flowers in eyepopping yellow and orange to brighten the day.

Rattling His Cage! Cake

Pans: Monkey, p. 165; 11 in. x 15 in. x 2 in. Sheet, p. 161; Cooling Grid, p. 171

Tips: 3, 12, 14, p. 134

Colors:* Sky Blue, Lemon Yellow, Rose, Leaf Green, Violet, Ivory, Golden Yellow, Brown, Black, Red-Red, p. 139

Fondant: White Ready-To-Use Rolled Fondant (36 oz.), Gum-Tex, p. 148; 20 in. Fondant Roller, Roll-N-Cut Mat, p. 152; Brush Set, p. 146; Dots Texture Press, p. 147

Recipes: Buttercream Icing, p. 128; Thinned Fondant Adhesive, p. 127

Also: 2013 Pattern Book (monkey face), p. 143; 101 Cookie Cutters (small and medium rounds), p. 173; 6 in. Cookie Treat Sticks, p. 171; Cake Boards, Fanci-Foil Wrap, p. 186; large marshmallow

See p. 114 for a list of commonly used decorating items you may need.

2 days in advance: Make rattle. Tint 4 oz. fondant violet; knead in ¼ teaspoon Gum-Tex.

Roll out ⅛ in. thick. Use cutters from set to cut one small and one medium circle. Use wide end of tip 3 to cut hole in center of small circle. Trim cookie stick to 5 in. long. Wrap with a strip of fondant, ¾ in. x 5 in.; let dry 24 hours. Roll out white and violet fondant ⅛ in. thick. Use knife to cut a white strip ¼ in. x 3 in. attach to medium circle with damp brush. Use narrow end of tip 12 to cut 5 violet circles; attach to strip. Attach circles to stick with thinned fondant adhesive; leave 3 in. of stick exposed for handle. Let dry.

Bake and cool 2-layer sheet cake; trim layers to 1½ in. high for a 3 in. high cake. Place on double-thick foil-wrapped board cut ¾ in. larger than cake on all sides. Ice cake smooth. Tint 8 oz. fondant each rose, yellow, blue and green. Roll out ⅛ in. thick as needed. Cut two strips, 3 in. x 7 in., in each color; reserve excess fondant. Imprint strips with texture press. Cut strips to 1 in. x 3 in. (13 of each color needed). Attach to cake sides with tip 3 dots of icing, alternating colors as you go; trim as needed. Roll out reserved fondant. Cut five small circles in each color; attach to cake top, trimming at edges as needed.

Bake and cool monkey cake; trim to 1 in. high. Place on cut-to-fit foil-wrapped board. Ice background areas smooth in white, face in tan. Using pattern and toothpick, mark face and features. Using tip 3, pipe outline eyebrows; outline and fill in eyes, nose and mouth (pat smooth with finger dipped in cornstarch). Pipe tip 3 outlines around inner ears, face and background areas; fill in face with tip 14 stars. Position monkey on sheet cake. Cover cake with tip 14 stars. Position rattle, supporting top with a marshmallow. Pipe tip 12 outlines over rattle to form fingers. Outline fingers with tip 3; cover with tip 14 stars. Serves 66.

*Combine Violet with Rose for violet shown. Combine Ivory with Golden Yellow for tan shown. Combine Brown with Black and Red-Red for brown shown.

Chipper Chimp Cookies

Cookie: 3-Pc. Jungle Pals Colored Metal Cutter Set, p. 205; 4-Pc. Circles Nesting Metal Cutter Set, p. 172; Cookie Sheet, Cooling Grid, p. 171

Tips: 1, 2, 3, p. 134

Colors:* Sky Blue, Lemon Yellow, Rose, Leaf Green, Ivory, Golden Yellow, Brown, Black, Red-Red, p. 139

Recipes: Color Flow Icing, Roll-Out Cookies, p. 128

Also: Color Flow Mix, p. 141

See p. 114 for a list of commonly used decorating items you may need.

Prepare and roll out dough. For each treat, cut one monkey head and one circle using largest cutter from set. Bake and cool cookies. Outline circle cookies with tip 3 and full-strength white icing; flow in with thinned white icing (p. 120). Immediately pipe tip 3 dots using thinned icing in assorted colors. Let dry.

Outline monkey head, face, ears and inner ears with tip 2 and full-strength brown icing. Flow in separate areas with thinned brown and tan icings. Let dry. Pipe tip 1 outline eyebrows and smile, dot eyes and nose. Pipe tip 3 dot cheeks. Let cookies dry overnight. Attach monkey to circle cookie with icing dots. Let set. Each serves 1.

*Combine Ivory with Golden Yellow for tan face shown. Combine Brown with Black and Red-Red for brown shown.

▲ On-Time Arrival Cake

Pans: 6 in. x 2 in. Round, p. 161; Airplane, p. 166; Cooling Grid, p. 171

Tips: 1A, 2A, 7, 10, 16, p. 134

Colors:* Violet, Rose, Leaf Green, Lemon Yellow, Sky Blue, Brown, Red-Red, Black, Copper (for skin tone shown), p. 139

Fondant: White Ready-To-Use Rolled Fondant (24 oz.), Gum-Tex, p. 148; 20 in. Fondant Roller, Roll-N-Cut Mat, p. 152; Yellow, Leaf Green, Orchid Pink, Sapphire Blue Pearl Dust, Brush Set, p. 153; Star, Round, Oval, Alphabet/Number Cut-Outs Fondant Cutters, p. 151; Rotary Cutter, p. 149

Recipe: Buttercream Icing, p. 128

Also: 2.5 in. Globe Pillar Set, p. 193; Fine Tip FoodWriter Edible Color Marker (black), p. 174; Piping Gel, p. 141; White Candy Melts Candy, p. 175; 6 in. Lollipop Sticks, p. 178; 14 in., 8 in. Cake Circles, Fanci-Foil Wrap, p. 186

See p. 114 for a list of commonly used decorating items you may need.

1 to 2 days in advance: Make fondant trims (p. 124).

Bake and cool four 1-layer round cakes and airplane cake. Position cakes on foil-wrapped circles (use cut-to-fit double-thick 14 in. circles for airplane). Cut four 3 in. pillars; insert into round cakes, 1½ in. from cake edge. Cover cakes with tip 1A ball clouds.

For airplane, ice cockpit area smooth. Cover remainder of cake with tip 16 stars. Pipe tip 7 dots, 1 in. apart, on wings and tail. Attach propeller with dots of icing. Position baby's head, steering wheel, bear and blocks, securing with icing. Attach curved arm to steering wheel. Attach rattle to other hand with melted candy dot; insert arm into cake. Attach stars to clouds with icing. Position airplane over rounds. Serves 36.

*Combine Violet with Rose for violet shown. Combine Brown with Red-Red for brown shown.

▼ Our Garden Girl Cake

Pans: 8 in. x 2 in. Round, p. 161; Standard Muffin, p. 162; Cooling Grid, p. 171

Tips: 1M, 3, p. 134

Colors: Leaf Green, Lemon Yellow, Rose, Sky Blue, Orange, Black, Copper (for skin tone shown), p. 139

Fondant: White Ready-To-Use Rolled Fondant (24 oz.), Gum-Tex, p. 148; 9 in. Fondant Roller, Roll-N-Cut Mat, 10-Pc. Gum Paste/Fondant Tool Set, p. 152; Fondant Shaping Foam, p. 155; Deluxe Brush Set, p. 153; Garden Shapes, Leaf Cut-Outs Fondant Cutters, p. 151

Recipes: Buttercream Icing, p. 128; Thinned Fondant Adhesive, p. 127

Also: Modern Garden Party Cupcake Wraps, p. 182; White Standard Baking Cups, p. 181; Butterfly Icing Decorations, p. 201; Border Punch Set with Scallop Cutting Insert, Grass Cutting Insert, p. 145; 2.5 in. Globe Pillar Set, p. 193; Piping Gel, p. 141; Candy Melting Plate, p. 178; Cake Circles, p. 186; Rotary Cutter, p. 145; 10 in. cake pedestal

See p. 114 for a list of commonly used decorating items you may need.

In advance: Make baby topper (p. 125). **Also:** Make cupped flowers (p. 125). Reserve excess fondant.

Bake and cool 2-layer cake. Ice cake smooth. Tint 8 oz. fondant green; also use reserved pink and orange. Roll out fondant ⅛ in. thick as needed. For flower stems, cut 13 green strips, ³⁄₁₆ in. wide in lengths from 2 in. to 3½ in. Cut 26 green leaves using smallest Cut-Out from set. Place on medium foam and score veins using small veining tool from set.

Use garden shapes Cut-Out to cut three pink and three orange tulips. Place on thin foam and add petal lines using small veining tool. Use dots of icing to attach stems and leaves to cake sides, approximately 2 in. apart, at varying heights. Attach tulips and cupped flowers using dots of icing. For grass border, cut three strips, 1½ in. x 18 in. Cut using punch with grass insert. Trim bottom of strip for grass measuring ⅞ in. high at highest point. Attach around cake using dots of icing.

Cut a 6 in. diameter green circle. Use rotary cutter to cut a wavy edge. Position on cake top. Position baby topper. Roll a green log ⅛ in. diameter x 1½ in. long for flower stem; attach in and under baby's hand. Attach cupped pink flower, bow and hair curl using fondant adhesive.

Bake and cool cupcakes. Ice tops with tip 1M swirl. Position butterfly wings. Roll ⅜ in. ball of reserved orange fondant into 1 in. long tapered body. Attach over wings using dots of icing. Position cupcake wrap. Position cupcakes around cake. Cake serves 20; each cupcake serves 1.

▲ Buttoned Up Blossom Cupcakes

Pans: Standard Muffin, p. 162; Cooling Grid, p. 171

Tip: 2A, p. 134

Colors:* Teal, Moss Green, Burgundy, Red-Red, Violet, Rose, p. 139

Fondant: White Ready-To-Use Rolled Fondant (1 oz. makes 8 treats), p. 148; Fabric Designs Gum Paste & Fondant Mold, p. 150

Recipe: Buttercream Icing, p. 128

Also: Daisy Cake Picks, p. 190; Green Dots, Pink Dots, Teal Dots, Purple Dots Standard Baking Cups, p. 181

See p. 114 for a list of commonly used decorating items you may need.

Tint ¼ oz. fondant each teal, green, pink and violet to match cups. Use fondant mold to make buttons. Let dry. Assemble daisy picks. Attach button to daisy with icing.

Bake and cool cupcakes. Ice cupcakes smooth to match baking cup color. Insert picks, trimming as needed. Each serves 1.

*Combine Burgundy with Red-Red for pink shown. Combine Violet with Rose for violet shown.

◀ Baby's Bunting Cookie Pops

Cookie: 4-Pc. Circles Nesting Metal Cutter Set, p. 172; Round Cut-Outs Fondant Cutters, p. 151; Cookie Sheet, Cooling Grid, p. 171

Tip: 2, p. 134

Colors:* Christmas Red, Red-Red, p. 139

Recipes: Color Flow Icing, Roll-Out Cookies, p. 128

Also: Color Flow Mix, p. 141; 4 in. Lollipop Sticks, p. 178, ¼ in. wide red satin ribbon (10 in. per treat)

See p. 114 for a list of commonly used decorating items you may need.

Prepare and roll out dough. For each treat, cut one cookie using smallest circle cookie cutter and one using medium round Cut-Out. Bake and cool. Outline with tip 2 and full-strength icing; let dry. Flow in with thinned icing. Let dry. With full-strength icing, pipe tip 2 outline stitching and attach cookies to stick. Tie bow around stick. Each serves 1.

*Combine Christmas Red with Red-Red for red shown.

▼ The Family's Growing! Cake

Pans: 18 in. x 3 in. Half Round, p. 163; Cooling Grid., p. 171

Tips: 3, 4, p. 134

Colors:* Kelly Green, Lemon Yellow, Copper (for skin tone shown), Black, Brown, p. 139

Fondant: White Ready-To-Use Rolled Fondant (60 oz.), Gum-Tex, p. 148; 20 in. Fondant Roller, Roll-N-Cut Mat, p. 152; Leaf Cut-Outs Fondant Cutters, p. 151; Leaf Green Pearl Dust, Brush Set, p. 153

Recipes: Buttercream Icing, p. 128; Thinned Fondant Adhesive, p. 127

Also: 2013 Pattern Book (hands, peapod curves), p. 143; 6 in. Cake Circle, Cake Boards, Fanci-Foil Wrap, p. 186; 4-Pc. Circles Nesting Metal Cutter Set, p. 172; 6 in. Lollipop Sticks, p. 178; Dark Green Candy Melts Candy, p. 175; Parchment Paper, p. 158; 20 in. x 11 in. plywood or foamcore board (½ in. thick)

See p. 114 for a list of commonly used decorating items you may need.

3 days in advance: Make baby. Tint 6 oz. fondant copper and a 1 in. ball brown. Knead 1 teaspoon Gum-Tex into copper and ¼ teaspoon into brown. Roll out copper fondant ⅛ in. thick. Using knife and 6 in. cake circle as a guide, cut head. Use pattern to cut two hands (reverse pattern for second hand). Let dry on cornstarch-dusted board. Reserve remaining copper fondant. Roll a brown log, ¼ in. diameter x 2½ in. long; shape into a swirl for hair curl. Let dry.

Also: Make peas. Tint 53 oz. fondant green. Knead 1 teaspoon Gum-Tex into 6 oz. green fondant. Roll out ⅛ in. thick. Using smallest circle cutter, cut four peas. Brush peas with leaf green Pearl Dust. Using largest leaf Cut-Out, cut four leaves (reverse cutter for two). For vine, roll a log, ⁵⁄₁₆ in. diameter x 11½ in. long; shape into spiral. Let all dry on cornstarch-dusted board. Reserve remaining green fondant.

Bake and cool 1-layer half-round cake; trim to 2 in. high. Trace cake curve pattern on parchment; line up straight edge and cut curve with knife. Reverse pattern to cut other side of cake. Prepare and cover cake with green fondant. Roll out remaining green fondant ⅛ in. thick. Lay and shape fondant over back of 18 in. half round pan. Using fondant peapod curve pattern, cut away top to create front layer of peapod and remove. Transfer remaining piece to cake, attaching with damp brush.

Add detail to head. Roll a ½ in. copper ball; attach for nose. Use tip 3 to pipe outline eyes and pipe in mouth (pat smooth with finger dipped in cornstarch). Attach hair curl with thinned fondant adhesive. Attach head, hands and peas; trim head as needed.

Attach leaves together in overlapping fashion with melted candy. Cut lollipop stick in half; attach leaf pairs with melted candy, leaving 2 in. extended at bottom. Let dry. Insert in cake. For vine, attach swirl to 6 in. stick with melted candy, leaving 2½ in. extended at bottom. Let dry. Bend extended end of stick slightly; insert in cake. Pipe tip 4 message. Serves 46.

*Combine Kelly Green with Lemon Yellow for green shown.

▶ Pea Wee Candies

Colors:* Kelly Green, Lemon Yellow, Brown, Orange, p. 139

Fondant: White Ready-To-Use Rolled Fondant (3 oz. per treat), p. 148; 9 in. Fondant Roller, Roll-N-Cut Mat, p. 152

Candy: Dessert Shells Candy Mold, p. 176; White, Light Cocoa (1 pk. each makes 5 treats), Candy Melts Candy, Primary (yellow, orange), Garden (green, black) Candy Color Sets, p. 175; Candy Dipping Set, Decorator Brush Set, p. 178

Recipe: Basic Truffles, p. 123

Also: 2013 Pattern Book (peapod), p. 143; Piping Gel, p. 141

See p. 114 for a list of commonly used decorating items you may need.

Prepare truffle recipe using light cocoa candy; reserve 1 wafer for each treat to tint dark skin tone heads. For peas, roll nine balls, ⅝ in., for each treat. For each head, roll one ball, 1⅛ in. Use candy colors to tint 2 oz. melted white candy light orange for light skin tone shown, 8 oz. green with a little yellow; mix remaining 2 oz. melted white candy with melted cocoa candy for dark skin tone shown. Dip pea truffles in green candy, head truffles in skin tone candy. Chill until firm on waxed paper-covered boards. Mold green dessert shells (p. 123); chill until firm.

Tint ¼ oz. fondant each light orange and light brown to match heads, Tint 4 oz. fondant green to match green candy. Make peapods (p. 125). Tint 1 oz. white candy black. Pipe eyes, mouth and nose with melted candy in cut parchment bag. Using fondant to match head, roll two logs for arms, ⅜ in. x 1 in.; flatten one end slightly and cut slits for fingers. Attach to shell with melted candy. For hat, shape a cone from a ¾ in. ball of green fondant; attach with melted candy. Position peas and head in peapod, supporting as needed with melted candy. Each serves 1.

*Combine Kelly Green with Lemon Yellow for green fondant shown.

▼ Baby-Bump Silhouette Cake

Pans: 4-Pc. Oval Set (second largest and smallest used), p. 160; Cooling Grid, p. 171
Tip: 8, p. 134
Color: Pink, p. 139
Sugar Sheets! **Edible Decorating Paper/Tools:** Black, Bright Pink (1 sheet each), White (2 sheets), p. 144; Rotary Cutter, Flower Mini Punch, Dab-N-Hold Edible Adhesive, p. 145
Also: 2013 Pattern Book (silhouette), p. 143; Piping Gel, p. 141; Brush Set, p. 153; Cake Boards, Fanci-Foil Wrap, p. 186
See p. 114 for a list of commonly used decorating items you may need.

Bake and cool 1-layer cake using second largest pan; place on foil-wrapped board 1 in. larger than cake. Ice cake smooth in pink. Pipe tip 8 bead bottom border. For lattice, use rotary cutter to cut 25 strips, ⅜ in. wide, from long edge of white edible paper. Attach to cake top with edible adhesive to create parallel diagonal lines, ⅝ in. apart, in one direction across cake top; trim ends as needed. For longest lines, overlap strips in center area. Position remaining strips as above in opposite direction to create lattice.

Use rotary cutter and smallest pan as a guide to cut a bright pink cameo; position on cake top. Use pattern and knife to cut black silhouette; attach to oval. Use mini punch to cut 16 white flowers. Attach around oval with edible adhesive, 1 in. apart. Serves 15.

▲ Store-Hopping Stork Cake

Pans: 3-Pc. Paisley Set (smallest used), p. 160; 3-D Sports Ball Set, p. 165; Cookie Sheet, Cooling Grid, p. 171
Tips: 4, 12, 17, 21, 47, 48, p. 134-135
Colors: Sky Blue, Rose, Lemon Yellow, Orange, p. 139
Recipes: Buttercream Icing, Roll-Out Cookies, p. 128
Also: 2013 Pattern Book (hair tuft, beak, tail, wing, feet, presents), p. 143; Piping Gel, p. 141; Cake Boards, Cake Circles, Fanci-Foil Wrap, p. 186; 16 in. x 25 in. plywood or foamcore board (¼ in. thick), ⅜ in. wide satin ribbon (2 ft.), dental floss
See p. 114 for a list of commonly used decorating items you may need.

In advance: Make cookies. Prepare and roll out dough. Use patterns to cut one of each size present, hair tuft, beak, tail, wing and two each feet, 7 in. x ¾ in. legs and 1 in. x ¾ in. foot supports. Bake and cool cookies.

Bake and cool 1-layer paisley and half ball cakes. Position on foil-wrapped base board, allowing 8 in. below body for legs. Cover cakes with tip 17 stars. Pipe tip 12 dot eye and tip 4 dot pupil.

Position wing, tail and hair tuft cookies. Cover wing with tip 17 pull-out feathers, tail with tip 17 elongated shells and hair curl with tip 21 c-scroll. Ice beak and feet cookies smooth. Sandwich leg and foot support cookies with icing; ice smooth.

Position beak and legs. Position foot supports next to legs; position feet on supports. Ice presents smooth. For ribbons, pipe tip 48 diagonal stripes on large package and tip 47 (smooth side up) vertical stripe on small package. Pipe tip 4 dots; flatten with fingertip dipped in cornstarch. Tie loop bow with 5 in. long tail; secure loops with dental floss. Position on boards running bow tail under beak and presents. Cakes serve 11; each cookie serves 1.

◀ Dotty Ducky Cookies

Cookie: Chick Comfort Grip Cutter, p. 239; Cookie Sheet, Cooling Grid, p. 171
Tips: 2, 3, p. 134
Colors: Lemon Yellow, Sky Blue, Rose, p. 139
Candy: White Candy Melts Candy (1 oz. makes 4 to 5 treats); Primary (yellow, blue), Garden (violet) Candy Color Sets, p. 175
Recipes: Royal Icing, Roll-Out Cookies, p. 128
Also: Kids Party Designs Gum Paste & Fondant Mold, p. 150; Meringue Powder, p. 141; Cake Boards, p. 186
See p. 114 for a list of commonly used decorating items you may need.

Prepare and roll out dough. Cut cookies using chick cutter. Bake and cool. Outline with tip 2 and full-strength tinted icing; flow in with thinned icing. Immediately pipe tip 3 dots using thinned white icing. Let dry on waxed paper-covered boards.

Tint melted candy in assorted colors using color sets. Mold candy bows in bow cavity of mold (p. 123). Chill until firm; unmold carefully. Attach to cookies with melted candy. Each serves 1.

▶ Baptismal Blessings Cake

Pans: 11 in. x 15 in. x 2 in. Sheet, p. 161; Cooling Grid, p. 171
Tips: 1, 2, 3, 4, 6, 48, p. 134-135
Color: Royal Blue, p. 139
Recipes: Buttercream, Color Flow Icings, p. 128
Also: 2013 Pattern Book (scroll with cross plaque), p. 143; Cake Boards, Fanci-Foil Wrap, p. 186; Parchment Paper, p. 158; Parchment Triangles, p. 136; Color Flow Mix, p. 141; sugar cubes
See p. 114 for a list of commonly used decorating items you may need.

At least 3 days in advance: Make Color Flow plaque (p. 120). Trace pattern on parchment paper. Turn over paper and tape to cake board. Outline plaque and cross with tip 3 and full-strength Color Flow; let set. Flow in with thinned Color Flow in cut parchment bag, leaving cross area open. Let dry 48 hours. Decorate using full-strength icing. Pipe tip 1 scrolls and dots around cross. Pipe tip 2 message; outline plaque with tip 6, ¼ in. from edge; overpipe with tip 4, then tip 3. Let dry.

Bake and cool 1-layer cake. Ice cake smooth with blue buttercream icing. Starting 2 in. from each corner, pipe tip 48 stripes, 1 in. apart and 3 in. from top edge. Pipe a diagonal stripe in each corner. Pipe tip 4 bead bottom border. Carefully peel parchment from plaque. Position sugar cubes on cake to support plaque. Position plaque, securing to sugar cubes with a tip 2 dot of full-strength Color Flow icing. Serves 27.

◀ Sacred Celebration Cake

Pans: Cross, p. 238; Cooling Grid, p. 171
Tips: 1, 2, p. 134
Color: Sky Blue, p. 139
Fondant: White Ready-To-Use Rolled Fondant (96 oz.), p. 148; 20 in. Fondant Roller, Roll-N-Cut Mat, p. 152; Brush Set, p. 153; Fondant Smoother, p. 152
Recipes: Buttercream, Royal Icings, p. 128
Also: 2013 Pattern Book (host letters), p. 143; Border Punch Set with Scallop Cutting Insert, p. 145; Round Comfort-Grip Cutter, p. 172; Meringue Powder, Piping Gel, p. 141; Cake Boards, Fanci-Foil Wrap, p. 186
See p. 114 for a list of commonly used decorating items you may need.

2 to 3 days in advance: Make host topper. Roll out fondant ⅛ in. thick. Cut using round cutter. Let dry overnight on cornstarch-dusted board. Use pattern and toothpick to mark letters. Outline with tip 2 and full-strength blue royal icing; let dry. Flow in with thinned royal icing; let dry.

Also: Prepare board. Cut two cake boards ¼ in. larger than pan on all sides. Tint 48 oz. fondant blue. Prepare and cover board with 30 oz. blue fondant (p. 120).

Bake and cool cake. Prepare and cover cake with white fondant (p. 119). Place on board. Roll out reserved blue fondant ¹⁄₁₆ in. thick. For cross, cut a strip 2 in. x 12 in. Use border punch to cut scallop outer edges, leaving a strip 1½ in. wide. Attach vertically using damp brush. Cut two strips, 3½ in. x 2 in. Scallop edges as above; attach horizontally. For bottom border, cut three strips, 1 in. x 18 in. Scallop top edge only.

Attach around base of cake, trimming as needed. Use tip 1 and royal icing to pipe outline scallops with zigzags; pipe dots. Attach topper with dots of icing. Serves 12.

◀ Pure Grace Cake

Pans: 6 in. x 2 in., 10 in. x 2 in. Square, p. 161, Cooling Grid, p. 171
Tips: 1, 2, 3, p. 134
Color: Rose, p. 139
Recipes: Buttercream, Color Flow Icings, p. 128
Also: 2013 Pattern Book (oval plaque, lace points, hanging border), p. 143; Color Flow Mix, p. 141; White Sugar Pearls, p. 157; 8 in. Cookie Treat Sticks, p. 171; Cake Boards, Fanci-Foil Wrap, p. 186; Piping Gel, p. 141; Dowel Rods, p. 194; Cake Marker, p. 137; 10 in. diameter pedestal cake stand, craft foam block
See p. 114 for a list of commonly used decorating items you may need.

3 days in advance: Make oval topper with lace points (p. 125). **2 days in advance:** Make hanging border pieces. To make 20 border pieces, tape pattern to cake board; cover with waxed paper. Spray with vegetable pan spray to help pieces release when dry; wipe lightly with tissue. Outline with tip 2 and full-strength Color Flow icing; let set. Flow in with thinned Color Flow icing. Make extras to allow for breakage and let dry 24 hours. Decorate with full-strength Color Flow icing. Pipe tip 1 cornelli lace. Edge curved sides only with tip 2 beads. Attach sugar pearls to points with tip 2 icing dots. Let dry 24 hours. Peel off waxed paper.

Bake and cool 2-layer cakes; ice cakes smooth in buttercream icing. Prepare for stacked construction (p. 120) but do not stack. Mark scallop points on 10 in. cake 3 in. from bottom edge, 2 in. apart. Mark scallop points on 6 in. cake 1 in. from bottom edge, 2 in. apart. Mark ¾ in. deep scallops between marked scallop points. Stack cakes.

Pipe tip 1 cornelli lace inside scallop areas. Pipe tip 2 zigzag on scallop edges. On 10 in. cake, pipe a 1 in. tip 2 line from each scallop point. Attach sugar pearl to end with tip 2 dot. Attach sugar pearls to top and sides of 6 in. cake with dots of icing.

At party: Position cake on pedestal, securing with buttercream icing. Pipe tip 3 line of buttercream icing ¼ in. from bottom edge of 10 in. cake. Attach border pieces around cake. Pipe tip 3 beads along straight edge of pieces. Insert topper. Serves 42.

▶ A Flowering of Faith Cake

Pans: Cross, p. 238; Cooling Grid, p. 171
Color: Rose, p. 139
Fondant: White Ready-To-Use Rolled Fondant (88 oz.), p. 148; 20 in. Fondant Roller, Roll-N-Cut Mat, p. 152; Macrame Designs Gum Paste & Fondant Mold, p. 150; White Pearl Dust, Brush Set, p. 153; Fondant Smoother, p. 152
Recipe: Buttercream Icing, p. 128
Also: Cake Boards, Fanci-Foil Wrap, p. 186; Piping Gel, p. 141
See p. 114 for a list of commonly used decorating items you may need.

In advance: Prepare board. Cut two cake boards ¼ in. larger than pan on all sides. Tint 36 oz. fondant rose. Prepare and cover board with 30 oz. rose fondant (p. 120).

Bake and cool cake. Place on board. Prepare and cover cake with white fondant (p. 119). Using reserved rose fondant and macrame mold, make four quilted border strips. Brush with Pearl Dust and attach to cake top with damp brush, trimming as needed. Using white fondant and macrame mold, make eight rope strips; attach around edge of rose cross with damp brush, trimming as needed.

Using white fondant and macrame mold, make five fans and one large ring. Attach at center of rose cross, in flower formation, with damp brush. Using white fondant and macrame mold, make eight rope strips; attach for bottom border with damp brush. Serves 12.

◄ Blossoming La Quinceañera Cake

Pans: 6 in., 8 in., 10 in., 12 in., 14 in. x 2 in. Round, p. 161; Soccer Ball, p. 165; Cooling Grid, p. 171

Tip: 3, p. 134

Colors: Lemon Yellow, Orange, p. 139

Fondant/Gum Paste: White Ready-To-Use Rolled Fondant (222 oz.), Ready-To-Use Gum Paste (16 oz.), p. 148; 20 in. Fondant Roller, 20 in. Fondant Roller Guide Rings, Roll-N-Cut Mat, Fondant Smoother, p. 152; Fabric Designs Gum Paste & Fondant Mold, p. 150; Brush Set, p. 153; Round Cut-Outs Fondant Cutters, p. 151

Recipes: Buttercream, Royal Icings, p. 128; Gum Glue Adhesive, p. 127

Also: 2013 Pattern Book (petals), p. 143; Meringue Powder, p. 141; Towering Tiers Cake Stand (5.5 in. center posts, 8 in., 10 in., 12 in., 14 in., and 16 in., plates, cake corer, top nut, center post foot, five base feet used), p. 193; Cake Boards, Cake Circles, p. 186; Parchment Paper, p. 158; heavy-duty aluminum foil

See p. 114 for a list of commonly used decorating items you may need.

3 days in advance: Make cake side dots. Cover cake boards with parchment paper. Use thinned royal icing to pipe 104 puddle dots (p. 119), ½ in. diameter. Make extras to allow for breakage. Let dry.

Also: Make gum paste mega flowers. To make large flower forming cups, line soccer ball pan with aluminum foil. Carefully remove foil, maintaining pan shape. Dust insides with cornstarch.

Tint gum paste: 6 oz. yellow and 9 oz. orange; reserve 1 oz. white. Roll out ¹⁄₁₆ in. thick as needed. Use medium round Cut-Out to cut a yellow circle; position in center of foil cup. Use pattern and knife to cut seven orange petals for 6 in. cake. Position inside foil cup and attach over circle using gum glue adhesive. Cut another yellow circle. Attach over center. Repeat for additional cake sizes, using white circles for yellow flowers. Let dry in foil cups 2 to 3 days.

Bake and cool five 2-layer cakes. Prepare and cover with fondant (p. 119). Prepare for towering tiers construction (p. 121). Use buttercream icing to pipe tip 3 bead bottom borders. Use fabric mold to make about 47 large fondant ribbons. Center and attach around cake sides using damp brush; trim as needed. Use tip 3 icing dots to attach puddle dots to ribbons, about 1½ in. apart.

At reception: Assemble tiers. Attach flowers to cake sides using 1 in. balls of fondant and damp brush. Serves 196.

◀ Lofty Purpose Cupcake Tower

Pans: Dimensions Large Cupcake, p. 167; Standard Muffin, p. 162; Cooling Grid, p. 171

Tips: 1A, 2, 4, 6, 10, p. 134

Colors:* Royal Blue, Violet, p. 139

Fondant/Gum Paste: White Ready-To-Use Rolled Fondant (40 oz.), Ready-To-Use Gum Paste (16 oz.), Gum-Tex, p. 148; 9 in. Fondant Roller, Roll-N-Cut Mat, Fondant Smoother, p. 152; Gold Pearl Dust, Pure Lemon Extract, p. 141; Flower Cut-Outs Fondant Cutters, p. 151

Recipes: Buttercream, Royal Icings, p. 128

Also: Towering Tiers Cake Stand (8 in., 10 in., 12 in., 14 in., 16., and 18 in. plates, top nut, center post foot, five base feet, 4.25 in. center posts used), p. 193; White Pearl Swirls Cupcake Wraps (4 pks.), p. 182; Assorted Primary Standard Baking Cups (3 pks.), p. 180; Meringue Powder, p. 141; Cake Boards, p. 186; colored paper

See p. 114 for a list of commonly used decorating items you may need.

2 days in advance: Make star toppers. Trace largest flower Cut-Out on paper and enlarge at 200% for large cupcake topper. Flatten a cupcake wrap and attach to sheet of paper. Enlarge at 200% for large cupcake topper.

Tint 24 oz. fondant royal blue. Add 1 tablespoon Gum-Tex. Roll out ⅛ in. thick. Use knife and flower pattern to cut large topper. Place on parchment-covered board. Use royal icing and tip 10 to pipe star; use tip 6 to pipe center monogram.

Use largest flower Cut-Out to cut 65 standard star toppers. Place on parchment-covered boards. Use royal icing and tip 4 to pipe stars; use tip 2 to pipe center monogram. Let dry 24 hours.

Paint all stars and monograms with gold Pearl Dust/lemon extract mixture (p. 118). Let dry 24 hours.

Bake and cool large cupcake and 65 standard cupcakes using blue baking cups. Tint 16 oz. fondant navy to match baking cups. Prepare and cover bottom of large cupcake with navy fondant (p. 119). Spatula ice top of large cupcake with buttercream icing; cover cupcake tops with a tip 1A icing swirl.

Roll out gum paste ⅛ in. thick. Use wrap pattern to cut out large cupcake wrap; attach around cake using tip 6 dots of icing. Position all toppers, supporting as needed with dots of icing. Position on stand. Cake serves 12; each cupcake serves 1.

* Combine Royal Blue with Violet for navy shade shown (large cupcake base).

▼ Reaching the Rainbow Cake

Pans: Topping Off Success, p. 243; 9 in. x 13 in. x 2 in. Sheet, p. 161; Cooling Grid, p. 171
Tips: 2, 21, p. 134
Sugar Sheets! **Edible Decorating Paper/Tools:** Red, Bright Blue, Bright Yellow, Bright Green, Black Alphabet (one sheet each), p. 144; Punch Set with Oval Cutting Insert, Spiral Cutting Insert, p. 145
Candy: Black (4 pks.), Yellow (4 oz.) Candy Melts Candy, p. 175; Decorator Brush Set, p. 178
Recipe: Buttercream Icing, p. 128
Also: Red, Blue, Yellow, Green Color Mist Food Color Spray, p. 139; Gold Pearl Dust, p. 153; Plastic Dowel Rods, p. 194; Cake Boards, Fanci-Foil Wrap, p. 186; 15 in. x 20 in. plywood or foamcore board (¼ in. thick)

See p. 114 for a list of commonly used decorating items you may need.

In advance: Make candy plaque (p. 123). Melt 35 oz. black candy and pour into Topping Off Success pan. Tap to settle; refrigerate until firm. Unmold onto soft cloth. Cut cake board to fit plaque; wrap with foil (p. 114). Attach plaque to board with melted candy. Use melted yellow candy and tip 2 to pipe tassel and fringe; chill until firm, then brush with gold Pearl Dust (p. 118). Using remaining black candy, melt and pipe button at center of cap; chill until firm.

Also: Prepare 15 in. x 20 in. board and wrap with foil.

Bake and cool two 1-layer sheet cakes. Position side by side on prepared base board for an 18 in. x 13 in. cake. Ice cake smooth. Cut dowel rod into four 2 in. lengths. Insert rods where plaque will sit. Spray cake top quarters with various colors of Color Mist food color spray, starting each color at outside corner and moving toward center.

Use punch with spiral insert to cut 32 spirals in each color edible paper; attach eight to matching cake top quarter and reserve remainder. Position plaque and message letters. Pipe tip 21 shell bottom border. Twist remaining spirals; insert into bottom border. Serves 36.

▶ Display Your Degree Cake

Pans: 6 in. x 2 in., 10 in. x 2 in. Round, p. 161; Cooling Grid, p. 171
Colors: Christmas Red, Golden Yellow, Black, p. 139
Fondant: White (4 oz.), Black (18 oz.), Red (14 oz.) Ready-To-Use Rolled Fondant, Gum-Tex, p. 148; 20 in. Rolling Pin, Roll-N-Cut Mat, p. 152; Gold, Ruby Red Pearl Dust, Pure Lemon Extract, p. 141; Fondant Trimmer, p. 152; Diamond Mini Punch, p. 145; Dots Texture Press, p. 147; Storage Board, p. 152
Recipe: Buttercream Icing, p. 128
Also: 2013 Pattern Book (Graduates), p. 143; Black Candy Melts Candy, p. 175; 11¾ in. Lollipop Sticks, p. 178; Bamboo Dowel Rods, p. 194; Cake Boards, Fanci-Foil Wrap, p. 186

See p. 114 for a list of commonly used decorating items you may need.

2 days in advance: Make topper. Knead ⅛ teaspoon Gum-Tex into 3 oz. black fondant. Roll out ⅛ in. thick. Use pattern and knife to cut out silhouette. Let dry two days on cornstarch-dusted board. Attach lollipop stick to back with melted candy, leaving 4 in. extended at bottom to insert into cake.

Bake and cool 2-layer cakes; ice cakes smooth. Prepare for stacked construction (p. 120). Tint 4 oz. fondant yellow. Roll out all fondant ⅛ in. thick as needed. Cut 29 black strips, ¾ in. x 4 in.; store on storage board to prevent drying (reserve excess fondant). Cut 10 red squares, 3 in. x 3 in. Imprint with texture press. Cut into 29 strips, 1 in. x 4 in. Brush with red Pearl Dust. Brush backs of all strips with damp brush and attach to cake sides, alternating red and black. Trim as needed.

Cut ½ in. wide yellow fondant strips, 35 in. long for 10 in. cake, 20 in. long for 6 in. cake. Attach around cakes with damp brush for bottom border, trimming as needed. Paint with gold Pearl Dust/lemon extract mixture (p. 118). Roll out reserved black fondant. Use mini punch to make 100 diamonds. Attach to bottom borders, ⅛ in. apart with damp brush. Insert topper. Serves 40.

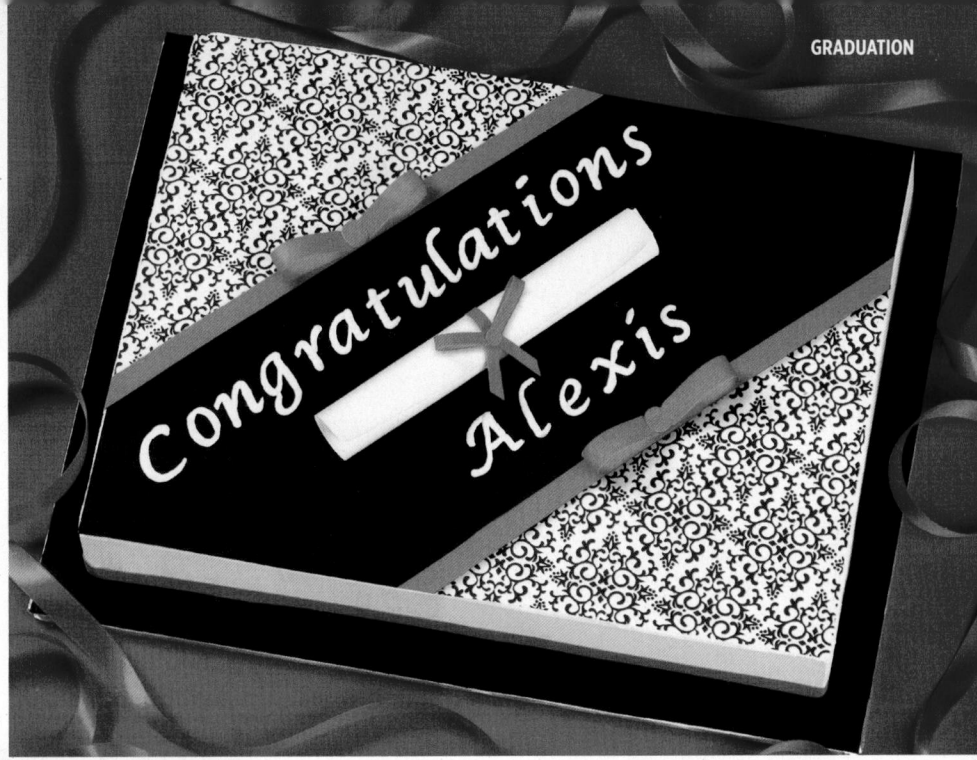

◄ The Definition of Success Cake

Pans: 9 in. x 2 in. Non-Stick Square, Cooling Grid, p. 169
Colors: Royal Blue, Lemon Yellow, Christmas Red, Leaf Green, p. 139
***Sugar Sheets!* Edible Decorating Paper/Tools:** Black (2), Streamers (1), p. 144; Rotary Cutter, p. 145
Fondant: White Ready-To-Use Rolled Fondant (12 oz.), p. 148; 9 in. Fondant Roller, Roll-N-Cut Mat, p. 152; Brush Set, p. 153
Recipe: Buttercream Icing, p. 128
Also: A-B-C and 1-2-3 Plastic Cutter Set, p. 173; Piping Gel, p. 141; Cake Boards, Fanci-Foil Wrap, p. 186
See p. 114 for a list of commonly used decorating items you may need.

Cut cake board to a 10¾ in. square; wrap with foil.

Bake and cool 1-layer cake. Ice cake smooth. Position on prepared board. For cake sides, use rotary cutter to cut 2 in. x 9 in. strips from streamers edible paper; attach with piping gel, trimming as needed. Cut four black strips, ¾ in. x 9 in., for cake top border, position on cake top, trimming as needed. Cut 2 in. wide strips from long edge of black sheets. Attach around outer edge of cake board with piping gel, trimming as needed. Divide fondant and tint four primary colors. Roll out ½ in. thick. Use cutters from set to cut each letter. Attach to cake top with piping gel. Serves 10.

▲ Wrap Up The Future Cake

Pans: 11 in. x 15 in. x 2 in. Sheet, p. 161; Cooling Grid, p. 171
Tips: 2A, 4, 12, p. 134
***Sugar Sheets!* Edible Decorating Paper/Tools:** Damask, White, Red (1 each), Black (3), p. 144; Rotary Cutter, p. 145
Recipes: Buttercream Icing, p. 128
Also: 2013 Pattern Book (triangle), p. 143; Piping Gel, p. 141; Brush Set, p. 153; Cake Boards, Fanci-Foil Wrap, p. 186
See p. 114 for a list of commonly used decorating items you may need.

Bake and cool 1-layer cake; ice cake smooth.

Position cake on a 13 in. x 17 in. foil wrapped board. Using triangle pattern, cut two triangles from damask edible paper. Use triangles as a guide for cutting black center strip. Position black strip and damask triangles on cake top. Cut ½ in. wide strips from long edge of red edible paper. Attach over damask/black seams with piping gel, trimming ends as needed. Use rotary cutter to cut 1⅛ in. wide strips of black edible paper. Attach around outer edge of board with piping gel, trimming as needed. Cut four red strips, ½ in. x 4 in., for bow loops. Fold and attach ends using damp brush. Let dry on sides for 15 minutes then attach to ribbons. Cut two red circles using narrow end of tip 2A. Attach for center knots. For bottom border, cut ½ in. wide red strips; attach. Pipe tip 4 message.

For diploma, cut an 8 in. x 8 in. white square. Roll up and slightly curl out ends. Secure at center with piping gel. Cut a red strip, ¼ in. x 2½ in.; wrap around diploma, securing with piping gel. Position on cake. Cut two red strips, ¼ in. x 3 in. for bow loops. Fold and attach ends using damp brush. Let dry on sides for 15 minutes then attach to ribbon. Cut two red strips, ¼ in. x 1½ in. for streamers; trim ends at an angle and attach to bow with piping gel. Cut a red circle using narrow end of tip 12. Trim to oval shape and attach for knot. Serves 27.

▼ Extra-Curricular Cookies

Pans: Cookie Sheet, Cooling Grid, p. 171
Tip: 4, p. 134
***Sugar Sheets!* Edible Decorating Paper/Tools:** Red, Damask (1 red sheet makes 4 treats, 1 damask sheet makes 24 treats), p. 144; Slide-N-Cut Edge Cutter, Dab-N-Hold Edible Adhesive, p. 145
Candy: Yellow (1 oz. makes 24 to 26 treats), Black Candy Melts candy (1 pk. makes 24 to 26 treats), p. 175; Graduation Lollipop Mold, p. 243; Decorator Brush Set, p. 178
Recipes: Buttercream Icing, Roll-Out Cookies, p. 128
Also: Detail Embosser, p. 149
See p. 114 for a list of commonly used decorating items you may need.

In advance: Make grad caps using painting or piping method (p. 123) and filling mold cavities only halfway. Chill until firm.

Prepare and roll out dough. Cut 4¾ in. square cookies using embosser with wavy cutting wheel. Bake and cool. Use Slide-N-Cut to cut 4¼ in. squares from red edible paper. Ice cookies smooth; position edible paper squares. Use Slide-N-Cut to cut 4¼ in. x ¾ in. damask strips; attach to red square, with edible adhesive ⅝ in. from left edge. Pipe tip 4 monogram. Attach cap with melted candy. Each serves 1.

Unbridled Texture!

Wedding is all about texture this year. You'll see it happening in every cake here, with molded accents, piping or patterns. The great thing is, Wilton products make it easy to add texture. Use items like fondant molds or texture presses to add fun details that bring personality to the cake.

Whisper White Cake

Pans: 6 in., 8 in., 10 in., 14 in. x 2 in. Square, p. 161; Cooling Grid, p. 171
Tips: 1, 2, p. 134
Fondant/Gum Paste: White Ready-To-Use Rolled Fondant (352 oz.), Ready-To-Use Gum Paste (16 oz.), p. 148; 20 in. Fondant Roller, 20 in. Fondant Roller Guide Rings, Roll-N-Cut Mat, Fondant Smoother, p. 152; Brush Set, p. 153; Wave Flower Former Set, p. 142; Flower Forming Cups, p. 155; Flower Cut-Outs Fondant Cutters, p. 151
Recipes: Royal Icing, p. 128; Thinned Fondant Adhesive, p. 127
Also: 2013 Pattern Book (side scrolls), p. 143; 7.5 in. Twist Legs (1 pk.), 10 in. Crystal-Clear Plate, p. 193; Meringue Powder, Piping Gel, p. 141; Dowel Rods, p. 194; Cake Boards, Fanci-Foil Wrap, p. 186; Spatula, p. 137; Parchment Paper, p. 158; Parchment Triangles, p. 136; 11 in. x 11 in. foamcore board (¼ in. thick), 20 in. x 20 in. foamcore board (½ in. thick)

See p. 114 for a list of commonly used decorating items you may need.

3 days in advance: Make flowers. Mix 16 oz. fondant with 16 oz. gum paste (reserve excess mixture for base panels). Roll out ¹⁄₁₆ in. thick. Cut 19 flowers using largest Cut-Out. Dry in 3 in. flower forming cups. Cut 25 flowers using medium Cut-Out. Dry in 2½ in. cups. Cut 225 flowers using smallest Cut-Out. Dry on wave flower formers. Make extras to allow for breakage. **Also:** Make base panels. Roll out reserved fondant/gum paste mixture ⅛ in. thick. Cut four panels each 2½ in. x 17½ in. wide. Use knife to equally trim ends at an angle leaving a 14¼ in. wide top edge. Let dry on cornstarch-dusted boards. **And:** Prepare and cover base boards with 90 oz. fondant, including reserved mixture (p. 119). **And:** Decorate flowers. Use royal icing to pipe tip 1 outline on petals of all flowers. Let dry.

Bake and cool four 3-layer cakes (trim one layer to 1 in. high for 5 in. high cakes). Prepare and cover with rolled fondant (p. 119). Prepare bottom cake for push-in pillar construction (p. 120); set on 20 in. base board. Using royal icing, attach angled base panels to bottom tier, positioning 17½ in. edge on board 2¼ in. from cake. Pipe tip 2 lines over corner seams. Beginning at the center, pipe tip 2 lines ¼ in. apart at the top, gradually widening at the bottom to fill angle at corners. Attach 50 small flowers to each side above panels in a wavy pattern.

Prepare top three cakes for stacked construction (p. 120); position on 11 in. base board. Use piping gel with parchment paper to transfer side scroll pattern to sides of 6 in. cake (p. 119). Use royal icing to cover marks with tip 1 swirls and random dots. Decorate sides of other three tiers with tip 1 clusters of 6-petal bead flowers, leaves, dots and swirls. Shape a fondant mound 2 in. x 5 in.; position on 6 in. cake. Use thinned fondant adhesive to attach seven large, 13 medium and 25 small flowers. Insert twist legs in marked areas. Attach 12 large and 12 medium flowers around legs, using fondant balls to vary angles.

At reception: Assemble cakes. Serves 180.**

▼ Frilly Fantasy Cake

Pans: 6 in., 8 in., 10 in. x 3 in. Round, p. 163; Cooling Grid, p. 171
Tips: 12, 127D, p. 134-135
Color: Rose, p. 139
Ornament: Two Rings, p. 191
Recipe: Buttercream Icing, p. 128
Also: Cake Circles, Fanci-Foil Wrap, p. 186; Disposable Decorating Bags, p. 136; Spatula, p. 137; Dowel Rods, p. 194
See p. 114 for a list of commonly used decorating items you may need.

Bake and cool three 2-layer cakes (trim layers to 2½ in. high for 5 in. high cakes). Ice cakes smooth in rose. Prepare cakes for stacked construction (p. 120). Starting at the top of each tier, pipe five rows of tip 127D ruffles. Pipe tip 12 bead bottom borders. Position topper on cake.† Serves 62.**

▲ Pastel Palette Cake

Pans: 6 in., 8 in., 10 in. x 2 in. Round, p. 161; Cooling Grid, p. 171
Tips: 1, 126, 127, p. 134-135
Colors:* Leaf Green, Rose, Lemon Yellow, Golden Yellow, p. 139
Recipes: Buttercream, Royal Icings, p. 128
Also: 3-Pc. Icing Comb Set, p. 137; Flower Nail No. 7, Flower Nail Templates, Pre-Cut Icing Flower Squares, Wave Flower Former Set, p. 142; White Sparkling Sugar, p. 156; Parchment Paper, p. 158; Disposable Decorating Bags, p. 136; Meringue Powder; Piping Gel, p. 141; Brush Set, p. 153; Dowel Rods, p. 194; Cake Circles, p. 186
See p. 114 for a list of commonly used decorating items you may need.

1 to 2 days in advance: Make royal icing flowers. Use flower nail, apple blossom/primrose template and flower squares to make eight tip 126 and seven tip 127 white wild roses (p. 118). (Make extras to allow for breakage.) Pipe tip 1 dot centers. Brush petal edges with piping gel; sprinkle with sparkling sugar. Let dry 24 hours on parchment-covered boards.

Bake and cool three 2-layer cakes. Ice smooth in buttercream in assorted colors, icing thicker on sides. Comb sides using square comb from set (p. 119). Prepare for stacked construction (p. 120). Attach flowers with icing. Serves 62.**

*Combine Lemon Yellow with Golden Yellow for yellow shown.

◀ Ruffled in Romance Cake

Pans: 6 in., 8 in., 14 in. x 2 in. Round, p. 161; Cooling Grid, p. 171
Tips: 2, 8, 16, 45, 127D, p. 134-135
Colors:* Lemon Yellow, Ivory, p. 139
Ornament: First Kiss, p. 191
Recipes: Buttercream, Royal Icings, p. 128
Also: Dowel Rods, p. 194; Cake Circles, Cake Board, Fanci-Foil Wrap, p. 186; Disposable Decorating Bags, p. 136; Parchment Paper, p. 158; Spatula, p. 137; Meringue Powder, p. 141

See p. 114 for a list of commonly used decorating items you may need.

1 day in advance: Make flowers. Use royal icing to pipe approximately 75 tip 16 drop flowers on parchment paper-covered board. Pipe tip 2 dot centers. Make extras to allow for breakage and let dry overnight.

Bake and cool 2-layer 6 in. and 14 in. cakes and 3-layer 8 in. cake (bake three 2 in. layers for a 6 in. high cake). Ice smooth 6 in. and 14 in. tiers in yellow buttercream and 8 in. tier in white buttercream. Prepare cakes for stacked construction (p. 120).

Pipe tip 45 cornelli lace-look ruffle (p. 125) on 8 in. cake in white buttercream, holding narrow edge of tip against cake with remainder of tip upright from cake side. On 14 in. cake, pipe tip 127D ruffle bottom border. On 6 in. cake, pipe tip 8 bead bottom border. Attach drop flowers 1¾ in. apart on 6 in. and 14 in. cakes with tip 2 dots of buttercream. Position topper.† Serves 102.**

*Combine Lemon Yellow with Ivory for yellow shade shown.

†Always place a separator plate, or cake board cut to fit, on the cake where you position any figurine or topper. This protects both the cake and your keepsake. For extra stability, secure your figurine to the plate with double-stick craft tape.

**The smallest tier is often saved for the first anniversary. The number of servings given does not include the smallest tier.

▶ Grand Monogram Cake

Pans: 12 in. x 2 in. Round, p. 161; Cooling Grid, p. 171
Tips: 1, 2, 3, 4, 5, 199, p. 134
Color: Kelly Green, p. 139
Fondant: White Ready-To-Use Rolled Fondant (72 oz.), p. 148; 20 in. Fondant Roller, 20 in. Fondant Roller Guide Rings, Roll-N-Cut Mat, Fondant Smoother, Fondant Trimmer, p. 152; Brush Set, p. 153
Recipes: Buttercream, Royal Icings, p. 128
Also: 2013 Pattern Book (scrollwork), p. 143; 4-Pc. Circles Nesting Metal Cutter Set, p. 172; 50-Pc. A-B-C and 1-2-3 Plastic Cutter Set, p. 173; Disposable Decorating Bags, p. 137; Meringue Powder, Piping Gel, p. 141; 14 in. Round Silver Cake Base, p. 187; Cake Circles, Fanci-Foil Wrap, p. 186; Parchment Paper, p. 158; 1½ in. wide white ribbon (38 in. long)

See p. 114 for a list of commonly used decorating items you may need.

In advance: Prepare base board. Tint 70 oz. fondant green. Prepare and cover base with 20 oz. fondant (p. 120). Reserve excess fondant.

Bake and cool 2-layer cake. Prepare and cover with reserved tinted fondant (p. 119); reserve excess fondant. Position cake on board. Attach ribbon around bottom, securing ends with double-stick craft tape. Transfer scroll pattern to cake top using piping gel method (p. 119); reverse pattern for one side.

Using royal icing, outline scrolls with tip 5; let set. Overpipe with tip 4, then tip 3, then tip 2, letting each outline set before adding the next. Use tip 4 to pipe a new outline ⅛ in. out from first scroll. Overpipe as above using tips 3, 2 and 1. Move out ⅛ in. and pipe a tip 3 outline; overpipe with tips 2 and 1. Move out ⅛ in. and pipe a tip 2 outline; overpipe with tip 1. Move out ⅛ in. and pipe a tip 1 outline. Pipe tip 1 dots around last outline. Roll out reserved green fondant ¼ in. thick. Cut circle using largest cutter from set; attach to cake top with damp brush.

Roll out white fondant ⅛ in. thick. Cut letter using plastic cutter from set. Attach to circle with damp brush. Outline and overpipe letter as above using tips 3, 2 and 1 for first outline, tips 2 and 1 for next outline, tip 1 for last outline and dots, each group ⅛ in. apart. Pipe tip 199 star bottom border in royal icing. Use tip 3 to pipe s-shaped scroll over each pair of stars. Overpipe scrolls with tips 2 and 1. Pipe tip 1 dots on base board, ⅛ in. from border. Serves 56.

◀ Wedding Scentsations! Mini Cakes

Pans: 9 in. x 13 in. x 2 in. Sheet, p. 161; Cooling Grid, p. 171
Color: Rose, p. 139
***Sugar Sheets!* Edible Decorating Paper/Tools:** White (1 sheet makes 35 treats), Bright Pink (1 sheet makes 20 treats), p. 144; Punch Set with Oval Cutting Insert, Layered Hearts Cutting Insert Set, Rotary Cutter, Dab-N-Hold Edible Adhesive, p. 145
Fondant: White Ready-To-Use Rolled Fondant (4 oz. per treat), p. 148; 20 in. Fondant Roller, 20 in. Fondant Roller Guide Rings, Roll-N-Cut Mat, p. 152; Silver Pearl Dust, Pure Lemon Extract, Brush Set, p. 153; Fabric Designs Gum Paste & Fondant Mold, p. 150; Fine Tip Primary Colors FoodWriter Edible Color Markers, p. 153
Recipes: Buttercream Icing, p. 128; Thinned Fondant Adhesive, p. 127
Also: Cake Boards, p. 186; Parchment Paper, p. 158; Spatula, p. 137; large marshmallows
See p. 114 for a list of commonly used decorating items you may need.

1 day in advance: Prepare silver trims. Use mold to make white fondant bows for each treat. Place on parchment-covered boards. Paint with silver Pearl Dust/lemon extract mixture (p. 118). Also paint one marshmallow per treat with mixture. Let all dry.

Bake and cool cake using firm-textured batter, such as pound cake. Cut into 2 in. squares. Tint remaining fondant rose. Prepare and cover treats with rolled fondant (p. 119). Attach marshmallow and bow with thinned fondant adhesive. For labels, use rotary cutter to cut 1½ in. squares from white edible paper. Use punch with medium heart insert to cut bright pink edible paper hearts. Attach to white squares using edible adhesive. Print initial with black edible marker. Attach to treat with edible adhesive. Each serves 1.

▶ Promised in Pink Cake

Pans: 6 in., 8 in., 10 in. x 2 in. Square, p. 161; Cooling Grid, p. 171
Color: Rose, p. 139
Fondant: White Ready-To-Use Rolled Fondant (160 oz.), Gum-Tex, p. 148; 20 in. Fondant Roller, 20 in. Fondant Roller Guide Rings, Roll-N-Cut Mat, p. 152; White Pearl Dust (2), Pure Lemon Extract, Brush Set, p. 153; Fondant Ribbon Cutter, p. 149
Recipes: Buttercream Icing, p. 128; Thinned Fondant Adhesive, p. 127
Also: A-B-C and 1-2-3 Plastic Cutter Set, p. 173; 8 in. Cookie Treat Sticks, p. 171; Parchment Triangles, p. 136; Parchment Paper, p. 158; Piping Gel, p. 141; Dowel Rods, p. 194; Cake Boards, Fanci-Foil Wrap, p. 186; 12 in. x 12 in. plywood or foamcore board (½ in. thick)
See p. 114 for a list of commonly used decorating items you may need.

2 to 3 days in advance: Make fondant ribbons for cake sides. Add 2 teaspoons Gum-Tex to 24 oz. white fondant. Roll out ⅛ in. thick. Cut strips using ribbon cutter with straight and wavy wheels and ¼ in. spacer. Trim strips to make 128 ribbons, 4 in. long; make extras to allow for breakage. Set on parchment-covered boards. Paint with white Pearl Dust/lemon extract mixture (p. 118). Let dry 24 hours. Turn over and paint other side; let dry.

Also: Make topper. Roll out white fondant ⅛ in. thick. Use ribbon cutter with wavy wheel to cut a rectangle 6 in. x 5 in. Cut initial with cookie cutter. Tint 136 oz. fondant rose; knead ¼ teaspoon Gum-Tex into 4 oz. rose fondant and reserve remainder. Use ribbon cutter with straight wheel to cut rectangle, 3½ in. x 4½ in. Attach letter to rose rectangle, then attach to white rectangle with damp brush. Paint white areas with Pearl Dust mixture; let dry. Attach topper to two cookie sticks using thinned fondant adhesive, leaving 4 in. extending at bottom. Let dry.
And: Prepare and cover base board (p. 120) with 24 oz. rose fondant. Reserve remaining fondant.

Bake and cool three 2-layer cakes. Prepare and cover cakes with reserved rose fondant (p. 119). Prepare cakes for stacked construction (p. 120). Starting at corners, use toothpick to lightly mark ¾ in. spacing for side ribbons. Line straight edge of ribbons with piping gel in a cut parchment bag; attach to cake sides and corners. Insert topper. Serves 82.**

**The smallest tier is often saved for the first anniversary. The number of servings given does not include the smallest tier.

◄ Daisy Lattice Cake

Pans: 6 in. x 2 in. Round, 8 in. x 2 in. Square, p. 161; Cooling Grid, p. 171
Tips: 1, 2, 3, p. 134
Colors:* Christmas Red, Creamy Peach, p. 139
Fondant: White Ready-To-Use Rolled Fondant (6 oz.), Gum-Tex, p. 148; 9 in. Fondant Roller, Roll-N-Cut Mat, p. 152; Brush Set, p. 153
Recipes: Buttercream, Royal Icings, p. 128; Thinned Fondant Adhesive, p. 127
Also: 2013 Pattern Book (assorted daisies, swirls), p. 143; Parchment Triangles, p. 136; Parchment Paper, p. 158; Meringue Powder, Piping Gel, p. 141; Dowel Rods, p. 194; Cake Boards, Cake Circles, Fanci-Foil Wrap, p. 186

See p. 114 for a list of commonly used decorating items you may need.

3 days in advance: Make daisies. Tint fondant. Add 1 teaspoon Gum-Tex. Roll out ⅟₁₆ in. thick. Use knife and patterns to cut one each of two largest daisies and two each of two smallest daisies. Let dry 24 hours on cornstarch-dusted cake boards. Using white royal icing, pipe tip 1 lattice over petals (p. 125); outline petals with tip 2. Pipe tip 2 dot center (pat dot smooth with finger dipped in cornstarch). Let dry.

Bake and cool two 2-layer cakes; ice smooth. Prepare for stacked construction (p. 120). Use piping gel to transfer swirl patterns to cake sides (p. 119). Outline and pipe in using tip 1 and buttercream icing; pat smooth. Pipe tip 3 bead bottom borders in buttercream. Use icing to attach one each of three daisy sizes to top tier; attach remaining daisies on bottom tier. Serves 24.**

*Combine Christmas Red with Creamy Peach for pink shown.

► Coral Reef-ined Cake

Pans: 6 in. x 3 in. Round, p. 163; 10 in. x 2 in. Round, p. 161; 3-D Sports Ball Set, p. 165; Cooling Grid, p. 171
Tip: 3, p. 134
Colors:* Garden Tone Icing Color Set (aster mauve used), Peach, Ivory, Brown, p. 139
Fondant: White Ready-To-Use Rolled Fondant (53 oz.), Gum-Tex, p. 148; Sea Life Designs Gum Paste & Fondant Mold, p. 150; 9 in., 20 in. Fondant Roller, 20 in. Fondant Roller Guide Rings, Roll-N-Cut Mat, 10-Pc. Gum Paste/Fondant Tool Set, p. 152; Shaping Foam, p. 155; White, Silver Pearl Dust, Pure Lemon Extract, Brush Set, p. 153
Recipe: Buttercream Icing, p. 128
Also: 4-Pc. Circles Nesting Metal Cutter Set, p. 172; White Candy Melts Candy, p. 175; Girl Power 2-Pack Candy Mold Set, p. 178; Cake Circles, Fanci-Foil Wrap, p. 186; Disposable Decorating Bags, p. 136; Dowel Rods, p. 194; 8 in. Lollipop Sticks, p. 178

See p. 114 for a list of commonly used decorating items you may need.

2 to 3 days in advance: Make fondant accents. Tint 1 oz. fondant each ivory, aster mauve and peach. Add ⅛ teaspoon Gum-Tex to each color and to 2 oz. white; marbleize (p. 119). Using sea life mold, make 18 various shells and starfish. Let dry on cornstarch-dusted surface. Mold ring using 2 oz. white fondant and girl power mold; let dry. For coral, tint 3 oz. fondant each light ivory and very light aster mauve with peach. Add ½ teaspoon Gum-Tex to each. Using sea life mold, make 12 coral shapes in each color. Make clam shell (p. 125). Let dry. Paint ring with silver Pearl Dust/lemon extract mixture (p. 118). Let dry.

Bake and cool two 1-layer cakes; ice smooth. Tint 14 oz. fondant dark pink, 18 oz. dark ivory, 3 oz. medium ivory, 2 oz. light ivory. Prepare and cover cakes with fondant (p. 119), 6 in. with dark pink, 10 in. with dark ivory. Prepare cakes for stacked construction (p. 120). Using sea life mold, make medium ivory chain border strips for bottom border and 20 light ivory sand dollars. Attach to cake with damp brush. Attach 10 coral pieces to side of 6 in. cake with tip 3 dots of icing.

Cut 10 lengths of 3 in. from lollipop sticks; attach with melted candy to remaining coral pieces, leaving 2 in. extended at bottom. Let set. Insert in top of 10 in. tier. Attach shells and starfish with tip 3 dots of icing. Position one clam shell half on cake top. Attach remaining clam shell to two lollipop sticks using melted candy, leaving 4 in. extended. Let set. Insert in cake top. Roll a 1½ in. ball of medium ivory fondant; flatten slightly and cut slit in top. Position in bottom clam shell half. Insert ring. Serves 19.**

◀ A Forever Moment Cake

Pans: 6 in., 10 in., 14 in. x 2 in. Square, p. 161; Cooling Grid, p. 171
Fondant: White Ready-To-Use Rolled Fondant (24 oz.), Chocolate Ready-To-Use Rolled Fondant (36 oz.), p. 148; 9 in. & 20 in. Fondant Rollers, 20 in. Fondant Roller Guide Rings, Roll-N-Cut Mat, p. 152; Baroque Designs Gum Paste & Fondant Mold, p. 150; Brush Set, Pure Lemon Extract, White Pearl Dust, p. 153
Ornament: First Kiss, p. 191
Recipe: Chocolate Buttercream Icing, p. 128
Also: Piping Gel, p. 141; Dowel Rods, p. 194; Cake Boards, p. 186; 16 in. Square Silver Cake Base, p. 187
See p. 114 for a list of commonly used decorating items you may need.

In advance: Prepare and cover base board with chocolate fondant (p. 120).

Bake and cool three 2-layer cakes. Ice smooth. Prepare for stacked construction (p. 120). Use baroque mold and white fondant to make about 84 large pearl chains. Attach to top, side and bottom edges using damp brush; trim as needed. Paint all pearls with white Pearl Dust/lemon extract mixture (p. 118). Position topper at reception.† Serves 148.**

**The smallest tier is often saved for the first anniversary. The number of servings given does not include the smallest tier.

†Always place a separator plate, or cake board cut to fit, on the cake where you position any figurine or topper. This protects both the cake and your keepsake. For extra stability, secure your figurine to the plate with double-stick craft tape.

▶ Lotus in Focus Cake

Pans: 6 in., 8 in., 10 in. x 2 in. Round, p. 161; 3-D Sports Ball Set, p. 165; Cooling Grid, p. 171
Tip: 12, p. 134
Fondant/Gum Paste: Ready-To-Use Gum Paste (8 oz.), White Ready-To-Use Rolled Fondant (40 oz.), p. 148; 9 in., 20 in. Fondant Roller, 20 in. Fondant Roller Guide Rings, Roll-N-Cut Mat, p. 152; Folk Designs Gum Paste & Fondant Mold, p. 150; Brush Set, p. 153
Recipe: Chocolate Buttercream Icing, p. 128
Also: 2013 Pattern Book (lotus petal), p. 143; Piping Gel, p. 141; 12 in. Round Silver Cake Base, p. 187; Circle Metal Cutter, p. 172; Cake Circles, p. 186; Dowel Rods, p. 194; White Candy Melts Candy, p. 175; Disposable Decorating Bags, p. 137; heavy-duty aluminum foil
See p. 114 for a list of commonly used decorating items you may need.

2 to 3 days in advance: Make flower topper. Use ball pan half to shape two foil curves for drying petals. Roll out gum paste 1/16 in. thick. Use pattern and knife to cut 15 petals. Let dry on cornstarch-dusted curves of foil and pans, placing three or four in each.

For topper base, roll out gum paste 1/8 in. thick; use cookie cutter to cut circle. Assemble flower. Attach bottom layer of seven petals to base with melted candy, overlapping slightly; let set. Attach center layer of five petals with melted candy; support petals with facial tissue. Let set.

Attach top layer of three petals as above. Roll a 1 in. fondant ball and flatten to 1/4 in. thick. Attach for flower center; let set. **Also:** Prepare and cover base board with 18 oz. fondant (p. 120).

Bake and cool three 2-layer cakes; ice smooth. Prepare for stacked construction (p. 120). Using folk art mold and fondant, make 265 heart blossoms. Attach to cake, starting with top row, 1 in. apart, with damp brush; attach descending rows at an angle. Attach flower to cake top with tip 12 dots of icing. Serves 62.**

◀ We Are Gathered Here Cake

Pans: 6 in., 8 in., 10 in., 12 in. x 2 in. Round, p. 161; Cooling Grid, p. 171
Tip: 21, p. 134
Fondant: Chocolate Ready-To-Use Rolled Fondant (236 oz.), Gum-Tex, p. 148; 20 in. Rolling Pin, 20 in. Rolling Pin Guide Rings, Roll-N-Cut Mat, Fondant Trimmer, p. 152; Dots Texture Press, p. 147; Fabric Designs Gum Paste & Fondant Mold, p. 150; Brush Set, p. 153
Recipes: Chocolate Buttercream Icing, p. 128; Thinned Fondant Adhesive, p. 127
Also: 2013 Pattern Book (heart topper), p. 143; 14 in. Round Silver Cake Base, p. 187; Cake Circles, p. 186; Dowel Rods, p. 194; Cake Marker, p. 137; Piping Gel, p. 141; 8 in. Cookie Treat Sticks, p. 171
See p. 114 for a list of commonly used decorating items you may need.

2 days in advance: Make heart topper. Add ½ teaspoon Gum-Tex to 9 oz. chocolate fondant; roll out ¼ in. thick. Cut out heart using pattern and knife; reserve remainder. Let dry overnight on cornstarch-dusted cake circle.

Roll out reserved fondant ³⁄₁₆ in. thick. Cut two strips, 1 in. x 18 in. Imprint with texture press. Shape ruffles (p. 125). Attach to back of heart with thinned fondant adhesive. Make a fondant ribbon rose (p. 119) using a strip 1 in. x 18 in. Imprint with texture press and shape rose; let dry.

Make 32 fondant buttons using fabric mold. Attach rose and buttons to heart with thinned fondant adhesive. Let dry. Attach heart to cookie treat stick using adhesive; let dry.

Also: Prepare and cover cake base with 24 oz. chocolate fondant (p. 120).

Bake and cool four 2-layer cakes. Prepare and cover cakes with rolled fondant (p. 119). Prepare for stacked construction (p. 120). Use cake marker to mark 2 in. above bottom edge around each cake. Assemble cakes on base board.

Pipe tip 21 shell bottom borders on all cakes. Roll out fondant ⅛ in. thick; make imprinted ruffles as above using strips 2 in. x 12 in. Finished ruffled strips should measure 2 in. x 8 in. Attach to cake sides, above and below markings, with piping gel and brush; be sure to align top ruffle with top edge of cake and align top and bottom ruffle strips.

Use fabric mold and fondant to make 11 large ribbons. Attach where top and bottom ruffles meet with piping gel. Use fabric mold and fondant to make approximately 96 buttons. Attach to bands, 1 in. apart, with piping gel. Insert heart topper. Serves 118.**

▶ Chocolate Charmers Petit Fours

Pans: 11 in. x 15 in. x 2 in. Sheet, p. 161; Cooling Grid, p. 171
Tip: 21, p. 134
Fondant: Chocolate Ready-To-Use Rolled Fondant (½ oz. per treat), p. 148; 9 in. Fondant Roller, Roll-N-Cut Mat, p. 152; Lines Texture Press, p. 147; Brush Set, p. 153
Also: 101 Cookie Cutters, p. 173; Cake Leveler, p. 158; Light Cocoa Candy Melts Candy (1 pk. makes 6-8 treats), p. 175; Piping Gel, p. 141; Chocolate Ready-To-Use Decorator Icing, p. 141; Disposable Decorating Bags, p. 136; Parchment Paper, p. 158; I Do, Mr. & Mrs., Double Heart Wedding Fun Pix, p. 190; Spatula, p. 137
See p. 114 for a list of commonly used decorating items you may need.

Bake and cool cake using firm-textured batter, such as pound cake; level to 1½ in. high. Cut circles using knife and medium round cutter as a guide. Ice bottom smooth with melted candy; let set.

Place candy side down on cooling grid over parchment paper. Cover with melted candy (p. 123); let dry. Roll out chocolate fondant ³⁄₁₆ in. thick. With knife, cut strips 2 in. x 8 in. for each treat; imprint with texture press. Trim strips to 1½ in. x 7½ in.; attach to treats using piping gel and brush.

Pipe tip 21 swirl of chocolate icing on each treat; insert pick. Each serves 1.

◀ Drifting Dogwoods Cake

Pans: 6 in., 8 in. x 3 in. Round, p. 163; Standard Muffin, p. 163; Cooling Grid, p. 171
Tips: 1, 4, p. 134
Colors:* Moss Green, Violet, Royal Blue, p. 139
Fondant/Gum Paste: White Ready-To-Use Rolled Fondant (82 oz.), Ready-To-Use Gum Paste (16 oz.), p. 148; 9 in., 20 in. Fondant Rollers, 20 in. Rolling Pin Guide Rings, Roll-N-Cut Mat, Fondant Trimmer, p. 152; Gum Paste Flower Cutter Set, Flower Impression Set, p. 154; 10-Pc. Gum Paste/Fondant Tool Set, p. 152; Brown, Red, Spruce Green Color Dust, White Pearl Dust, Brush Set, p. 153; Shaping Foam, Flower Forming Cups, p. 155; p. 152; Gum Paste Wire and Tape, p. 155
Recipes: Buttercream, Royal Icings, p. 128; Gum Glue Adhesive, p. 127
Also: 2013 Pattern Book (pleats), p. 143; Meringue Powder, p. 141; White Standard Baking Cups, p. 181; Disposable Decorating Bags, p. 136; Spatula, p. 137; Cake Circles, Fanci-Foil Wrap, p. 186; Piping Gel, p. 141; Dowel Rods, p. 194; Fresh Flower Cake Spikes, p. 191; 7 in. high cake pedestal, light blue tulle (5 ft. x 5 ft.)
See p. 114 for a list of commonly used decorating items you may need.

2 days in advance: Make flowers. Tint 1 oz. gum paste light green, 2 oz. blue. Use cutter and instructions from gum paste cutter set to make 55 white dogwood flowers with green centers; let dry overnight in large flower forming cups and additional cups molded from foil. Make five additional dogwood flowers on 22-gauge wire, 6 in. long, following daisy instructions from set to attach wire to center and pull through flower. When dry, brush petals with white Pearl Dust, petal indents with brown/red Color Dust mixture and flower centers with spruce green Color Dust. Use ejector and instructions from set to make 30 small blue blossoms. Let dry. Pipe tip 1 dot centers in white royal icing. **Also:** Prepare and cover double-thick cake circles trimmed to 9 in. diameter for base board with 14 oz. rolled fondant (p. 120).

Bake and cool 2-layer cakes (trim to 2½ in. layers for 5 in. high cakes) and 28 cupcakes. Ice smooth in buttercream. Prepare cakes for stacked construction (p. 120) but do not stack. Using pattern, make and attach 46 overlapping fondant pleats (p. 125). Assemble cake on tulle-draped pedestal. Place a dogwood flower on each cupcake. Attach unwired flowers and blossoms to cake and tulle with royal icing. Twist wired flowers together; arrange in flower spike and insert in cake top. Position cupcakes. Cake serves 24**; each cupcake serves 1.

*Combine Royal Blue with Violet for blue shown.

▶ Lace Embrace Cake

Pans: Petal Pan Set (9 in., 15 in. x 2 in. used), p. 160; Cooling Grid, p. 171
Tips: 1, 2, 5, p. 134
Fondant: White Ready-To-Use Rolled Fondant (36 oz.), Gum-Tex, p. 148; 20 in. Fondant Roller, 20 in. Fondant Roller Guide Rings, Fondant Trimmer, p. 152
Ornament: Clear Bianca, p. 191
Recipes: Buttercream, Royal Icings, p. 128
Also: 2013 Pattern Book (heart; small, medium and large half-circles), p. 143; 10 in., 16 in. Cake Circles, Fanci-Foil Wrap, p. 186; 7.5 in. Twist Legs, 6 in. Plate from Crystal-Clear Cake Divider Set, p. 193; 6 in. Lollipop Sticks, p. 178; Meringue Powder, Piping Gel, p. 141; Disposable Decorating Bags, p. 136; Parchment Paper, p. 158; Spatula, p. 137
See p. 114 for a list of commonly used decorating items you may need.

3 days in advance: Make lace pieces (p. 125) using half-circle patterns. You will need 384 small, 18 medium and 210 large lace pieces; make extras to allow for breakage and let dry. **Also:** Make fondant heart. Knead ½ teaspoon Gum-Tex into 6 oz. fondant. Roll out ⅛ in. thick. Using pattern and knife, cut out heart. Lightly imprint inner heart outline using toothpick. Let dry on cornstarch-dusted board. Decorate heart with royal icing. Attach lollipop stick to back of heart, extending 3½ in. from bottom; let dry. Using tip 2, attach large lace pieces around heart edge; let dry. Pipe tip 2 bead border on inner heart edge and tip 5 bead border on edge. Let dry. **And:** Prepare cake circles and base board. Using pans as a guide, cut cake circles to match petal shape (one for each cake). Cut base board 1 in. larger on all sides than 15 in. Prepare and cover base board with rolled fondant (p. 120).

Bake and cool 2-layer cakes; ice smooth in buttercream. Place 15 in. cake on prepared board. Starting at top of cake, insert small lace pieces ⅛ in. deep at a 45° angle downward with edges touching side to side (each horizontal row with six pieces per petal division). Space rows ½ in. apart, working toward bottom of cake. For 9 in. cake, insert large lace pieces as above (each row with three pieces per petal division); leave three bottom rows open for placement at reception. Pipe tip 5 bead top borders.

At reception: Assemble cakes. Position five large lace pieces around each pillar. Insert three bottom rows of lace pieces in 9 in. cake. Position topper.† Insert heart topper. Serves 64.**

†Always place a separator plate, or cake board cut to fit, on the cake where you position any figurine or topper. This protects both the cake and your keepsake. For extra stability, secure your figurine to the plate with double-stick craft tape.

◄ A Moveable Meadow Cake

Pans: 6 in., 8 in., 10 in. x 2 in. Round, p. 161; Cooling Grid, p. 171
Tip: 4, p. 134
Color: Moss Green, p. 139
Fondant/Gum Paste: White Ready-To-Use Rolled Fondant (96 oz.), Ready-To-Use Gum Paste (12 oz.), p. 148; Gum Paste Flower Cutter Set, p. 154; Shaping Foam, p. 155; 10-Pc. Gum Paste/Fondant Tool Set, p. 152; White Pearl Dust, Pure Lemon Extract, Brush Set, p. 153; 9 in., 20 in. Fondant Rollers, 20 in. Fondant Roller Guide Rings, Roll-N-Cut Mat, Fondant Trimmer, p. 152
Recipes: Buttercream Icing, p. 128; Gum Glue Adhesive, p. 127
Also: Cake Circles, p. 186; 12 in. Round Silver Cake Base p. 187; Disposable Decorating Bags, p. 136; Spatula, p. 137; Piping Gel, p. 141; 7.5 in. Twist Legs (2 pks.), 6 in., 8 in. Plates from Crystal-Clear Cake Divider Set (1 each), p. 193, craft foam block, spaghetti
See p. 114 for a list of commonly used decorating items you may need.

2 days in advance: Make flowers. Tint 2 oz. gum paste green; leave remainder white. Using cutter, small blossom ejector and instructions from gum paste set, make 122 white stephanotis flowers with green calyxes; use a 6 in. piece of thin spaghetti for stem rather than wire. Make extras to allow for breakage and let dry 24 hours in craft foam block. Paint stems with moss green icing color/lemon extract mixture (p. 118). Let dry. Brush flowers with white Pearl Dust; let set. **Also:** Tint 96 oz. fondant green. Prepare and cover base board with 18 oz. fondant tinted green (p. 120). Reserve remaining fondant.

Bake and cool 2-layer cakes. Prepare and cover with tinted fondant (p. 119). Prepare cakes for separator plate and pillar construction (p. 120), but do not assemble cakes. Sponge bottom 2 in. of cakes with thinned buttercream in deep moss green (p. 126). Pipe tip 4 bead bottom borders.

At reception: Insert twist legs in 10 in. and 8 in. cakes. Insert 60 flowers in 10 in. cake, 40 in. 8 in. cake and 22 in 6 in. cake. Assemble cakes. Serves 62.**

**The smallest tier is often saved for the first anniversary. The number of servings given does not include the smallest tier.

► Revelling in Roses Cake

Pans: 6 in., 8 in. x 3 in. Round, p. 163; 12 in. x 2 in. Round, p. 161; Cooling Grid, p. 171
Fondant: White Ready-To-Use Rolled Fondant (180 oz.), p. 148; 20 in. Fondant Roller, 20 in. Fondant Roller Guide Rings, Roll-N-Cut Mat, Fondant Smoother, 10-Pc. Gum Paste/Fondant Tool Set, Fondant Trimmer, p. 152; Shaping Foam, p. 155
Recipe: Buttercream Icing, p. 128
Also: 14 in. Round Silver Cake Base, p. 187; Cake Circles, p. 186; Dowel Rods, p. 194; Brush Set, p. 153; Piping Gel, p. 141; Spatula, p. 137
See p. 114 for a list of commonly used decorating items you may need.

Bake and cool three 2-layer cakes (trim 6 in. and 8 in. layers to 2½ in. high for 5 in. high cakes). Prepare and cover cakes with rolled fondant (p. 119). Prepare for stacked construction (p. 120); and assemble cakes on base board. For roses, roll out fondant ⅟₁₆ in. thick. Use large fondant cutter to cut strips, ⅜ in. wide x 24 in. long. Thin top edge of strips on shaping foam using large ball tool. Brush a small section on top of cake with piping gel. Loosely roll up each strip to form roses on prepared cake section, varying the look to create gently rippled petal line on top. Continue down sides of cake to cover completely; you will need approximately 125 roses. Serves 80.**

▼ Garden Greeters Petit Fours

Pans: 9 in. x 13 in. x 2 in. Sheet, p. 161; Cooling Grid, p. 171
Colors:* Moss Green, Violet, Rose, Lemon Yellow, Golden Yellow, p. 139
Fondant: White Ready-To-Use Rolled Fondant (20 oz.), Gum-Tex, p. 148; 9 in. Fondant Roller, Roll-N-Cut Mat, p. 152; Fern Designs Gum Paste & Fondant Mold, p. 150; Round Cut-Outs Fondant Cutters, p. 151; Purple, Goldenrod Color Dust, Pure Lemon Extract, Brush Set, p. 153
Also: Graceful Tiers Cake Stand, p. 192; White Ready-To-Use Decorator Icing (1 can covers 8 to 10 treats), p. 141; White Candy Melts Candy, p. 175; Spatula, p. 137; Cake Leveler, p. 188; Parchment Triangles, p. 136, spaghetti
See p. 114 for a list of commonly used decorating items you may need.

1 day in advance: Make butterflies and dragonflies. Tint 5 oz. fondant each medium violet and medium yellow; knead ½ teaspoon Gum-Tex into each. Use mold to make 20 each butterflies and dragonflies. Let dry. Paint details using goldenrod (butterflies) or purple (dragonflies) Color Dust/lemon extract mixture in (p. 118). Attach insects to 3 in. pieces of spaghetti using melted candy in cut parchment bag. Let set.

Bake and cool two sheet cakes using firm-textured batter, such as pound cake. Level to 1½ in. high. Cut circles for 30 petit fours using knife and largest Cut-Out as a guide. Place on cooling grid over pan and cover with heated icing (p. 123); let dry. Tint 8 oz. fondant dark green and 2 oz. light green. For treat sides, mold 120 leaves each large dark green and small light green; reserve remaining fondant. Place ferns under plastic wrap after molding to prevent drying. Attach four ferns in each size to sides of each treat using damp brush. Insert insects in treat tops. For stand, use reserved dark green fondant to mold four large and 14 medium ferns; use light green fondant to mold six tendrils. Before pieces dry, attach to stand using melted candy. Attach remaining butterflies and dragonflies randomly to stand. Each serves 1.

*Combine Violet with Rose for violet shown. Combine Lemon Yellow with Golden Yellow for yellow shown.

▲ Cascade of Cupcakes

Pans: Standard Muffin, p. 162; Cooling Grid, p. 171
Tip: 2A, p. 134
Color: Moss Green, p. 139
Fondant/Gum Paste: Ready-To-Use Gum Paste (60 oz.), p. 148; 9 in. Fondant Roller, Roll-N-Cut Mat, Gum Paste Flower Cutter Set, Flower Impression Set, p. 154; 10-Pc. Gum Paste/Fondant Tool Set, p. 152; Fondant Shaping Foam, Flower Forming Cups, Flower Drying Rack, Color Stamen Set (4 pks., yellow only used), Gum Paste Wire and Tape, p. 155; Wave Flower Former Set, p. 142; Deep Pink, Orange, Purple, Periwinkle Blue, Goldenrod, Spruce Green, White Color Dust, Brush Set, p. 153
Recipes: Buttercream Icing, p. 128; Gum Glue Adhesive, p. 127
Also: Fanci Flow Fountain Set, p. 190; 8 in. (28), 10 in. (2) Decorator Preferred Smooth Edge Plates, 3 in., 5 in. (7 pks. each), 7 in. (1 pk.) Grecian Pillars, p. 194; Grass Standard Shaped Baking Cups (3 pks.), p. 180; Spatula, p. 137; White Standard Baking Cups (2 pks.), p. 181; Disposable Decorating Bags, p. 136; heavy-duty aluminum foil, cotton ball
See p. 114 for a list of commonly used decorating items you may need.

1 week in advance: Make gum paste flowers following instructions in cutter set book unless otherwise noted. Tint 8 oz. gum paste green for calyxes and leaves; flowers will be white with Color Dust highlights (mix equal parts white with Color Dust shade noted). Make 54 large roses on 4 in. long 20-gauge wires; brush 18 each with deep pink, orange and goldenrod Color Dust. Let dry upside down on drying rack. Make 36 briar roses without calyxes, using a ½ in. diameter gum paste ball for center and inserting eight stamens rather than thread. Brush centers with goldenrod and petals with deep pink Color Dust. Let dry in 3 in. flower forming cups (mold additional cups from foil). Make 40 2-layer daisies without wires. Brush centers with goldenrod Color Dust and 20 flowers each with deep pink and goldenrod Color Dust. Let dry in 3 in. flower forming cups. Make 40 fantasy flowers (p. 126). Make 140 leaves. Roll out green gum paste ¹⁄₁₆ in. thick; cut leaves using large rose leaf cutter from set. Imprint leaves in rose leaf mold from flower impression set and let dry in varied positions on cornstarch-dusted wave flower formers.

Bake and cool cupcakes: 84 in white cups, 49 in grass cups. Spatula ice cupcakes in white cups. Pipe tip 2A swirl on cupcakes in grass cups.

At reception: Assemble 10 in. plates on 7 in. pillars, half of 8 in. plates on 5 in. pillars and remaining on 3 in. pillars. Position 7 in. pillar setup in center. Position fountain on plate, surrounded by 5 in., then 3 in. setups. Position six white cups each on 8 in. plates; position grass cups on table. With scissors, cut off wires from flowers; position 12 roses around fountain base, securing with icing. Position remaining flowers on cupcakes. Each serves 1.

◀ Marriage Monograms Mini Cupcakes

Pans: Mini Muffin Pan, p. 162; Cooling Grid, p. 171
Tip: 12, p. 134
Colors:* Rose, Violet, Orange, Red-Red, Golden Yellow, Lemon Yellow, p. 139
Fondant: White Ready-To-Use Rolled Fondant (½ oz. makes 10 treats), Gum-Tex, p. 155; 4-Pc. Letters & Numbers Gum Paste/Fondant Mold Set, p. 148
Recipe: Buttercream Icing, p. 128
Also: Lavender, Red, Pink, Yellow, Peach Petal Mini Cups, p. 180; Disposable Decorating Bags, p. 136
See p. 114 for a list of commonly used decorating items you may need.

In advance: Make fondant letters. Tint 1 in. balls of fondant to match baking cup colors. Knead ⅛ teaspoon of Gum-Tex into each color (use orange for peach cups). Use mold to make letters. Unmold and let dry on cornstarch-dusted board at least 24 hours.

Bake and cool cupcakes in mini cups. Pipe tip 12 swirl; insert matching color letter. Each serves 1.

*Combine Golden Yellow with Lemon Yellow for yellow shown. Combine Violet with Rose for violet shown.

◀ **Enveloped in Love Cake**

Pans: 6 in., 8 in., 10 in. x 2 in. Round, p. 161; Cooling Grid, p. 171
Tip: 5, p. 134
Color: Teal, p. 139
Fondant: White Ready-To-Use Rolled Fondant (124 oz.), Gum-Tex, p. 148; 9 in., 20 in. Fondant Roller, 20 in. Fondant Roller Guide Rings, Roll-N-Cut Mat, p. 152; Macrame Designs Gum Paste & Fondant Mold, p. 150; 4-Pc. Letters & Numbers Gum Paste/Fondant Mold Set, p. 151; White Pearl Dust, Pure Lemon Extract, Brush Set, p. 153
Recipes: Buttercream Icing, p. 128; Thinned Fondant Adhesive, p. 127
Also: 2013 Pattern Book (cone topper), p. 143; 12 in. Round Silver Cake Base, p. 187; Cake Boards, Fanci-Foil Wrap, p. 186; Disposable Decorating Bags, p. 136; Dowel Rods, p. 194; 4 in. diameter jar (6 in. high)
See p. 114 for a list of commonly used decorating items you may need.

2 days in advance: Make cone topper. Tint 88 oz. fondant light teal. Add 1 teaspoon Gum-Tex to 10 oz. of tinted fondant; reserve remainder for covering cakes. Roll out ⅛ in. thick. Cut topper shape using pattern and knife. Wrap around 4 in. cornstarch-dusted jar, overlapping ends and securing with damp brush. Let dry.

Bake and cool three 2-layer cakes. Prepare and cover with reserved fondant (p. 119). Prepare cakes for stacked construction (p. 120). Pipe tip 5 bead bottom border on 8 in. and 10 in. cakes. Roll a white fondant rope, 18 in. long x ½ in. diameter; attach to bottom of 6 in. cake with damp brush. Using macrame mold and white fondant, mold 226 large and 80 medium circles. Trim 30 medium circles with wide end of tip 5 to make small circles. Attach large circles to 8 in. cake top with damp brush, working upward to cover entire 6 in. cake. Attach circles to 8 in. and 10 in. cake sides, placing large, then medium, then small and leaving progressively more space in between. Position topper on cake; secure with thinned fondant adhesive. Attach remaining circles to topper. Using alphabet mold and white fondant, make message. Attach with damp brush. Paint circles with white Pearl Dust/lemon extract mixture (p. 118). Serves 62.

▼ Silver Scrollwork Cake

Pans: 4-Pc. Heart Set (largest pan used), p. 160; Cooling Grid, p. 171
Colors:* Royal Blue, Black, p. 139
Fondant: White Ready-To-Use Rolled Fondant (125 oz.), Gum-Tex, p. 148; 20 in. Fondant Roller, 20 in. Fondant Roller Guide Rings, Roll-N-Cut Mat, Fondant Trimmer, p. 152; Decorative Press Set, Silver Pearl Dust, Pure Lemon Extract, Brush Set, p. 153
Recipes: Buttercream Icing, p. 128; Thinned Fondant Adhesive, p. 127
Also: 2013 Pattern Book (cake side scrolls, top scroll, heart), p. 143; Piping Gel, p. 141; Cake Boards, Fanci-Foil Wrap, p. 186; 17 in. square foamcore board, ¼ in. thick
See p. 114 for a list of commonly used decorating items you may need.

In advance: Make scrolls. Copy pattern to make 17 or 19 side scrolls; tape to cake boards and cover with waxed paper. Add ½ teaspoon Gum-Tex to 14 oz. white fondant; soften fondant with shortening. Use press with circle insert to press logs. Arrange over patterns, trimming as needed. Paint with silver Pearl Dust/lemon extract mixture (p. 118). Let dry.
Also: Prepare base board. Cut foamcore board 1 in. larger than pan on all sides. Tint 90 oz. fondant blue. Prepare and cover board with 24 oz. rolled fondant (p. 120). Reserve excess fondant.

Bake and cool 2-layer cake (trim layers to 1½ in. high for a 3 in. high cake). Prepare and cover with reserved blue fondant (p. 119). Position cake on base board. Use vegetable shortening to soften remaining blue fondant. Use press with circle insert to press logs for bottom border; you will need 48 in. Brush ends with damp brush and roll slightly to smooth. Attach around cake with thinned fondant adhesive. Roll out 24 oz. white fondant ⅛ in. thick; cut center heart using pattern. Attach to cake with damp brush. Soften remaining white fondant with shortening; press several logs and attach as above to form a 40 in. long rope border; attach around edge of white heart with thinned fondant adhesive. Press additional white logs; using pattern, form top scroll and 3½ in. high letters; attach. Attach scrolls to cake sides, ½ in. apart. Paint white logs with silver Pearl Dust/lemon extract mixture. Let dry. Serves 72.

*Combine Royal Blue with a little Black for blue shown.

◄ Cookie Couplet

Cookie: 6-Pc. Heart Nesting Plastic Cutter Set, p. 173; Cookie Sheet, Cooling Grid, p. 171
Color: Royal Blue, p. 139
Fondant: White Ready-To-Use Rolled Fondant (1 oz. per treat), p. 148; Decorative Press Set, Silver Pearl Dust, Pure Lemon Extract, Brush Set, p. 153
Recipes: Royal Icing, Roll-Out Cookies, p. 128; Thinned Fondant Adhesive, p. 127
Also: Meringue Powder, p. 141; Cake Boards, p. 186; Parchment Paper, p. 158
See p. 114 for a list of commonly used decorating items you may need.

In advance: Make cookies. Prepare and roll out dough. Cut cookies using largest heart cutter from set; bake and cool. Place on cooling grid over parchment. Cover with thinned icing (p. 123). Let dry overnight.

Use vegetable shortening to soften 1 oz. fondant for each cookie. Use press set with 3-hole insert to press logs, you will need 14 in. for each cookie. Brush ends with damp brush as needed. Use thinned fondant adhesive to attach around edge of heart; shape and attach a 1¼ in. wide swirl and 1¼ in. high initials and a ¼ in. diameter center dot. Paint with Pearl Dust/lemon extract mixture (p. 118). Let dry. Each serves 1.

▲ Starry Night Cake

Pans: 6 in., 8 in. x 3 in. Round, p. 163; Cooling Grid, p. 171
Tip: 1, p. 134
Color: Teal, p. 139
Fondant: White Ready-To-Use Rolled Fondant (68 oz.), p. 148; 9 in., 20 in. Fondant Rollers, Roll-N-Cut Mat, p. 152; Fondant Trimmer, p. 152; White Pearl Dust, Brush Set, p. 153
Ornaments: Clear Bianca, p. 191; Hanging Gems (3 pks.), p. 190
Recipe: Buttercream Icing, p. 128
Also: White Sugar Pearls, p. 157; Cake Circles, p. 186; Dowel Rods, p. 194; Spatula, p. 157; Disposable Decorating Bags, p. 136
See p. 114 for a list of commonly used decorating items you may need.

Bake and cool two 2-layer cakes (trim layers to 2½ in. high for 5 in. high cakes). Tint 60 oz. fondant teal. Prepare and cover cakes with rolled fondant (p. 119). Prepare for stacked construction (p. 120). Roll out remaining white fondant ⅛ in. thick. Cut 1 in. high strips for cake borders, 20 in. long for 6 in. cake, 26 in. long for 8 in. cake. Attach strips to cakes with damp brush; trim as needed. Brush strips with white Pearl Dust. Pipe tip 1 bead petal flowers, 2 in. apart on cake sides. Attach sugar pearls for flower centers with tip 1 dot of icing.

At reception: Assemble cakes on pedestal. Position topper.† Slide hanging gems below cake on stand. Serves 24.**

**The smallest tier is often saved for the first anniversary. The number of servings given does not include the smallest tier.

†Always place a separator plate, or cake board cut to fit, on the cake where you position any figurine or topper. This protects both the cake and your keepsake. For extra stability, secure your figurine to the plate with double-stick craft tape.

Nature Sketch Cake

Pans: 3-Pc. Diamond Set, p. 160; Cooling Grid, p. 171
Tips: 2, 5, p. 134
Colors:* Orange, Christmas Red, Leaf Green, Lemon Yellow, Black, p. 139
Fondant/Gum Paste: White Ready-To-Use Rolled Fondant (120 oz.), Black Ready-To-Use Rolled Fondant (36 oz.), Ready-To-Use Gum Paste (6 oz.), p. 148; 20 in. Fondant Roller, 20 in. Fondant Roller Guide Rings, Roll-N-Cut Mat, 10-Pc. Gum Paste/Fondant Tool Set, p. 152; Flower Impression Set, Gum Paste Flower Cutter Set, p. 154; Shaping Foam, Flower Forming Cups, p. 155; Goldenrod, Red, Orange, Lime Green Color Dust, Pure Lemon Extract, Brush Set, p. 153; Leaf Cut-Outs Fondant Cutters, p. 151
Recipes: Buttercream Icing, p. 128; Gum Glue Adhesive, p. 127
Also: Piping Gel, p. 141; Cake Boards, Fanci-Foil Wrap, p. 186; Disposable Decorating Bags, p. 136; Dowel Rods, p. 194; 22 in. x 17 in. plywood or foamcore board (½ in. thick)
See p. 114 for a list of commonly used decorating items you may need.

2 days in advance: Make gum paste flowers. Tint gum paste: 5½ oz. red, ½ oz. green. Following flower cutter set instructions, make three large Gerbera daisies using large daisy/Gerbera and small daisy cutters and Gerbera center from flower impression set. Make two medium Gerbera daisies using medium daisy cutters and Gerbera center from flower impression set. Position in large flower forming cups dusted with cornstarch. Attach centers using gum glue adhesive. Let dry 48 hours.

Paint petals with red and orange Color Dust/lemon extract mixture (p. 118) and centers with goldenrod and lime green Color Dust/lemon extract mixture. **Also:** Prepare base board (p. 119). Cut board 1 in. larger on all sides than largest pan. Prepare and cover with 36 oz. black fondant.

Bake and cool three 2-layer cakes. Prepare and cover with white fondant (p. 119). Prepare for stacked construction (p. 120). Pipe tip 5 bead bottom borders. Roll out white fondant ⅛ in. thick. Use leaf Cut-Outs to cut four large and 10 medium leaves. Attach using damp brush. Use tip 2 to outline leaves and to pipe stems and veins. Attach flowers using thinned fondant adhesive. Serves 98.**

*Combine Christmas Red with Orange for red shown. Combine Leaf Green with Lemon Yellow for green shown.

Cornelli Crest Cake

Pans: 4-Pc. Oval Set (3 smallest pans used), p. 160; Cooling Grid, p. 171
Tips: 1, 2, 3, p. 134
Color: Black, p. 139
Gum Paste/Fondant: Ready-To-Use Gum Paste, (6 oz.) p. 148; Gum Paste Flower Cutter Set, p. 154; Shaping Foam, Flower Drying Rack, Rose Bases, Gum Paste Wire and Tape, p. 155; Fresh Flower Spikes, p. 191; White (8 oz.), Black (132 oz.) Ready-To-Use Rolled Fondant, p. 148; 9 in., 20 in. Fondant Rollers, 20 in. Fondant Roller Guide Rings, Roll-N-Cut Mat, 10-Pc. Gum Paste/Fondant Tool Set, p. 152; Global Designs Gum Paste & Fondant Mold, p. 150; Brush Set, p. 153
Recipes: Buttercream Icing, p. 128; Gum Glue Adhesive, p. 127
Also: 2013 Pattern Book (small, medium, large triangles), p. 143; Piping Gel, p. 141; Cake Boards, Fanci-Foil Wrap, p. 186; Disposable Decorating Bags, p. 136; Dowel Rods, p. 194; Spatula, p. 137; 16 in. x 13 in. plywood or foamcore board (½ in. thick)
See p. 114 for a list of commonly used decorating items you may need.

3 days In advance: Make three gum paste roses using large rose cutter and directions from cutter set. **Also:** Cover base board. Using second largest pan from set as a guide, cut board ¾ in. larger than pan all around perimeter. Prepare and cover with 24 oz. black fondant (p. 119). Reserve remaining fondant.

Bake and cool 2-layer cakes. Prepare and cover with black fondant (p. 120); reserve excess fondant. Prepare for stacked construction (p. 120). Use small and large triangle patterns to mark triangle sections on front and back of top and bottom tiers. Roll out white fondant ⅛ in. thick. Use medium triangle pattern to cut two triangles; attach to middle tier, front and back.

Pipe tip 2 cornelli lace over cake sides between triangles; use white icing on top and bottom tiers, black icing on middle tier. Using black icing, pipe tip 3 bead bottom borders; pipe tip 2 bead borders on remaining sides of all triangles. Use global mold to make four white and two black 4-petal flowers. Attach to triangles using damp brush. Use contrasting icing and tip 1 to decorate flowers with outlines, beads and dots.

At reception: Place roses in flower spikes; insert in cake top. Serves 71.**

▼ A Feast of Roses Cake

Pans: 6 in., 10 in., 14 in. x 2 in. Round, p. 161; Mini Ball, p. 165; Cooling Grid, p. 171
Tips: 2, 5, p. 134
Fondant: Red (150 oz.), White (36 oz.) Ready-To-Use Rolled Fondant, Gum-Tex, p. 148; 20 in. Fondant Roller, 20 in. Fondant Roller Guide Rings, Roll-N-Cut Mat, Fondant Trimmer, p. 152; Baroque Designs Gum Paste & Fondant Mold, p. 150; Ruby Red Pearl Dust, Pure Lemon Extract, Brush Set, p. 153
Recipe: Buttercream Icing, p. 128
Also: 16 in. Round Silver Cake Base, p. 187; Cake Boards, p. 186; White Sugar Pearls, p. 157; Dowel Rods, p. 194; Punch Set with Oval Cutting Insert, p. 145; Piping Gel, p. 141; Disposable Decorating Bags, p. 136; Spatula, p. 137
See p. 114 for a list of commonly used decorating items you may need.

1 day in advance: Make flowers. Knead 2 teaspoons Gum-Tex into 24 oz. white fondant; roll out ⅛ in. thick. Make 135 ribbon roses (p. 119) using strips ¾ in. x 8 in. Let dry 24 hours on cornstarch-dusted boards. **Also:** Prepare and cover base board with 24 oz. red fondant (p. 120).

Bake and cool three 2-layer round cakes and mini ball cake. Prepare and cover rounds with reserved red fondant and mini ball with white fondant (p. 119). Prepare for stacked construction (p. 120). Position cakes on base board. Roll out white fondant ⅛ in. thick. Using punch with insert, cut 13 ovals for 6 in. cake, 21 for 10 in. cake and 30 for 14 in. cake. Attach at bottom borders with damp brush. Use baroque mold to make small white paisley heart accents; attach to ovals with damp brush. Using tip 2, edge ovals with piping gel; attach sugar pearls. Paint edges of ribbon roses with ruby red Pearl Dust/lemon extract mixture (p. 118); attach around base of each round and on mini ball cake with tip 5 dots of icing. Serves 128.**

▲ Petal Impressions Cake

Pans: 6 in., 10 in., 14 in. x 2 in. Square, p. 161; 3-D Sports Ball Set, p. 165; Cooling Grid, p. 171
Tips: 1, 3, p. 134
Colors:* Black, Christmas Red, Leaf Green, Lemon Yellow, p. 139
Fondant/Gum Paste: White (192 oz.), Black (48 oz.) Ready-To-Use Rolled Fondant, Ready-To-Use Gum Paste (4½ oz.), p. 148; 9 in., 20 in. Fondant Rollers, 20 in. Fondant Roller Guide Rings, Roll-N-Cut Mat, Fondant Smoother, 10-Pc. Gum Paste/Fondant Tool Set, p. 152; Baroque Designs Gum Paste & Fondant Mold, p. 150; Fondant Shaping Foam, p. 155; Flower Impression Mat, Gum Paste Flower Cutter Set, p. 154; Brush Set, Red, Goldenrod Color Dust, Pure Lemon Extract, p. 153
Recipes: Buttercream, Royal Icings, p. 128; Thinned Fondant Adhesive, p. 127
Also: 2013 Pattern Book (large scalloped petal), p. 143; Meringue Powder, Piping Gel, p. 141; Disposable Decorating Bags, p. 136; Dowel Rods, p. 194; Cake Boards, Fanci-Foil Wrap, p. 186; 16 in. Square Silver Cake Base, p. 187
See p. 114 for a list of commonly used decorating items you may need.

2-3 days in advance: Make gum paste fantasy flower topper (p. 126). **Also:** Prepare and cover base board with black fondant (p. 120). Reserve remaining fondant.

Bake and cool 2-layer cakes. Prepare and cover with white fondant (p. 119). Prepare for stacked construction (p. 120). Randomly imprint flowers using cutters from set for individual petals. Use dogwood cutter for 4-petal flowers; use orchid throat cutter for 5-petal flowers. Stack cakes. Roll out white fondant ³⁄₁₆ in. thick. Cut four ribbons, 19 in. x 3 in.; use damp brush to attach ribbons down center of cake sides, trimming ends as needed. Use baroque mold and reserved black fondant to make 13 small pearl chains. Attach to ribbon centers, trimming as needed. Using tip 2 and thinned black royal icing, decorate imprinted flowers with brush embroidery (p. 119). Pipe tip 2 vines between flowers. At reception, use small ball of fondant to position fantasy flower on cake top. Serves 148.**

*Combine Lemon Yellow with Leaf Green for yellow shown.

**The smallest tier is often saved for the first anniversary. The number of servings given does not include the smallest tier.

◀ Ring Bearing Bites

Pans: Silicone Bite-Size Treat Mold, p. 168; Cookie Sheet, Cooling Grid, p. 171
Tips: 2A, 3, p. 134
Fondant: White Ready-To-Use Rolled Fondant (3 oz. per treat), Gum-Tex, p. 148; 9 in. Fondant Roller, Roll-N-Cut Mat, p. 152; Jewelry Designs Gum Paste & Fondant Mold, p. 150; Silver, White, Gold Pearl Dust, Pure Lemon Extract, Brush Set, p. 153
Recipe: Quick Pour Fondant, p. 127
Also: Cake Board, p. 186
See p. 114 for a list of commonly used decorating items you may need.

2 days in advance: Make rings. Knead ⅛ teaspoon Gum-Tex into ¼ oz. fondant for each ring. Roll out ⅛ in. thick. Cut ring using wide end of tip 2A; cut opening using wide end of tip 3. For each diamond, use jewelry mold and fondant to make two round gems; attach flat sides together with damp brush. Let dry on cornstarch-dusted board.

Bake and cool cakes using firm-textured batter like pound cake, in silicone mold supported by cookie sheet. Place on cooling grid over cookie sheet; cover with thinned icing (p. 123). Let set. Roll a ⅞ in. ball of fondant; flatten and taper sides into a 1⅜ in. pillow shape. Position on treat. Use knife to cut a ⅛ in. x ½ in. slit in fondant to hold ring. Use jewelry mold to make dotted trim border. Attach around treat using damp brush; trim as needed. Use Pearl Dust/lemon extract mixture to paint (p. 118) gold border, silver ring and white diamond; let dry. Insert ring in pillow, securing with icing. Attach diamond to ring with icing. Each serves 1.

▶ Bring On The Bling Cake

Pans: 6 in. x 2 in. Round, 8 in., 12 in. x 2 in. Square, p. 161; Non-Stick Cookie Sheet, p. 169
Tips: 1, 6, p. 134
Colors: Black, Christmas Red, Brown, p. 139
Fondant/Gum Paste: White (72 oz.), Black (94 oz.) Ready-To-Use Rolled Fondant, Gum-Tex, Ready-To-Use Gum Paste (16 oz.), p. 148; 9 in., 20 in. Fondant Rollers, 20 in. Fondant Roller Guide Rings, Roll-N-Cut Mat, Fondant Smoother, Fondant Trimmer, p. 152; White, Gold Pearl Dust, Pure Lemon Extract, Brush Set, p. 153; Wave Flower Former, p. 142; Jewelry Designs Gum Paste & Fondant Mold, p. 150
Recipes: Buttercream Icing, p. 128; Thinned Fondant Adhesive, Gum Glue Adhesive, p. 127
Also: 2013 Pattern Book (diamond and scrolls for topper), p. 143; White, Red Cake Sparkles, p. 157; Piping Gel, p. 141; White, Black Candy Melts Candy, p. 175; Spatula, p. 137; 6 in. Cake Circle, 13 in. x 19 in. Cake Boards, p. 186; 14 in. Square Cake Base, p. 187; 4-Pc. Circles Nesting Metal Cutter Set, p. 172; Gold Color Mist Food Color Spray (3), p. 139; Disposable Decorating Bags, p. 136; Dowel Rods, p. 194
See p. 114 for a list of commonly used decorating items you may need.

2 days in advance: Make diamond ring topper (p. 126). **Also:** Make cake side gems. Tint 9 oz. white fondant red: 63 oz. light tan. Use jewelry mold to make 201 tan square gem bases and 201 red square gems. Brush gem bases with gold Pearl Dust. Let dry. Mix crushed red cake sparkles with white Pearl Dust. Brush red gems with piping gel; cover with mixture; let dry. Attach gems to bases with piping gel. **And:** Prepare and cover base board with 24 oz. tan fondant (p. 120). Reserve remaining tan fondant for covering cake. Spray board with gold Color Mist food color spray.

Bake and cool 2-layer cakes. Prepare for stacked construction (p. 120). Prepare and cover cakes with fondant (p. 119). Spray light tan tier with gold Color Mist food color spray. Pipe tip 6 bead bottom borders. Attach diagonal rows of three gems to black cakes with piping gel. Use jewelry mold to make eight large bead borders with black fondant; trim each to 4 in. lengths. Use piping gel to attach to each side. Use mold to make four brooches with red fondant. Brush with white Pearl Dust. Attach to 8 in. cake with thinned fondant adhesive. Position ring topper on cake. Cake serves 104.**

▶ Golden Garden Cake

Pans: 16 in. x 2 in. Round, p. 161; 6 in., 8 in., 10 in. x 3 in. Round, 18 in. x 3 in. Half Round, p. 163; 4-Pc. Hexagon Set (largest pan used), p. 160; 3-D Sports Ball Set, p. 165; Heating Core (recommended), p. 163; Cooling Grid, p. 171
Tips: 3, 4, p. 134
Colors:* Brown, Black, p. 139
Fondant/Gum Paste: White Ready-To-Use Rolled Fondant (512 oz.), Ready-To-Use Gum Paste (32 oz.), p. 148; 9 in., 20 in. Fondant Rollers, 20 in. Fondant Roller Guide Rings, Roll-N-Cut Mat, Fondant Trimmer, 10-Pc. Gum Paste/Fondant Tool Set, p. 152; Fondant Shaping Foam, p. 155; Wave Flower Former Set, p. 142; Gum Paste Flower Cutter Set, Flower Forming Cups, p. 154; Brush Set, Gold Pearl Dust, Deep Pink, White Color Dust, Pure Lemon Extract, p. 153
Recipes: Buttercream Icing, p. 128; Thinned Fondant Adhesive, Gum Glue Adhesive, p. 127
Also: 4-Pc. Circles Nesting Metal Cutter Set, p. 172; Pearl, Gold Color Mist Food Color Spray (2 each), p. 139; Piping Gel, p. 141; Dowel Rods, p. 194; Cake Boards, Cake Circles, Fanci-Foil Wrap, p. 186; Parchment Paper, p. 158; 20 in. diameter plywood base board (½ in. thick)
See p. 114 for a list of commonly used decorating items you may need.

3 days in advance: Make gum paste flowers and leaves. Reserve 4 oz. gum paste. Divide remainder into fourths and tint light tan, medium tan, light brown and medium brown (7 oz. each). Roll out ¹⁄₁₆ in. thick as needed. Make three ribbon roses (p. 119) using a strip 2½ in. x 9 in., folded horizontally in half, for each. Let dry on cornstarch-dusted board.

Use flower cutter set to make cascading flowers (p. 126). Paint flowers and leaves with gold Pearl Dust/lemon extract mixture (p. 118) or spray with gold Color Mist food color spray. Let dry. Mix pink Color Dust with some white to lighten. Brush on to highlight petals and leaves as desired. **Also:** Prepare and cover base board with 48 oz. fondant tinted medium tan (reserve excess fondant). Spray with gold Color Mist food color spray. Let dry.

Bake and cool: 2-layer 6 in., 8 in. and 10 in. rounds (trim layers to 2½ in. high for 5 in. high cakes); 3-layer 15 in. hexagon (trim one layer to 1 in. high for a 5 in. high cake); 2-layer 16 in. round (4 in. high); and four 18 in. half rounds (you will need four layers 2 in. high for a 4 in. high cake). Prepare and cover cakes with rolled fondant (p. 119). Spray with pearl Color Mist food color spray; let dry. Prepare for stacked construction (p. 120).

Pipe tip 4 bead bottom borders. Roll out medium tan fondant ⅛ in. thick. Cut circle using second largest cutter from set. Attach to front of hexagon tier using thinned fondant adhesive. Paint with gold Pearl Dust/lemon extract mixture. Pipe tip 3 initial; pat smooth with finger dipped in cornstarch. Attach flowers and leaves using balls of fondant and thinned fondant adhesive. Serves 378.**

*Combine Brown with a little Black for light and medium brown shown.

**The smallest tier is often saved for the first anniversary. The number of servings given does not include the smallest tier.

Cake Couture!

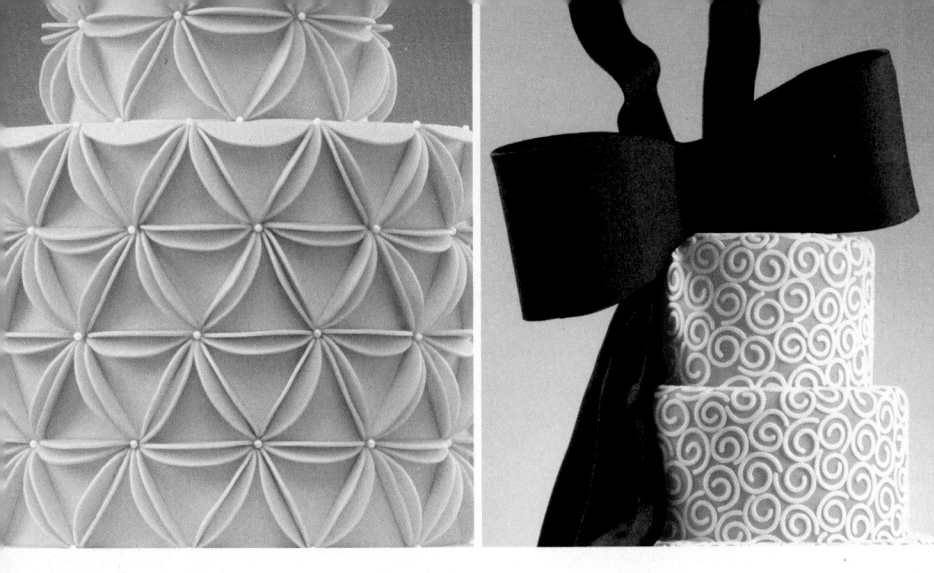

Personalization, color and style have taken cake design to an all-time high. In other words, cake has become fashionable! More than ever before, cakes can play off exciting looks in fabrics, jewelry and art. With the great colors and patterns in our *Sugar Sheets!* edible decorating paper, our amazing fondant tools and other Wilton products, it was inevitable that we would be able to design fashion-forward cakes that create red-carpet excitement for any celebration. Welcome to our cake couture collection for 2013!

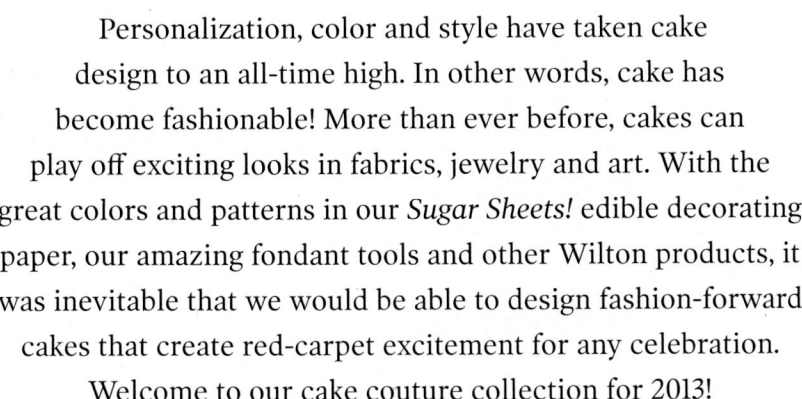

▶ Buttoned Up Classic Cake

Pans: 6 in. x 2 in., 8 in. x 2 in., 10 in. x 2 in. Square, p. 161
Tip: 12, p. 134
Colors:* Lemon Yellow, Leaf Green, Orange, Rose, p. 139
Fondant: White Ready-To-Use Rolled Fondant (132 oz.), p. 148;
9 in, 20 in. Fondant Rollers, Roll-N-Cut Mat, p. 149; Fabric Designs,
Jewelry Designs Gum Paste and Fondant Molds, p. 150; Silver
Pearl Dust (3), Brush Set, Pure Lemon Extract, p. 153
Recipe: Buttercream Icing, p. 128
Also: Cake Boards, Fanci-Foil Wrap, p. 186; Dowel Rods, p. 194;
4-Pc. Circles Nesting Metal Cutter Set, Circle Metal Cutter, p. 172; 11 in. x 11 in. foamcore
board (¼ in. thick)
See p. 114 for a list of commonly used decorating items you may need.

Bake and cool 2-layer cakes. Tint 24 oz. fondant rose, 36 oz. orange, 48 oz. green. Prepare
and cover cakes with rolled fondant (p. 119); reserve remaining fondant. Prepare cakes for
stacked construction (p. 120).

For large buttons, roll out white fondant ¼ in. thick. Cut circles with third largest cutter
from nesting set. Imprint inner circle using circle metal cutter. Use narrow end of tip 12 to
make button holes, ¼ in. apart. Paint buttons with silver Pearl Dust/lemon extract mixture
(p. 118). Attach to center of front cake side using damp brush.

For bottom borders, use fabric mold and white fondant to mold small ribbon strips. Brush
with silver Pearl Dust/lemon extract mixture; let dry. Attach to bottom borders using
damp brush. You will need four strips for 6 in. cake, five strips for 8 in. cake and six strips
for 10 in. cake.

For center strips, use jewelry mold and white fondant to make mesh border strips. Paint
with silver Pearl Dust/lemon extract mixture; let dry. You will need 12 strips. Attach to cake
sides with damp brush, trimming as needed to fit. For small buttons, use fabric mold and
white fondant to make 81 small 2-hole buttons. Paint with silver Pearl Dust/lemon extract
mixture; let dry. Attach buttons to strips with damp brush, ⅝ in. apart. Serves 60.

*Combine Leaf Green with Lemon Yellow for green shown.

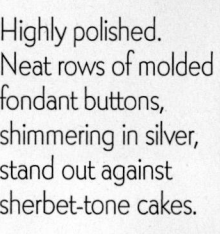

Highly polished.
Neat rows of molded
fondant buttons,
shimmering in silver,
stand out against
sherbet-tone cakes.

◀ Corsage Colorama Cake

Pans: 6 in. x 2 in., 10 in. x 2 in. Round, p. 161; Mini Ball, p. 162
Colors:* Rose, Orange, Lemon Yellow, Golden Yellow, Leaf Green, p. 139
Fondant/Gum Paste: White Ready-To-Use Rolled Fondant (96 oz.),
Ready-To-Use Gum Paste (32 oz.), p. 148; 9 in. and 20 in. Fondant Rollers, 20 in.
Fondant Roller Guide Rings, Roll-N-Cut Mat, Storage Board, Fondant
Smoother, p. 152; Pattern Embosser, p. 149; Fondant Shaping Foam, p. 155;
Brush Set, p. 153; Fondant Trimmer, p. 152
Recipes: Buttercream Icing, p. 128; Gum Glue Adhesive, p. 127; favorite
crisped rice cereal treats
Also: 4-Pc. Circles Nesting Metal Cutter Set, p. 172; Pastry Brush, p. 159; White
Candy Melts Candy, p. 175; Piping Gel, p. 141;
Bamboo Dowel Rods, p. 194; 16 in. Round
Silver Cake Base, p. 187; Cake Circles, Fanci-
Foil Wrap, p. 186; 12 oz. foam bowls—5⅞ in.
dia. (6 needed)
**See p. 114 for a list of commonly used
decorating items you may need.**

Larger than life! The
wonder of nature is
magnified on richly
colored jumbo roses,
which beckon you
to examine every
fascinating fold.

Two days in advance: Make jumbo roses
(p. 127). **Also:** Prepare base board. Tint 96 oz.
fondant green. Prepare and cover cake base with
24 oz. fondant (p. 120). Reserve excess fondant.

Bake and cool 2-layer round cakes. Prepare
and cover with reserved green fondant (p. 119); reserve remaining fondant.
Prepare cakes for stacked construction (p. 120).

Roll out remaining green fondant ⅛ in. thick. Cut a strip 4 in. x 20 in. Imprint
dots using pattern embosser. Attach around sides of 6 in. cake using damp
brush. Trim as needed. Cut a strip 4 in. x 33 in. Repeat as above to cover
sides of 10 in. cake. To allow room for roses, position 10 in. cake on prepared
cake base 1¼ in. from back edge. Position 6 in. cake at back left of 10 in.
cake with cake sides aligned vertically.

At party: Position roses, supporting and angling as needed with balls of
fondant. Serves 40.

*Combine Lemon Yellow with Golden Yellow for yellow shown. Leaf Green with Lemon Yellow
for green shown.

◀ Bedazzled Cake

Pans: 6 in. x 3 in., 8 in. x 3 in. Round, p. 163; Cooling Grid, p. 171

Colors:* Creamy Peach, Orange, Leaf Green, Royal Blue, p. 139

Fondant/Gum Paste: Ready-To-Use Gum Paste (16 oz.), White Ready-To-Use Rolled Fondant (24 oz.), p. 148; 9 in. Fondant Roller, Roll-N-Cut Mat, Storage Board, p. 152; Jewelry Designs Gum Paste and Fondant Mold, p. 150; Leaf Green, Sapphire Blue, Orchid Pink, Yellow, Gold (2), Silver (2) Pearl Dust, Pure Lemon Extract, Brush Set, p. 153

Recipe: Buttercream Icing, p. 128

Also: 2013 Pattern Book (heart topper, scallops), p. 143; Cake Circles, p. 186; Cake Leveler, p. 158; White Candy Melts Candy (1 pk.), p. 175; 8 in. Cookie Treat Sticks, p. 171; Piping Gel, p. 141; Dowel Rods, p. 194; 10 in. round cake pedestal

See p. 114 for a list of commonly used decorating items you may need.

A masterpiece of mosaic-looking fashion with jeweled belt and bracelet borders and a stylized heart topper.

3 days in advance: Make heart topper. Tint 16 oz. gum paste orange. Roll out ⅛ in. thick. Use pattern and knife to cut out heart; reserve remaining gum paste. Let heart dry 24 hours on cornstarch-dusted surface. Flip over and let dry another 24 hours.

Also: Make scallops for cake pedestal. Roll out gum paste ⅛ in. thick. Use pattern and knife to cut nine scallops. Place scallops under storage board flap. To shape scallops, dust cake pedestal lightly with cornstarch. Center 8 in. cake board on cake pedestal. Using cake board as a guide, position 1 in. of scallop ends on pedestal plate, then bend down scallops to drape down from pedestal. Let dry on pedestal for 2 days, then remove.

And: Make jewels. Use jewelry mold and white fondant to make 252 square gem backs and 104 round gem backs. Tint 2 oz. fondant each light blue and light green. Use jewelry mold to make 126 square gems in white and 63 each in blue and green. Use jewelry mold to make 52 round gems in white and 26 each in blue and green. Paint 126 of the square and 52 of the round gem backs with gold Pearl Dust/lemon extract mixture (p. 118); paint remaining backs with silver Pearl Dust/lemon extract mixture. Let dry. Paint 26 of the white round gems and 63 of the white square gems with orchid pink Pearl Dust/lemon extract mixture and remaining white gems with yellow Pearl Dust/lemon extract mixture. Brush blue and green gems with matching color Pearl Dust only. Attach pink and yellow gems to silver backs and blue and green gems to gold backs with piping gel. Let dry. Attach nine round gems to each scallop, alternating back colors. **And:** Complete heart topper. Bend lollipop stick to follow curve of heart topper; attach with melted candy, leaving 4 in. extended to insert in cake. Chill until set. Attach round gems to heart topper with piping gel.

Bake and cool 2-layer cakes (trim layers to 2½ in. for 5 in. high tiers). Prepare cakes for stacked construction (p. 120). Ice smooth in orange.

Attach two rows of square gems to top and bottom edges of cakes with icing, alternating backing colors. Attach scallops to cake pedestal with piping gel, positioning ends against base of cake. Carefully trim if needed.

At party: Insert topper in cake. Serves 32.

*Combine Creamy Peach with Orange for orange shade shown.

◀ Plaid in
Play Cake

Pans: 6 in. x 2 in., 8 in. x 2 in., 10 in. x 2 in.
Square, p. 161; Cooling Grid, p. 171
Colors:* Teal, Red-Red, Orange, Black, Lemon
Yellow, Golden Yellow, p. 139
Fondant: White (114 oz.), Red (64 oz.), Black
(38 oz.) Ready-To-Use Rolled Fondant,
Gum-Tex, p. 148; 9 in., 20
in. Fondant Rollers, 20
in. Fondant Roller Guide
Rings, Roll-N-Cut Mat,
Fondant Smoother, p. 152;
Brush Set, p. 153; Wave
Flower Former Set, p. 142
Recipe: Buttercream Icing,
p. 128
Also: 2013 Pattern Book
(buckle), p. 143; Cake
Boards, Fanci-Foil Wrap,
p. 186; Spatula, p. 137;
Dowel Rods, p. 194; Slide-
N-Cut Edge Cutter, p. 145;
Cake Leveler, p. 158; 12 in. x 12 in. plywood or
foamcore board (½ in. thick)
**See p. 114 for a list of commonly used
decorating items you may need.**

Fasten your seat belts! It's a tartan tier cake that shows the traditional pattern in a brilliant new color mix. The belt of fondant around the center tier cinches the look.

1 day in advance: Make buckle inserts. Add
Red-Red to 6 oz. red fondant for deep red on
belt and inserts. Knead ¼ teaspoon Gum-Tex
into 2 oz. of deep red; roll out ⅛ in. thick. Use
edge cutter to cut four strips, 2 in. x 2½ in. Let
dry on large side of cornstarch-dusted wave
flower former. Reserve remaining red fondant.
Also: Prepare base board. Prepare and cover
base board with 24 oz. black fondant (p. 120).
Reserve remaining black fondant.

Bake and cool 3-layer cakes. (trim one layer
to 1 in. high for 5 in. high cakes). Tint 108 oz.
fondant dark teal. Prepare and cover 6 in. and
10 in. cakes with teal fondant and 8 in. cake
with reserved red fondant. Prepare cakes for
stacked construction (p. 120) but do not stack.

Mark 2 in. divisions at top and bottom of teal
cakes with toothpick. Tint 6 oz. fondant yellow.
Roll out yellow and reserved red and black
fondant ¹⁄₁₆ in. thick. Use edge cutter to cut
¼ in. wide red strips and ⅛ in. wide black and
yellow strips, each 5 in. long. Starting at one
corner, attach a red strip diagonally from top
to bottom with damp brush, connecting at first
and third markings. Attach a black strip, ⅛ in.
from red. Attach a yellow strip against the red
strip. Attach another group of strips diagonally
from the next top marking, running in the
opposite direction. Continue attaching groups
of strips in lattice fashion around the cakes.

Stack cakes. Roll out remaining black fondant
¼ in. thick. Use pattern and knife to cut
4 buckles; remove center. Attach buckles
centered on cake sides with piping gel. Roll out
reserved deep red fondant ⅛ in. thick. Cut four
2 in. wide x 5 in. long strips with edge cutter.
Attach from cake corners to meet buckles with
piping gel. Attach belt inserts in buckle centers
with piping gel. Serves 60.

*Combine Red-Red with Orange for red shown. Combine
Lemon Yellow with Golden Yellow for yellow shown.

▶ Bugle Call Cake

Pans: 6 in. x 2 in., 8 in. x 2 in., 10 in. x 2 in. Round, p. 161; Cooling Grid, p. 171

Tip: 2, p. 134

Colors: * Royal Blue, Kelly Green, Lemon Yellow, p. 139

Fondant/Gum Paste: White Ready-to-Use Rolled Fondant (92 oz.), Ready-to-Use Gum Paste (16 oz.), p. 148; 20 in. Fondant Roller, Roll-N-Cut Mat, Fondant Smoother, p. 152; Gold Pearl Dust, Pure Lemon Extract, Brush Set, p. 153

Recipes: Buttercream, Royal Icings, p. 128; Thinned Fondant Adhesive, p. 127

Also: 12 in. Silver Round Cake Base, Cake Circles, p. 186; Dowel Rods, p. 194; Spatula, p. 137; Disposable Decorating Bags, p. 136; Blue Candy Melts Candy, p. 175; Meringue Powder, p. 141; 6 in. Lollipop Sticks, p. 178; Piping Gel, p. 141; drawing compass, white paper

See p. 114 for a list of commonly used decorating items you may need.

4 days in advance: Make cones. Using compass, trace the following circles on paper: five each 5 ¼ in., 4 ¾ in., 4 ¼ in. and 2 ¼ in. dia.; four each 3 ¾ in., 3 ¼ in., 2 ¾ in. and 1 ¾ in. dia. Cut out circles, retaining one of each size to use as patterns. Roll remaining circles into cones; tape edges. Tint gum paste blue; roll out ¹⁄₁₆ in. thick. Using circle patterns, cut a gum paste circle for each paper cone (cut extras to allow for breakage). Roll gum paste circles into cones; secure edges with damp brush. Let dry overnight on matching size paper cones dusted with cornstarch. Using royal icing, pipe tip 2 scrolls on cones. Let dry. Paint scrolls with gold Pearl Dust/lemon extract mixture (p. 118). Carefully remove paper cones. **Also:** Make topper. Attach three cones, 5¼ in., 4¾ in., and 4¼ in., together using melted candy. Chill until firm. Attach lollipop stick to back center with melted candy, leaving 3 in. extended to insert in cake. Chill. Attach three cones, 2¼ in. to front with melted candy. Chill. Attach two cones, 1¾ in. to front with melted candy.

And: Prepare and cover base board (p. 120) with 24 oz. lime green fondant.

Bake and cool 2-layer cakes. Prepare and cover cakes with fondant (p. 119). Prepare cakes for stacked construction (p. 120), positioning cakes offset to back center of base board.

Attach cones to cakes with thinned fondant adhesive in descending sizes as follows: For 6 in. cake, attach one each of six largest cones, starting at left center of cake. For 8 in. cake, attach one each of seven largest cones, aligning largest cone between second and third largest cones on 6 in. cake. For 10 in. cake, attach one of each size cone, aligning largest cone between second and third largest cones on 8 in. cake.

At party: Insert topper. Serves 62.

*Combine Kelly Green with Lemon Yellow for lime green shade shown.

> Celebrate with a fanfare! A cascade of cornelli-covered horns plays blue notes over lime-green layer cakes.

We've bottled glamour in a gilded candy atomizer accessorized with metallic studs and heart pendants.

◀ Eau De La Torte Cake

Pans: 8 in. x 2 in. Round, 10 in. x 2 in. Square, p. 161; 3-D Sports Ball Set, p. 165; Non-Stick Medium Cookie Sheet, p. 169
Colors: Rose, p. 134
Fondant: White (24 oz.), Black (12 oz.) Ready-To-Use Rolled Fondant, Gum-Tex, p. 148; 9 in., 20 in. Fondant Rollers, 20 in. Fondant Roller Guide Rings, Roll-N-Cut Mat, Fondant Smoother, p. 152; Folk Designs, Jewelry Designs Gum Paste and Fondant Molds, p. 150; Gold (3), Silver Pearl Dust, Pure Lemon Extract, Brush Set, p. 153; Storage Board, p. 152
Recipe: Buttercream Icing, p. 128
Also: White Candy Melts Candy (4 pks.), p. 175; Piping Gel, p. 141; 4-Pc. Circles Nesting Metal Cutter Set, p. 172; Cake Circles, Fanci-Foil Wrap, p. 186; Wooden Dowel Rods, Hidden Pillars, p. 194; Cake Dividing Chart, Cake Marker, p. 137; Cake Leveler, p. 158; 11 in. x 11 in. plywood or foamcore board (½ in. thick), small knife
See p. 114 for a list of commonly used decorating items you may need.

3 to 4 days in advance: Make perfume bottle topper (p. 126).

Also: Mold trims for cake. Use jewelry mold to make 201 round gems. Use folk mold to make four large hearts. Paint 115 round gems and four hearts with gold Pearl Dust/lemon extract mixture and remaining round gems with silver Pearl Dust/lemon extract mixture. Let all pieces dry.

Also: Make bow (p. 126). Tint 7 oz. fondant rose. Knead 1 teaspoon Gum-Tex into rose fondant. Roll out ⅛ in. thick. Cut and assemble bow using two 1½ in. x 6 in. strips for loops, one 1½ in. x 2 in. strip for knot and two 1½ in. x 5 in. strips for streamers. Let dry, supporting loops with facial tissue. Let bow and streamers dry on cornstarch-dusted ball pan half. Reserve remaining rose fondant.

Bake and cool 3-layer cakes (for 10 in. cake, trim one layer to 1 in. high for a 5 in. high cake). Ice cakes smooth in rose. Prepare cakes for stacked construction (p. 120).

Roll out black fondant ⅛ in. thick. Cut a 10 in. circle; center on bottom of 8 in. cake pan. Smooth over edge to create a 1 in. border; trim as needed. Lift off and position on 8 in. cake and smooth. Divide 8 in. cake sides into eighths below border. Mark for scallops 1 in. deep. Attach silver gems at scallop markings and bottom border with icing. Trim a hidden pillar to 5 in. tall and insert in center of 8 in. cake for candy ball support.

Attach gold gems to 10 in. cake sides, ¼ in. apart, vertically and horizontally. Roll out reserved rose fondant ¹⁄₁₆ in. thick. Cut 12 strips, ¼ in. x 5 in. Center one strip on each cake side, attaching with icing. Attach a strip on either side of center strip, ¼ in. apart. Attach gold heart to each group with icing.

At party: Position perfume bottle on top of 8 in. cake. Insert handle on rod through hole. Secure with melted candy. Attach bow and streamers with melted candy; let set. Cake serves 48.

▶ White Hot Splendor Cake

Pans: 4-Pc. Hexagon (3 smallest used), p. 160
Fondant: Black (126 oz.), White (18 oz.) Ready-To-Use Rolled Fondant, Gum-Tex, p. 148; 9 in., 20 in. Fondant Rollers, 20 in. Fondant Roller Guide Rings, Roll-N-Cut Mat, Fondant Smoother, p. 152; Leaf Cut-Outs Fondant Cutters, p. 151; 10-Pc. Gum Paste/Fondant Tool Set, Storage Board, p. 152; Wave Flower Former Set, Shaping Foam, p. 155; White Pearl Dust, Pure Lemon Extract, Brush Set, p. 153
Recipe: Buttercream Icing, p. 128
Also: Cake Boards, Fanci-Foil Wrap, p. 186; Dowel Rods, p. 194; Piping Gel, p. 141; 15 in. hexagon plywood or foamcore board (1½ in. thick)
See p. 114 for a list of commonly used decorating items you may need.

3 to 4 days in advance: Prepare base board. Using bottom of 15 in. pan as a guide, cut board in hexagon shape. Cover base board with 24 oz. black fondant (p. 120). Reserve remaining fondant.

Bake and cool 2-layer cakes. Prepare and cover cakes with black fondant (p. 119). Prepare cakes for stacked construction (p. 120).

Add 2 teaspoons Gum-Tex to 18 oz. white fondant. Roll out fondant ¹⁄₁₆ in. thick, working with 3 oz. at a time. Use largest Cut-Out to cut 142 leaves. Place leaves under storage board flap until ready to use. Imprint veins on leaves using small end of veining tool. Place leaves on wave flower former for 10 to 20 minutes to create shape, turning some leaves over and placing in different positions to vary shape. Paint leaves with white Pearl Dust/lemon extract mixture (p. 118).

For 6 in. cake top, shape and position a 1½ in. x 1 in. mound of black fondant. Attach leaves to mound with damp brush, overlapping to create flame look. Starting at the top edge of each side panel on 6 in. cake, attach your first batch of leaves with piping gel. Overlap and shape leaves slightly to create a wave effect. Support leaves with facial tissue, if needed to hold shape. Continue making and attaching batches of leaves as above, continuing down to base board. Serves 64.

Fondant leaves become flickering flames, racing up three black tiers to ignite a cake top bonfire.

▶ Loopside Down Cake

Pans: 8 in. x 2 in., 10 in. x 2 in. Round, p. 161

Colors:* Rose, Black, p. 139

Fondant/Gum Paste: White (96 oz.), Red (36 oz.), Black (48 oz.) Ready-To-Use Rolled Fondant, Ready-To-Use Gum Paste (16 oz.), p. 148; 9 in., 20 in. Fondant Rollers, 20 in. Fondant Roller Guide Rings, Roll-N-Cut Mat, Fondant Smoother, Storage Board, p. 152; Brush Set, p. 153

Recipes: Buttercream Icing, p. 128; Gum Glue Adhesive, p. 127

Also: 2013 Pattern Book (bow loop), p. 143; Punch Set with Oval Cutting Insert, Spiral Cutting Insert, Rotary Cutter, p. 145; Piping Gel, p. 141; 6 in. Cookie Treat Sticks, p. 171; Black Candy Melts Candy (1 pk.), p. 175; Dowel Rods, p. 194; Cake Circles, Cake Boards, Fanci-Foil Wrap, p. 186; Parchment Triangles, p. 136; 18 in. dia. foamcore board (½ in. thick), 6 in. dia. craft foam circle (4 in. thick)

See p. 114 for a list of commonly used decorating items you may need.

The natural order is reversed! Midnight black fashion elements tower over rose fondant cakes studded with spirals.

3 to 4 days in advance: Make bow pieces (p. 126). Tint 16 oz. gum paste black. Roll out ⅛ in. thick. Use pattern to cut two bow loops. Brush ends with gum glue adhesive, fold into loops and pinch slightly to secure. Cut two streamers 1½ in. wide x 11 in. long. Lift and shape bottom 9½ in. for flowing effect leaving 1½ in. straight for attaching to back of bow. Support streamer curves with cotton balls and loop openings with facial tissue. Let dry 48 hours on cornstarch-dusted surface. Reserve remaining gum paste.

Also: Assemble bow using melted candy. Roll out reserved gum paste ⅛ in. thick. For knot, cut a strip 1½ in. wide x 6 in. long. Wrap around bow ends and secure bow in back with candy. Reserve remaining gum paste. Let dry 24 hours. Roll out remaining gum paste ⅛ in. thick. For streamer supports, cut two strips ¾ in. x 2¼ in. Attach across back of bow on either side of knot. Attach one cookie stick across both loops to support strips. Attach streamers to strips at an angle with flat sections behind bow loops. Attach another cookie stick vertically behind knot leaving 4 in. extended at bottom to insert into top tier.

And: Prepare and cover base board with 36 oz. red fondant (p. 120).

Bake and cool 2-layer 8 in. and 10 in. cakes. Tint 78 oz. fondant rose. Prepare and cover cakes and 6 in. craft foam circle with rolled fondant (p. 119). Prepare cakes and circle for stacked construction (p. 120). Position on covered base board.

Roll out white fondant ¹⁄₁₆ in. thick as needed. Use punch with spiral insert to cut about 375 spirals. Let dry 5 to 10 minutes after cutting for easier lifting. Place under storage board flap until ready to position on cakes. Attach using damp brush, beginning at top center and working down, trimming spirals near base board as needed.

For drape, roll out black fondant ¼ in. thick. Cut a tapered section 28 in. long, 8 in. wide at the top and 12 in. wide at the bottom. Pleat and gather to make top just 1½ in. to 2 in. wide. Position train starting at center of top tier. Form graceful folds and pleats as drape extends to base board. Roll ends under for draped effect.

At party: Insert bow in front of train. Serves 48.

▼ Floral Origami Cake

Pans: 6 in. x 2 in., 10 in. x 2 in., 14 in. x 2 in. Round, p. 161
Color: Rose, p. 139

This 3-D bouquet is created from fondant circles, which are pleated into triangles and placed in alternating directions.

Fondant: White Ready-To-Use Rolled Fondant (88 oz.), Gum-Tex, p. 148; 9 in., 20 in. Fondant Rollers, 20 in. Fondant Roller Guide Rings, Roll-N-Cut Mat, p. 152; Brush Set, p. 153; Storage Board, p. 158
Recipe: Buttercream Icing, p. 128
Also: 16 in. Round Silver Cake Base, p. 187; Cake Circles, p. 186; Dowel Rods, p. 194; Circle Metal Cutter, p. 172; Piping Gel, p. 141; Pink Sugar Pearls, p. 157; Spatula, p. 137

See p. 114 for a list of commonly used decorating items you may need.

In advance: Prepare cake base. Tint fondant rose. Prepare and cover cake base with 24 oz. fondant (p. 120). Reserve remaining fondant.

Bake and cool 2-layer cakes for 6 in. and 14 in. tiers and four 1-layer cakes for an 8 in. high 10 in. tier. Ice cakes smooth in rose. Prepare for stacked construction (p. 120). Position on base board.

Divide reserved rose fondant into four equal portions. Knead in 2 teaspoons Gum-Tex to every portion. Make dimensional triangles (p. 127). You will need 235 triangles, making six at a time. Starting at the bottom of cake, attach triangles side by side with piping gel, alternating wide side up, then down. Continue making and attaching triangles until all cake sides are covered. Attach sugar pearls to center points with piping gel. Serves 131.

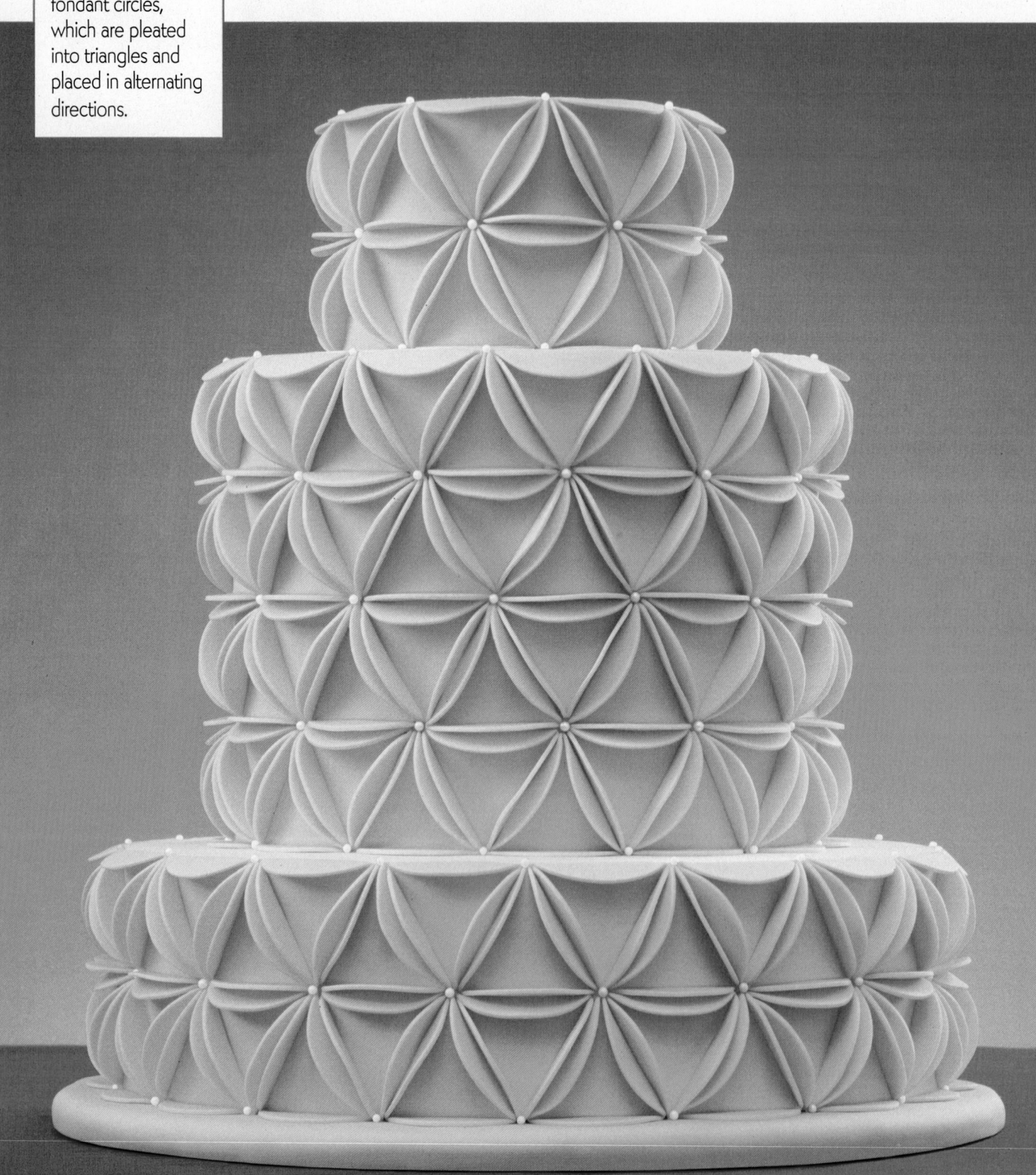

◀ Thrills and Frills Cake

Pans: Hexagon Pan Set (three smallest used), p. 160

Sugar Sheets! **Edible Decorating Paper/Tools:** Zebra (4), p. 144; Rotary Cutter, p. 145

Fondant: White (129 oz.), Black (24 oz.) Ready-To-Use Rolled Fondant, Gum-Tex, p. 148; 9 in., 20 in. Fondant Roller, 20 in. Fondant Roller Guide Rings, Roll-N-Cut Mat, Fondant Smoother, 10-Pc. Gum Paste/Fondant Tool Set, p. 152; Shaping Foam, p. 155; Deluxe Brush Set, p. 153

Recipe: Buttercream Icing, p. 128

Also: Cake Boards, Fanci-Foil Wrap, p. 186; Dowel Rods, p. 194; Pink Color Mist Food Color Spray, p. 139; Piping Gel, p. 141; 16 in. x 16 in. foamcore or plywood board (½ in. thick)

See p. 114 for a list of commonly used decorating items you may need.

The contrast is wild! Hot pink zebra striped panels are played against richly textured honeycomb ruffles.

In advance: Prepare base board. Using bottom of 15 in. pan as a guide, cut board in a hexagon shape. Prepare and cover board with black fondant (p. 120).

Bake and cool 2-layer cakes. Prepare and cover cakes with white fondant (p. 119). Prepare cakes for stacked construction (p. 120). Spray zebra edible paper with pink food color spray. Let dry. Using rotary cutter, cut rectangles from zebra edible paper, three 3⅛ in. x 4 in. for 6 in. cake, three 4⅛ in. x 4 in. for 9 in. cake and three 6⅛ in. x 4 in. for 12 in. cake. Attach rectangles to alternating hexagon panels with piping gel.

Make ruffles. Add 1 teaspoon Gum-Tex to 27 oz. fondant. Roll out 1⁄16 in. thick. Cut four strips at a time, ⅜ in. x 24 in. As you work on one strip, store others under plastic wrap. Place strip on thin shaping foam; thin one edge with large ball tool. Brush open panels of 12 in. cake with piping gel. Attach first group of strips to panel, thinned edge out, starting at bottom of panel. Position strips tightly together, folding over to create new rows and attaching the next strip where the previous strip ends. Support ruffles with facial tissue if needed. Continue cutting and attaching strips to fill open panels of all cakes. Serves 64.

▶ Drapes Take Shape! Cake

Pans: 8 in. x 2 in., 12 in. x 2 in. Round, p. 161; 3-D Sports Ball Set, p. 165

Tip: 2, p. 134

Fondant: Chocolate Ready-To-Use Rolled Fondant (192 oz.), p. 148; 9 in., 20 in. Fondant Rollers, 20 in. Fondant Roller Guide Rings, Roll-N-Cut Mat, Fondant Smoother, 10-Pc. Gum Paste/Fondant Tool Set, p. 152; Graceful Vines Fondant Imprint Mat, p. 151; Macrame Designs Gum Paste & Fondant Mold, p. 150; Brush Set, p. 153

Recipes: Snow-White Buttercream, Chocolate Buttercream Icing, p. 128; favorite crisped rice cereal treats

Also: 2013 Pattern Book (large and small petals), p. 143; Cake Dividing Chart, p. 137; Light Cocoa Candy Melts Candy (1 pk.), p. 175; Meringue Powder, Piping Gel, p. 141; Cake Leveler, Pastry Brush, p. 158; 2.5 in. Globe Pillar and Base Set, p. 193; Bamboo and Plastic Dowel Rods, p. 194; 16 in. Round Silver Cake Base, p. 187; Cake Circles, p. 186; Disposable Decorating Bags, p. 136; Spatula, p. 137

See p. 114 for a list of commonly used decorating items you may need.

In advance: Make topper (p. 126).

And: Prepare and cover cake base with 24 oz. fondant (p. 120).

Bake and cool a 2-layer 8 in. cake and 3-layer 12 in. cake (trim one layer to 1 in. high for a 5 in. high tier). Prepare and cover cakes with fondant (p. 119). Position cakes on base and prepare for stacked construction (p. 120). Insert 4 in. plastic dowel rod in center of 8 in. cake to support topper. Use macrame mold to make four quilted border sections. Attach for bottom border of 8 in. cake with piping gel, trimming as needed.

Use cake divider to divide 12 in. cake in tenths, marking cake at top. Roll 10 2 in. balls of fondant into tapered 5 in. long logs. Attach at marks with piping gel, wide end down. Roll out fondant 1⁄16 in. thick. Imprint design using graceful vines mat. Cut 10 rectangles, 8 in. x 7 in. Form vertical pleats by placing three plastic dowel rods under fondant alternating with two bamboo dowel rods on top. Remove rods and pinch top of rectangle closed to create a triangular drape. Attach over fondant logs with piping gel, curling bottom edges under slightly for puddle effect. Use snow white buttercream icing and tip 2 to pipe over imprinted designs.

At party: Position topper. Serves 60.

Add cream to your cocoa. The 2-tiered chocolate cake features raised embroidery details overpiped in white on a distinctive hourglass-shaped topper and billowing fondant drapes.

▶ Flowing
Feathers Cake

Pans: 6 in. x 2 in., 10 in. x 2 in., 12 in. x 2 in. Round, p. 161; Cooling Grid, p. 171
Colors: Sky Blue, p. 139
Fondant: White Ready-to-Use Rolled Fondant (192 oz.), Gum-Tex, p. 148; 9 in., 20 in. Fondant Rollers, 20 in. Fondant Roller Guide Rings, Roll-N-Cut Mat, Fondant Smoother, p. 152; Baroque Designs Gum Paste and Fondant Mold, p. 150; 10-Pc. Gum Paste & Fondant Tool Set, Storage Board, p. 152; White, Silver, Sapphire Blue Pearl Dust, Pure Lemon Extract, Brush Set, p. 153
Recipe: Buttercream Icing, p. 128
Also: 2013 Pattern Book (straight and curved topper feathers, large and small bottom tier feathers), p. 143; Blue Candy Melts Candy (1 pk.), p. 175; 11¾ in. Lollipop Sticks, p. 178; 2 in. Globe Pillar and Base Set, p. 193; Cake Leveler, p. 158; Cake Circles, Fanci-Foil Wrap, p. 186; Cake Dividing Chart, p. 137; 6 in. Decorator Preferred Smooth Edge Plate, Dowel Rods, p. 194; Parchment Triangles, p. 136; Spatula, p. 137; Piping Gel, p. 141; 18 in. round plywood or foamcore board (½ in. thick), craft foam block

See p. 114 for a list of commonly used decorating items you may need.

2 days in advance: Make feather topper (p. 127).

Also: Prepare base board. Tint 120 oz. fondant light blue. Prepare and cover base board (p. 120) with 36 oz. fondant. Reserve remaining light blue fondant. **And:** Prepare globe pillar bases. Roll out light blue fondant ⅛ in. thick. Cut rectangles 6½ in. x 2 in.; cover globes with fondant, securing with piping gel. Use baroque mold and light blue fondant to make six various leaf shapes for each globe. Attach with piping gel. Reserve remaining fondant.

Bake and cool 3-layer 6 in. cake, 2-layer 10 in. cake and 1-layer 12 in. cake (trim one 6 in. layer to 1 in. high for a 5 in. high cake). Position a 10 in. cake circle centered on top of 12 in. cake. Use cake circle as a guide to cut angled sides from 10 in. at top of cake to 12 in. at bottom. Position 6 in. cake on smooth edge plate. Prepare cakes for globe pillar construction (p. 120); prepare 10 in. and 12 in. cakes for stacked construction (p. 120). Prepare and cover cakes with reserved light blue fondant (p. 119), stacking and covering 10 in. and 12 in. cakes as one bottom tier. Position on prepared base board.

Use cake divider to divide base of bottom tier into 10ths. Roll 5 oz. of light blue fondant into a log, ½ in. dia.; press to fill in space between base of bottom tier and board at an angle.

Tint 40 oz. fondant dark blue. Roll out ¹⁄₁₆ in. thick. Use large bottom tier feather pattern

Dripping with pearls and plumage, featuring a crested topper and a bed of feathers fanning down the bottom tier.

to cut 10 feathers. Vein and cut v-shaped sides as for topper. Brush with sapphire blue Pearl Dust. Attach at cake divisions with piping gel. Cut and prepare another group of 10 large bottom tier feathers as above, but brush with white Pearl Dust. Attach in open areas with piping gel. Use small bottom tier feather pattern to cut 10 feathers. Vein and cut

v-shaped sides as above. Brush with sapphire blue Pearl Dust. Attach feathers with piping gel aligining with first group of blue dusted feathers and overlaying 2½ in. on cake top.

Use baroque mold and white fondant to make approximately 50 large pearl chains. Paint with silver Pearl Dust/lemon extract mixture

(p. 118). With a dry brush, apply more silver Pearl Dust to enhance the shine. Using piping gel, randomly attach chains in different lengths around globes.

At party: Position 6 in. cake. Attach pearl chains in various lengths, securing with piping gel. Insert topper feathers. Serves 60.

▼ Ribbon Roses Grow Wild! Cake

Pans: 6 in. x 2 in., 12 in. x 2 in. Round, p. 161

Tip: 6, p. 134

Colors:* Rose, Violet, p. 139

Sugar Sheets! Edible Decorating Paper/Tools: Damask (4 sheets), p. 144; Rotary Cutter, p. 145

Fondant/Gum Paste: White Ready-To-Use Rolled Fondant (168 oz.), Ready-To-Use Gum Paste (32 oz.), p. 148; 9 in., 20 in. Fondant Rollers, Roll-N-Cut Mat, Fondant Smoother, p. 149; Lilac Purple, Orchid Pink Pearl Dust, Brush Set, Pure Lemon Extract, p. 153; Storage Board, p. 152

Recipe: Buttercream Icing, p. 128

Also: 2013 Pattern Book (heart topper, pleat) p. 143; Violet Color Mist Food Color Spray, p. 139; Piping Gel, p. 141; White Candy Melts Candy (1 pk.), p. 175; 8 in. Cookie Treat Sticks, p. 171; Dowel Rods, p. 194; Cake Circles, Fanci-Foil Wrap, p. 186; Disposable Decorating Bags, p. 136; Spatula, p. 137; Cake Leveler, p. 158; 24 in. dia. plywood or foamcore board (½ in.

thick), gallon size zip-close plastic bags, thin cardboard

See p. 114 for a list of commonly used decorating items you may need.

2 or more days in advance: Prepare heart topper base. Roll out gum paste ¼ in. thick. Use pattern to cut out open heart. Let dry on cornstarch-dusted board. **Also:** Make gum paste pleats (p. 127). **And:** Prepare and cover base board with 96 oz. fondant tinted rose (p. 120).

And: Make 575 fondant ribbon roses (p. 119), using strips 1 in. x 6 x ¹⁄₁₆ in. thick. Paint top edge with lilac and pink Pearl Dust/lemon extract mixture (p. 118). Brush bottom edge with damp brush. Roll and gather fondant, pinching bottom edge to secure. You will need to make all of your roses before you begin assembly. As you work, bag and seal your roses so they remain soft and pliable until needed (roses will stay fresh for two to three days).

To complete heart, attach 32 roses using melted candy. Position roses close together, packing as tightly as needed to fit. Chill to set candy. Slightly curve the top 3 in. of a cookie stick to conform

to heart; attach to back of heart, leaving 5 in. extended at bottom to insert into cake.

Bake and cool 3-layer cakes (trim 12 in. cake for a 5 in. high tier). Prepare for stacked construction (p. 120). Ice smooth in white and position on prepared board.

Spray damask edible paper with violet food color spray; let dry. Use right half of pleat pattern to cut 20 panels from damask edible paper (each sheet makes five). Brush with piping gel and attach to right side of pleats. Let dry.

Use icing to attach pleats around cake, positioning top edge on cake side about 3 in. above base of cake. Attach roses to cake using tip 6 icing dots. Begin at pleats and work up. Pack as needed for a nice, tight fit.

At party: Insert heart topper. Serves 52.

*Combine Rose with Violet for violet shown.

A plush garden of ribbon roses creates a distinctive contrast with the sharply pleated damask panels below.

Our 2013 Yearbook Cover Cake

Flamboyantly Floral!

When you're looking for a cake that shouts "start the fun", you can't do better than our cover design for 2013. It has all the elements you want in a celebration cake—bright and colorful, with fun accents that really catch your eye!

Colorful Curls!

Having those bright rose curls at the base creates a "big reveal" feeling, as if we are opening a surprise package.

Fun Flowers!

Gerbera daisies are big and bold with a wide-open shape that can bring a celebration to life.

Punchy Print!

Animal prints are trend-right, and they are really a great way to add a fashion touch to your cake!

Pans: 6 in. x 2 in., 8 in. x 2 in. Round, p. 161
Colors:* Rose, Orange, Lemon Yellow, Golden Yellow, Leaf Green, p. 139
Sugar Sheets! **Edible Decorating Paper/Tools:** Zebra (3), p. 144; Rotary Cutter, p. 145
Fondant/Gum Paste: Ready-To-Use Gum Paste (38 oz.), White Ready-To-Use Rolled Fondant (8 oz.), p. 148; 9 in. Fondant Roller, Roll-N-Cut Mat, Storage Board, 10-Pc. Gum Paste/Fondant Tool Set, p. 152; Gum Paste Flower Cutter Set, p. 154; Shaping Foam, Flower Forming Cups, p. 155; Flower Impression Set, p. 154; Brush Set, p. 153
Recipes: Buttercream Icing, p. 128; Gum Glue Adhesive, p. 127
Also: Green Sugar Pearls, p. 157; White Candy Melts Candy (1 pk.) p. 175; 11¾ in. Lollipop Sticks, p. 178; Piping Gel, Pure Lemon Extract, p. 141; Cake Circles, p. 186; Dowel Rods, p. 194

See p. 114 for a list of commonly used decorating items you may need.

2 days in advance: Make 13 gerbera daisies. Tint gum paste: ½ oz. light yellow, 4 oz. each rose, orange and dark yellow, 5 oz. lime green. Roll out all colors except light yellow ¹⁄₁₆ in. thick. Using cutter and instructions from flower cutter set, make three or four gerbera daisies in each color with light yellow centers. Attach sugar pearls to cover flower center with piping gel. Let dry. Make six stems using lollipop sticks painted with leaf green and lemon yellow icing color/lemon extract mixture. Let dry. Attach various color daisies to stems with melted candy. Let set. **Also:** Make 26 curls.

Combine 10 oz. gum paste with 10 oz. fondant; tint rose. Roll out ⅛ in. thick. Use rotary cutter to cut seven strips each, 1 in. x 8½ in. and 1 in. x 6½ in.; cut 12 strips, 1 in. x 7½ in. Curl one end of strip so that 8½ in. strips are 3¾ in. high, 7½ in. strips are 3 in. high and 6½ in. strips are 2½ in. high. Stand on a long edge, support curls with facial tissue. Let dry on cornstarch-dusted surface.

Bake and cool 2-layer cakes. Ice smooth. Prepare for stacked construction (p. 120).

Using rotary cutter, cut five strips, 4 in. high from long edge of zebra edible paper. Attach to cake sides with piping gel; trim if needed.

Attach seven daisies without stems to 6 in. cake side with melted candy; let set. Attach curls to 8 in. cake side with melted candy, positioning groups in ascending then descending heights.

At party: Insert daisies on stems in cake top, trimming and curving stems as needed. Serves 32.

*Combine Lemon Yellow with Golden Yellow for yellow shown. Combine Leaf Green with Lemon Yellow for green shown.

Join the Fun!

Experience what more than 4 million people have already discovered in The Wilton Method of Cake Decorating Courses.

You'll learn the latest techniques and tips, grow your skills and accomplish new levels of decorating sophistication—all while having fun with fellow classmates. Plus, a Wilton Method Instructor will help you every step of the way.

Whether you are new to cake decorating or want to enhance your skills, Wilton offers the perfect course just for you.

Course 1

Decorating Basics

Discover the excitement of creating amazing cakes in Course 1–Decorating Basics!

Your Wilton Method Instructor will lead you through the essential steps for making colorful flowers, beautiful borders and impressive accents.

Plus, you and other students will encourage and support each other along the way!

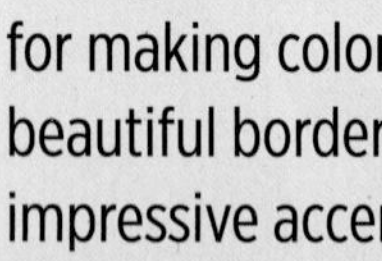

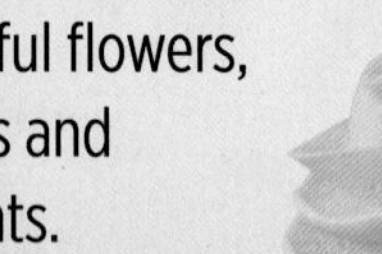

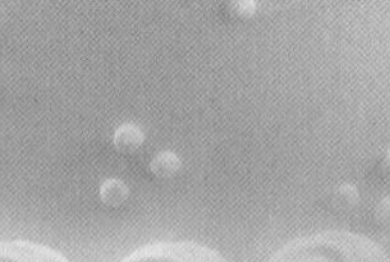

Flowers and Cake Design

Course 2

Design professional-looking cakes that everyone will be asking you to make! Learn how to create fantastic icing flowers, such as lilies, violets, daffodils and The Wilton Rose.

Gum Paste and Fondant

Course 3

Learn techniques and hints on these popular, shapable icings. You'll shape life-like flowers and amazing accents, like carnations, mums and bows.

Advanced Gum Paste Flowers

Course 4

Take your cake decorating to the next level! You'll sculpt incredible gum paste decorations, like Gerbera daisies, Stargazer lilies and more.

NEW!

Sign up today for one of our fun-filled, 4-session courses at a location near you!

Visit **www.wilton.com** for details.

Step-By-Step
Decorating Guide

Commonly Used Decorating Items

The best way to start any decorating project is to have all the items you'll need to use close at hand. When you're gathering the products listed in your project instructions, make sure you have the following items as well.

FOR ALL DECORATING:
- Knife
- Spoon
- Aluminum foil
- Waxed paper
- Zip-close plastic bags
- Cornstarch
- Solid vegetable shortening
- Granulated sugar
- Confectioners' sugar

- Plastic ruler
- Tape (or double-stick tape)
- Scissors
- Toothpicks
- Facial tissue
- Cotton balls

FOR CANDY MAKING:
- Warming tray
- Vegetable peeler

CAKE PREPARATION

The best cakes for decorating have a light, golden brown surface. Here is how to bake, level, torte and ice consistently great cakes.

BAKING CAKES

Prepare the pan:
Use Bake Easy! non-stick spray or Cake Release pan coating and a pastry brush—no flour needed. Or use solid vegetable shortening and flour.

To bake cakes without forming a crown, use Wilton Bake-Even Strips. Just saturate with water, run fingers down strips to remove excess moisture and wrap around the sides of your pan. See www.wilton.com for more information.

Mix the batter:
Preheat your oven to temperature specified in recipe for 10 to 15 minutes.

Measure ingredients before you begin.

For liquids, measure at eye level in clear standard liquid measuring cups. For dry ingredients, level off using measuring cups for dry ingredients. Avoid packing in cup.

Scrape the sides and bottom of the bowl for even mixing.

Fill the pans:
Fill prepared pans half to ⅔ full.

Bake immediately after mixing as near to center of oven as possible.

Allow at least 1 in. of space on all sides and between pans.

Avoid opening the oven door during the first 20 minutes of baking.

Test cakes for doneness:
To test, insert our Cake Tester (p. 159) near center of the cake. The cake is done if the Cake Tester comes out clean.

Remove cakes from oven and cool in pans for 10 minutes on a cooling grid.

Remove cakes from pans:
Place parchment or waxed paper over the cake.

Place a second cooling grid on top of the cake and invert the cake while sandwiched between the two grids.

Remove top grid and cake pan. Cool completely on remaining grid. The paper prevents the wire grid from breaking the crust or leaving imprints.

CUTTING CAKE BOARDS

Round and sheet cakes:
No need to cut a board! Simply use a Wilton Cake Board that is 2 in. larger than your cake. (For 8 in. round cakes, buy a 10 in. circle.)

Shaped and square cakes:
Cut a board to fit. Turn pan upside down and trace outline onto board. Cut board with a craft knife, leaving ¼ in. extra around outline unless specified otherwise in project instructions.

WRAPPING CAKE BOARDS

Trace your board onto Fanci-Foil Wrap. For shaped cakes, make the outline 3 in. to 4 in. larger than the board. For round and sheet cakes, make the outline about 2 in. larger than the board. Cut Fanci-Foil along the outline.

Place board, white side down, on top of cut foil. Cut deep slits at several points along foil edge, creating tabs of foil to wrap neatly

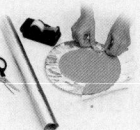

around the board. Tape tabs to board. To hold cake in place, spread a thin layer of icing on wrapped board before positioning cake.

LEVELING AND TORTING CAKES

After cooling the cake and before decorating, you'll need to level the top. You may also want to cut the cake into layers to add a tasty filling. Either task can be done using a Wilton Cake Leveler or a serrated knife.

Cake Leveler method:
Position ends of the cutting wire (or feet on ULTIMATE Cake Leveler, not pictured) into the notches at desired height.

With legs standing on the work surface, cut into the crusted edge using an easy sawing motion, then gently glide wire or blade through the cake. If torting, reposition the height of your leveler as needed.

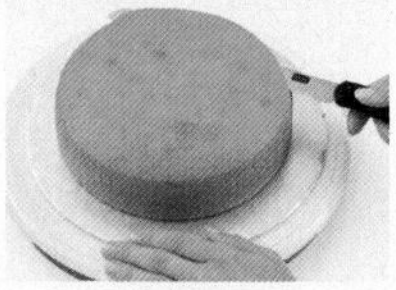

Serrated knife method:

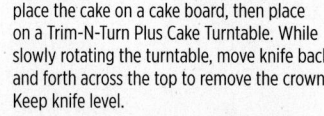

For leveling, place the cake on a cake board, then place on a Trim-N-Turn Plus Cake Turntable. While slowly rotating the turntable, move knife back and forth across the top to remove the crown. Keep knife level.

For torting, divide cake sides and mark equal horizontal points with dots of icing or toothpicks all around. Place cake on board, then on cake turntable. Place one hand on top of the cake. While slowly rotating the turntable, move knife back and forth to cut the cake along the measured marks. Repeat for each additional layer.

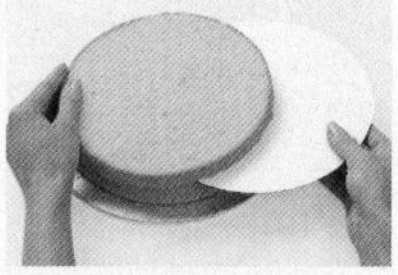

To separate the torted layers, carefully slide the top layer onto a cake board to keep it rigid and safe from breakage. Repeat for each additional layer.

FILLING TORTED CAKES

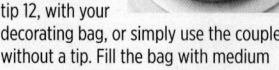

Use a large round tip, like tip 12, with your decorating bag, or simply use the coupler without a tip. Fill the bag with medium consistency buttercream icing.

Start with the bottom layer, torted side up. Pipe a dam of icing just inside the edge of the cake (about ¾ in. high and ¼ in. from the outside edge). Fill with icing, preserves or pudding.

Place next layer on top; repeat. Finish with top layer, torted side down.

ICING THE CAKE

For the best-looking iced cakes, you need to keep crumbs out of the icing. Follow these

guidelines to make it easy:

- Thin your icing with 2 tablespoons of corn syrup, water or milk for easier spreading.
- Never allow the spatula to touch the cake surface or to pull icing from the cake surface.
- Try "crumb coating": Lightly ice the cake first, allow a light crust to form, then add a top icing cover.
- Try our Icing Smoother (p. 137). it's sized specifically for standard cake heights to easily smooth icing with comfort and control.

Using a spatula
Place the cake on its cake board on a decorating turntable. Place a large amount of thin consistency icing on the center of the cake.

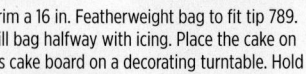

Spread icing across the top, pushing toward edges. Smooth the top using the edge of the spatula. Sweep edge of spatula from the rim of the cake to its center. Lift off spatula and remove excess icing.

Cover cake sides with icing. Smooth sides by holding the spatula upright with the edge against the icing, slowly spinning the turntable without lifting the spatula from the icing's surface. Return excess icing to the bowl and repeat until sides are smooth.

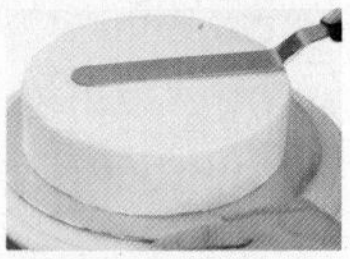

Rotate the cake slightly and repeat the procedure, starting from a new point on the rim until you have covered the entire top. Smooth the center of the cake by leveling the icing with the edge of your spatula.

More hints:
- For easier smoothing, dip spatula in hot water, wipe dry and glide across entire surface.
- Set the cake aside and let icing crust over for at least 15 minutes before decorating. When crusted, place parchment paper on the cake top and gently smooth with the palm of your hand.

Using tip 789 
Extra-wide tip works fast—especially on cake sides!

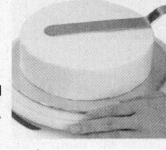

Trim a 16 in. Featherweight bag to fit tip 789. Fill bag halfway with icing. Place the cake on its cake board on a decorating turntable. Hold bag at a 45° angle and lightly press tip against cake. Squeeze a ribbon of icing in a continuous spiral motion to cover cake top, with last ribbon forcing icing over edge.

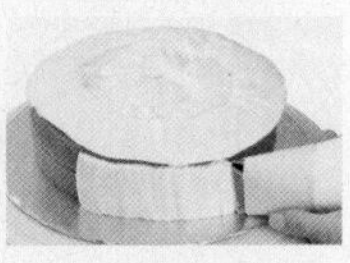

To ice the sides, squeeze icing as you turn the cake slowly. Repeat until the entire cake side is covered.

Smooth sides and top with spatula (see **Using a spatula**).

ICING INDEX

Different icings have different qualities, which make them best for certain types of decorating tasks. Here's a rundown of the six main types of icing used in most Wilton decorating projects.

Buttercream-Style Icings

Tasks: Icing cakes smooth, piping borders, writing, flowers, etc.

Qualities: Softer and more spreadable than most icings. The traditional choice for flavor and versatility.

Types:
• Homemade—See Buttercream and Snow-White Buttercream recipes, p. 128.
• Wilton Ready-To-Use Decorator Icing—Available in white or chocolate, p. 141.
• Wilton Creamy White Buttercream Icing Mix—Same taste and texture as homemade, p. 141.

Special Information:
• Buttercream flowers are soft enough to be cut with a knife.
• Snow-white buttercream flowers have a translucent look when air-dried.
• All buttercream-style icings taste and look great for most decorating.

Consistency: All buttercream icings can be adjusted to the consistency you want. Our buttercream recipes are thin-to-stiff depending on the amount of corn syrup or sugar added (sugar stiffens). Wilton Ready-To-Use Icing in 1 lb. cans is stiff; you can make roses right from the can; thin with corn syrup if desired. Our 4.5 lb. tub is thin-to-medium consistency so you can spread on a cake without thinning.

Coloring: Buttercream icings (except chocolate) yield all colors. Snow-white and white ready-to-use icings may yield truer colors due to their pure white base color. Most colors deepen upon setting. Chocolate buttercream is recommended when black or brown icing is needed.

Storage: Buttercream can be refrigerated in an airtight container for two weeks. Before using, bring icing to room temperature and stir with a spatula. Iced cakes store at room temperature for two to three days.

Royal Icing

Tasks: Flower making, figure piping, making flowers on wires. Great for decorating cookies and gingerbread houses.

Qualities: Dries candy-hard for lasting decorations. Great for making decorations ahead of time.

Types:
• Homemade, p. 128—Made with Wilton Meringue Powder, p. 141.
• Wilton Ready-To-Use Royal Icing Mix—So convenient; just add water, p. 141.

Special Information:
• Bowls and utensils must be kept grease-free to maintain stability.
• Cover icing with damp cloth to prevent crusting.

Consistency: Thin-to-stiff, depending on the amount of water added. Thinned royal icing may be used for covering cookies or filling in outlined areas.

Coloring: Yields deep colors. Some colors may fade in bright light. Requires more icing color than buttercream to achieve the same intensity.

Storage: Store at room temperature in an airtight container for two weeks.

Wilton Whipped Icing Mix (p. 141)

Tasks: Icing cakes. Great for most decorations—stars, roses, borders, garlands and writing. Toppings on pies, puddings, tarts.

Qualities: Holds shape like no other mix. Light and delicate vanilla flavor.

Special Information:
• Exclusive Wilton formula.
• Just add ice water, whip and you're ready to decorate!
• For chocolate whipped icing, add ½ cup sifted cocoa powder.

Consistency: Velvety smooth. Can create peaked effects.

Coloring: Yields any color.

Storage: Can be refrigerated in an airtight container. Iced cakes store at room tempature for 2 to 3 days.

Rolled Fondant

Tasks: Cover cakes with a perfectly smooth surface. Ideal for creating hand-shaped decorations, stand-up bows, molded borders and more.

Qualities: Flexible, easy-to-shape. Like edible clay for your cake! Light, delicate vanilla or chocolate flavor.

Types:
• Homemade, p. 127.
• Wilton Ready-To-Use Rolled Fondant. Available in white or chocolate, plus a variety of colors, p. 148.

Special Information:
• When covering cakes with fondant, lightly cover surface with apricot glaze or buttercream icing to seal in moisture.
• Heighten the flavor by kneading in your favorite extract.

Consistency: Dough-like. Roll out before applying to cake or cutting decorations.

Coloring: White produces pastels to deep colors. Wilton pre-colored fondant is available in many shades.

Storage: Excess fondant can be stored two months in an airtight container wrapped in plastic wrap. Do not refrigerate or freeze. Iced cakes store at room temperature for three to four days.

Gum Paste

Tasks: Making detailed flowers with very thin petals.

Qualities: Can be rolled out very thin yet hold its shape. Dries hard. Gum paste flowers, trims and accents are meant for decoration only.

Types:
• Homemade, p. 127—Use Wilton Gum-Tex and Glucose, p. 141.
• Wilton Ready-To-Use Gum Paste, p. 148.

Special Information:
• Gum paste picks up dust and lint very easily. Be sure your hands and work surfaces are very clean before handling.
• Shortening helps keep gum paste pliable. Before kneading, rub a thin coat of vegetable shortening on your hands and work surface to avoid sticking.

Consistency: Dough-like. Roll out before cutting decorations.

Coloring: White produces pastels to deep colors.

Storage: Gum paste dries out quickly. Keep wrapped in plastic wrap and stored in a plastic bag. Keeps up to two weeks at room temperature. If storing longer, cover with a thin coating of vegetable shortening, wrap tightly with plastic wrap, place in a plastic bag in a covered container and refrigerate.

Color Flow Icing

Tasks: Create detailed icing decorations which can be placed on cakes and cookies.

Qualities: Dries hard, with a shiny finish. You can "draw" almost any design by outlining pattern areas with full-strength Color Flow, then filling in with thinned Color Flow.

Type:
• Homemade, p. 128—Use Wilton Color Flow Mix, p. 141.

Special Information:
• Moist icings break down Color Flow decorations. Position Color Flow decorations on your cake shortly before serving or place on sugar cubes.
• Color Flow designs take a long time to dry. Allow at least two or three days in advance when making decorations.
• Bowls and utensils must be kept grease-free to maintain texture.
• Cover icing with damp cloth to prevent crusting

Consistency: Thin or full-strength.

Coloring: Produces pastels to deep colors.

Storage: Store at room temperature in an airtight container for two weeks.

COLORING ICING

You can create virtually any color using Wilton Icing Colors, p. 139. The concentrated colors won't affect your icing consistency. To get consistent color in the shade you want, keep the hints below in mind. Visit www.wilton.com for more hints, a color mixing chart, and bag striping effects.

• Begin with white icing. For dark brown or black, begin with chocolate icing to reduce the amount of color needed. For large areas of red, use No-Taste Red, p. 139.
• Icing colors intensify in buttercream about one to two hours after mixing. Royal icing requires more color than buttercream to achieve the same intensity.
• To maintain color consistency, always mix enough of each icing color to complete your cake, including flowers and borders. It can be difficult to duplicate the exact shade of any color.

To color:

Dip a toothpick into the color, then swirl it into the icing.

Add color a little at a time until you achieve the shade you desire.

Always use a new toothpick each time you add color. Avoid getting icing in your jar of color. Blend icing well with a spatula.

It's easy to create a wide variety of skin tones using various Wilton Icing Colors. If you wish to reach a shade lighter or darker than what is indicated, add slightly less or more of the icing color. Color listings for projects in this book reflect skin tone shown; feel free to choose your own shade.

Skin Tone Shades

Copper	Ivory with a touch of Red	Brown	Brown with a touch of Red	More Brown with a touch of Red

FILLING DECORATING BAGS

Hold bag with one hand and fold down the top with the other hand to form a generous cuff over your hand. Or, use our Decorating Bag Sleeve (p. 136), which makes it easy to fill the bag without holding it.

Fill bag about half full with icing. Do not overfill the bag! Icing may squeeze out from the top.

Squeeze bag with spatula between your thumb and finger while removing spatula.

Close bag by unfolding the cuff and twisting the bag closed. This forces the icing down into the bag.

Use a Wilton Icing Bag Tie, (p. 136), to secure the bag and ensure that the icing does not squeeze out of the top.

Place the twisted part of the bag between your thumb and forefinger. Close your hand around the bag so that you can squeeze the icing in the bag between your palm and fingers.

CAKE BAKING AND SERVING GUIDES

The charts below are based on baking recommendations from the Wilton Test Kitchen; your results may vary depending on oven performance or altitude in your area. Always check for doneness at the shortest bake time listed.

Serving amounts are based on party-sized portions of 1.5 in. x 2 in. or smaller wedding-sized portions of approximately 1 in. x 2 in. Cakes from 3 in. to 6 in. high, baked in the same size pan, would yield the same number of servings because they follow the same pattern of cutting. Cakes shorter than 3 in. would yield half the number of servings indicated for that pan. Number of servings are intended as a guide only.

Icing amounts are very general and will vary with consistency, thickness applied and tips used. Icing amounts allow for top and bottom borders.

4 IN. HIGH CAKES

The figures for 2 in. pans are based on a 2-layer, 4 in. high cake. Fill pans ½ to ⅔ full.

PAN SHAPE	SIZE	NUMBER SERVINGS PARTY	NUMBER SERVINGS WEDDING	CUPS BATTER 1 LAYER, 2 IN.	BAKING TEMP. (F.)	BAKING TIME MINUTES	APPROX. CUPS ICING TO ICE AND DECORATE
Round	4 in.	8	8	¾	350°	22-26	1½
	6 in.	12	12	2¼	350°	35-40	2½
	8 in.	20	24	4	350°	37-42	3½
	9 in.	24	32	5	350°	40-45	4
	10 in.	28	38	6	350°	40-45	5
	12 in.	40	56	8	350°	45-50	6
	14 in.	63	78	11½	325°	50-55	8½
	16 in.	77	100	16	325°	55-60	9½
Square	6 in.	12	18	3	350°	40-45	3½
	8 in.	20	32	6	350°	45-50	4½
	10 in.	30	50	9	350°	50-55	6
	12 in.	48	72	11½	325°	55-60	7½
	14 in.	63	98	16	325°	55-60	9
	16 in.	80	128	22	325°	60-70	11½
Heart	6 in.	8	14	2	350°	30-35	3
	8 in.	18	22	4	350°	40-45	4
	9 in.	20	28	4¼	350°	40-45	5½
	10 in.	24	38	6½	350°	45-50	7
	12 in.	34	56	9¼	325°	55-60	8½
	14 in.	48	72	13½	325°	55-60	9½
	16 in.	64	94	17	325°	60-65	13
Petal	6 in.	6	8	1½	350°	30-35	3
	9 in.	14	18	3¾	350°	35-40	4½
	12 in.	38	40	7¼	350°	45-50	6
	15 in.	48	64	10⅔	325°	55-60	8
Hexagon	6 in.	10	12	2	350°	35-40	2½
	9 in.	20	26	4½	350°	40-45	4
	12 in.	34	40	8	350°	50-55	5½
	15 in.	48	70	14	350°	55-60	7
Oval	7.75 in. x 5.5 in.	9	13	2¾	350°	30-35	2½
	10.75 in. x 7.8 in.	20	26	5	350°	40-45	4
	13.5 in. x 9.8 in.	30	45	8¼	325°	50-55	5½
	16.5 in. x 12.4 in.	44	70	13¼	325°	50-55	7½
Sheet	7 in. x 11 in.	24	32	5½	350°	40-45	5
	9 in. x 13 in.	36	50	10	350°	45-50	7
	11 in. x 15 in.	54	74	11½	325°	50-55	9
	12 in. x 18 in.	72	98	16	325°	55-60	11
Paisley	9 in. x 6 in.	9	13	2¾	350°	35-40	4½
	12.5 in. x 9.5 in.	28	38	7	350°	45-50	7
	16.5 in. x 12.5 in.	40	56	10½	325°	55-60	9
Diamond	10.25 in. x 7.4 in.	12	18	3	350°	30-35	3
	15 in. x 11 in.	20	32	6	350°	45-50	6
	19.25 in. x 14.25 in.	42	66	11	325°	55-60	9½
Pillow	6.75 in. x 6.75 in.	13	19	2½	350°	33-38	3
	10 in. x 10 in.	30	40	5½	350°	39-44	6½
	13.25 in. x 13.25 in.	64	72	10	350°	41-46	9½

3 IN. HIGH CAKES (using 3 in. high pans)

The figures for 3 in. pans are based on a 1-layer cake which is torted and filled to reach 3 in. high; fill pans ½ full.

PAN SHAPE	SIZE	NUMBER SERVINGS PARTY	NUMBER SERVINGS WEDDING	CUPS BATTER 1 LAYER, 2 IN.	BAKING TEMP.	BAKING TIME MINUTES	APPROX. CUPS ICING TO ICE AND DECORATE
Round	6 in.	12	12	3	350°	45-50	3½
	8 in.	20	24	5	350°	55-60	4
	10 in.	28	38	8	350°	55-60	4½
	12 in.	40	56	10	350°	55-60	5¼
	14 in.	63	78	15	325°	70-75	6¼
	16 in.	77	100	18	325°	60-65	7
	18 in. Half, 3 in. layer	110*	146*	12**	325°	60-65	7½
Contour	9 in.	11	17	5¾	350°	55-60	3

For any pans 3 in. deep and 12 in. diameter or larger, we recommend using a heating core (p. 163) to insure even baking. Use two cores for 18-in. pans.

*Two half rounds.   **For each half round pan.

For additional pan information, visit **www.wilton.com**

THREE ESSENTIALS OF CAKE DECORATING

Every decoration you make is the result of three things working together: the consistency of your icing, the position of the bag (how you are holding it) and the amount and type of pressure you apply to the bag.

ICING CONSISTENCY

The icing consistency you want depends on what type of decorations you are doing. Just a few drops of liquid in your icing can make a big difference in your decorating results. Many factors can affect your icing consistency, such as humidity, temperature, ingredients and equipment.

For buttercream icing, as a general guideline, if you feel your icing is too thin, add a little more confectioners' sugar. If you feel your icing is too thick, add a little more liquid as directed below. For royal icing, if adding more than ½ cup confectioners' sugar to thicken icing, add 1 to 2 more teaspoons of meringue powder.

Option 1: Stiff Icing
Used for decorations, such as flowers with upright petals, like the rose.

Use this test to check the consistency:

- Place 1 cup of icing in a 9 oz. cup, 3¾ in. tall and about 2¾ in. dia.
- Insert a straight spatula all the way into the center of the icing and jiggle the cup.
- When the icing is stiff consistency, the spatula will not move.

Option 2: Medium Icing
Used to create stars, dimensional decorating, borders and flowers with petals that lie flat.

To convert stiff consistency to medium consistency, add 1 teaspoon of water for each cup of stiff consistency icing (2½ teaspoons of water for the full recipe). Mix until well blended.

- Use the same test as for stiff consistency.
- When the icing is medium consistency, the spatula will move slightly and start to lean when you jiggle the cup.

Option 3: Thin Icing
Used for writing and printing, leaves, icing a cake.

To convert stiff consistency to thin consistency, add 2 teaspoons of water for each cup of stiff consistency icing (5 teaspoons of water for the full recipe). Mix until well blended.

- Use the same test as for stiff consistency.
- When the icing is thin consistency, the spatula will fall over when you jiggle the cup.

When making thin consistency icing for writing and printing, add ½ teaspoon of piping gel per cup of thin consistency icing. It will add stretch to the icing to make writing and printing easier.

BAG POSITION
(HOLDING THE BAG)

The way your decorations curl, point and lie depends on the way you hold and move the bag. Bag position is described in terms of both angle and direction.

Angle

Refers to the position of the bag relative to the work surface. There are two basic angles.

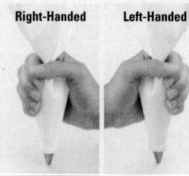

90° angle is straight up, perpendicular to the work surface. It is used when making stars or drop flowers.

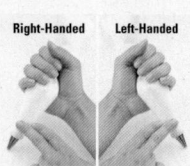

45° angle is halfway between vertical and horizontal. It is used for writing, borders and many flowers.

Bag Direction

The angle of the bag to the work surface, when holding it at 45°, is only half the story of bag position. The other half is the direction in which the back of the bag is pointed.

Correct bag position is easiest to learn when you think of the back of the bag as the hour hand of a clock. When you hold the bag with the tip in the center of the clock, you can sweep out a circle with the back end of the bag. Pretend the circle you formed in the air is a clock face. The hours on the clock face correspond to the direction you point the back end of the bag.

Right-Handed

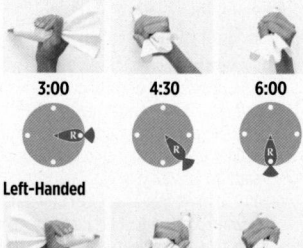

3:00   4:30   6:00

Left-Handed

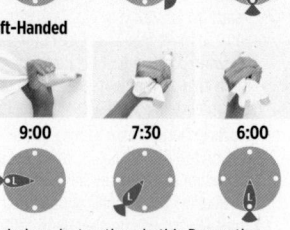

9:00   7:30   6:00

Technique instructions in this Decorating Guide will list the correct direction for holding the bag, when the bag direction differs for left-handed decorators, that direction will be listed in parentheses. (Example: When right-handers hold bag at 3:00, left-handers hold bag at 9:00.)

Right-handed decorators always decorate from left to right. Left-handed decorators always decorate from right to left, except for writing.

Most decorating tip openings are the same shape all the way around—so there is no right side or wrong side up when squeezing the bag. For tips such as petal, ruffle, basketweave and leaf, which have irregularly shaped openings, you must watch tip position as well as bag position. Instructions will state correct tip position if needed.

PRESSURE CONTROL
(SQUEEZING THE BAG)

The size and uniformity of your decorations depends on the amount of pressure you apply to the bag and the steadiness of the pressure. Learn to apply pressure so consistently that you can move the bag in a free and easy glide while just the right amount of icing flows through the tip.

Heavy Pressure   Medium Pressure   Light Pressure

TIP TECHNIQUES

Your icing turned out great! Now you are ready to learn how to pipe beautiful shapes on your cake. Stars, shells, dots, lines and other techniques are the foundation of your decorating knowledge. See how to pipe each one, step by step. Each technique includes the correct angle, pressure and movement to use for a uniform look.

ROUND TIPS

Dot

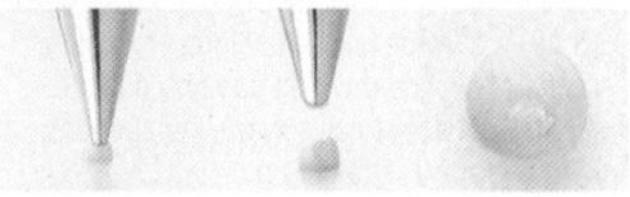

Use for: Flower centers, faces, figure piping, border effects.

Hint: When making large dots, lift the tip as you squeeze to allow icing to fill out completely.

Decorate with: Round tip 3 and medium consistency Icing. Hold bag at 90° straight up, with tip slightly above surface.

1. Squeeze bag and keep point of tip buried in icing until the dot is the size you want.
2. Stop pressure, pull tip up and to the side to help prevent points in dots.

Ball

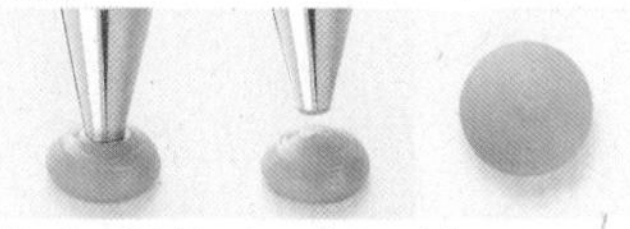

Use for: Bold borders; figure piping.

Hint: Vary the basic look by adding stars, dots or spirals on the ball shapes.

Decorate with: Round tip 8 and medium consistency icing. Hold bag at 90° straight up with tip slightly above surface.

1. Squeeze the bag, applying a steady, even pressure. As the icing begins to build up, raise the tip with it, but keep the tip buried in the icing.
2. Stop squeezing as you bring the end of the tip to the surface.
3. Lift the tip up and pull away from your piped ball. Use the edge of the tip to shave off any point so that your ball is nicely rounded.

Bead

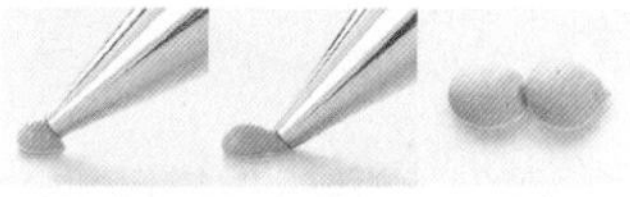

Use for: Borders or framing decorations; accents for letters.

Hint: If you can pipe a shell, you can pipe a bead. The movements are similar.

Decorate with: Round tip 5 and medium consistency icing. Hold bag at 45° at 3:00 (9:00) with tip slightly above surface.

1. Squeeze as you lift tip slightly so that icing fans out.
2. Relax pressure as you draw the tip down and bring the bead to a point. Stop squeezing and pull tip away.
3. To make a bead border, start the next bead a little behind the previous one so that the fanned out end covers the tail of the preceding bead to form an even chain. To pipe a bead heart, simply pipe one bead, then a second, joining the tails. Smooth together using a decorator brush.

Outline

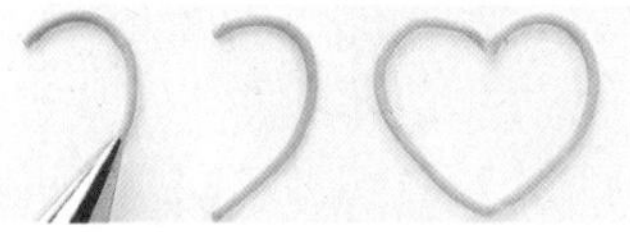

Use for: Characters, designs, Color Flow plaques, piping facial features on character cakes.

Hint: Can be done with round or star tips, depending on whether perfectly round or ridged outlines are desired.

Decorate with: Round tip 3 and thin consistency icing. Hold bag at 45° at 3:00 (9:00), with tip slightly above surface.

1. Touch tip to surface. Lift tip slightly; squeeze and guide tip along surface.
2. Stop squeezing. Touch tip to surface. Pull away.

Printing

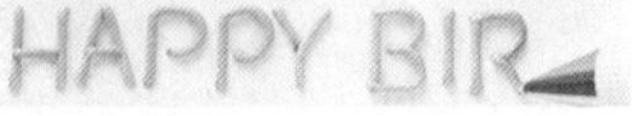

Use for: Names and messages on cakes, cupcakes, cookies.

Hint: Adding piping gel to thinned icing will help your lines flow without breaking. Add ½ teaspoon piping gel per cup.

Decorate with: Round tip 3 and thin consistency icing. Right handers hold bag at 45° at 6:00 for vertical lines, 3:00 for horizontal and curving lines. Left handers hold bag at 45° at 6:00 for vertical lines, 45° at 9:00 for horizontal and curving lines. Hold tip lightly touching surface.

1. Letters can be piped freehand or after marking with a toothpick or imprinting with a message press. With message press, let icing crust slightly before imprinting.
2. Raise tip slightly and with steady even pressure, squeeze out a straight line, lifting the tip off the surface to let the icing string drop.
3. Stop squeezing, touch tip to surface, and pull tip away. Be sure that the end of the tip is clean before you go on to another line.

Writing

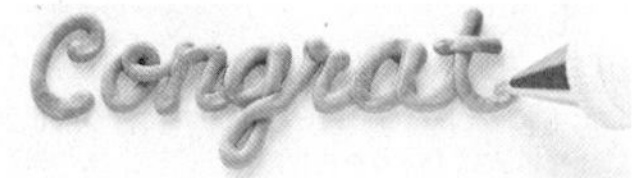

Use for: Names and messages on cakes, cupcakes, cookies.

Hint: You'll find you have more control if you let the icing draw out slightly over the surface as you write.

Decorate with: Round tip 5 and thin consistency icing with ½ teaspoon piping gel added per cup. Hold bag at 45° at 3:00 (9:00). Left handers may have to adjust the bag position to fit their writing style.

1. Squeeze with a steady, even pressure. Glide tip along the surface in a smooth, continuous motion.
2. Remember to keep your wrist straight, moving your entire forearm as a single unit. Use your arm, not your fingers, to form each line, letter or word.
3. After you begin to master the curves and swings of the letters, lift the tip up slightly as you write.

Drop Strings

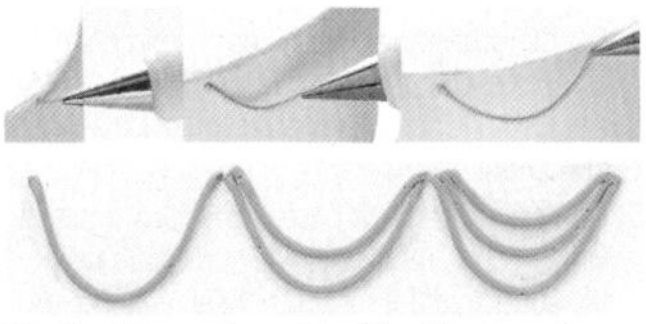

Use for: Swags for cake sides. You can pipe a row of single strings or multiple strings in rows of two or three.

Hint: The trick to beautiful drop strings is to pull the bag toward you as the string drapes down. If you "draw" the string with the tip, you won't achieve a pretty curve and strings tend to break.

Decorate with: Round tip 3 and stiff consistency icing slightly thinned with corn syrup. Hold bag at shoulder level at 4:30 (7:30). Hold tip lightly touching surface to attach strings.

1. With a toothpick mark horizontal divisions on cake in the width you desire. For multiple rows of strings, mark the cake for the deepest row and pipe that row. Touch tip to first mark and squeeze, pausing momentarily so that icing sticks to the surface.
2. While squeezing, pull the bag toward you. Continue squeezing to allow the icing to drape naturally into an arc. Icing will drop by itself—do not move the tip down with the string. The end of the tip should be the same distance from the surface as the width from point to point on your cake.
3. Stop pressure before you touch tip to second mark to end string. Repeat on remaining marks, keeping drop strings uniform in length and width.
4. For double drop strings, return to the first drop string point. Squeeze the bag and drop a string with a slightly shorter arc than in the first row.
5. Join the end of this string to the end of the corresponding string in the first row. Repeat the process to complete the row. If desired, pipe triple drop strings, with a slightly shorter arc than in the second row. Join the ends of strings to the ends of the corresponding first and second row strings.

STAR TIPS

Star

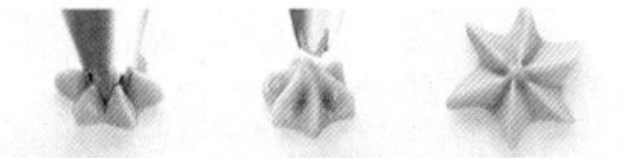

Use for: Borders, details such as buttons and facial features, flower centers.

Hint: After squeezing out a star, be sure to stop pressure completely before you pull your tip away. This will give you a perfectly formed star shape, without peaks.

Decorate with: Star tip 16 and medium consistency icing. Hold bag at 90° straight up with tip about ⅛ in. above the surface.

1. Squeeze the bag to form a star. Increase or decrease pressure to change star size.
2. Stop pressure completely.
3. Pull tip straight up and away.

For pull-out stars: gradually decrease pressure as you pull away. Stop pressure and pull tip away. Work from the bottom to the top of the area to be covered with pull-out stars.

Star Fill In

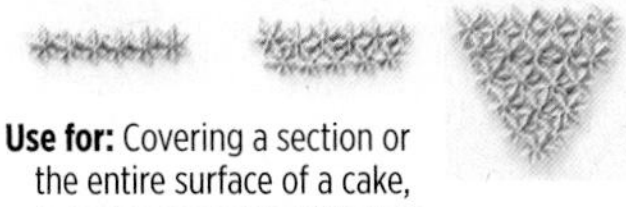

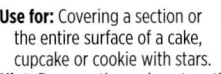

Use for: Covering a section or the entire surface of a cake, cupcake or cookie with stars.

Hint: Because these close-together stars require so much piping from the same bag, it's a good idea to keep replenishing the icing. Replenish icing when it gets soft to prevent stars from being poorly defined.

Decorate with: Star tip 16 or triple star tip 2010, which covers large areas quickly and easily; use medium consistency icing. Hold bag at 90° straight up with tip ¼ in. above surface.

1. Pipe stars evenly and close together.
2. Adjust the tip position slightly each time so that the points of the stars interlock and cover the area without gaps.
3. If using tip 16, pipe a row of stars beneath the first, again adjusting tip position to close any gaps.
4. Continue to fill in entire area.

Zigzag

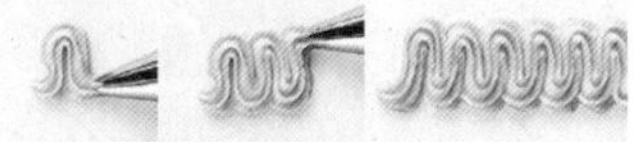

Use for: Filling in outlined areas, borders, swags, covering cake sides.

Hint: When piping zigzags, think about two motions simultaneously. The movement of your arm determines the height of the waves and the distance between them. The pressure on your bag determines the thickness of the line. Strive for uniform thickness and even spacing as you go.

Decorate with: Star tip 16 and medium consistency icing. Hold bag at 45° at 3:00 (9:00) with tip lightly touching surface.

1. Steadily squeeze and glide tip along the surface in an up and down motion.
2. Continue piping up and down with steady pressure.
3. To end, stop pressure and pull tip away. For more elongated zigzags, move your hand to the desired height while maintaining a steady pressure. For a more relaxed look, increase the width as you move the bag along.

Shell

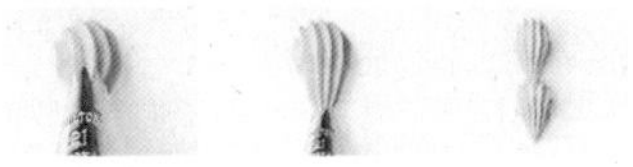

Use for: Borders, fleurs de lis, character details.

Hint: Lift the tip only slightly when piping, to avoid a bumpy look.

Decorate with: Star tip 21 and medium consistency icing. Hold bag at 45° at 6:00 with tip slightly above the surface.

1. Squeeze hard, letting icing fan out generously as it forces the tip up.
2. Gradually relax pressure as you lower tip. Pull the bag toward you until tip reaches the surface.
3. Relax pressure and pull tip along the surface to form a point.
4. To make a shell border, start your next shell so that the fanned end just covers the tail of the preceding shell to form a chain.

Rosette

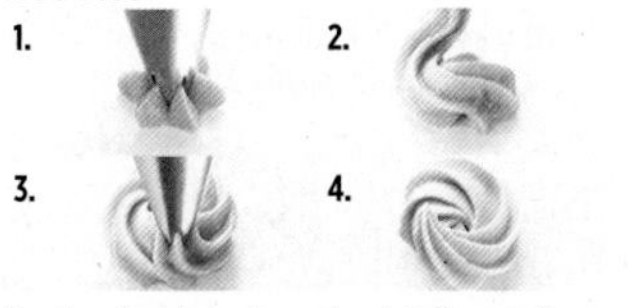

Use for: Borders, character details, candleholders on cake or cupcake tops.

Hint: Rosettes can be used in place of piped roses on the side of your cake—for the effect of a rose without the work. Try finishing rosettes with a center star or dot.

Decorate with: Star tip 16 and medium consistency icing. Hold bag at 90° straight up with tip slightly above surface.

1. Squeeze out icing to form a star.
2. Without releasing pressure, raise tip slightly as you drop a line of icing on top of the star in a tight, complete rotation. Begin at 9:00 (3:00), move to 12:00, then 3:00 (9:00) and continue to 6:00.
3. Stop pressure at 6:00 but continue to move the tip back to the starting point to make a complete rotation.
4. Pull tip away, continuing the circular motion so that the tail maintains the circular shape of the rosette. For a rosette border, pipe a line of uniform rosettes, touching one another.

PETAL TIPS

Ruffle

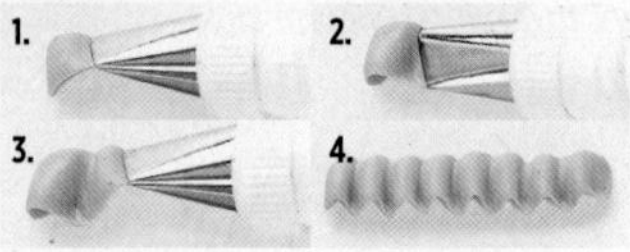

Use for: Borders, framing plaques, clothing trim, swags, designs.

Hint: Moving your hand quickly up and down will give you a tight ruffle. For a looser look, move more slowly across the surface. Practice different looks to perfect your pressure control.

Decorate with: Petal tip 104 and medium consistency icing. Hold bag at 45° at 3:00 (9:00), with wide end of tip lightly touching surface and narrow end facing away from surface.

1. As you keep the wide end against the cake, move wrist up to pull up icing.
2. Move wrist down to complete one curl of the ruffle.
3. Repeat up and down motion.
4. Raise and lower the narrow end as you move around the cake. Repeat this motion for the entire ruffle.

MULTIPLE TIPS

Swirl Drop Flower

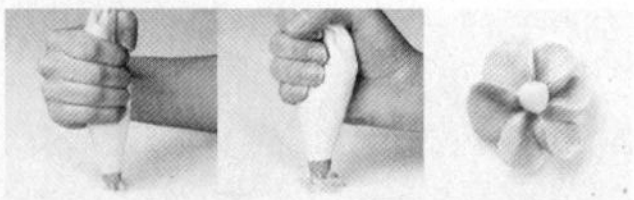

Use for: Bouquets, borders, designs.

Hint: The swirled look of the petals happens when you twist your wrist the proper way. Practice your wrist movement, keeping your knuckles in the position described below. You can also create a star flower by not moving your wrist and letting icing build up as you squeeze.

Decorate with: Drop flower tip 2D for petals and round tip 3 for center; medium consistency buttercream (or royal icing for flowers made in advance). Hold bag at 90° straight up with tip lightly touching the surface.

1. Before piping, turn your hand ¼ turn so the back of your hand is away from you and your knuckles are at 9:00 (3:00). Lightly touch the surface with tip 2D.
2. As you squeeze out icing, slowly turn your hand until the back of your hand returns to its natural position, with knuckles at 12:00.
3. Stop squeezing, lift tip away.
4. For flower center, hold the bag straight up and squeeze out a tip 3 dot of icing. Keep the tip buried as you squeeze.
5. Stop squeezing, Pull tip up and off to the side, shaving off the point on the dot.

USING A FLOWER NAIL

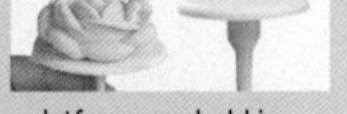

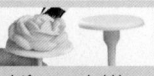

The nail is a revolving platform you hold in your hand to conveniently build roses and other flowers. It allows you to work close up, to turn for easy piping and to remove your completed flowers without damage, to dry. The key to making the flower on the nail is to coordinate the turning of the nail with the formation of each petal.

Attach a square of waxed paper or a pre-cut flower square (p. 142) on the flat surface of the flower nail using a dot of icing. Pipe your flower directly on the waxed paper. Hold the flower nail between the thumb and forefinger of your left (right) hand (use other fingers to support nail) and roll it slowly counterclockwise (clockwise for lefties) as you press out icing with the decorating bag held in the right (left) hand. Your right (left) hand moves in and out, or up and down, as it holds the decorating bag and tip at just the right angle (in most cases 45°) and keeps the icing flowing at an even speed. After piping, slide the waxed paper with flower off the nail to dry flat or on flower formers (p. 142).

FLOWER-MAKING TECHNIQUES

Explore beautiful flowers and leaves, which add lovely color to your cake design. Create the magnificent rose—the most popular icing flower of all. With practice, your flowers will have the just-picked look of real garden flowers.

FLOWER NAIL FLOWERS

The Wilton Rose

Hint: If you are going to be placing your roses on your cake immediately, waxed paper squares are not needed. Slide flower from nail onto cake, using a spatula.

Decorate with: For base, round tip 12; for petals, petal tip 104 and flower nail No. 7 for larger roses. Use stiff consistency royal or buttercream icing. Hold bag at 90° straight up for base, with tip slightly above flower nail; hold bag at 45° at 4:30 (7:30) for petals, wide end of tip touching base.

Rose Base

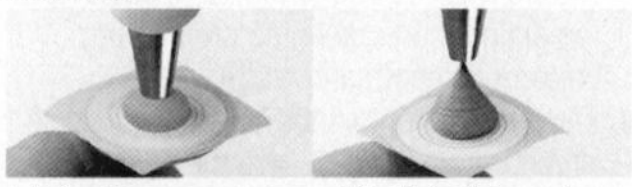

1. Using heavy pressure and tip 12, build up a base, remembering to keep your tip buried as you squeeze. Start to lift the tip higher, gradually raise the tip, and decrease the pressure.
2. Stop pressure, pull up and lift away. The rose base should be 1½ times as high as the rose tip opening.

Center Bud

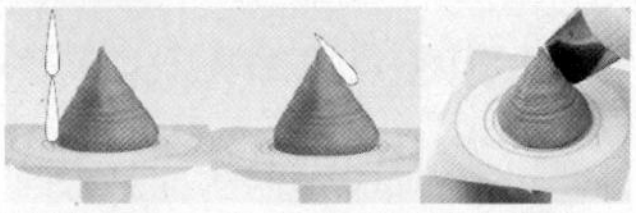

3. Make the center bud, using tip 104. Hold nail containing base in your left (right) hand and bag in right (left) hand. The wide end of the tip should touch the cone of the base at or slightly below the midpoint. The narrow end of the tip should point up and angled in over top of base.
4. Now you must do three things at the same time: Squeeze the bag, move the tip and rotate the nail. As you squeeze the bag, move the tip up from the base, forming a ribbon of icing. Slowly turn the nail counterclockwise (clockwise for lefties) to bring the ribbon of icing around to overlap at the top of the mound, then back down to starting point. Move your tip straight up and down only; do not loop it around the base.
5. Now you have a finished center bud.

Top Row of three petals

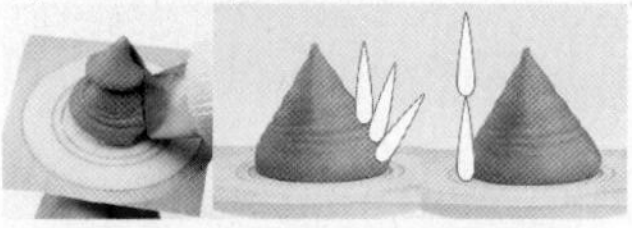

6. Touch the wide end of tip 104 to the midpoint of bud base, narrow end straight up.
7. Turn nail, keeping wide end of tip on base so that petal will attach. Move tip up and back down to the midpoint of mound, forming the first petal.
8. Start again, slightly behind end of first petal, and squeeze out second petal. Repeat for the third petal, ending by overlapping the starting point of the first petal. Rotate the nail ⅓ turn for each petal.

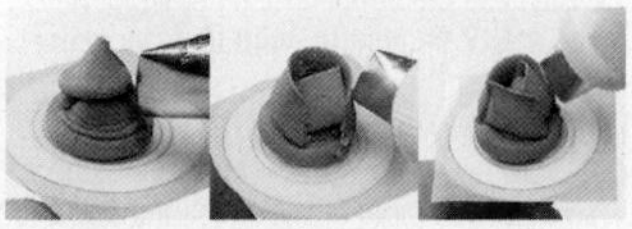

Middle Row of five petals

9. Touch the wide end of tip 104 slightly below center of a petal in the top row. Angle the narrow end of tip out slightly more than you did for the top row of petals. Squeeze bag and turn nail moving tip up, then down to form first petal.
10. Repeat for a total of five petals, rotating the nail ⅕ turn for each petal.
11. The last petal end should overlap the first's starting point.

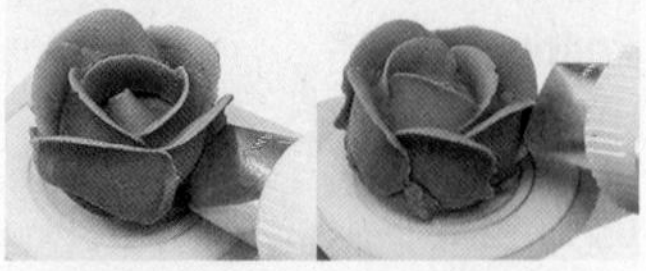

Bottom Row of seven petals.

12. Touch the wide end of tip below the center of a middle row petal, again angling the narrow end of tip out a little more. Squeeze bag and turn nail to end of fingers, moving tip up, then down to form first petal.
13. Repeat for a total of seven petals, rotating the nail ⅐ turn for each petal.
14. The last petal end should overlap the first's starting point.
15. Slip waxed paper and completed rose from nail. This is the completed Wilton Rose.

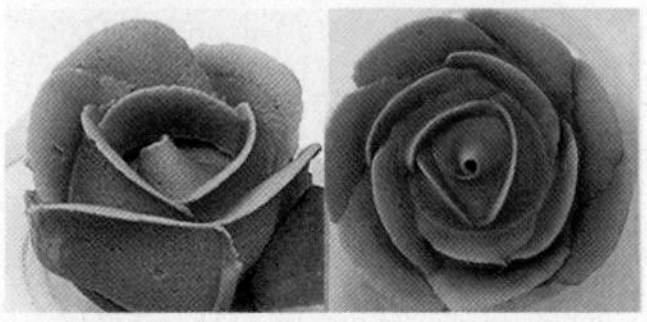

Rosebud

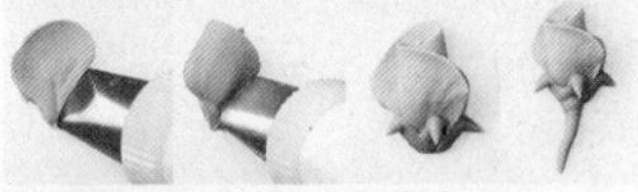

Hint: This flat flower can be piped directly on the cake in your favorite colors.

Decorate with: Flower Nail No. 7 and petal tip 104 for petals, round tip 3 for sepals and calyx. Use buttercream—stiff consistency for petals, thin consistency for sepals and calyx. For petals, hold bag at 45° at 4:30 (7:30); for sepals and calyx, hold bag at 45° at 6:00.

Back Petal

1. Wide end of tip 104 is touching the surface. Narrow end of tip is about ¼ in. off the surface. As you squeeze, move tip along the surface away from you in a straight line about ⅛ in. long. Pause the motion but continue squeezing to let the icing fan out. As you return to the original position, release pressure about halfway back. Move tip to the starting point, stop pressure and pull tip away.

Top Petal

2. Hold the bag as you did for the back petal. Opening of tip is parallel to the cupped edge of the back petal. Icing from tip must attach to the inside edge of cupped side of base petal at the very top. Apply medium pressure but DO NOT move the bag. When second petal is complete, stop pressure. Touch tip down to the surface and pull towards you

Center Sepal

3. Using tip 3, begin at base of rosebud. Squeeze with steady pressure as you slowly move up the surface of the rosebud. Relax pressure as you pull bag away from the flower to form a point.

Side Sepals

Repeat as for center sepal. Place where flower meets the surface.

Calyx

4. Insert tip 3 into base of the center sepal. Squeeze, letting icing build up. Slowly draw tip toward you, relaxing pressure as you move away from the flower. Stop pressure, pull tip away.

Wild Roses

Hint: Flower will be about the size of your flower nail head (No. 7). For a more cupped shape, increase the angle you hold the tip—be sure to dry in flower formers to keep the curved shape.

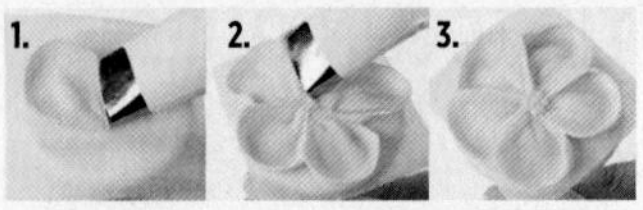

Decorate with: Petal tip 103 for petals. Round tip 1 for stamens. Use medium consistency royal icing. For petals, hold bag at 45° at 3:00 (9:00) with wide end of tip lightly touching center of nail, narrow end pointing out and raised ⅛ in. above nail surface. For stamens, hold bag at 90° straight up.

1. Use tip 103 at a 45° angle. Touch nail with wide end of tip, keeping narrow end just slightly above nail surface. Begin at center of flower nail and squeeze out first petal, turning nail ⅕ turn as you move tip out toward edge of nail. Relax pressure as you return to center of nail, curving tip slightly upward to create a cupped shape. Stop squeezing as wide end touches center of nail and lift up.
2. Repeat step 4 more times.
3. Pipe tiny pull-out dot stamens with tip 1.

FLORAL GREENERY

Leaves

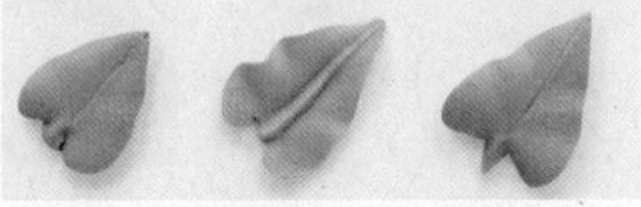

Basic Leaf	Veined Leaf	Large Leaf
Tip 352	Tip 67	Tip 366

Use for: Bouquets, borders, accents.

Hint: Add piping gel to your icing to keep your leaves from breaking.

Decorate with: Tips 352, 67 or 366. Use thin consistency buttercream icing. Hold bag at 45° at 6:00, with tip lightly touching surface, wide opening parallel to surface.

1. Squeeze hard to build up the base and, at the same time, lift the tip slightly.
2. Relax pressure as you pull the tip toward you, drawing the leaf to a point.
3. Stop squeezing and lift away.

Vines

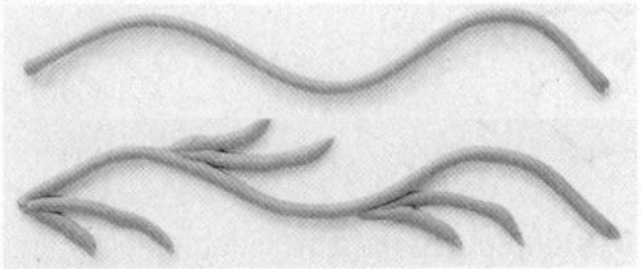

Use for: Bouquets, cake sprays.

Hint: In a flower spray, your eye is drawn to the point where vines meet—the focal point. This is where you will place the most flowers. Always use an odd number of main vines.

Decorate with: Tip 3. Use thin consistency buttercream icing. Hold bag at 45° at 3:00 (9:00), with tip lightly touching surface.

1. Touch your tip lightly to the surface as you start to squeeze, then lift slightly above the surface as you draw out the stem.
2. Move tip gently up and down to form "hills and valleys." To end the line, stop squeezing and pull the tip along the surface.
3. Add secondary curved stems, starting at main stem, stopping pressure as you pull to a point.

PEARL DUST & COLOR DUST COLOR EFFECTS

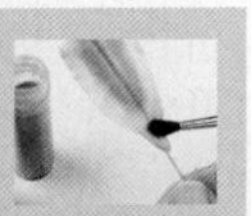

You can lighten any Pearl or Color Dust color by adding white. Brushing wet, mixed with Wilton Lemon Extract (p. 153) creates a more vivid look. Some projects may take more than one coat of "paint" for even coverage; let each coat dry completely before starting a new one. Since the extract can evaporate quickly, mix small amounts of paint at a time and use immediately. Use a brush to paint wet or apply dry. For fine detail, a small round head brush works best. For large areas, use a wider, flat brush.

To make a "paint": In a small bowl, mix ¼ teaspoon Pearl Dust or Color Dust with ¼ teaspoon lemon extract. Dissolve the dust completely into the extract before painting. For larger projects, start with ½ teaspoon Pearl Dust or Color Dust and ½ teaspoon lemon extract.

OTHER DECORATING TECHNIQUES

Brush Embroidery

Add textured flowers and leaves with the soft look of lace using this easy icing technique. Works best using the square tip brush from the Wilton Brush Set (p. 153).

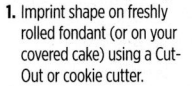

1. Imprint shape on freshly rolled fondant (or on your covered cake) using a Cut-Out or cookie cutter.
2. Thin royal or buttercream icing with piping gel. Using tip 2 or 3, outline shape. For large designs, outline one section of the design, brush out lines following step 3, then continue with the next design section.

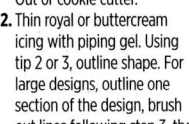

3. Before each outline can dry, immediately brush out lines of icing toward center of pattern area with damp brush. Work in quick, short strokes. Clean brush with water after brushing each design to create distinct lines of icing.

Combing

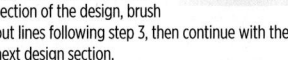

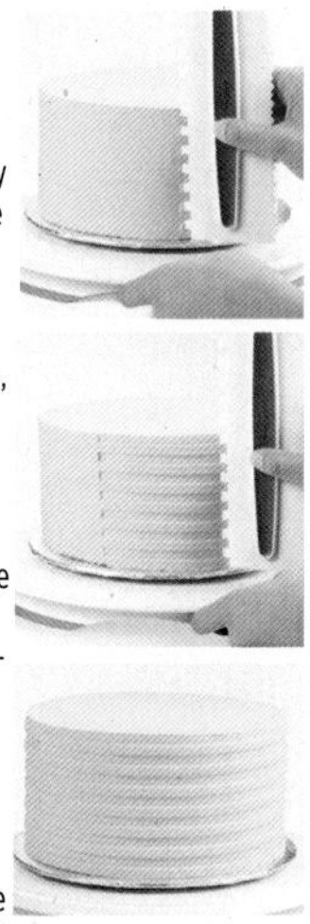

Use for: Creating a textured surface for cake sides.

Hint: Comb immediately after icing cake, while icing is soft. Using a turntable helps to keep the movement of your comb smooth, so your surface will be perfect.

Practice with: Icing Comb Set (p. 137); Trim-N-Turn Plus Cake Turntable (p. 138)

Decorate with: Medium-to-thin buttercream icing

Cover the cake with a slightly thicker coating of icing so the comb's ridges will not touch the cake. Hold comb at a 45° angle. Turn the turntable as you run the comb edge over the surface. Use different combs and edges to add different contoured effects to your iced cake. Choose the type of effect you want—wide or narrow—then run that edge around your cake to form ridges.

Puddle Dots

Thin royal icing (or Color Flow), adding ½ teaspoon water per ¼ cup of icing. Icing is ready for flowing when a small amount dripped back into mixture takes a count of 10 to disappear. On waxed paper-covered boards, pipe a ball, ¼ in. to 1¼ in. diameter, depending on project instructions, using thinned icing in a cut parchment bag or bag and tip. Let dry 48 hours. Decorate following project instructions.

Tinting Shredded Coconut

Place desired amount of coconut in plastic bag, add a little color with a toothpick and knead until color is evenly blended. Dry on waxed paper.

Smoothing Icing with Finger

When piping some facial features or details, such as dot eyes or piped in shapes, you may want to smooth out the area for a clean look. To do this, gently pat the area with your finger dipped in cornstarch. .

Fondant Ribbon Roses

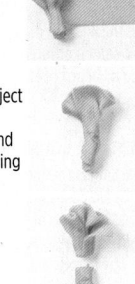

Roll out fondant ⅛ in. on Roll-N-Cut Mat lightly dusted with cornstarch. Cut strip following dimensions stated in project instructions. Begin rolling from one end of strip, gradually loosening roll as flower gets larger, attaching with damp brush. Use veining tool between spirals to open up petals; let dry on cornstarch-dusted board or candy melting plate.

Molding with Fondant and Gum Paste Molds

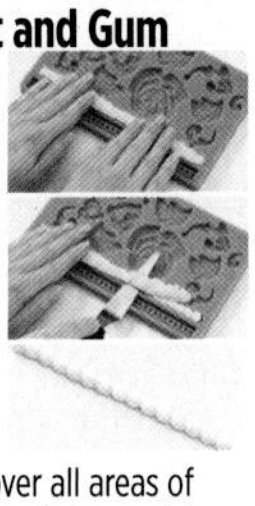

It's easy to create detailed shapes in exciting designs that are ready to place on your cake.

Lightly dust mold cavities with cornstarch. Fill cavity with fondant or gum paste. Press down on fondant or gum paste with fingers to cover all areas of the cavity. To evenly distribute the material, you can also press with Shaping Foam. Trim excess fondant or gum paste using spatula or palette knife from 10-Pc. Gum Paste Tool Set. Turn mold over and flex to release shapes. Follow project instructions for placing design on your cake. Or let dry as needed.

Fondant Curlicues

Toothpicks, lollipop sticks or dowel rods may be used for various sizes.

1. Roll out fondant ¹⁄₁₆ in. thick on Roll-N-Cut Mat lightly dusted with cornstarch. Cut into thin strips.
2. Loosely wrap strips around a lollipop stick several times to form curls. Let set 5 to 10 minutes.
3. Slide curl off lollipop stick and let dry.

Sealing Globe Pillar Opening with Fondant

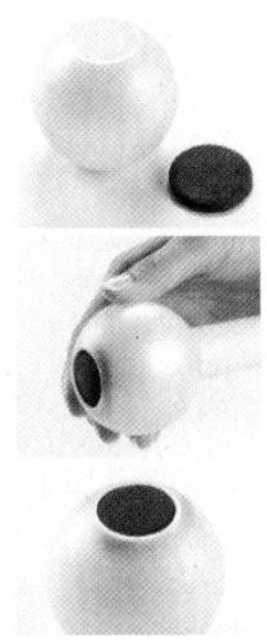

To make perfectly round 3-D heads and bodies you need to seal the top globe opening before covering with fondant.

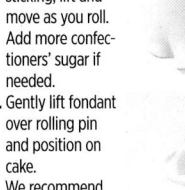

1. Roll out fondant ⅛ in. thick; cut 1½ in. circle or with medium Round Cut-Out Fondant Cutter (p. 151).
2. Brush around inside hole of Globe Pillar with piping gel or thinned fondant adhesive. Insert circle piece of fondant and push to cover hole with end of 9 in. fondant roller.
3. Smooth around outside edges.

Transferring Patterns To Cakes

1. Make a copy of pattern. Turn copy over and trace pattern on back to create a reverse pattern. Tape pattern, reverse side up, on flat surface.
2. Cover pattern with waxed paper and outline with piping gel.
3. Carefully lay outlined pattern, gel side down, on iced cake that has crusted. Using a decorator brush, gently trace over gel lines. To remove, lift pattern straight up from cake.

USING ROLLED FONDANT

The dough-like consistency of fondant makes it the perfect medium for creating ruffles and braids, stately molded accents, distinctive borders, fun trims and beautiful flowers. Decorators agree that fondant is an icing that is truly easy to work with. It's even easier with Wilton Ready-To-Use Rolled Fondant (p. 148)—no mixing, no mess!

COVERING THE CAKE

Just follow our instructions for the right ways to knead, roll out and lift the fondant, and you'll find that covering a cake is easy. For instructions on covering square, petal and other cake shapes, see the *Celebrate With Fondant* book, available on p. 143.

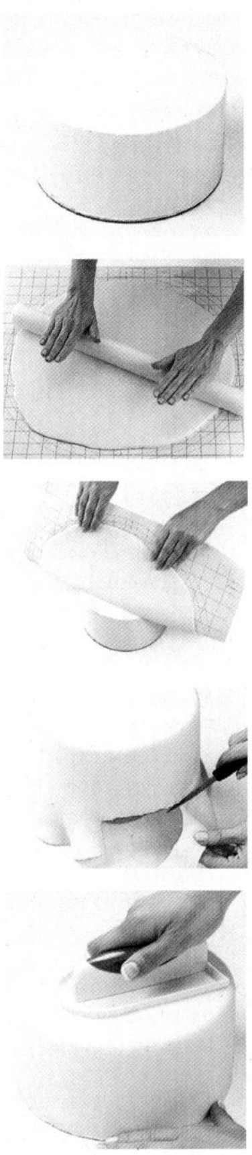

1. Prepare cake by lightly covering with buttercream icing.
2. Before rolling out fondant, knead it until it is a workable consistency. If fondant is sticky, knead in a little confectioners' sugar. Lightly dust your smooth work surface or the Roll-N-Cut Mat and your rolling pin with confectioners' sugar to prevent sticking. Roll out fondant sized to your cake (see "Fondant Amounts," at right). To keep fondant from sticking, lift and move as you roll. Add more confectioners' sugar if needed.
3. Gently lift fondant over rolling pin and position on cake. We recommend using the Fondant Smoother because the pressure of your hands may leave impressions on the fondant.
4. Smooth and shape fondant on top and sides of cake using Fondant Smoother (p. 152). Beginning in the middle of the cake top, move the Fondant Smoother outward and down the sides to smooth and shape fondant to the cake and remove air bubbles. If an air bubble appears, insert a pin on an angle, release air and smooth the area again. Use the straight edge of the Fondant Smoother to mark fondant at the base of cake. Trim off excess fondant using the fondant cutter, a spatula or sharp knife.

MARBLEIZING FONDANT

Using Icing Color: Roll fondant into a ball, kneading until it's soft and pliable. Using a toothpick, add dots of icing color in several spots. Knead fondant slightly until color begins to blend in, creating marbleized streaks. Roll out fondant to desired shape.

Using Pre-Tinted Fondant and White Fondant: Roll a log each of tinted and white fondant. Twist one log around the other several times. Knead fondant slightly until color begins to blend in, creating marbleized streaks. Roll out fondant to desired shape.

FONDANT AMOUNTS

Use this chart to determine how much ready-to-use rolled fondant to buy. Wilton fondant is available in 24 oz. (1 lb., 8 oz.) or 80 oz. (5 lb.) packages. Amounts listed do not include decorations.

CAKE SHAPE	CAKE SIZE	FONDANT
Round 4 in. high	6 in.	18 oz.
	8 in.	24 oz.
	10 in.	36 oz.
	12 in.	48 oz.
	14 in.	72 oz.
	16 in.	108 oz.
	18 in.	140 oz.
Round 3 in. high	6 in.	14 oz.
	8 in.	18 oz.
	10 in.	24 oz.
	12 in.	36 oz.
	14 in.	48 oz.
	16 in.	72 oz.
	18 in.	108 oz.
Sheet 2 in. high	7 in. x 11 in.	30 oz.
	9 in. x 13 in.	40 oz.
	11 in. x 15 in.	60 oz.
	12 in. x 18 in.	80 oz.
Oval 4 in. high	7.75 in. x 5.5 in.	24 oz.
	10.75 in. x 7.8 in.	36 oz.
	13.5 in. x 9.8 in.	48 oz.
	16.5 in. x 12.4 in.	72 oz.
Heart 4 in. high	6 in.	18 oz.
	8 in.	26 oz.
	9 in.	32 oz.
	10 in.	36 oz.
	12 in.	48 oz.
	14 in.	72 oz.
	16 in.	96 oz.
Petal 4 in. high	6 in.	18 oz.
	9 in.	30 oz.
	12 in.	48 oz.
	15 in.	72 oz.
Square 4 in. high	6 in.	24 oz.
	8 in.	36 oz.
	10 in.	48 oz.
	12 in.	72 oz.
	14 in.	96 oz.
	16 in.	120 oz.
Hexagon 4 in. high	6 in.	18 oz.
	9 in.	36 oz.
	12 in.	48 oz.
	15 in.	84 oz.
Paisley 4 in. high	9 in. x 6 in.	20 oz.
	12.5 in. x 9.5 in.	48 oz.
	16.5 in. x 12.5 in.	72 oz.
Diamond 4 in. high	10.25 in. x 7.4 in.	24 oz.
	15 in. x 11 in.	36 oz.
	19.25 in. x 14.25 in.	60 oz.
Pillow	6.75 in. x 6.75 in.	16 oz.
	10 in. x 10 in.	28 oz.
	13.25 in. x 13.25 in.	48 oz.

HOW TO COLOR AND FLAVOR FONDANT

You can easily tint our White Ready-To-Use Rolled Fondant (p. 148) or the Rolled Fondant recipe (p. 127) using Wilton Icing Colors (p. 139). Using a toothpick, add icing color, a little at a time, and knead into fondant until color is evenly blended. Wilton Ready-To-Use Rolled Fondant has a mellow flavor, which can be enhanced using Wilton No-Color Butter Flavor, Imitation Vanilla Extract or Imitation Almond Extract (p. 141). Knead flavor into fondant until well blended.

COVERING BASE BOARDS WITH FONDANT

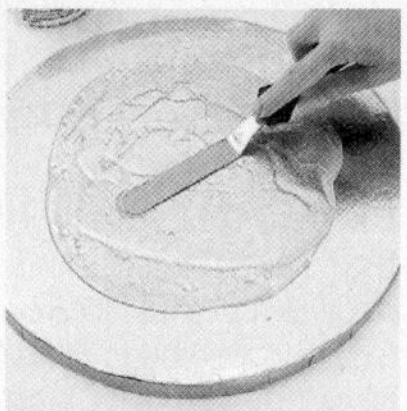

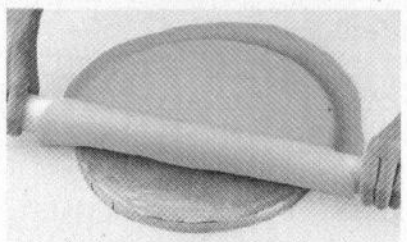

Cut cake boards 2 in. larger in diameter than your cake, unless otherwise directed, then roll out fondant about 1 in. larger than board size. Wrap board with foil.

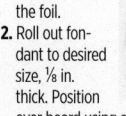

1. Lightly coat board with piping gel to help the fondant stick to the foil.

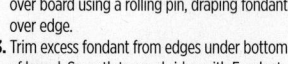

2. Roll out fondant to desired size, ⅛ in. thick. Position over board using a rolling pin, draping fondant over edge.
3. Trim excess fondant from edges under bottom of board. Smooth top and sides with Fondant Smoother.

COVERING LARGE CAKES

In most cases, the smaller your cake, the easier it will be to cover with rolled fondant. However, there is an easy way to position and smooth fondant on cakes that are 12 in. dia. or larger. Follow the steps below to lift fondant onto the cake without tearing.

1. Cover cake lightly with buttercream icing. Roll out fondant sized to fit your cake.
2. Slide a large cake circle that has been dusted with confectioners' sugar under the rolled fondant. Lift the circle and the fondant and position over cake. Gently shake the circle to slide the fondant off and into position on the cake. Smooth and trim as described above.

COLOR FLOW

Working With Color Flow

1. Trace your design pattern onto parchment paper, then tape paper onto a cake circle or the back of a cookie pan. Cover with waxed paper; smooth and tape. Using tip 2 and parchment bag half-filled with full-strength Color Flow, squeeze, pull and drop icing string following pattern outline. Stop, touch tip to surface and pull away. If you will be using the same color to fill in, let outline dry a few minutes until it "crusts."
To prevent bleeding of different colors, let outline dry 1 to 2 hours before filling in.
2. Thin Color Flow mixture with water following recipe directions (p. 128). Cut opening in parchment bag to the size of tip 2. Fill in design with thinned Color Flow.
3. Let decorations air dry thoroughly, at least 48 hours. To remove, cut away waxed paper from board, then turn over and peel waxed paper off the Color Flow piece.

Hint: To easily remove dried Color Flow, pull waxed paper backing over the edge of a table with one hand, while holding decoration with other hand. Waxed paper will pull off naturally. Or, with dried Color Flow resting on cookie sheet, place cardboard sheet over Color Flow, lift and turn over so that top of decoration rests on cardboard. Lift off waxed paper.

Since any moist icing will break down Color Flow, either position Color Flow decorations on cake shortly before serving or place on sugar cubes, attaching with full-strength Color Flow.

TIERED CAKE CONSTRUCTION

There are many methods of constructing tiered cakes. Here are some used in this book. Visit **www.wilton.com** for more construction methods.

TO PREPARE CAKE FOR ASSEMBLY

Place base tier on a sturdy base plate of three or more thicknesses of corrugated cardboard. For heavy cakes, use foil-covered Wilton Silver Cake Bases or a foamcore or plywood base, ½ in. thick. Base can be covered with Fanci-Foil Wrap and trimmed with Tuk-N-Ruffle or use Ruffle Boards (p. 186). Each tier of your cake must be on a cake circle or board cut to fit. Place a few strokes of icing on boards to secure cake. Fill and ice layers before assembly.

Adding Dowel Rods (p. 194) to Tiered Cakes

Use the upper tier for size reference when determining dowel rod placement. All the dowel rods must be placed within the area you will mark (see steps below) to provide adequate support.

1. Center a cake board the same size as the tier above it on base tier and press it gently into icing to imprint an outline. Remove. Use this outline to guide the insertion of the dowel rods.

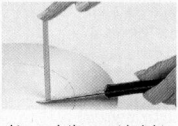

2. Insert one dowel rod into cake straight down to the cake board. Make a knife scratch on the rod to mark the exact height. Pull dowel rod out.

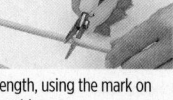

3. Cut the suggested number of rods (see note below) the exact same length, using the mark on the first one as a guide.

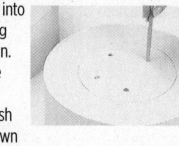

4. Insert rods into tier, spacing evenly 1½ in. in from the imprinted outline. Push straight down until each touches the cake board. Repeat this procedure for every stacked or pillared tier on the cake.

NOTE: The larger and more numerous the tiers, the more dowels needed. If the tier above is 10 in. or less, use six ¼ in. bamboo dowels. Use eight dowel rods for 16 in. and 18 in. cakes; on these larger tiers, use ¾ in. plastic dowel rods in the base tier. When using white plastic dowel rods that are wider and provide more support, the number needed may be less.

Stacked Construction

Stacking is the most architectural method of tiered cake construction. Tiers are placed directly on top of one another and pillars are not used. Cakes are supported and stabilized by dowel rods and cake boards.

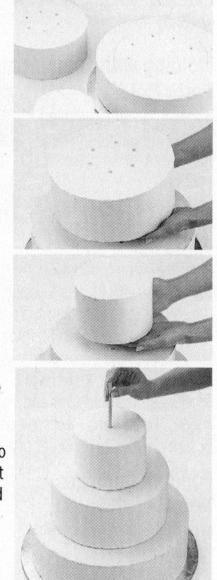

1. Dowel rod all tiers except top tier.
2. Position the middle tier on the base tier, centering exactly.*
3. Repeat with the top tier.
4. To stabilize tiers further, sharpen one end of a long dowel rod and push it through all tiers and cake boards to the base of the bottom tier. To decorate, start at the top and work down.

Separator Plate (2-Plate) and Pillar Construction

This most dramatic method features two, three or more single cakes towered together. Use separator plates and pillars (p. 194). Check pillars and plates for correct fit before constructing your cake.

1. Set cake tiers on separator plates 2 in. larger in diameter than cakes.
2. Dowel rod cakes and position separator plates on tiers with feet up. (Note: Connect only same size separator plates with pillars.)

3. Position pillars over feet on separator plates.

4. Carefully set cake plate on pillars. Continue adding tiers this way.**

Push-In Pillar Construction

Simple assembly—no dowel rods needed! Use any type of Wilton push-in pillars and plates (p. 194). Check pillars and plates for correct fit before constructing your cake.

1. Mark tier for push-in pillar placement. Use the separator plate for the next tier above, gently pressing it onto the tier, feet down, making sure it is centered. Lift plate away. The feet will leave marks on the icing to guide the position of pillars when you assemble the tier. Repeat this process for each tier, working from largest to smallest tier. The top tier is left unmarked.  
2. Place each tier on its separator plate, securing with icing.
3. Position push-in pillars at marks, and insert into tiers. Push straight down until pillars touch the cake plate.
4. To assemble, start with the tier above the base tier. Place the feet of the separator plate on the pillar openings. Continue adding tiers in the same way until the cake is completely assembled.**

Globe Pillar Set Construction

These elegant pearl-look globes (p. 193) are available in separate sets of four 2 in., 2½ in. or 3 in. globes. The 3 in. globes are to be used to support the base cake only. They have a reinforced center channel which eliminates the need for pillars. The 2 in. and 2½ in. sets should be used with 9 in. "Hidden" Pillars (included in set); do not use these sets to support the base cake. Your cake design may use a base board instead of the 3 in. globes to support the base cake as shown below.

1. Position base cake on a thick base board. Using the separator plate which will hold the cake above, mark base cake for pillar placement (see Push-In Pillar Construction, above). Lift plate away.
2. Insert pillars through cake centered over marked

*Finely shredded coconut or confectioners' sugar, placed in area where cake circles and plastic plates will rest, helps prevent icing on the cake from sticking.
**Assemble cakes when you arrive at the reception or party.

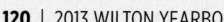

area to rest on
its separator
plate or base
board. Place
the correct size
globe (2½ in.
for cake shown
here) over the
pillars. Mark pillars where
they extend
above globes.
The cut pillars
should be equal
to the height of
the base
cake plus the
height
of each globe.

3. Trim pillars at
   markings with
   craft knife or
   serrated edge
   knife.
4. Insert pillars
   in base cake.
   Position globes over pillars.
5. Position the tier above on globes.
6. Add additional sets for more tiers.

Towering Tiers Cake & Dessert Stand Construction (p. 193)

Final cake assembly should be done at the cake's final location. Moving the cake once assembled is not recommended. Do not cut cakes directly on the stand; remove first from the stand.

Prepare Cake Boards:

Cake tiers will use the same size cake boards as cake. Each board will need a 1½ in. diameter hole cut in the center to accommodate the

---

center post of the stand. To do that, make a waxed paper pattern for each cake to be used. To find the exact center of the board, fold the pattern in half, and then again in half to make quarters. Snip the point of the paper to make a small center hole. Place a center column piece over the small hole and trace. Cut out hole and test the size to make sure it fits over the column. Adjust if necessary. Place the pattern on the cake board, trace the hole and cut out. Test the size again to make sure the board fits over the column. Adjust if necessary. Save paper patterns for cake tiers.

Prepare Cake Tiers:

Ice cake tiers and position on prepared cake boards (with holes). All cake tiers (except for the top tier) will need to have a center hole cut out. Using your waxed paper patterns from the cake boards, mark the center hole on the top of the cake. Using the Cake Corer Tool, gently push the corer into the center of the cake all the way to the bottom and twist a half turn.
(See photo 1.) Keep the corer straight, remove it from the cake, leaving a hole in the center of the tier. Repeat for all the cake tiers.

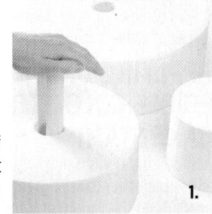
1.

Stand and Cake Assembly:

Short center posts are ideal for cupcakes and small individual desserts. Tall center posts should be used for cake tiers up to 5 in. high. First, decide which plates and center columns

---

2.

will be used for the cake setup. The largest plate of the cake setup will be the base tier. For the 16 in. and 18 in. plates, assemble by sliding the half plate sections together and interlocking them on the plate support. (See photo 2.) Use 14 in. plates or smaller as is. Screw the base feet to the bottom of the base plate. Place center post foot on the bottom of the plate or plate assembly (if using a 16 in. or 18 in. plate). (See photo 3.) Place a center

3.

post section on the top of plate and screw into center post foot to secure. Once the base assembly is complete, add the first cake tier. Slide the base cake with board over the center post. (See photo 4.) Place the next sized plate on the center post currently in place. (See photo 5.) Attach another center post. (See photo 6.)

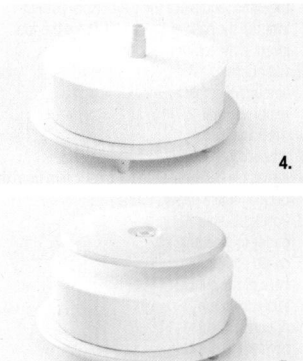
4.

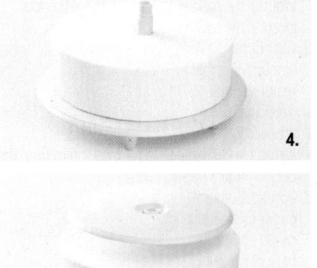
5.

Slide the next cake over center post onto plate. Continue until all tiers are in position. For the top tier, add the top tier plate and screw on the top nut to the center post. Position top cake tier on the plate. (See photo 7.)

6.

To display cupcakes, first assemble the entire stand using the short posts and the desired number of plates. Start with the largest plate at the bottom and build up to the smallest plate. Position cupcakes on the stand.

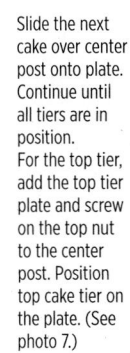
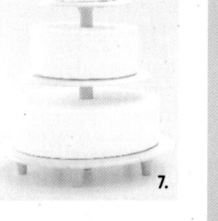
7.

Alternate 2-Plate Set-Ups

Wilton wire separator sets are an easy way to add the drama of height to your cake design. Both the Garden Gazebo Separator Set and the Leaf and Vine Separator Set (p. 193) include two 8 in. separator plates and a 6.25 in. diameter by 6 in. high decorative separator ring.

Assembly is a breeze:

1. Dowel rod base cake as for 2-Plate & Pillar Construction.
2. Position one plate from set on base cake feet side up; position separator ring.
3. Position top cake tier on remaining plate and position on separator ring.

Garden Gazebo Separator Set   Leaf and Vine Separator Set

STORING CAKES

Take some final precautions and store your cake the best way possible. After all, your time, effort and creativity have made it very special! Beware of the following factors, which can affect the look of your decorated cake.

Sunlight and fluorescent lighting will alter icing colors. Keep your cake stored in a covered box and out of direct sunlight and fluorescent lighting.

Humidity can soften royal icing, fondant and gum paste decorations. If you live in a climate with high humidity, prepare your royal icing using only pure cane confectioners' sugar (not beet sugar or dextrose), add less liquid and add 1 more teaspoon meringue powder (p. 141) to the recipe.

Heat can melt icing and cause decorations to droop. Keep your decorated cake as cool as possible and stabilize buttercream icing by adding 2 teaspoons meringue powder per recipe. Protect your cake by placing it in a clean, covered cake box. Avoid using foil or plastic wrap to cover a decorated cake—these materials can stick to icing and crush delicate decorations. The icing that covers your cake determines how it should be stored—in the refrigerator, at cool room temperature, or frozen, if storing for longer than three days. If you want to store your iced cake in a different way than noted, make a small test cake.

Icing type determines care. See Icing Index on p. 115 for storage information.

NOTE: Cakes with thoroughly dried royal icing decorations should be stored according to the type of icing that covers the cake. However, if royal icing decorations are to be put on a cake that will be frozen, it is recommended that these decorations be placed on the cake after thawing so that they don't bleed from condensation or become soft.

TRANSPORTING TIERED CAKES

Following some simple guidelines ensures that your cake will arrive safely—whether you are traveling hundreds of miles or just a few.

Before Moving Cakes

Be certain the cake is constructed on a sturdy base made of three or more thicknesses of corrugated cardboard. Base tiers of very heavy cakes should be placed on a foamcore or plywood base, ½ in. thick. Cakes on pillars must be transported unassembled. Toppers, candles and ornaments should be removed from cakes when they are being moved. For stacked cakes, move the entire assembled cake. Or, for a larger quantity of tiers, transport unassembled and assemble at the reception. Be sure to have with you the equipment and icings you will need to finish any decorating needed after assembly at the reception.

Boxing the cake makes transportation easier. Place the boxes on carpet foam or a non-skid mat on a level surface to prevent shifting.

In Pan

Take tiers apart if constructed in Center Column or Push-In Leg method. Leave columns or legs in place. Position the plates on crumpled foil or in shallow pans if they do not sit level. Remove pillars from tier plates; plates stay in position.

In Box

Place the cakes in clean, covered, sturdy

---

boxes that are sized to the base board of each cake. This prevents shifting within the box and possibly crushing the sides of the cake. If the box is too big, roll pieces of masking tape sticky side out and attach to the inside bottom of the box. Position the cake base on top of the tape, securing the base in the box. For taller decorations, prop up box top and sides, secure with masking tape.

On Non-Skid Foam

If tiers cannot be boxed, they can be transported on large pieces of non-skid foam. Place the foam on the floor of the vehicle, then carefully place the tiers centered on each piece of foam. Remove any ornament or fragile decorations before transporting.

At Your Destination

Before you bring in the cake from your car, walk the path you will have to travel to the setup site. Be alert for any bumps along the way and note any tight spaces you will have to maneuver around. Make sure the cake table is level—it's a good idea to bring a level to check this on setup day. Request a cart on wheels to move the cake into the reception area. This is easier and safer than carrying by hand. Remove the cakes from the boxes on the reception table by cutting the sides of the boxes and sliding the cakes out. Bring along a repair kit, including extra icing, prepared decorating bags and tips, flowers and spatulas, just in case it is necessary to make any repairs. Once the cake is assembled, take a picture to establish that the cake was in perfect condition when you left it.

SUGAR SHEETS!™ EDIBLE DECORATING PAPER DECORATING TECHNIQUES

It's a new way to decorate everyone will love! The Punch. Cut. Decorate! *method features Wilton Sugar Sheets! edible decorating paper, punches and cutting tools that make it easy to create decorations in dazzling colors and shapes.*

Shape flexible edible paper into bows and fans, curve and cut to form stand-up flower shapes and punch to create multi-colored layered shapes that bring new excitement to your sweet treats. The cutting tools also make it easy to cleanly cut captivating shapes from edible paper, gum paste or rolled fondant. Use individually or layer and lay flat on top of your treats.

Best of all, Sugar Sheets! edible decorating paper is ideal for "off-cake" decorating. This means you can perfect the look you want before you place it on the cake. Just cut or punch your shapes, build your decoration, add a colorful effect or message and position on the cake.

Follow the easy techniques here to start the decorating excitement. Discover hundreds of exclusive ideas at wilton.com. Get ready to Punch. Cut. Decorate!

USING SINGLE SHAPE PUNCH SET AND CUTTING INSERTS WITH EDIBLE PAPER

Our tools are designed to cut a variety of exciting shapes easily every time! After you've cut one shape, just replace the insert to cut a different one for the ultimate in cake creativity! You can also use punches and inserts to cut shapes from gum paste or rolled fondant.

1. Remove protective silicone cap to separate the top and bottom cutting inserts. Lift the top of the punch and place the flat bottom cutting insert in the base of the punch. Place the top insert in the top of the punch.
2. Cut out the amount of edible paper you will need and place unused portion in resealable package. Remove plastic film from the back of edible paper.
3. Position edible paper to meet the raised edge in the back of the punch. For best results and cleanest cut, do not punch right to the edge of the sheet. Leave a small amount of clearance around the shape.
4. With slow, even pressure, push down top of punch to cut shape.
5. Your cut piece will be below the bottom of the punch.
6. Lift punch away from your cut piece.
7. Use your edible paper piece immediately or store under a Gum Paste Storage board or plastic wrap to keep the piece flexible until ready to place on cake.

USING BORDER PUNCH SET AND BORDER CUTTING INSERTS WITH EDIBLE PAPER

Use these fun border shapes to frame your cakes or as accents for clothes, animal features, clouds and more!

1. Remove protective silicone cap to separate the top and bottom cutting inserts. Lift the top of the punch and place the flat bottom cutting insert in the base of the punch. Place the top insert in the top of the punch.
2. Cut out the amount of edible paper you will need and place unused portion in resealable package. Remove plastic film from the back of edible paper.
3. Position edible paper to meet the raised edge in the back of the punch. Push down top of punch to cut border. For best results and cleanest cut, do not punch right to the edge of the sheet. Leave a small amount of clearance around the shape.
4. Reposition edible paper in punch, aligning uncut edge with punch. Push down top of punch to cut a continuous border.
5. Your cut border piece will look like this.
6. Use the cut pieces, or use the part of the edible paper that is still in the negative space) to assemble borders, trimming as needed.

CUTTING A TWO-SIDED BORDER

For decorations that will go on the top or sides of your cake, a double-edged piece works beautifully. Try it for clouds, zigzag accents and more.

1. After cutting one border edge of your edible paper, turn the

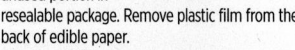

piece around so the straight edge of the piece meets the raised edge in the back of the punch. Push down top of punch to cut second edge.
2. Attach your piece to your treat, trimming as needed.

DRAWING WITH FOODWRITER EDIBLE COLOR MARKERS

Make edible paper decorations personal—draw designs and mark messages in cool colors with FoodWriter edible color markers. FoodWriter edible markers are also great for tracing shapes on your edible paper pieces, which helps make cutting precisely a breeze.

1. Choose the color that will look best with your edible paper piece. Start drawing borders or designs with a FoodWriter edible color marker.
2. Complete design, filling in areas if desired.
3. Print name or write message using a different color of edible marker

APPLYING DAB-N-COLOR EDIBLE COLOR TO CAKE STAMP

Add exciting designs and messages to your edible paper, fondant or gum paste decorated treats using the variety of Wilton Cake Stamps and Dab-N-Color edible colors! Be sure to wash and throughly dry stamps before using. We suggest testing your stamp on a scrap piece of edible paper or a sheet of paper before applying.

1. Squeeze a few drops of edible color onto stamp or a small container or plate. Gently wipe or brush on a thin layer of color to cover stamp surface. Do not over-saturate stamp.
2. Press stamp down onto edible paper, fondant or gum paste with even pressure. Lift stamp straight up and away from surface. If stamping names or messages on cake tops, use the Spell-N-Stamp Cake Stamping Block (p. 147) for precise spacing and even pressure.
3. Let color dry at least 10-15 minutes before applying to your treat.

APPLYING CAKE STAMP TO EDIBLE PAPER FOR CAKE SIDES

Adding Wilton Cake Stamp designs to your edible paper-covered cake definitely makes for even sweeter accents. Keep plastic backing on edible paper strips while stamping. Remove backing before attaching to cake.

1. Apply all stamp designs onto edible paper before placing onto cake.
2. Let color dry at least 10-15 minutes before attaching to cake. Attach edible paper to sides of cake using piping gel.
3. This is the completed stamped cake design.

APPLYING CAKE STAMP TO FONDANT-COVERED CAKE

Apply your Wilton Cake Stamp directly onto your fondant-covered cake. Or, you can stamp onto rolled out fondant and then cover your cake. Apply Dab-N-Color edible color to cake stamp according to directions above.

1. For stamping on the side of a cake, follow stamping directions above. For stamping on round cakes, you may need to gently rock the stamp from one side to the other to evenly stamp the image.

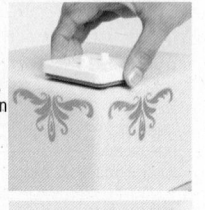

2. For stamping on the top of a cake, press stamp down with even pressure. Lift stamp straight up and away from surface.
3. This is the completed stamped cake design.

RUFFLED RIBBON ROSE WITH EDIBLE PAPER

This flower will charm everyone, with its intricate gathered layers of petals. You'd never think it was so easy to make, but thanks to edible paper, rolling and pinching each layer is a breeze!

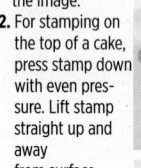

1. Cut a strip to size listed in your project instructions using rotary cutter. Here we've used 1 in. x 8 in. strips.
2. Brush bottom edge with piping gel.
3. Begin rolling from one end, gently gathering and pinching bottom edge.
4. Continue wrapping more loosely as you go.
5. You can stop with a small flower using one strip...
6. Or, create a larger flower by adding a second strip. Brush end of strip to attach to original flower and continue wrapping loosely and pinching bottom edge as before.
7. Your flower is ready!

USING DAB-N-HOLD EDIBLE ADHESIVE

Use Dab-N-Hold edible adhesive to apply edible paper to fondant or crusted buttercream icing, create layered decorations and more. Dab small dots on your edible paper and spread with brush as needed. Attach and allow to dry.

CANDY MAKING TECHNIQUES

USING CANDY MELTS CANDY

To Melt

Chocolate Pro Electric Melting Pot (p. 175): The most convenient way to melt—no microwave or double boiler needed! Melts large amounts of Candy Melts candy in minutes.

Double boiler method: Fill lower pan with water to below level of top pan. Bring water to simmer, then remove from heat. Put Candy Melts candy in top pan and set in position on lower pan. Stir constantly, without beating, until smooth and completely melted.

Microwave method: In microwave-safe container, microwave 1 package Candy Melts candy at 50% power or defrost setting for 1 minute. Stir thoroughly. Continue to microwave and stir at 30 second intervals until smooth and completely melted. Candy Melts candy may also be melted in Candy Decorating Bags (p. 178). Melt as described above, squeezing bag between heating intervals to blend Candy Melts candy together. When completely melted, snip off end of bag and squeeze melted Candy Melts candy into molds. Throw away bag when empty.

NOTE: Candy Melts candy will lose its pouring and dipping consistency if overheated, or if water or other liquid is added. If coating is overheated, add 1 teaspoons vegetable shortening per 12 oz. Candy Melts candy.

To Mold (1 color candies)

Pour melted candy into clean, dry mold; tap lightly to remove air bubbles. Place mold on level surface in refrigerator until bottom of mold appears frosty or until candy is firm. Pop out candy. For lollipops, fill molds, tap to remove air bubbles, then position sticks in mold. Rotate sticks to thoroughly cover with candy so they remain securely in place. Chill until firm, then unmold.

To Color

Add Candy Colors (p. 175) to melted Candy Melts candy a little at a time. Mix thoroughly before adding more color. Colors tend to deepen as they're mixed.

Multi-colored candy

"Painting" Method: Before filling mold cavity, use a decorator brush dipped in melted Candy Melts candy to paint features or desired details; let set. Fill mold and chill until firm as described above.

Piping Method: Use a parchment or Candy Decorating Bag filled halfway with melted candy. Cut small hole in tip of bag and gently squeeze to add candy detail to mold; let set. Fill mold and chill until firm as described above.

SPECIALTY TECHNIQUES

Candy Shells

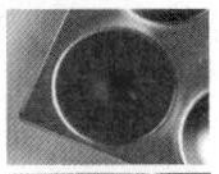

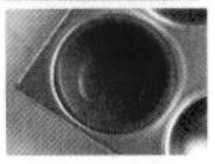

Fill pan cavity to the top edge with melted candy. Tap on counter to remove air bubbles. Let chill for 8 to 10 minutes or until a ⅛ in. to ¼ in. shell has formed. Pour out excess candy then return shell to refrigerator to chill completely. Carefully unmold shells (if you have difficulty removing shells, place pan in freezer for 2 to 3 minutes, then unmold). Smooth top edges by sliding across warmed cookie sheet or warming plate. Excess candy can be reheated and reused.

Candy Shells in Candy Molds

Fill each cavity less than ½ full with melted candy. Using a decorator brush, paint the candy onto the sides of each mold to top edge so that no light can be seen through the shell. Place mold in refrigerator for a few minutes to harden candy shell. Fill candy shell with truffle mixture or favorite candy filling. Seal top with additional melted candy. Refrigerate until firm. Unmold.

Candy Shells in Baking Cups

Spoon or pipe 1 to 2 tablespoons of melted candy into the bottom of a standard baking cup. Brush candy up sides, to desired height, forming an even edge. Chill 5 to 8 minutes. Repeat process if a thicker shell is needed. Chill until firm. Carefully peel baking cup off candy shell.

Covering Cakes and Cookies with Candy Melts Candy or Poured Icings

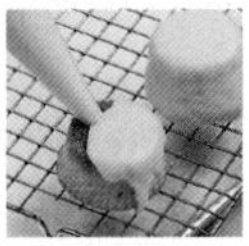

For Candy Melts candy, melt following package directions. For icing recipes, follow recipe directions to reach pouring consistency. For canned icing, heat in microwave at Defrost setting (30% power) for 20 to 30 seconds; stir. Repeat until consistency of icing will pour. Place cooled cakes or cookies on cooling grid positioned over parchment-lined cookie sheet or pan. Pour or pipe candy or icing on center of item, continue covering top so that candy or icing drips down and covers sides. Let dry.

CANDY RECIPES

Candy "Clay"

1 package (12 oz.) Candy Melts Candy (p. 175)
¼ cup light corn syrup

Melt candy following package directions. Add corn syrup and stir to blend. Turn out mixture onto waxed paper and let set at room temperature to dry. Wrap well and store at room temperature until needed. Candy clay handles best if hardened overnight.

To Use: Candy clay will be very hard at the start; knead a small portion at a time until workable. If candy clay gets too soft, set aside at room temperature or refrigerate briefly. When rolling out candy clay, sprinkle work surface with cornstarch or cocoa (for cocoa clay) to prevent sticking. Roll to approximately ⅛ in. thick.

To Tint: White candy clay may be tinted using Candy Color or Icing Color. Knead in color until well blended.

To Store: Prepared candy clay will last for several weeks at room temperature in an airtight container.

Basic Ganache and Truffles

1 package (12 oz.) Candy Melts Candy (p. 175)
⅓ cup heavy whipping cream

Chop candy (you can use a food processor). Heat whipping cream in saucepan just to boiling point. Do not boil. Remove from heat and add chopped candy, stir until smooth and glossy.

Whipped Ganache: Follow recipe above, using ⅔ cup whipping cream. Allow mixture to set and cool to room temperature (mixture will have the consistency of pudding; this may take 1-2 hours). Whip on high speed with an electric mixer until light and soft peaks form.

Truffles: Add 1 tablespoon liqueur for flavor, if desired. Stir until smooth and creamy. Refrigerate until firm. Roll into 1 in. dia. balls. Can be used as center for dipped candies, served plain or rolled in nuts, coconut or cocoa powder. Store truffles in refrigerator up to 3 weeks. Makes about 2 dozen (1 in.) balls.

Ganache Glaze: If mixture is too thick, add 1 to 2 tablespoons whipping cream. Position cake on cooling grid over parchment-lined pan. Pour glaze onto center and work out toward edges.

NOTE: Cake may be iced first in buttercream. Let icing set, then pour on ganache glaze. If cake has a perfect surface, no other icing is needed.

DECORATING TECHNIQUES FOR THE 2013 WILTON YEARBOOK CAKES

We've organized our decorating techniques to make everything easier to find. Special techniques for this book are presented in the same order as our projects, beginning with the Birthday Section projects on page 4 up through our Special Section, ending at page 111.

#1 Candle

(see A Great First Impression Cake, p. 11)

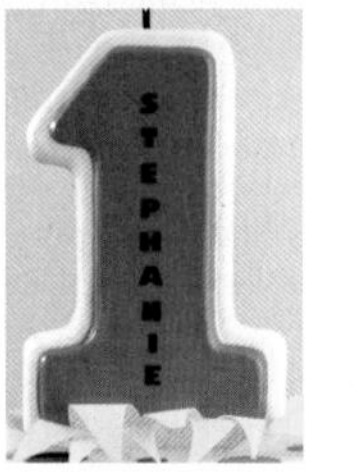

Pour 12 oz. melted red candy into #1 pan. Tap to settle; chill until firm. Fill pan with 24 oz. melted white candy. Tap to settle; chill until firm. Unmold onto soft cloth. Attach edible paper letters with piping gel.

Monkeys

(see Monkey-Go-Round Canopy Cake, p. 12)

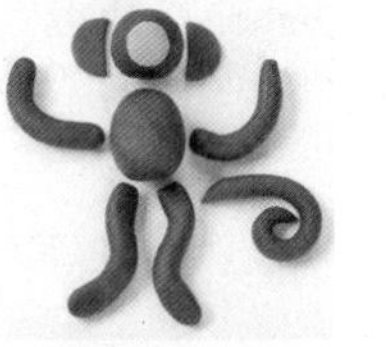

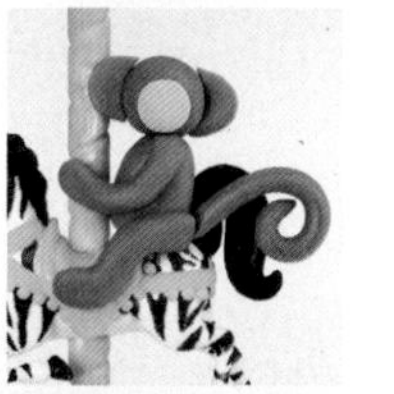

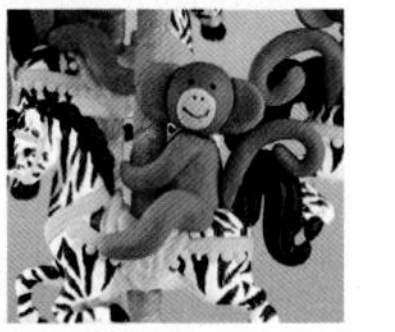

Shape and attach the following features for each monkey in brown fondant with damp brush: ¾ in. x 1 in. torso, ⅝ in. x 1¾ in. legs, ¼ in. x 1½ in. arms, ¼ in. x 2½ in. tail, ¾ in. ball head. For ears, roll out brown fondant ⅛ in. thick. Cut a circle using wide end of tip 2; cut in half and attach. For muzzle, roll out light brown fondant ⅛ in. thick. Cut a circle using narrow end of tip 2A; attach. Draw eyes, nose and mouth with black edible marker.

Dump Truck Candy Plaque

(see Tricked-Out Truck Cake, p. 15)

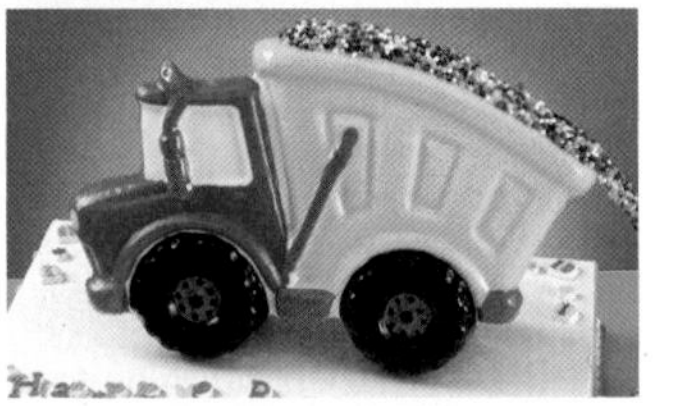

Use candy colors to tint 3 oz. black, 2 oz. gray (use black color), 10 oz. red and 18 oz. yellow. Reserve 9 oz. white. Use piping method to fill in areas of pan; chill until firm after each addition. Pipe gray wheel, rims and white window. Pipe black tires, bolts and axles. Pipe yellow dump bed and red cab. Pipe gray exhaust pipe and dump rod. When completely set, unmold onto soft cloth. Place plaque on parchment paper-covered surface. Pipe white candy on top edge of dump bed; immediately sprinkle with jumbo nonpareils. Let set. Cut two dowel rods to 7½ in. long. Attach to back of plaque, behind wheels, with melted candy, leaving 2 in. extended to insert into cake. For topping stream, slightly curve a lollipop stick and place on waxed paper covered board. Using white candy in cut bag, pipe a ½ in. x 4½ in. curved line over stick. Immediately sprinkle with jumbo nonpareils. Chill until firm.

Make cookies: Prepare and roll out dough. Use boy cutter to cut four kids. Use knife to cut two triangle easels, 1 in. x 2 in., for each cookie. Bake and cool cookies. Decorate on waxed paper-covered boards using royal icing. Use tip 3 to outline and pipe in shirts, pants, and shoes. Pat smooth with finger dipped in cornstarch. Pipe tip 2 zigzag and dot trims on clothes. Pipe tip 2 dot eyes, outline mouths, hair and bows. Let dry. Attach easels to back of cookies with melted candy. Let set.

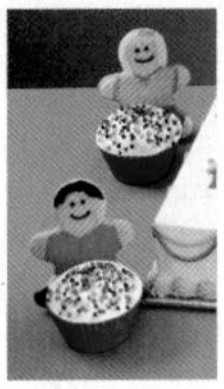

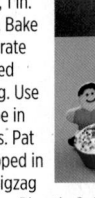

Fondant Trims

(see Frolic in the Flowers Cake, p. 17)

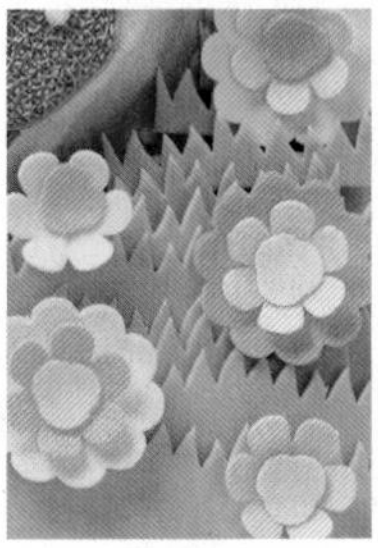

Add 1 teaspoon Gum-Tex to reserved green fondant. Roll out ⅛ in. thick. Cut six strips, 1¾ in. x 13 in. Use border punch with grass insert to cut grass design on one long edge of each strip. Reserve scraps from punch. Let dry on cornstarch-dusted boards. Roll out reserved green fondant ½ in. thick. Use knife to cut 1½ in. wide grass supports: cut six each 2⅞ in., 2¾ in., 2¼ in. and 2 in. high; cut four each 1¾ in., 1½ in., 1¼ in., ¾ in., ½ in. and ¼ in. high. For fantasy flowers, tint fondant: 4 oz. each rose, yellow, orange. Knead ¼ teaspoon Gum-Tex into each. Roll out colors ⅛ in. thick. Use punch with layered flower inserts to cut nine large, 23 medium and 23 small flowers in various colors. Place large flowers in 3 in. forming cup, medium flowers in 2½ in. cup and small flowers in melting plate cavities. Attach flowers in two or three layers with piping gel, combining colors for each; let dry. For clouds, roll out white fondant ⅜ in. thick. Cut three freeform clouds, 2½ in. x 4 in., 2 in. x 3 in. and 1½ in. x 2 in. Let dry on cornstarch-dusted board.

Candy Flower Plaque and Candy Leaves

(see Shading Ladybugs Cake, p. 17)

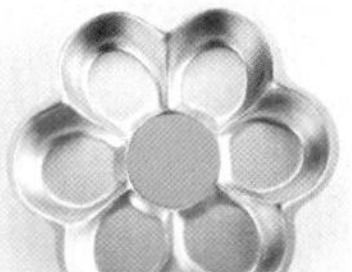

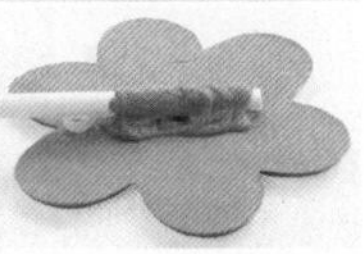

Flower: Pipe melted candy into cake pan using cut parchment bags; chill until firm after each addition. Use yellow candy for center, orange for petals. Chill until firm. Unmold onto soft cloth. Attach plastic dowel rod to back of flower with melted candy, extending 7½ in. at

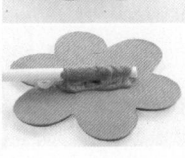

(continued on p. 124)

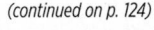

DECORATING TECHNIQUES FOR THE 2013 WILTON YEARBOOK CAKES

(continued from p. 123)

bottom. Position coupler ring as a spacer between extended section of dowel rod and flower to create a slight gap; this will enable you to insert dowel rod in center post on cake without dislodging flower. Chill until firm. Remove coupler ring.

Candy Leaves: Paint melted candy on real lemon leaves for a beautiful natural look that adds to your candy floral creations! The detailed veining gives these leaves an unmatched realism.

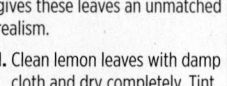
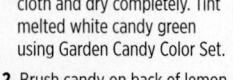
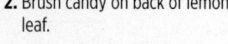

1. Clean lemon leaves with damp cloth and dry completely. Tint melted white candy green using Garden Candy Color Set.
2. Brush candy on back of lemon leaf. 
3. When dry, peel off leaf from candy. 

Candy Television and Game Controller

(see Video Kid Cake, p. 20)

Melt black candy. Mold screen in 9 in. x 13 in. x 2 in. pan. Fill to ⅜ in. deep; tap to settle, chill until firm. Mold candy base in large loaf pan. Fill to ½ in. deep.; tap to settle. Cut hidden pillar to 3 in. long. Stand in candy, centered and 1 in. from long side. Chill until firm. Unmold and remove pillar from candy base, leaving hole for candy pillar support.

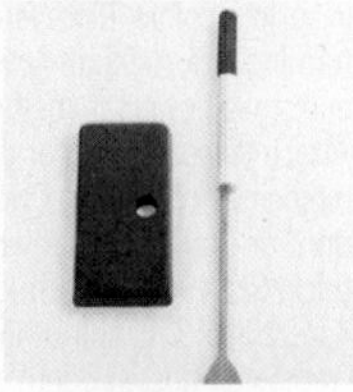

To make candy pillar support, tape a 3 in. pillar length to a full 6 in. pillar with masking tape, creating a 9 in. length. Be sure to line up ridges. Pipe a puddle of candy on waxed paper and stand pillar in puddle. Chill until set. Fill with melted candy using a cut disposable bag. Tap to settle; chill until firm. Using a wooden spoon handle, carefully push candy pillar out of hidden pillar. Attach candy pillar to center back of screen using

melted candy, extending 3 in. beyond bottom of screen. Let set. Insert into candy base, securing with melted candy. Let set.

For screen, place white edible paper over pattern. Use black edible marker to trace design. Paint details using edible colors (add white for lighter shades). Brush screen with piping gel and attach paper

Mold controller using geometric cutter from classic set. Place cutter on non-stick pan; fill to ⅜ in. deep. Tap to settle, chill until firm. Bring to room temperature and cut shape horizontally in half. Attach two lollipop sticks with melted candy to back of pointed ends, extending 3 in. to insert into cake.

Dragon Cookies

(see Camelot Cake and Cookies, p. 22)

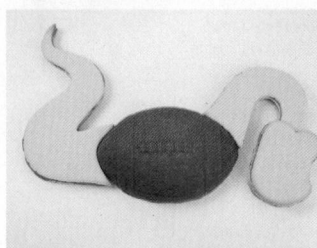

Stack tail and head/neck cookies with icing; attach single head. Position all cookies except legs on prepared base board. Use tip 4 to pipe in mouth; pat smooth with finger dipped in cornstarch. Pipe in tip 2 teeth; pat smooth. Use tip 4 to outline stomach and neck sections, spacing sections 1 in. apart on stomach area, ¾ in. apart on neck. Pipe in sections with tip 16 stars. Cover tail, back and top of neck with tip 104 ruffle scales. Pipe tip 12 ball eyes; pat smooth. Pipe tip 3 dot pupils; pat smooth. Ice nostril area smooth. Use tip 12 to outline, building up nostrils and eyebrows for dimension. Cover head with tip 16 stars. Use tip 4 to outline feet; fill in with tip 16 stars. Cover top of legs with tip 104 ruffle scales. Position leg cookies.

Clouds

(see Buzz's Blastoff Cake, p. 29)

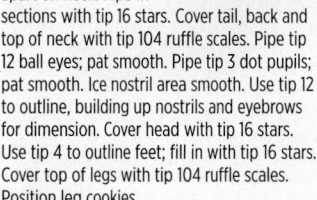

Spray outside pan from bottom of arms and down sides with non-stick spray. Prepare cereal treat mixture; mold into cloud shapes on parchment-covered board. Immediately press cloud shapes against sprayed area of pan to cover an area 5 in. x 18 in. and 2½ in. thick, tapering to ¼ in. wide. Let cool. Roll out white fondant ⅛ in. thick; cut a 22 in. x 6½ in. strip; cover clouds, shaping over raised areas with fingers and trimming as needed. Let set. Slide pan away and remove clouds.

Spidey

(see Hanging with Spider-Man Cake, p. 37)

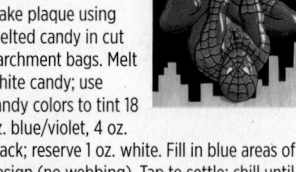

Make plaque using melted candy in cut parchment bags. Melt white candy; use candy colors to tint 18 oz. blue/violet, 4 oz. black; reserve 1 oz. white. Fill in blue areas of design (no webbing). Tap to settle; chill until firm. Fill in whites of eyes and black spider on chest; chill until firm. Melt red candy; fill in plaque to ¾ in. deep. Tap to settle; chill until firm. Unmold onto waxed paper-covered board. Use melted black candy and tip 2 to pipe webbing and figure details. Chill until firm.

Fondant Features

(see The Departed Has Arrived Cake, p. 42)

Tint fondant as follows: 1 oz. marbleized with ivory and 1½ oz. black. Reserve 14 oz. white fondant. Make the following fondant trims and attach with icing: For eyes, roll two 1 oz. balls of ivory marbleized fondant. Roll out white fondant 1/16 in. thick. Use pattern to cut eyelids. Roll out black fondant 1/16 in. thick. Use pattern to cut mouth.

For eyebrows, roll two 2½ in. x ½ in. dia. ropes of black fondant. For lips, roll two 5 in. x ¼ in. dia. ropes of white fondant. Score lines with knife. Roll out white fondant ⅛ in. thick. Using knife, cut triangles for teeth from 5/16 in. to 1 in. long. Roll a 1½ in. ball of white fondant and shape into nose. For nostrils, roll black fondant 1/16 in. thick. Using small end of tip 2A, cut one circle. Cut circle in half; attach nostrils with damp brush. Reserve remaining black fondant.

Zombie Arms

(see Knife of the Party Cupcake Display, p. 43)

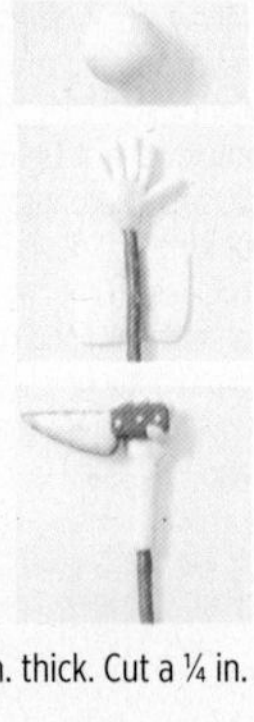

For hand, roll a ⅝ in. ball of fondant. Flatten top half; wrap bottom half around tip of pretzel stick. Taper and smooth around stick with fingers; rounded top should extend 1 in. from tip of stick. Use scissors to cut ⅝ in. slits for fingers. Smooth fingertips with fingers. For arm portion, roll out fondant ⅛ in. thick. Cut a ¼ in. square.

Brush square with piping gel; wrap around pretzel stick or a 3 in. lollipop stick for topper left arm. Smooth seams with fingers. Wrap fingers around knife icing decorations. Let dry.

Remove icing decorations. In candy melting plate, combine White-White with Black icing color and lemon extract to make light gray. Brush on arms. Let dry overnight.

Fondant Trims

(see Yule Jewel Gingerbread House, p. 56)

Mold trims using jewelry mold as follows. Mold two brooches. Paint center with lilac purple Pearl Dust/lemon extract mixture (p. 118), border with silver Pearl Dust/lemon extract mixture. Mold 24 faceted gems. Paint with orchid pink Pearl Dust/lemon extract

mixture. Mold 24 faceted gem bases. Paint with silver Pearl Dust/lemon extract mixture. Mold 129 square gems. Paint with Pearl Dust/lemon extract mixture: 71 leaf green, 27 lilac purple, 31 orchid pink. Make 89 square gem bases. Paint with silver Pearl Dust/lemon extract mixture. Attach 36 green and 4 pink square gems to trees with thinned fondant adhesive. Attach remaining gems to bases. Mold 213 round gems. Paint with white Pearl Dust/lemon extract mixture. Mold ten square chain borders. Trim eight to 6½ in. long. Cut remaining two strips into 2 in. long sections. Paint with silver Pearl Dust/lemon extract mixture. Mold three chain link borders. Trim to make five strips 1½ in. long; one strip 2 in. long; two strips 2¾ in. long. Paint with silver Pearl Dust/lemon extract mixture.

Box Lid

(see Heart Full of Love Candy Box, p. 59)

You can use pans as candy molds to make solid decorative plaques. If your pan has detail, it may be painted or filled in desired colors as you would for any candy mold.

Pour melted candy into center of pan cavity. Tap pan gently on counter to eliminate bubbles. Candy should be ¼ to ¾ in. thick, depending on project instructions. Place pan in refrigerator for about 30 to 40 minutes until firm (check occasionally; if candy becomes too chilled, it may crack). Unmold onto hand or soft towel (tap gently if necessary).

Fondant Trims

(see On-Time Arrival Cake, p. 70)

Tint fondant: 4 oz. each brown, skintone; 3 oz. light green; 2 oz. each light blue, pink, yellow, 1 oz. violet; reserve remaining white. Roll out ⅛ in. thick unless otherwise specified. Attach pieces using a damp brush unless otherwise specified. Let dry on cornstarch-dusted, waxed paper-covered boards.

Blocks: Add ¼ teaspoon Gum-Tex to 2¼ oz. white fondant. Roll out. Cut 30 squares, 1 in. Let dry 24 hours. Assemble into blocks, using five squares per block (bottoms are open) and attaching edges with melted candy. Roll out fondant colors 1/16 in. thick. Cut strips, ¼ in. x 1 in.; attach for borders, trimming as needed. Cut letters using alphabet Cut-Outs; attach.

Banner: Roll out violet. Cut a 1 in. x 6 in. long strip. Trim ends at an angle. Print message with black edible marker. Let dry 24 hours on crumpled facial tissues to create wavy effect. Attach two lollipop sticks to back using melted candy, leaving 3 in. extended at left side to insert into cake.

Bear: Add ¼ teaspoon Gum-Tex to brown fondant. Roll a 1¼ in. dia. ball for head. Roll and flatten small balls for ¾ in. wide oval muzzle and ½ in. dia. ears (indent with end of brush); attach. Use black

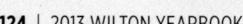

FoodWriter to draw eyes, nose and mouth. Shape a ¼ in. x 1½ in. high tapered oval for body. Roll two tapered logs for arms, ½ in. dia. x 2 in. long; flatten hand slightly and cut slit for thumbs. Roll a log for legs, ¾ in. dia. x 3 in. long; flatten ends for feet. Wrap around bottom of body, positioning one leg on each side and securing at center back. Assemble bear.

Baby: Prepare globe base (p. 119). Roll out skin tone fondant ⅛ in. thick. Cut a 6 in. dia. circle. Wrap globe, smoothing with hands. Trim away excess. Draw eyes and 1¾ in. wide smile with black edible marker. Roll two logs for arms, ½ in. dia. x 3 in. long. Slightly flatten hand end and cut slits for fingers. For raised arm, insert a 6 in. lollipop stick 2½ in. deep. Curve fingers slightly. Slightly curve opposite arm.

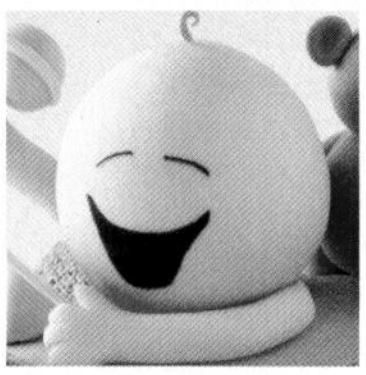

Rattle: Using light green fondant, roll a ¾ in. ball for top, ½ in. flattened disk for handle, ⅛ in. diam. x ¾ in. long log for stem. Cut hole in center of handle using narrow end of tip 10. Cut ⅛ in. wide yellow strips to trim ball and a 1/16 in. wide strip for handle trim. Attach pieces with melted candy.

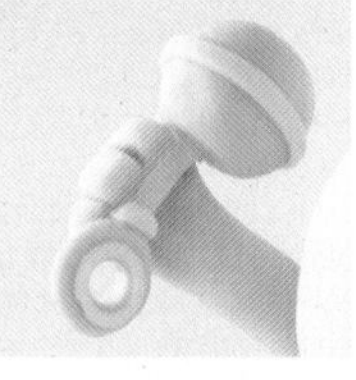

Propeller: Roll out yellow fondant. Cut four blades using medium oval Cut-Out. Arrange on board. Cut large circle for axle using smallest round Cut-Out; attach. Cut circle for axle cap using narrow end of tip 2A; attach with thinned fondant adhesive.

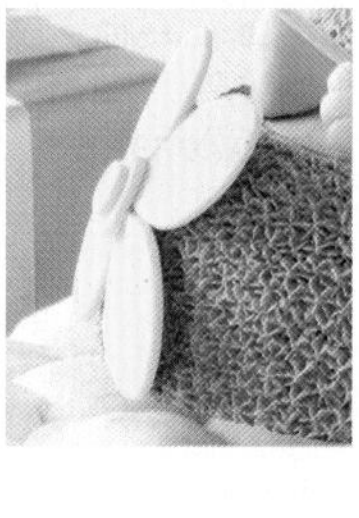

Steering Wheel: Roll out green fondant. Cut wheel using medium round Cut-Out. Roll a 1 in. ball for base; flatten bottom and shape a 1 in. high angled base. Attach wheel.

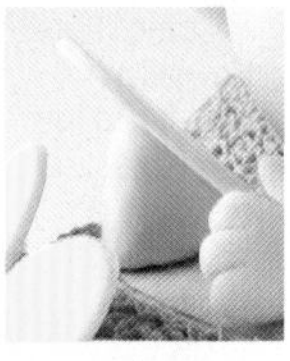

Stars: Roll out green, pink and yellow fondant. Cut five stars in each color, varying sizes by using large or medium star Cut-Outs. Brush with matching Pearl Dust (p. 118).

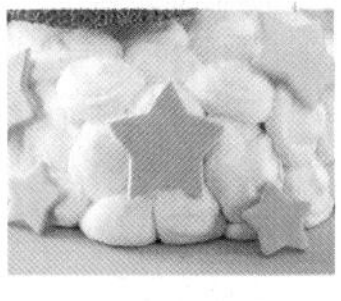

Baby Topper & Cupped Flowers

(see Our Garden Girl Cake, p. 71)

Baby Topper:
Tint fondant: 8 oz. skin tone; ⅛ oz. black; reserve small amount of white. Roll out ⅛ in. thick as needed. Prepare globe pillar (p. 119). Cut a 6 in. dia circle to cover head, a 2½ in. x 8 in. strip to cover top of body. Brush globes with piping gel and wrap with fondant, using hands to smooth. Use knife to cut away fondant from open holes. Cut a 1½ in. x 8½ in. white strip; attach for diaper using damp brush. Cut pillar to 4½ in. long. Slide globes onto pillar. For arms, roll ⅝ in. dia.x 3 in. long logs; flatten end of hands and cut slits for fingers. Attach with piping gel. For ears, roll out some skin tone fondant; cut two circles using wide end of tip 3. Trim off ⅓; shape and attach to head. Roll tiny ball nose; attach. Roll and flatten small balls for cheeks; attach. Roll thin logs for eyes and smile; attach. For feet, shape two ovals ¾ in. wide x 1½ in. long x 1¼ in. thick. Flatten and taper; attach with piping gel. Roll and attach tiny ball toes in graduated sizes. Let dry. For yellow hair curl, roll a ⅛ in. dia. x 1¾ in. long log. Shape into curl and let dry flat. For bow, cut a ½ in. x 3½ in. strip. Fold ends to center to form loops and attach using damp brush. For knot, cut a ¼ in. x 1 in. strip. Wrap around center; secure with damp brush. Let dry on side. Reserve excess fondant.

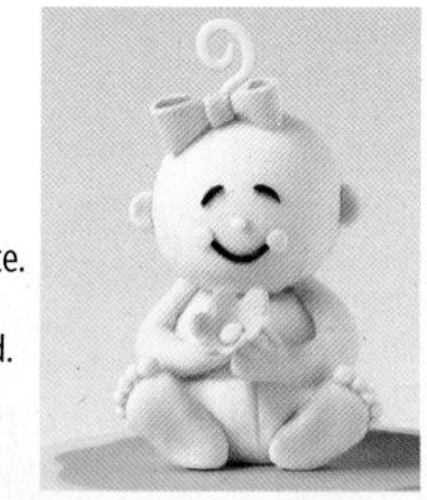

Cupped Flowers:
Tint fondant: 1 oz. blue, 1¼ oz. yellow; 1½ oz. orange; 1½ oz. rose. Roll out ⅛ in. thick as needed. For cupped flowers, use medium Cut-Out to cut one pink, three blue and four yellow. Place on thick shaping foam and cup using small ball tool from set. Let dry in cornstarch-dusted melting plate. For centers, roll ¼ in. dia. fondant balls in contrasting colors. Attach with piping gel. After assembled on cake, attach prepared cupped flower, curl and bow.

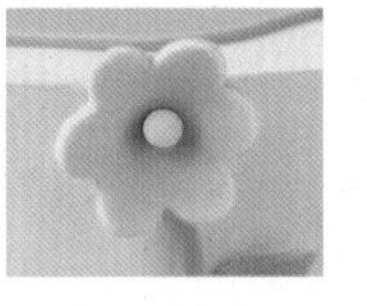

Pea Pods

(see Pea Wee Candies, p. 72)

Roll two green logs, 3/16 in. dia. x 1¼ in. long; curl one log for stem, wrap the other around lollipop stick for tendril. Let dry on cornstarch-dusted board. Shape two green cones, 1¼ in. long x 1 in. wide, for each treat. Attach to ends of dessert shell with piping gel, shaping into an upward curve. Roll out remaining green fondant ⅛ in. thick. Use pattern and knife to cut peapod. Position dessert shell at center of fondant; brush outside of shell with piping gel. Pull fondant up and over sides of shell; trim as needed. Cut a ⅝ in. slit on each end; gently pinch and separate. Attach tendril and stem with melted green candy.

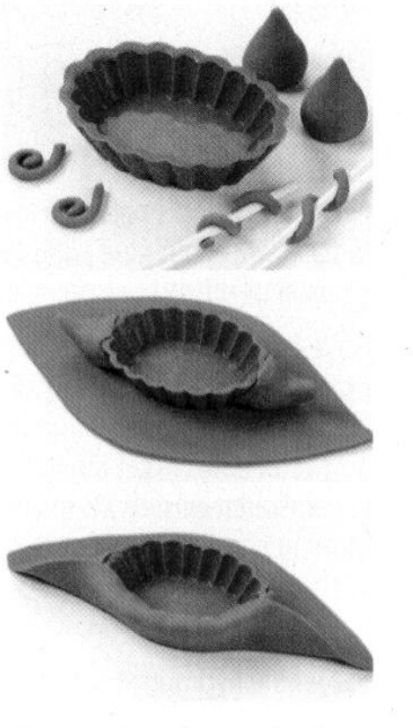

Oval Topper with Lace Points

(see Pure Grace Cake, p. 75)

Tape oval pattern to cake board; cover with waxed paper. Outline with tip 2 and full-strength color flow; let set. Flow in with thinned color flow. Let dry 24 hours. Decorate remaining details and lace points with full-strength color flow. Pipe tip 2 initial; let dry 24 hours. To make 25 lace points, tape pattern to cake board; cover with waxed paper. Spray with vegetable pan spray to help pieces release when dry; wipe lightly with tissue. Outline pattern with tip 2. Pipe tip 2 dots on extended pattern lines. Make extras to allow for breakage and let dry 24 hours. Make a hole in craft block with cookie stick. Peel off waxed paper from oval and attach stick to back, leaving 5 in. extended at bottom. Let dry. Insert topper in craft block. Attach 2 to 3 lace points at a time. Pipe a tip 2 line of icing on edge of oval; position lace points. Continue attaching lace points around entire oval. Overpipe edge of oval with tip 2 beads. Let dry 24 hours.

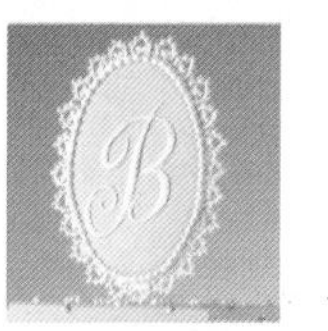

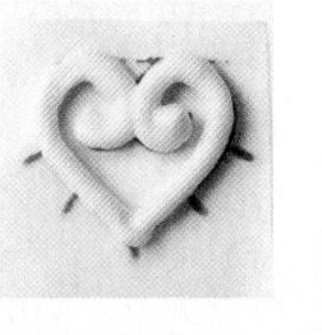

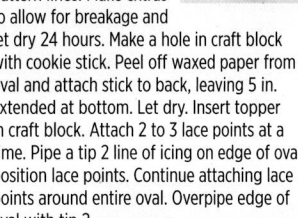

Triangles

(Wrap Up The Future Cake, p. 79)

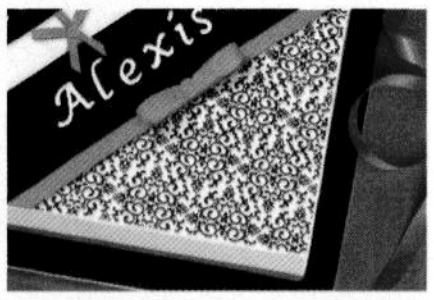

Cut two triangles from damask edible paper using rotary cutter and pattern. Trim 1 in. off long edge of one sheet of black edible paper. Position a whole black sheet and the cut black sheet side by side on cake top. Position damask triangles at top left and bottom right corners of cake top.

Cornelli Lace-Look Ruffle

(see Ruffled in Romance Cake, p. 83)

Pipe tip 45 cornelli lace-look ruffle in white buttercream, holding narrow edge of tip against cake with remainder of tip upright from cake side.

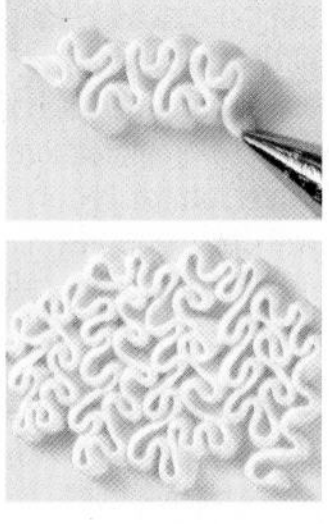

Lattice Petals

(see Daisy Lattice Cake, p. 85)

1. Starting in the center of the petal, pipe tip 1 diagonal strings in royal icing, ⅛ in. apart.
2. From the opposite side, pipe tip 1 diagonal strings in the other direction, ⅛ in. apart, covering the area.
3. Outline the petal with tip 1.

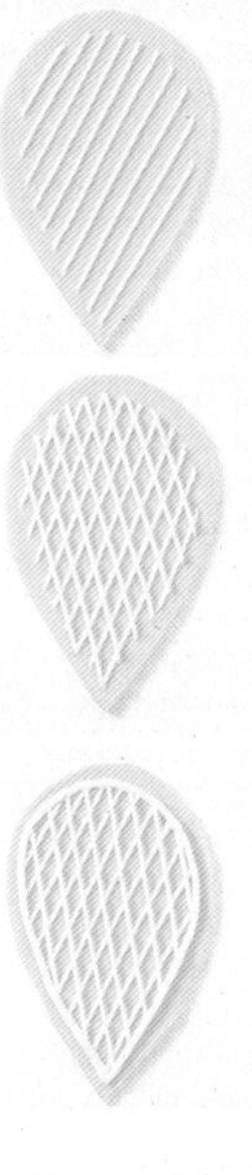

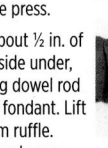

Clam Shell

(see Coral Reef-ined Cake, p. 85)

Add 1 teaspoon Gum-Tex to 5 oz. white fondant. Tint very light ivory; add a few dots of aster mauve and gently knead to marbleize with a streaked look. Roll out ⅛ in. thick. Cut two circles using large circle cutter. Cut a straight edge on each circle ½ in. from end. Mark center of straight edge 2¾ in. wide. Cut angles from markings 1½ in. long, to taper sides upward for fan shape. Shape shell pieces on thin foam with narrow veining tool, starting on straight edge and fanning outward. Let dry on outside of sports ball pan half dusted with cornstarch, veined side up. Paint shell halves with white Pearl Dust/lemon extract mixture (p. 118).

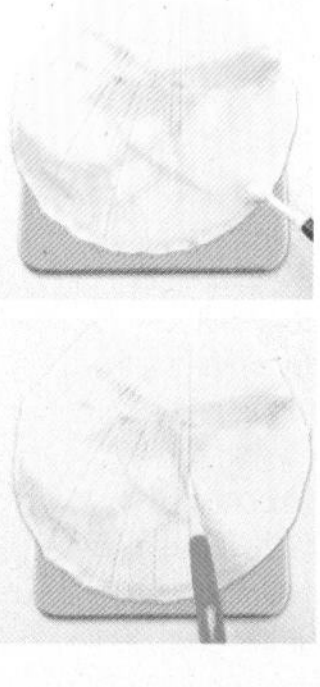

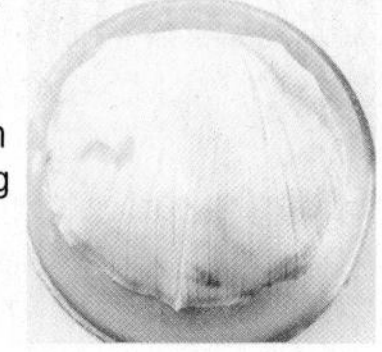

Fondant Ruffle Strips

(see We Are Gathered Here Cake, p. 87)

Cut strips following dimensions in project instructions. Imprint using texture press.

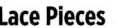

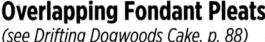

Roll about ½ in. of short side under, placing dowel rod under fondant. Lift to form ruffle. Pleat and press opposite edge down to secure.

Place dowel rod ¾ in. from first ruffle. Lift, pleat and press to form second ruffle. Continue lifting, pleating and pressing to end of strip. Roll end under and press to secure.

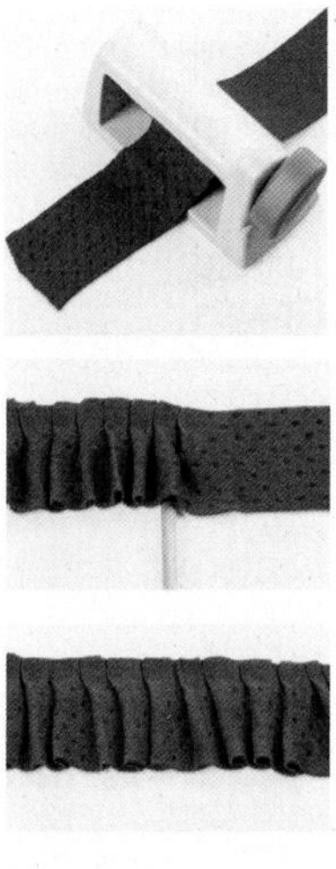

Lace Pieces

(see Lace Embrace p. 88)

Copy half-circle patterns and tape to cake boards. Cover with waxed paper; lightly spray with pan spray and wipe with tissue. Using tip 1 and royal icing, outline half circles and scrolls inside patterns, making sure scrolls touch and reach outside edge. Pipe tip 1 bead border over curved outside edge.

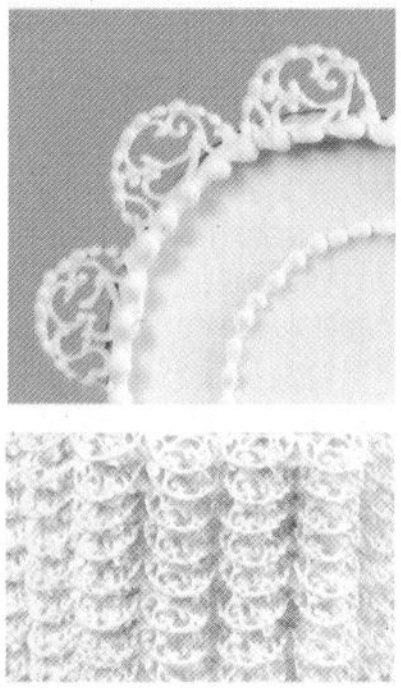

Overlapping Fondant Pleats

(see Drifting Dogwoods Cake, p. 88)

Roll out fondant 3/16 in. thick. Use pattern and fondant trimmer to cut 46 notched pleats (27 for 8 in. cake, 19 for 6 in. cake).

Fold notched side over ¾ in. Trim at point as needed.

Attach first pleat to 8 in. cake, with pointed end overlapping top, pointing toward center. Continue to attach pleats in overlapping fashion with damp brush, starting 1 in. from left edge of previous pleat. Complete 8 in. cake, then stack 6 in. cake on top and pleat as above.

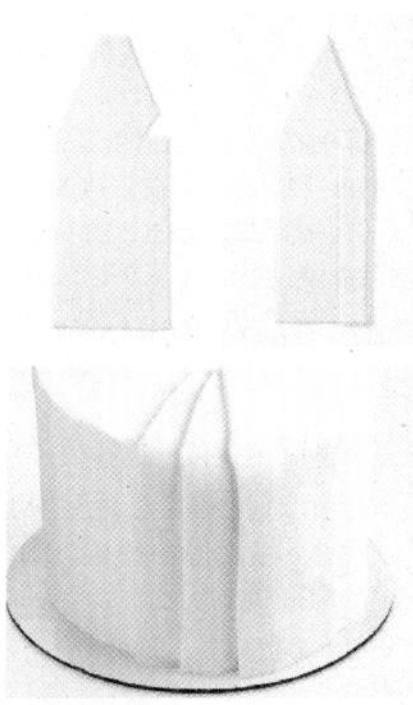

DECORATING TECHNIQUES FOR THE 2013 WILTON YEARBOOK CAKES

Sponging on Fondant

(see A Moveable Meadow Cake, p. 89)

Thin buttercream icing. Dampen a new sponge and lightly dip into icing. Using a quick pulling motion, blot icing on cake surface to produce a spackled effect. Different spackled effects can be achieved using crushed waxed paper or paper towel.

Fantasy Flowers

(see Cascade of Cupcakes, p. 90)

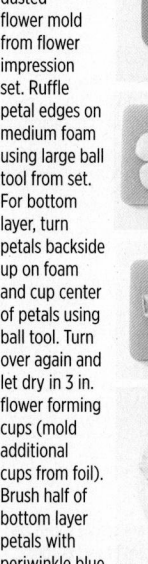

Roll out gum paste 1/16 in. thick. Cut two petal sets for each flower using large rose cutter from set. Imprint details on cornstarch-dusted flower mold from flower impression set. Ruffle petal edges on medium foam using large ball tool from set. For bottom layer, turn petals backside up on foam and cup center of petals using ball tool. Turn over again and let dry in 3 in. flower forming cups (mold additional cups from foil). Brush half of bottom layer petals with periwinkle blue, half with purple Color Dust. For top layer, ruffle petal edges as above. Brush top layer of petals with Color Dust. Place front side up on thick foam; cup centers and attach to bottom layer petals with gum glue adhesive. For centers, press a 3/8 in. gum paste ball in daisy center mold of flower impression set. Dust with goldenrod Color Dust and attach to flower with gum glue adhesive. Let dry.

Gum Paste Fantasy Flower Topper

(see Petal Impressions Cake, p. 95)

Tint gum paste: 4 oz. red, 1/2 oz. yellow. Roll out red 1/16 in. thick as needed. Use pattern to cut five large petals; use large ball tool and medium shaping foam to ruffle edges. Use small rose cutter from gum paste flower cutter set to cut

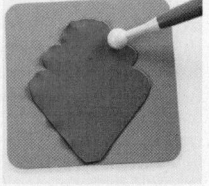

base. Dust inside of 3-D Sports Ball pan half with cornstarch. Position base in center. Center one large petal over one section of base; secure with fondant adhesive. Attach remaining large petals, overlapping edges slightly as you go. For smaller inner flower, follow steps above using orchid throat cutter to cut five petals and small calyx to cut base. Attach inside large flower, using pieces of tissue to lift and support petals. Use yellow gum paste and flower impression set to mold dogwood center; attach. Let dry 48 hours. Paint flower with red Color Dust/lemon extract mixture (p. 118); dust center with goldenrod Color Dust.

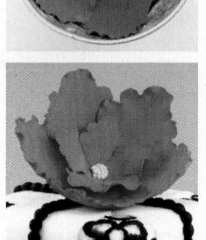

Diamond Ring Topper

(see Bring On The Bling Cake, p. 96)

For band, roll out gum paste 3/8 in. thick. Cut a strip 7/8 in. x 16 in. Shape into a circle, attaching ends with gum glue adhesive. Let dry on cut side on cornstarch-dusted board. For scrolls, roll out gum paste 1/8 in. thick. Cut two strips, 1/2 in x 5 in. Lay on cut side on scroll patterns. Roll out remaining gum paste 1/16 in. thick. For prongs, cut four strips, 3/8 in. x 2 1/8 in. Let dry on large side of wave flower former. For diamond, use pattern to cut four triangle bottoms, four trapezoid sides and one square top. Let dry 1 day. Chill pieces before attaching as follows with melted candy: Attach edges of triangles to form a 3-D pyramid; chill until firm. Attach wide edges of trapezoids to flat edges at bottom of pyramid; chill. Attach square top; chill. Overpipe seams with tip 1 and melted candy. Mix crushed white Cake Sparkles with white Pearl

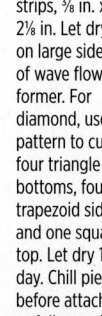

Dust. Brush diamond with piping gel; cover with mixture. Paint remaining ring pieces with gold Pearl Dust/lemon extract mixture (p. 118). Attach scrolls to band and prongs to diamond corners with melted candy. Attach diamond to top of ring. Let dry. For cake topper base, mold a black candy disk, 1/4 in. thick, using second smallest circle cutter on non-stick cookie sheet; chill until firm. Attach to topper with melted candy; chill.

Cascading Flowers

(see Golden Garden Cake, p. 97)

For all flowers, roll out gum paste 1/16 in. thick as needed. Cut pieces using cutters from Gum Paste/Fondant Cutter Set.

Make two large flowers. Cut a base using large rose cutter. Cut five petals using small calla lily cutter; attach to base with gum glue adhesive. Let dry in cornstarch-dusted ball pan half.

Make 13 fantasy flowers using various petal combinations cut with small and large rose, hydrangea, large blossom and dogwood cutters. Let individual pieces dry in cornstarch-dusted 2 1/2 in. and 3 in. flower forming cups. When dry, attach petals in two or three layers for each flower with thinned fondant adhesive.

Make nine hydrangeas, nine large blossoms, nine large rose leaves and 10 hydrangea leaves. Vein some leaves with veining tool on thin foam. Let pieces dry at least two days on wave flower formers.

Jumbo Gum Paste Roses

(see Corsage Colorama Cake, p. 100)

For rose bases, prepare cereal treat mixture. Make three cones: 2 in. dia. (at base) x 2 1/2 in. high. Brush bottoms with melted candy; let set on waxed paper-covered board. Brush tops with melted candy to seal completely; chill until firm.

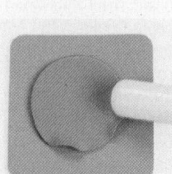

Divide gum paste and tint 10 oz. each: yellow, orange, pink. Roll out 1/16 in. thick as needed.

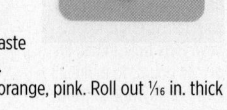

For rosebud and first petal row, cut three petals using smallest circle cutter from set. Soften outer edges by setting petal on medium shaping foam and rolling with 9 in. fondant roller. Brush bottom of one petal with gum glue adhesive and wrap around tip of cone to form bud. Attach two remaining petals, overlapping slightly, to complete first row.

For second row, cut five petals using smallest circle cutter. Soften edges and attach as above. For third row, cut five petals using second smallest circle cutter. Soften edges then shape over outside of mini ball pan; let set for 5 minutes, then attach. Repeat for fourth row, cutting six petals with second smallest cutter; attach.

For each rose, cut a 2 1/2 in. dia. circle out of bottom of a foam bowl. Insert rose base through hole in bowl to support your rose petals. Place bowl with rose into an uncut bowl. Support with facial tissue as needed. Let dry 48 hours.

Dimensional Petals

(see Floral Origami Cake, p. 106)

Roll out fondant 1/16 in. thick, working one portion at a time. Cut circles using metal cutter. Place circles under storage board flap until ready to use. Divide circle into 3 sections; indent triangle shape on each circle 5/8 in. in from edge with plastic ruler. Fold circle edges up to form triangle.

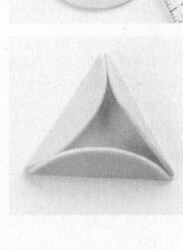

Topper

(see Drapes Take Shape! Cake, p. 107)

For top section, cover top hole of one globe with a 2 in. circle of fondant. Roll out fondant 1/16 in. thick. Imprint design using Graceful Vines Mat. Use pattern to cut eight small petals. Starting at bottom center, use piping gel to attach petals to globe, alternating points up, then down. Trim excess as needed.

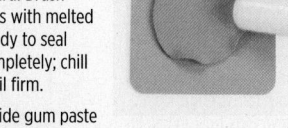

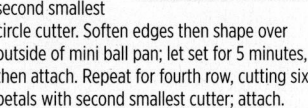

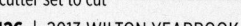

For topper base, prepare cereal treat mixture. Press into both halves of lightly greased sports ball pan. Insert 9 in. pillar from globe set through center of one half to meet bottom of pan. Use end of same pillar to mark center opening on other half; cut out treat mixture from center. Spread melted candy over top of half with pillar. Immediately unmold other half and insert over pillar, securing halves together and reshaping as needed. Let set then unmold. Use pastry brush to coat ball and 1¾ in. of pillar with melted candy for a smooth surface. Let set. Use fondant to build up and taper up to 1¾ in. of pillar. Position top section on pillar, securing with melted candy. Let set.

Roll out fondant ¹⁄₁₆ in. thick and imprint design using mat as above. Use pattern to cut seven large petals. Starting at bottom center, attach to base and pillar with piping gel, overlapping slightly. Use melted candy to attach to cake circle cut to 4 in. dia. Use icing and tip 2 to pipe over imprinted designs.

Perfume Bottle Topper

(see Eau De La Torte Cake, p. 104)

Make two candy shells (p. 123), ¼ in. thick, in ball pan halves. Heat tip of knife and cut opening in top center of one shell, ¼ in. dia. Flatten bottom of second shell by running over warm pan. Run edges of shells over warm pan and assemble halves with melted candy. Make bottle trims using white fondant. Use jewelry mold to make three square chain borders. Attach border strips over center seam with piping gel; trim as needed. Use folk mold to make one large heart. Attach heart to border strip.

For handle, roll out fondant ⅛ in. thick. Cut circle using second largest cutter. Use folk mold to make one large medallion. Attach medallion to center of fondant circle with piping gel. Let dry. Trim dowel rod to 9 in. Use jewelry mold to make an additional square chain border. Trim border to 1 in. and attach around dowel rod, 3 in. from end, with melted candy. Use jewelry mold to make 19 round gems. Attach to edge of circle with piping gel.

Attach circle to 3 in. area above dowel rod with melted candy. Paint topper and handle with gold Pearl Dust/lemon extract mixture (p. 118); let dry.

Fondant Bows

(see Eau De La Torte Cake, p. 104 and Loopside Down Cake, p. 105)

Cut strips for bow loops and streamers (if needed), using dimensions listed in project instructions. Your bow may use more loops than shown here or it may omit the center knot. Set streamers aside on cornstarch-dusted waxed paper. Fold strips over to form loops. Brush ends lightly with damp brush. Align ends and pinch slightly to secure. Support loops with crushed facial tissue. Let dry. Cut strip for knot, if needed, following dimensions in project instructions. Wrap strip around the ends of two loops to create knot look, attaching with damp brush. Attach streamers following project instructions.

Feather Topper

(see Flowing Feathers Cake, p. 108)

Knead 1 teaspoon Gum-Tex into 8 oz. fondant. Tint dark blue. Roll out ¹⁄₁₆ in. thick. Use topper patterns to cut out one large and two curved feathers. Use small veining tool to score center vein and pull out side veins, curving some downward. Use quilting/cutting wheel to cut slightly curved v-shaped feathers on each side. Attach lollipop stick to back of each feather with melted candy in a cut parchment bag, extending 3 in. at bottom to insert in cake. Chill until firm. Brush feathers with sapphire blue Pearl Dust. Gently shape feathers with fingers for a natural look (gently curve lollipop sticks for curved feathers). Let dry upright in craft block.

Gum Paste Pleats

(see Ribbon Roses Grow Wild! Cake, p. 109)

Cut 20 thin cardboard forms, 5 in. x 8 in. long. Fold in half length wise. Cut 20 spacers 1 in. x 3½ in., tape to bottom edges of form to hold angle. Tint remaining gum paste violet. Roll out ¹⁄₁₆ in. thick. Use pattern to cut 20 pleats; make extras to allow for breakage. Fold gently and position on drying forms; let dry 24 hours.

ROLLED FONDANT AND GUM PASTE RECIPES

Fondant is rolled out and used as a covering for any firm-textured cake, pound cake or fruit cake, which is first covered with a light layer of buttercream icing to help fondant adhere to the cake. Apricot glaze may also be used. Cakes covered with rolled fondant can be decorated with royal or buttercream icing. Wilton also offers convenient Rolled Fondant and Gum Paste (p. 148). It's ready to use, with no mixing.

Rolled Fondant

1 tablespoon plus 2 teaspoons unflavored gelatin
¼ cup cold water
½ cup Glucose (p. 148)
2 tablespoons solid vegetable shortening
1 tablespoon Glycerin (p. 139)
Icing color and flavoring, as desired
8 cups sifted confectioners' sugar (about 2 lbs.)

Combine gelatin and cold water; let stand until thick. Place gelatin mixture in top of double boiler and heat until dissolved. Add glucose, mix well. Stir in shortening and just before completely melted, remove from heat. Add glycerin, flavoring and color. Cool until lukewarm. Next, place 4 cups confectioners' sugar in a bowl and make a well. Pour the lukewarm gelatin mixture into the well and stir with a wooden spoon, mixing in sugar and adding more, a little at a time, until stickiness disappears. Knead in remaining sugar. Knead until the fondant is smooth, pliable and does not stick to your hands. If fondant is too soft, add more sugar; if too stiff, add water (a drop at a time). Use fondant immediately or store in airtight container in a cool, dry place. Do not refrigerate or freeze. When ready to use, knead again until soft. This recipe makes approx. 36 oz., enough to cover a 10 x 4 in. round cake.

Chocolate Fondant

1 package (12 oz.) Dark Cocoa Candy Melts Candy (p. 175)
⅓ cup light corn syrup
24 oz. White Ready-To-Use Rolled Fondant (p. 148)
Brown or Black Icing Color (p. 139, optional)

Melt Candy Melts candy following package directions. Add corn syrup; stir to blend. Turn out mixture onto waxed paper; let stand at room temperature to dry and harden several hours. Wrap well and store at room temperature until ready to continue with recipe.

Knead small portions of candy mixture until soft and pliable. Knead softened mixture into fondant until smooth and evenly colored. If darker color is desired, knead in icing color.

Extra-Firm Rolled Fondant

Use this recipe for a fondant with the extra body and pliability ideal for making drapes, swags and elaborate decorations.

1 to 2 teaspoons Gum-Tex (p. 148)
24 oz. Ready-To-Use Rolled Fondant (p. 148)

Knead Gum-Tex into fondant until smooth. Store in an airtight container or tightly wrapped in plastic.

Apricot Glaze

Ideal for preparing a cake for fondant or for crumb-coating cakes before icing.

1 cup apricot preserves

Heat preserves to boiling, strain. Brush on cake while glaze is still hot. Let dry. Glaze will dry to a hard finish in 15 minutes or less. Makes enough to cover a 10 in. x 4 in. cake.

Thinned Fondant Adhesive

Use this mixture when attaching dried fondant to other fondant decorations or for attaching freshly cut fondant pieces to lollipop sticks or florist wire.

1 oz. Ready-To-Use Rolled Fondant (p. 148) (1½ in. ball)
¼ teaspoon water

Knead water into fondant until it becomes soft and sticky. To attach a fondant decoration, place mixture in decorating bag fitted with a small round tip, or brush on back of decoration. Recipe may be doubled.

Quick-Pour Fondant Icing

6 cups sifted confectioners' sugar (about 1½ lbs.)
½ cup water
2 tablespoons light corn syrup
1 teaspoon Wilton Imitation Almond Extract (p. 141)
Wilton Icing Colors (p. 139)

Cakes should be covered with apricot glaze (see recipe) or a thin coating of buttercream icing. Let set 15 minutes before covering with fondant.

Place sugar in saucepan. Combine water and corn syrup. Add to sugar and stir until well mixed. Place over low heat. Don't allow temperature to exceed 100°F. Remove from heat, stir in flavor and icing color. To cover, place cake or cookies on cooling grid over a drip pan. Pour fondant into center and work towards edges. Touch up bare spots with spatula. Let set. Excess fondant can be reheated. Makes about 2½ cups.

Gum Paste

Clay-like gum paste can be rolled thinner than fondant for finer detail. Gum paste dries hard and is meant for decoration only; remove from cake before serving.

1 tablespoon Gum-Tex (p. 148)
3 cups sifted confectioners' sugar (about ¾ lb.)
1 heaping tablespoon Glucose (p. 148)
4 tablespoons warm water
1 cup sifted confectioners' sugar (save until ready to use)

In a large bowl, mix Gum-Tex into 3 cups confectioners' sugar. Make a well in the center and set aside. Mix water and glucose in a glass measuring cup and blend; heat in microwave on high for about 30 seconds until mixture is clear. Pour into well of 3 cups confectioners' sugar and mix until well blended (mixture will be very soft). Place mixture in a plastic bag and seal tightly; let mixture rest at room temperature for 8 hours or overnight. Knead remaining confectioners' sugar into gum paste when you are ready to use it. As you work it in, gum paste will whiten and soften.

Gum Glue Adhesive

This easy-to-make mixture is used to attach gum paste decorations to each other. Just brush it on to your decorations. To make, break ¼ teaspoon of gum paste into very small pieces. Dissolve pieces in 1 tablespoon water. Let rest about 1 hour. Mixture will be ready to use even if some pieces have not dissolved. Store unused portions covered in the refrigerator for up to 1 week.

RECIPES

The cakes, cookies and other desserts in this Yearbook were made using our favorite kitchen-tested recipes. Follow these instructions for decorated desserts that look and taste their best!

ICING RECIPES

Buttercream Icing
(Medium consistency)*
½ cup solid vegetable shortening
½ cup (1 stick) butter or margarine, softened
1 teaspoon Wilton Imitation Clear Vanilla Extract**
4 cups sifted confectioners' sugar (about 1 lb.)
2 tablespoons milk

In large bowl, cream shortening and butter with electric mixer. Add vanilla. Gradually add sugar, one cup at a time, beating well on medium speed. Scrape sides and bottom of bowl often. When all sugar has been mixed in, icing will appear dry. Add milk and beat at medium speed until light and fluffy. Keep bowl covered with a damp cloth until ready to use. For best results, keep icing bowl in refrigerator when not in use. Refrigerated in an airtight container, this icing can be stored 2 weeks. Rewhip before using. Makes about 3 cups.

For thin (spreading) consistency icing, add 2 tablespoons light corn syrup, water or milk.

For Pure White Icing (stiff consistency), omit butter; substitute an additional ½ cup vegetable shortening for butter and ½ teaspoon Wilton Imitation Clear Butter Flavor (p. 141). Add up to 4 tablespoons light corn syrup, water or milk to thin for icing cakes.

Chocolate Buttercream Icing
Add ¾ cup cocoa powder (or three 1 oz. squares unsweetened chocolate, melted) and an additional 1-2 tablespoons milk to buttercream icing. Mix until well blended.

Chocolate Mocha Icing: Substitute brewed strong coffee for milk in Chocolate Buttercream recipe.

Darker Chocolate Icing: Add an additional ¼ cup cocoa powder (or 1 additional 1 oz. square unsweetened chocolate, melted) and 1 additional tablespoon milk to Chocolate Buttercream Icing.

Snow-White Buttercream Icing (Stiff consistency)*
⅔ cup plus 3 tablespoons water, divided
¼ cup Wilton Meringue Powder**
12 cups sifted confectioners' sugar (about 3 lbs.), divided
1¼ cups solid vegetable shortening
3 tablespoons light corn syrup
¾ teaspoon salt
¾ teaspoon Wilton Imitation Almond Extract**
¾ teaspoon Wilton Imitation Clear Vanilla Extract**
½ teaspoon Wilton Imitation Clear Butter Flavor**

In large bowl, combine ⅔ cup water and meringue powder; whip with electric mixer at high speed until peaks form. Add 4 cups sugar, one cup at a time, beating at low speed after each addition. Add remaining 8 cups sugar and 3 tablespoons water, shortening and corn syrup in 3 additions, blending well after each. Add salt and flavorings; beat at low speed until smooth. Makes about 7 cups.

For thin (spreading) consistency icing, add up to 4 more tablespoons each water and corn syrup.

NOTE: Recipe may be doubled or halved.

Royal Icing
3 tablespoons Wilton Meringue Powder**
4 cups sifted confectioners' sugar (about 1 lb.)
6 tablespoons water [1]
Beat all ingredients at low speed for 7-10

minutes (10-12 minutes at high speed for portable mixer) until icing forms peaks. Makes about 3 cups.

Thinned Royal Icing: To thin for pouring, add 1 teaspoon water per cup of royal icing. Use grease-free spoon or spatula to stir slowly. Add ½ teaspoon water at a time until you reach proper consistency.

Color Flow Icing Recipe
(full-strength for outlining)
¼ cup + 1 teaspoon water
4 cups sifted confectioners' sugar (about 1 lb.)
2 tablespoons Wilton Color Flow Mix**

With electric mixer, using grease-free utensils, blend all ingredients on low speed for 5 minutes. If using hand mixer, use high speed. Color Flow icing "crusts" quickly, so keep bowl covered with a damp cloth while using. Stir in desired icing color. Makes about 2 cups.

Thinned Color Flow: To fill in an outlined area, the recipe above must be thinned with ½ teaspoon of water per ¼ cup of icing (just a few drops at a time as you near proper consistency). Use grease-free spoon or spatula to stir slowly. Color Flow is ready for filling in outlines when a small amount dropped into the mixture takes a count of ten to disappear.

NOTE: Color Flow designs take a long time to dry, so plan to do your Color Flow piece at least 2 or 3 days in advance.

Poured Cookie Icing
This icing dries to a shiny, hard finish. Great to use as icing or to outline and fill in with tip 2 or 3.
1 cup sifted confectioners' sugar
2 teaspoons milk
2 teaspoons light corn syrup

Place sugar and milk in bowl. Stir until thoroughly mixed. Add corn syrup; mix well. For filling in areas, use thinned icing (add small amounts of light corn syrup until desired consistency is reached). Makes about ½ cup.

COOKIE RECIPES

Giant Sugar Cookie
1 cup (2 sticks) butter, softened
1½ cups granulated sugar
1 egg
1½ teaspoons Wilton Pure Vanilla Extract
½ teaspoon Wilton Imitation Almond Extract (optional)
2¾ cups all-purpose flour
1 teaspoon salt

Preheat oven to 325°F. Lightly spray pan with vegetable pan spray.

In large bowl, beat butter and sugar with electric mixer at medium speed until well blended. Beat in egg and extracts; mix well. Combine flour and salt; add to butter mixture. Beat until well blended. Press dough into prepared pan.

Bake 28-30 minutes or until light brown around edges. Cool in pan 5 minutes. Turn pan over; lightly tap pan to remove cookie. Cool completely on cooling grid. Makes 1 giant cookie.

Linzer Cookies
(Using Linzer Cutter Sets, p. 174)
2 cups all-purpose flour
⅔ cup (about 2 oz.) finely ground almonds
¼ teaspoon ground cinnamon
¼ teaspoon salt
1 cup (2 sticks) butter, softened
⅔ cup granulated sugar
1 egg
½ teaspoon Wilton Pure Vanilla Extract
½ cup seedless raspberry jam
Confectioners' sugar (optional)

In small bowl, combine flour, almonds, cinnamon and salt; set aside. In large

bowl, beat butter and sugar with electric mixer until light and fluffy. Add egg and vanilla; mix well. Add flour mixture; mix only until incorporated. Divide dough into 2 pieces; press into small disks, about 1 inch thick. Wrap separately in plastic wrap and refrigerate 2 hours or until firm enough to roll.

Preheat oven to 350°F. On floured surface, roll out one disk of dough ⅛ in. thick (keep remaining dough chilled). Cut half of the dough using the cutter with your chosen insert (this is top cookie). Cut an equal number of cookies using the cutter without the insert (this is the bottom cookie). Transfer to parchment paper lined baking sheets. Dough scraps can be formed into a disk, chilled for at least 30 minutes and rerolled.

Bake 10 to 12 minutes or until a light golden brown. Cool on cookie sheet 2 minutes. Remove from sheet and cool completely. Invert bottom cookies; spread with approximately 1 teaspoon of jam. Dust the top cookies with confectioners' sugar if desired; gently sandwich cookies together. Makes about 20 sandwich cookies.

Roll-Out Cookies
1 cup (2 sticks) unsalted butter, softened
1½ cups granulated sugar
1 egg
1½ teaspoons Wilton Imitation Clear Vanilla Extract**
½ teaspoon Wilton Imitation Almond Extract**
2¾ cups all-purpose flour
1 teaspoon baking powder
1 teaspoon salt

Preheat oven to 350°F. In large bowl, beat butter and sugar with electric mixer until light and fluffy. Beat in egg and extracts. Combine flour, baking powder and salt; add to butter mixture 1 cup at a time, mixing after each addition. Do not chill dough. Divide dough into 2 balls. On a floured surface, roll each ball into a circle approximately 12 in. wide and ⅛ in. thick. Dip cookie cutter in flour before each use. Bake cookies on ungreased cookie sheet 8-11 minutes or until cookies are lightly browned. Makes about 3 dozen cookies. Recipe may be doubled.

Spritz Cookies
1½ cups (3 sticks) butter, softened
1 cup granulated sugar
1 egg
2 tablespoons milk
1 teaspoon Wilton Imitation Clear Vanilla Extract**
½ teaspoon Wilton Imitation Almond Extract**
3½ cups all-purpose flour
1 teaspoon baking powder

Preheat oven to 350°F. In large bowl, beat butter and sugar with electric mixer until light and fluffy. Add egg, milk, and extracts; mix well. Combine flour and baking powder; gradually add to butter mixture, mixing to make a smooth dough. Do not chill. Place dough into cookie press and press cookies onto ungreased cookie sheet. Bake 10-12 minutes or until lightly browned around edges. Remove cookies from cookie sheet; cool on cooling grid. Makes 7-8 dozen cookies.

Sugar Cookies
(for pan-shaped cookies)
1 cup (2 sticks) butter, softened
1½ cups granulated sugar
1 egg
1½ teaspoons Imitation Clear Vanilla Extract**
½ teaspoon Imitation Almond Extract (optional)**

2¾ cups all-purpose flour
1 teaspoon salt

Preheat oven to 350°F. Lightly spray pan or mold cavities with vegetable pan spray. In large bowl, beat butter and sugar with electric mixer at medium speed until well blended. Beat in egg and extracts; mix well. Combine flour and salt; add to butter mixture. Beat until well blended. Press dough into prepared mold or pan, filling to ¼ in. deep. Bake 12-15 minutes or until light brown around edges. Cool in pan 10 minutes. Carefully remove cookies. Cool completely on cooling grid. Makes about 3 dozen cookies.

SPECIALTY RECIPES

Chocolate Whoopie Pies
½ cup (1 stick) butter, softened
1 cup firmly-packed brown sugar
1 egg
1 teaspoon Wilton Pure Vanilla Extract**
2 cups all-purpose flour
⅓ cup cocoa powder
1 teaspoon baking powder
1 teaspoon baking soda
½ teaspoon salt
1 cup buttermilk
Wilton Cake Release Pan Coating (p. 158)

Preheat oven to 350°F. Lightly spray pan with pan coating.

In large bowl, beat butter and sugar with electric mixer on medium speed until light and fluffy (about 3 minutes). Add egg and vanilla; beat until well combined.

In another bowl, sift together flour, cocoa powder, baking powder, baking soda and salt. Add half of dry ingredients to butter mixture and mix on low speed. When almost mixed, stop mixer and add buttermilk. Mix until well blended. Stop mixer and add remaining dry ingredients. Mix until well combined.

Spoon 2 tablespoons batter into each whoopie pie pan cavity. Spread evenly to edges. Cavity should be about ⅔ full. Bake for 8-10 minutes or until top of cakes spring back when touched. Allow cakes to cool in pan for 8 minutes. Cool completely before filling. Makes 12 Whoopie Pies (24 cakes).

Whoopie Pie Filling
6 tablespoons butter, softened
1½ cups confectioners' sugar, sifted
⅛ teaspoon salt
1 jar marshmallow crème (about 7 oz.)
1 teaspoon Wilton Pure Vanilla Extract**

In large bowl, beat butter with electric mixer until creamy. Add sugar and salt; mix well. Add marshmallow crème and vanilla; blend well. Use immediately to fill Whoopie Pies or refrigerate, covered, for up to 1 week. Bring back to room temperature and beat lightly before using. Makes 2½ cups of filling (enough for 12 pies).

Vanilla Sugar Cookies on a Stick
1 cup (2 sticks) unsalted butter, softened
1½ cups granulated sugar
1 egg
1½ teaspoons Wilton Imitation Clear Vanilla Extract**
½ teaspoon Wilton Imitation Almond Extract**
2¾ cups all-purpose flour
2 teaspoons baking powder
1 teaspoon salt

Preheat oven to 400°F. In large bowl, beat butter with sugar with electric mixer until light and fluffy. Beat in egg and extracts. Mix flour, baking powder and salt; add to butter mixture 1 cup at a time, mixing after each addition. Do not chill dough. Spray pan with vegetable pan spray. Position

stick in pan. Press dough into pan cavities. Bake 10-12 minutes or until cookies are lightly browned. Makes about 12 cookies.

Favorite Cake Ball Pops
1 box favorite cake mix
1 box (3.4 oz.) instant pudding and pie filling mix
4 eggs
1 cup water
⅓ cup vegetable oil
½ cup Wilton White Ready-To-Use Decorator Icing**
1 package (12 oz.) Wilton Candy Melts Candy (p. 175)
Lollipop Sticks (p. 178) or Cookie Treat Sticks (p. 171)

Preheat oven to 350°F. Spray 13 x 9 x 2 in. Sheet Pan or two 8 x 2 in. or 9 x 2 in. Round Pans with vegetable pan spray. In large bowl, combine cake mix, pudding mix, eggs, water and oil. Beat at medium speed with electric mixer 2 minutes. Pour into prepared pan.

Bake 30 to 35 minutes for round pans, 35 to 40 minutes for sheet pan, or until toothpick inserted in center comes out clean. Cool in pan 10 minutes; remove from pan to cooling grid and cool completely. Divide cake in half; freeze one half for future use.

In large bowl, use hands to crumble cake until no large chunks remain. Add icing; mix with fingers until well combined. Form mixture into cake balls. Chill in refrigerator at least 2 hours. Melt Candy Melts candy according to package directions. Dip sticks into melted Candy Melts candy and insert into cake balls; let set. Wait until candy is completely firm before dipping the pops completely in melted Candy Melts candy.

For SMALL pops, 1 tablespoon makes a 1¼ in. dia. ball. One recipe makes 48 small cake balls.

For MEDIUM pops, 2 tablespoons make a 1½ in. dia. ball. One recipe makes 24 medium cake balls.

For LARGE pops, 3 tablespoons make a 1¾ in. dia. ball. One recipe makes 16 large cake balls. Makes four 6-7 oz. servings.

Yellow Sponge Cake
¾ cup sifted cake flour
½ teaspoon baking powder
⅛ teaspoon salt
5 eggs
½ teaspoon cream of tartar
1 teaspoon Wilton Pure Vanilla Extract**
½ cup granulated sugar

Preheat oven to 400°F. Line 10.5 in. x 15.5 in. x 1 in. jelly roll pan with parchment paper.

In small bowl, sift together flour, baking powder and salt; set aside. Separate eggs; beat whites until foamy. Add cream of tartar and beat until stiff but not dry. In clean bowl, beat egg yolks 1 minute; add vanilla extract and gradually add sugar, beating until pale yellow and doubled in volume. Add flour mixture, beating until just combined. Fold ⅓ of egg whites into yolk mixture to loosen; fold in remaining whites until no streaks remain. Pour batter into pan, spreading evenly from center out.

Bake in center of oven 8-10 minutes or until top is lightly browned and center springs back when touched. Loosen sides. Turn out of pan onto parchment paper sprinkled with 1 tablespoon granulated sugar. Carefully remove parchment from bottom of cake. Roll cake from short side and let cool seam side down.

[1] When using large countertop mixer or for stiffer icing, use 1 tablespoon less water.

*Changes in Wilton's traditional recipes have been made due to Trans Fat Free Shortening replacing Hydrogenated Shortening.

** p. 141

2013 PRODUCT SHOPS

Welcome to the most complete selection of cake decorating products anywhere! Here you'll find all the great Wilton tools, ingredients, accents and more you need to create every design in this Yearbook.

When you're ready to buy, we make it a breeze! Use one of these easy ways to charge your order at your convenience:

ORDER ONLINE
24 HOURS A DAY/
7 DAYS A WEEK

FAX TOLL-FREE
888-824-9520
24 HOURS A DAY/
7 DAYS A WEEK

PHONE TOLL-FREE
800-794-5866
8:00 a.m.-4:30 p.m.,
Monday-Friday CST
(RETAIL CUSTOMERS ONLY)

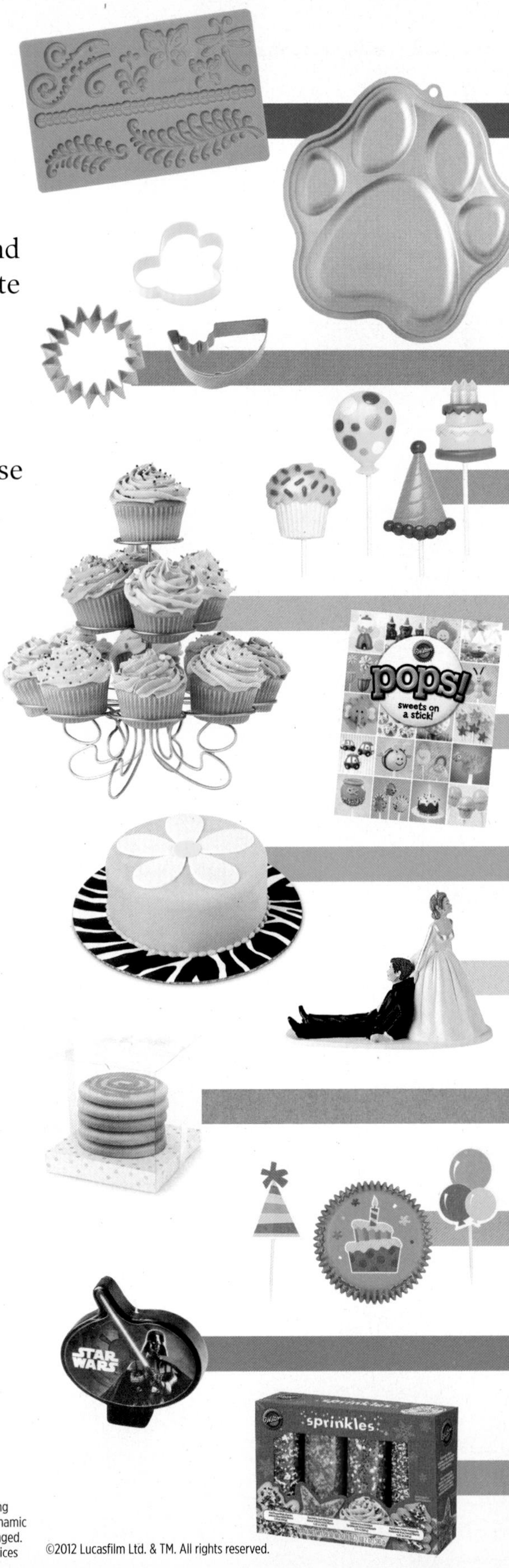

MAIL YOUR ORDER
Use the convenient retail order form in this book.

Cake Decorating

Wilton makes it easy to create amazing cakes and treats with our high-quality cake decorating tools, accessories, tips, icing colors and ready-to-use icing.

DECORATING CADDIES & SETS

Everything has its place! Our durable, convenient caddies keep all your tools and tips at your fingertips, so you have everything you need for your projects and Wilton Method courses.

DECORATOR PREFERRED TOOL CADDY

This amazing tool caddy was made with the decorator in mind! The removable lid stacks under the caddy for optimal space saving. Convenient top tray holds tips, icing colors and more. Large bottom compartment includes adjustable dividers to personalize and organize your space, so you always know where your tools are. And, the snap locks on either side add security during transport. Plus, cleanup is a breeze—simply wipe clean with a damp cloth. Caddy measures 8.25 in. x 16.25 in. x 6.25 in.
409-3077 $49.99

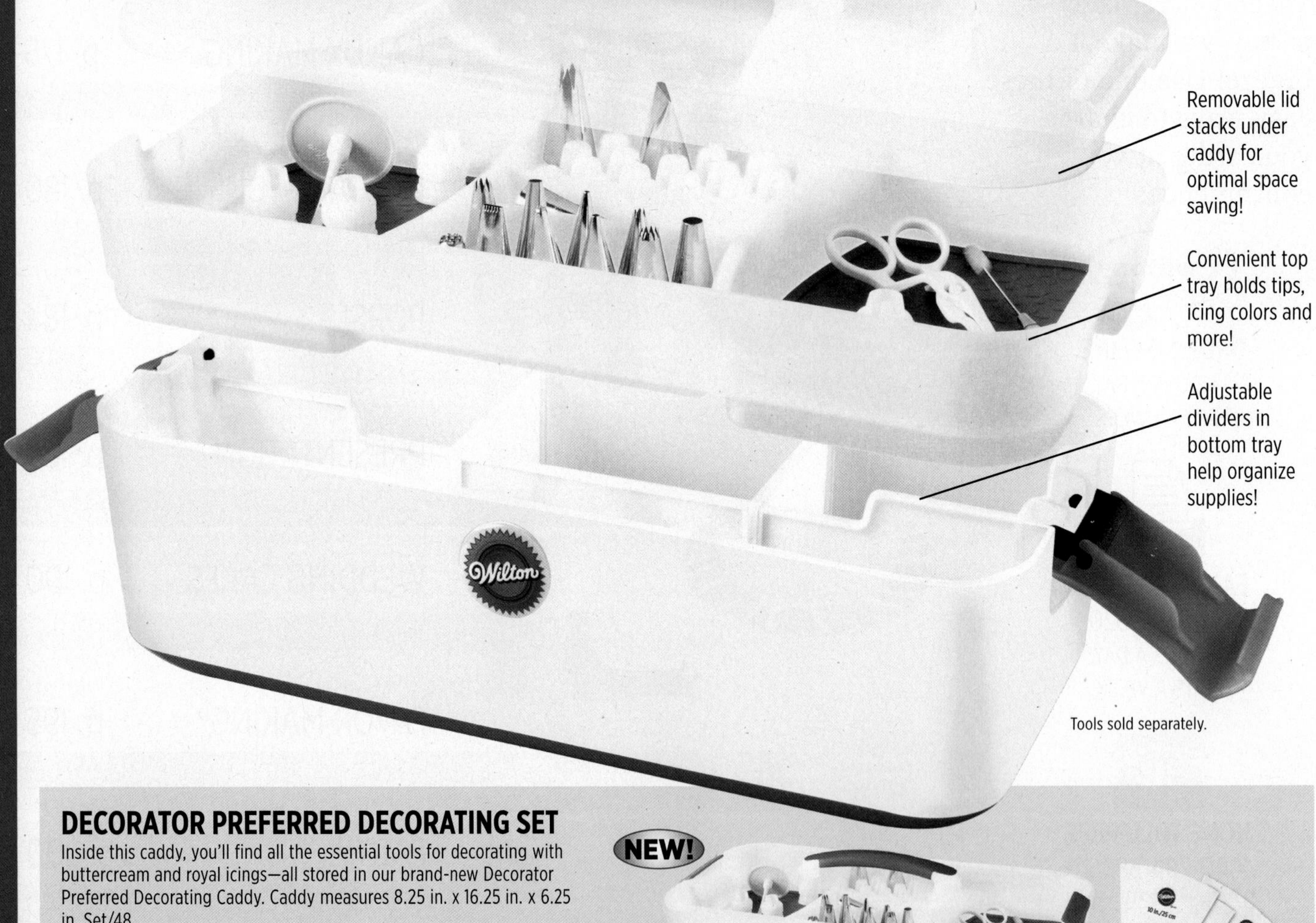

NEW!

Removable lid stacks under caddy for optimal space saving!

Convenient top tray holds tips, icing colors and more!

Adjustable dividers in bottom tray help organize supplies!

Tools sold separately.

DECORATOR PREFERRED DECORATING SET

Inside this caddy, you'll find all the essential tools for decorating with buttercream and royal icings—all stored in our brand-new Decorator Preferred Decorating Caddy. Caddy measures 8.25 in. x 16.25 in. x 6.25 in. Set/48.
2109-3127 $99.99

NEW!

LOOK AT ALL YOU GET! GREAT SAVINGS!

- 16 Decorating Tips: Round 3, 5, 12; Star 18, 21, 32, 1M; Basketweave 48; Leaf 352, 69; Petal 103, 125; Drop Flower 225, 109; Multi-Opening 233; Bismark 230
- 9 in. and 13 in. Angled Spatulas
- 4 Standard Couplers
- 2 Bake-Even Strips
- 16 in. Professional Decorating Bag
- 2 — 10 in. Professional Decorating Bags
- 12 — 12 in. Disposable Decorating Bags
- 1.5 in. Flower Nail
- Tip Brush
- Flower Lifter
- 6 Silicone Tip Covers

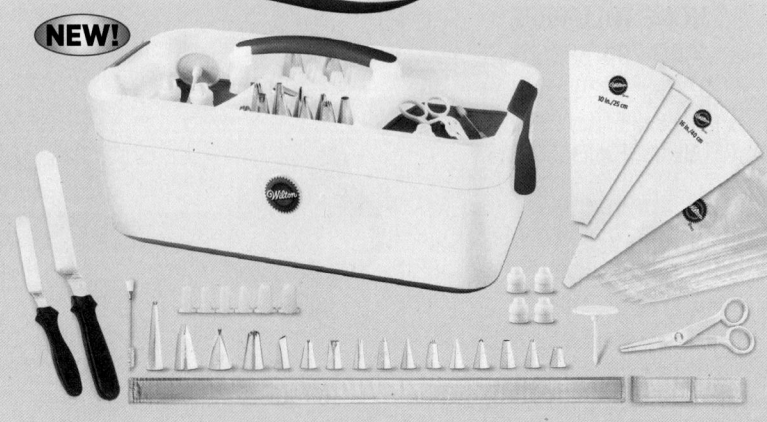

ULTIMATE TOOL CADDY

It's the storage solution designed specifically for cake decorators! Perfect for keeping your decorating space neat—or take it with you for touching up your cake at the event. The Ultimate Tool Caddy features three levels of organization to help you find your tools and accessories with ease. Caddy measures 14.75 in. x 12.75 in. x 8 in. Patent Pending.

409-3071 $59.99

Top level: Tip & Accessory Organizer Compartments

The 36 pegs hold virtually any size tip, including wired drop flower tips, and let you stack to hold more! Two tip accessory compartments hold couplers, brushes and more.

Middle level: Flip-top and Icing Color Drawers

Two slide-out drawers feature three compartments with snap-open tops. The perfect space for Cut-Outs fondant cutters, stamens, flower nails, decorating bags, candles and more. Icing color drawer holds up to 24—0.5 oz. jars or 10 each 1 oz. and 0.5 oz. jars.

Bottom level: Oversized Drawer

Large pull-out drawer is ideal for oversized items. Create customized spaces with three dividers! Use the recessed lid to hold cake leveler.

Plus:

Spatula slots on both sides for straight and angled spatulas.

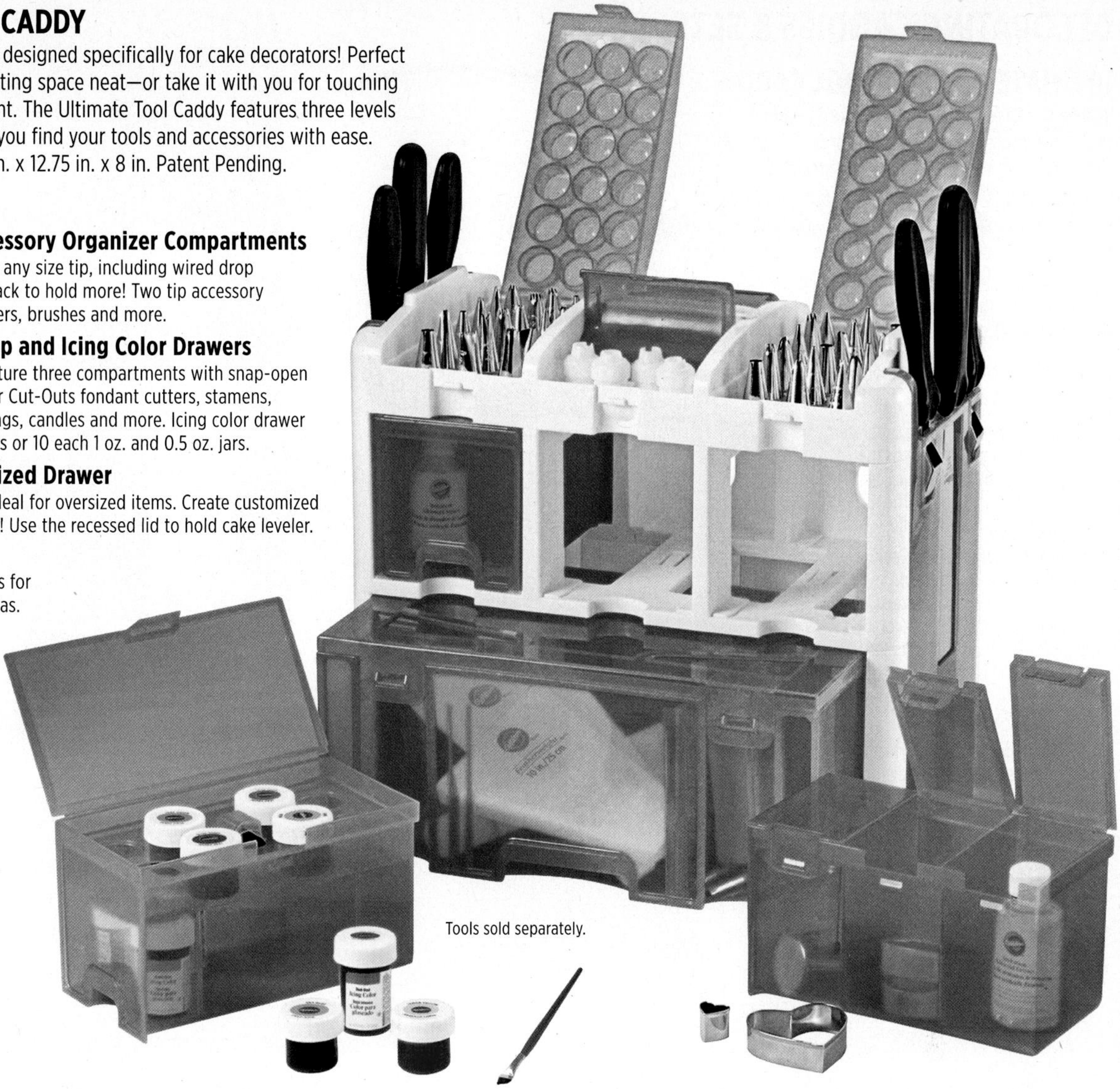

Tools sold separately.

ULTIMATE DECORATING SET

With the Ultimate Decorating Set, you get the world's best decorating caddy, loaded with the world's best cake decorating tools from Wilton. It's our most extensive collection of the essential tools for every decorating need from buttercream and royal icing, to gum paste and fondant decorating! With this set, you can do it all! Caddy measures 14.75 in. x 12.75 in. x 8 in. Set/177.

2109-0309 $199.99

Everything you need for Wilton Method Decorating Courses 1, 2 & 3!

$**250** value!

PLUS — The ULTIMATE Tool Caddy to store it all neatly!

LOOK AT ALL YOU GET!

For Buttercream and Royal Icing:
- 17 Decorating Tips: Round 1, 3, 5, 12; Star 1M, 14, 16, 18, 21; Petal 59s, 101, 104; Leaf 352, 366; Bismarck 230; Drop Flower 2D; Multi-Opening 233
- 9 in. and 11 in. Straight Spatulas
- 9 in. and 13 in. Angled Spatulas
- 2 — 10 in. Featherweight Decorating Bags
- 50 — 12 in. Disposable Decorating Bags
- 6 — 15 in. Parchment Triangles
- 4 Standard Couplers
- 6 Silicone Tip Covers
- 4-Pc. Decorating Nail Set
- 2 — 2-Pc. Lily Nail Sets
- 180 Lily Stamens
- 48 Flower Nail Template Stickers
- 6 Foil Squares
- Wave Flower Former Set
- 6 Flower Forming Cups
- Tip/Coupler Dishwasher and Storage Bag
- Practice Board with Stand and Patterns

For Fondant and Gum Paste:
- Button Flower Fondant Cut & Press Set
- Fondant Ribbon Cutter/ Embosser Set
- Pansy Cutter
- Thick and Thin Fondant Shaping Foam
- 3 Decorating Brushes
- Dusting Pouch
- Thick and Thin Modeling Tools
- Ball Tool
- Veining Tool
- 2 Dowel Rods
- 2-Pc. Mum Cutter Set
- 3-Pc. Round Cut-Outs Set
- 5-Pc. Stepsaving Rose Flower Cutter Set
- Calla Lily Cutter
- 6 Calla Lily Formers
- Straight Scallop Cutter
- 9 in. Rolling Pin with 4 Rings (two ⅛ in., two ¹⁄₁₆ in.)
- Fondant Smoother
- 8 in. Cake Circle

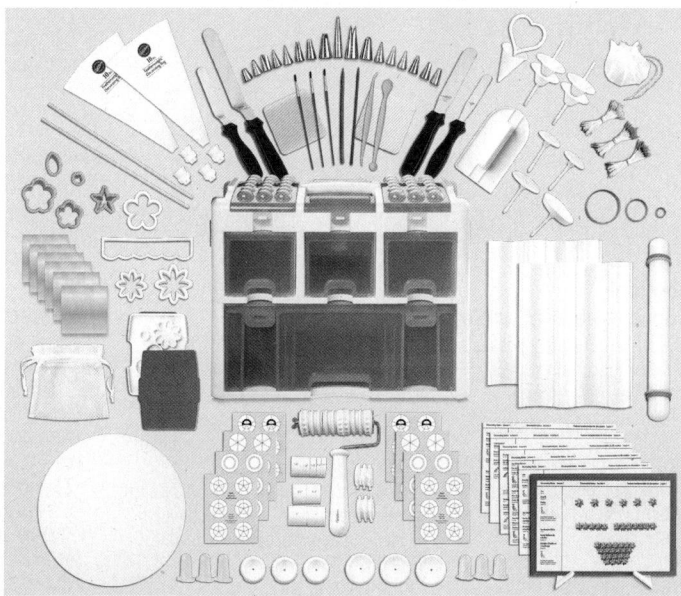

DECORATING CADDIES & SETS

ULTIMATE ROLLING TOOL CADDY

Wilton has taken the ULTIMATE Tool Caddy to new heights! This premier decorator's organizational tool contains a multitude of storage options with the convenience of on-the-go transportation. It rolls in and out of a closet or pantry with its rotating wheels and extending handle for easy storage. Caddy measures 19.5 in. x 17 in. x 9 in.
409-3078 $149.99

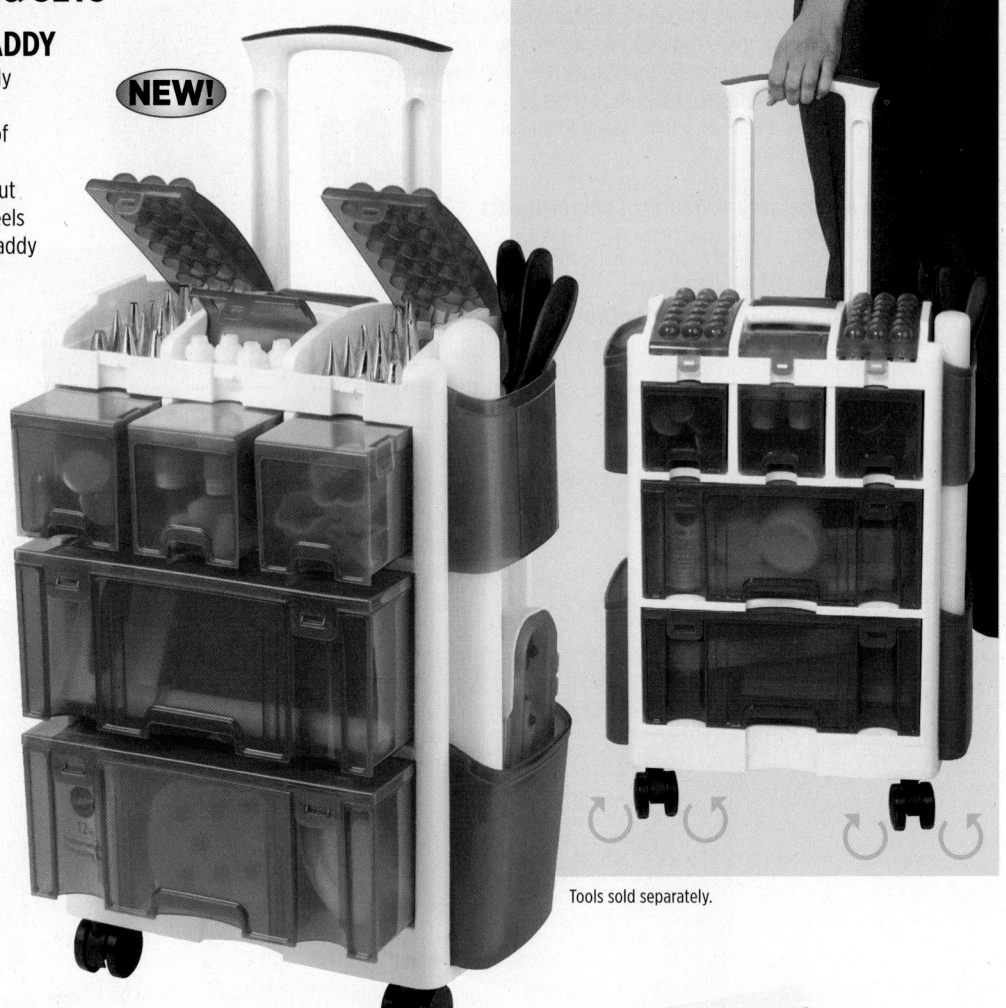

NEW!

Look at all the Ultimate Rolling Tool Caddy can hold:

- **Top compartments:** Two tip organizer compartments feature 36 pegs that hold standard and drop flower tips. Two adjacent accessory compartments hold couplers, tip brushes and more.

- **3 small slide-out drawers:** Feature compartments with individual snap-open tops, which provide ample storage for fondant cutters, stamens, decorating bags and more. Plus, one drawer holds up to 24—0.5 oz. Wilton Icing Colors or 10 each 1 oz. and 0.5 oz. Wilton Icing Colors, and features a lift-out tray.

- **2 large pullout drawers:** Perfect for oversized items and can be divided into two or three customized spaces with the included dividers

- **Side panel:** Compartments are perfect for a 20 in. rolling pin, mats, decorating bags and more.

- **Back panel:** Holds Wilton Yearbook of Cake Decorating, course books and more.

Tools sold separately.

DECORATING SETS

Convenient sets of decorating essentials give you instant versatility! Each features Wilton precise, high-quality tips for achieving many of the most popular techniques.

12-Piece Cupcake Decorating Set
Create fun-looking cupcakes with this decorating set! Includes:
- 4 Decorating Tips (12, 1M, 22 and Bismarck 230).
- 8 — 12 in. Disposable Decorating Bags.
- Step-by-step, illustrated instructions.
Set/12.
2104-6667 $8.99

18-Piece Cake Decorating Set
Perfect for Wilton character cakes! Includes:
- 4 Decorating Tips (4, 12, 18 and 103).
- 6 — 12 in. Disposable Decorating Bags.
- 2 Standard Couplers.
- 5 liquid color packets (0.067 fl. oz each: yellow, red, green, orange and blue).
- Step-by-step, illustrated instructions.
Set/18.
2104-2530 $7.99

25-Piece Cake Decorating Set
A great decorating set for beginner cake decorators. Includes:
- 5 Decorating Tips (3, 16, 32, 104 and 352).
- 4 Icing Colors (0.5 oz each: Lemon Yellow, Pink, Sky Blue and Leaf Green).
- 12 — 12 in. Disposable Decorating Bags.
- 2 Standard Couplers.
- 1.25 in. Flower Nail.
- Step-by-step, illustrated instructions.
Set/25.
2104-2536 $12.99

53-Piece Cake Decorating Set
The works! Decorate many advanced wedding, floral and basketweave cakes as well as basic cakes. Includes:
- 18 Decorating Tips (2, 3, 5, 7, 12, 16, 18, 21, 32, 48, 67, 101, 103, 104, 129, 225, 349 and 352).
- 24 — 12 in. Disposable Decorating Bags.
- 2 Standard Couplers.
- 5 Icing Colors (0.5 oz each: Golden Yellow, Moss Green, Rose Petal Pink, Cornflower Blue and Violet).
- 1.25 in. Flower Nail.
- 8 in. Angled Spatula.
- Storage Tray.
- 40-page "Cake Decorating Beginner's Guide."
Set/53.
2104-2546 $32.99

ORDER TOLL FREE: 800-794-5866

Tools sold separately.

DECORATOR PREFERRED CARRY-ALL TOTE

Designed for the decorator on-the-go, this stylish, oversized durable canvas bag carries practically anything you may need for a Wilton Method of Cake Decorating course or cake setups.

You'll be amazed at all the Carry-All Tote Features:
- The sturdy base keeps the tote standing upright whether empty or filled.
- The convenient separators divide the tote into three compartments to hold items, such as the Tool, Tip and Icing Color Organizers (sold separately).
- The smaller inner side pockets are perfect for pens, FoodWriter edible color markers or other decorating tools.
- Zipper pockets and pouches are perfect for cell phones, car keys and credit cards.
- Padded, roomy inner pouch is large enough for a tablet, Wilton Yearbook of Cake Decorating and decorating inspirations.
- Plus, grease-resistant lining zips open easily and wipes clean with a damp cloth. Tote measures 13 in. x 14.75 in. x 9 in.

409-3076 $49.99

DECORATING ORGANIZERS

When you hear the snap when closing these organizers, you know your decorating tools are safe! All fit snuggly in the Decorator Preferred Carry-All Tote (sold above).

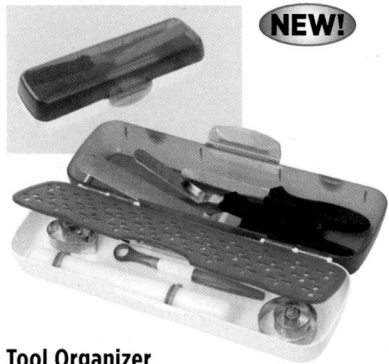

Tool Organizer
Holds all the tools from Course 1—Decorating Basics and up to a 13 in. spatula (sold separately). The hinged divider snaps into place to separate clean and dirty tools, and lays flat when open to maximize work space. 14 in. x 5.25 in.

405-8785 $14.99

Supplies sold separately.

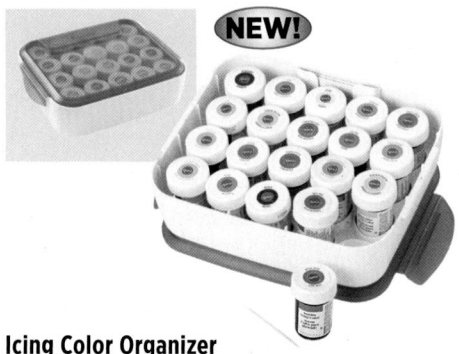

Icing Color Organizer
Keep your icing colors organized and level. This convenient tray holds up to 20—0.5 oz. and/or 1 oz. Wilton Icing Colors. Separate storage compartment conveniently holds toothpicks for easy use. Storage tray nests on lid to maximize workspace, and is angled for easy viewing and selection of colors. Stacks conveniently with Tip Organizer (sold separately). 9 in. x 7 in. x 2.6 in.

405-8783 $12.99

Icing Colors sold separately.

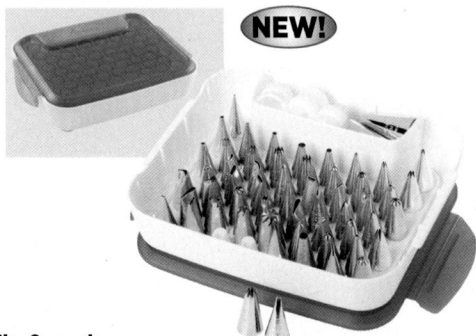

Tip Organizer
Always have a wide selection of decorating tips readily available with the Wilton Tip Organizer. Holds 55 standard-sized tips and allows for nesting of up to three tips. Separate compartment holds couplers, flower nails and oversized tips. The storage tray nests on its lid to maximize space and is angled for easy viewing. Stacks conveniently with Icing Color Organizer (sold separately). 1.75 in. x 8.75 in. x 7 in.

405-8784 $12.99

Tips sold separately.

DECORATING TIPS & ACCESSORIES

Presenting the best quality tips on the market, used by decorators throughout the world. Wilton tips are made to hold their shape and create precise decorations year after year. Dishwasher safe tips are tested for consistent performance in the Wilton Test Kitchen. All tips work with standard bags and couplers, unless otherwise indicated.

Dishwasher Tip Tray

Durable, top-rack dishwasher-safe tray allows water and detergent to flow through for thorough tip cleaning. Snap-on lid securely keeps tips in place while cleaning. Holds 10 standard decorating tips (sold separately). 5.5 in. x 3.75 in. x 1 in.
417-1189 $9.99

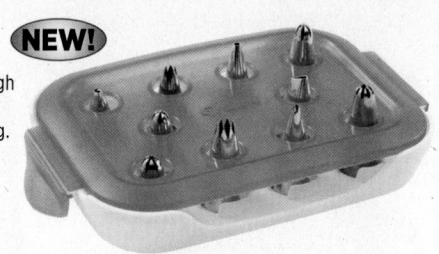

NEW!

ROUND TIPS

Outline, lettering, dots, stringwork, balls, beads, lattice, lacework.

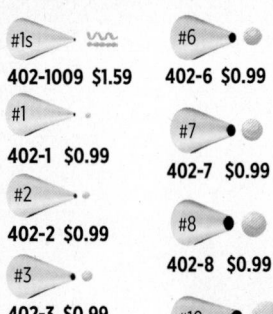

#1s	#6
402-1009 $1.59	402-6 $0.99
#1	#7
402-1 $0.99	402-7 $0.99
#2	#8
402-2 $0.99	402-8 $0.99
#3	#10
402-3 $0.99	402-10 $0.99
#4	
402-4 $0.99	
#5	#12
402-5 $0.99	402-12 $0.99

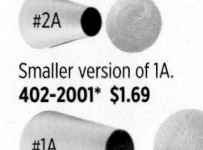

#2A
Smaller version of 1A.
402-2001* $1.69

#1A
Bold borders, figure piping.
402-1001* $1.89

#230
Fill eclairs and bismarcks.
402-230 $2.19**

#55
402-55 $0.99

#301
For flat lettering.
402-301 $0.99

DROP FLOWER TIPS

Small (106-225); medium (131-194); large (2C-1G, great for cookie dough).

#106	#131
402-106 $1.69	402-131 $1.69
#107	#190
402-107 $1.69	402-190** $1.89
#108	#224
402-108** $1.69	402-224 $1.69
#109	#225
402-109** $1.89	402-225 $1.69
#129	
402-129 $1.69	

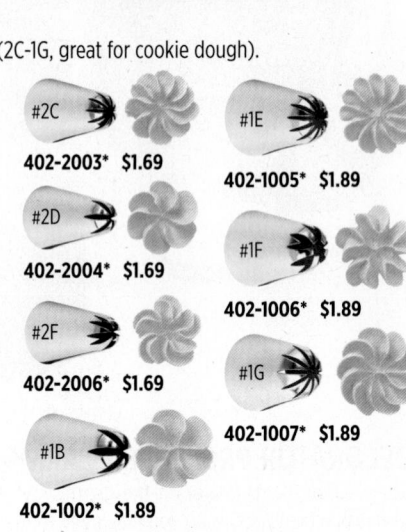

#2C	#1E
402-2003* $1.69	402-1005* $1.89
#2D	#1F
402-2004* $1.69	402-1006* $1.89
#2F	#1G
402-2006* $1.69	402-1007* $1.89
#1B	
402-1002* $1.89	

CLOSED STAR TIPS

Create deeply grooved shells, stars and fleurs de lis.

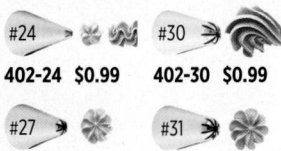

#35
402-35 $0.99

#24	#30	#133
402-24 $0.99	402-30 $0.99	402-133 $0.99
#27	#31	#54
402-27 $0.99	402-31 $0.99	402-54 $0.99

SPECIALTY TIPS

Shells, squares, curved ribbon, ropes and swirls.

#79	#83	#105
402-79 $0.99	402-83 $0.99	402-105 $0.99
#81	#96	
402-81 $0.99	402-96 $0.99	

MULTI-OPENING TIPS

Rows and clusters of strings, beads, stars (use 233 for grass).

#134	#233
402-134** $1.89	402-233 $1.69
#234	TRIPLE STAR
402-234* $1.89	Triple Star* 402-2010 $2.89

OPEN STAR TIPS

Star techniques, drop flowers; use 6B and 8B with pastry dough, too. The finely cut teeth of 199 and 363 create decorations with many ridges.

#13	#16	#18
402-13 $0.99	402-16 $0.99	402-18 $0.99
#14	#17	#20
402-14 $0.99	402-17 $0.99	402-20 $0.99

#21	#199
402-21 $0.99	402-199 $1.69
#22	#363
402-22 $0.99	402-363 $1.69
#32	#1M (2110)
402-32 $0.99	402-2110* $1.69

#4B
402-4400** $1.69
#6B
402-6600** $1.69
#8B
402-8800** $1.89

*Fits large coupler.

**Tip does not work with coupler. Use with bag only or parchment. Cake Icer tip should be used with bags 16 in. or larger.

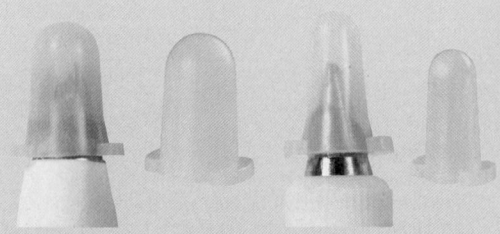

Silicone Decorating Tip Cover Set

With convenient silicone covers, icing won't dry out in your bag between uses. Fit snugly over all standard and most large tips. Top-rack dishwasher safe. Pk./6.
414-916 $6.49

Decorating Couplers

Couplers make it easy to change decorating tips on the same icing bag.

Standard
Fits all decorating bags and standard tips.
411-1987 $0.79

Large
Use with large decorating tips and 14 in. to 18 in. Featherweight bags.
411-1006 $1.79

Tip Brush

Great for cleaning small tip openings. Plastic bristles. 0.25 in. x 4 in. long.
418-1123 $1.59

Tip Saver

Restores bent tips to proper shape; opens clogged tips. Heavy-duty plastic.
414-909 $3.49

TIP SETS

Be ready for virtually any decorating need with these generous sets. Each includes a great variety of tips stored upright in a convenient locking case.

Deluxe
Includes:
• Round Tips 2, 4, 7, 10
• Star Tips 13, 16, 17, 18, 199 (open), 30 (closed)
• Leaf Tips 65, 66, 67, 352
• Petal & Drop Flower Tips 61, 97, 101, 102, 103, 104, 106, 107, 225
• Specialty Tips: Basketweave 46, 47; Multi-Opening 233
• Tip Coupler
• 1.25 in. Flower Nail
• Tipsaver Case
Set/28.
2104-6666 $28.99

Master
Includes:
• Round Tips 1, 2, 3, 4, 6, 7, 10, 12
• Star Tips 13, 16, 17, 18, 22, 32, 199 (open), 24, 27, 30, 31, 54 (closed)
• Leaf 65, 66, 67, 68, 69, 70, 73, 352
• Petal & Drop Flower Tips 59, 61, 97, 101, 102, 103, 104, 123, 125, 150, 106, 108, 109, 129, 225, 2C, 2D
• Specialty Tips: Basketweave 134, 233, 96, 45, 46, 47, 48
• 2 Couplers
• 2 — 1.25 in. Flower Nails
• Tipsaver Case
Set/56.
2104-7778 $49.99

PETAL TIPS
Realistic flower petals, dramatic ruffles, drapes, swags and bows.

#59s/59° — 402-594 $0.99
#59 — 402-59 $0.99
#61 — 402-61 $0.99
#62 — 402-62 $0.99
#97 — 402-97 $0.99
#101s — 402-1019 $1.59
#101 — 402-101 $0.99
#102 — 402-102 $0.99

#103 — 402-103 $0.99
#104 — 402-104 $0.99
#150 — 402-150 $1.69
#123 — 402-123* $1.69
#124 — 402-124* $1.69
#125 — 402-125* $1.69

#126 — 402-126* $1.69
#127 — 402-127* $1.69

#127D
Giant Rose** 402-1274 $1.89

RUFFLE TIPS
Plain, fluted, shell-border, special effects.

#86 — 402-86 $0.99
#88† — 402-88† $0.99
#100 — 402-100 $0.99
#353 — 402-353 $1.59
#340 — 402-340 $1.59
#402 — 402-402* $1.69

†For left-handers.   •Fits large coupler.

LEAF TIPS
Ideal for shell-motion borders, too.

#65s — 402-659 $1.59
#66 — 402-66 $0.99
#68 — 402-68 $0.99
#73 — 402-73 $0.99

#352 — 402-352 $1.59
#70 — 402-70 $0.99
#65 — 402-65 $0.99
#67 — 402-67 $0.99
#69 — 402-69 $0.99

#74 — 402-74 $0.99
#349 — 402-349 $1.59
#113 — 402-113* $1.69
#366 — Makes leaves for larger flowers. 402-366* $1.89

BASKETWEAVE TIPS
Tips 44, 45 make only smooth stripes; rest of basketweave tips and Cake Icer make both smooth and ribbed stripes.

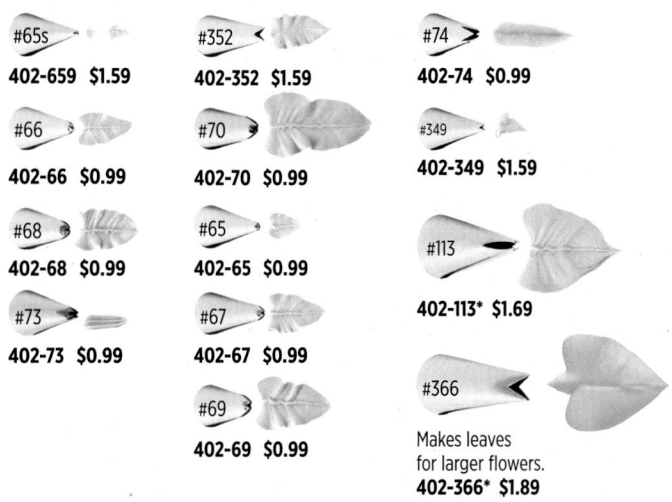

#44 — 402-44 $0.99
#45 — 402-45 $0.99
#46 — 402-46 $0.99
#47 — 402-47 $0.99
#48 — 402-48 $0.99
#1D — 402-1004** $1.89
#2B — 402-2002* $1.69

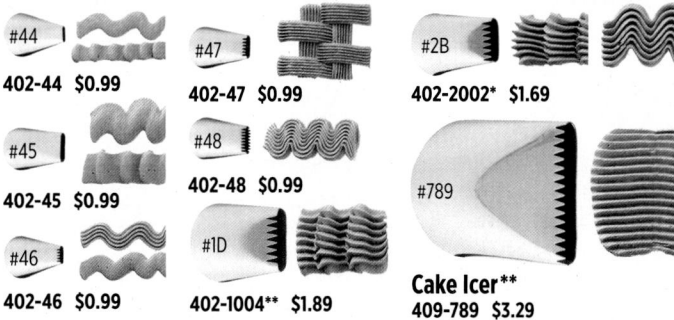

#789 — Cake Icer** 409-789 $3.29

LEFT-HANDED TIP SETS

 PARA ZURDOS

Achieve the same beautiful flowers as right-handed decorators! Tips fit standard bags and couplers.

Drop Flower
Includes Left tips 106 and 107 for making small swirled flowers. Set/2.
#106L
#107L
418-613† $3.29

Petal
Includes Left tip 59° for violets, Left tip 97 for Victorian roses and Left tip 116** for large Wilton Roses. Set/3.
#59°L
#97L
#116L
418-612† $3.29

DECORATING BAGS & ACCESSORIES

Wilton offers a large selection of decorating bags and accessories perfect for use with buttercream and royal icings.

NEW!

Decorating Bag Holder

Keep icing bags organized and in easy reach of your decorating workspace. Openings hold up to six decorating bags from 8 in. to 16 in. (sold separately). The built-in, snug flower nail grips grasp nails for easy one-handed use. Stable legs smoothly lock into place and fold to maximize storage space. Silicone feet prevent the holder from sliding on the work surface. 6.5 in. x 11.25 in. x 4.5 in.
417-1186 $14.99

NEW!

Deluxe Practice Board

Our Deluxe Practice Board will give you the confidence and skills to create incredible cake designs. Features include:
- Ample area for practicing Wilton bag and tip techniques.
- Storage area for practice sheets and creative inspiration.
- Large, clear decorating window opens easily to slip in practice sheets.
- Sturdy lid locks in 4 different positions to closely simulate the side of a cake, or use closed for the top of cake.
- More than 80 bag and tip techniques for buttercream and royal icings with easy-to-use cake decorating instructions.

13 in. x 10.75 in.
406-1075 $29.99

Decorating Bag Sleeve

Great tool to fill decorating bags. The corners create a stable frame for holding bags and can be used to dry reusable decorating bags. Folds flat for easy storage. Each: 10 in. x 4 in. Set/3.
417-1185 $6.99

DECORATING BAGS

From parchment triangles to our convenient disposable or premium reusable Featherweight styles, Wilton bags are made to our strict specifications for consistent quality.

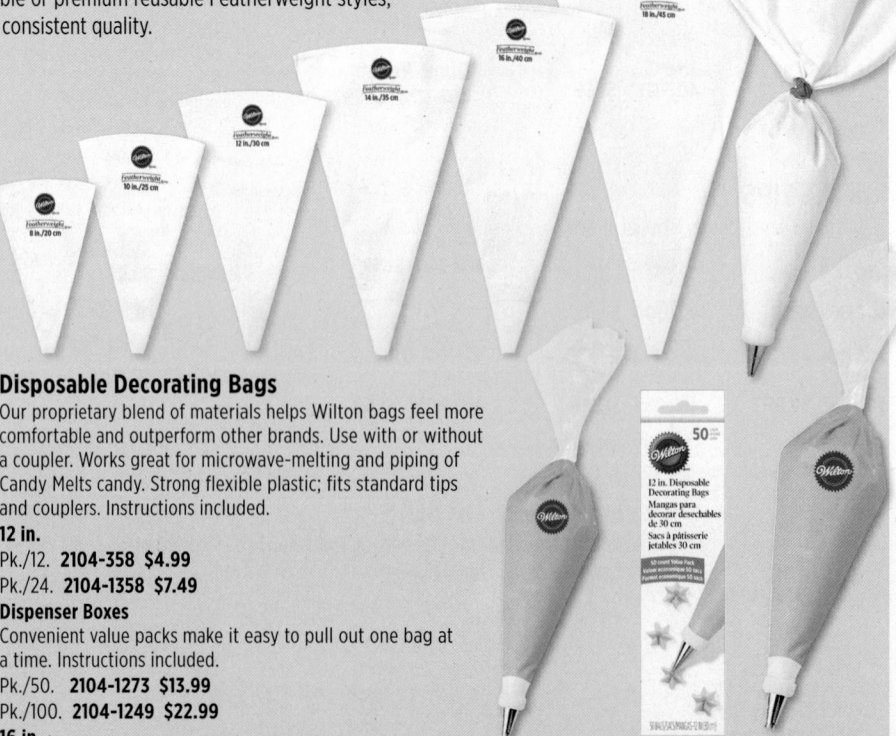

Featherweight Decorating Bags

The best quality bags for decorating with strong resilient seams to help them last for years! Featherweight bags feel soft and comfortable in the hand—the polyester material becomes softer the more the bags are used. Lightweight, strong and flexible, they'll never get stiff. Coated to prevent grease from seeping through. Dishwasher safe. Instructions included; sold singly.

8 in. 404-5087 $3.29	14 in. 404-5140 $6.79
10 in. 404-5109 $4.79	16 in. 404-5168 $8.49
12 in. 404-5125 $5.79	18 in. 404-5184 $9.49

Parchment Triangles

Make use-and-toss decorating bags ideal for small amounts of icing or brush striping. Excellent wet strength for candy or a variety of icings. Also great for smoothing iced cakes and transferring patterns. 15 in. Pk./100.
2104-1508 $7.99

Icing Bag Ties

Wrap around the twist of decorating bag to prevent icing from oozing out. Pk./12.
417-173 $4.49

Disposable Decorating Bags

Our proprietary blend of materials helps Wilton bags feel more comfortable and outperform other brands. Use with or without a coupler. Works great for microwave-melting and piping of Candy Melts candy. Strong flexible plastic; fits standard tips and couplers. Instructions included.

12 in.
Pk./12. **2104-358 $4.99**
Pk./24. **2104-1358 $7.49**
Dispenser Boxes
Convenient value packs make it easy to pull out one bag at a time. Instructions included.
Pk./50. **2104-1273 $13.99**
Pk./100. **2104-1249 $22.99**
16 in.
Decorate longer without refilling the bag—great for piping borders on large cakes or icing cupcakes. Use with Cake Icer Tip 789. Pk./12. **2104-1357 $5.99**

Cake Dividing Chart

A great tool to use when paired with the Cake Marker (sold below). This reusable chart measures precise divisions of iced cakes helping decorators to divide cakes into symmetrical, even sections. Ideal for guiding string work, garlands and many other decorating techniques.
20 in. x 20 in.
409-2554
$9.99

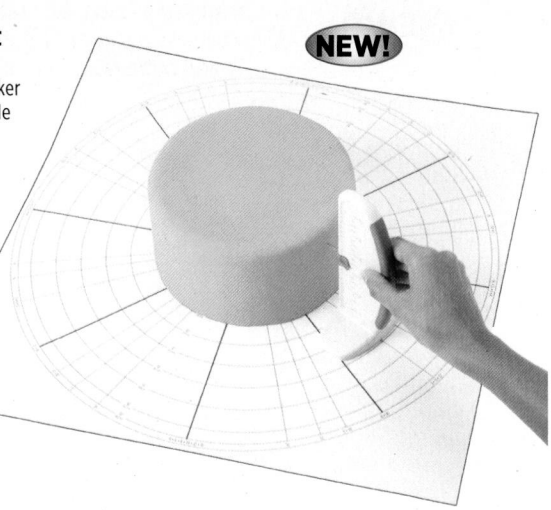

Icing Smoother

Sleek, stainless steel blade helps to create perfectly smooth cake tops and sides just like a baker's blade. It's sized specifically for standard cake heights, and the flat bottom creates a surface to rest along the cake side. The hand grip is specifically molded for a secure grasp.
9 in. x 3 in.
417-1648 $9.99

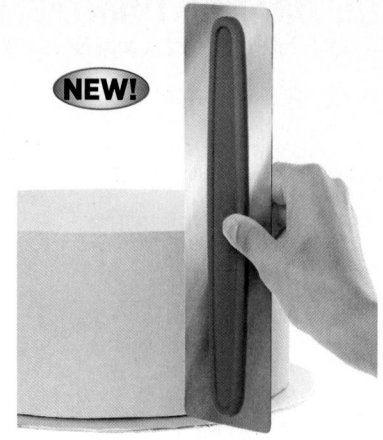

Cake Marker

Mark cake sides for perfect placement of accents or borders. Three adjustable marker pins snap into place and slide along the ruler edge to mark cake sections. 6.75 in. x 2.625 in. Patent Pending.
409-2545 $5.99

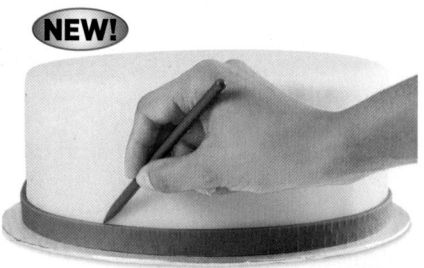

Cake Measuring Tape Set

Measure cakes for easy placement of accents and borders using our Cake Measuring Tape. Simply wrap the tape around your cake and use a marking tool (sold separately) to plan your design. Each tape: 26 in. long. Set/2.
417-1156 $7.99

3-Pc. Icing Comb Set

Add a professional finish to your buttercream-iced cakes! This set offers six different textures—ridges, swirls and waves—which makes creating texture a breeze. The hand grip is specifically molded for a secure grasp, and it keeps your fingers from dragging into the cake sides. The combs snap together for storage. Each: 9 in. x 3 in. Set/3.
417-1154 $14.99

SPATULAS

The stainless steel blades offer strength and flexibility for icing cakes, cupcakes and more. Decorate with greater comfort, more control and less fatigue.

WHITE HANDLES
Nylon weighted handles give you greater control.

Straight
Great for spreading and smoothing fillings, all-around kitchen use.
9 in. **409-6045 $7.99**
11 in. **409-6046 $9.99**
15 in. **409-6047 $13.99**

Tapered
Easily ices hard-to-reach spots.
9 in. **409-6057 $7.99**

Angled
Ideal angle for smoothing cake sides and spreading fillings.
9 in. **409-6040 $7.99**
13 in. **409-6041 $9.99**
15 in. **409-6042 $13.99**

Cake Knife/Spatula
This stainless steel knife is perfect for torting cakes: Cuts layers cleanly and has the width to transfer layers without breakage. Use the smooth edge for spreading icing or filling on cake layers. Lightweight nylon handle. 15 in. long.
409-6048 $9.99

BLACK HANDLES
Contoured handle with finger pad provides an excellent grip and superior control.

Cupcake **NEW!**
Round blade is perfect for icing cupcakes and small treats.
8.25 in. **409-6000 $5.99**

Square Head **NEW!**
Square end allows for a clean angle when icing the sides of cake.
11 in. **409-6039 $6.99**

Straight Blade
9 in. **409-6006 $4.29**
11 in. **409-6018 $6.29**
15 in. **409-6030 $10.49**

Angled Blade
9 in. **409-6012 $4.79**
13 in. **409-6024 $6.79**
15 in. **409-6036 $10.49**

Tapered Blade
9 in. **409-6003 $4.29**

DECORATING TURNTABLES

A quality cake turntable is a must for easy decorating.

The 6.5 in. high dome is the perfect height to protect decorated cakes. Also features a smooth rotating turntable and removable serving tray!

ULTIMATE Trim-N-Turn Caddy

With our ULTIMATE Trim-N-Turn Caddy your cakes always arrive safe and secure! Patent Pending.
Features include:
• Dome clearance of 6.5 in.; the perfect height to protect decorated cakes.
• Smooth turntable rotation.
• Plate locks when transporting.
• Removable serving tray lets you present in style.
• Holds up to a 10 in. dia. cake board.
2105-0474 $69.99

NEW!

Remove base for easy serving!

Trim-N-Turn ULTRA Cake Turntable

Combines an extra-high, smooth-turning platform with non-slip detail for secure performance.
Features include:
• Platform turns in either direction for easy icing, borders, combing and leveling.
• Great for left-hand or right-hand users.
• Non-slip design with soft-grip ring molded into platform to keep cake in place.
• 3 in. raised base with arched sides for easy grip.
• Hidden ball bearing track for smooth turning.
• Lock platform with ease using the pull-out tab.
• 12 in. platform removes from base for easy cleaning.
• Holds cakes up to 11 in. with platform visible—holds larger cakes if needed.
307-301 $22.99

Trim-N-Turn PLUS Cake Turntable

Smooth-turning performance puts your cake in the ideal position for decorating beautiful borders and icing sides perfectly smooth.
Features include:
• Non-slip base raised for better control.
• Arched sides for easy lifting.
• Removable 12 in. platform for easy cleaning.
• Hidden ball-bearing track for smooth turning.
• Holds cakes up to 11 in. with platform visible—holds larger cakes if needed.
307-303 $14.99

Tilt-N-Turn ULTRA Cake Turntable

The ultimate in turntable design. It's perfect for placing cut-out designs, piping borders, writing and more. Ideal for both left- and right-handed decorators. Patent Pending.
Features include:
• 18 different locking plate positions.
• 12 in. top plate detaches completely from turntable base
• Smooth plate rotation.
• Non-slip soft grip design molded into plate surface securely keeps cake in place.
• 5 in. high, durable construction with balanced weight and non-slip feet.
• Large push button for easy plate release and adjustment.
• Holds cakes up to 11 in. with platform visible—holds larger cakes if needed.
307-121 $79.99

It tilts! Decorate any part of your cake conveniently!

Remove base for easy serving!

ICING COLORS

Produce deep, rich color with just a small amount using this fast-mixing gel. Exclusive concentrated gel formula helps decorators achieve the exact shade desired without changing icing consistency. 1 oz. single bottles. Certified Kosher.

Each $2.29

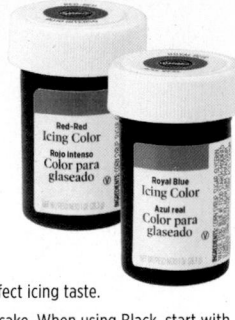

*Note: Large amounts of these colors may affect icing taste.

Use No-Taste Red for large areas of red on a cake. When using Black, start with chocolate icing to limit the amount of color needed.

Ivory 610-208	Buttercup Yellow 610-216	
Golden Yellow 610-159	Lemon Yellow 610-108	

Copper 610-450	Creamy Peach 610-210	Orange 610-205	Red-Red* 610-906	Christmas Red* 610-302	Red (no-taste) 610-998	Rose 610-401
Burgundy 610-698	Pink 610-256	Violet 610-604	Delphinium Blue 610-228	Cornflower Blue 610-710	Royal Blue 610-655	Sky Blue 610-700
Teal 610-207	Kelly Green 610-752	Leaf Green 610-809	Moss Green 610-851	Juniper Green 610-234	Brown 610-507	Black* 610-981

ICING COLORS SETS

Have a variety of colors at your fingertips with our sets. Certified Kosher.

4 Colors Primary
Contains Lemon Yellow, Sky Blue, Christmas Red and Brown. 0.5 oz. jars. Set/4.
601-5127 $5.49

8 Colors
Contains Lemon Yellow, Orange, Pink, Christmas Red, Violet, Sky Blue, Leaf Green and Brown. 0.5 oz. jars. Set/8.
601-5577 $10.99

12 Colors
Our most popular collection creates the spectrum of popular colors plus light and dark skin tones. Contains Lemon Yellow, Golden Yellow, Pink, No-Taste Red, Burgundy, Violet, Royal Blue, Teal, Kelly Green, Copper, Brown and Black. 0.5 oz. jars. Set/12.
601-5580 $14.99

4 Colors Pastel
Contains Creamy Peach, Rose Petal Pink, Moss Green and Cornflower Blue. 0.5 oz. jars. Set/4.
601-25588 $5.49

4 Colors Garden Tone
Contains Buttercup Yellow, Delphinium Blue, Aster Mauve, Juniper Green. 0.5 oz. jars. Set/4.
601-4240 $5.49

White-White Icing Color
Stir in to whiten icing made with butter or margarine. Perfect for wedding cakes. 2 fl. oz. Certified Kosher.
603-1236 $2.99

Glycerin
Add to dried out icing color, fondant or gum paste to restore consistency. 2 fl. oz. Certified Kosher.
708-14 $2.29

FOODWRITER EDIBLE COLOR MARKERS

Decorate on Wilton Cookie Icing, Fondant, Color Flow and royal icing designs. Or add dazzling color to countless foods, like toaster pastries, cheese, fruit slices, bread and more. Each set includes five 0.07 oz. FoodWriter edible markers. Certified Kosher.

Each Set $8.49

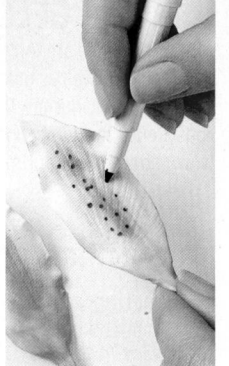

EXTRA-FINE TIP

Extra Fine Tip Set 609-105
For fine detailing.

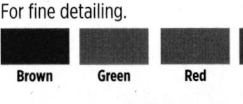

Brown	Green	Red	Blue	Black

FINE TIP **BOLD TIP**

Fine Tip Primary Colors Set 609-100
Bold Tip Primary Colors Set 609-115

Yellow	Green	Red	Blue	Black

Fine Tip Neon Colors Set 609-116

Purple	Orange	Pink	Light Green	Black

COLOR MIST FOOD COLOR SPRAY

Easy-to-use spray gives the versatility and dazzling effects of an airbrush in a convenient can! Use it to transform plain iced cake with sensational color, or add splashes of holiday color to iced cookies and cupcakes. No mess, taste-free formula. Colors match Wilton Icing Colors above. 1.5 oz. Certified Kosher. **Each $3.79**

NEW! Gold 710-5520 $4.29

NEW! Silver 710-5521 $4.29

NEW! Pearl 710-5522 $4.29

3 new colors for a shimmering metallic finish!

Red 710-5500	Blue 710-5501
Yellow 710-5502	Green 710-5503
Violet 710-5504	Pink 710-5505
Black 710-5506	
Orange 710-5507	

ICINGS & GELS

All Wilton icings are formulated for easy decorating as well as great taste. Our convenient, ready-to-use icings are the perfect medium consistency for decorating, so you don't need to worry about mixing or measuring.

TUBE ICINGS, GELS

Decorating Icings

The same high-quality as our Ready-To-Use Icings, in a convenient tube. Ideal for small areas of color on character cakes. Use with the Tip Set or Coupler Ring Set (below) and any standard-size, Wilton metal tip (not included). Colors match Wilton Icing Colors (p. 139). 4.25 oz. Certified Kosher.
Each $2.29

Red 704-218	**Royal Blue** 704-248
Violet 704-242	**Leaf Green** 704-224
Yellow 704-236	**Kelly Green** 704-227
Orange 704-212	**Chocolate** 704-254
Pink 704-230	**White** 704-200
	Black 704-206

Coupler Ring Set

Attach Wilton standard-size metal decorating tips onto Wilton tube icings to create any technique. Set/4.
418-47306 $2.29

Tip Set

Tips easily twist onto Wilton tube icings. Includes star, round, leaf and petal tips. Set/4.
418-621 $2.19

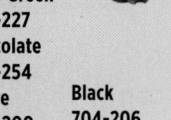

Decorating Gels

Add colorful highlights to your decorating with these transparent gels. Create a beautiful stained-glass effect and add distinctive writing and printing. Colors match Wilton Icing Colors (p. 139). 0.75 oz. Certified Kosher.
Each $1.79

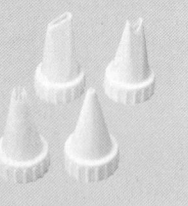

Red 704-318	**Orange** 704-312
Pink 704-330	**Royal Blue** 704-348
Violet 704-342	**Kelly Green** 704-324 / **White** 704-302
Yellow 704-336	**Brown** 704-354 / **Black** 704-306

SPARKLE GEL

NEW!

Squeeze on sparkling color effects with our ready-to-use gel. Great for dots, messages, water effects and fondant accents. Resealable 3.5 oz. tubes. Certified Kosher.
Each $2.99

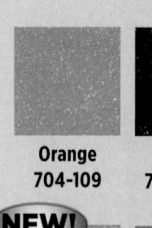

NEW!

Orange 704-109	Black 704-1061	White 704-107	Gold 704-1060	Red 704-112
Light Green 704-1019	**Blue** 704-110	**Yellow** 704-108	**Green** 704-111	**Pink** 704-356

Light Blue 704-1013

COOKIE ICING

Use this quick-setting, microwavable icing to cover your cookies with a smooth finish. Easy to use: Heat and squeeze onto cookies using the convenient cap. Sets smooth in just 1 hour. 10 oz. bottle covers about 12 (3 in.) cookies. Certified Kosher. **$4.99**

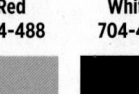

Yellow 704-487	Pink 704-486	Red 704-488	White 704-481
Green 704-493	**Blue** 704-444	**Orange** 704-496	**Black** 704-205

READY-TO-DECORATE ICING

Add an exciting finishing touch to treats without mixing or mess. Just slip one of the four free tips over the nozzle and start the fun. Tips include: small round tip, large round tip, leaf tip and star tip. Colors match Wilton Icing Colors (p. 139). 6.4 oz. Certified Kosher.
Each $4.79

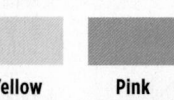

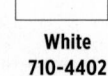
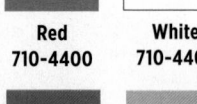

Yellow 710-4409	Pink 710-4406	Red 710-4400	White 710-4402	
Green 710-4401	**Violet** 710-4408	**Blue** 710-4407	**Orange** 710-4410	**Black** 710-4404

ICING WRITER

Squeeze colorful accents onto fondant and Wilton Cookie Icing with this easy-to-control, ready-to-use icing! Dries to a smooth, satin finish. 3 oz. bottle. Certified Kosher.
Each $2.99

Yellow 710-2226	Pink 710-2230	Red 710-2225
White 710-2228	**Green** 710-2229	**Violet** 710-2231 / **Blue** 710-2227

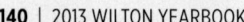

MIXES & READY-TO-USE ICINGS

Create delicious icings for decorating cakes and treats with Wilton mixes.

Buttercream Icing Mix
Our convenient mix has the delicious taste and creamy texture of homemade buttercream icing. Makes 1½ to 2 cups. Enough to ice a 1-layer 8 in. cake. Certified Kosher Dairy.
710-112 $3.99

Royal Icing Mix
A convenient mix for creating hard-drying flowers and other decorations! Makes 2 cups—enough icing for about 280 drop flowers or 88 small roses. Certified Kosher.
710-1219 $5.99

Whipped Icing Mix
Our light, whipped icing provides the ideal texture for decorating in an easy-to-make, delicious mix. Light and delicate vanilla flavor. Makes 5 cups, enough to ice and decorate one 2-layer 9 in. round cake or 9 in. x 13 in. sheet cake. Certified Kosher Dairy.
710-1241 $5.99

Meringue Powder
Primary ingredient for royal icing. Stabilizes buttercream, adds body to boiled icing and meringue. Replaces egg whites in many recipes. Resealable top opens for easy measuring. 4 oz. can makes five recipes of royal icing; 8 oz. can makes 10 recipes. 16 oz. can makes 20 recipes. Certified Kosher.
4 oz. 702-6007 $5.99
8 oz. 702-6015 $8.99
16 oz. 702-6004 $17.99

READY-TO-USE ICINGS

Wilton makes the only ready-to-use icing that is the perfect consistency for decorating. The pure white color is best for creating true vivid colors using Wilton Icing Colors. Rich and creamy with a delicious homemade taste.

Creamy Decorator Icing
Ideal medium consistency for use in Wilton Method of Cake Decorating courses in a convenient tub. Has a great vanilla flavor and is easy to color. Yields 9 cups of icing, which will cover three 2-layer 8 in. cakes, four 9 in. x 13 in. cakes or 60 cupcakes. 4.5 lb. Certified Kosher
704-680 $17.99

Decorator Icing
Ideal stiff consistency for making roses and flowers with upright petals. 16 oz. can.
Each $3.79
White 710-118
Chocolate 710-119

Color Flow Mix
Create dimensional flow-in designs for your cake. Great for covering and decorating cookies! 4 oz. can makes 10 — 1½ cup batches. Certified Kosher.
701-47 $8.99

Piping Gel
Perfect for writing messages and adding decorative accents. Use clear or tint with icing color. 10 oz. Certified Kosher.
704-105 $4.29

FLAVORINGS

Wilton flavors are concentrated—only a drop or two adds delicious taste to icings, cakes, beverages and other recipes.

Clear Flavorings
Recommended and used in Wilton Method Classes, these delicious flavors won't change your icing color. Certified Kosher.

Imitation Clear Vanilla Extract
2 fl. oz.
604-2237 $1.99
8 fl. oz.
604-2269 $4.99

Imitation Clear Butter Flavor
2 fl. oz.
604-2040 $1.99
8 fl. oz.
604-2067 $4.99

Imitation Clear Almond Extract
2 fl. oz.
604-2126 $1.99

Pure Lemon Extract
Great for painting with Wilton Pearl Dust and Color Dust! Dries quickly on your fondant or gum paste flowers for natural-looking color highlights. 2 fl. oz. Certified Kosher.
604-2235 $1.99

Pure Vanilla Extract
Unmatched flavor and aroma enhances cakes, puddings, pie fillings, custards and more. 4 fl. oz. Certified Kosher.
604-2270 $7.99

FLOWER MAKING TOOLS & ACCESSORIES

Wilton offers essential tools to create classic Wilton Flowers.

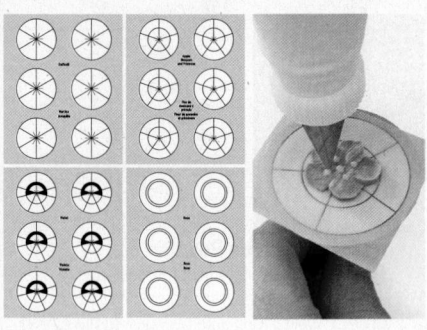

Flower Nail Templates
Convenient stickers guide you to create perfectly formed flowers! Includes four template styles used to create five popular icing flowers. Set/48.
414-1000 $3.99

Flower Nail No. 7
For basic flower making. Provides the control you need when piping icing flowers. Stainless steel. 1.5 in. wide.
402-3007 $1.49

Lily Nail Set
Includes 0.5 in., 1.25 in., 1.625 in. and 2.5 in. dia. cups. Plastic. Set/8.
403-9444 $2.49

Decorating Nail Set
A great selection of sizes for creating virtually any size nail flower! Includes 1.5 in., 2 in., 2.5 in. Flower Nails and 2.25 in. x 2.5 in. Cupcake Nail. Stems insert easily in nails to create a secure platform. Top-rack dishwasher safe. Plastic. Pk./4.
417-107 $6.99

Pre-Cut Icing Flower Squares
Perfectly sized waxed paper squares attach to flower nail with a dot of icing for easy piping and transfer of flowers. Pk./50.
414-920 $1.99

Flower Lifter
Easily transfers buttercream flowers from nail to cake without damage. Angled design keeps your hands from touching the cake. Detachable blades for easy cleaning. Plastic. 5.25 in. long.
417-1199 $3.49

STAMENS
Finish your royal icing or gum paste flowers with these lovely stamen styles. Cut stamens to desired size and insert in flower center.

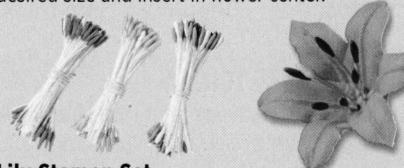

Lily Stamen Set
Create lifelike lilies with trim-to-fit lily stamen clusters in three natural colors! Includes 10 each pink, yellow and brown. 2.125 in. long. Pk./30.
1005-4451 $3.49

Color Stamen Set
Includes 60 each yellow, white and orange. 2.125 in. long. Pk./180.
1005-4452 $3.49

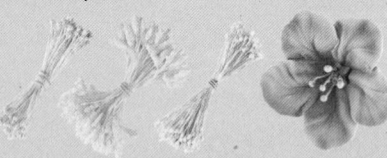

Flower Stamen Assortment
May be tinted (except pearl) with Wilton Icing Colors added to vanilla. Includes 60 each pearl, fluffy and glitter. 2.5 in. long. Pk./180.
1005-410 $3.49

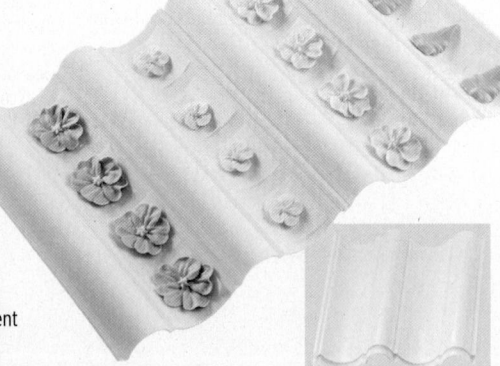

Wave Flower Former Set
Convenient connecting platform dries flowers, leaves and other decorations in royal icing, gum paste or fondant. Wave shape makes it easy to dry concave or convex shapes; large drying area is great for ribbons, bows and streamers. 14.5 in. x 9 in. assembled. Plastic. Set/2. Patent Pending.
1907-1320 $6.99

MAKE-ANY-MESSAGE PRESS SETS
Create concise writing, letters and decorative accents for your cake tops with the help of our various press sets.

Italic
Press words up to 10.5 in. wide, letters 0.75 in. high. Includes letter holder. Set/58.
2104-2277 $8.99

Classic
Press words up to 10.5 in. wide, letters 0.75 in. high. Includes letter holder. Set/56.
2104-10 $8.99

Cake Stencils Variety Pack
It's so easy—just place on your iced cake, then sprinkle with Wilton Cake Sparkles, add exciting Wilton sugars in a rainbow of colors or use Color Mist food color spray. Also works beautifully with Wilton Rolled Fondant. Includes Happy Birthday, Flower, Swirl and Heart designs. Pk./4.
417-148 $7.99

DESSERT DECORATORS

It's easy to add beautiful decorations to any dessert or appetizer in minutes!

Designed for comfortable one-hand decorating and effortless tip positioning, this is the most convenient dessert tool you'll ever use. Create beautiful decorations: shells, stars, rosettes, leaves.
415-850 $34.99

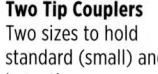

Rotating Cylinder
Just turn to place the tip in the correct position.

Ergonomic Design
Easy, comfortable grip for right or left hand.

Stainless Steel Cylinder
Stainless steel won't transfer flavors; maintains temperature of fillings.

Fits Virtually Any Tip/Coupler
Use with the tips included or with most other Wilton tips.

Pull-Out Plunger
Inner ring pushes filling smoothly through cylinder.

Convenient Thumb Lever
The ideal distance from cylinder for comfortable one-handed decorating.

Durable Construction
Cylinder and plunger are housed in an impact-resistant sleeve for years of great decorating performance.

Easy To Fill and Clean
Most parts detach with ease; wash in warm, soapy water.

Dessert Decorator Pro includes all this:

Two Tip Couplers
Two sizes to hold standard (small) and large tips.

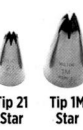

Tip 366 Leaf | Tip 4B Star | Tip 125 Petal | Tip 21 Star | Tip 1M Star | Tip 230 Bismarck

Six Durable Nickel-Plated Tips
Quality metal tips produce perfectly shaped decorations every time.

Tip/Coupler Dishwasher and Storage Bag
Just place nylon mesh bag with tips and couplers in dishwasher silverware rack.

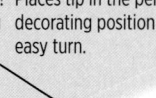

Tips in bag for size reference only. Tips included are shown at left.

Recipes and Instructions
Includes delicious recipes and easy decorating instructions.

Dessert Decorator Plus

It's the easy-to-use tool for beautifully decorated desserts! One hand does it all: elegant shells, stars and leaves, beautiful script messages, pretty bows and flowers. **415-0906 $14.99**

See-through Barrel
Know how much icing is left! Parts detach easily for filling and cleaning.

Ergonomic Design
Finger-grip barrel is easy to handle in right or left hand.

Rotating Cylinder
Places tip in the perfect decorating position with an easy turn.

Pull-Out Plunger
Inner ring pushes icing through cylinder.

Convenient Thumb Lever
Lets you hold tool and decorate with one hand.

Dessert Decorator Plus includes all this:

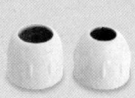

2 Tip Couplers
Two sizes hold standard (small) and large tips.

5 Precision Tips
Produce perfectly shaped decorations every time.

Round Tip | Star Tip | Petal Tip | Leaf Tip | Filling Tip

Instruction Sheet
See how to create every decoration shown!

CAKE DECORATING PUBLICATIONS

Wilton, the No. 1 in cake decorating, offers you a wide variety of publications to increase your skills and knowledge.

NEW!

"Cake Decorating Beginner's Guide"
Wilton shows beginners everything they need to know. Includes:
• How to bake and ice perfect cakes.
• How to mix any color icing with ease.
• Step-by-step decorating instructions.
Soft cover, 40 pages.
902-1232 $3.99

"Cake Decorating Basics" DVD
See the essentials of creating amazing cakes. Includes:
• Tools to icing.
• Baking perfect cakes.
• Decorating stars, shells, flowers and more.
60 minutes.
901-120 $19.99

"Celebrate With Fondant"
It's the first book to feature fondant created the Wilton way! Includes:
• More than 40 terrific cake ideas
• Alternate ways to decorate each design
• Step-by-step instructions
Soft cover, 120 pages.
902-911 $14.99

"Decorating Cakes—A Reference & Idea Book"
Learn Wilton tried-and-true decorating techniques. Includes:
• 30 exciting cakes with complete instructions and product listing.
• 103 techniques with instructions.
• In-depth sections on baking cakes, preparing icing and more.
Soft cover, 116 pages.
902-904 $14.99

"2013 Pattern Book"
Duplicate many of the beautiful cake designs featured in the "2013 Yearbook" and on the Wilton website. Includes:
• More than 133 decorating outlines to transfer to your cake or treats.
• Easy-to-follow instructions.
Soft cover, 48 pages.
408-2013 $9.99

Sugar Sheets!™

EDIBLE DECORATING PAPER

Use edible, flexible *Sugar Sheets!* edible decorating paper to cut or punch virtually any shape or border design. There's no preparation, no mess. Just peel, punch or cut and place your decorations in minutes. *Sugar Sheets!* have a light, sweet flavor that works with buttercream or fondant-covered treats. 8 in. x 11 in. Certified Kosher. **Each $3.99**

SOLID COLORS

NEW! Orange 710-2965	**NEW!** Brown 710-2966
Light Pink 710-2950	Light Blue 710-2954
Bright Pink 710-2952	Bright Blue 710-2956
Light Green 710-2957	Bright Green 710-2958
Light Yellow 710-2955	Bright Yellow 710-2947
Red 710-2953	Black 710-2961
Purple 710-2949	White 710-2960

PATTERNS

NEW! Multi Stars 710-2971	**NEW!** Streamers 710-2973	**NEW!** Floral 710-2969	**NEW!** Wild Stripes 710-2972	**NEW!** Scrolls 710-2975

NEW! Mod Dots 710-2970	Zebra 710-2943	Damask 710-2941	Pink Hearts 710-2951

EDIBLE PRE-CUT STICKERS

Just peel and place pre-cut letters and numbers or frames onto treats. Personalize frames with a colorful design or initial using Wilton Cake Stamps and Dab-N-Color edible color. Certified Kosher. **Each $3.99**

Alphabet Black
Each sheet includes 87 letters, 20 numbers; each approx. 0.625 in.
710-2944

Alphabet Primary
710-2945

NEW!

Frames
Includes 12 pre-cut circles measuring 2.25 in. dia.
710-2981

EDIBLE PRE-CUT BORDERS & STICKERS

NEW!

It's an easy way to add colorful, edible details to treats. Just peel and place on cakes, cupcakes, cookies, brownies and more. Includes 12 stickers and 8 border strips. Certified Kosher. **Each $3.99**

Gift 710-2976	**Cupcake** 710-2977	**Flower** 710-2978	**Candy** 710-2979

ORDER TOLL FREE: 800-794-5866

SUGAR SHEETS! TOOLS & ACCESSORIES

Let your creativity flow with the help of these convenient tools. Perfect for use with *Sugar Sheets!* edible decorating paper, fondant and gum paste!

PUNCH SET & CUTTING INSERTS

Punch set includes base and oval cutting insert. Silicone cap holds plastic top and bottom inserts together for easy storage and protects the cutting blade. For food use only. Patent Pending.

Additional cutting inserts sold below.

Punch Set with Oval Cutting Insert
1907-1120
$14.99

Cutting Inserts

Designs range from 1.25 in. x 1.5 in to 2.25 in. x 2 in. **Each $5.99**

| Square Caption 1907-1041 | Balloon 1907-1042 | Scalloped Heart 1907-1012 | Spiral 1907-9702 | Daisy 1907-1013 | Sunburst 1907-1015 | Butterfly 1907-1014 | Leaf 1907-9703 |

NEW! NEW!

Cutting Insert Sets

Designs range from 0.5 in. x 0.5 in. to 2.4 in x 2 in. Set/3. **Each $14.99**

| Layered Hearts 1907-1121 | Layered Circles 1907-1122 | Layered Flowers 1907-1123 | Layered Stars 1907-1125 |

BORDER PUNCH SET & CUTTING INSERTS

Border punch set includes base and scallop cutting insert. Silicone cap holds plastic top and bottom inserts together for easy storage and protects the cutting blade. For food use only. Patent Pending.

Additional cutting inserts sold below.

Border Punch Set with Scallop Cutting Insert
1907-1127
$14.99

Cutting Inserts

Designs range from 0.25 in. to 0.75 in. high. **Each $5.99**

| Lace 1907-1128 | Waves 1907-1129 | Hearts 1907-1132 | |
| Flowers 1907-1131 | Diamonds 1907-1130 | Bubbles 1907-1133 | Grass 1907-1049 |

NEW!

Slide-N-Cut Edge Cutter

Cuts even strips of *Sugar Sheets!* edible decorating paper, fondant or gum paste. Slide the cutting arm to the position you want, and lock into place. Includes straight and wavy cutting blades. For food use only. 9 in. x 12 in. cutting surface. Patent Pending.
1907-1117
$29.99

Mini Punches

NEW!

Cut fun edible confetti and colorful mini accents from *Sugar Sheets!* edible decorating paper, fondant or gum paste! For food use only. Designs range from 0.3 in. to 0.5 in. Patent Pending. **Each $6.99**

★	●	∷	♥	❀	◆
Star 1907-1032	Round 1907-1033	Multi Round 1907-1034	Heart 1907-1030	Flower 1907-1031	Diamond 1907-1035

Decorative Scissors

Create hand-cut edible shapes! Great for *Sugar Sheets!* edible decorating paper, gum paste or rolled fondant. Stainless steel blades lock in place and easily disassemble for cleaning. Intended for food use only. 2.75 in. x 6.5 in. **Each $6.99**

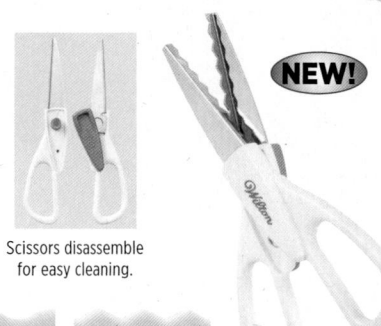

NEW!

Scissors disassemble for easy cleaning.

| Scallop 1907-1029 | Waves 1907-1028 | Zigzag 1907-1027 |

Rotary Cutter

Hand cut accents from *Sugar Sheets!* edible decorating paper, fondant or gum paste! Easy to control with an ergonomic, soft-grip handle and smooth, easy-cutting stainless steel blade. Protective blade cover included. For food use only. 4 in. x 1.75 in.
1907-1119 $5.99

Circle Cutter

Cut circles easily and quickly from *Sugar Sheets!* edible decorating paper, fondant or gum paste! Place cutter on your material and rotate the blade to make uniform rounds from 5 in. to 12.5 in. For food use only. 9 in. x 2.25 in. Patent Pending.
1907-1118 $14.99

Tweezers

Lift and transfer *Sugar Sheets!* edible decorating paper, fondant and gum paste decorations easily! Two head styles available, reverse action, and silicone grip. 3.25 in. x 1.25 in. **Each $5.99**

| Fine 1907-1134 | Wide 1907-1335 |

Dab-N-Hold Edible Adhesive

NEW!

Spreads thin, attaches fast and easy! Use to apply *Sugar Sheets!* edible decorating paper pieces to fondant or crusted buttercream icing, create layered decorations and more! 2 fl. oz. Certified Kosher.
610-927 $5.99

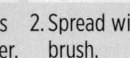

1. Dab small dots on edible paper. 2. Spread with brush. 3. Attach to treat and let dry.

SUGAR SHEETS! TOOLS & ACCESSORIES

CAKE STAMP SETS

Put your personal stamp on cakes and treats with these fun stamp sets! Use with Dab-N-Color edible colors to stamp an unforgettable finishing touch on *Sugar Sheets!* edible decorating paper, fondant or gum paste designs. For food use only. **Each Set $12.99**

6-Pc. Stamp Sets
Designs range from 2.5 in. x 3.5 in.

Flowers
417-1177

Animals
417-1117

Party Fun
417-1180

Flourishes
417-1179

4-Pc. Stamp Sets
Stamps are sized to fit large punch shapes for easy designs. Designs range from 1.25 in. x 1.25 in.

Balloons
417-1176

Hearts
417-1174

Flowers
417-1173

Butterflies
417-1175

0123
456
789

10-Pc. Classic Numbers
Largest number stamp approx. 0.8 in. x 1.5 in.
417-5117 $9.99

ABCDEFGH
IJKLMNOP
QRSTUV
WXYZ

26-Pc. Classic Alphabet
Largest letter stamp approx. 1.2 in. x 1.4 in.
417-1168 $24.99

Dab-N-Color Edible Color

A rainbow of vivid shades creates dazzling stamped designs and painted highlights on *Sugar Sheets!* edible decorating paper, fondant and gum paste. For stamping, just dab a small amount of color onto stamp or dispense color into a container and gently brush or wipe on color to cover stamp surface. 2 fl. oz. Certified Kosher. **Each $4.99**

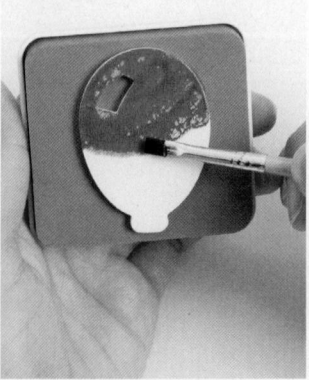

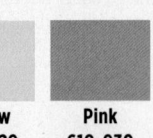
White
610-928

Yellow
610-929

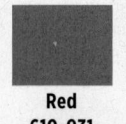
Pink
610-930

Red
610-931

Orange
610-937

Purple
610-932

Blue
610-933

Green
610-934

Brown
610-935

Black
610-936

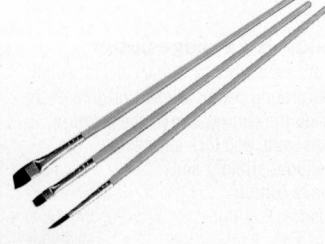

Brush Set
Fine-bristle brushes in three tip designs (round, square and bevel) help you achieve different painted effects. Set/3.
1907-1207 $3.29

TEXTURE PRESSES

Patterned wheels create fun, embossed decorations on *Sugar Sheets!* edible decorating paper, fondant or gum paste! Add texture to a variety of accents. For food use only. 5.5 in. x 2.5 in.; 3.5 in. wheels.
Each $12.99

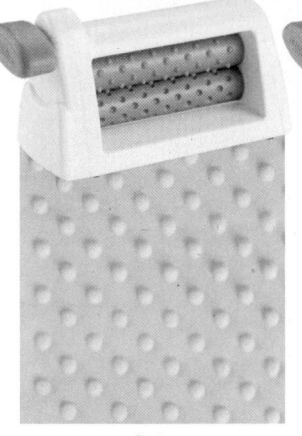

Dots
1907-1037

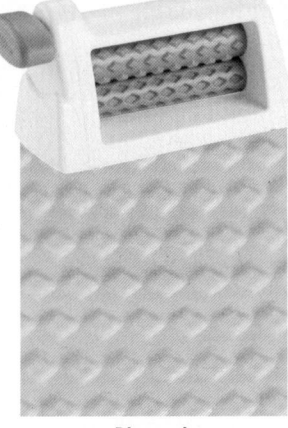

Diamonds
1907-1038

Lines
1907-1036

NEW!

CAKE STAMPING BLOCKS

Conveniently holds Wilton Cake Stamps (sold separately) for customized messaging and stamping on *Sugar Sheets!* edible decorating paper, rolled fondant and gum paste!

NEW!

Small Cake Stamping Block
417-1170
$5.99

Large Cake Stamping Block
417-1171
$9.99

Spell-N-Stamp Cake Stamping Block
The versatile square and round message area creates a look perfect for your cake shape. 6.5 in. x 9.75 in.
417-1172 $12.99

Stamps shown reversed for readability.

NEW!

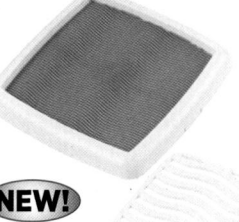

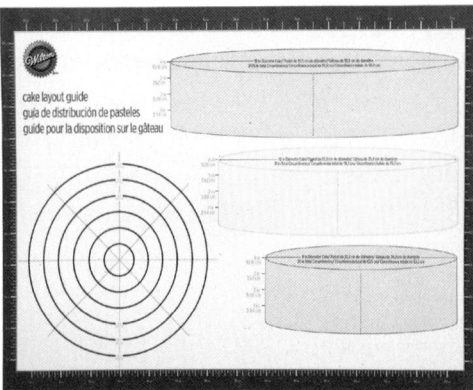

2-Pc. Stamp Cleaning Tray Set
The cleaning tray features a wavy ridged surface perfect for cleaning stamps. The separate drying rack is great for air drying after cleaning. Tray and rack snap together for easy storage. 7.25 in. x 7.25 in. x 0.75 in.
1907-1039 $12.99

Storage Board
Place cut pieces under flaps until you're ready to work. Ample space for storing multiple petals and leaves when making flowers. 8 in. x 10 in.
409-2544 $6.99

Cake Layout Guide
Plan the look of your cake before you place your decorations! The 30 in. x 24 in. surface includes a cake top circle marked for rounds up to 12 in. and 4 in. cake side layouts. Laminated plastic.
409-2546 $12.99

READY-TO-USE ROLLED FONDANT
Our fondant is ready to roll and shape, making it the easiest way to create an elegant fondant cake!

WHITE FONDANT PACKS
The 24 oz. package covers an 8 in. 2-layer cake plus decorations; the 80 oz. package covers a 2-layer 6 in., 8 in. and 10 in. round tiered cake plus decorations. Pure white. Certified Kosher.

24 oz.
710-2076 **$7.29**

80 oz.
710-2180 **$23.99**

COLORED FONDANT MULTI PACKS
Each 17.6 oz. package contains four 4.4 oz. packs. Certified Kosher.
Each Pack $11.99

Primary Colors
Green, Red, Yellow, Blue.
710-445

Neon Colors
Purple, Orange, Yellow, Pink.
710-446

Pastel Colors
Blue, Yellow, Pink, Green.
710-447

Natural Colors
Light Brown, Dark Brown, Pink, Black.
710-448

COLORED FONDANT PACKS
Pre-colored and ready-to-use. 24 oz. package. Certified Kosher.

Black
710-2190
$10.99

Red
710-2191
$10.99

Blue
710-2182
$9.99

Yellow
710-2183
$9.99

Pink
710-2181
$9.99

Green
710-2184
$9.99

Chocolate
710-2078
$9.99

GUM PASTE
Design breathtaking gum paste roses, daisies, apple blossoms, tulips and other flowers in advance for decorating cakes.

Ready-To-Use Gum Paste
Create beautiful hand-molded flowers right from the package. Just tint, roll out and cut to create incredible floral bouquets for your cakes. Easy instructions included. 1 lb. Certified Kosher.
707-130 $10.99

Gum Paste Mix
Just add water and knead. Workable, pliable paste molds beautiful flowers and designs. 16 oz. Certified Kosher.
707-124 $6.99

GUM PASTE INGREDIENTS
Essential ingredients for making gum paste from scratch.

Gum-Tex
6 oz. Certified Kosher.
707-117 $8.49

Glucose
8.5 fl. oz. Certified Kosher.
707-2598 $4.49

ORDER TOLL FREE: 800-794-5866

GUM PASTE/FONDANT TOOLS & ACCESSORIES

Make all your gum paste and fondant flowers, borders and embellishments come to life with the various, quality Wilton tools and accessories.

NEW!

Ribbon Cutter

Cut a variety of ribbon widths and designs in fondant and gum paste with our Fondant Ribbon Cutter.

Includes:
- Three spacers: 1 in., ½ in. and ¼ in.
- Four cutting wheels: straight, wavy, zigzag.
- Two locks: ensures wheels and spacers do not shift.
- Roller handle with easy-button release and comfortable grip.
- Storage case keeps all parts together for easy storage.

Set/25.
1907-1019 $29.99

Angled, space-saving storage tray lets you easily view spacers and cutting wheels.

Includes

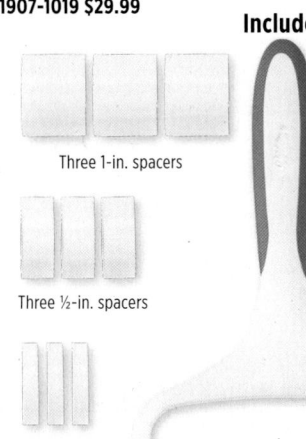

Three 1-in. spacers

Three ½-in. spacers

Three ¼-in. spacers

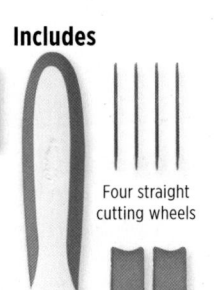

Roller handle with easy-button release

Four straight cutting wheels

Four wavy cutting wheels

Two locks

Four zigzag cutting wheels

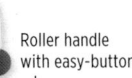

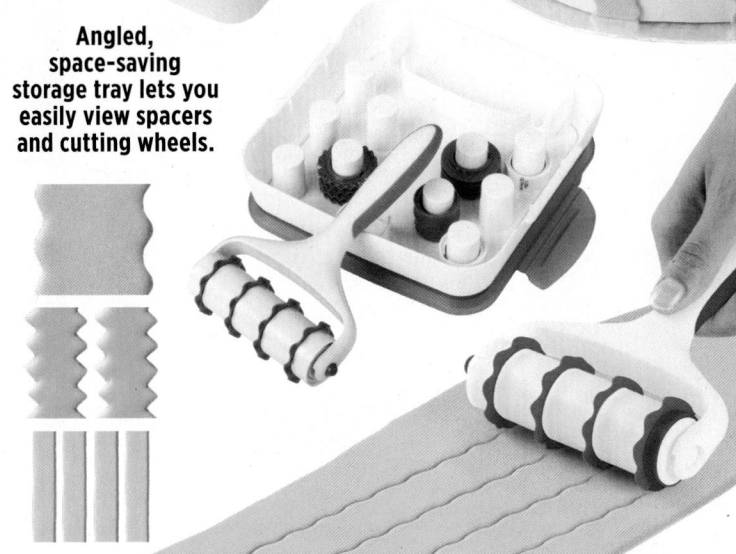

Pattern Embosser

NEW!

Create a seamless, 4 in. wide pattern on fondant or gum paste with our Pattern Embosser.

Includes:
- Three classic patterns: dots, lace and woven.
- Rollers easily snap onto handle.
- Storage case keeps all parts together for easy storage.

Set/5.
1907-1017 $39.99

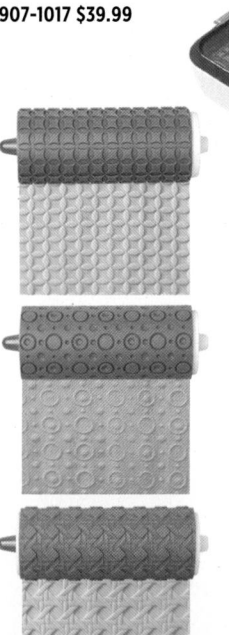

Create a seamless, 4 in. wide pattern on fondant or gum paste.

Detail Embosser

NEW!

Add detail quickly with our Detail Embosser.

Includes:
- Two easy-to-remove wheels; each wheel has three embossing designs.
- Six patterns: dash, bead, zigzag and wavy, stitch and dot.
- Roller handle with easy-button release and comfortable grip.
- Storage case keeps workspace organized.

Set/4.
1907-1018 $19.99

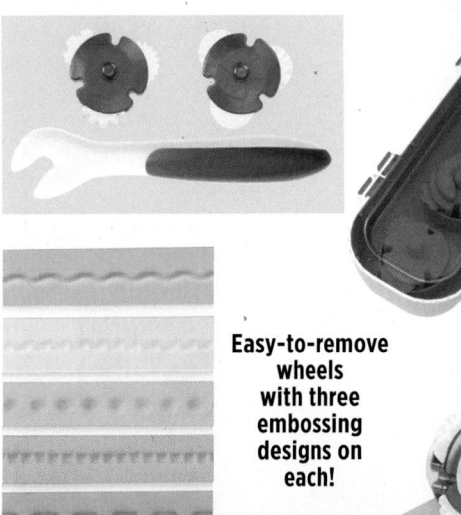

Easy-to-remove wheels with three embossing designs on each!

GUM PASTE/FONDANT TOOLS & ACCESSORIES

GUM PASTE & FONDANT MOLDS

Create amazing detail quickly with our theme silicone molds! Molds contain detailed impression areas, which imprint texture and dimension on gum paste or fondant shapes. **Each $9.99**

Kids Party
409-2553

Macrame
409-2549

Folk
409-2550

Jewelry
409-2551

Sea Life
409-2552

Fern
409-2548

Nature
409-2565

Fabric
409-2563

Global
409-2564

Baroque
409-2562

ORDER TOLL FREE: 800-794-5866

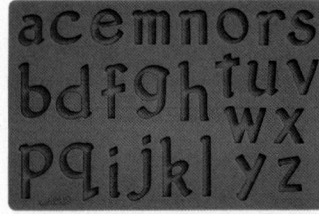

NEW!

Molds shown reversed for readability.

Letters/Numbers Gum Paste & Fondant Mold Set

With this set, it's easy to put the finishing touches on your cakes with a beautiful three-dimensional message or monogram. Just fill silicone molds with fondant or gum paste, press and smooth, and release. Great for two-tone letters and numbers, a perfect way to personalize cake and cupcakes. Includes 26 capital letters, 26 lower case letters, numbers 0-9 and "?". Set/4.
409-2547 $29.99

FONDANT IMPRINT MATS

Imprint a beautifully recessed pattern to cover your cake! Just smooth your rolled fondant over the silicone mat, place on your cake and peel back the mat. The recessed design imprinted in the fondant adds beautiful definition, so even white cakes stand out. Also great for textured fondant ribbons and edging. 20 in. x 20 in.
Each $19.99

Graceful Vines
409-414

Happy Birthday
409-417

Star Power
409-416

Floral Fantasy
409-415

CUT-OUTS FONDANT CUTTERS

With Cut-Outs Fondant Cutters, it's easy to make fun shapes for your fondant cakes and cupcakes. Just roll out fondant and/or gum paste, press down with the stainless steel Cut-Out and lift away. Remove shapes with a small spatula.

Crinkle
Circle, Square, Triangle, Heart. 1.25 in. Set/4.
417-444 $3.79

Fancy
Flower, Leaf, Oval, Heart 1.5 in. to 2 in. Set/4.
417-445 $3.79

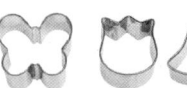

Garden
Butterfly, Tulip, Bell, Flower 1.25 in. to 1.75 in. Set/4.
417-443 $3.79

Ovals
0.625 in. to 2.25 in. Set/3.
417-438 $2.99

Rounds
0.75 in. to 2.25 in. Set/3.
417-432 $2.99

Squares
0.625 in. to 2.25 in. Set/3.
417-431 $2.99

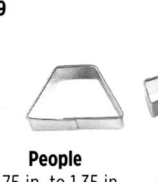

People
0.75 in. to 1.35 in. Set/6.
417-441 $4.49

Hearts
0.75 in. to 2.25 in. Set/3.
417-434 $2.99

Stars
0.625 in. to 2.1 in. Set/3.
417-433 $2.99

Flowers
0.625 to 2.1 in. Set/3.
417-435 $2.99

Funny Flowers
0.75 in. to 2.3 in. Set/3.
417-436 $2.99

Leaves
1 in. to 3 in. Set/3.
417-437 $2.99

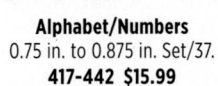

Alphabet/Numbers
0.75 in. to 0.875 in. Set/37.
417-442 $15.99

GUM PASTE/FONDANT TOOLS & ACCESSORIES

Fondant Trimmer

Comfortably designed, nylon fondant trimmer makes all your cutting easy and precise. Provides a clean cut for fondant and gum paste, and is safe to use on most surfaces. Wheel removes from handle for easy cleaning. Wheel: 3 in.; Handle: 7 in.
1907-1051 $9.99

NEW!

Cut-N-Spin Rotating Cutting Board

Turn as you cut to create gum paste and fondant shapes conveniently! Hand wash. 12 in. x 12 in.
409-2561 $19.99

Storage Board

Place cut pieces under flaps until you're ready to work. Ample space for storing multiple petals and leaves when making flowers. Use the back side to roll out fondant for small details. 8 in. x 10 in.
409-2544 $6.99

7-Pc. Deluxe Gum Paste Tool Set

Cut, shape and position delicate gum paste decorations and fondant details with more control using the essential tools in this seven-piece set! Four dual-action tools feature contoured handles with comfortable grip. Angled spatula, tweezers and scissors are sized especially for handling small gum paste pieces. Includes cutting tool, quilling tool, knife/needle tool and cutter brush. Convenient case. Set/7.
1907-1011 $29.99

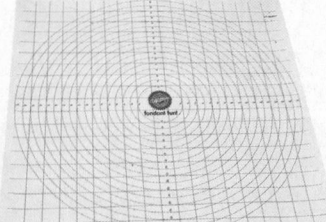

Roll-N-Cut Mat

For precise measuring, rolling and cutting of fondant or dough. Pre-marked circles for exact sizing. Square grid helps you cut precise strips. Non-stick surface for easy release. 20 in. square with circles from 3 in. to 19 in. dia.
409-412 $9.99

9 in. Fondant Roller

Roll out fondant evenly for easy cutting and shaping with this three-piece, non-stick roller. Just the right size for preparing small amounts of fondant. Perfect for use with fondant, gum paste and our variety of Cut-Outs fondant cutters. Includes 1/8 in. and 1/16 in. rings. 9 in. x 1 in. dia.
1907-1205 $6.99

Fondant Smoother

Smooths fondant-covered cakes to a beautiful surface. Contoured handle is comfortable to hold. Softly rounded base edge prevents marking fondant surface. The squared back helps to create a clean angle between sides and base of cake. 3.25 in. x 5.75 in.
1907-1016 $7.99

NEW!

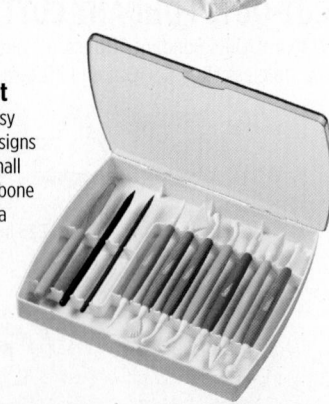

Dusting Pouches

Essential for rolling out gum paste or fondant! Fabric pouch dusts surfaces with a cornstarch/confectioners' sugar mixture to prevent your rolling pin from sticking. 7 in. dia. Pk./4.
417-106 $3.29

10-Pc. Gum Paste/Fondant Tool Set

Precise tools feature comfortable grips for easy handling. Colored grips and numbered tip designs make tools easy to identify. Includes large/small veining tool, shell tool/knife, large/small dogbone tool, serrated quilting/cutting wheel, umbrella tool with five and six divisions, scriber/cone tool, large/small ball tool, palette knife and modeling sticks #1 and #2 and convenient case. Set/10.
1907-1107 $29.99

20 in. Fondant Roller

Its extra-wide, smooth design is perfect for rolling out fondant to cover cakes. The non-stick surface makes handling large pieces of fondant easy. (Mat sold at left.) 20 in. x 1.5 in. dia.
1907-1210 $22.99

20 in. Fondant Roller Guide Rings

Slip these easy-to-use guide rings onto the ends of your 20 in. Fondant Roller to achieve the perfect thickness every time. Includes 1/16 in. (blue), 1/8 in. (orange) 3/16 in. (gold) rings. Set/3.
1907-1010 $4.99

Water Brush

Just fill with water and brush to attach fondant and gum paste decorations. Perfect for rehydrating your *Sugar Sheets!* edible decorating paper.
7 in. x 0.75 in.
1907-1111
$7.99

Deluxe Brush Set

Create amazing color effects with the wide range of brush shapes and sizes in this set. Quality nylon bristles in wide and narrow shapes give you exceptional control. Brushes are also ideal for attaching shapes using gum glue adhesive, striping decorating bags with color and more. Set/7.
1907-1112 $8.99

Brush Set

Fine-bristle brushes in three tip designs (round, square and bevel). Set/3.
1907-1207 $3.29

Decorative Press Set

Squeeze with ease to make exciting decorations from gum paste or rolled fondant! Shapes include circle, basketweave, teardrop, three-hole, star and semicircle. Comes apart for easy cleaning. For food use only. Set/6.
1907-1116 $19.99

Extra Fine Tip
FoodWriter Edible Color Markers

The ideal tip size and color palette for adding details to gum paste flowers! Also great for fondant decorating—drawing facial details, writing messages and outlining designs. Set includes five 0.07 oz. FoodWriter edible color markers. Certified Kosher. Set/5.
609-105 $8.49

Brown	Green	Red	Blue	Black

EXTRA-FINE TIP

COLOR ACCENTS

Brush edible accents onto your fondant, gum paste or royal icing decoration with a soft brush, or mix with Wilton Pure Lemon Extract to paint vibrant color on to your decoration.
Each $4.49

Color Dust

Give flower decorations a deep matte finish, or create natural shading that adds depth. Certified Kosher (except Deep Pink and Purple). 0.05 oz. bottle.

White 703-100	Red 703-101	Deep Pink 703-103	Orange 703-104	Purple 703-105
Brown 703-106	Periwinkle Blue 703-107	Goldenrod 703-108	Spruce Green 703-109	Lime Green 703-110

Pearl Dust

Give your decorations a beautiful, glittering finish. Creates rich, lustrous highlights on flowers, bows, letters and more. Certified Kosher (except Orchid Pink and Lilac Purple). 0.05 oz. bottle.

Leaf Green 703-215	Lilac Purple 703-221	Sapphire Blue 703-222	Ruby Red 703-223	Gold 703-216
Yellow 703-213	Bronze 703-214	Orchid Pink 703-217	Silver 703-218	White 703-219

Pure Lemon Extract

Mix with Wilton Pearl Dust and Color Dust for brilliant painted applications! Dries quickly on fondant or gum paste decorations for natural-looking color highlights. The pure lemon flavor is excellent in your favorite recipes, too! 2 fl. oz. Certified Kosher.
604-2235 $1.99

Fondant Decorative Punch Set

Punch out fondant accents with elegant openwork shapes. As you punch, the disk imprints a detailed design that adds a pretty touch of texture. The comfortable angled handle holds eight design disks. Disks turn to lock into place. Set/9.
1907-1204 $9.99

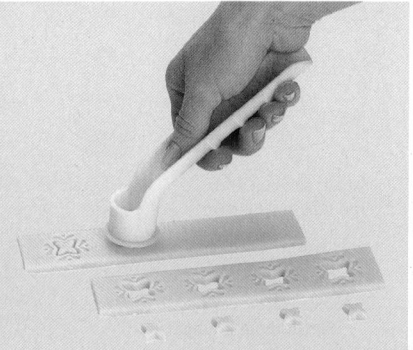

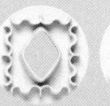

Large Tulip with Leaves	Dutch Blossom	Paisley with Dots	Wide Diamond with Scrolls	Small Tulip with Leaves	Snapdragon with Leaves	4-Leaf Clover with Dots	Narrow Diamond with Scrolls

GUM PASTE/FONDANT FLOWER TOOLS & ACCESSORIES

Along with our cutters and ejectors, you'll want to own the complete line of quality Wilton gum paste and fondant tools and accessories to make your flowers come to life.

GUM PASTE FLOWER CUTTER SET

Cut petals and leaves used to make exquisite gum paste flowers, like stargazer lilies, roses and cymbidium orchids with the great variety of cutters and ejectors included. Cutters are comfortable to hold, with a contoured top and precise cutting edges. Ejectors cut blossom and hydrangea shapes then imprint beautiful texture on both sides using the custom Impression Strip. The full-color trilingual instruction book includes step-by-step instructions for 13 of the most popular gum paste flowers. Set/25.

2109-0054 $29.99

Includes all of this:
19 Cutters • 4 Ejectors • 2 Accessories

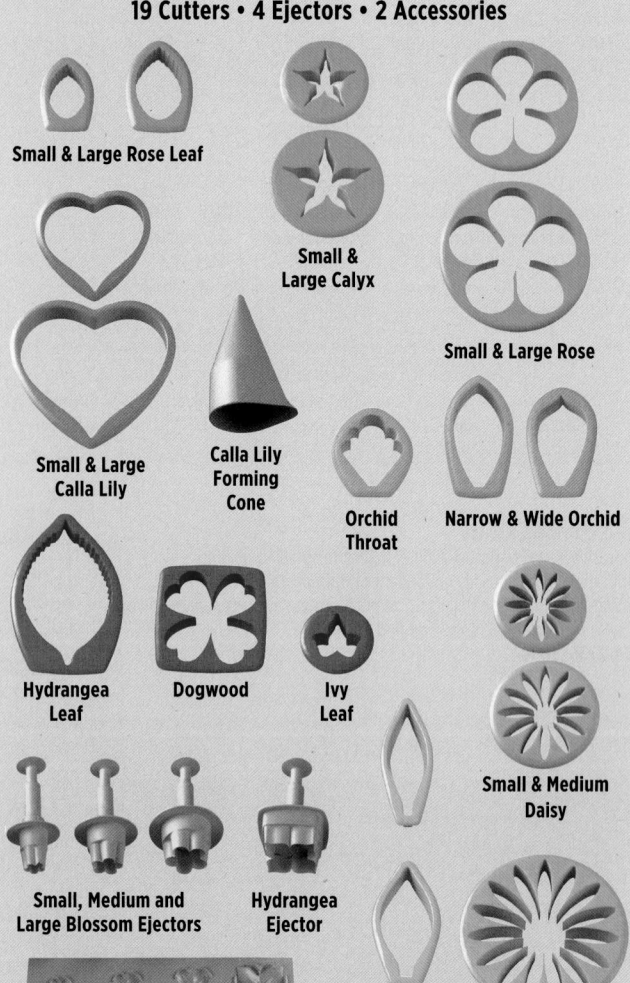

Small & Large Rose Leaf

Small & Large Calyx

Small & Large Rose

Small & Large Calla Lily

Calla Lily Forming Cone

Orchid Throat

Narrow & Wide Orchid

Hydrangea Leaf

Dogwood

Ivy Leaf

Small & Medium Daisy

Small, Medium and Large Blossom Ejectors

Hydrangea Ejector

Narrow & Wide Lily

Large Daisy/Gerbera

Ejector Impression Strip

Flower Impression Set

Give your gum paste flowers incredible texture and detail! This two-piece silicone mold set is the perfect complement to the Wilton Gum Paste Flower Cutter Set. On back, a wire stem groove creates a ridge for easy wire assembly on your flowers. Set/2.

409-2560 $14.99

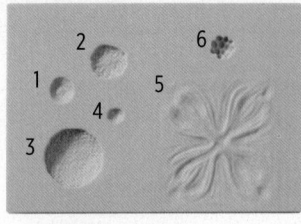
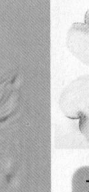

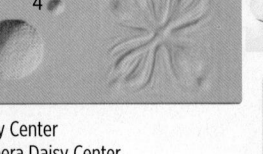

1. Daisy Center
2. Gerbera Daisy Center
3. Sunflower Center
4. Small Daisy Center
5. Dogwood
6. Dogwood Center
7. Ivy Leaf/Hydrangea Leaf/Rose Leaf
8. Calla Lily/Cymbidium Orchid Throat/Cymbidium Orchid Petals/Cymbidium Orchid Leaves/Stargazer & Tiger Lily Petals/Stargazer & Tiger Lily Leaves

Calla Lily Former Set

Cut, shape and dry beautiful, deeply cupped gum paste calla lilies with the cutter and formers in this set. Step-by-step instructions make it easy! Includes one cutter, six formers and complete instructions. Set/7.

417-1109 $5.99

Daisy Cutter Set

Just roll out fondant and/or gum paste, press down with cutter and lift away. Remove shapes with a small spatula. Durable plastic. 0.75 in. to 2.5 in. Set/3.

417-439 $2.99

Sweet Pea Cutter Set

Create these favorite gum paste bouquet flowers with the two precision cutters in this set. Includes step-by-step instructions to show you how. Cutters: 0.875 in. and 1.125 in. Set/3.

417-1153 $2.49

NEW!

Floral Garland Cutter/Ejector Set

Quickly and easily cuts and positions fondant or gum paste flowers on cakes. Includes ejector, five cutters and instructions. Set/7.

1907-1001 $10.99

Stepsaving Rose Bouquets Flower Cutter Set

Create gorgeous fondant and gum paste roses and forget-me-nots using book and cutters in this set. Cutters include large and small rose, rose leaf, calyx and forget-me-not. Set/6.

1907-1003 $9.99

Wave Flower Former Set

Use this convenient connecting platform to dry flowers, leaves and other decorations in royal icing, gum paste or fondant. Wave shape makes it easy to dry concave or convex shapes; large drying area is great for ribbons, bows and streamers. 14.5 in. x 9 in. assembled. Patent pending. Set/2.
1907-1320 $6.99

Rose Bases

Plastic bases let you wrap around a strip of gum paste to form the perfect rose base. Bottom opening for adding florist wire. Includes 12 each 1 in. x 0.5 in. and 1.125 in. x 0.75 in.
1005-4453 $5.99

Fondant Shaping Foam

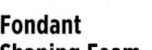

Thick, medium and thin squares are the ideal soft surface for shaping flowers, leaves and other fondant or gum paste cutouts. Use the thin and medium squares for thinning petal edges with a ball tool, carving vein lines on leaves and making ruffled fondant strips. Use the thick square for cupping flower centers. Each square is 4 in. x 4 in.; thin is 0.0625 in. high, medium is 0.125 in. high, thick is 0.5 in. high. Set/3.
1907-9704 $3.29

Flower Forming Cups

Curved round shape is ideal for drying gum paste, fondant and royal icing flowers and leaves. Openings in bottom center make it easy to pull wires through and adjust for the perfect drying position.

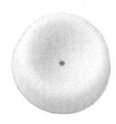 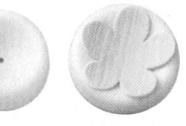

Flower Forming Cups
Includes 2.5 in. and 3 in. dia. cups. Set/6.
1907-118 $5.49

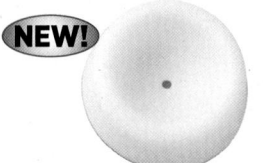

NEW!

Large Forming Cups
4 in. dia. x 0.75 in. high. Set/4.
1907-1076 $5.99

Flower Drying Rack

Space-saving, multi-level rack lets you dry wired flowers upside down so they retain their shape and petal position. Assembled 12.4 in. high x 13 in. dia.
409-2543 $5.99

STAMENS

Finish your royal icing or gum paste flowers with these lovely stamen styles. Cut stamens to desired size and insert in flower center. **Each Pack $3.49**

Lily Stamen Set
Includes 10 each pink, yellow and brown. 2.125 in. long. Pk./30.
1005-4451

Color Stamen Set
Includes 60 each yellow, white and orange. 2.125 in. long. Pk./180.
1005-4452

Flower Stamen Assortment
Includes 60 each pearl, fluffy and glitter. May be tinted (except pearl) with Wilton Icing Colors added to vanilla. 2.5 in. long. Pk./180.
1005-410

Gum Paste Wire and Tape
Create natural-looking stems using 20-, 22- and 26-gauge wire for flowers, then wrap with self-sticking green florist tape. Includes 32 wires and 30 yds. of ½ in. wide tape.
1907-1113 $6.99

FONDANT CUT & PRESS SETS

Give your cake the perfect finish! Create a beautifully textured fondant and/or gum paste design in seconds with the Fondant Cut & Press Set. It's easy: Just roll out fondant, gum paste or a 50/50 mixture, cut with the rectangular cutting edge, then place on inside of press bottom, cover with top and press to imprint design. Includes two-piece cutter/press and instructions. **Each Set $6.99**

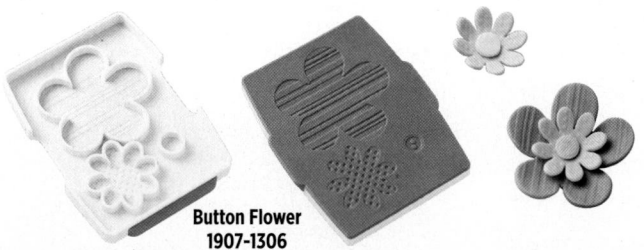

Button Flower
1907-1306

Rose Leaf
1907-1300

SPRINKLES & SUGARS

You've never had more exciting ways to top your treats! Wilton makes decorating quick, easy and colorful with a great variety of toppings to give your iced cakes, cupcakes and cookies the perfect finishing touch.

NEW!

Sprinkles Essentials Set
Top cookies, cupcakes, cakes and your treats with this great variety of basic sprinkles. Contains chocolate jimmies, white nonpareils, rainbow jimmies and rainbow nonpareils. Total net weight 18 oz. Certified Kosher.
710-167 $12.99

SPRINKLES
Great shapes and colors add a dash of excitement to cakes, cupcakes, ice cream and more. Certified Kosher.
Each $2.29

Rainbow Nonpareils	White Nonpareils	Cinnamon Drops	Chocolate Flavored Jimmies	Rainbow Jimmies
3 oz.	3 oz.	3 oz.	2.5 oz. **710-774**	2.5 oz.
710-772	**710-773**	**710-769**	6.25 oz.	**710-776**
			710-168 $4.49	6.25 oz.
				710-994 $4.49

JUMBO SPRINKLES
These big and bold decorations are perfect for cupcakes, mini cakes, jumbo and king-sized cupcakes, brownies and cookies. Certified Kosher. **Each $4.49**

Jumbo Daisies	Jumbo Confetti	Jumbo Hearts	Jumbo Stars	Jumbo Nonpareils
3.25 oz.	3.25 oz.	3.25 oz.	3.25 oz.	4.8 oz.
710-028	**710-029**	**710-032**	**710-026**	**710-033**

SPARKLING SUGARS
Easy-pour sugars have a coarse texture and a brilliant sparkle that makes cupcakes, cookies and cakes really shine. Certified Kosher.

  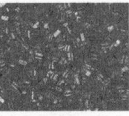  

Blue	Yellow	Pink	White	Rainbow
5.25 oz.	5.25 oz.	5.25 oz.	8 oz.	8 oz.
710-039	**710-036**	**710-038**	**710-992**	**710-991**
$3.99	**$3.99**	**$3.99**	**$4.49**	**$4.49**

Blue	Yellow	Orange
710-750	**710-754**	**710-759**

COLORED SUGARS
Fill in brightly colored designs on cakes, cupcakes and cookies. 3.25 oz. bottle. Certified Kosher. **Each $2.29**

Pink	Red	Lavender	Light Green	Dark Green	Black
710-756	**710-766**	**710-758**	**710-752**	**710-764**	**710-762**

CRUNCHES
Add delicious flavor and a colossal crunch! Sprinkle over iced cupcakes or brownies. Certified Kosher. **Each $4.99**

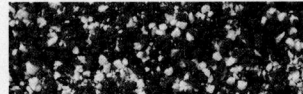  

Cookies 'N Cream	Rainbow Chip	Turtle
5 oz.	Certified Kosher Dairy. 5.25 oz.	5 oz.
710-9702	**710-9704**	**710-9703**

6-MIX ASSORTMENTS
Assorted fun shapes in an easy-pour flip-top bottle. Certified Kosher.
Each $4.99

Flowerful Medley
Contains confetti, colorful leaves, daisies, pastel hearts, wild flowers, butterflies. 2.54 oz. total.
710-4122

Animals and Stars
Contains cows, stars, dinosaurs, stars and moons, bears, dolphins. 2.4 oz. total.
710-4123

Nonpareils
Contains pink, orange, green, red, yellow, purple. 3 oz. total.
710-4125

Jimmies
Contains pink, orange, green, red, yellow, blue. 3.18 oz. total.
710-4127

4-MIX ASSORTMENTS
Assorted sugars in an easy-pour flip-top bottle. 4.4 oz. total. Certified Kosher. **Each $4.99**

Bright Sugars
Contains yellow, light green, lavender, pink.
710-651

Primary Sugars
Contains red, dark green, blue, yellow.
710-650

ORDER TOLL FREE: 800-794-5866

EDIBLE ACCENTS

Adds glimmering touches to treats. Perfect for use on iced cakes, cupcakes and cookies—or sprinkle on drinks for twinkling toasts! Thousands of pieces in every jar! Certified Kosher. **Each $5.99**

Silver Stars	Gold Stars	Silver Hearts	Gold Hearts	Pink Hearts
0.04 oz.	0.04 oz.	0.06 oz.	0.06 oz.	0.06 oz.
703-201	**703-200**	**703-204**	**703-203**	**703-205**

CAKE SPARKLES

Brilliant edible glitter in a variety of colors. Great for stencilling, snow scenes and highlighting messages. 0.25 oz. Certified Kosher. **Each $3.29**

Blue 703-1314

Yellow 703-1272

Orange 703-1308

Pink 703-1260

Red 703-1284

Purple 703-1266

Green 703-1278

Silver 703-1285

White 703-1290

Black 703-1302

PEARLIZED SPRINKLES

Add the soft, shimmering look of Sugar Pearls in six glistening shades. Or, shake on the sparkle with dazzling pearlized sugars and jimmies! Certified Kosher, except for Silver Pearlized Jimmies.

NEW!

Black Sugar Pearls 4.8 oz. 710-1129 $4.99

Green Sugar Pearls	Yellow Sugar Pearls	Pink Sugar Pearls	Blue Sugar Pearls
5 oz.	5 oz.	5 oz.	5 oz.
710-1130 $4.99	**710-1131 $4.99**	**710-1132 $4.99**	**710-1133 $4.99**

White Sugar Pearls	Gold Pearlized Sugar	Silver Pearlized Sugar	Sapphire Pearlized Sugar
5 oz.	5.25 oz.	5.25 oz.	5.25 oz.
710-044 $4.99	**710-041 $4.49**	**710-042 $4.49**	**710-047 $4.49**

Emerald Pearlized Sugar	Ruby Pearlized Sugar	White Pearlized Jimmies	Silver Pearlized Jimmies
5.25 oz.	5.25 oz.	4.5 oz.	4.23 oz.
710-048 $4.49	**710-046 $4.49**	**710-045 $4.49**	**710-1127 $4.49**

DIMENSIONAL ICING DECORATIONS

Create impressive decorated cakes easily with our icing decorations. Perfect way to dress up brownies, cupcakes and other treats. **Each Pack $5.99**

NEW!

Multi Flower
Four large, 1.5 in.; six small, 0.875 in. Pk./10.
710-8888

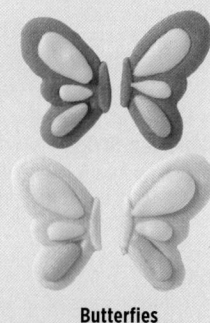

Candy Eyeballs
Perfect additions to faces on pops, cookies, cupcakes and more. Shown actual size, 0.43 in. dia.; 0.88 oz. Approx. 62 pieces.
710-0017 $3.99

Red Roses

Small	Medium	Large
0.75 in. Pk./12.	1.25 in. Pk./8.	1.75 in. Pk./6.
710-7152	**710-7151**	**710-7150**

White Roses

Small	Medium	Large
0.75 in. Pk./12.	1.25 in. Pk./8.	1.75 in. Pk./6.
710-7155	**710-7154**	**710-7153**

Purple Posies	Daisies	Pink Posies	Leaves	Butterfies
Four large, 1.25 in.; six small, 1 in. Pk./10.	Four large, 1.25 in.; six small, 0.875 in. Pk./10.	Four large, 1.25 in.; six small, 0.875 in. Pk./10.	Four large, 1.25 in.; six small, 0.875 in. Pk./10.	Create 10 butterflies with 20 wings, each 1.125 in. high x 0.625 in. wide. Pk./10.
710-1101	**710-7157**	**710-7158**	**710-1100**	**710-7160**

BAKING ACCESSORIES

An amazing cake begins with Wilton baking accessories.

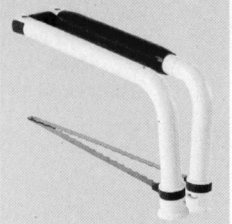

ULTIMATE Cake Leveler folds in half for convenient storage.

ULTIMATE Cake Leveler

This feature-packed leveler makes it easier than ever to create perfectly straight cake tops and layers. The ULTIMATE Cake Leveler has it all: safe, precise cutting; easy height adjustment and convenient storage! Blade adjusts from ¾ in. to 3 in. high. Complete instructions included. Patent Pending.
415-800 $24.99

For cakes up to 16 in. wide!

New wavy wire for cleaner cutting!

Small Cake Leveler

Make your cake top perfectly level for precise decorating—just place adjustable wire in notches to desired height up to 2 in. and glide through the cake. Makes torting easy, too! For cakes up to 10 in. wide.
415-0165 $9.99

Bake Easy! Non-Stick Spray

This convenient, non-stick spray helps your cakes release perfectly with fewer crumbs for easier icing and a flawless look for decorating. Use for all mixes and recipes, versatile for all types of baking and cooking. 6 oz.
702-6018 $3.49

Cake Release Pan Coating

No need to grease and flour your baking pan—Cake Release pan coating coats in one step. Cakes release perfectly every time without crumbs, giving you the ideal surface for decorating. In convenient dispensing bottle. 8 oz. Certified Kosher.
702-6016 $3.49

Non-Stick Parchment Paper

Use Wilton silicone-treated, non-stick parchment to line baking pans and cookie sheets—a non-fat alternative that saves cleanup time. Roll out cookie dough between two sheets, dough won't stick and will easily transfer to your cookie sheet. You can even reuse it for the next batch. Oven-safe to 400°F, great for conventional ovens, microwaves and the freezer. Double roll is 41 square feet, 15 in. wide. Certified Kosher.
415-680 $5.99

Bake-Even Strips

Cakes bake perfectly level and moist without cracking, when you wrap these strips around the outside of the pan before baking. Oven-safe, instructions and clips included.

Small Set
Two 1½ in. high strips, 30 in. long. Enough for two 8 in. or 9 in. round pans. Set/2.
415-260 $8.99

Large Set
Four 1½ in. high strips, 36 in., 43 in., 49 in. and 56 in. long. Enough for one each: 10 in., 12 in., 14 in., 16 in. round pans. Set/4.
415-262 $18.99

6-Pc. Covered Mixing Bowl Set

Perfect for preparing decorating icings. Clear lids snap on tight to keep icing the right texture. Includes one each 1-, 2- and 3-quart nesting bowls with easy-grip handles and easy-pour spouts for better control. Rubberized base keeps bowls from sliding on countertops. Measurements clearly marked for precise mixing. Dishwasher safe. Set/6.
417-469 $14.99

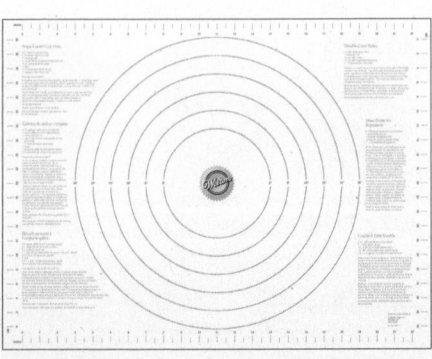

Pastry Mat

Non-stick mat with pre-marked measurements for easy rolling and precise cutting! Includes circles for pie, tart and pizza crusts from 6 in. to 16 in. dia., pre-marked inches and centimeters for exact cutting of lattice strips. Delicious cookie and pie crust recipes are printed on the mat. Non-stick surface for easy release. 18 in. x 24 in.
409-413 $9.99

ORDER TOLL FREE: 800-794-5866

BETTER BAKING TOOLS

Essential tools designed to do more! Wilton Better Baking Tools are designed with exclusive features that make baking easier:

Scoop-It Batter Spoons
Fill jumbo, standard and mini baking cups ²/₃ full every time! Also great for muffins and pancake batter. Egg-shape design makes pouring easy and mess free. Flexible edge helps scrape batter from bowl. Cupcake-shaped plastic ring holds spoons together. Nests for compact storage.
2103-1112 $5.99

NEW!

Scoop-It Measuring Spoons
Set/5.
2103-325 $5.99

Scoop-It Measuring Cups
Set/4.
2103-324 $7.99

2-Cup Liquid Measure
Patent Pending.
2103-334 $7.99

4-Cup Liquid Measure
Patent Pending.
2103-335 $9.99

Egg Separator
Has a countertop cup design to collect and measure egg whites—makes pouring into recipes a breeze. Separate eggs with less mess! Ideal for egg white omelets; cup holds up to 10 egg whites.
2103-391 $6.99

Cake Tester
Reusable pick comes out clean when cake is ready. Includes storage cover.
2103-434 $3.99

Cake Lifter
2103-307 $9.99

Baker's Blade
Pat. No. D587,538.
2103-310 $7.99

12 in. Rolling Pin
Has removable handles making it fully submersible and dishwasher safe.
2103-301 $24.99

Silicone Spoon Scraper
Pat. No. D584,927.
2103-328 $6.99

Silicone Stand Mixer Scraper
Pat. No. D587,537.
2103-329 $6.99

Silicone Universal Scraper
Pat. No. D586,630.
2103-327 $6.99

Cyclone Whisk
Has an innovative center spiral that incorporates more air into batters. Pat. No. D582,223.
2103-317 $9.99

Baker's Pastry Blender
Features a unique patented clip that slides along the wires to remove butter and dough.
2103-313 $6.99

Tilt-N-Mix 3-Pc. Bowl Set
2103-306 $29.99

KITCHEN TOOLS

Make decorating and kitchen tasks easier! Lightweight, comfortable tools with contoured handles and quality blades of stainless steel and silicone heads suited for the task.

Pastry Wheel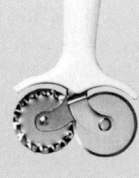
Create crisp straight or graceful scalloped edges with this smooth-rolling pastry wheel. Comfortable handle with finger/thumb guard. 6.5 in. long.
2103-315 $8.99

Pastry Brush
Flexible silicone bristles are great for brushing on Cake Release pan coating, shortening or hot glazes. More durable than nylon bristles. Comfortable ergonomic handle. 8.5 in. long.
409-6056 $5.99

Cookie Spatula
Angled stainless steel blade moves cookies from pan to plate with ease. Slides easily under cookies—great for serving brownies and bar cookies, too. Comfortable ergonomic handle with thumbrest. 9 in. long.
409-6054 $6.99

Cake and Pie Server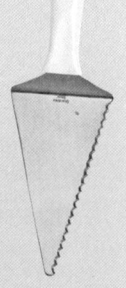
Slice and serve with greater control. The comfortable ergonomic handle with thumb rest and angled blade makes lifting every slice easier. Serrated stainless steel blade cuts even the first slice cleanly. 9 in. long.
409-6058 $6.99

Bakeware

In Wilton decorating classes, we've shown millions of students that to get a beautiful cake for decorating, you have to start with a quality pan. That's why Wilton designs bakeware with more features to promote perfect baking every time.

ALUMINUM PAN SETS

Create a classic tiered cake with confidence when you start with Wilton even-baking aluminum pan sets. For generations, decorators have counted on Wilton quality pans to bake the light golden-brown surface essential for beautiful tiers. The precise lines and seamless baking surface of each pan help you achieve a perfect cake for decorating. Each pan is 2 inches deep, except where noted.

3-Pc. 3 in. Deep Round Set
Popular sizes for stacked tiers in a generous depth designed for 2-layer 5 in. cakes. Includes 6 in., 10 in., 14 in. Set/3.
2105-6114 $44.99

4-Pc. 3 in. Deep Round Set
Extra-tall design helps you create impressive 2-layer wedding tiers, 5 in. high. Includes 8 in., 10 in., 12 in., 14 in. Set/4.
2105-2932 $49.99

4-Pc. Round Set
Our most popular collection offers the versatility of constructing classic wedding tiers or creating individual round party cakes. Includes 6 in., 8 in., 10 in., 12 in. Set/4.
2105-2101 $39.99

4-Pc. Oval Set
An elegant shape ideal for cascading arrangements. The large 16.5 in. pan also works well as a base for round tiers. Includes 7.75 in. x 5.5 in., 10.75 in. x 7.8 in., 13.5 in. x 9.8 in. and 16.5 in. x 12.38 in. Set/4.
2105-2130 $49.99

4-Pc. Hexagon Set
A great choice for fondant-covered designs. The sharp lines create a strong presence for weddings, religious occasions, graduations and more. Includes 6 in., 9 in., 12 in., 15 in. Set/4.
2105-3572 $49.99

3-Pc. Diamond Set
Create a contemporary look for weddings, showers, anniversaries and more—the unique diamond design is ideal for rolled fondant cakes. Includes 10.25 in. x 7.4 in., 15 in. x 11 in. and 19.25 in. x 14.25 in. Set/3.
2105-4204 $49.99

3-Pc. Square Set
A favorite graduated grouping, highlighted by a 16 in. pan for a dramatic base tier. Includes 8 in., 12 in., 16 in. Set/3.
2105-2132 $49.99

4-Pc. Heart Set
A perfect fit for anniversaries, showers, Valentine's Day and more. Includes 6 in., 10 in., 12 in., 14 in. Set/4.
2105-606 $49.99

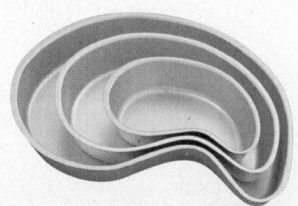

3-Pc. Paisley Set
Create a beautiful tiered cake with graceful curves. Ideal for cascading floral arrangements—perfect for weddings, showers and more. Includes 9 in. x 6 in., 12.5 in. x 9.5 in. and 16.5 in. x 12.5 in. Set/3.
2105-4039 $49.99

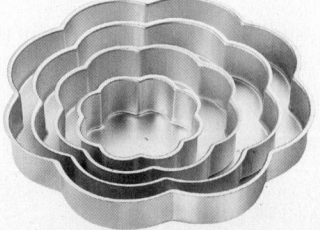

4-Pc. Petal Set
The lively curves of this best-selling tiered set tie in perfectly with floral-themed weddings and showers. Includes 6 in., 9 in., 12 in., 15 in. Set/4.
2105-2134 $49.99

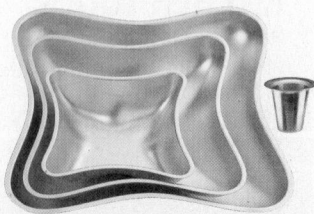

4-Pc. Pillow Set
Create a romantic tiered wedding cake in a classic ring pillow shape. Each pan will need to be baked twice, iced and stacked together to achieve the full pillow effect. Includes 6.75 in. x 6.75 in., 10 in. x 10 in. and 13.25 in. x 13.25 in. pans plus heating core for even baking in the largest pan. Set/4.
2105-0575 $49.99

*Heating Core (p. 163) is recommended for pans which are 10 in. diameter or larger and 3 in. deep.

ORDER TOLL FREE: 800-794-5866

PERFORMANCE PANS

Decorators and bakers know they can depend on these classic aluminum pans: durable, even-heating and built to hold their shape through years of use. These are also great all-purpose pans you'll use for casseroles, entrees, baked desserts and more.

Rounds
Put together your own set to create classic tiers or bake an individual round cake. Each pan is 2 in. deep.

6 in.
2105-2185 $7.99

8 in.
2105-2193 $8.99

10 in.
2105-2207 $9.99

12 in.
2105-2215 $12.99

14 in.
2105-3947 $16.49

16 in.
2105-3963 $19.99

2-Pan Round Set
9 in.
2105-7908 $14.99

Squares
You'll call on this shape constantly for cakes, brownies and entrees! Each pan is 2 in. deep.

6 in.
507-2180 $8.99

8 in.
2105-8191 $10.99

10 in.
2105-8205 $12.99

12 in.
2105-8213 $16.49

14 in.
2105-8220 $20.99

16 in.
2105-8231 $22.99

Sheets
Perfect for casseroles, entrees and more. Each pan is 2 in. deep.

9 in. x 13 in.
2105-1308 $12.99

11 in. x 15 in.
2105-158 $17.99

12 in. x 18 in.
2105-182 $19.99

Covered Baking Pan
Clear, durable cover makes it easy to transport desserts. 11 in. x 15 in.
2105-3849 $22.99

SPECIALTY PANS
Make delicious desserts with these aluminum pans.

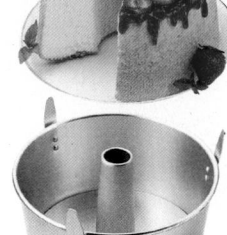

Classic Angel Food
Removable inner core sleeve, cooling legs.

7 in. x 4.5 in. deep.
Takes ½ standard mix.
2105-9311 $15.99

10 in. x 4 in. deep.
Takes one standard mix.
2105-2525 $18.99

Fancy Ring Mold
Ideal for pound cakes, mousse and more! Takes one standard mix. 10 in. dia. x 3 in.
2105-5008 $13.99

Springform Pans
Strong construction and an easy-release design that releases a perfect cheesecake every time. Built tough with strong springlocks that hold up year after year. The removable waffle-textured bottom design keeps crusts from sticking while distributing heat evenly. Springlock releases sides. Each pan is 3 in. deep.

6 in.
2105-4437 $13.99

8 in.
2105-8464 $14.99

9 in.
2105-5354 $15.99

10 in.
2105-8465 $16.99

MINI SHAPED PANS
Six cavity pans make uniquely shaped mini cakes. One cake mix makes 12 to 14 mini cakes.

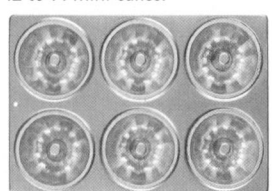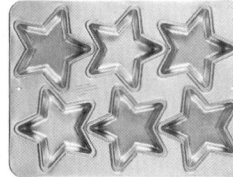

Mini Fluted Mold
Pan is 14.75 in. x 9.75 in.; individual cavities are 4 in. x 1.25 in. deep.
2105-2097 $20.99

Mini Star
Pan is 14.5 in. x 11 in.; individual cavities are 4.75 in. x 1.25 in. deep.
2105-1235 $14.99

WONDER MOLD PANS
Create an elegant 3-D shape for decorating fabulous dress designs.

Mini Wonder Mold
Pair with the Wilton Classic Wonder Mold for a color-coordinated bridal party centerpiece. One cake mix makes 4 to 6 cakes. Pan is 10 in. x 10 in. x 3 in. deep. Individual cakes are 3.5 in. x 3 in. Aluminum.
2105-3020 $13.99

Classic Wonder Mold
Use with our Teen Doll Pick to make the doll of your dreams. Takes 5 to 6 cups of firm-textured batter. Heat-conducting rod assures even baking. Kit contains pan, rod, stand, 7 in. brunette doll pick and instructions. Aluminum/plastic. Pan is 8 in. dia. x 5 in. deep.
2105-565 $19.99

For a full listing of the doll picks shown, please see p. 209 in our Party section.

ALUMINUM COOKIE SHEETS & PANS

Extra-thick aluminum heats evenly for perfectly browned bottoms. Versatile sheets are great for baking appetizers, turnovers and more.

Jumbo Sheet
Large batches of cookies slide off with ease.
14 in. x 20 in.
2105-6213
$19.99

Insulated Sheet
Two quality aluminum layers sandwich an insulating layer of air for perfect browning without burning.
14 in. x 16 in.
2105-2644
$20.99

Jelly Roll and Cookie Pans
Wilton pans are 1 in. deep for fuller-looking desserts.

10.5 in. x 15.5 x 1 in.
2105-1269 $14.49

12 in. x 18 x 1 in.
2105-4854 $16.49

ALUMINUM MUFFIN PANS

With so many great Wilton muffin pans to choose from, you'll be making muffins and cupcakes more often. You'll love our mini pans for the perfect brunch muffins and the jumbo-sized pan for bakery-style muffins and cupcakes.

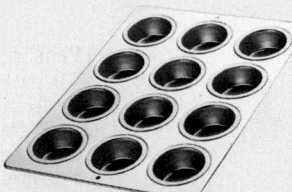

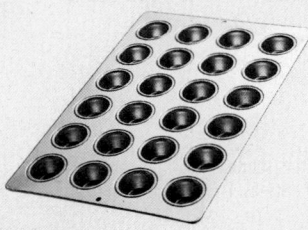

Jumbo Muffin
Make super-sized cupcakes and muffins.
Six cups, each 4 in. dia. x 2 in.
2105-1820 $18.99

White Jumbo Baking Cups (shown on p. 181)
Paper. 2.25 in. dia. Pk./50.
415-2503 $1.99

Standard Muffin
Most popular size for morning muffins, after-school cupcakes and desserts. 12 cups, each 3 in. dia. x 1 in.
2105-9310 $18.99

White Standard Baking Cups (shown on p. 181)
Paper. 2 in. dia. Pk./75.
415-2505 $1.99

Mini Muffin
Great for mini cheesecakes, brunches, large gatherings. Cups are 2 in. dia. x 0.75 in.
12-Cup **2105-2125 $12.99**
24-Cup **2105-9313 $19.99**

White Mini Baking Cups (shown on p. 181)
Paper. 1.25 in. dia. Pk./100.
415-2507 $1.99

ALUMINUM LOAF PANS

It's all in the crust. Wilton Loaf Pans bake bread with hearty, crisp crusts and soft, springy centers. Our superior anodized aluminum promotes better browning, resulting in the perfect texture for all your breads.

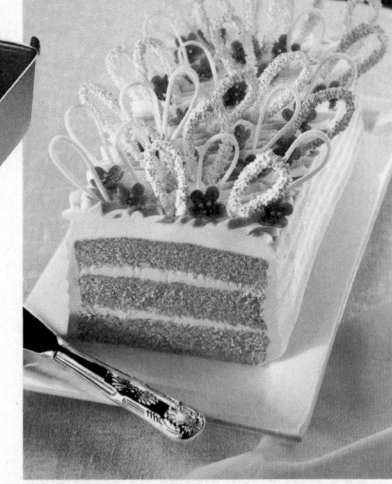

Petite Loaf
Great for single-sized dessert cakes, frozen bread dough. Nine cavities, each 2.5 in. x 3.38 in. x 1.5 in.
2105-8466 $11.99

Petite Loaf Baking Cups (not shown)
For gift breads. White paper. Fits Petite Loaf Pan. Pk./50.
415-450 $1.59

Mini Loaf
Everyone loves personal-sized nut breads or cakes. Six cavities are 4.5 in. x 2.5 in. x 1.5 in.
2105-9791 $11.99

Long Loaf
Legs provide support for cooling angel food cakes, breads or classic cakes.
16 in. x 4 in. x 4.5 in. deep.
2105-1588 $15.49

ADJUSTABLE BAKEWARE ORGANIZER

No more struggling to find the pan you need! The Adjustable Bakeware Organizer keeps your pans separated and easy to grab.

Powder-coated wires adjust to organize cookie sheets, pizza pans, cutting boards and more. Mounts vertically or horizontally to maximize your cabinet space. Includes six adjustable wires, four mounting screws and base. Assembled dimensions: 10 in. x 8.5 in. x 8.75 in.
2555-1084 $14.99

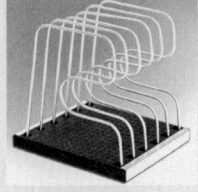

ORDER TOLL FREE: 800-794-5866

DECORATOR PREFERRED®

PROFESSIONAL ALUMINUM BAKEWARE

Built with the most features to help decorators bake their best! Compare these benefits:

- **Straight Sides**—Bake perfect 90° corners for the precise look wedding cakes require.

- **Grip Lip Edges**—Extra-wide rims make heavy filled pans easy to handle.

- **Pure Aluminum**—The best material for baking cakes—creates a light, golden brown cake surface, beautiful for decorating.

- **Superior Thickness**—Thicker than ordinary bakeware, built to distribute heat evenly for more consistent baking.

- **Hand-Crafted Construction**—Sheets and squares are hand welded for excellent detail and durability.

- **Limited Lifetime Warranty**—Superior construction and performance designed and guaranteed to last a lifetime.

Squares

8 in. x 2 in.
2105-6142 $11.99

12 in. x 2 in.
2105-6144 $19.99

10 in. x 2 in.
2105-6143 $16.49

Sheets

9 in. x 13 in. x 2 in.
2105-6146 $18.99

12 in. x 18 in. x 2 in.
2105-6148 $25.49

11 in. x 15 in. x 2 in.
2105-6147 $20.99

Rounds
Includes the hard-to-find 18 in. x 3 in. Half Round; bake and ice two halves to create one 18 in. round cake.

3-inch

6 in.
2105-6106 $9.99

8 in.
2105-6105 $10.99

10 in.
2105-6104 $12.99

12 in.
2105-6103 $16.49

14 in.
2105-6102 $19.99

18 in. Half Round
2105-6100 $26.99

Heating Core
Distributes heat to bake large cakes evenly. Recommended for pans 10 in. dia. or larger, and 3 in. deep. Releases easily from cake. 3.5 in. x 3.5 in. x 4 in. dia.
417-6100 $8.99

Contour
Create cakes with an elegant, rounded top edge. This is the perfect shape for positioning rolled fondant.
9 in. x 3 in.
2105-6121 $14.49

Hearts
Bake a heart-shaped cake for showers, weddings, anniversaries and more. Each pan is 2 in. deep.

6 in.
2105-600 $7.99

8 in.
2105-601 $9.99

10 in.
2105-602 $10.99

12 in.
2105-607 $12.99

CHROME-PLATED COOLING GRIDS

Sturdy design will never rust. Low profile design fits neatly into cabinets.

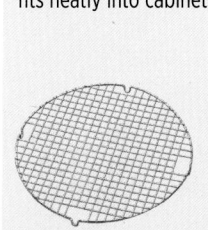

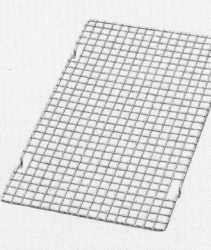

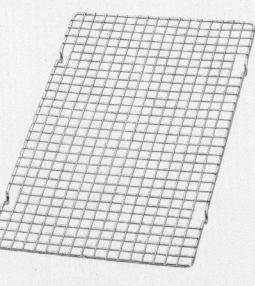

13 in. Round
2305-130 $8.99

10 in. x 16 in. Rectangle
2305-128 $6.99

14.5 in. x 20 in. Rectangle
2305-129 $9.99

3-Tier Stackable
Use singly or stack to save space while cooling three cake layers, pies and tarts or batches of cookies at the same time. Individual grids are 13.5 in. x 9.75 in. x 3 in. high; stacked grids are 9.75 in. high.
2305-151 $14.49

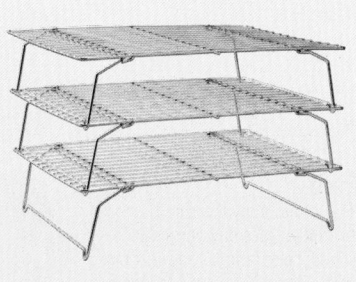

NOVELTY SHAPED PANS
Your cakes can really take shape with any of our aluminum pans.

Crown
Perfect for birthdays, school parties, Mother's and Father's Day! One-mix pan is 14.25 in. x 10.5 in. x 2 in. deep.
2105-1015 $13.99

Princess Carriage
Give it the royal treatment decorated in her favorite colors for birthdays and showers. One-mix pan is 13.75 in. x 12 in. x 2 in. deep.
2105-1027 $13.99

3-D Rubber Ducky Set
A big splash for birthdays, baby showers and school celebrations. Two-piece pan takes 5 to 5 1/3 cups of firm-textured batter. Bake halves separately then ice together. Assembled cakes are 9 in. x 5 in. x 7 in. high. Set/2.
2105-2094 $19.99

#1
Great for kids' birthdays, first anniversary, contest winners, first place teams—or just to let someone know he/she is #1! One-mix pan is 12.75 in. x 8.5 in. x 2 in. deep.
2105-1194 $13.99

Baby Buggy
It's a precious carriage design fit for royalty. One-mix pan is 11.25 in. x 11.25 in. x 2 in. deep.
2105-3319 $13.99

Noah's Ark
Celebrate baby showers, first birthdays and special occasions with an ark full of animals and a rainbow of good wishes. One-mix pan is 11.25 in. x 9.5 in. x 2 in. deep.
2105-0249 $13.99

3-D Mini Bear Set
Includes baking stand, four clips and instructions. Two-piece pan takes one cup of batter; standard pound cake mix makes about four cakes. Assembled cakes are 4 in. x 3.25 in. x 4.75 in. high. Set/8.
2105-489 $15.99

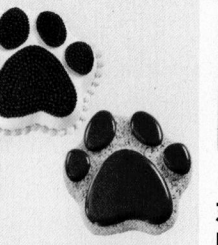

Paw Print
The pan that goes hand-in-hand with celebrations for animal lovers of all ages! One-mix pan is 10.25 in. x 10.75 in. x 2 in. deep.
2105-0252 $13.99

3-D Mini Bear Set
Makes cute teddy bear cakes for fun treats on a stick. One cake mix makes approximately 53 mini bear cakes. Assembled cakes measure 2.25 in. x 2.25 in. x 1.5 in. deep. Set/8.
2105-0545 $21.99

3-D Bear Set
Three decorating ideas on the box! Two-piece pan takes 6 2/3 cups of firm-textured batter. Includes six clips, heat-conducting core and instructions. Pan is 9 in. x 6.75 in. x 8.5 in. high. Set/10.
2105-603 $29.99

Teddy Bear
This cutie will be busy all year round with birthdays, school parties and baby showers. One-mix pan is 13.5 in. x 12.25 in. x 2 in. deep.
2105-1193 $13.99

Ballerina Bear
Decorate her to match your own little ballerina or cheerleader! One-mix pan is 14.5 in. x 10 in. x 2 in. deep.
2105-1028 $13.99

Pony
This proud pony is a sure bet for birthdays, race day parties and school celebrations. One-mix pan is 13.75 in. x 10.5 in. x 2 in. deep.
2105-1011 $13.99

Lady Bug
It's a pan that adapts to any environment—try it as a birthday bee, a Valentine love bug or even a friendly fly. One-mix pan is 12 in. x 10 in. x 2 in. deep.
2105-3316 $13.99

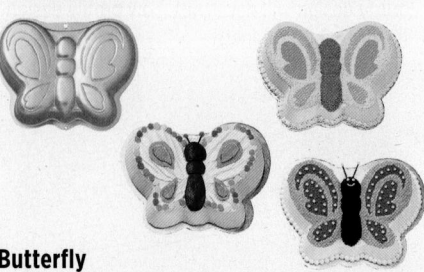

Butterfly
A butterfly cake is the perfect way to captivate! One-mix pan is 11 in. x 8.5 in. x 2 in. deep.
2105-2079 $13.99

Monkey

Kids will just love him at birthday parties, school celebrations and jungle-themed events. One-mix pan is 12.75 in. x 11.25 in. x 2 in. deep.

2105-1023 $13.99

Dinosaur

Our prehistoric pal has a fun-loving look that's just right for kids' birthdays, school functions and animal-themed celebrations. One-mix pan is 12.75 in. x 11 in. x 2 in. deep.

2105-1022 $13.99

Elephant

Makes a great guest at birthday parties, school celebrations, baby showers and other special events. One-mix pan is 12 in. x 9.25 in. x 2 in. deep.

2105-0576 $13.99

Soccer Ball

A great way to reward a season or a game well done! One-mix pan is 8.75 in. x 8.75 in. x 3.5 in. deep.

2105-2044 $13.99

Baseball Mitt

The perfect treat for opening day, birthdays and team gatherings. One-mix pan is 10 in. x 10.25 in. x 2 in. deep.

2105-0561 $13.99

3-D Sports Ball Set

Use this four-piece set to create a perfect sports cake centerpiece. Includes two 6 in. diameter half-ball pans and two metal baking stands. Each pan half takes 2.5 cups batter. Set/4.

2105-6506 $13.99

Helmet

It's easy to create the ideal victory celebration cake with school colors, stats or the final score. One-mix pan is 12.75 in. x 10.5 in. x 2 in. deep.

2105-1029 $13.99

First and Ten Football

Touching down at Super Bowl parties, award dinners, homecomings and much more. One-mix pan is 12 in. x 7.75 in. x 3 in. deep.

2105-6504 $13.99

Mini Ball

Ice two mini balls and push together for a 3-D effect. One cake mix makes 10 to 12 mini balls. Six cavities, each 3.5 in. x 3.5 in. x 1.5 in. deep.

2105-1760 $13.99

Guitar

Celebrate school band concerts, kid and adult birthdays! One-mix pan is 16.5 in. x 8.5 in. x 2 in. deep.

2105-570 $13.99

Star

Brighten birthdays, opening nights, even law enforcement occasions. One-mix pan is 12.75 in. x 12.75 in. x 1.8 in. deep.

2105-2512 $13.99

Stand-Up House

Haunted houses, Easter hutches, Christmas cottages, schools and dog houses are a few ideas for this pan. Cakes can stand up or lay flat. One-mix pan is 9 in. wide x 8.75 in. high x 3 in. deep.

2105-2070 $16.99

SweetHeart

A gently curving shape gives the classic heart a more romantic flair. Charm guests for birthdays, Mother's Day, Valentine's Day, showers and more. One-mix pan is 10.25 in. x 11 in. x 2 in.

2105-1197 $13.99

Heart

For graceful expressions of love on Valentine's Day or anytime. One-mix pan is 9 in. x 2 in. deep.

2105-5176 $8.99

Book

Tell a delicious story for grads, newlyweds and milestone birthdays. Serves up to 30. Three-mix pan is 15 in. x 11.5 in. x 2.75 in. deep.

2105-2521 $19.99

NOVELTY SHAPED PANS

3-D Choo-Choo Train Set
Two-piece pan snaps together to
create a cake 10 in. x 4 in. x 6 in. high.
Takes 4¾ cups firm-textured batter. Set/2.
2105-2861 **$16.99**

3-D Cruiser
Bake exciting 3-D cakes,
ready to customize for all occasions. Pan takes 6½ cups
batter and is 11 in. x 6.75 in. x 4 in. deep.
2105-2043 **$13.99**

Airplane
Makes a perfect landing at birthdays,
welcome home parties, retirement celebrations and
more. One-mix pan is 12.25 in. x 11.5 in. x 2 in. deep.
2105-0250 **$13.99**

Dump Truck
It carries loads of fun party
memories, whether hauling cookie gifts or colorful
candies. One-mix pan is 8 in. x 12 in. x 2 in. deep.
2105-0562 **$13.99**

Train
Load with delicious cargo!
One-mix pan is 14 in. x 7.25 in. x 2 in. deep.
2105-2076 **$13.99**

Firetruck
When the occasion calls for a five-alarm celebration.
One-mix pan is 15.5 in. x 8.5 in. x 2 in. deep.
2105-2061 **$13.99**

Pirate Ship
Birthdays, movie
parties and school celebrations
provide a bounty of decorating opportunities. One-mix
pan is 13.2 in. x 11.25 in. x 2 in. deep.
2105-1021 **$13.99**

Tractor
Down on the farm
has never been so much fun.
One-mix pan is 13.5 in. x 9.5 in. x 2 in. deep.
2105-2063 **$13.99**

Cupcake
Bake and decorate it to look like
your favorite party cupcake—only
bigger! 9.75 in. x 9.5 in. x 2 in. deep.
2105-3318 **$13.99**

Enchanted Castle
Wonderful for molded sugar
or ice cream. 11.5 in. x 11.75 in.
x 2 in. deep.
2105-2031 **$13.99**

Dancing Daisy
It's the perfect shape for cakes,
molded gelatin and ice cream,
brunch breads and more. 12 in. x
12 in. x 2 in. deep.
2105-1016 **$13.99**

Sunflower
Ideal for cakes, mousse, gelatin
and salad molds. 10 in. round x
2 in. deep.
2105-1019 **$13.99**

Find hundreds of decorating ideas using Wilton novelty shaped pans!

www.wilton.com

ORDER TOLL FREE: 800-794-5866

Dimensions®
DECORATIVE BAKEWARE

You'll create one-of-a-kind cakes with amazing detail and definition, thanks to our heavyweight cast aluminum designs. Dimensions' extra-thick construction and premium non-stick coating mean these uniquely sculpted shapes will release from the pan perfectly. Limited Lifetime Warranty.

2-LAYER CAKE PANS
Assemble shaped top and bottom cake halves with a thin layer of icing.

Large Cupcake
Finished cake 8.25 in. x 7.5 in.;
10-cup total capacity.*
Pat. Nos. D575,097 and D591,552.
2105-5038 $30.99

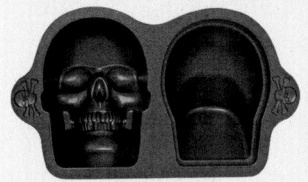

3-D Skull
Finished cake 6.5 in. x 5.5 in.
x 7.5 in.; 10-cup total capacity.*
Pat. No. D625,546.
2105-1181 $34.99

Multi-Cavity Mini Pumpkins
Finished cakes 3.4 in. x
3.4 in.; 5-cup total capacity.*
Pat. No. D574,663.
2105-1183 $30.99

**Multi-Cavity
Mini Cupcakes**
Finished cakes 3.8 in. x 4 in.;
6-cup total capacity.*
Pat. No. D577,535 and
Patent Pending.
2105-5043 $30.99

Large Pumpkin
Finished cake: 6.75 in. x 6 in.;
10-cup total capacity.*
Pat. No. D577,951.
2105-1184 $34.99

Perennial
9.5 in. x 3.2 in.; 9-cup capacity.*
Pat. No. D530,563.
2105-5031 $30.99

Tulip
9.5 in. x 4 in.; 11-cup capacity.*
Pat. No. D526,529.
2105-5032 $30.99

Cascade
9.5 in. x 4.75 in.; 11-cup capacity.*
Pat. No. D478,249.
2105-1199 $30.99

Belle
9 in. x 3.75 in.; 11-cup capacity.*
Pat. No. D478,250.
2105-1186 $30.99

Crown of Hearts
11 in. x 2.5 in.; 11-cup capacity.*
Pat. No. D486,992.
2105-5011 $30.99

Queen of Hearts
9 in. x 3.25 in.; 11-cup capacity.*
Pat. No. D478,466.
2105-5001 $30.99

6-Cavity Mini Hearts
Each 4 in. x 2 in.; 7-cup total
capacity.* Pat. No. D487,211.
2105-5012 $30.99

4-Cavity Mini Snowflakes
Each 5 in. x 2.25 in.; 7-cup total
capacity.* Pat. No. D543,413.
2105-5028 $30.99

*For cakes, fill pans ½ to ⅔ full.

NON-STICK FILLED CAKE PAN SETS
The patented recessed design creates a contour you can fill with ice cream, fruit, mousse and more—just bake, fill, flip and frost! The premium non-stick coating provides easy unmolding. Each includes bonus recipe booklet with delicious ideas and complete instructions. Non-stick steel.

Mini Tasty-Fill
Four 4 in. x
1.25 in. pans.
Set/4.
**2105-155
$11.99**

Fanci-Fill
Two 8.75 in. x 2 in.
pans. Set/2.
**2105-150
$19.99**

**Heart
Tasty-Fill**
Two 8.5 in. x
2.75 in. pans.
Set/2.
2105-157 $17.99

ORDER ONLINE: WWW.WILTON.COM

SILICONE BAKEWARE

Discover the convenience and easy release of flexible silicone bakeware!
- Perfect for baking, molding, more
- Silicone oven safe to 500° F
- Freezer, microwave and dishwasher safe
- Place bakeware on cookie sheet for easy oven removal

EASY-Flex SILICONE BAKEWARE
Flexible pans and tools for great baking performance

Standard Baking Cups
2 in. dia.; six red, six blue. Convenient fill line. Pk./12.
415-9400 $9.99

6-Cup Muffin
2105-4802 $9.99

Baking Mat
Line cookie sheets—protects against burned bottoms and cleans up with ease! Or, use as a pastry mat.
10 in. x 15 in.
2105-4808 $9.99
11 in. x 17 in.
2105-4809 $12.99

12-Cup Mini Muffin
2105-4829 $9.99

TREAT MOLDS

Make treats in favorite party shapes using these colorful, easy-release molds. Always place silicone bakeware on a cookie sheet for easy removal from oven. One cake mix makes 20 to 24 cakes. Individual cavities are 2.5 in. x 2.5 in. x 1.25 in. deep. **Each $9.99**

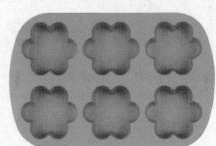
Mini Flowers
2105-4825

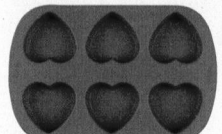
Mini Hearts
2105-4824 $9.99

Mini Stars
2105-4819 $9.99

BROWNIE FUN!

Bake and decorate the most delicious brownies you've ever served using this line of products!

"Brownie Fun!"

"Brownie Fun!" is packed with more than 140 easy-to-make designs and delicious recipes for brownies and mini treats. Includes:
- Fun shapes like flowers, footballs, burgers, space aliens and volcanos.
- Find elegant ideas for weddings, showers and other special occasions.
- Learn how to mix, bake and decorate perfect brownies.
- Shop complete line of brownie products.
Soft cover, 112 pages.
902-1105 $14.99

BROWNIE MOLDS

Shaped brownies on a stick are the perfect, fun-to-eat treat for parties and favors! Always place silicone bakeware on a cookie sheet for easy removal from oven. Silicone molds are dishwasher safe.

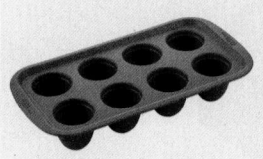
Round Pops
One 8 in. x 8 in. size brownie mix makes 24 brownies. Individual cavities are 1.75 in. x 1.75 in. x 1.75 in. deep.
2105-4925 $9.99

Bite-Size Treat
One 8 in. x 8 in. size brownie mix makes 40 to 42 brownies. Individual cavities are 1.5 in. x 1.5 in. x .75 in. deep.
2105-4923 $9.99

Blossom Brownie
One 8 in. x 8 in. size brownie mix makes six brownies.
2105-4924 $9.99

BROWNIE TOOLS

Easy-to-handle brownie tools from Wilton make decorating, mixing, cutting and serving brownies a breeze!

Hearts
Pat. No. D597,800.
2308-1471

Mini
Pat. No. D597,799.
2308-1474

Combo Cutters
Make multiple shapes with just one cut. Stainless steel combo cutters are divided into a neat, space-saving square, which maximizes the number of treats you get from one pan. Each cutter approx. 4 in. x 2.5 in. x 2.75 in. deep.
Each $3.99

Brownie Lifter
Move your brownies from pan to plate looking great! Its tapered nylon blade is set at the perfect angle for getting under brownies without breakage. 9 in. long.
570-1160 $6.99

Batter Blender
Mix thick brownie batter faster and with less effort. Silicone head is great for stirring, scraping and spreading batter. Scalloped tip breaks up clumps. 11 in. long. Pat. No. D600,510.
570-1158 $7.99

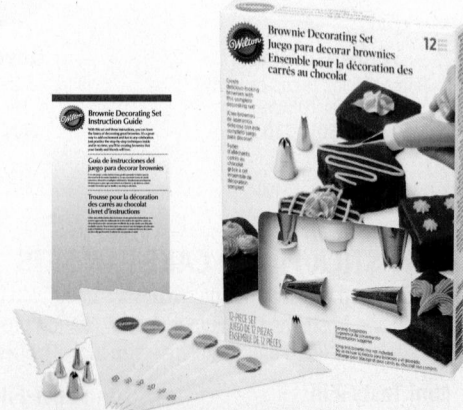
12-Piece Brownie Decorating Set
The ideal set for discovering the fun of cake and brownie decorating! Create most of the fun icing techniques in the "Brownie Fun!" book with the tips included—rosettes, stars, drop flowers, messages and more. Includes tips 5, 21, 352 and 2D, standard coupler, decorating triangle, six disposable decorating bags and instruction sheet.
2104-2533 $8.99

ORDER TOLL FREE: 800-794-5866

NON-STICK DOUGHNUT & WHOOPIE PIE PANS

Surprise your family with two tasty treats baked in these quality, non-stick pans. Create traditional cake doughnuts in two sizes with the Standard and Mini Doughnut Pans; perfect for brunches. Bake fun-filled sandwich cakes in your favorite flavors with our Whoopie Pie Pan. Recipes and instructions included. Non-stick heavy-duty steel construction. 10-year limited warranty.

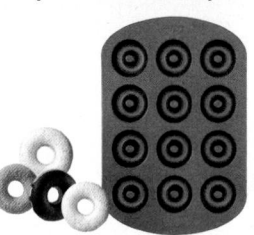  

12-Cavity Mini Doughnut
Makes 12 individual mini doughnuts 1.75 in. dia. x 0.5 in deep.
2105-0614 $9.99

6-Cavity Doughnut
Makes six individual full-sized doughnuts 3.25 in. dia. x 1 in. deep.
2105-0565 $9.99

12-Cavity Whoopie Pie
Makes 12 round cakes for six whoopie pies 3 in. x 3 in. x 0.625 in. deep.
2105-0615 $11.99

CHECKERBOARD CAKE PAN SET

Bake multi-colored cakes perfect for holidays and special events! Set includes plastic batter dividing ring, three non-stick, steel pans and complete baking instructions. Pans feature oversized handles for safe lifting. Each takes 5½ cups. Visit www.wilton.com to find checkerboard ideas for every occasion. Each pan: 9 in. x 1.5 in. high. Set/4.
2105-9961 $15.99

NON-STICK BAKEWARE

Our premium non-stick bakeware combines superior non-stick performance, serving convenience and elegant design, to provide the highest level of baking satisfaction.

- Oversized handles for safe lifting of the pan
- Pan dimensions permanently stamped into handles
- Heavy-duty steel construction prevents warping
- Easy cleanup

MUFFIN & LOAF PANS

Regular Muffin
6-Cup
2105-405 $11.99

Mini Muffin
12-Cup
2105-403 $8.99

2105-405

Regular Muffin
12-Cup
2105-406 $16.99

Jumbo Muffin
6-Cup
2105-955 $6.99

King-Size Muffin
6-Cup
2105-9921 $9.99

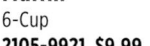
2105-9921

Large Loaf
9.25 in. x 5.25 in. x 2.75 in.
2105-402 $9.99

4-Cavity Mini Loaf
5.75 in. x 3 in. x 2.2 in.
2105-444 $21.49

2105-402

CAKE & PIE PANS

Round Cake
9 in. x 1.5 in.
2105-408 $9.99

Square Cake
9 in. x 9 in. x 2 in.
2105-407 $10.99

2105-408

Biscuit/Brownie
11 in. x 7 in. x 1.5 in.
2105-443 $11.99

Oblong Cake
13 in. x 9 in. x 2 in.
2105-411 $14.99

Covered Oblong Cake
13 in. x 9 in. x 2 in.
2105-423 $19.99

2105-411

Pie w/Fluted Edges
9 in. x 1.5 in.
2105-438 $9.99

COOLING GRIDS

Cookies and cakes won't stick with our slick non-stick coating.

Round
13 in.
2305-230 $10.49

Rectangle
10 in. x 16 in.
2305-228 $9.99
14.5 in. x 20 in.
2305-229 $14.49

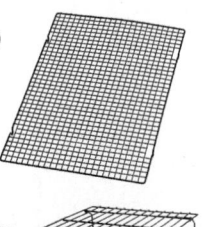

3-Pc. Stackable
Individual grids are 13.5 in. x 9.75 in. x 3 in. high; stacked grids are 9.75 in. high.
2105-459 $11.99

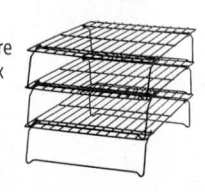

COOKIE PANS & SHEETS

Small Cookie
13.25 in. x 9.25 in. x 0.5 in.
2105-436 $13.99

Medium Cookie
15.25 in. x 10.25 in. x 0.75 in.
2105-412 $14.99

2105-412

Large Cookie/Jelly Roll
17.25 in. x 11.5 in. x 1 in.
2105-413 $16.99

Jumbo Air Insulated Sheet
18 in. x 14 in.
2105-422 $23.99

2105-422

SPRINGFORM PANS

Round
4 in. x 1.75 in.
2105-453 $6.99

Round
6 in. x 2.75 in.
2105-447 $11.99

Round
9 in. x 2.75 in.
2105-414 $16.99

2105-435

Round
10 in. x 2.75 in.
2105-435 $17.99

Heart
4 in. x 1.75 in.
2105-457 $9.99

Heart
9 in. x 2.75 in.
2105-419 $21.49

2105-419

SPECIALTY PANS

Dessert Shell Pan
Individual cavities are 3.5 in. dia. x 1.5 in. deep.
2105-8600 $8.99

2105-8600

9 in. Square Covered Brownie Pan
9 in. x 9 in. x 2 in.
2105-9199 $7.99

2105-9199

Fluted Tube
9.75 in. x 3.4 in.
2105-416 $16.99

6-Cavity Mini Fluted Tube
4.2 in. x 2 in.
2105-445 $21.49

2105-445

Angel Food
9.4 in. x 4.25 in.
2105-415 $19.99

14 in. Pizza Crisper
14 in. x 0.5 in.
2105-420 $16.99

2105-420

TART/QUICHE PANS

Round
9 in. x 1.2 in.
2105-442 $11.99

Round
11 in. x 1.2 in.
2105-450 $13.99

2105-450

Round 3-Pc. Set
8 in. x 1.2 in., 9 in. x 1.2 in., and 10 in. x 1.2 in.
2105-451 $26.99

Cookie Making

Create unforgettable cookies! Wilton has exactly what you need: high-quality pans and cookie sheets, easy-to-use presses, colossal cutter sets, fun stencils, colorful icings and unique toppings!

COOKIE PRESSES

Make dozens of cookies in no time with one of our feature-packed presses! From our Comfort Grip Press, designed for easy handling and filling, to our powerful cordless Cookie Master Plus, spritz cookie-making has never been easier!

Cookie Pro ULTRA II

Making traditional spritz cookies has never been so easy! Cookie Pro Ultra II is designed to be the easiest-to-fill, most comfortable press you've ever used. And, with 12 terrific shapes, plus four fun mini cookie designs, your cookie jar will be quickly filled with impressive-looking cookies all year round. Complete instructions and delicious recipes included. Set/17.
2104-4018 $24.99

12 Disks in Festive Shapes

Plus 4 BONUS Disks For Mini Cookies!

COOKIE MASTER *Plus*
Cordless Cookie Press

Our cordless cookie press is so powerful and easy to operate, you and your kids will use it all year to create cookies, appetizers, desserts and more. Exclusive patented reverse action means there's no need to take press apart for refilling. Ergonomic design is shaped to fit in your hand for excellent comfort.

Includes 12 aluminum disks in classic and seasonal shapes, four accent tips for decorating and filling and two bonus recipe booklets—sweet and savory. Uses four AA batteries (not included). Patent Nos. D484,755; 6,701,828. Set/19.
2104-4008 $39.99

4 Accent Tips

12 Disk Designs

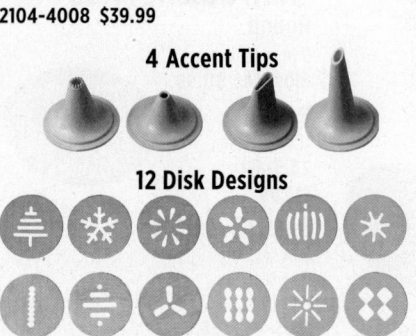

COMFORT GRIP
Cookie Press

Experience a classic press that is truly comfortable. Its ergonomic handle feels great, and the easy-squeeze action releases perfectly shaped dough. Clear barrel takes the guesswork out of refilling. Fluted bottom raises press off the cookie sheet for better-defined shapes. Includes 12 cookie disks in a variety of shapes and our classic Spritz Cookie recipe. Set/13.
2104-4011 $12.99

12 Disk Designs

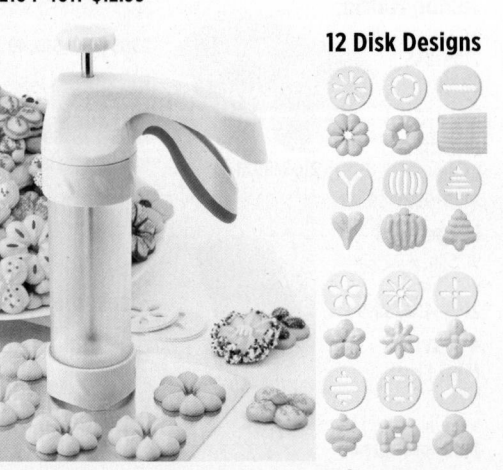

COOKIE BAKEWARE AND ACCESSORIES

Bake delicious cookies using Wilton's bakeware and accessories.

COOKIE TREAT PANS

Cookie treats on a stick are so easy! Just press cookie dough into pan, insert a cookie stick, then bake, cool and decorate. Also great for rice cereal treats and candy. Recipe included. Each pan makes four individual treats. Aluminum. **Each $9.99**

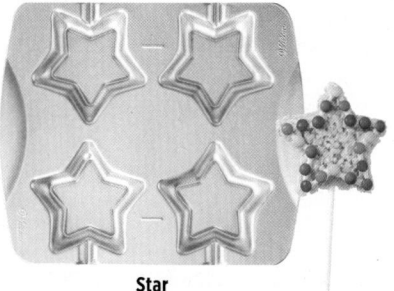

Star
Cavities: 4.25 in. x 4 in. x .5 in.
2105-0274

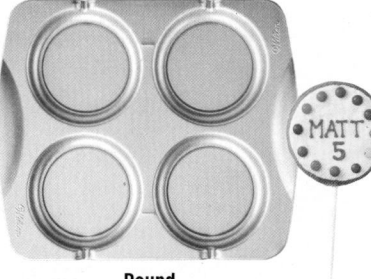

Round
Cavities: 4.25 in. x .5 in.
2105-0271

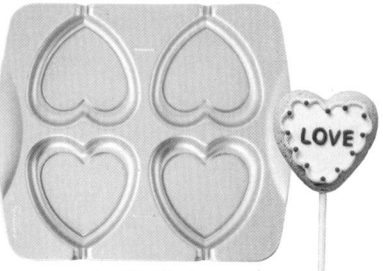

Heart
Cavities: 4.25 in. x 4 in. x .5 in.
2105-0272

Blossom
Cavities: 4.25 in. x 4 in. x .5 in.
2105-0273

Cookie Treat Sticks
For fun cookie pops.
6 in. Pk./20.
1912-9319 $1.99
8 in. Pk./20.
1912-9318 $2.99

Clear Party Bags
Each pack contains 25 bags and 25 ties. 4 in. x 9.5 in.
1912-1240 $2.09

GIANT COOKIE PANS

Create a jumbo cookie that will be a big hit for any occasion. Specially designed for one package of refrigerated dough, these pans are also great for brownies and pizza! Each shape is approx. 0.75 in. deep. Use with recipes that call for a standard 13 in. x 9 in. pan. Aluminum. **Each $7.99**

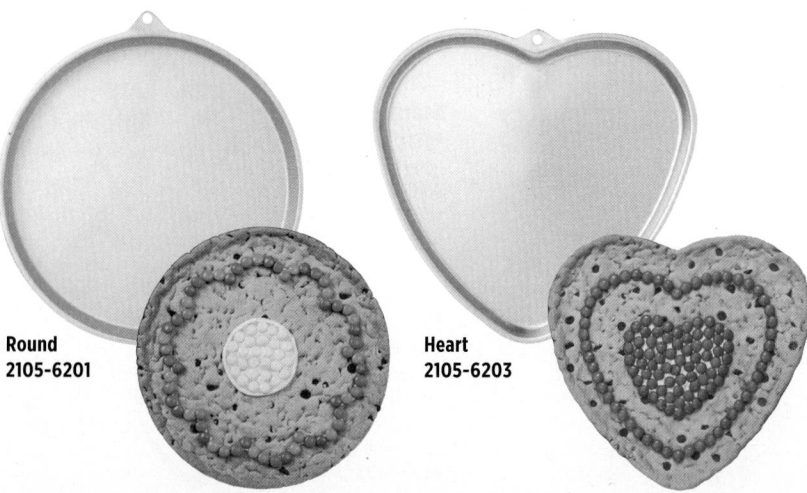

Round
2105-6201

Heart
2105-6203

Cookie Sheets
Extra-thick aluminum heats evenly for perfect browning.

Aluminum
Jumbo size. 14 in. x 20 in.
2105-6213 $19.99

Insulated Aluminum
Two quality aluminum layers sandwich an insulating layer of air for perfect browning. 16 in. x 14 in.
2105-2644 $20.99

Cooling Grids
Chrome
Sturdy design will never rust.
13 in. Round
2305-130 $8.99
10 in. x 16 in.
2305-128 $6.99
14.5 in. x 20 in.
2305-129 $9.99

Non-Stick
Cookies and cakes won't stick with our slick non-stick coating.
13 in. Round
2305-230 $10.49
10 in. x 16 in.
2305-228 $9.99
14.5 in. x 20 in.
2305-229 $14.49

3-Pc. Stackable Chrome-Plated
Use singly or stack to save space. Individual grids: 13.5 in. x 9.75 in. x 3 in. high; stacked: 9.75 in. high.
2305-151 $14.49

See p. 160-169 for the full line of Wilton Bakeware.

Parchment Paper
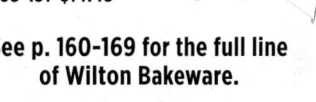
Use Wilton silicone-treated non-stick parchment to line baking pans and cookie sheets—a non-fat alternative that saves cleanup time. Oven-safe to 400°F, great for conventional oven, microwave and freezer. Double roll is 41 square feet, 15 in. wide. Certified Kosher.
415-680 $5.99

Cookie Scoop **NEW!**
Perfect for easy scooping and consistently round cookies. Stainless steel. Capacity 4 teaspoons.
417-1112 $5.99

Cookie Spatula
Angled blade moves cookies from pan to plate with ease. Great for serving brownies and bar cookies, too. Comfortable ergonomic handle with thumb rest. Stainless steel. 9 in. long.
409-6054 $6.99

Jumbo Cookie Spatula
Generously sized spatula is great for handling multiple or oversized cookies, brownies, pastries and large treat bars. The easy-grip handle helps balance large cookies and desserts. Stainless steel. 11 in. long.
570-2018 $6.99

ORDER ONLINE: WWW.WILTON.COM

2013 WILTON YEARBOOK | 171

COMFORT-GRIP CUTTERS

Easy-grip, stainless steel cutters with extra-deep sides are perfect for cutting cookies, brownies, sheet cakes and more. The cushion grip gives you comfortable control. Recipe included. Top-rack dishwasher safe. Each approx. 4 in. x 4 in. x 1.75 in. **Each $3.19**

Heart
2310-616

Round
2310-608

Flower
2310-613

Double Heart
2310-647

Teddy Bear
2310-609

Daisy
2310-619

Butterfly
2310-614

Star
2310-605

METAL CUTTERS

Our metal cutters are built to last, cut cleanly and release with ease. Each approx. 3 in. **Each $0.69**

Daisy
2308-1007

Circle
2308-1010

Chick
2308-1000

Heart
2308-1003

Star
2308-1008

Gingerbread Boy
2308-1002

Bear
2308-1009

Bell
2308-1006

Cross
2308-1018

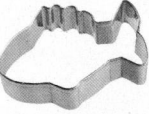
Fish
2308-1017

Butterfly
2308-1015

METAL CUTTER SETS

Multi-piece sets add variety to the shapes you can cut. Recipe included.

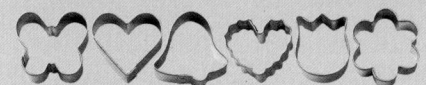

Mini Romantic
Butterfly, heart, bell, crinkled heart, tulip, blossom. Each approx. 1.5 in. Set/6.
2308-1225 $3.29

Mini Noah's Ark
Lion, horse, ark, elephant, bear, giraffe. Each approx. 1.5 in. Set/6.
2308-1206 $3.29

Mini Geometric Crinkle
Square, circle, heart, diamond, triangle, oval. Each approx. 1.5 in. Set/6.
2308-1205 $3.29

Bug Buddies
Caterpillar, dragonfly, spider, butterfly, bee, ladybug. Each approx. 3 in. Set/6.
2308-1245 $5.29

Classic
Geometric, crinkle diamond, heart, half moon, star, flower. Each approx. 3 in. Set/6.
2308-1235 $5.29

Hearts
Seven different heart cutter designs. Sizes range from 1.5 in. to 3 in. Set/7.
2308-1237 $5.29

NESTING METAL CUTTER SETS

Generous rolled edges and deep sides make these cutters easy to use. Recipe included. Set/4. **Each Set $4.79**

Butterflies
Four graduated sizes up to 5 in.
2308-1119

Circles
You'll use every size in this classic shape! Four graduated sizes up to 5 in.
2308-0914

Blossoms
Flowers in four graduated sizes up to 5 in.
2308-1204

Stars
For holidays and more! Four graduated sizes up to 5 in.
2308-1215

Nesting From The Heart
Two crinkled, two smooth. Four graduated sizes up to 5 in.
2308-1203

ORDER TOLL FREE: 800-794-5866

COLORED METAL CUTTER SETS

Coated metal multi-piece sets represent popular themes. Recipe included. Each approx. 3 in.

NEW!

 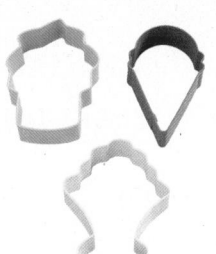   

Summer Picnic
Bee, sun, watermelon slice. Set/3.
2308-0212 $3.69

Ice Cream
Cake cone, sugar cone, sundae. Set/3.
2308-0992 $3.69

Summer
Sandal, margarita, sunglasses. Set/3.
2308-0993 $3.69

Garden
Watering can, flower pot, spade. Set/3.
2308-0094 $3.69

Tea Party
Tea pot, tea cup, cupcake. Set/3.
2308-0092 $3.69

Flower
Tulip, daisy, butterfly. Set/3.
2308-0948 $3.69

  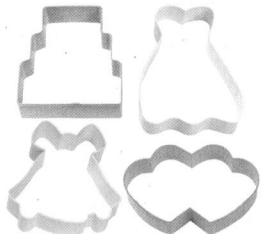 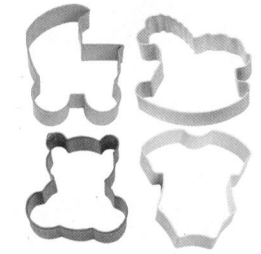 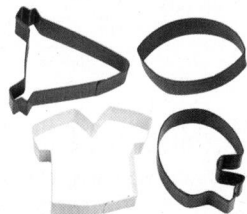

Party
Present, party hat, cake, cupcake. Set/4.
2308-0909 $4.79

Pet
Paw, dog, doghouse, bone. Set/4.
2308-0910 $4.79

Wedding
Cake, dress, bells, double heart. Set/4.
2308-1071 $4.79

Baby
Carriage, rocking horse, teddy bear, romper. Set/4.
2308-1067 $4.79

Football
Pennant, football, jersey, helmet. Set/4.
2308-1263 $4.79

PLASTIC CUTTER SETS

Wilton has a wide variety of cutter shapes, and we've gathered your favorites in convenient sets. Great for cookies, brownies, gelatin treats, crafts and more.

101 Cookie Cutters
With this set, you're covered! Make cookies featuring popular holiday and theme shapes, like sports, flowers, animals and more. Or, use the complete alphabet and numeral collections to create the perfect cookie message. Recipe included. Average cutter size approx. 3.5 in. x 3.5 in. Recipe included. Set/101.
2304-1050 $14.99

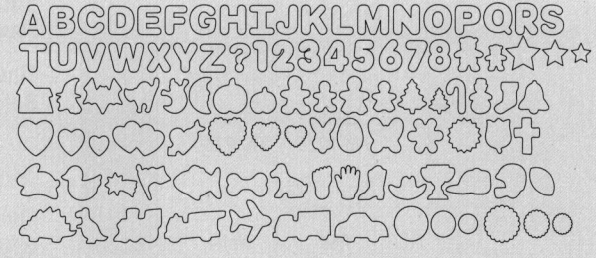 

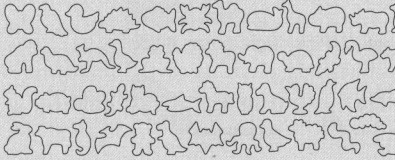

Animal Pals
Everyone will go wild for this menagerie of favorite animal shapes. Includes fish, dog, cat, birds, butterflies, reptiles and more. Recipe included. Average cutter size approx. 3.5 in. x 3.5 in. Set/50.
2304-1055 $9.99

A-B-C and 1-2-3
Complete alphabet and numeral collection! Great for learning games, too. Recipe included. Average cutter size approx. 3.5 in. x 3.5 in. Set/50.
2304-1054 $9.99

PLASTIC NESTING CUTTER SETS

Your favorites in graduated shapes. Designed to nest for easy storage. Discover all the fun ways to use our cutters—for bread shapes, stencils, crafting and so much more. **Each Set $2.99**

Blossom
Six graduated sizes up to 4.5 in. Set/6.
2304-116

Heart
Six graduated sizes up to 4.2 in. Set/6.
2304-115

Star
Six graduated sizes up to 4.6 in. Set/6.
2304-111

LINZER COOKIE CUTTER SETS

Make European-inspired jam-filled cookies for a fun treat. Metal fluted cookie cutters have six interchangeable center shapes that let the filling show through. Recipe included. Each cookie approx. 3 in. Set/7.
Each Set $7.99

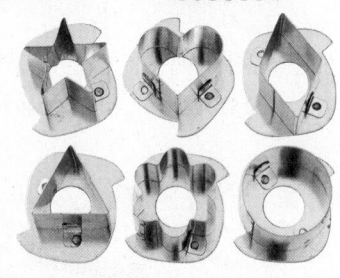

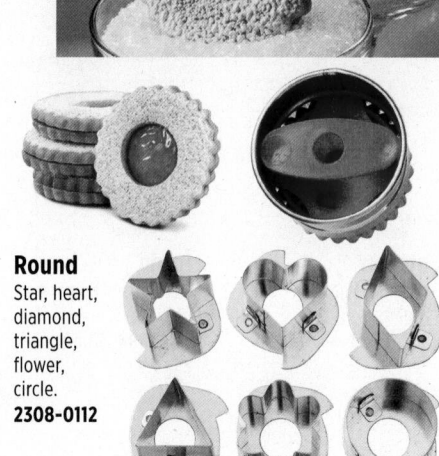

Square
Star, heart, diamond, triangle, flower, circle.
2308-0113

Round
Star, heart, diamond, triangle, flower, circle.
2308-0112

Find a variety of delicious cookie recipes at **wilton.com**

ICINGS & COLORS

Add extra touches that make cookies more delicious! Squeeze on the fun with Wilton Cookie Icing and Icing Writer for colorful decorations with a satin finish. Or, let kids draw designs and messages in cool colors with FoodWriter edible color markers.

COOKIE ICING

Use this quick-setting, microwavable icing to cover your cookies with a smooth finish. Just heat and squeeze onto cookies using the convenient cap. Sets smooth in 1 hour. 10 oz. bottle covers about 12 (3 in.) cookies. Certified Kosher.
Each $4.99

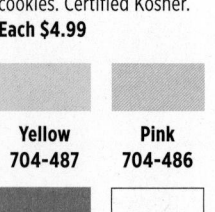

Yellow	Pink
704-487	704-486
Red	White
704-488	704-481

Green	Blue	Orange	Black
704-493	704-444	704-496	704-205

ICING WRITER

Squeeze colorful accents onto Wilton Fondant and Cookie Icing with this ready-to-use icing! It's easy to control; just squeeze the bottle and icing flows smoothly from the built-in round tip. Dries to a smooth, satin finish. 3 oz. bottle. Certified Kosher.
Each $2.99

Yellow	Pink
710-2226	710-2230
Red	White
710-2225	710-2228

Green	Violet	Blue
710-2229	710-2231	710-2227

FOODWRITER EDIBLE COLOR MARKERS

Use edible markers to add dazzling color to countless foods. Decorate on Wilton Cookie Icing, Fondant, Color Flow and royal icing designs. Brighten everyday foods, like toaster pastries, cheese, fruit slices, bread and more. Each set includes five markers. Certified Kosher. Set/5. **Each Set $8.49**

Extra Fine Tip Set 609-105
For fine detailing.

Brown	Green	Red	Blue	Black

Fine Tip Primary Colors Set 609-100
Bold Tip Primary Colors Set 609-115

Yellow	Green	Red	Blue	Black

Fine Tip Neon Colors Set 609-116

Purple	Orange	Pink	Light Green	Black

Extra-Fine Tip	Fine Tip	Bold Tip

SPRINKLES & SUGARS

6-MIX COLORED SPRINKLE ASSORTMENTS

Assorted colors in an easy-pour, flip-top container. Top cupcakes, ice cream and other goodies. Certified Kosher. **Each Container $4.99**

Nonpareils
Contains pink, orange, green, red, yellow, purple. 3 oz. total.
710-4125

Jimmies
Contains pink, orange, green, red, yellow, blue. 3.18 oz. total.
710-4127

4-MIX COLORED SUGAR ASSORTMENTS

Brighten up plain cookies fast! Sprinkle these colored sugars on your treats before baking or after cookies are iced. Certified Kosher. **Each Container $4.99**

Bright
Contains pink, yellow, light green, lavender. 4.4 oz. total.
710-651

Primary
Contains red, dark green, blue, yellow. 4.4 oz. total.
710-650

ORDER TOLL FREE: 800-794-5866

Candy Making

Making delicious candy treats is as easy as melt, mold and serve! Use our easy-to-melt Candy Melts candy and detailed molds for beautiful candy perfect for favors, gifts and special surprises!

CANDY MELTS

Delicious, creamy, easy-to-melt wafers are ideal for all your candy making—molding, dipping or drizzling. Artificial vanilla flavor unless otherwise indicated.

12 oz. (unless otherwise noted).
Certified Kosher Dairy.
Each $3.29

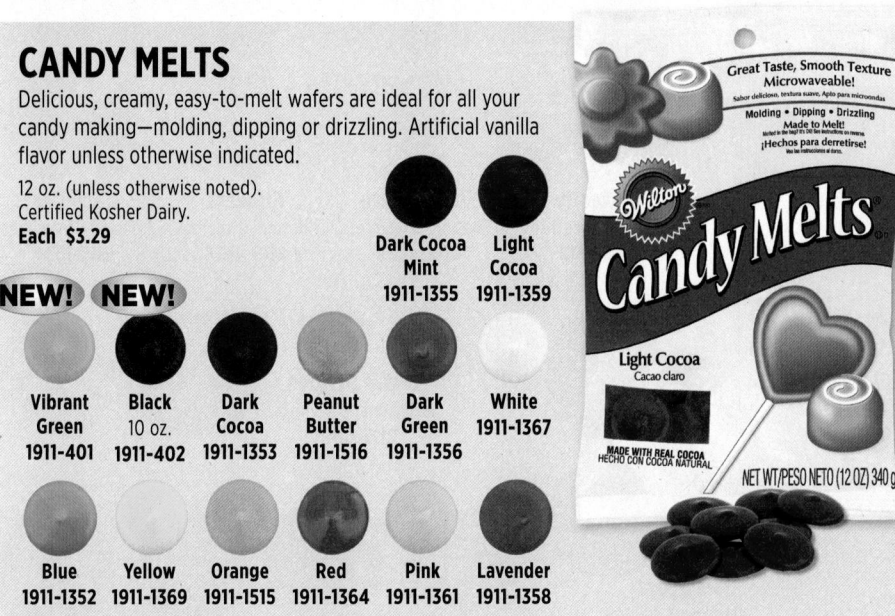

Dark Cocoa Mint 1911-1355
Light Cocoa 1911-1359

NEW! **NEW!**

Vibrant Green 1911-401
Black 10 oz. 1911-402
Dark Cocoa 1911-1353
Peanut Butter 1911-1516
Dark Green 1911-1356
White 1911-1367

Blue 1911-1352
Yellow 1911-1369
Orange 1911-1515
Red 1911-1364
Pink 1911-1361
Lavender 1911-1358

Colorburst Candy Melts
Brilliant flecks of color are blended into each easy-melting wafer, for candies that will look great for showers, receptions, holidays and more. 10 oz. bag. Certified Kosher Dairy. **Each $3.29**

Pastels 1911-490

Brights 1911-491

"Candy Making Beginner's Guide"

With the "Candy Making Beginner's Guide," you'll learn how easy and fun it is to create delicious candy treats. Includes:
- Quick ideas on how to melt Candy Melts candy so you can get right into the fun!
- Easy techniques on how to mold, paint and pipe candy.
- Delicious dipping ideas for candy-coated treats.
- Fun candy projects for any celebration.
- Delicious recipes, such as truffles, fillings, clusters and bark.

Soft cover, 40 pages
902-1231 $3.99

CANDY COLOR SETS

Concentrated oil-based colors blend easily with Candy Melts candy.
Each Set $4.49

Primary
Yellow, orange, red and blue 0.25 oz. jars. Certified Kosher. Set/4. **1913-1299**

Garden
Pink, green, violet and black 0.25 oz. jars. Certified Kosher. Set/4. **1913-1298**

Candy Dips

Designed for fun, easy dipping of pops, treats, fruit, cookies and more with little prep. Quick melting right in the container using your microwave. 10 oz. Certified Kosher Dairy.
Each $3.49
Light Cocoa 1911-511
White 1911-510

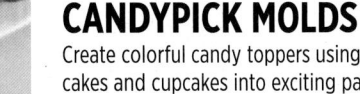

Candy Decorating Pen Set

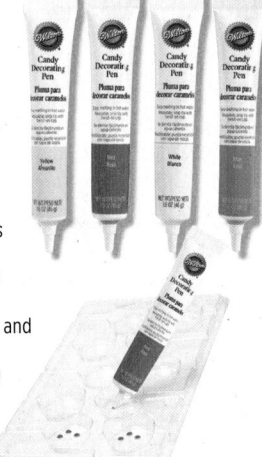

Just melt candy pens in hot water and squeeze into detailed areas of candy mold. The snip-off tip makes it easy to control the flow. Includes 1.6 oz. tubes of yellow, red, white and blue. Set/4.
1914-1285 $11.99

CHOCOLATE PRO ELECTRIC MELTING POT

It's the fast and fun way to melt candy like a pro.
- Melting base stays cool to the touch.
- Easy-pour spout helps prevent spills.
- Removeable non-stick pot holds 2½ cups.
- Non-skid feet keep it steady.
- Dip fruit, potato chips and pretzels for a candy-coated treat.
- Create flavored chocolate sauces for ice cream or silky ganache glaze to pour over cakes.

120 volts. cUL listed.
2104-9004 $34.99

CANDYPICK MOLDS

Create colorful candy toppers using Candy Melts candy to transform plain cakes and cupcakes into exciting party treats!
Each $1.99

Princess
2 designs, 8 cavities.
2115-2113

Pirate
2 designs, 8 cavities.
2115-2112

Big Top
2 designs, 8 cavities.
2115-2117

ORDER ONLINE: WWW.WILTON.COM

PRETZEL MOLDS

Easy to mold! Add your favorite melted Candy Melts candy, position pretzel rod and chill to set. **Each $1.99**

Princess
2 designs, 6 cavities.
2115-2123

Jungle Pals
2 designs, 6 cavities.
2115-2125

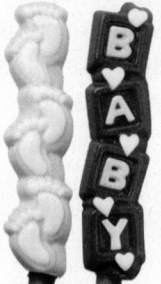

Baby
2 designs, 6 cavities.
2115-2101

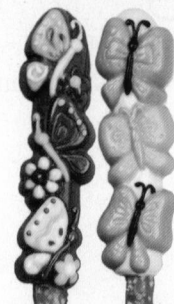

Butterfly
2 designs, 6 cavities.
2115-1032

Smiley Face
1 design, 6 cavities.
2115-4437

Flowers
1 design, 6 cavities.
2115-4436

Race Car
2 designs, 6 cavities.
2115-1034

COOKIE CANDY MOLDS

It's a breeze to add a great tasting and colorful candy design to your favorite store-bought cookies. Great for sandwich cream cookies or any round cookie 2 in. dia. or less.
Each $1.99

NEW!
Daisy/Flower
2 designs, 8 cavities.
2115-0004

NEW!
Dot & Stripes
2 designs, 8 cavities.
2115-0006

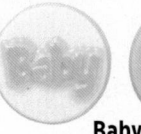

Baby
2 designs, 8 cavities.
2115-2124

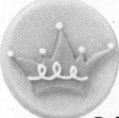

Princess
2 designs, 8 cavities.
2115-2133

Flowers
2 designs, 8 cavities.
2115-1351

Hearts
2 designs, 8 cavities.
2115-1352

Animals
4 designs, 8 cavities.
2115-1354

Sports
4 designs, 8 cavities.
2115-1353

CLASSIC CANDY MOLDS

Wilton has a great selection of traditional shapes to create elegant gift assortments and party trays.

Square **NEW!**
Mold traditional shaped candy perfect for gift giving or favors. 1 design, 10 cavities.
2115-0002 $1.99

Faceted **NEW!**
A definite "gem" of a candy mold. Leave solid or fill.
1 design, 10 cavities.
2115-0003 $1.99

NEW!
3-D Cupcake Look Container
Make a colorful cupcake-shaped candy container. Fill with candy pieces, mousse and more. Makes 3 built treats.
2115-0001 $2.99

Dessert Accents
Finish your signature dessert with flair—top it with a dramatic candy shape using this exciting mold. Swirls, scrolls, zigzags, triangles and leaves add 5-star style. 5 designs, 10 cavities.
2115-2102 $1.99

Dessert Shells
2-piece mold.
1 design, 3 cavities.
2115-1035 $2.99

Dessert Dome
Create versatile candy shell domes, perfect for serving fruit and sorbets or making filled candies. Two-piece mold makes dome halves 1.2 in., 1.6 in. and 2.6 in. dia.; 3 designs, 6 cavities.
2115-2122 $2.99

Truffles
1 design, 14 cavities.
2115-1521 $1.99

Peanut Butter Cups
1 design, 11 cavities.
2115-1522 $1.99

Deep Heart Truffles
1 design, 8 cavities.
2117-100 $1.99

Cordial Cups
Mold a candy "glass" for dessert liqueurs, or fill with whipped cream and float in cocoa or coffee.
1 design, 6 cavities.
2115-1535 $1.99

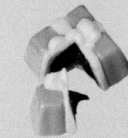

Mint Discs
1 design, 18 cavities.
2115-1739 $1.99

Gift Truffles
1 design, 15 cavities.
2115-1728 $1.99

CANDY & LOLLIPOP MOLDS

More fun shapes and greater detail make Wilton Candy Molds the perfect way to create candy. You can do it all, from exciting kids' party treats to elegant wedding and shower favors. For specific holiday designs, see our Seasonal Section, p. 220-245.
Each $1.99

Stars
1 design,
12 cavities.
2115-1554

Roses in Bloom
1 design,
10 cavities.
2115-1738

Hearts
1 design,
15 cavities.
2115-1712

Dancing Daisies Lollipop
1 design,
9 cavities.
2115-1430

Rubber Ducky
1 design,
6 cavities.
2115-1565

Smiley Face Lollipop
1 design,
10 cavities.
2115-1715

Mini Baby Icons
5 designs,
20 cavities.
2115-1537

Baby Shower
4 designs,
11 cavities.
2115-1710

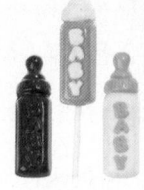

Baby Bottles Lollipop
1 design,
6 cavities.
2115-1560

Seashells
5 designs, 11 cavities.
2115-1561

Baby Treats
5 designs, 5 cavities.
2115-4447

Sea Creatures Lollipop
5 designs, 5 cavities.
2115-1414

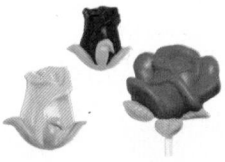

Roses & Buds Lollipop
3 designs, 9 cavities.
(4 lollipop, 5 candy).
2115-1708

Wedding Shower Lollipop
5 designs, 10 cavities. (4 lollipop,
6 candy).
2115-1711

LARGE LOLLIPOP MOLDS

Mold large, detailed lollipops with our Candy Melts candy and these molds. Perfect for party favors, school treats and more.
Each $1.99

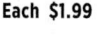

Monkey
3 designs, 3 cavities.
2115-2100

Big Top
3 designs, 3 cavities.
2115-2116

3-D Cake
Makes a spectacular wedding or shower favor when you pair it with our Lollipop Wrapping Kit, p. 179. 2 designs, 3 cavities.
2115-0005 $2.99

NEW!

Pirate
3 designs, 3 cavities.
2115-2111

Sports
4 designs, 4 cavities.
2115-4432

Pinwheel
2 designs,
3 cavities.
2115-4443

Double Heart
2 designs, 4 cavities.
2115-4440

Party/Birthday
4 designs, 4 cavities.
2115-4434

Fairy Tale
3 designs, 3 cavities.
2115-1033

FUN FACE LOLLIPOP MOLDS

Make kids smile with lollipop mouths, mustaches and animal snouts that are as much fun to play with as they are to eat. It's the perfect way to start the fun at birthday parties!
Each $1.99

Mustache
3 designs,
3 cavities.
2115-2118

Animal Nose
3 designs,
3 cavities.
2115-2119

Smile Factor
3 designs,
3 cavities.
2115-2120

Monster Mouth
3 designs,
3 cavities.
2115-2121

CANDY MAKING

CANDY MOLD SETS

Be ready for any celebration with this great variety of theme molds!

2-PACK CANDY MOLD SETS

A variety of shapes in one great set! Fits your celebration themes.
Each Pack $2.99

Girl Power
10 designs,
10 cavities.
Pk./2.
2115-1604

**Garden
Goodies
Lollipop**
10 designs,
10 cavities.
Pk./2.
2115-1607

Baby
10 designs,
10 cavities.
Pk./2.
2115-1605

10-PACK CANDY MOLD SET

Includes 72 total shapes and 114 total cavities for fun candy messages, sports treats, flowers and more. Pk./10. **2115-1724 $9.99**

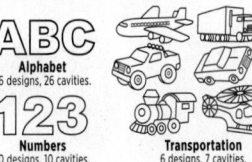 

ABC
Alphabet
26 designs, 26 cavities.

123
Numbers
10 designs, 10 cavities.

Transportation
6 designs, 7 cavities.

Sports Champ
7 designs, 7 cavities.

Celebration
5 designs, 10 cavities.

Hearts
1 design, 15 cavities.

Peanut Butter Cups
1 design, 11 cavities.

Snack Time
6 designs, 12 cavities.

Fruit Lollipop
5 designs, 5 cavities.

Garden Flowers
5 designs, 11 cavities.

CANDY MAKING ACCESSORIES

Wilton has the tools to help you achieve candy-making success—from melting and molding to decorating and more!

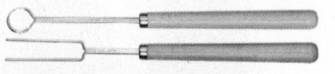

Metal Candy Dipping Set
Professional-quality stainless steel with wooden handles. 8.75 in. long. Set/2.
1904-925 $10.99

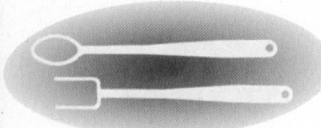

Candy Dipping Set
Easy-handling spoon and fork each 7.75 in. long. Set/2.
1904-3230 $3.49

Candy Thermometer
Yields precise measurement essential for preparing hard candy, nougat and more.
1904-1200 $14.99

Candy Melting Plate
Microwave up to 11 candy colors at one time with less mess! Plastic with non-slip grip edge. Includes decorating brush.
1904-8016 $3.49

Easy-Pour Funnel
Push-button controls flow of candy. Nylon. 5 in. x 4 in. dia.
1904-552 $4.49

LOLLIPOP STICKS
Create the perfect pop with sticks in every size.

Bamboo Sticks
Sustainable, durable bamboo is perfect for gift pops, caramel apples and more. 5 in. Pk./30.
1912-1931 $4.29

Paper Sticks
Sturdy paper sticks. Not for oven use.

4 in. Pk./50.
1912-1006 $1.99

6 in. Pk./35.
1912-1007 $1.99

8 in. Pk./25.
1912-9320 $1.99

11.75 in. Pk./20.
1912-1212 $3.99

Decorator Brush Set
Plastic, durable bristles with easy-to-hold handle. Set/3.
2104-9355 $1.99

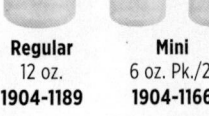

Squeeze Bottles
Fill your mold without mess! Convenient bottles available in two sizes.
Each $1.99

Regular
12 oz.
1904-1189

Mini
6 oz. Pk./2.
1904-1166

Candy Decorating Bags
The convenient way to melt small amounts of Candy Melts candy and pipe color detail in your molds! Or, drizzle candy designs over molded candies and desserts. Flexible 12 in. plastic bags. Pk./12.
2104-4825 $4.49

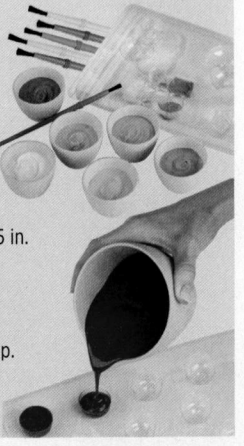

STAY-WARM CERAMIC MELTING CUPS & BOWLS
Microwave-safe ceramic pieces retain heat, keeping candy melted longer. Ideal for filling all types of Wilton molds. Great for heating and pouring dessert toppings, too.

Melting Cups
Holds heat up to ½ hour. Includes six cups (2 in. x 1.5 in. deep each) and six decorating brushes. Set/12.
1904-1067 $10.99

Melting Bowls
Holds heat up to 1 hour. Each bowl 4 in. x 3.5 in. deep. Set/2.
1904-1076 $10.99

CANDY PRESENTATION

Your homemade candy deserves a beautiful presentation. Wilton has everything you need to wrap and package your candy gifts.

Lollipop Pocket Kits

NEW!

Dress up your candy lollipops in one of these fun wraps! Fantastic to use for showers, weddings, candy bouquet centerpieces and more. Each includes: 8 wraps, ribbons, adhesives; 1 print-your-own sheet. Lollipop sticks and candy sold separately. Wraps approx. 4 in. dia. Pk./8.
Each Pack $3.99

Cupcake
415-0956

Pink Flower
415-0959

Silver Star
415-0958

Red Heart
415-0957

CANDY CUPS

Crisply pleated just like professionals use.
Each Pack $1.79

Glassine
White glassine-coated paper.
1 in. Dia.
Pk./100. **1912-1243**
1.25 in. Dia.
Pk./75. **1912-1245**

Foil
Wax-laminated paper on foil.
Pk./75. **Each Pack $1.79**
Red **415-314**
Blue **415-313** Gold **415-306**
Pink **415-315** Silver **415-307**

Love Chocolate Boxes
Bright, fun pattern makes your gift even sweeter! Holds ½ lb. Pk./3.
1904-4242 $2.29

Classic Boxes
Attractive gift giving for any occasion.
1 lb. Candy Boxes
White. Pk./3.
1904-1172 $2.99
½ lb. Candy Boxes
Pk./3. **Each $2.29**
White **1904-1150**
Red **1904-1152**

"Home Made" Box Seals
Embossed seals add a "homemade" touch whenever you give baked goods! Pk./24.
1904-8936 $1.29

Pretzel Boxes
Your tempting pretzels show through the front window. Tented design holds pretzels upright to protect against breakage. 3 in. x 2 in. x 9.5 in. high. White. Pk./3.
1904-2000 $2.99

Truffle Boxes
An elegant look with a lock-close top that forms a perfect "bow." Holds 2 to 3 pieces of candy. Pk./4.
Each Pack $2.29
White **1904-1154**
Gold **1904-1156**

Drawstring Lollipop Bags
Fill with your favorite candies, then pull the drawstring to close. Also great for cookies, nuts and other treats.
4.5 in. x 5.5 in. Pk./15.
1912-9469 $2.29

Lollipop Wrapping Kit
Includes 18 sticks (4 in.), 18 bags (3 in. x 4 in.) and 18 twist ties.
1904-1193 $2.29

Clear Treat Bags
3 in. x 4 in. Pk./50.
1912-2347 $2.89
4 in. x 6 in. Pk./100.
1912-1294 $4.19

Pretzel Bags
See-through bags are ideal for showing off your candy-coated pretzels—great for favors and gifts. Includes 20 plastic bags, 20 twist ties. 2.25 in. x 9.75 in. Pk./20.
1912-5911 $2.29
MegaPack
Pk./75.
1912-5912 $3.99

Large Jewel Tone Foil Wraps
Wrap larger candies in beautiful, bright foil squares! 6 in. x 6 in. Pk./12.
2113-1119 $2.29

Foil Wrappers
Bright, shiny coverings for candy and lollipops!
4 in. x 4 in. squares. Pk./50.
Each Pack $1.99
Gold **1904-1197**
Silver **1904-1196**
Red **1904-1198**

CHOCOLATE PRO CHOCOLATE FOUNTAIN

The Chocolate Pro Chocolate Fountain makes it easy to enjoy delicious, hand-dipped desserts any time!

- Holds 4 lbs. of melted chocolate.
- Three adjustable feet, plus bubble level, allow perfect leveling from all angles.
- Tiers come apart for easy cleaning.
- Graceful canopy style creates an elegant flow from all three levels.
- Bowl is designed to keep chocolate melted and flowing.

120 volts; cUL listed.
2104-9008 $109.99

Chocolate Pro Melting Chocolate Wafers

The best real melting chocolate for fountains and fondues. Made from premium ingredients for superior melting and a delicious taste. Ideal texture and rich flavor for making dipped desserts. No tempering needed! No oil needed! 2 lbs.
Each $17.99

Milk Chocolate
2104-2618

NEW!

White Chocolate
2104-2619

Cupcake Fun!

What makes everyday cupcakes more fun? It's our exciting products! From a rainbow of baking cup colors to different display and gifting options, we make baking, decorating and serving one-of-a-kind cupcakes a pleasure!

Cupcake Decorating Set
Create fun-looking cupcakes with this decorating set. Includes:
- 4 standard decorating tips (12, 1M, 22 and Bismarck 230).
- 8 — 12 in. disposable decorating bags.
- Step-by-step, illustrated instructions.

Set/12.
2104-6667 $8.99

"Cupcake Fun!"
Packed with more than 150 exciting cupcake and treat ideas, "Cupcake Fun!" is everything you need to create the ultimate cupcake celebration! Includes:
- Ideas for all occasions and celebrations in addition to captivating shapes, from coffee cups to flying saucers.
- Foolproof baking steps.
- Delicious recipe section, including key lime cupcakes, mocha icing and more.
- Complete line of cupcake products.

Soft cover, 128 pages.
902-795 $12.99

SPECIALTY BAKING CUPS
Exciting shapes and designs help your cupcakes make a grand entrance for any occasion. Standard size, 2 in. dia.; Mini size, 1.25 in. dia.

Petal Cups
A pretty pastel flower in full bloom! Perfect for shower, Mother's Day and birthday cupcakes. Standard size, Pk./24.; Mini size, Pk./48.
Each Pack $3.99

Petal Cups now available in Mini Size!  **NEW!**

| **Red** Standard 415-1380 Mini 415-0466 | **Pink** Standard 415-1375 Mini 415-95046 | **Peach** Standard 415-1376 Mini 415-0467 | **Yellow** Standard 415-1443 Mini 415-0465 | **Lavender** Standard 415-1442 Mini 415-95045 | **White** Standard 415-1379 Mini 415-0468 |

Shaped Cups
Colorful cups have the look of layered flowers and green fields. Standard size, Pk./24.; Mini size, Pk./48.
Each Pack $3.99

NEW!

| **White Rose** Standard 415-1439 | **Grass** Standard 415-7051 | **Grass** Mini 415-0469 |

Ruffled Cups
Gently flared edges and a softly puckered texture make these a great alternative to crisply pleated cups. Pk./24.
Each Pack $3.99

| **Rose** 415-1391 | **Pink** 415-1396 | **Yellow** 415-1393 | **Teal** 415-1390 | **Lavender** 415-1395 | **White** 415-1389 |

Pleated Cups
A peaked, softly pleated style in rich colors creates a bold, breezy presentation. Pk./15. **Each Pack $3.99**

| **Yellow** 415-1382 | **Blue** 415-1381 | **Purple** 415-1383 |

Blossom Cups*
Pretty petals frame your cupcake in colors to match your celebration look. Pk./12. **Each Pack $3.99**

| **Pink** 415-1595 | **Yellow** 415-0177 |

Blue 415-0178

| **Lavender** 415-0179 | **White** 415-0176 |

*Do not place in muffin pans. Place directly on cookie sheet and fill halfway with batter.

MULTI-COLORED ASSORTMENTS
Always have colorful baking cups on hand for any celebration or simply "just because."

NEW!

Monochrome $2.09
White, black, silver. Pk./75.
Standard 415-0374

NEW!

Rainbow $4.99
Yellow, blue, red, white, green, purple. In reusable tube. Pk./150.
Standard 415-1623

NEW!

Bright Rainbow $4.99
Yellow, blue, pink, white, green, purple. In reusable tube. Pk./150.
Standard 415-1624

Pastel $1.99
Pink, yellow, blue-green.
Standard Pk./75. **415-394**
Mini Pk./100. **415-2123**

Jewel $2.09
Gold, purple, teal.
Standard Pk./75. **415-1078**
Mini Pk./100. **415-1111**

Primary $2.09
Red, yellow, blue.
Standard Pk./75. **415-987**
Mini Pk./100. **415-1110**

ORDER TOLL FREE: 800-794-5866

ColorCups NEW!

Always bright, colorful and fun!

Let your celebration colors stay true! Baking cups are foil-lined to keep colors on the outside bright and fun for every celebration. Place on a cookie sheet or bake in a standard-sized muffin pan. Standard size, 2 in. dia. Pk./36. **Each Pack $2.99**

Blue
415-0480

Red
415-0481

Hearts
415-0499

Flowers
415-0500

Pink Dots
415-0486

Yellow Dots
415-0487

Black Dots
415-0488

Red Dots
415-0490

Pink/Purple/ Orange Stripes
415-0492

Celebrate Pink
415-0495

Celebrate Blue
415-0496

Pink/Purple/ Orange Dots
415-0483

Yellow/Blue/ Orange/Green Dots
415-0485

Zebra
415-0516

Leopard
415-0517

Damask
415-0518

BAKING CUPS

With colorful Wilton designs, your cupcakes and muffins become part of the party! There's a baking cup pattern or color to suit every celebration! Standard size, 2 in. dia., Pk./75; Mini size, 1.25 in. dia., Pk./100, unless otherwise indicated. **Each Pack $2.09** (except where noted)

NEW!

Green Dots
Standard 415-0154

NEW!

Teal Dots
Standard 415-0156

NEW!

Pink Dots
Standard 415-0158

NEW!

Red Dots
Standard 415-0148

NEW!

Black Dots
Standard
415-7068

NEW!

Purple Dots
Standard
415-0162

NEW!

Retro Dots
Standard
415-1878

NEW!

Color Wheel
Standard
415-1868

NEW!

Gingham
Standard
415-0377

Snappy Stripes
Standard 415-5381
Mini 415-5380

Bubble Stripes
Standard 415-114
Mini 415-115

Be My Cupcake
Standard 415-127
Mini 415-128

Cupcake Heaven
Standard 415-422
Mini 415-426

Dazzling Dots
$1.59
Standard Pk./50.
415-582
Mini Pk./75. **415-1141**

Transportation
Standard
415-1147

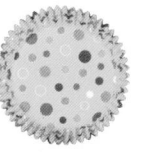
Sweet Dots
Standard   Mini
415-1052   415-1183

Modern Garden Party
Standard   Mini
415-0170   415-0171

Pink Party
Standard   Mini
415-0166   415-0167

SILVER CELEBRATE

Perfect for birthdays, anniversaries, weddings and more.

Standard
415-1544
$2.09

Cupcake Combo
24 Standard size cups, 24 picks
415-1546 $2.29

Silver Foil
Each Pack $1.99
Wax-laminated paper on foil.
Standard Pk./24.
415-207
Mini Pk./36.
415-1414

Gold Foil
Each Pack $1.99
Wax-laminated paper on foil.
Standard Pk./24.
415-206
Mini Pk./36.
415-1413

White
Each Pack $1.99
Jumbo Pk./50.
415-2503
Standard Pk./75.
415-2505
Mini Pk./100.
415-2507

UNBLEACHED NEW!

Let your decorated cupcake be the center of attention in these unbleached paper cups.
Each Pack $2.09

Standard Pk./75.
415-1864

Mini Pk./100.
415-1865

CUPCAKE FUN!

CUPCAKE BOXES

Display and gift your cupcake creations with our window boxes. Each box includes an insert with recessed space to hold standard-sized cupcakes safely in place. Easy folding assembly; great for favors! Choose single, 3-, 4- or 6-cupcake size. Ribbon not included.

4-CUPCAKE BOX
Each Pack $5.29 (except where noted)

NEW!

Sweet Pink
415-0946
$5.99

NEW!

Kraft
415-0953

Primary
415-0941

Pastel
415-1361

White
415-1215

Silver
415-1359
$5.99

Cupcake Heaven
415-1206

1-CUPCAKE BOX
Holds one standard cupcake. Pk./3. **Each Pack $3.29**

NEW!

Black & White Dots
415-0950

NEW!

Zebra
415-1897

NEW!

White
415-0436

Cupcake Heaven
415-289

3-CUPCAKE BOX
Holds three standard cupcakes. Pk./3.
$5.99

NEW!

Pastel
415-0955

6-CUPCAKE BOX
Holds six standard cupcakes. Pk./2.
Cupcake Heaven
415-1207 $5.29

CUPCAKE WRAPS

Set cupcakes apart with these captivating, openwork wraps. Precisely cut paper designs are the ideal way to enhance your treats, whether the tops are decorated, swirled or iced smooth.

2 in. dia. Fits standard-sized cupcakes; baking cups sold separately. Pk./18.
Each Pack $3.49

Pink Party
415-0169

Modern Garden Party
415-0173

White Pearl Fence
415-0111

Lavender Swirls
415-0181

Red Foil Swirls
415-0180

White Pearl Swirls
415-0182

Black Swirls
415-0112

SILICONE BAKING CUPS

Discover the convenience and easy release of flexible silicone! Reusable, oven-safe cups in fun colors and exciting shapes are perfect for baking and serving. All have convenient batter fill line. **Each Pack $9.99**

Silly-Feet!
Orange, yellow, blue, purple. Cups are 2 in. dia. 2.3 in. high with feet. Pk./4.
415-9428

Pastel Round
Three each: pink, yellow, green, blue. 2 in. dia. Pk./12.
415-9410

Flower Fun Cups
Six yellow, six pink. 2 in. wide. Pk./12.
415-9450

Square
Six blue, six green. 2 in. wide. Pk./12.
415-9424

Heart
Six pink, six red. 2 in. wide. Pk./12.
415-9409

ORDER TOLL FREE: 800-794-5866

CUPCAKES-N-MORE DESSERT STANDS

The look is fresh and fun, featuring wire spirals to securely hold each cupcake or treat. The twisting, towering design is perfect for any setting: showers, kids' birthdays, weddings, holidays and more.

13-Count Standard
Holds 13 standard-sized cupcakes.*
9.25 in. high x 9 in. wide.
307-831 $14.99

19-Count Standard
Holds 19 standard-sized cupcakes.
18 in. high x 12 in. wide.
307-666 $22.99

23-Count Standard
Holds 23 standard-sized cupcakes.*†
12 in. high x 13 in. wide.
307-826 $32.99

24-Count Mini
Holds 24 mini-sized cupcakes.*
10.5 in. high x 9 in. wide.
307-250 $16.99

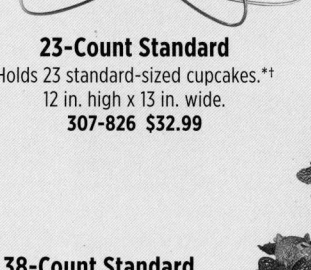

38-Count Standard
Holds 38 standard-sized cupcakes.*
15 in. high x 18 in. wide.
307-651 $44.99

*Pat. No. 7,387,283. †Pat. No. D516,385.

3-Tier Treat Stands
Give cupcakes the perfect showcase for the party with easy-to-assemble, three-level stands. Securely holds 24 standard-sized cupcakes. Corrugate cardboard. Baking cups not included. 10.5 in. high.

NEW!

Damask
1512-0863 $6.99

Baby Feet
12 in. wide x 17.5 in. high.
1004-1492 $6.99

White
1512-127 $5.99

4-Tier Stacked Dessert Tower
Four plastic stacking sections with angled tiers for the best view of decorated desserts. Holds 36 standard-sized cupcakes. Sections easily disassemble and nest for storage; assembled tower is 16.25 in. high x 12 in. wide. Pat. No. D560,974.
307-856 $19.99

Collapsible for easy storage

3-in-1 Caddy
It's the most convenient way to take along cakes, cupcakes, muffins and more! The 3-in-1 Caddy features an exclusive reversible cupcake tray which holds 12 standard-sized or 24 mini-sized cupcakes. Or, remove the tray to carry up to a 9 in. x 13 in. decorated cake on the sturdy locking base. The see-through cover has higher sides to protect icing flowers and tall decorations. You can also use the caddy at home to keep pies, cookies and brownies fresh for days after baking. 18 in. x 14 in. x 6.75 in. high. Pat. No. D572,539.
2105-9958 $19.99

CUPCAKE FUN!

Pops!

Give the party more pizzazz with Pops! Wilton has sensational ways to bake, decorate and serve sweet treats on a stick. Start the fun with our exciting "Pops! Sweets on a Stick!" publication and discover all the decorating possibilities!

"Pops! Sweets on a Stick!"
Discover more than 250 decorating ideas for sweets on a stick. Includes:
- Gallery of designs from people pops to fun flowers.
- Variety of favor and reception ideas.
- Delicious recipes for cake ball pops, sugar cookies on a stick, plus dipping and decorating techniques.
- Impressive presentation suggestions.
- Complete product section.

Soft cover; 112 pages.
902-1055 $14.99

Candy Dips
Designed for fun, easy dipping of pops, treats, fruit, cookies and more with little prep. Quick melting right in the container using your microwave. 10 oz. **Each $3.49**

White 1911-510
Light Cocoa 1911-511

See page 175 for the complete assortment of Wilton Candy Melts candy.

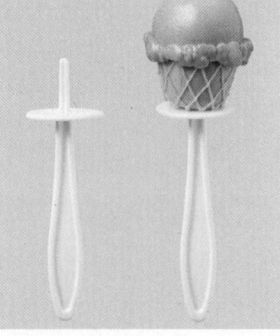

Pops Sticks
8 in. long plastic sticks. Insert pop or treat onto stick end with platform. Pk./6.
2103-1122 $3.99

Paper Sticks
Sturdy paper sticks in four sizes. Not for oven use.

4 in. Pk./50. **1912-1006 $1.99**
6 in. Pk./35. **1912-1007 $1.99**
8 in. Pk./25. **1912-9320 $1.99**
11.75 in. Pk./20. **1912-1212 $3.99**

Pops Decorating Stand
Securely holds pops upright for decorating. Also, ideal for letting candy set on pops undisturbed. Holds up to 44 pops. Corrugate. Assembly instructions included. 12 in. dia. x 3.75 in. high.
1512-136 $3.99

POPS DECORATIONS

Transform your pops into friendly faces to delight all your guests. With our shaped sprinkles, icing decorations and Fun Pix, it's easy to populate your party!

MAKE-A-FACE ICING DECORATIONS
Put a face on pops, cookies, mini cupcakes and more. Makes nine faces of three types of treats. Certified Kosher. Approx. .5 in. to 1.5 in. Pk./9. **Each Set $2.29**

People
710-1005

Animals
710-1004

SPRINKLE SETS
Create hair, noses, ears and more to bring your pops to life. Convenient, individual flip-top containers. 3.74 oz. total weight. **Each Set $3.99**

People Faces
Contains diamonds, jimmies, circles.
710-056

Jungle Pals Pops Fun Pix
Insert into your pops for instant, party-ready treats. Made of clear plastic. 2.75 in. x 2.5 in. Pk./8.
2113-1122 $2.29

Candy Eyeballs
Add faces on pops, cookies, cupcakes and more. Shown actual size, 0.43 in. dia. 0.88 oz. Approx. 62 pieces.
710-0017 $3.99

Animal Faces
Contains triangles, jimmies, ovals.
710-055

BAKEWARE

Bake delicious pops using Wilton's bakeware and accessories.

SILICONE MOLDS

Flexible silicone is perfect for baking, molding and so much more. Freezer, refrigerator, microwave and dishwasher safe—oven safe to 500°F.
Each $9.99

Heart Pops Mold
One mix makes approx. 16 pops. Four cavities, each 2 in. x 5 in. x 0.75 in. deep.
2105-0588

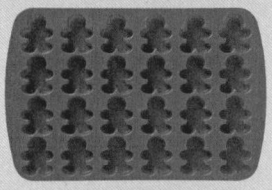

Boy Mold
One mix makes approx. 80 pops. 24 cavities, each 1.75 in. x 1.6 in. x 0.75 in. deep.
2105-0553

Star Pops Mold
One mix makes approx. 16 pops. Four cavities, each 2.25 in. x 5 in. x 0.5 in. deep.
2105-0546

Round Pops Mold
One 8 in. x 8 in. size brownie mix makes 24 pops. Eight cavities, each 1.75 in. x 1.75 in. x 1.75 in. deep.
2105-4925

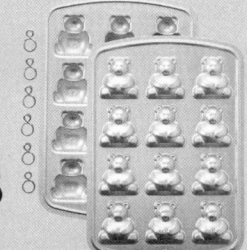

Cookie Treat Sticks
Oven-safe.
6 in. Pk./20.
1912-9319 $1.99
8 in. Pk./20.
1912-9318 $2.99

Mini 3-D Bear Set
One mix makes about 50 pops. Two-piece aluminum pan bakes cakes 2.25 in. x 2.25 in. x 1.25 in. Set/8.
2105-0545 $21.99

POPS PRESENTATION

Give pops with pizzazz using these fun presentation pieces. Pops and decorations where shown not included.

POPS DOILIES & WRAPS

Fancy bases present pops with a touch of sophistication. Insert stick through hole in doily or wrap.

Doilies
24 doilies, 3.25 in. dia.
1904-1001 $1.99

Ruffles
Eight sets, 4 in. dia.
2113-1102 $2.29

Hearts
Eight sets, 4.25 in. and 3.5 in. dia.
2113-1100 $2.29

Pops Favor Bags
12 bags 4.25 in. x 7 in.; 12 ribbons, 12 in.
1912-1341 $1.99

Jewel Tone Foil Wraps
Wrap pops in bright foil squares! Gold, blue, pink. 6 in. x 6 in. Pk./12.
2113-1119 $2.29

Pops Gift Boxes
Two window boxes 8 in. x 6.25 in. x 6.25 in.; two clear seals 1 in. dia.
415-1502 $5.29

Pops Flower Pot Kit
Two containers 6 in. x 5.25 in.; two bags 7.5 in. x 2 ft; 2 ribbons 1.5 ft; two tags 2 in. dia.
415-1503 $5.29

Pops Display Stand
Decorate to match your celebration. Holds 28 pops. Corrugate. Assembly instructions included. 12 in. dia. x 9.5 in. high; two border strips 1.25 in. wide; 10 in. and 12 in. dia.
1512-138 $5.99

Presentation

Delicious-looking cakes, cupcakes, brownies and more deserve to be served in style. Wilton offers boards, bases, doilies, gift-giving containers and bags that add an instant sophistication or pop of color and fun.

CAKE BOARDS, BASES & ACCESSORIES

Your cake or treats will look their best when presented with quality, greaseproof Wilton boards and circles.

FASHION CAKE BOARDS

Greaseproof cake boards show off your 10 in. cakes or treats in style. 12 in. dia. Pk./3. **Each Pack $4.99**

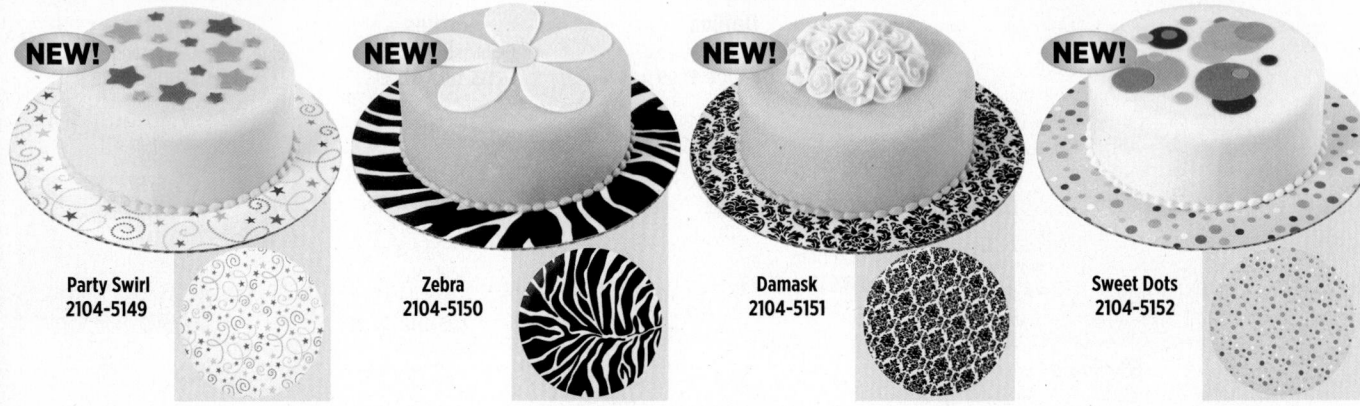

Party Swirl
2104-5149

Zebra
2104-5150

Damask
2104-5151

Sweet Dots
2104-5152

Cake Boards

Shaped cakes look best on boards cut to fit! Strong corrugated cardboard, generously sized in rectangular shapes. Perfect for sheet and square cakes. For shaped cakes, use the pan as a pattern and cut out board to fit cake (see p. 114). Greaseproof coating.

10 in. x 14 in. Rectangle Pk./6. **2104-554 $5.99**
13 in. x 19 in. Rectangle Pk./6. **2104-552 $5.99**

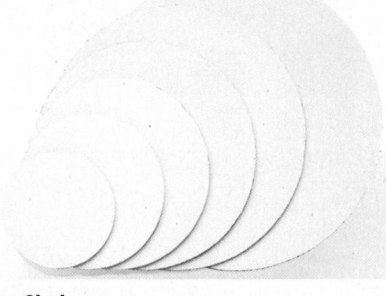

Cake Circles

Corrugated cardboard for strength and stability. Greaseproof coating.

6 in. Round Pk./10. **2104-64 $3.99**
8 in. Round Pk./12. **2104-80 $4.99**
10 in. Round Pk./12. **2104-102 $5.99**
12 in. Round Pk./8. **2104-129 $5.99**
14 in. Round Pk./6. **2104-145 $6.49**
16 in. Round Pk./6. **2104-160 $6.99**

Show-N-Serve Cake Boards

Scalloped edge has the look of intricate lace. Greaseproof coating.

10 in. Round Pk./10. **2104-1168 $4.99**
12 in. Round Pk./8. **2104-1176 $5.49**
14 in. Round Pk./6. **2104-1184 $5.99**
14 in. x 20 in. Rectangle Pk./6. **2104-1230 $6.99**

Ruffle Boards

Ready-to-use cake board and ruffle in one. Bleached white board and all-white ruffling complement any cake.

8 in. (for 6 in. round cake) **415-950 $2.79**
10 in. (for 8 in. round cake) **415-960 $3.29**
12 in. (for 10 in. round cake) **415-970 $4.49**
14 in. (for 12 in. round cake) **415-980 $4.99**
16 in. (for 14 in. round cake) **415-990 $5.99**
18 in. (for 16 in. round cake) **415-1000 $8.49**

Tuk-N-Ruffle

A pretty touch that attaches to edge of your serving tray or board with royal icing or tape. White.

60 ft. bolt per box.
802-1008 $17.99

6 ft. pkg.
802-1991 $3.99

Fanci-Foil Wrap

Serving side has a non-toxic, grease-resistant surface. Continuous roll: 20 in. x 15 ft.

White
804-191
$8.99

Gold
804-183
$8.99

Silver
804-167
$8.99

ORDER TOLL FREE: 800-794-5866

SILVER CAKE BASES

Convenient 0.5 in. thick silver foil-covered bases are grease-resistant and reusable. Strong to hold heavy decorated cakes without an additional serving plate. Perfect for all types of cakes and craft creations.

Round Bases

10 in. Pk./2.
2104-1187 $7.99
12 in. Pk./2.
2104-1188 $8.99
14 in. Pk./2.
2104-1189 $10.99
16 in. Pk./2.
2104-1190 $12.99

Square Bases

14 in. Pk./2.
2104-0969 $10.99
16 in. Pk./2.
2104-0970 $12.99

DOILIES

Add instant elegance to cake plates, dessert trays, entrées and sandwich buffets. Use under table centerpieces and plants, for decorations and crafts, too.

DAMASK
Beautiful, decorative design.
Each Pack $2.99

ZEBRA
Trend-right pattern.
Each Pack $2.99

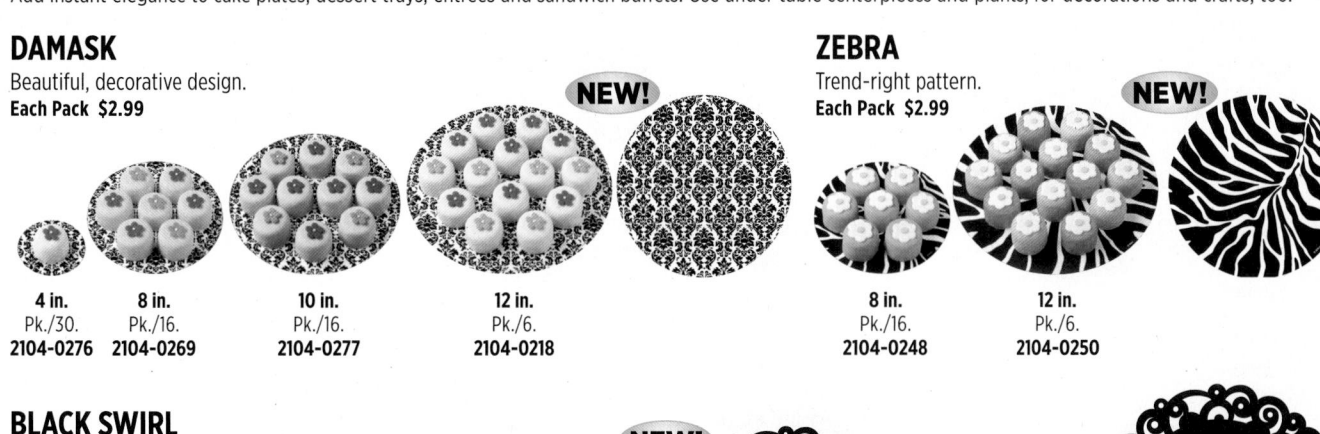

DAMASK

4 in.
Pk./30.
2104-0276

8 in.
Pk./16.
2104-0269

10 in.
Pk./16.
2104-0277

12 in.
Pk./6.
2104-0218

ZEBRA

8 in.
Pk./16.
2104-0248

12 in.
Pk./6.
2104-0250

BLACK SWIRL
Simple and stylish for treats and cakes.
Each Pack $3.99

4 in.
Pk./30.
2104-5153

8 in.
Pk./16.
2104-0219

10 in.
Pk./16.
2104-5154

12 in.
Pk./6.
2104-0220

GREASEPROOF WHITE
A classic style that adds elegance to your treats.
Each Pack $1.99

10 in. x 14 in.
Rectangle
Pk./6.
2104-90224

14 in.
Pk./4.
2104-90214

12 in.
Pk./6.
2104-90212

10 in.
Pk./10.
2104-90210

8 in.
Pk./16.
2104-90208

6 in.
Pk./20.
2104-90206

4 in.
Pk./30.
2104-90204

PRESENTATION

TREAT CONTAINERS

Your homemade treats are even more welcome when packaged in our boxes, bags and accessories. We make it easy to present your delicious foods with pride!

Large Treat Boxes
Window boxes show off your delicious treats and small cakes. 4 in. x 8 in. x 8 in. Pk./3.
415-9490
$5.29

Rectangle Boxes
Window boxes show off your delicious treats. 8 in. x 3.25 in. x 3.25 in. high. Pk./3.
415-1433 $5.29

Compartment Boxes
Three boxes (6.25 in. x 6.25 in. x 2 in. high) with 12 removable trays (3.2 in. x 3.2 in. x 1.8 in. high).
415-1431 $5.29

Treat Baskets
Roomy handled basket is ideal for your gifts. Great for muffins, mini loaves and more. 6.5 in. x 6.5 in. x 3 in. Pk./2.
415-104 $5.29

Small Treat Kits
Create the perfect gift with window boxes. Great for candies or 3.5 in. cookies. Includes seals and sticker sheet. 4.5 in. x 4.5 in. x 1.5 in. Pk./3.
415-102 $3.29

Popcorn Treat Boxes
Classic shape stands up tall to hold popcorn, nuts and other snacks. 3.75 in. x 2.25 in. x 5.25 in. high. Pk./4.
1904-1141 $3.29

Hexagon Treat Boxes
Self-closing top forms a pretty petal box top. Great for cookies, candy and favors. 4 in. x 6.25 in. high. Pk./4.
415-105 $5.29

Stripes Cookie Totes
What a fun way to give and enjoy your famous cookies! Resealable handle bags have a see-through window to show off those tempting treats. 9.5 in. x 6.75 in. x 3 in. deep. Pk./3.
1912-0880
$3.49

Treat Cups
Present all your uniquely shaped desserts in these great treat cups. Greaseproof coating for added strength and easy cleanup. Not recommended for baking.

Each Pack $1.99

Round
2.5 in. x .5 in. Pk./18.
415-908

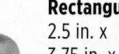

Rectangular
2.5 in. x 3.75 in. x 0.75 in. Pk./12.
415-909

CLEAR TREAT BAGS

Find the perfect size to wrap up any treats.

10 in. x 16 in. Treat Bag Kit
Wrap up bread loaves, smaller bowls and plates of treats. Includes four each 10 in. x 16 in. bags; 18 in. ribbons and gift tags.
1912-1142 $3.29

16 in. x 20 in. Treat Bag Kit
Ideal size for Treat Baskets above. Great for a cookie platter, pie, scones and more. Includes three each 16 in. x 20 in. bags; 18 in. ribbons and gift tags.
1912-1143 $4.29

Clear Mini Plate Kit
Wrap up your homemade cookies with clear bags and a silver foil board that helps them arrive safely. Includes eight each 3.75 in. x 12 in. bags; 12 in. ribbons; 3.5 in. dia. plates. Pk/8.
1912-0881 $2.99

PLATTERS

Colorful shaped platters are perfect for seving treats or an 8 in. cake! Pk./3.
Each Pack $5.99

12 in. Cupcake Platter
2104-5141

12 in. Flower Platter
2104-5142

12 in. Heart Platter
Red, pink.
2104-5143

13 in. Star Platter
Red, silver, blue.
2104-5144

SILVER PLATTERS

Features a shining, silver-tone surface and elegant scalloped shape.
Each Pack $8.99

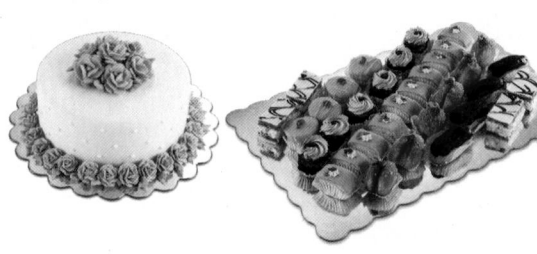

12 in. Round
Pk./8.
2104-1166

14 in. Round
Pk./6.
2104-1167

13 in. x 19 in. Rectangle
Pk./4.
2104-1169

PARTY BAGS

Fill with candy, cookies and other goodies; great for gifts and surprises, too! Includes 20 each plastic bags and ties. 4 in. x 9.5 in. Pk./20, unless otherwise noted. **Each Pack $2.09**

Celebrate
1912-0115

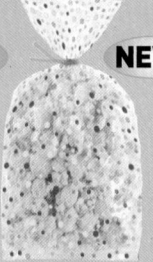

Sweet Dots
1912-0116

Damask
1912-0117

Confetti
1912-0118

Clear Shaped Party Bags
4.5 x 7.25 in.
Each pack contains 100 bags and ties.
1912-1112 $4.19

Clear Party Bags
4 in. x 9.5 in. Each pack contains 25 bags and ties.
1912-1240 $2.09

Mega pack
50 ct.
1912-1239 $3.19

4 in. x 6 in. Mini Bags
Mega pack 100 ct.
1912-1294 $4.19

Snappy Stripes
1912-1089

Colorful Stars
1912-2362

Dazzling Dots
1912-1090

Red
1912-2357

Baby Feet
1912-1100

Drawstring Bags
Six plastic bags with ribbon drawstrings. 6 in. x 9 in. Pk./6.
1912-0864 $2.99

Foil Bags
Eight bright, 2-ply plastic, foil-lined bags, Eight ties included. 6 in. x 9 in. Pk./8.
1912-0865 $2.99

Clear Drawstring Bags
6 in. x 9 in. Pk./6.
1912-0915 $2.99

PRESENTATION

ORDER ONLINE: WWW.WILTON.COM

Wedding Cakes

The beautiful cake designs Wilton is famous for are just the beginning of your dream wedding presentation. Richly detailed Wilton cake décor, toppers, accents, stands and separators complement your design to capture the moment forever.

CAKE DÉCOR

It's easy to make a statement—whether it's elegance, whimsy or sparkle—with our gorgeous cake décor accents.

NEW!

CAKE PICKS

Add dimension to cakes and cupcakes with beautiful paper daisy and butterfly picks! Daisy: 3 in. dia. x 3 in. high. Butterflies: 3.25 in. wide x 2.25 in. long x 3 in. high. Pk./12.
Each Pack $9.99

Daisy
120-1177

Warm Butterfly
120-1173

Elegant Butterfly
120-1172

Cool Butterfly
120-1174

NEW!

FUN PIX

Dress up cupcakes, brownies, ice cream and more. 3.25 in. high. Paper. Pk./12.
Each Pack $2.99

I Do
2113-0332

Mr. & Mrs.
2113-0334

Doubleheart
2113-0333

HANGING GEMS

NEW!

Sparkling faux gems add elegance to every cake design. Plastic gems: 3 in. long, picks: 2.5 in. long. Pk./8.
Each Pack $9.99

Heart
120-1185

Diamond
120-1186

CAKE PICKS

Stunning picks with the look of silver or gold draw attention to your celebration! Perfect for cake tops, bouquets, floral arrangements and centerpieces. Beautifully appointed with rhinestones; crafted of painted resin.

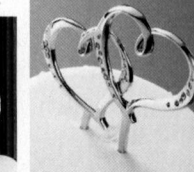
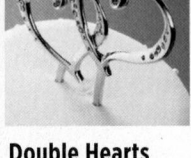

Silver 25th
5 in. high x
4 in. wide.
1008-758 $14.99

Gold 50th
5.25 in. high x
4.25 in. wide.
1008-762 $14.99

Double Hearts
5 in. high x
4.5 in. wide.
1006-985 $14.99

Heart Cake Decor
2 in. pick. 3.75 in. wide x 3 in. high.
Pk./6.
120-1024 $19.99

NEW!

Fanci Flow Fountain
Add beauty and drama of flowing water and light to your cake design. With its classic crystal-looking water cascades, adjustable water control and easy assembly, the Wilton Fanci Flow Fountain is the perfect accent for any celebration. Assembled: 13 in. high x 9 in. dia.
306-1147 $79.99

CAKE TOPPERS

Discover the unmatched detail that has made Wilton figurines the perfect finishing touch for generations. The rich, sculpted crafting, realistic detailing and romantic designs make these figurines perfect wedding day keepsakes.

First Kiss
Material: Bonded marble.
Height: 6.75 in.
Base: 3 in. dia.
202-258 $24.99

Clear Bianca
Material: Acrylic.
Height: 5.5 in.
Base: 3.75 in. x 3.5 in.
202-424 $24.99

Threshold of Happiness
Material: Resin. Height: 5 in. Base: 3.25 in. x 2 in.
202-202 $24.99

Our Day
Material: Resin.
Height: 4.75 in.
Base: 2 in. x 1.75 in.
202-409 $6.99

Lasting Love
Material: Resin.
Height: 4.5 in.
Base: 2.25 in. x 1.75 in.
202-302 $6.99

Simple Joys
Material: Plastic, fabric flowers, fabric. Height: 8 in.
Base: 4.5 in. dia.
103-150 $24.99

HUMOROUS CAKE TOPPERS

Add a lighthearted touch to the celebration. Great for pre-wedding events, such as showers, these figurines are sure to bring a smile to the face of anyone who has ever planned a wedding!

Oh No You Don't
Material: Resin. Height: 4.25 in.
Base: 6 in. x 3 in.
115-102 $19.99

Now I Have You
Material: Resin. Height: 4.25 in.
Base: 4.25 in. x 3.75 in.
115-101 $19.99

Ball and Chain
Material: Resin. Height: 2.25 in. Base: 3.5 in.
1006-7143 $19.99

Two Rings
Material: Plastic, resin.
Height: 5.5 in.
Base: 3.75 in. dia.
1006-1121 $34.99

CAKE ACCESSORIES

Complete your wedding cake design with any of our dramatic cake accessories.

Crystal Bridge and Stairway Set
Bridge the gap between lavish tiers. Includes two stairways (16.75 in. long) and one platform (4.75 in. x 5 in.). Plastic. Set/3.
205-2311 $19.99

Flower Display Cups
Blossom-shaped display cups keep flowers in place while displayed on the cake surface. Bottom spike holds cup in place on fondant or buttercream icing; top spike can hold a ball of fondant for easy insertion of stems. Plastic. Pk./3.
205-8504 $6.99

Fresh Flower Cake Spikes
Spike is topped by a silicone cap to prevent spills and hold flowers in place. Also ideal holders for wired icing flowers and artificial flower displays. Plastic. Pk./6.
205-8501 $6.99

CAKE STANDS

Stunning Wilton Cake Stands are the best way to show off your special cake. Take a look—there's one perfectly suited to your wedding cake size and design.

Cake and Treat Display Set

Three different stand sizes and removable scroll legs allow multiple combinations of cake setups. The elegant white finish and clear plates complement any cake design. Set includes: three coated metal support rings (8.25 in. dia. x 8.25 in. high; 10.25 in. dia. x 6.25 in. high; 12.25 in. dia. x 4 in. high), three clear plastic plates (8 in., 10 in., 12 in. dia.), coated metal scrolled legs [three each small (3.5 in.), medium (6.75 in.) and large (8.25 in.)]. Set/15.

307-352 $39.99
Replacement Plates Set/3. **302-7925 $10.99**

3-Tier Pillar Cake Stand

A distinctive display, featuring locking pillars in a secure base, providing dramatic tier heights and stable support. Its unique design and clean construction complement any setting: great for cakes, mini cakes, appetizers and more. Set includes: 15.75 in. off-white plastic base; three pillars (5.75 in., 12.75 in. and 19.5 in. high); three plate supports and plates (10 in., 12 in. and 14 in. plates); assembly instructions. Set/11.

307-350 $59.99

Cakes-N-More 3-Tier Party Stand

Contemporary stairstep stand with crystal-clear plates and chrome-plated finish puts the focus where it belongs—on your stunning cake and desserts! Set includes: three cake plates (8 in., 10 in. and 12 in.); six stand legs (4 in., 7 in. and 7.75 in. high); center stand support ring; assembly instructions. Set/13.

307-859 $34.99
Replacement Plates Set/3. **302-7925 $10.99**

Round Floating Tiers Cake Stand

The beautiful illusion of floating tiers makes a grand display for your cakes. Disassembles for easy storage. Set includes: metal tier support rings; ring support bars; connector bar; white separator plates (8 in., 12 in. and 16 in.); all hardware; assembly instructions. Set/9.

307-710 $79.99
Replacement plates are available at www.wilton.com

Candlelight Cake Stand

Elegant scrollwork and soft candlelight show off your cake design. Flameless votives are convenient and safe. (Average battery life: 24 hours.) Stand supports 40 lbs., use with 14 in. smooth or scallop edge separator plate (not included). Set includes: 21.5 in. dia. x 5 in. high stand; four flameless votives (with four replaceable CR2032 batteries included); four glass holders; assembly instructions. Set/5.

307-351 $44.99

Graceful Tiers Cake Stand

The three-tiered, scrollwork stand features crystal-clear plates perfect for cakes, cupcakes, muffins and more. Set includes: cream-colored, coated metal stand (14.5 in. wide x 29.5 in. high); three clear separator plates (8 in., 10 in. and 12 in. dia.); one wrench; all hardware; assembly instructions. Set/11.

307-841 $59.99
Replacement Plates Set/3.
302-7925 $10.99

Fancy Scrolls Cake Stand

The perfect way to display your party cakes or fancy desserts. Slide the two scrolled base pieces together to form the base and place the 12 in. plate on top for a secure cake presentation. After the party, the base pieces easily disassemble and lock into the plate for compact storage. 5 in. high. Set/3.

307-854 $14.99

CAKE ASSEMBLY SETS

Take your wedding cake to new heights with any of our assembly sets. Each design adds beauty to a variety of styles.

Globe Pillar and Base Sets

The 2 in. and 2.5 in. Pillar Sets are positioned between tiers, as globes fit over hidden pillars to provide strong support. The 3 in. base set features a reinforced center channel, which fits over separator plate feet to hold your base cake. Sets include four globes and four 9 in. pillars. Globe Base Set includes four pillar globe bases.

2 in. Globe Pillar Set/8. **303-822 $8.99**
2.5 in. Globe Pillar Set/8. **303-824 $10.99**
3 in. Globe Base Set/4. **303-825 $10.99**
9 in. Replacement Pillars Set/4. **303-4005 $4.99**

Roman Column Tier Set

Perfect pillar and plate set for use with the Fanci Flow Fountain. Set includes: six 13.75 in. Roman columns and two 18 in. round Decorator Preferred separator plates. Set/8.
301-1981 $44.99

Leaf and Vine Wire Separator Set

Entwined vines and the classic white finish looks beautiful with a variety of cake styles and the assembly is easy! Set includes: white coated metal separator ring; 6.25 in. dia. x 6 in. high; two smooth-edge separator plates, 8 in. dia. Set/3.
303-454 $19.99

Garden Gazebo Wire Separator Set

Elegant gazebo and the classic white finish is stunning with a variety of cake styles and the assembly is easy! Set includes: white coated metal separator ring, 6.25 in. dia. x 6 in. high; two smooth-edge separator plates, 8 in. dia. Set/3.
303-453 $19.99

Towering Tiers Cake Stand

Clean, contemporary design highlights this multi-tiered display, perfect for cakes and cupcakes! The alternate setup with shorter divisions between plates is ideal for cupcakes and fancy desserts. Set includes: 2-pc. 18 in. plate; 2-pc. 16 in. plate; two plate supports (for use with the 18 in. and 16 in. plates); 14 in., 12 in., 10 in. and 8 in. plates; top nut; center post foot; five base feet; five (4.25 in. high) short center posts (for cupcake display); five (5.5 in. high) tall center posts (for cake display); Cake Corer; assembly instructions. Set/24.
307-892 $99.99

Holds up to 125 cupcakes!

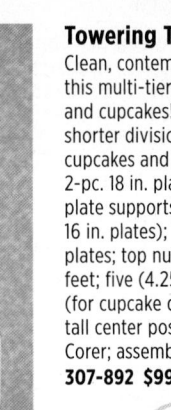

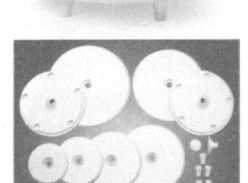

Replacement parts are available at www.wilton.com.

Crystal-Clear Cake Divider Set

Sparkling twist legs push through the cake, rest on plate below and beautifully accent your cake design (dowel rods not needed). Set includes: 6 in., 8 in., 10 in., 12 in., 14 in. and 16 in. separator plates; 24 7.5 in. twist legs. Set/30.
301-9450 $52.49

Additional Plates

6 in.	302-9730	$3.19
8 in.	302-9749	$4.19
10 in.	302-9757	$5.29
12 in.	302-9765	$7.39
14 in.	302-9773	$9.49
16 in.	302-9780	$11.59

7.5 in. Twist Legs
Pk./4. **303-9794 $4.19**

9 in. Twist Legs
Pk./4. **303-977 $5.29**

SEPARATOR PLATES

Wilton Separator Plates provide superior stability with beautiful design. Our Decorator Preferred Plates are built for unmatched stability with patented Circles of Strength design.

Decorator Preferred Smooth Edge Plates

6 in.	302-4101	$2.99
8 in.	302-4102	$3.99
10 in.	302-4103	$4.99
12 in.	302-4104	$5.99
14 in.	302-4105	$6.99
16 in.	302-4106	$9.99
18 in.	302-4107	$12.99

Decorator Preferred Square Plates

6 in.	302-1801	$3.99
8 in.	302-1802	$4.99
10 in.	302-1803	$5.99
12 in.	302-1804	$6.99
14 in.	302-1805	$7.99
16 in.	302-1806	$10.99
18 in.	302-1807	$13.99

Decorator Preferred Scalloped Plates

6 in.	302-6	$2.99	12 in.	302-12	$5.99
7 in.	302-7	$2.99	13 in.	302-13	$6.29
8 in.	302-8	$3.99	14 in.	302-14	$6.99
9 in.	302-9	$4.29	15 in.	302-15	$7.99
10 in.	302-10	$4.99	16 in.	302-16	$9.99
11 in.	302-11	$5.29	18 in.	302-18	$12.99

Crystal-Look Plates

Wilton Crystal-Look plates have an elegance like no other with ridged sides that look like cut crystal.
Use with Crystal-Look pillars (sold below).

7 in.	302-2013	$4.99
9 in.	302-2035	$5.99
11 in.	302-2051	$6.99
13 in.	302-2078	$8.99
*17 in.	302-1810	$16.49

*Use only with 13.75 in. Crystal-Look pillars (sold below).

Fillable Pillars

Fill pillars with colorful gems, ribbon or decorative stones to personalize your cake design! Pillars are designed to be used with Wilton Decorator Preferred Separator Plates. Sets include four pillars, eight pedestals. Not recommended to be filled with any type of liquid. Pk./12.

4 in.	6 in.
303-801	303-802
$7.99	$9.99

SEPARATOR PILLARS

Pair with our separator plates to give your wedding cake added height.

   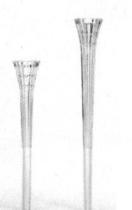 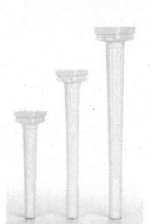

"Hidden" Pillars

Separate cake tiers and create a floating illusion. Pushed into tiers as dowel rods, they fit onto all Decorator Preferred separator plates. Trimmable, hollow plastic. 6 in. high. Pk./4.
303-8 $3.19

Crystal-Look Pillars

Contemporary cut crystal look. Pk./4.
3 in. **303-2171 $3.99**
5 in. **303-2196 $4.99**
7 in. **303-2197 $5.99**
*13.75 in. (not shown)
303-2242 $4.99
*Sold singly. Use only with 17 in. Crystal-Look plate (sold above).

Grecian Pillars

Elegantly scrolled and ribbed. Pk./4.
3 in.
303-3606 $3.99
5 in.
303-3703 $4.99
7 in.
303-3705 $5.99

Crystal-Look Spiked Pillars

For single plate cake construction. Pk./4.
7 in.
303-2322 $4.99
9 in.
303-2324 $5.99

Grecian Spiked Pillars

For single plate cake construction. Wide base increases stability. Pk./4.
5 in. **303-3708 $2.99**
7 in. **303-3710 $3.99**
9 in. **303-3712 $4.99**

Baker's Best Disposable Pillars with Rings

For single plate cake construction. Pk./4.
7 in.
303-4000 $3.79
9 in.
303-4001 $3.99

Roman Columns

Handsome pillars may be used with 16 in. and 18 in. plates. Pk./2.
10.25 in.
303-8136 $6.99
13.75 in.
303-2130 $7.99

DOWEL RODS AND PEGS

Provide support for all tiered cakes with our dowel rods.

Bamboo Dowel Rods

Made of eco-friendly bamboo, the renewable resource! Easy to cut. Length: 12 in.; dia.: 0.25 in. Pk./12.
399-1010 $3.19

Plastic Dowel Rods

Heavy-duty hollow plastic provides strong, stable support. Cut with serrated knife or strong shears to desired length. Length: 12.25 in.; dia.: 0.75 in. Pk./4.
399-801 $2.59

Plastic Pegs

Insure that cake layers and separator plates atop cakes stay in place. Pegs do not add support; dowel rod cake properly before using. Length: 4 in. Pk./12.
399-762 $1.49

WEDDING PUBLICATIONS

A great source of information for planning your special day.

"Wilton Wedding Cakes"

Set your imagination free with 38 exquisite cakes inside the *Wilton Wedding Cakes—A Romantic Portfolio* publication. Includes:
• Patterns, techniques and recipes.
• Step-by-step instructions so you can re-create each cake to perfection.
• Comprehensive construction guide.
• Ornament, favor suggestions and tiered cake accessories.
Soft cover, 144 pages.
902-907 $16.99

"Wilton Tiered Cakes"

Wilton Tiered Cakes publication has the most contemporary looks in reception cakes. Includes:
• 38 amazing cake designs.
• How to mix colors on a wedding cake using textured fondant or floral accents.
• Cute teddy bear tower with fondant baby blocks used as separators.
• Complete instructions, techniques, construction and cutting techniques.
• Wilton products.
Soft cover, 128 pages.
902-1108 $14.99

"Wilton Wedding Style"

Wilton Wedding Style shows you the full spectrum of wedding color possibilities from white to bright. Includes:
• Color-theme sections show you how to incorporate your signature color into every part of your wedding.
• 100-plus ideas for invitations, favors, tabletop décor and more.
• 18 dream cakes, plus petits fours, cupcakes and edible favors.
• Step-by-step project instructions with materials checklists.
• Hundreds of decorating ideas for ceremonies and receptions.
Soft cover, 124 pages.
902-1101 $14.99

Favor Making

Give guests a memorable favor tailored specifically for your celebration theme, colors and style. Wilton has a wide selection of favor kits, boxes, accents and candy that will suit your special event.

CLEAR FAVOR BOX KITS

It's all the essentials you need...simply fill with a cupcake, mini cake or cookies. Includes 20 each boxes, ribbons and printable labels. Assembly instructions included. Baking cups sold separately. Assembled box approx. 3.5 in. x 3.5 in. x 3.5 in. Pk./20.
Each Pack $24.99

White Pearl
415-0435

NEW!

Silver
415-0390

Black
415-0391

Pastel Dots
415-0412

Pink Dots
415-0410

Blue Stripes
415-0411

COOKIE ENVELOPE KITS

Wrap up your cookie pops in a sweet-themed envelope perfect for any celebration. Includes 20 each wraps, bags, ribbons, printable labels and seals. Lollipop sticks sold separately. Assembly instructions included. Assembled envelope approx. 4 in. x 4 in. Pk./20.
Each Pack $9.99

Black Damask
415-0399

White Pearl Stripes
415-0400

NEW!

Silver Dots
415-0401

Gold Damask
415-0402

Pink Dots
415-0419

Blue Stripes
415-0420

FAVOR MAKING

FAVOR BOX KITS

Add style and fun to your wedding festivities with favors that follow the trends. Take a look at the selection of Wilton Favor Candy on page 198 to fill your favors.

Flowers
415-0386

Birds
415-0387

Die-Cut Wrapped Boxes

Beautiful, intricate favor boxes add a touch of elegance to any event. Includes 24 each boxes, wraps, ribbons and printable tags. Box approx. 1.5 in. x 2.5 in. x 2.5 in. Pk./24.
Each Pack $19.99

Popcorn Boxes

Clever favor boxes inspired by popcorn boxes make fun favors for your party! Includes boxes, bags, ribbons and pre-printed stickers. Assembly instructions included. Box approx. 2.25 in. x 1.5 in. x 1.5 in.

Pk/25. **Each Pack $9.99**

 Blue
415-0501

 Pink
415-0502

Pk/50. **Each Pack $19.99**

 Gold
415-0521

Red
1006-4038

Silver
415-0522

Purple
1006-0664

 **Green**
1006-0666

Pink
1006-0753

White
1006-4039

Blue
1006-0665

Bright Pink
1006-0675

Black
1006-0755

Divider Boxes

Change the candy colors to reflect your celebration theme. Candy sold separately. Includes 40 dividers and 20 each boxes, ribbons and printable labels. Assembled box approx. 0.5 in. x 3 in. x 3 in. Pk./20.
Each Pack $19.99

Silver 415-0403	White 415-0405
Black 415-0404	Gold 415-0406

Cones

Includes 50 each cones, pre-printed tags, ribbons and strings. Pk./50.
Each Pack $19.99
Silver 1006-1165
Gold 1006-0722

Paper Lantern Boxes

Includes 50 each boxes and ribbons. Flameless votive not included. Pk./50.
Each Pack $19.99
White 1006-1177
Black 1006-4042

FAVOR BOXES

Stately designs for you to dress up any way you like. Favor candy sold separately.

Rattle Boxes

Pretty pastel covers with a fun die cut design set the tone for the celebration. Includes 25 each boxes and ribbons. Assembled box approx. 2.25 in. x 2.25 in. x 2.25 in. Pk./25.
Each Pack $9.99
Blue 415-0504
Pink 415-0505
Assorted 415-0506

Square Boxes

Includes 100 boxes. Ribbons not included. Pk./100.
Each Pack $19.99

Gold 415-0519	Bright Pink 1006-0633	
Silver 415-0520	Purple 1006-0634	Green 1006-0636
Pink 1006-0632	Blue 1006-0635	Black 1006-0638

Flirty Fleur

Paper. Box approx. 2.25 in. wide x 2.25 in. high. Pk./10.
1006-936 $4.99

SPECIALTY SHAPED FAVOR KITS

Add a unique twist to your party with these novelty shaped favor kits. Wilton Favor Candy sold on page 198.

NEW!

Cylinders
Includes 20 each cylinders, ribbons and printable labels. Assembled favor approx. 1.5 in. dia. x 4.75 in. high. Pk./20.
Each Pack $24.99
White/Pearl Stripes 415-0388
Black/White Stripes 415-0389
Pink/White Stripes 415-0407
Blue/White Stripes 415-0408

Tins
Includes 25 each tins, printable round labels and rectangular strips. Tin approx. 2 in. dia. Pk./25.
1006-8038 $19.99

Hearts
Includes 24 each containers, ribbons, tulle circles and printable tags. Heart approx. 2.5 in. wide x 1 in. deep. Pk./24.
1006-924 $24.99

Umbrellas
Includes 24 each containers, ribbons and printable tags. Umbrella approx. 2.5 in. wide x 1 in. deep. Pk./24.
120-520 $24.99

Love Potion Bottles
Includes funnel and 24 each bottles with corks, ribbons and printable labels. Bottle approx. 2.75 in. high. Pk./24.
1006-1009 $24.99

Martini Glasses
Includes 24 each containers, ribbons, tulle circles and printable tags. Glass approx. 3.5 in. high. Pk./24.
120-518 $24.99

Champagne Bottles
Includes 24 each containers, ribbons and printable labels. Bottle approx. 4 in. high. Pk./24.
120-519 $24.99

Goblets
Includes 24 each containers, ribbons, tulle circles and printable tags. Goblet approx. 2.75 in. high. Pk./24.
1006-923 $24.99

Baby Bottles
Multicolor pastel assortment. Includes 24 each containers, ribbons and printable tags. Bear accent not included. Bottle approx. 4 in. high. Pk./24.
1006-577 $24.99

Rattles
Multicolor pastel assortment. Includes 20 each containers, ribbons and printable tags. Rattle approx. 4 in. high. Pk./20.
1006-572 $24.99

Baby Blocks
Multicolor pastel assortment. Includes 20 each containers, ribbons and printable tags. Tulle not included. Block approx. 1.75 in. x 1.75 in. x 1.75 in. square. Pk./20.
1006-284 $24.99

Pails
White. Includes 18 each containers, ribbons and printable tags. Tulle and safety pin accent not included. Pail approx. 2 in. high. Pk./18.
1006-916 $24.99

FAVOR MAKING

FAVOR BAG KITS

These beautiful bags hold favors for shower, wedding and anniversary celebrations. Perfect for mints, almonds or small gifts. Favor candy sold separately.
Each Pack $4.99

Flirty Fleur
Paper. Includes 10 each bags and ribbons. Bag approx. 3.25 in. wide x 6 in. high x 1.75 in. deep. Pk./10.
1006-941

Sweet Heart
Paper. Includes 10 each bags and ribbons. Bag approx. 3.25 in. wide x 6 in. high x 1.75 in. deep. Pk./10.
1006-940

FAVOR CANDY

Fun shapes, beautiful colors and great flavors—Wilton candy makes the perfect filler for favors, treat bags and candy dishes.

Heart
1006-2991

Thank You
1006-2992

Baby Feet
1006-2994

White Pearls
Sweet, tart flavor. 15 oz. bag.
1006-0673 $6.29

Pastel Pearls
Sweet, tart flavor. 15 oz. bag.
1006-0674 $6.29

Hearts
Sweet, tart flavor. 12 oz. bag.
1006-9053 $6.29

Bling Rings
Individually wrapped. Sweet, tart flavor. Each 1 in. wide x 1.12 in. high. Pk./30.
1006-6173 $4.29

Celebration Candy
Features fun images and a light, sweet flavor. Individually wrapped. Approx. 1 in. dia. Pk./40. **Each Pack $4.29**

Pillow Mints
10 oz. bag. Pastel.
1006-857 $4.29
48 oz. bag. Pastel.
1006-8027 $20.99
48 oz. bag. White.
1006-8028 $20.99

Mint Drops
Pastel. Certified Kosher Dairy. 14 oz. bag.
1006-788 $6.29
32 oz. bag.
1006-3710 $13.99

Jordan Almonds
Certified Kosher.
16 oz. bag. Assorted.   **1006-779 $7.99**
44 oz. bag. Assorted.   **1006-1133 $21.99**
16 oz. bag. White.   **1006-778 $7.99**
44 oz. bag. White.   **1006-1134 $21.99**

Wedding Bells
Sweet, tart flavor. 12 oz. bag.
1006-1140 $6.29

Baby Feet
Sweet, tart flavor. 12 oz. bag.
1006-9047 $6.29

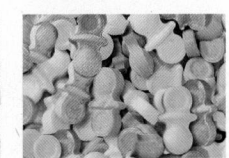
Mini Pacifiers
Sweet, tart flavor. 12 oz. bag.
1006-540 $6.29

FAVOR ACCENTS

Add fun or flair to favor and table decorations.

Engagement Rings
Metal. Faux diamond approx. 0.25 in. Pk./12.
1006-115 $1.99

Sweet Heart Charms
Stamped tin. 1.25 in. x 0.75 in. Pk./12.
1006-411 $1.99

Thank You Tags
Stamped tin. 1.75 in. dia. Pk./12.
1006-987 $1.99

Ducky*
Yellow. 0.85 in. high. Pk./20.
1004-2850
Each $2.99

Safety Pins*
1.5 in. high. Pk./20.
Each Pack $1.99
Pink 1103-21
Blue 1103-26

Shower Rattles
Includes pink, lavender, blue, yellow, mint green. 3.75 in. high. Pk./6.
1103-29 $2.99

Newborn Baby Figurines*
1 in. high. Pk./6.
1103-62 $1.99

Mini Clothes Pins*
Includes pink, lavender, blue, yellow, mint green. 1.3 in. high. Pk./20.
1103-27 $1.99

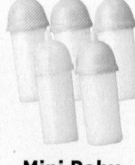
Mini Baby Bottles*
Includes pink, lavender, blue, yellow, mint green. 3.75 in. high. Pk./20.
1103-16 $1.99

Pacifiers*
Includes pink, lavender, blue, yellow, mint green. 0.75 in. high. Pk./20.
1003-1086 $2.99

⚠ *WARNING: CHOKING HAZARD
Small parts. Not for children under 3 years.

CANDY FAVOR KITS

Add something sweet to each guest's plate with our pre-wrapped candy favors. Give them alone or use them to top treats, like cupcakes!

CANDY HEARTS

Light, sweet flavor. Includes 12 each pre-wrapped candy hearts, ribbons, pre-printed thank-you tags and bonus print-your own tags. Pk./12.
Each Pack $9.99

Pastel
1006-0774

Black/White
1006-0773

Pink
1006-0772

LOLLIPOPS

Light, sweet flavor. Includes 24 each pre-wrapped lollipops, ribbons, pre-printed thank-you tags and bonus print-your own tags. Pk./24.
Each Pack $9.99

NEW!

Pastel
1006-2975

Black/White
1006-2976

Pink
1006-2977

Blue
1006-2978

LOLLIPOP POCKET KITS

Dress up your candy lollipops in one of these fun wraps. Fantastic to use as shower or wedding favors, or to display in a candy bouquet centerpiece. Includes 20 each wraps, ribbons, adhesives and printable tags, unless otherwise noted*. Lollipops and sticks sold separately. Wrap approx. 4 in. dia. Pk./20.
Each Pack $9.99

NEW!

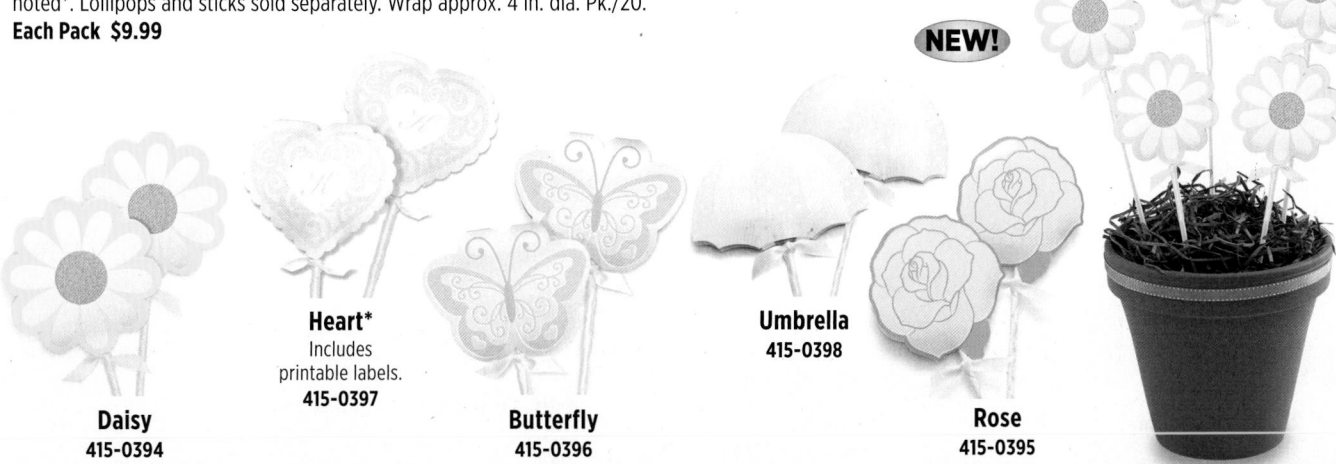

Daisy
415-0394

Heart*
Includes
printable labels.
415-0397

Butterfly
415-0396

Umbrella
415-0398

Rose
415-0395

FAVOR MAKING

Party

You've written the guest list—now start your decorating list here! From baking cups to candles, cake toppers to treat bags, Wilton has the exciting and colorful party designs you want, and they will all impress your guests!

THEME PARTY PRODUCTS

Give your party personality! See how easy it is to pull your look together with the great selection of Wilton theme party products. You'll discover favorite subjects, including jungle animals, colorful flowers, over-the-hill tombstones and sports for every season. Find candles, party bags, baking cups, candy molds, cake pans and more—all with the Wilton touch of fun design and detail.

CELEBRATION

Party hats, cakes and gifts—these shapes set the tone for a birthday blast!

Layered Cupcake Fun Pix

NEW!

Dress up cupcakes, brownies, ice cream and more. Paper, 3.25 in. high. Pk./12.
2113-1395 $2.49

Cupcake Combo

Quick and colorful way to serve cupcakes that set the tone for your celebration. Contains 24 each 2 in. dia. baking cups and and 3 in. high paper party picks, 12 each of two designs. Pk./24.
415-1176 $2.29

Icing Decorations

Edible sugar shapes to decorate cupcakes, cookies and cakes. Certified Kosher.
Each Pack $2.29

Cupcake Pan

Bake and decorate it to look like your favorite party cupcake—only bigger! Create endless color and flavor combinations. Aluminum. One-mix pan is 9.75 in. x 9.5 in. x 2 in. deep. **2105-3318 $13.99**

Candles

Approx. 1.5 in. high. Set/4.
2811-860 $3.99

⚠ WARNING: Never leave burning candles unattended. Burn within sight. Keep away from drafts. Do not burn candles on or near anything that can catch fire. Burn candles out of reach of children and pets. Always leave at least 4 in. (10 cm) between burning candles.

Baking Cups

Colorful paper. Standard size, 2 in. dia., Pk./75; mini size, 1.25 in. dia., Pk./100.
Each Pack $2.09
Standard 415-986
Mini 415-1164

Cupcake Stand Kit

Bright, 3-tier stand with fun decorative topper holds 24 cupcakes. Includes 12 in. x 17 in. high stand, 24 each 2 in. dia. cups and 3 in. high picks.
1510-134 $10.99

Party/Birthday Lollipop Mold

4 designs, 4 cavities.
2115-4434 $1.99

Happy Birthday
0.5 in. to 1.625 high Pk./20.
710-2735

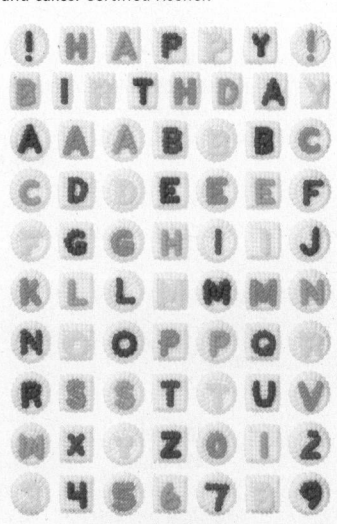

Alphabet/Numerals
0.25 in. to 0.5 high Pk./71.
710-2734

4-Pc. Colored Metal Cutter Set

Cupcake, party hat, gift, cake. Coated metal. Each approx. 3 in. to 3.5 in. Set/4.
2308-0909 $4.79

ORDER TOLL FREE: 800-794-5866

MODERN GARDEN PARTY

Plant the seeds for a sunny celebration when you serve treats using this contemporary garden look.

NEW!

Layered Butterfly & Flower Fun Pix
Dress up cupcakes, brownies, ice cream and more. Paper, 3.25 in. high. Pk./12.
2113-1396 $2.49

Jumbo Butterfly Sprinkles
Add a dash of excitement to cakes, cupcakes, ice cream and more. 3.5 oz.
710-1128 $4.49

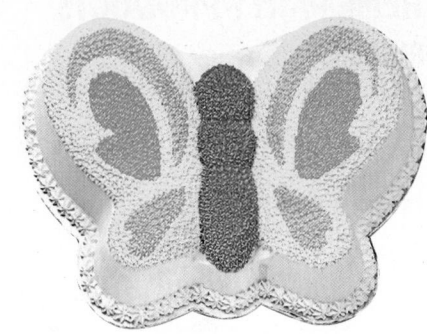

Cupcake Combo
Quick and colorful way to serve cupcakes that set the tone for your celebration. Contains 24 each 2 in. dia. baking cups and 3 in. high paper party picks, 12 each of two designs. Pk./24.
415-0172 $2.29

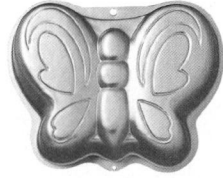

Butterfly Pan
A butterfly cake or molded salad is the perfect way to captivate! Aluminum. One-mix pan is 11 in. x 8.5 in. x 2 in. deep.
2105-2079 $13.99

Baking Cups
Colorful paper. Standard size, 2 in. dia., Pk./75; mini size, 1.25 in. dia., Pk./100.
Each Pack $2.09
Standard 415-0170
Mini 415-0171

Treat Bags
Fill with candy, cookies and other goodies; great for gifts and surprises, too!

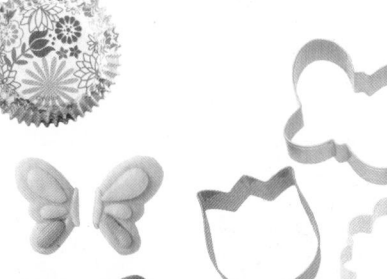

Cupcake Wraps
Includes 18 wraps (2 in. dia.). Baking cups sold separately. Pk./18.
415-0173 $3.49

Icing Decorations
Perfect for topping cakes, cupcakes and cookies! 0.75 in. x 1.125 in. high. Pk./10.
710-7160 $5.99

3-Pc. Colored Metal Cutter Set
Tulip, butterfly, daisy. Coated metal. Each approx. 3 in. Set/3.
2308-0948 $3.69

Party Bags
Includes 20 each plastic bags and ties. Bag: 4 in. x 9.5 in. Pk./20.
1912-0863 $2.09

Drawstring Bags
Includes six plastic bags with ribbon drawstrings. Bag: 6 in. x 9 in. Pk./6.
1912-0864 $2.99

PINK PARTY

Make your party the hot spot with hot pink cups, bags and picks!

Baking Cups
Colorful paper. Standard size, 2 in. dia., Pk./75; mini size, 1.25 in. dia., Pk./100.
Each Pack $2.09
Standard 415-0166
Mini 415-0167

Cupcake Wraps
Includes 18 wraps (2 in. dia.). Baking cups sold separately. Pk./18.
415-0169 $3.49

Cupcake Combo
Quick and colorful way to serve cupcakes that set the tone for your celebration. Contains 24 each 2 in. dia. baking cups and 3 in. high paper party picks, 12 each of two designs. Pk./24.
415-0168 $2.29

Party Bags
Fill with candy, cookies and other goodies; great for gifts and surprises, too! Includes 20 each plastic bags and ties. Bag: 4 in. x 9.5 in. Pk./20.
1912-0860 $2.09

THEME PARTY PRODUCTS

PRINCESS

The royal treatment for any birthday girl begins here with colorful treats and cakes that rule!

Princess Carriage Pan
Create a birthday celebration fit for a princess! Or, decorate a classic carriage cake for the bridal shower. Aluminum. One-mix pan is 12.25 in. x 9.5 in. x 2 in. deep.
2105-1027 $13.99

Romantic Castle Cake Set
Everything you need to transform your tiered cake into a fantasy castle. Includes three sizes of detailed turret towers with removable peak pieces, lattice windows, a paneled door and roof pieces. Complete assembly and decorating ideas included. For design ideas visit www.wilton.com. Set/32.
301-910 $20.99

Layered Fun Pix
Dress up cupcakes, brownies, ice cream and more. Paper, 3 in. high. Pk./12.
2113-1386 $2.49

Candles
Approx. 2.25 in. high. Set/4.
2811-1001 $3.99

⚠ WARNING: Never leave burning candles unattended. Burn within sight. Keep away from drafts. Do not burn candles on or near anything that can catch fire. Burn candles out of reach of children and pets. Always leave at least 4 in. (10 cm) between burning candles.

Cupcake Stand Kit
Bright, 3-tier stand with fun decorative topper holds 24 cupcakes. Includes 12 in. x 17 in. high stand, 24 each 2 in. dia. cups and 3 in. high picks.
1510-1008 $10.99

Cupcake Combo
Quick and colorful way to serve cupcakes that set the tone for your celebration. Contains 24 each 2 in. dia. baking cups and 3 in. high paper party picks. Pk./24.
415-1313 $2.29

Icing Decorations
Edible sugar shapes to decorate cupcakes, cookies and cakes. Certified Kosher. Pk./24.
710-1079 $2.29

Pretzel Mold
2 designs, 6 cavities.
2115-2123 $1.99

Cookie Candy Mold
Great for sandwich cream cookies or any round cookie 2 in. dia. or less. 2 designs, 8 cavities.
2115-2133 $1.99

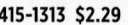
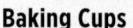

Baking Cups
Colorful paper. Standard size, 2 in. dia., Pk./75; mini size, 1.25 in. dia., Pk./100.
Each Pack $2.09
Standard 415-1142
Mini 415-1145

3-Pc. Colored Metal Cutter Set
Castle, crown, slipper. Coated metal. Each approx. 3 in. to 3.5 in. Set/3.
2308-0915 $3.69

Cupcake Wrap Kit
Includes 12 wraps (2 in. dia.) and 24 pix, 12 each of two designs (3 in. high). Baking cups sold separately. Pk./12.
415-1561 $3.49

CandyPick Mold
Create colorful candy toppers to transform plain cakes and cupcakes into exciting party treats! It's easy, using your favorite Candy Melts colors and this fun detailed mold. 2 designs, 8 cavities.
2115-2113 $1.99

Fairy Tale Lollipop Mold
3 designs, 3 cavities.
2115-1033 $1.99

ORDER TOLL FREE: 800-794-5866

SMILEY FACE

This friendly face has a way of making everyone happy at birthdays, housewarmings and welcome home parties.

Smiley Stars
2811-6325

Smiley Flames
2811-6326

Pretzel Mold
1 design, 6 cavities.
2115-4437 **$1.99**

Chunky Candles
Thicker candles to energize any cake! They feature bold textured spirals and a fun, handcarved shape on top. 3.25 in. high. Pk./4.
Each Pack $3.99

Lollipop Mold
1 design, 10 cavities.
2115-1715 **$1.99**

Candles
1.5 in. high. Set/6.
2811-9351 **$3.99**

⚠ WARNING: Never leave burning candles unattended. Burn within sight. Keep away from drafts. Do not burn candles on or near anything that can catch fire. Burn candles out of reach of children and pets. Always leave at least 4 in. (10 cm) between burning candles.

FLOWER FUN

Pick this daisy for Mother's Day, wedding showers and birthdays for any garden lover.

Jumbo Daisy Sprinkles
Add a dash of excitement to cakes, cupcakes, ice cream and more. 3.5 oz.
710-0036 **$4.49**

Dancing Daisy Pan
One perfect flower makes bunches of great cakes and desserts! Aluminum. One-mix pan is 12 in. x 12 in. x 2 in. deep.
2105-1016 **$13.99**

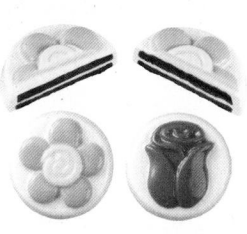

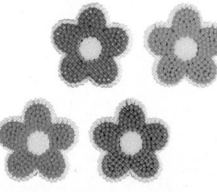

Lollipop Mold
1 design, 9 cavities.
2115-1430 **$1.99**

Flowers Cookie Candy Mold
Great for sandwich cream cookies or any round cookie 2 in. dia. or less. 2 designs, 8 cavities.
2115-1351 **$1.99**

Daisy
2310-619

Flower
2310-613

Comfort-Grip Cutters
Easy-grip stainless steel cutters with extra-deep sides. Recipe included. Approx. 4 in. x 4 in. x 1.75 in.
Each $3.19

Icing Decorations
1.125 in. dia. Certified Kosher. Pk./12.
710-553 **$2.29**

PARTY

THEME PARTY PRODUCTS

BIG TOP

Ladies and gentlemen, children of all ages—the greatest way to celebrate your special occasion is under the Big Top! Bright colors and fun designs delight kids and adults alike.

Primary Colors Cupcake Stand Kit
Bright, 3-tier stand with fun decorative topper holds 24 cupcakes. Includes 12 in. x 17 in. high stand, 24 each 2 in. dia. cups and 3 in. high picks.
1510-135 $10.99

Elephant Pan
This perky pachyderm is sure to please all your party guests. Aluminum. One-mix cake pan is 12.25 in. x 9 in. x 2 in. deep.
2105-0576 $13.99

CandyPick Mold
Create colorful candy toppers to transform plain cakes and cupcakes into exciting party treats! It's easy, using your favorite Candy Melts candy colors and this fun detailed mold. 2 designs, 8 cavities.
2115-2117 $1.99

Large Lollipop Mold
3 designs, 3 cavities.
2115-2116 $1.99

PIRATES

Give kids a party to treasure with cakes and cupcakes that carry high seas excitement.

Cupcake Combo
Quick and colorful way to serve cupcakes that set the tone for your celebration. Contains 24 each 2 in. dia. baking cups and 3 in. high paper party picks. Pk./24.
415-1015 $2.29

Pirate Ship Pan
Your ship has come in with this favorite kids' shape and its cargo of great decorating ideas on the label! Aluminum. One-mix pan is 13.2 in. x 11.25 in. x 2 in. deep.
2105-1021 $13.99

Large Lollipop Mold
3 designs, 3 cavities.
2115-2111 $1.99

CandyPick Mold
Create colorful candy toppers to transform plain cakes and cupcakes into exciting party treats! It's easy, using your favorite Candy Melts candy colors and this fun detailed mold. 2 designs, 8 cavities.
2115-2112 $1.99

ORDER TOLL FREE: 800-794-5866

JUNGLE PALS

Kids will just love these adorable creatures for birthdays, school parties and special events.

Layered Fun Pix
Dress up cupcakes, brownies, ice cream and more. Paper, 3 in. high. Pk./12.
2113-1387 $2.49

Baking Cups
Colorful paper. Standard size, 2 in. dia., Pk./75; mini size, 1.25 in. dia., Pk./100.
Each Pack $2.09
Standard 415-1324
Mini 415-1013

Candle Picks
Approx. 2 in. high. Set/4.
2811-1012 $3.99

⚠ WARNING: Never leave burning candles unattended. Burn within sight. Keep away from drafts. Do not burn candles on or near anything that can catch fire. Burn candles out of reach of children and pets. Always leave at least 4 in. (10 cm) between burning candles.

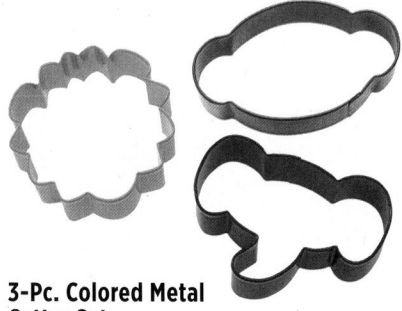

3-Pc. Colored Metal Cutter Set
Lion, elephant and monkey. Coated metal. Each approx. 3 in. to 3.5 in. Set/3.
2308-0916 $3.69

Cupcake Wrap Kit
Includes 12 wraps (2 in. dia.) and 24 pix, 12 each of two designs (3 in. high). Baking cups sold separately. Pk./12.
415-1564 $3.49

Monkey Pan
Kids will just love him at birthday parties, school celebrations and jungle-themed events. Aluminum. One-mix pan is 12.75 in. x 11.25 in. x 2 in. deep.
2105-1023 $13.99

Jungle Animals Topper Set
1.75 in. to 3 in. high. Set/4.
2113-2095 $4.29

Monkey Large Lollipop Mold
3 designs, 3 cavities.
2115-2100 $1.99

Pretzel Candy Mold
2 designs, 6 cavities.
2115-2125 $1.99

Cupcake Stand Kit
Bright, 3-tier stand with fun decorative topper holds 24 cupcakes. Includes 12 in. x 17 in. high stand, 24 each 2 in. dia. cups and 3 in. high picks.
1510-7768 $10.99

Animals Cookie Candy Mold
Great for sandwich cream cookies or any round cookie 2 in. dia. or less. 4 designs, 8 cavities.
2115-1354 $1.99

THEME PARTY PRODUCTS

SPORTS

Here's the perfect game plan for your next party, whatever sport you favor. Action-packed, colorful ways to serve cakes, cupcakes or treats.

Mini Ball Pan
Ice two mini balls and push together for a 3-D effect. One cake mix makes 10 to 12 mini balls. Aluminum. Six cavities, each 3.5 in. x 3.5 in. x 1.5 in. deep.
2105-1760 **$13.99**

Cupcake Combo
Quick and colorful way to serve cupcakes that set the tone for your celebration. Contains 24 each 2 in. dia. baking cups and 3 in. high paper party picks. Pk./24.
415-1314 $2.29

Round Comfort-Grip Cutter
Easy-grip stainless steel cutter with extra-deep sides. The cushion grip gives you comfortable control. Recipe included. Approx. 4 in. x 4 in. x 1.75 in.
2310-608 $3.19

Cookie Candy Mold
Great for sandwich cream cookies or any round cookie 2 in. dia. or less. 4 designs, 8 cavities.
2115-1353 $1.99

Large Lollipop Mold
4 designs, 4 cavities.
2115-4432 $1.99

BASKETBALL

Slam dunk winners! Create thrilling cakes and candies.

Topper Set with Decals
Includes one topper, six candleholders, six 2 in. high candles, one sheet of decals. Set/14.
2811-8423 $5.49

⚠ WARNING: Never leave burning candles unattended. Burn within sight. Keep away from drafts. Do not burn candles on or near anything that can catch fire. Burn candles out of reach of children and pets. Always leave at least 4 in. (10 cm) between burning candles.

Candle
1.75 in. high. Set/6.
2811-9323 $3.99

Soccer Ball Pan
Aluminum. One-mix pan is 8.75 in. x 8.75 in. x 3.5 in. deep.
2105-2044 $13.99

Basketball Topper Set
Includes one forward, two centers, three guards and one hoop, 2.25 to 4 in. high. Set/7.
2113-2237 $3.29

⚠ WARNING: CHOKING HAZARD Small parts. Not for children under 3 years.

SOCCER

A great way to reward a season or a game well played!

Topper Set with Decals
Includes one topper, six candleholders, six 2 in. high candles, one sheet of decals. Set/14.
2811-8421 $5.49

Baking Cups
Colorful paper. Standard size, 2 in. dia. Pk./50.
415-296 $1.59

Icing Decorations
1.125 in. dia. Certified Kosher. Pk./9.
710-477 $2.29

Candle
1 in. high. Set/6.
2811-9322 $3.99

⚠ WARNING: Never leave burning candles unattended. Burn within sight. Keep away from drafts. Do not burn candles on or near anything that can catch fire. Burn candles out of reach of children and pets. Always leave at least 4 in. (10 cm) between burning candles.

Soccer Ball Pan
Aluminum. One-mix pan is 8.75 in. x 8.75 in. x 3.5 in. deep.
2105-2044 $13.99

Soccer Topper Set
Seven players and two nets, 1.75 in. to 2 in. high. Set/9.
2113-9002 $3.29

 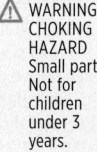

⚠ WARNING: CHOKING HAZARD Small parts. Not for children under 3 years.

ORDER TOLL FREE: 800-794-5866

BASEBALL/SOFTBALL

From Little League to World Series celebrations, cover the bases with 3-D cakes and hit candles and toppers.

Topper Set with Decals
Includes one topper, six candleholders, six 2 in. high candles, one sheet of decals. Set/14.
2811-8425 $5.49

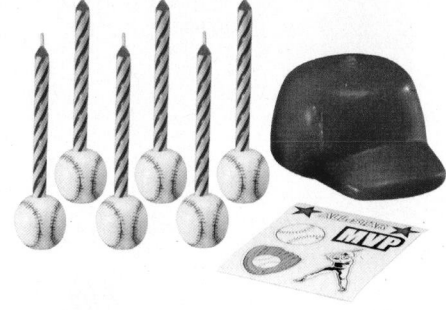

3-D Sports Ball Pan Set
Includes two 6 in. dia. half-ball pans and two metal baking stands. Each pan half takes 2½ cups batter. Aluminum. Set/4.
2105-6506 $13.99

Baking Cups
Colorful paper. Standard size, 2 in. dia. Pk./50.
415-298 $1.59

Icing Decorations
1.375 in. x 1.25 in. Certified Kosher. Pk./9.
710-475 $2.29

Candle
2.75 in. high. Set/6.
2811-750 $3.99

Baseball Topper Set
Batter, catcher, three fielders and pitcher, 2.1 in. to 2.75 in. high. Set/6.
2113-2155 $3.29

⚠ WARNING: Never leave burning candles unattended. Burn within sight. Keep away from drafts. Do not burn candles on or near anything that can catch fire. Burn candles out of reach of children and pets. Always leave at least 4 in. (10 cm) between burning candles.

⚠ WARNING: CHOKING HAZARD
Small parts. Not for children under 3 years.

FOOTBALL

Touching down at Super Bowl parties, homecomings, award dinners and much more.

Topper Set with Decals
Includes one topper, six candleholders, six 2 in. high candles, one sheet of decals. Set/14.
2811-8424 $5.49

⚠ WARNING: Never leave burning candles unattended. Burn within sight. Keep away from drafts. Do not burn candles on or near anything that can catch fire. Burn candles out of reach of children and pets. Always leave at least 4 in. (10 cm) between burning candles.

Mini Football Silicone Mold
Freezer, refrigerator, microwave and dishwasher safe—oven safe to 500°F. One mix makes 20 to 24 footballs. Six cavities, each 2.5 in. x 1.5 in. deep.
2105-4842 $9.99

First and Ten Football Pan
Aluminum. One-mix pan is 12 in. x 7.75 in. x 3 in. deep.
2105-6504 $13.99

Baking Cups
Colorful paper. Standard size, 2 in. dia.. Pk./75.
415-5152 $2.09

Icing Decorations
1 in. x 1.5 in. Certified Kosher. Pk./9.
710-478 $2.29

Candle
2 in. high. Set/6.
2811-757 $3.99

Football Topper Set
Eight players and two goal posts, 1½ in. to 4½ in. high. Set/10.
2113-2236 $3.29

4-Pc. Colored Metal Cutter Set
Coated metal. Pennant, football, jersey, helmet. Recipe included. Approx. 3 in. Set/4.
2308-1263 $4.79

⚠ WARNING: CHOKING HAZARD
Small parts. Not for children under 3 years.

THEME PARTY PRODUCTS

GOLF
Great ways to top cakes with perfect form.

Golf Topper Set
Includes 4.5 in. high golfer plus three each: 2.5 in. wide greens, 4 in. high flags, 5 in. clubs and golf balls. Set/13.
1306-7274 $3.29

Topper Set with Decals
Includes one topper, six candleholders, six 2 in. high candles. one sheet of decals. Set/14.
2811-8420 $5.49

⚠ WARNING: CHOKING HAZARD Small parts. Not for children under 3 years.

⚠ WARNING: Never leave burning candles unattended. Burn within sight. Keep away from drafts. Do not burn candles on or near anything that can catch fire. Burn candles out of reach of children and pets. Always leave at least 4 in. (10 cm) between burning candles.

HOCKEY
When the goal is a great cake, here's the topper set to use!

Topper Set With Decals
Includes one topper, six candleholders, six 2 in. high candles, one sheet of decals. Set/14.
2811-8422 $5.49

⚠ WARNING: Never leave burning candles unattended. Burn within sight. Keep away from drafts. Do not burn candles on or near anything that can catch fire. Burn candles out of reach of children and pets. Always leave at least 4 in. (10 cm) between burning candles.

AGING GRACEFULLY
The secret of aging is keeping your sense of humor! These Wilton products help anyone face those big birthdays with a smile!

Cupcake Combo
Quick and colorful way to serve cupcakes. Contains 24 each 2 in. dia. baking cups and 3 in. high paper party picks, 12 each of two designs. Pk./24.
415-1315 $2.29

Candle Picks
1.75 in. high. Set/13.
2811-786 $2.29

Candle
2.25 in. high.
2811-553 $2.29

Icon Candles
2.5 in. high. Pk./10.
2811-8417 $2.29

⚠ WARNING: Never leave burning candles unattended. Burn within sight. Keep away from drafts. Do not burn candles on or near anything that can catch fire. Burn candles out of reach of children and pets. Always leave at least 4 in. (10 cm) between burning candles.

RUBBER DUCKY
This bathtime favorite will make the biggest splash for birthdays and baby showers.

Candy Mold
1 design, 6 cavities.
2115-1565 $1.99

Baking Cups
Colorful paper. Standard size, 2 in. dia., Pk./75; mini size, 1.25 in. dia., Pk./100.
Each Pack $2.09
Standard 415-1016
Mini 415-1017

Favor Accents
Tie onto favors, gifts and decorations. 0.85 in. high. Pk/20.
1004-2850 $2.99

⚠ WARNING: CHOKING HAZARD Small parts. Not for children under 3 years.

Candles
1.5 in. high. Set/6.
2811-9337 $3.99

⚠ WARNING: Never leave burning candles unattended. Burn within sight. Keep away from drafts. Do not burn candles on or near anything that can catch fire. Burn candles out of reach of children and pets. Always leave at least 4 in. (10 cm) between burning candles.

3-D Rubber Duck Pan Set
Five adorable designs included. Two-piece pan takes 5½ cups batter. Aluminum.
2105-2094 $19.99

ORDER TOLL FREE: 800-794-5866

CAKE TOPPERS

With Wilton toppers, a decorated cake is just minutes away! The excellent detail you expect from Wilton is evident in every design.

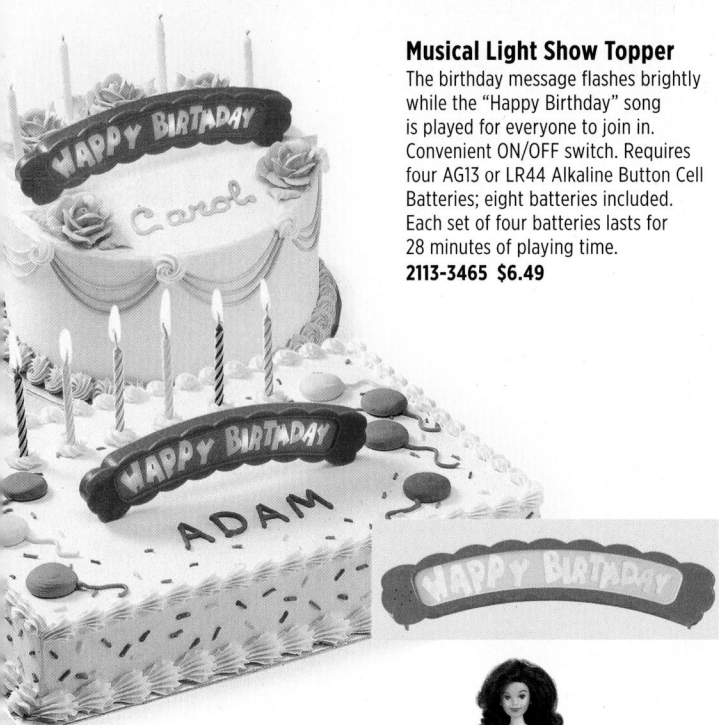

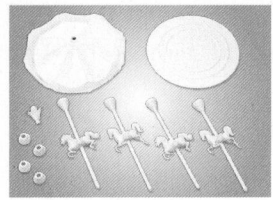

Musical Light Show Topper

The birthday message flashes brightly while the "Happy Birthday" song is played for everyone to join in. Convenient ON/OFF switch. Requires four AG13 or LR44 Alkaline Button Cell Batteries; eight batteries included. Each set of four batteries lasts for 28 minutes of playing time.

2113-3465 $6.49

Carousel Cake Display Set

Decorate a grand carousel to match your celebration cake—perfect for birthdays and holidays. Everything you need to transform your tiered cake into a nostalgic carousel is included: 10 in. base plate, carousel canopy top, four pillars, four horses and a blossom finial on top. Complete assembly and decorating ideas included.

301-1335 $24.99

DOLL PICKS

Beautiful faces for realistic doll cakes.

Mini Doll Pick Set
4.25 in. high with pick. Set/4.
1511-1019 $6.99

Brunette
2815-101

Blond
2815-102

Ethnic
2815-103

Teen Doll Pick
Her hair and face are prettier than ever—she'll give your Wonder Mold (p. 161) cakes a realism and sophistication unlike anything you've seen. 7.75 in. high with pick.
Each $3.49

Frustrated Fisherman Topper
4.5 in. high.
2113-2384 $3.79

NOVELTY CANDLES

Assorted
2811-1011
Blue
2811-1017
Red
2811-1019
Pink
2811-3696

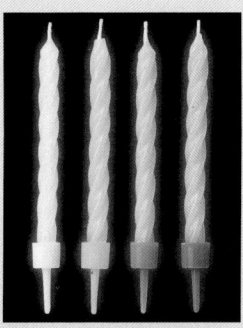

Musical Candle
Plays "Happy Birthday To You."
4.75 in. high.
2811-1231
$4.29

Color Flame
Candle and flame are colored the same! Color Flame Candles give your cake that extra dash of excitement and fun. Choose single-color packs or the assorted pack with four vivid colors: blue, red, orange and green. They make a plain iced cake a party treat to remember. 2 in. high. Pk./12.
Each Pack $2.99

Glow-in-the-Dark
These luminous candles will lend an extra touch of fun to any celebration. Assorted colors: white, yellow, green, blue. 2.5 in. high. Pk./10.
2811-165 $2.29

⚠ WARNING: Never leave burning candles unattended. Burn within sight. Keep away from drafts. Do not burn candles on or near anything that can catch fire. Burn candles out of reach of children and pets. Always leave at least 4 in. (10 cm) between burning candles.

CANDLES

Wilton has an unmatched variety of candle colors, shapes and themes. Find the right look for your celebration here!

Zebra Print
3 in. high. Set/12.
2811-1106 $2.29

Camouflage Chunky Candles
Thicker candles to energize any cake! They feature a fun handcarved shape on top. 2.25 in. high. Pk./4.
2811-1009 $3.99

CANDLE PICK SETS

Put your celebration message in lights! These bright candle picks are a unique and easy way to pick up the party theme on your cake top. Fun colors are just right for the occasion.
Each Set $2.99

Happy Birthday
3 in. high. Set/13.

Multi-Colored
2811-702

Pink/Purple
2811-706

Blue/Green
2811-707

Multi-Colored Numerals
3 in. high. Set/10.
2811-701

Multi-Colored Congratulations
3 in. high. Set/15.
2811-708

CANDLE SETS

Wilton gives you more choices! Top your cake with candles in the perfect colors—and check out our exciting designs. **Each Set $3.99**

Cupcake
1.25 in. high. Set/4.
2811-1004

Baby Things
Approx. 2 in. high. Set/4.
2811-855

Tropical Fish Candles
Approx. 1.5 in. high. Set/4.
2811-9333

Farm
Approx. 1.625 in. high. Set/4.
2811-9347

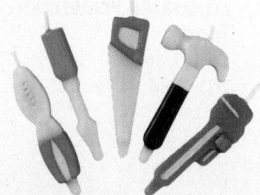

Home Improvement Tools
Approx. 2.25 in. high. Set/5.
2811-9136

Construction Vehicles
Approx. 1.75 in. long. Set/4.
2811-858

Race Cars
Approx. 1.75 in. high. Set/4.
2811-9135

Firefighting
Approx. 1.5 in. high. Set/4
2811-9339

Fiesta
Approx. 1.75 in. high. Set/4.
2811-9345

Beach Sandals
0.375 in. high, 0.875 in. long. Set/6.
2811-9352

Margaritas
1.25 in. high. Set/6.
2811-9343

Beer Cans
1.75 in. high. Set/6.
2811-9326

Champagne Bottles
2 in. high. Set/6.
2811-163

⚠ WARNING: Never leave burning candles unattended. Burn within sight. Keep away from drafts. Do not burn candles on or near anything that can catch fire. Burn candles out of reach of children and pets. Always leave at least 4 in. (10 cm) between burning candles.

ORDER TOLL FREE: 800-794-5866

CLASSICS

Wilton has the color and style of candle perfect for any event.

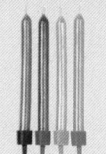

Pearlized Multicolor
Watch them shimmer from the moment you light them! 2.5 in. high. Pk./10.
2811-3665 **$2.29**

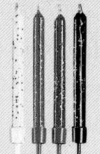

Glitter
2.5 in. high. Pk./10.
Each Pack $1.29
White 2811-248
Pink 2811-244
Blue 2811-246
Black 2811-247

Celebration
2.5 in. high. Pk./24.
Each Pack $0.79
White 2811-207
Pink 2811-213
Red 2811-209
Blue 2811-210
Black 2811-224

Assorted Celebration
Classic spirals in attractive two-tones. 2.5 in. high. Pk./24.
2811-215
$0.79

"Trick"
Blow 'em out—they relight! 2.5 in. high. Asst: White, Yellow, Pink, Blue. Pk./10.
2811-220 **$1.49**

Silver and Gold
2.25 in. high. Pk./10.
Each Pack $1.79
Silver 2811-9123
Gold 2811-9122

#1
2811-9101

Pink #1
2811-240

Blue #1
2811-241

Numerals
Festive way to mark age or year. Edged in green unless specified. 3 in. high.
Each $0.89

#2 2811-9102	#6 2811-9106	#0 2811-9100
#3 2811-9103	#7 2811-9107	? 2811-9110
#4 2811-9104	#8 2811-9108	
#5 2811-9105	#9 2811-9109	

RAINBOW COLORS

Shimmer
2.5 in. high. Pk./10.
2811-3663 **$2.29**

Tricolor
2.5 in. high. Pk./10.
2811-779 **$2.29**

Rounds
2.5 in. high. Pk./24.
2811-284 **$0.79**

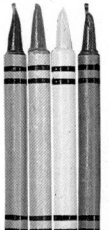

Crayons
3.25 in. high. Pk./8.
2811-226 **$1.79**

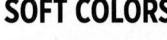

Party Thins
8 in. high. Pk./20.
2811-239
$1.29

Triangle "Trick" Sparklers
They relight! 2.5 in. high. Pk./9.
2811-278 **$1.49**

Wavy "Trick" Sparklers
They relight! 2.5 in. high. Pk./10.
2811-272 **$2.49**

Lattice
2.5 in. high. Pk./10.
2811-3656
$2.29

Curly
3 in. high. Pk./12.
2811-9127
$1.79

HOT COLORS

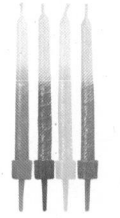

Shimmer
2.5 in. high. Pk./10.
2811-3662
$2.29

Tricolor
2.5 in. high. Pk./10.
2811-781
$2.29

Rounds
2.5 in. high. Pk./24.
2811-225
$0.79

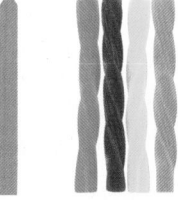

Twist
2.5 in. high. Pk./8.
2811-3659
$2.99

Triangle "Trick" Sparklers
They relight! 2.5 in. high. Pk./9.
2811-276 **$1.49**

Wavy "Trick" Sparklers
They relight! 2.5 in. high. Pk./10.
2811-270 **$2.49**

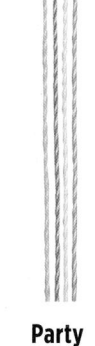

Lattice
2.5 in. high. Pk./10.
2811-3655 **$2.29**

Party Thins
8 in. high. Pk./20.
2811-237
$1.29

SOFT COLORS

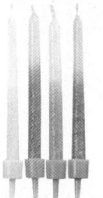

Shimmer
2.5 in. high. Pk./10.
2811-3664 **$2.29**

Tricolor
2.5 in. high. Pk./10.
2811-782 **$2.29**

Party Thins
8 in. high. Pk./20.
2811-255
$1.29

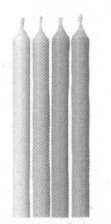

Rounds
2.5 in. high. Pk./24.
2811-291 **$0.79**

Triangle "Trick" Sparklers
They relight! 2.5 in. high. Pk./9.
2811-288 **$1.49**

TALLS

Slenders
6.5 in. high. Pk./24.
Each Pack $0.99

"Trick" Sparklers
Blow 'em out—they relight! 6.5 in. high. Pk./18.
Each Pack $1.49

Longs
Sized right for larger cakes or for making a bold statement on any cake. 5.8 in. high. Pk./12.
Each Pack $2.29

Assorted
2811-1188

Assorted
2811-1230

Red & Blue
2811-704

White
2811-773

Multicolor
2811-777

⚠ WARNING: Never leave burning candles unattended. Burn within sight. Keep away from drafts. Do not burn candles on or near anything that can catch fire. Burn candles out of reach of children and pets. Always leave at least 4 in. (10 cm) between burning candles.

PARTY

Famous Favorites

Invite today's hottest stars to your next celebration! Wilton has a great cast of today's favorite faces and themes on fun party products for cakes and cupcakes, including pans, toppers, treat stands and more.

NEW!

Transform your Padawan's Party into a galactic adventure with your favorite *Star Wars*™ characters!

Darth Vader™ Pan
Aluminum. One-mix pan is 11 in. x 11.5 in. x 2 in. deep.
2105-3035 $15.99

Darth Vader™ & Yoda™ Toppers
Plastic toppers add fun to cupcakes, brownies, cakes and other treats. 1.37 in. high. Set/8.
2113-3035 $4.49

Darth Vader™ Baking Cups
Standard size, paper. 2 in. dia. Pk./50.
415-3035 $1.79

Darth Vader™ Candle
Colorful details. Clean-burning. 3.25 in. high.
2811-3035 $4.49

Yoda™ & Darth Vader™ Icing Decorations
Edible sugar shapes to decorate cupcakes, cookies, ice cream and cake. Certified Kosher. Pk./12.
710-3035 $2.49

Darth Vader™ & Yoda™ Toppers Fun Pix
Dress up cupcakes, brownies, ice cream and more. Paper, 3 in. high. Pk./24.
2113-3036 $2.29

⚠ WARNING: Never leave burning candles unattended. Burn within sight. Keep away from drafts. Do not burn candles on or near anything that can catch fire. Burn candles out of reach of children and pets. Always leave at least 4 in. (10 cm) between burning candles.

ORDER TOLL FREE: 800-794-5866

Bring fun and imagination to your celebration! Girls just love the glam that *Barbie*™ brings to the party!

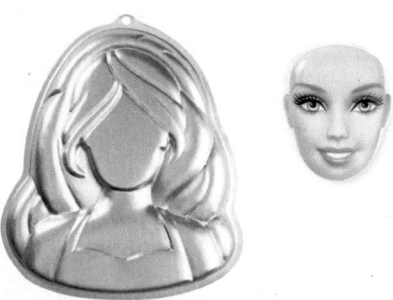

Pan
Aluminum. Includes plastic facemaker.
One-mix pan is 11.5 in. x 10.25 in. x 2 in. deep.
2105-6065 $15.99

Toppers
Plastic toppers add fun to cupcakes, brownies, cakes and other treats. 1.5 in. high. Set/8.
2113-6065 $4.49

Fun Pix
Dress up cupcakes, brownies, ice cream and more. Paper, 3 in. high. Pk./24.
2113-6066 $2.29

Baking Cups
Standard size, paper. 2 in. dia. Pk./50.
415-6065 $1.79

Candle
Handpainted with colorful details. Clean-burning. 2.8 in. high.
**2811-6065
$4.49**

Icing Decorations
Edible sugar shapes to decorate cupcakes, cookies, ice cream and cake. Certified Kosher. Pk./12.
710-6065 $2.49

Treat Bags
Fill with candy, cookies and other goodies. Great for gift cards and small surprises, too! 4 in. x 9.5 in. plastic bags with twist ties. Pk./16.
1912-6065 $2.09

FAMOUS FAVORITES

THOMAS & FRIENDS™

It's full steam ahead when you invite *Thomas The Tank Engine*™ to the celebration!

Pan
Aluminum. One-mix pan is 9.75 in. x 13.25 in. x 2 in. deep.
2105-4242 $15.99

Fun Pix
Dress up cupcakes, brownies, ice cream and more. Paper, 3 in. high. Pk./24.
2113-4243 $2.29

Icing Decorations

Edible sugar shapes to decorate cupcakes, cookies, ice cream and cake. Certified Kosher. Pk./12.
710-4242 $2.49

Baking Cups

Standard size, paper. 2 in. dia. Pk./50.
415-4242 $1.79

Toppers
Plastic toppers add fun to cupcakes, brownies, cakes and other treats. 1.3 in. high. Set/8.
2113-4242 $4.49

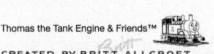
CREATED BY BRITT ALLCROFT

Based on the Railway Series by The Reverend W Awdry.
©2012 Gullane (Thomas) Limited. Thomas the Tank Engine & Friends and Thomas & Friends are trademarks of Gullane (Thomas) Limited. ©HIT Entertainment Limited.
HIT and the HIT logo are trademarks of HIT Entertainment Limited.

Candle
Handpainted with colorful details. Clean-burning. 2.6 in. high.
2811-4242 $4.49

⚠ WARNING: Never leave burning candles unattended. Burn within sight. Keep away from drafts. Do not burn candles on or near anything that can catch fire. Burn candles out of reach of children and pets. Always leave at least 4 in. (10 cm) between burning candles.

Treat Bags
Fill with candy, cookies and other goodies. Great for gift cards and small surprises, too! 4 in. x 9.5 in. plastic bags with twist ties. Pk./16.
1912-4242 $2.09

---

nickelodeon SPONGEBOB SQUAREPANTS™

Everyone's favorite underwater fry cook always brings extra enthusiasm to in the party!

SpongeBob Pan
Aluminum. One-mix pan is 11 in. x 12 in. x 2 in. deep.
2105-5135 $15.99

SpongeBob Toppers
Handpainted plastic toppers add excitement to cupcakes, brownies, cakes and other treats. 2 in. high. Set/6.
2113-5130 $4.49

SpongeBob Candle
Handpainted with colorful details. Clean-burning. 2.6 in. high.
2811-5135 $4.49

⚠ WARNING: Never leave burning candles unattended. Burn within sight. Keep away from drafts. Do not burn candles on or near anything that can catch fire. Burn candles out of reach of children and pets. Always leave at least 4 in. (10 cm) between burning candles.

©2012 Viacom International Inc. All Rights Reserved. Nickelodeon, SpongeBob SquarePants and all related titles, logos and characters are trademarks of Viacom International Inc.
Created by Stephen Hillenburg.

SpongeBob Treat Stand
Bright, 3-tier stand and decorative topper holds up to 24 cupcakes. Assembly instructions included. Cardboard. Baking cups not included. 11.75 in. x 15 in. high.
1512-5130 $6.99

SpongeBob & Patrick Fun Pix

Dress up cupcakes, brownies, ice cream and more. Paper, 3.5 in. high. Pk./24.
2113-5131 $2.29

SpongeBob & Patrick Icing Decorations
Edible sugar shapes to decorate cupcakes, cookies, ice cream and cake. Certified Kosher. Pk./9.
710-5130 $2.49

SpongeBob Baking Cups
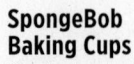
Standard size, paper. 2 in. dia. Pk./50.
415-5130 $1.79

SpongeBob Treat Bags
Fill with candy, cookies and other goodies. Great for gift cards and small surprises, too! 4 in. x 9.5 in. plastic bags with twist ties. Pk./16.
1912-5130 $2.09

ORDER TOLL FREE: 800-794-5866

Disney
MICKEY MOUSE CLUBHOUSE
Minnie Mouse Bow-tique

It's always fun when *Mickey* or *Minnie* join the party! Fun designs are perfect for kids and adults alike!

Pan
Create a fun *Minnie Mouse* cake, too! (instructions at www.wilton.com). Aluminum. One-mix pan is 13 in. x 12 in. x 2 in. deep.
2105-7070 $15.99

Toppers
Plastic toppers add fun to cupcakes, brownies, cakes and other treats. *Mickey* 1.5 in. high; *Minnie/Daisy* 1.44 in. high. Set/8.
Each $4.49
Mickey
2113-7070
Minnie/Daisy
2113-6363

Candles
Handpainted with colorful details. Clean-burning. 3 in. high. **Each $4.49**
Mickey 2811-7070
Minnie 2811-6363

⚠ WARNING: Never leave burning candles unattended. Burn within sight. Keep away from drafts. Do not burn candles on or near anything that can catch fire. Burn candles out of reach of children and pets. Always leave at least 4 in. (10 cm) between burning candles.

Fun Pix
Dress up cupcakes, brownies, ice cream and more. Paper, 3 in. high. Pk./24. **Each $2.29**
Mickey 2113-7071
Minnie/Daisy 2113-6364

Treat Stand
Bright, 3-tier stand and fun decorative topper holds up to 24 cupcakes. Assembly instructions included. Cardboard. Baking cups not included. 11.75 in. x 15 in. high.
1512-7070 $6.99

Baking Cups
Standard size, paper. 2 in. dia. Pk./50. **Each $1.79**
Mickey 415-7070
Minnie/Daisy 415-6363

Icing Decorations
Edible sugar shapes to decorate cupcakes, cookies, ice cream and cake. Certified Kosher. **Each $2.49**
Mickey Pk./9. 710-7070
Minnie Pk./12. 710-6363

Treat Bags
Fill with candy, cookies and other goodies. Great for gift cards and small surprises, too! 4 in. x 9.5 in. plastic bags with twist ties. Pk./16.
Each $2.09
Mickey 1912-7070
Minnie 1912-6363

FAMOUS FAVORITES

Pan
Aluminum. One-mix pan is 13.75 in. x 6.25 in. x 2.75 in.
2105-6400 $15.99

Any party is more exciting when it stars *Lightning McQueen!* All the fun details you love on the big screen are here.

Toppers
Handpainted plastic toppers add fun to cupcakes, brownies, cakes and other treats. 1.25 in. high. Set/6.
2113-6400 $4.49

Candle
Handpainted with colorful details. Clean-burning. 2.1 in. high.
2811-6405 $4.49

⚠ WARNING: Never leave burning candles unattended. Burn within sight. Keep away from drafts. Do not burn candles on or near anything that can catch fire. Burn candles out of reach of children and pets. Always leave at least 4 in. (10 cm) between burning candles.

©Disney • Pixar
Disney.com/Cars

Treat Stand
Bright, 3-tier stand and fun decorative topper holds up to 24 cupcakes. Assembly instructions included. Cardboard. Baking cups not included. 12 in. x 16.25 in. high.
1512-6405 $6.99

Icing Decorations
Edible sugar shapes to decorate cupcakes, cookies, ice cream and cake. Certified Kosher. Pk./9.
710-6400 $2.49

Fun Pix
Dress up cupcakes, brownies, ice cream and more. Paper, 3 in. high. Pk./24.
2113-6402 $2.29

Baking Cups
Standard size, paper. 2 in. dia. Pk./50.
415-6405 $1.79

Treat Bags
Fill with candy, cookies and other goodies. Great for gift cards and small surprises, too! 4 in. x 9.5 in. plastic bags with twist ties. Pk./16.
1912-6405 $2.09

Pan
Aluminum. One-mix pan is 10.5 in. x 11.75 in. x 2 in.
2105-4355 $15.99

Enter *Ariel's* world of enchantment under the sea! Her sweet look will captivate kids and bring all the thrills of *The Little Mermaid* story to your celebration.

Toppers
Handpainted plastic toppers add fun to cupcakes, brownies, cakes and other treats. 1.75 in. high. Set/6.
2113-4355 $4.49

Candle
Handpainted with colorful details. Clean-burning. 3 in. high.
2811-4355 $4.49

Fun Pix
Dress up cupcakes, brownies, ice cream and more. Paper, 3 in. high. Pk./24.
2113-4356 $2.29

Baking Cups
Standard size, paper. 2 in. dia. Pk./50.
415-4355 $1.79

Icing Decorations
Edible sugar shapes to decorate cupcakes, cookies, ice cream and cake. Certified Kosher. Pk./9.
710-4355 $2.49

⚠ WARNING: Never leave burning candles unattended. Burn within sight. Keep away from drafts. Do not burn candles on or near anything that can catch fire. Burn candles out of reach of children and pets. Always leave at least 4 in. (10 cm) between burning candles.

© Disney

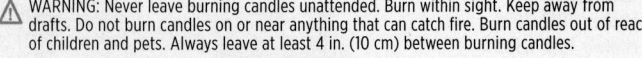
DisneyPrincess.com

Pan
Aluminum. One-mix pan is 13 in. x 10.25 in. x 2 in. deep.
2105-8080 $15.99

Toppers
Plastic toppers add fun to cupcakes, brownies, cakes and other treats. 1.5 in. high. Set/8.
2113-8080 $4.49

Candle
Handpainted with colorful details. Clean-burning. 3.25 in. high.
2811-8080 $4.49

⚠ WARNING: Never leave burning candles unattended. Burn within sight. Keep away from drafts. Do not burn candles on or near anything that can catch fire. Burn candles out of reach of children and pets. Always leave at least 4 in. (10 cm) between burning candles.

©Disney • Pixar
www.ToyStory.com

Treat Stand
Bright, 3-tier stand and fun decorative topper holds up to 24 cupcakes. Assembly instructions included. Cardboard. Baking cups not included. 11.75 in. x 15 in. high.
1512-8080 $6.99

Fun Pix
Dress up cupcakes, brownies, ice cream and more. Paper, 3.25 in. high. Pk./24.
2113-8081 $2.29

Icing Decorations
Edible sugar shapes to decorate cupcakes, cookies, ice cream and cake. Certified Kosher. Pk./12.
710-8080 $2.49

DISNEY • PIXAR TOY STORY

Send your celebration "To infinity, and beyond!" *Buzz Lightyear* is simply the coolest space ranger, and he is sure to please everyone at the party.

Baking Cups
Standard size, paper. 2 in. dia. Pk./50.
415-8080 $1.79

Treat Bags
Fill with candy, cookies and other goodies. Great for gift cards and small surprises, too! 4 in. x 9.5 in. plastic bags with twist ties. Pk./16.
1912-8080 $2.09

Pan
Aluminum. One-mix pan is 10.5 in. x 12 in. x 2 in.
2105-5110 $15.99

Toppers
Handpainted plastic toppers add fun to cupcakes, brownies, cakes and other treats. 2.25 in. high. Set/6.
2113-5110 $4.49

Candle
Handpainted with colorful details. Clean-burning. 3 in. high.
2811-5110 $4.49

⚠ WARNING: Never leave burning candles unattended. Burn within sight. Keep away from drafts. Do not burn candles on or near anything that can catch fire. Burn candles out of reach of children and pets. Always leave at least 4 in. (10 cm) between burning candles.

© Disney   DisneyFairies.com

Treat Stand
Bright, 3-tier stand holds up to 24 cupcakes. Assembly instructions included. Cardboard. Baking cups not included. 11.75 in. x 15.5 in. high.
1512-0993 $6.99

Fun Pix
Dress up cupcakes, brownies, ice cream and more. Paper, 3 in. high. Pk./24.
2113-5111 $2.29

Icing Decorations
Edible sugar shapes to decorate cupcakes, cookies, ice cream and cake. Certified Kosher. Pk./9.
710-5110 $2.49

DISNEY FAIRIES

Tinker Bell brings fun to the celebration with a captivating twinkle in her eye and that magical smile.

Baking Cups
Standard size, paper. 2 in. dia. Pk./50.
415-5115 $1.79

Treat Bags
Fill with candy, cookies and other goodies. Great for gift cards and small surprises, too! 4 in. x 9.5 in. plastic bags with twist ties. Pk./16.
1912-5115 $2.09

FAMOUS FAVORITES

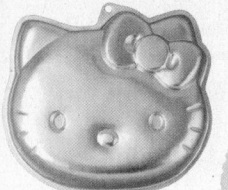

HELLO KITTY ®

Make birthday wishes come true with *Hello Kitty!*

Pan
Aluminum. One-mix pan is 10.5 in. x 9.25 in. x 2 in. deep.
2105-7575 $15.99

Toppers
Plastic toppers add fun to cupcakes, brownies, cakes and other treats. 1.4 in. high. Set/8.
2113-7575 $4.49

Candle
Handpainted with colorful details. Clean-burning. 2.2 in. high.
2811-7575 $4.49

⚠️ WARNING: Never leave burning candles unattended. Burn within sight. Keep away from drafts. Do not burn candles on or near anything that can catch fire. Burn candles out of reach of children and pets. Always leave at least 4 in. (10 cm) between burning candles.

©1976, 2012 SANRIO CO., LTD. Used Under License.

Treat Stand
Bright, 3-tier stand and fun decorative topper holds up to 24 cupcakes. Assembly instructions included. Cardboard. Baking cups not included. 11.75 in. x 15 in. high.
1512-7575 $6.99

Fun Pix
Dress up cupcakes, brownies, ice cream and more. Paper, 3 in. high. Pk./24.
2113-7576 $2.29

Icing Decorations
Edible sugar shapes to decorate cupcakes, cookies, ice cream and cake. Certified Kosher. Pk./12.
710-7575 $2.49

Baking Cups
Standard size, paper. 2 in. dia. Pk./50.
415-7575 $1.79

Treat Bags
Fill with candy, cookies and other goodies. Great for gift cards and small surprises, too! 4 in. x 9.5 in. plastic bags with twist ties. Pk./16.
1912-7575 $2.09

SPIDER SENSE SPIDER-MAN ™

When *Spidey* drops in for the party, kids will be captivated!

Pan
Aluminum. One-mix pan is 13 in. x 12.75 in. x 2 in.
2105-5062 $15.99

Candle
Handpainted with colorful details. Clean-burning. 3 in. high.
2811-5062 $4.49

⚠️ WARNING: Never leave burning candles unattended. Burn within sight. Keep away from drafts. Do not burn candles on or near anything that can catch fire. Burn candles out of reach of children and pets. Always leave at least 4 in. (10 cm) between burning candles.

Icing Decorations
Edible sugar shapes to decorate cupcakes, cookies, ice cream and cake. Certified Kosher. Pk./11.
710-5062 $2.49

Treat Stand
Bright, 3-tier stand and fun decorative topper holds up to 24 cupcakes. Assembly instructions included. Cardboard. Baking cups not included. 11.75 in. x 15 in. high.
1512-5062 $6.99

Baking Cups
Standard size, paper. 2 in. dia. Pk./50.
415-5062 $1.79

Treat Bags
Fill with candy, cookies and other goodies. Great for gift cards and small surprises, too! 4 in. x 9.5 in. plastic bags with twist ties. Pk./16.
1912-5062 $2.09

TM & © 2012 Marvel & Subs.

Elmo Pan
Aluminum. One-mix pan
is 13.5 in. x 10.5 in. x 2 in.
2105-3461 $15.99

Cupcake Toppers
Plastic toppers add fun to
cupcakes, brownies, cakes
and other treats. 1.5 in.
high. Pk./8.
2113-3461 $4.49

Elmo Birthday Candle
Handpainted with
colorful details.
Clean-burning.
3.12 in. high.
2811-3464 $4.49

Fun Pix
Dress up
cupcakes,
brownies, ice
cream and more.
Plastic,
3 in. high. Pk./12.
2113-3462 $2.29

Cupcake Stand
Bright, 3-tier stand and fun
decorative topper holds up to 24
cupcakes. Assembly instructions
included. Cardboard. Baking cups
not included. 11.75 in. x 15 in. high.
1512-3460 $6.99

Icing Decorations
Edible sugar shapes to decorate cupcakes, cookies,
ice cream and cakes. Certified Kosher. Pk./9.
710-3460 $2.49

⚠ WARNING: Never leave burning candles unattended.
Burn within sight. Keep away from drafts. Do not burn
candles on or near anything that can catch fire. Burn
candles out of reach of children and pets. Always
leave at least 4 in. (10 cm) between burning candles.

SESAME STREET®
123

**Birthdays are sweet
when you spend them on
Sesame Street!**

Baking Cups
Standard size,
paper. 2 in. dia.
Pk./50.
**415-3461
$1.79**

Treat Bags
Fill with candy,
cookies and other
goodies. Great for
gift cards and small
surprises, too!
4 in. x 9.5 in. plastic
bags with closures.
Pk./16.
**1912-3461
$2.09**

Dora Pan
Aluminum. One mix pan is
11 in. x 11 in. x 2 in. deep.
2105-6305 $15.99

Dora Toppers
Handpainted
plastic toppers
add excitement to
cupcakes, brownies,
cakes and other
treats. 2.25 in. high.
Set/6.
2113-6300 $4.49

Dora & Boots Candle
Handpainted with colorful
details. Clean-burning. 2.6 in. high.
2811-6305 $4.49

⚠ WARNING: Never leave burning candles
unattended. Burn within sight. Keep away
from drafts. Do not burn candles on or near
anything that can catch fire. Burn candles out
of reach of children and pets. Always leave at
least 4 in. (10 cm) between burning candles.

Dora Treat Stand
Bright, 3-tier stand and decorative topper holds
up to 24 cupcakes. Assembly instructions included.
Cardboard. Baking cups not included. 11.75 in. x 15
in. high.
1512-6300 $6.99

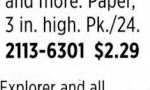

Dora & Boots Fun Pix
Dress up cupcakes,
brownies, ice cream
and more. Paper,
3 in. high. Pk./24.
2113-6301 $2.29

DORA the EXPLORER™

Dora invites you to celebrate
with a birthday adventure!

Dora Icing Decorations
Edible sugar shapes to
decorate cupcakes, cookies, ice cream and
cake. Certified Kosher. Pk./8.
710-6300 $2.49

Dora & Boots Baking Cups
Standard size,
paper. 2 in. dia. Pk./50.
415-6305 $1.79

Dora & Boots Treat Bags
Fill with candy, cookies
and other goodies.
Great for gift cards and
small surprises, too!
4 in. x 9.5 in. plastic
bags with twist ties.
Pk./16.
**1912-6305
$2.09**

FAMOUS FAVORITES

Seasonal

Enjoy celebrating the seasons and holidays with Wilton! We add color, sweetness and fun for every one, giving you great ways to make and serve cakes, cupcakes, treats and more.

HALLOWEEN
BAKEWARE

Jack-O-Lantern Cake Pan

NEW!

Non-stick pan bakes a frightfully fun jack-o-lantern cake with its features already cut out. Takes about 4½ cups of cake batter.
2105-0679
$9.99

Dimensions 3-D Skull Pan

Heavyweight cast aluminum conducts heat extremely evenly. Premium non-stick surface for easy release and cleanup. 10-cup total capacity. Finished cake 6.5 in. x 5.5 in. x 7.5 in. Patent No. D625546.
2105-1181 $34.99

NON-STICK MINI CAKE PANS

One mix makes 24 to 28 treats.

NEW!

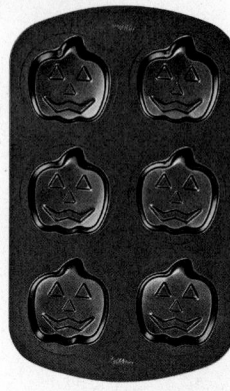

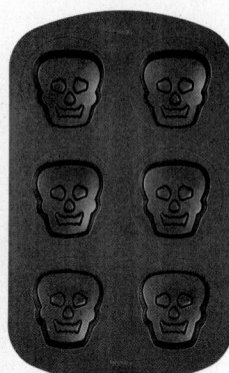

Coffin Dessert Shells
6 cavities, each 6 in. x 3.13 in. deep.
2105-0261 $14.99

Jack-O-Lantern
6 cavities, each 3.75 in. x 1.25 in. deep.
2105-1541 $11.99

Skulls
6 cavities, each 3.75 in. x 1.25 in. deep.
2105-1511 $11.99

Iridescents! Jack-O-Lantern Pan

This bright, colorful shape is as much fun for serving party treats as it is for baking! Designed for quick, easy cake decorating. Also ideal for crisped rice cereal treats, molded gelatin, bread dough and more. One-mix pan is 11.75 in. x 11.2 in. x 2 in. deep. Aluminum.
2105-2059 $9.99

MINI TREAT MOLDS

Discover the convenience of flexible silicone bakeware. Freezer, refrigerator, microwave and dishwasher safe—oven safe to 500°F. One mix makes 20 to 24 treats. Six cavities, each 2.5 in. x 1.5 in. deep. **Each $9.99**

Jack-O-Lantern Faces
2105-4939

Scary Skulls
2105-4899

COOKIE SHAPES PANS

NEW!

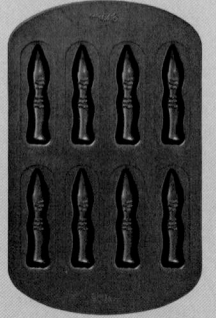

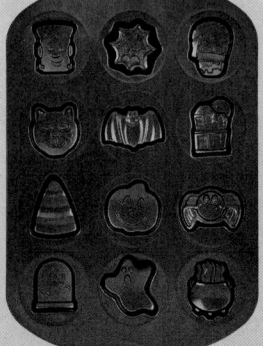

Bones
5 cavities, each approx. 5.75 in. x 1.25 in. x 0.5 in. deep.
2105-0260 $8.99

Fingers
8 cavities, each approx. 3.75 in. x 1 in. x 0.5 in. deep.
2105-0511 $8.99

Halloween
12 cavities, each approx. 2.75 in. x 2.25 in. x 0.25 in. deep.
2105-8131 $11.99

ORDER TOLL FREE: 800-794-5866

COOKIE

PRE-BAKED COOKIE KITS

No baking, just fun! Everything you need is included to make great haunted designs. **Each Kit $16.49**

Pre-Baked and Pre-Assembled Halloween Cookie House Kit

Perfect for home, school or parties, and it's so easy and fun to make! Kit includes:
• Pre-baked, pre-assembled cookie house (measures approx. 7 in. x 4 in. x 8 in. high)
• Orange and black decorating icing mixes
• Lots of colorful candy trims
• Two disposable decorating bags and round decorating tips
• Cardboard base
• Complete decorating instructions
2104-4319

Pre-Baked Haunted Mansion Cookie Kit

Easy to assemble and fun to decorate, it's the ideal family activity! Kit includes:
• 11 gingerbread house pieces (assembled house measures approx. 6 in. x 3.5 in. x 9.5 in. high)
• Black and gray decorating icing mixes
• Lots of colorful candy trims
• Two disposable decorating bags and round decorating tips
• Cardboard base
• Complete assembly and decorating instructions
2104-4321

CUTTER SETS

7-Pc. Coffin

Create ghoulishly good treats with our cookie cutter set packaged in a coffin container. Spider, cat, ghost, bat, pumpkin, coffin, tombstone. Each approx. 3 in. Set/7.
2308-0925
$7.99

4-Pc. Grippy

Safe, easy cutting with a comfortable grip and deep plastic sides. Cat, ghost, pumpkin, bat. Each approx. 3.5 in. Set/4.
2311-257 $4.49

COMFORT-GRIP CUTTERS

These easy-grip cutters with extra-deep, stainless steel sides are perfect for cutting so many favorite foods into spectacular shapes. The cushion grip gives you comfortable control even when cutting thick desserts. Recipe included. 4.5 in. x 4.5 in. x 1.5 in. deep. **Each $3.19**

NEW!

Pumpkin 2310-600

Bat 2310-661

Skull 2310-3620

Tombstone 2310-599

Ghost 2310-607

9-Pc. Halloween

Bat, ghost, cat, witch, moon, witch's broom, tombstone, house, pumpkin. Colored aluminum. Each approx. 3 in. to 3.75 in. Set/9.
2308-2501
$10.49

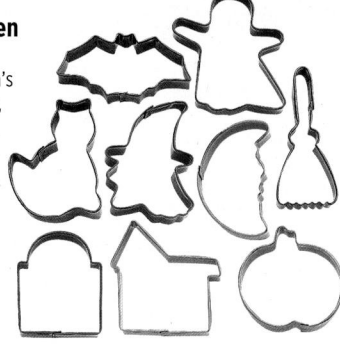

4-Pc. Witch

Boot, cauldron, hat, broom. Coated metal. Each approx. 3 in. Set/4.
2308-0921 $4.79

4-Pc. Spooky Shapes

Moon, pumpkin, witch, ghost. Coated metal. Each approx. 3 in. Set/4.
2308-1200 $4.79

3-PC. CUTTER SETS

Coated metal. Each approx. 3 in. Set/3. **Each $3.69**

NEW!

Bat/Jack-O-Lantern/Corn
Bat, jack-o-lantern, candy corn.
2308-0105

NEW!

Mad Scientist
Beaker, skull/crossbones, cauldron.
2308-0558

NEW!

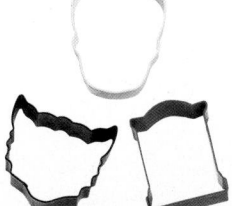

Vampire
Bat, coffin, fanged teeth.
2308-0559

Haunted Halloween
Skull, cat face, tombstone.
2308-1092

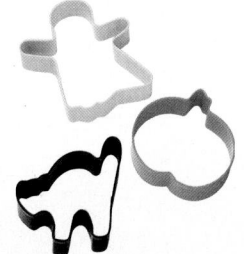

Halloween
Ghost, pumpkin, cat.
2308-1265

SEASONAL

COOKIE
METAL CUTTER SETS

5-Pc. Pumpkin Fun Face
The possibilities are endless on the different faces you can give your pumpkin cookies. Includes one pumpkin and three facial features. Largest is approx. 2 in. Set/5.
2308-0924 **$4.99**

7-Pc. Halloween Linzer Cookie
Traditional in design, the fluted round cookie cutter has six interchangeable center shapes—pumpkin, owl, bat, ghost, cat, witch hat—that let the cookie filling show through. Cookies approx. 3 in. Set/7.
2308-0920 **$7.99**

18-Pc. Halloween
Set of 18 metal cutters includes pumpkin, oak leaf, cat, coffin, tombstone, witch, maple leaf, apple, spider, witch's broom, moon, bat, candy corn, ghost, house, spider web, monster head, cauldron. Each approx. 3 in. Set/18.
2308-1131 **$10.49**

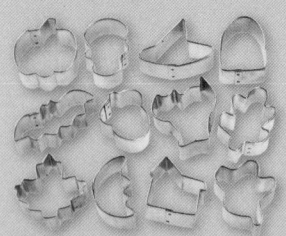
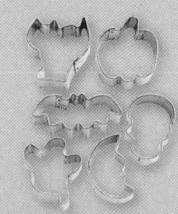

12-Pc. Halloween Mini
Pumpkin, skull, witch's hat, tombstone, bat, acorn, cat, oak leaf, maple leaf, moon, house, ghost. Each approx. 1.5 in. to 2.25 in. Set/12.
2308-1246 **$5.29**

6-Pc. Halloween Mini
Cat, pumpkin, bat, skull, ghost, moon. Each approx. 1.5 in. Set/6.
2308-1211 **$3.29**

4-Pc. Nesting
Four graduated sizes up to 4.5 in. Set/4. **$4.79**

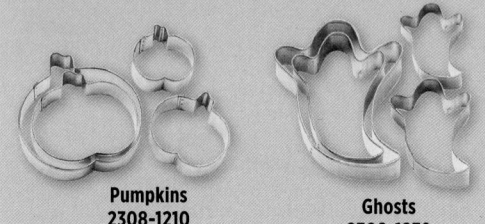

Pumpkins
2308-1210

Ghosts
2308-1238

PARTY

Baking Cups
Colorful paper. Standard size, 2 in. dia., Pk./75. Mini size, 1.25 in. dia., Pk./100.
Each $2.09

Pumpkin Stripe
Standard 415-0205
Trick or Treat
Mini 415-0541

Spooky Pop
Standard 415-0442
Mini 415-0443

Halloween in 3-D
Standard 415-0439
Mini 415-0440

Cupcake Combo
Contains 24 each 2 in. dia. baking cups and 3 in. high paper party picks 12 of each design. Pk./24.
Each $2.29

Pumpkin Stripe
415-0540

Spooky Pop
415-0444

Halloween in 3-D
415-0441

Party Bags
Fill with candy, cookies and other goodies. Great for gift cards and small surprises, too! Includes 20 each plastic bags and ties. Bags: 4 in. x 9.5 in. Pk./20.
$2.09

Pumpkin Stripe
1912-1351

Spooky Pop
1912-0034

Halloween in 3-D
1912-0033

Shaped Party Bags
Includes 15 each large plastic bags and ties. Bags: 6 in. x 9 in. Pk./15.
$2.09

Spider Treat Boxes
Holds candies, cookies or four cupcakes. Assembly instructions included. 3 in. x 6.25 in. x 6.25 in. deep. Pk./3.
415-0454 **$5.29**

Spooky Pop
1912-0035

Shaped Party Bags
Includes 15 each large plastic bags and ties. Bags: 6 in. x 9 in. Pk./15.
$2.09

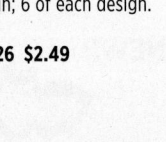

Eyes & Eyebrows Picks
Contains 12 paper party picks, 3 in. high; 6 of each design. Pk./12.
2113-1126 **$2.49**

Icing Decorations
Edible sugar shapes to decorate cupcakes, cookies, cakes and more. Pk./12.
Each Pack $5.99

Knife
710-017

Skull
710-1082

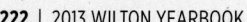

ORDER TOLL FREE: 800-794-5866

CANDY

CANDY KITS

Halloween Candy Kit for Pretzels
Create creepy pretzel treats.
Kit includes:
• 3 fun shaped molds: movie monster pretzel, shrieking sweets pretzel and frightful fun pretzel
• 12 oz. Candy Melts candy: 3 oz each light cocoa, white, orange and green
• 4 disposable decorating bags
• 1 decorating brush
• 20 pretzel bags with ties
Certified Kosher Dairy.
2104-0256 $9.99

Halloween Candy Making Kit
Colorful homemade candy makes the season more fun. Kit includes:
• 3 fun shaped molds: spooky spells candy and lollipop, midnight mischief lollipop and graveyard goodies candy
• 12 oz. Candy Melts candy: 3 oz each light cocoa, white, orange and green
• 20—6 in. lollipop sticks
• 4 disposable decorating bags
• 1 decorating brush
• 20 party bags with ties
Certified Kosher Dairy.
2104-0255 $9.99

CANDY MOLDS

Candy Corn/Pumpkin Lollipop Mold
3 designs, 3 cavities.
2115-1433 $1.99

Large Rat Candy Mold
1 design, 1 cavity.
2115-2163 $1.99

Large Skull Candy Mold
1 design, 1 cavity.
2115-2164 $1.99

Large Casket Candy Mold
1 design, 1 cavity.
2115-2165 $1.99

Haunted Manor Cookie Candy Mold
Great for sandwich cream cookies or any round cookie 2 in. dia. or less. 2 designs, 8 cavities.
2115-1357 $1.99

 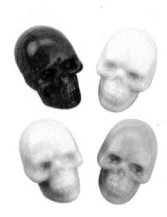  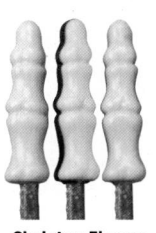   

Skeleton Bones Candy Mold
6 designs, 20 cavities.
2115-1424 $1.99

Skulls 3-D Candy Mold
1 design, 8 cavities.
2115-1421 $1.99

Creepy Tombstones 3-D Candy Mold
Makes 3 creepy tombstones with interchangeable bases.
2115-1415 $1.99

Skeleton Fingers Pretzel Mold
1 design, 6 cavities.
2115-1418 $1.99

Witch Fingers Pretzel Mold
2 designs, 6 cavities.
2115-1616 $1.99

Mummies Pretzel Mold
1 design, 6 cavities.
2115-1783 $1.99

Smiling Pumpkins Lollipop Mold
1 design, 7 cavities.
2115-1750 $1.99

Candy Melts
Ideal for molding, dipping or coating. Artificially vanilla flavored unless otherwise indicated. 12 oz. bag. Certified Kosher Dairy.
Each $3.29

Orange	1911-1515
Yellow	1911-1369
Dark Green	1911-1356
Dark Cocoa	1911-1353
Light Cocoa	1911-1359
Dark Cocoa Mint	1911-1355
White	1911-1367
Lavender	1911-1358

Vibrant Green
1911-401

Black
10 oz. bag.
1911-402

See pages 175-179 for more Wilton candy items.

Halloween Candy Necklace Kits*
It's the perfect party activity— each kit makes eight tasty necklaces!
Each $3.99

Skull & Bones
2104-4464

Pumpkin
2104-1274

*Recommended for children 3+ years.

SEASONAL

ORDER ONLINE: WWW.WILTON.COM

ICINGS & COLORS

See Color Guide below. All are certified Kosher.

Orange	Black	Violet	Green	White

Decorating Icing

Tubes can be used with our Tip Set or Coupler Ring Set (p. 140) and any standard-size Wilton metal tip. Colors match Wilton Icing Colors (p. 139). 4.25 oz.

Each $2.29

Orange	704-212
Black	704-206
Violet	704-242
Leaf Green	704-224
White	704-200

Decorating Gel

Transparent gels are great for writing messages and decorating cakes and cookies. Colors match Wilton Icing Colors (p. 139). 0.75 oz.

Each $1.79

Orange	704-312
Black	704-306
Violet	704-342
Green	704-324
White	704-302

Ready-to-Decorate Icing

Anyone can decorate with Wilton Ready-to-Decorate Icing! Our brilliant colors and four decorating tips make it a breeze to add an exciting finishing touch to treats—without mixing or mess. 6.4 oz.

Each $4.79

Orange	710-4410
Black	710-4404
Violet	710-4408
Green	710-4401
White	710-4402

Halloween Icing Colors Set

0.5 oz. jars of black and orange. Set/2.
601-3010 **$3.29**

Sparkle Gel

Squeeze on sparkling color effects with our ready-to-use gel. Great for dots, messages and fondant accents. Resealable 3.5 oz. tube. **Each $2.99**

Orange	704-109
Black	704-1061
Light Green	704-1019
White	704-107

Cookie Icing

Easy to use—just heat and squeeze onto cookies using the convenient cap. Sets smooth in just 1 hour. 10 oz. bottle covers approx. 12 cookies, 3 in. each.

Each $4.99

Orange	704-496
Black	704-205
Green	704-493
White	704-481

FoodWriter Edible Ink Markers Set

Add fun, dazzling color to foods. Decorate on Wilton Fondant, Color Flow, royal icing designs and cookie icing. Includes black and orange markers (0.07 oz. each). Set/2.
609-101 **$4.29**

Color Mist Food Color Spray

Gives decorators the versatility and dazzling effects of an airbrush in a convenient can! Use it to add sensational edible color to iced cookies and cupcakes. No mess, taste-free formula. 1.5 oz.

Each $3.79

Orange	710-5507
Black	710-5506
Violet	710-5504
Green	710-5503

Cupcake & Cookie Stencils

Just place one of the fun designs over your iced treat, then sprinkle with colored sugars or spray with Color Mist food color spray. Eight designs.
417-499 **$2.19**

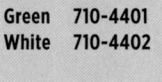

Candy Eyeballs

Perfect additions to faces on pops, cookies, cupcakes and more. Shown actual size, 0.43 in. dia.; 0.88 oz. Approx. 62 pieces.
710-0017 **$3.99**

SPRINKLES

Creepy Sprinkles Lab Set

Brew up some wickedly fun treats this Halloween when you top off desserts with our sprinkles-filled test tubes. Contains black/spooky green jimmies; bone sprinkles; orange sugar; black, orange and green jimmies. Total net weight: 4.41 oz. Set/4. Certified Kosher.
710-1055 **$5.99**

INDIVIDUAL BOTTLES

Plastic bottles for convenient pouring and storing. Certified Kosher, except Silver Pearlized Jimmies.

Jumbo Jack-O-Lanterns
3.5 oz. bottle.
710-2114 **$4.49**

Jumbo Skulls
3.5 oz. bottle.
710-2115 **$4.49**

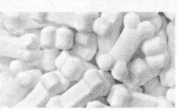
Jumbo Bones
3.53 oz. bottle.
710-1053 **$4.49**

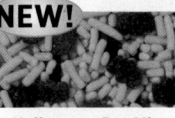
Halloween Bat Mix
3.75 oz. bottle.
710-1454 **$3.29**

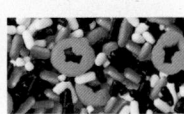
Hallow Pumpkin Mix
2.5 oz. bottle.
710-182 **$2.29**

Spider Mix
2.5 oz. bottle.
710-0030 **$2.29**

Silver Pearlized Jimmies
4.23 oz. bottle.
710-1127 **$4.49**

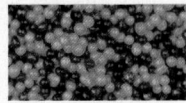
Halloween Nonpareils
3 oz. bottle.
710-593 **$2.29**
5 oz. bottle.
710-199 **$3.29**

Sugars

3.25 oz. bottle. Certified Kosher. **Each $2.29**

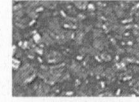
Orange
710-759

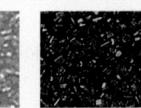
Black
710-762

Lavender
710-758

Light Green
710-752

Cake Sparkles

Edible accents, 0.25 oz. bottle. Certified Kosher. **Each $3.29**

Orange
703-1308

Black
703-1302

Purple
703-1266

Green
703-1278

White
703-1290

6-Mix Assortment

Contains Halloween nonpareils; Halloween confetti; hallow pumpkin mix; black, orange and purple sugars. 7.1 oz. Certified Kosher.
710-185 **$5.99**

ORDER TOLL FREE: 800-794-5866

AUTUMN
BAKEWARE

DIMENSIONS DECORATIVE BAKEWARE
Heavyweight cast aluminum conducts heat extremely evenly. Premium non-stick surface for easy release and cleanup.

Pumpkin
10-cup total capacity. Finished cake: 6.75 in. x 6 in. Pat. No. D577,951.
2105-1184 $34.99

Multi-Cavity Pumpkin Pan
5-cup total capacity. Finished cakes: 3.4 x 3.4 in. Pat. No. D574,663.
2105-1183 $34.99

MINI TREAT MOLD
Freezer, refrigerator, microwave and dishwasher safe; oven safe to 500°F.

Silicone Mini Leaf and Pumpkin Mold
One-mix makes 20 to 24 cakes. Six cavities, each 2.6 in. x 2.5 in. x 1.5 in. deep.
2105-4874 $9.99

CANDY

Pumpkin Candy Mold
1 design, 11 cavities.
2115-1558 $1.99

Pumpkin Harvest Pretzel Mold
2 designs, 6 cavities.
2115-1420 $1.99

Candy Melts
Artificially vanilla flavored unless otherwise indicated. 12 oz. bag. Certified Kosher Dairy.
Each $3.29

Red	1911-1364	Dark	
Light		Cocoa	1911-1353
Cocoa	1911-1359	Dark Cocoa	
Orange	1911-1515	Mint	1911-1355
Yellow	1911-1369	White	1911-1367
Dark		Peanut	
Green	1911-1356	Butter	1911-1516

See pages 175-179 for more Wilton candy items.

PARTY
MYSTIC AUTUMN

NEW!
Baking Cups
Paper. Standard size, 2 in. dia., Pk./75. Mini size, 1.25 in. dia., Pk./100.
Each Pack $2.09
Standard 415-0448
Mini 415-0449

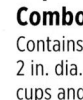

NEW!

Cupcake Combo
Contains 24 each 2 in. dia. baking cups and 3 in. high paper party picks, 12 of each design. Pk./24.
415-0450 $2.29

NEW!

Party Bags
Includes 20 each plastic bags and ties. Bags: 4 in. x 9.5 in. Pk./20.
1912-0038 $2.09

Icing Decorations
Certified Kosher.

3-D Pumpkins Pk./12.
710-0134 $5.99

Mini Pumpkins Pk./18.
710-538 $2.29

NEW!
Shaped Party Bags
Includes 15 each plastic bags and ties. Bags: 6 in. x 9 in. Pk./15.
1912-0039 $2.09

COOKIE

Maple Leaf Comfort-Grip Cutter
Approx. 4.5 in. x 1.5 in. deep.
2310-632 $3.19

Cupcake & Cookie Stencils
Place over baked treat, then sprinkle with colored sugars or spray with Color Mist food color spray (p. 224). Eight designs.
417-495 $2.19

SPRINKLES
Individual Bottles
Certified Kosher.

Micro Leaves Mix
3 oz. bottle.
710-1456 $4.49

Colorful Leaves Mix
2.5 oz. bottle.
710-787 $2.29

Cake Sparkles
Edible accents in 0.25 oz. bottle. Certified Kosher.
Each $3.29

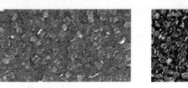

Red Sugar
3.25 oz. bottle.
710-766 $2.29

Dark Green Sugar
3.25 oz. bottle.
710-764 $2.29

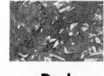
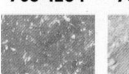
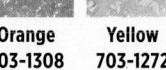

Red 703-1284
Dark Green 703-1278
Orange 703-1308
Yellow 703-1272

6-Mix Assortment
Contains yellow, red, orange and light green sugar, colorful leaves mix and chocolate jimmies. 7.2 oz. Certified Kosher.
710-751 $5.99

METAL CUTTER SETS

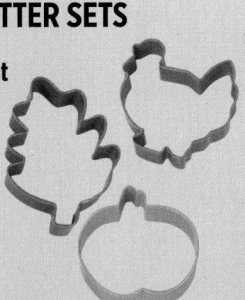

3-Pc. Harvest
Turkey, leaf, pumpkin. Coated metal. Each approx. 3 in. to 3.5 in. Set/3.
2308-1264 $3.69

9-Pc. Leaves and Acorns Nesting
Graduated acorns, oak and maple leaves (three each). Each approx. 1.75 in. to 3.75 in. Set/9.
2308-2000 $6.29

6-Pc. Harvest Mini
Oak leaf, maple leaf, apple, pumpkin, elm leaf, acorn. Each approx. 1.5 in. Set/6.
2308-1217 $3.29

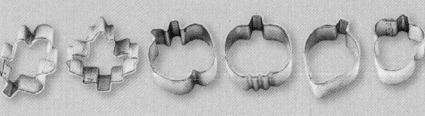

SEASONAL

BAKEWARE

NEW!

12-Cavity Whoopie Pie Pan

Bake fun-filled sandwich cakes in your favorite flavor. Recipes and instructions included. Non-stick heavy-duty steel construction. 12 cavities, each approx. 3 in. x 0.5 in. deep.
2105-0366 $11.99

Iridescents! Tree Pan

This bright, colorful shape is as much fun for serving party treats as it is for baking! Designed for quick, easy decorating. Also ideal for crisped rice cereal treats, molded gelatin, bread dough and more. Aluminum. One-mix pan is 14 in. x 10 in. x 2 in. deep.
2105-2081 $9.99

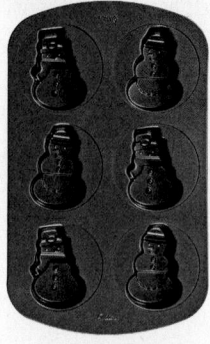

NON-STICK MINI CAKE PANS

Bake fun single-sized cakes, brownies and more. Non-stick steel releases treats easily. One mix makes 16 treats.
Each $11.99

Snowman/Woman
6 cavities, each approx. 2.8 in. x 3.7 in. x 1.3 in. deep.
2105-0574

Gingerbread Boys and Trees
6 cavities, each approx. 2.8 in. x 3.7 in. x 1.3 in. deep.
2105-1515

TREAT MOLDS

Discover the convenience of flexible silicone bakeware. Freezer, refrigerator, microwave and dishwasher safe—oven safe to 500°F. One mix makes approx. 80 bite-sized treats; 40 to 48 petite; 20 to 24 mini cakes treats.
Each $9.99

Bite-Size Gingerbread Boy
24 cavities, each 1.75 in. x 1.6 in. x .75 in. deep.
2105-4901

NEW!

3-D Tree
12 cavities, each 2 in. x 1 in. deep.
2105-0332

Mini Gingerbread Boy/Stocking/Tree
Six cavities, each 2.5 in. x 1.5 in. deep.
2105-4893

Petite Tree
12 cavities, each 2 in. x 1 in. deep.
2105-4898

Bite-Size Tree
24 cavities, each 2.25 in. x 1.75 in. x .75 in. deep.
2105-4902

COOKIE SHAPES PANS

Includes classic shapes for your single-serving holiday cookies and molded desserts. **Each $11.99**

NEW!

Word Banner
6 cavities, each approx. 5.5 in. x 3 in. x 0.5 in. deep.
2105-0287

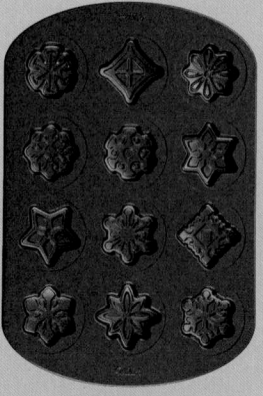

Snowflake Stars
12 cavities, each approx. 2.75 in. x 2.25 in. x 0.25 in. deep.
2105-0567

Holiday
12 cavities, each approx. 2.75 in. x 2.25 in. x 0.25 in. deep.
2105-8122

ORDER TOLL FREE: 800-794-5866

COOKIE
METAL CUTTER SETS
Put variety in your cookie making with fun Christmas multi-shape sets. Recipe included.

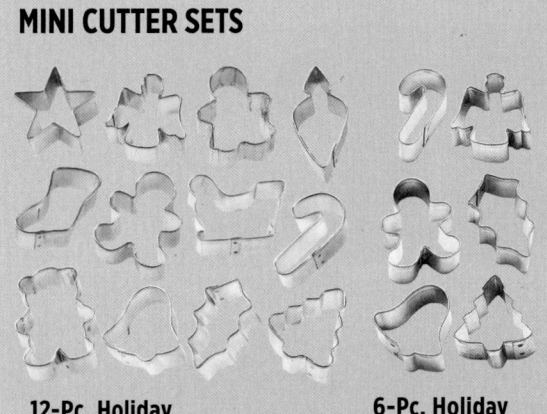

MINI CUTTER SETS

12-Pc. Holiday
Star, angel, gingerbread girl, ornament, stocking, gingerbread boy, sleigh, candy cane, teddy bear, bell, holly leaf, tree. Each approx. 1.5 in. Set/12.
2308-1250 $5.29

6-Pc. Holiday
Candy cane, angel, gingerbread boy, holly leaf, bell, tree. Each approx. 1.5 in. Set/6.
2308-1214 $3.29

18-Pc. Holiday
Snowflake, holly leaf, gingerbread girl, star, sleigh, tree, stocking, snowman, reindeer, ornament, candy cane, Santa hat, angel, bell, gift, wreath, gingerbread boy, mitten. Each approx. 3 in. Set/18.
2308-1132 $10.49

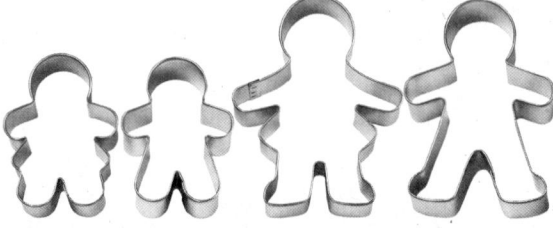

4-Pc. Gingerbread Family
Includes 2 parents and 2 children. Approx. 2.5 in. to 3.75 in. Set/4.
2308-0934 $4.79

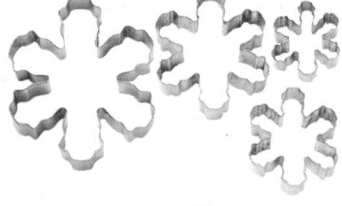

4-Pc. Nesting
Four graduated sizes up to 5 in. Set/4.
Each Set $4.79
Snowflakes
2308-1244
Gingerbread Boys
2308-1239

9-Pc. Holiday
Candy cane, gingerbread girl, stocking, angel, star, bell, snowman, tree, gingerbread boy. Colored aluminum. Each approx. 3 in. to 3.75 in. Set/9.
2308-2500 $10.49

4-Pc. Jolly Shapes
Stocking, star, tree candy cane. Coated metal. Each approx. 3 in. Set/4.
2308-1201 $4.79

3-PC. CUTTER SETS
Coated metal. Each approx. 3 in. Set/3. **Each $3.69**

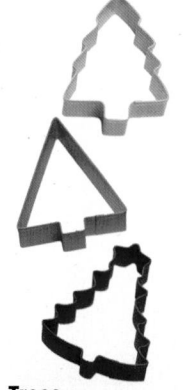

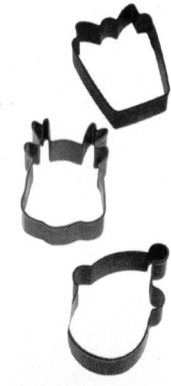

Delightfully Decadent
Holly leaf, bow, snowflake.
2308-0131

Frosted Fun
Gingerbread girl, candy cane, gingerbread boy.
2308-0132

Homemade for the Holidays
Train, bear, rocking horse.
2308-0133

Trees
Classic fir, triangle tree, startop tree.
2308-1103

Gingerbread
Boy, girl, house.
2308-1102

Snowflake Wishes
Gift, reindeer, Santa.
2308-1104

Christmas
Snowflake, tree, gingerbread boy.
2308-1266

SEASONAL

NEW!

Gingerbread Boy Giant Non-Stick Cookie Pan

It's easy and fun to bake and decorate a cookie big enough to feed your holiday crowd. It's also great for refrigerated cookie dough, refrigerated pizza dough and crisp rice cereal treats.
2105-059 $7.99

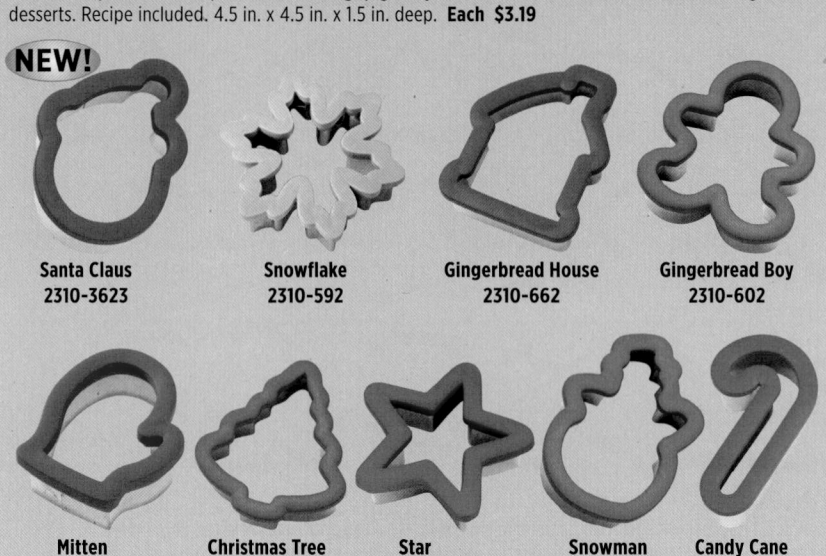

COMFORT-GRIP CUTTERS

These easy-grip cutters with extra-deep, stainless steel sides are perfect for cutting so many favorite foods into spectacular shapes. The cushion grip gives you comfortable control even when cutting thick desserts. Recipe included. 4.5 in. x 4.5 in. x 1.5 in. deep. **Each $3.19**

NEW!

| Santa Claus | Snowflake | Gingerbread House | Gingerbread Boy |
| 2310-3623 | 2310-592 | 2310-662 | 2310-602 |

| Mitten | Christmas Tree | Star | Snowman | Candy Cane |
| 2310-639 | 2310-604 | 2310-631 | 2310-634 | 2310-644 |

7-PC. LINZER COOKIE CUTTER SETS

Make European-inspired jam-filled cookies for a fun holiday treat. Fluted cookie cutters have six interchangeable center shapes that let the filling show through. Cookies approx. 3 in. Metal. Recipe included. Set/7. **Each $7.99**

Round
Star, heart, diamond, triangle, flower, circle.
2308-3800

Star
Tree, circle, star, candy cane, diamond, snowman.
2308-0918

4-Pc. Grippy Cutter Set
Safe, easy cutting, with a comfortable grip and deep plastic sides. Stocking, tree, star, gingerbread boy. Each approx. 3.5 in. Set/4.
2311-260 $4.49

Christmas Cookie Tree Cutter Kit

Kit includes:
- 10 plastic star cookie cutters in graduated sizes.
- Three disposable decorating bags.
- Round decorating tip.
- Cookie and icing recipes.
- Baking and decorating instructions for four designs. Assembled tree measures approx. 8 in. x 11 in. high.

2104-1555 $7.99

TOOLS

Jumbo Cookie Spatula
Generously sized spatula is great for handling multiple or oversized cookies, brownies, pastries and treat bars. Easy-grip handle helps balance large desserts. Stainless steel; dishwasher safe. 11 in. long.
570-1161 $6.99

Cookie Spatula
Angled blade moves cookies from pan to plate with ease. Great for serving brownies and bar cookies, too. Comfortable ergonomic handle with thumb rest. Stainless steel. 9 in. long.
409-6054 $6.99

NEW!

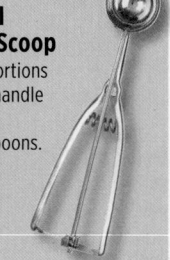

Cookie Scoop
Perfect for easy scooping and consistently round cookies. Stainless steel. Capacity 4 teaspoons.
417-1112 $5.99

Stainless Steel Large Cookie Scoop
Scoops uniform portions of dough; spring handle for easy release. Capacity 3 tablespoons.
417-139 $6.99

GINGERBREAD KITS

Gingerbread Mini Village

Kit includes:
- Four individual sets of gingerbread house panels (assembled houses measure between 3.25 in. and 5 in. high).
- Lots of colorful candy trim.
- White ready-to-use icing.
- Decorating bag and tip.
- Cardboard bases.
- Complete assembly and decorating instructions.

2104-1910 $16.49

Deluxe Gingerbread

Kit includes:
- Six pre-baked gingerbread house pieces (assembled house measures approx. 6.25 in. deep x 8.25 in. wide x 9 in. high).
- Two gingerbread boy cookies (3 in. high).
- Two gingerbread tree cookies (6 in. high).
- Two gingerbread easels for trees.
- Lots of colorful candy trim.
- White ready-to-use icing.
- Green ready-to-use icing.
- Two decorating bags and two tips.
- Complete assembly and decorating instructions.

2104-1911 $34.99

Gingerbread Cottage

Kit includes:
- Pre-baked gingerbread house pieces (assembled house measures approx. 8 in. x 7 in. x 6.5 in. high).
- Lots of colorful candy trim.
- Icing mix.
- Decorating bag and tip.
- Cardboard base.
- Complete assembly and decorating instructions.

2104-1907 $16.49

Pre-Assembled Gingerbread House

Kit includes:
- Pre-baked, pre-assembled gingerbread house (assembled house measures approx. 5.5 in. x 5.5 in. x 4.5 in. high).
- Lots of colorful candy trim.
- Icing mix.
- Decorating bag and tip.
- Cardboard base.
- Complete decorating instructions.

2104-1904 $16.49

Gingerbread House

Kit includes:
- Pre-baked gingerbread house pieces (assembled house measures approx. 5.25 in. x 5.5 in. x 4.75 in. high).
- Lots of colorful candy trim.
- Icing mix.
- Decorating bag and tip.
- Cardboard base.
- Complete assembly and decorating instructions.

2104-1903 $12.99

Gingerbread Boy Cookie Decorating

Kit includes:
- Eight pre-baked gingerbread boy cookies.
- Lots of colorful candy trim.
- White ready-to-use icing.
- Red and green fondant.
- Decorating bag and tip.
- Complete decorating instructions.

2104-1906 $12.99

Gingerpops Cookie

Kit includes:
- 20 pre-baked cookies (approx. 2.5 in. high).
- White ready-to-use icing.
- Black ready-to-use icing.
- Green ready-to-use icing.
- Red ready-to-use icing.
- White nonpareil sprinkles.
- Three decorating bags and round tips.
- Treat bag kit including 10 each: treat bags, lollipop sticks and sticker ties.
- Complete decorating instructions.

2104-1912 $12.99

Gingerbread Tree

Kit includes:
- Pre-baked cookies (assembled tree measures approx. 5.5 in. x 8.25 in. high).
- White and green icing mixes.
- Lots of colorful candy trim.
- Two disposable decorating bags and tips.
- Complete assembly and decorating instructions.

2104-1905 $12.99

"Cookie Exchange"

Whether you're hosting or simply attending, Wilton "Cookie Exchange" is filled with ideas to inspire you.
Includes:
- Hundreds of festive cookie designs, including a Gallery section with more than 150 easy ideas in six favorite seasonal shapes.
- Great recipes, including almond snowballs to crème de menthe bars.
- Baking basic section to ensure your cookies turn out just right.
- Helpful hosting section that includes how to plan the event.

Soft cover, 96 pages
902-1102 $14.99

13-Pc. Cookie Decorating Set

Create festive cookies with this essential decorating set!
Includes:
- 5 standard decorating tips (2, 3, 5, 18 and 352).
- 6 — 12 in. disposable decorating bags.
- 2-Pc. Cookie Stencil Set (Tree and Gingerbread Boy).
- Step-by-step, illustrated instructions.

2104-2538 $8.99

SEASONAL

PARTY

Baking Cups

Colorful paper. Standard size, 2 in. dia., Pk./75. Mini size, 1.25 in. dia., Pk./100.
Each Pack $2.09

Gingerbread Cottage
Standard **415-1883**
Mini **415-1884**

Secret Santa
Standard **415-0060**
Mini **415-0061**

Sweets & Treats
Standard **415-1886**
Mini **415-1887**

Pleated Poinsettia Cups

Poinsettia-shaped cup offers a quick and colorful way to serve cupcakes that set the tone for your celebration. 2 in. dia. paper cup. Pk./15.
415-1605 $3.99

Cupcake Combo

Contains 24 each 2 in. dia. baking cups and 3 in. high paper party picks 12 of each design. Pk./24.
Each Pack $2.29

Gingerbread Cottage
415-1892

Secret Santa
415-0062

Sweets & Treats
415-1891

TREAT BOXES

Medium
6.25 in. x 6.25 in. x 3 in. high. Ribbon not included. Pk./3.
415-1893 $5.99

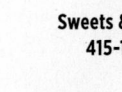

Party Bags

Fill with candy, cookies and other goodies. Great for gift cards and small surprises, too! Includes 20 each plastic bags and ties. Bags: 4 in. x 9.5 in. Pk./20.
Each Pack $2.09

Gingerbread Cottage
1912-0021

Secret Santa
1912-0085

Sweets & Treats
1912-0023

Sample
6.25 in. x 6.25 in. x 2 in. high. Pk./3.
415-1894 $5.29

Shaped Party Bags

Includes 15 each large plastic bags and ties. Bags: are 6 in. x 9 in. Pk./15.
Each Pack $2.09

Gingerbread Cottage
1912-0022

Secret Santa
1912-0086

Sweets & Treats
1912-0024

Tented
3 in. x 4 in. x 8.5 in. high. Ribbon not included. Pk./3.
415-1900 $4.49

Cookie Decorations

Edible sugar shapes sized just right for cookies. Great for cupcakes and other treats, too! Certified Kosher. Pk./24.
Each Pack $2.29

Mini Gingerbread
710-1139

Mini Holly
710-0993

Mini Candy Cane
710-0992

Mini Snowmen
710-0994

Icing Decorations

Edible sugar shapes to decorate cupcakes, cookies, cakes and more.

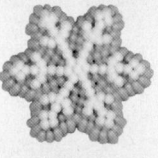

Snowflakes
Pk./12.
710-543 $2.29

ORDER TOLL FREE: 800-794-5866

CANDY

Santa Lollipop Mold
1 design, 9 cavities.
2115-1706 $1.99

Snowflake Large Lollipop Mold
3 designs, 3 cavities.
2115-1571 $1.99

Christmas Trees Pretzel Mold
1 design, 6 cavities.
2115-1747 $1.99

COOKIE CANDY MOLDS
Great for sandwich cream cookies or any round cookie 2 in. dia. or less. 2 designs, 8 cavities.
Each $1.99

NEW!

Snowflake
2115-2160

CANDY CANE MOLDS

Add a new twist to store-bought candy canes by molding a fun candy character on them! Fill mold cavities with your favorite melted Candy Melts candy, position candy cane and refrigerate to set. 2 designs, 2 cavities.
Each $1.99

Santa Claus
2115-1575

Frosty Friends
2115-1573

Holiday
2115-1359

Winter
2115-1360

NEW!

Christmas Candy Making Kit
Colorful homemade candy makes the season more fun.
Kit includes:
• 3 fun shaped molds: elves candy mold, North Pole lollipop mold, gifts candy mold.
• 12 oz. Candy Melts candy: 3 oz each light cocoa, white, red and green.
• 20—6 in. lollipop sticks.
• 4 disposable decorating bags.
• 1 decorating brush.
• 20 party bags with ties.
Kosher Dairy.
2104-0012 $9.99

NEW!

Christmas Candy Kit for Pretzels
Create festive pretzel treats.
Kit includes:
• 3 fun shaped molds: polar pals pretzel mold, tall tree pretzel mold and snowy sweets pretzel mold.
• 12 oz. Candy Melts candy: 3 oz each light cocoa, white, red and green.
• 4 disposable decorating bags.
• 1 decorating brush.
• 20 party bags with ties.
Kosher Dairy.
2104-0013 $9.99

Candy Cups
Perfect for holiday sweets!
1 in. dia. Pk./75.
Each Pack $1.79
Red Foil 415-314
Silver Foil 415-307
Gold Foil 415-306

Red/Green Candy Cups
Mixed, glassine paper.
1 in. Pk./72.
1912-1247 $1.79

CANDY MELTS
Artificially vanilla flavored unless otherwise indicated. 12 oz. bag. Certified Kosher Dairy.
Each $3.29

Red	1911-1364		
White	1911-1367	**Dark Cocoa**	1911-1353
Dark Green	1911-1356	**Dark Cocoa Mint**	1911-1355
Light Cocoa	1911-1359	**Yellow**	1911-1369

Peppermint Bark Kit
Spread a little holiday cheer! Makes five complete treats for gift giving.
Kit includes:
• 6 oz. Candy Melts dark cocoa candy.
• 6 oz. Colorburst Candy Melts candy cane candy.
• 2 disposable decorating bags.
• 5 each gift bags, silver cord ties and tags.
• 5 snowflake cutters.
Kosher Dairy.
2104-2266 $9.99

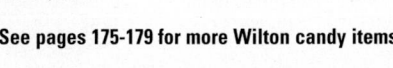

Christmas Candy Necklace Kits*
It's the perfect party activity—each kit makes six tasty necklaces! **Each $3.99**

Snowflake
2104-0213

Christmas Lights
2104-0214

*Recommended for children 3+ years.

Colorburst Candy Melts
Brilliant flecks of color are blended into each easy-melting wafer. 10 oz. bag. Certified Kosher Dairy.
Each $3.29

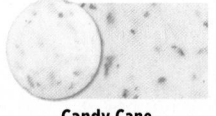
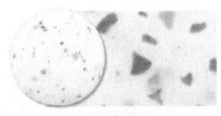
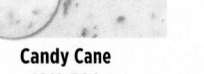

Candy Cane
1911-500

Brights
1911-491

See pages 175-179 for more Wilton candy items.

SEASONAL

ICINGS & COLORS

See Color Guide below. All are certified Kosher.

Red **Kelly Green** **Leaf Green** **White**

Decorating Icing

Tubes can be used with our Tip Set or Coupler Ring Set (p. 140) and any standard-size Wilton metal tip. Colors match Wilton Icing Colors (p. 139). 4.25 oz.

Each $2.29
Red   704-218
Kelly Green   704-227
Leaf Green   704-224
White   704-200

Sparkle Gel

Squeeze on sparkling color effects with our ready-to-use gel. Great for dots, messages and fondant accents. Resealable 3.5 oz. tube.

Each $2.99
Red   704-112
Green   704-111
White   704-107
Gold   704-1060
Light Blue   704-1013

Decorating Gel

Transparent gels are great for writing messages and decorating cakes and cookies. Colors match Wilton Icing Colors (p. 139). 0.75 oz.

Each $1.79
Red   704-318
Green   704-324
White   704-302

Cookie Icing

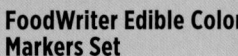

Easy to use—just heat and squeeze onto cookies using the convenient cap. Sets smooth in just 1 hour. 10 oz. bottle covers approx. 12 cookies, 3 in. each.

Each $4.99
Red   704-488
Green   704-493
White   704-481

Ready-to-Decorate Icing

Anyone can decorate with Wilton Ready-to-Decorate Icing! Our brilliant colors and four decorating tips make it a breeze to add an exciting finishing touch to treats—without mixing or mess. 6.4 oz.

Each $4.79
Red   710-4400
Green   710-4401
White   710-4402

FoodWriter Edible Color Markers Set

Add fun, dazzling color to foods. Decorate on Wilton Fondant, Color Flow, royal icing designs and cookie icing. Includes green and red markers (0.07 oz. each). Set/2.
609-102 $4.29

Christmas Icing Colors Set

0.5 oz. jars of red-red and kelly green. Set/2.
601-3011 $3.29

Color Mist Food Color Spray

Gives decorators the versatility and dazzling effects of an airbrush in a convenient can! Use it to add sensational edible color to iced cookies and cupcakes. No mess, taste-free formula. 1.5 oz.

Red   710-5500 $3.79
Green   710-5503 $3.79
Gold   710-5520 $4.29
Silver   710-5521 $4.29

Christmas Cupcake and Cookie Stencils

Just place one of the fun designs over your iced treat, then sprinkle with colored sugars or spray with Color Mist food color spray. Eight designs.
417-510 $2.19

SPRINKLES

NEW!

Holiday Sprinkles Set

Top cookies, cupcakes, cakes and your treats with this great variety of basic sprinkles. Contains red/green/white jimmies, red/white sparkling sugar, twinkling tree sprinkles and red/green/white nonpareils. Total net weight 18 oz. Certified Kosher.
710-177 $9.99

NEW!

Twinkling Treats Sprinkles Set

From colorful cookie trays to festive cupcakes, these dazzling sprinkles will make your holidays bright. Contains light bulb sprinkles, red/green/white nonpareils, and green and red sugars. Total net weight 6.95 oz.
710-0020 $5.99

INDIVIDUAL BOTTLES

All Certified Kosher except Silver Pearlized Jimmies.

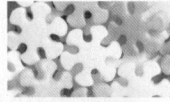
Jumbo Snowflakes
3.2 oz. bottle.
710-0117 $4.49

Holly Mix
3.35 oz. bottle.
710-1126 $4.49

Candy Cane
3.7 oz. bottle.
710-1107 $4.49

Holiday Confetti
2 oz. bottle.
710-172 $2.29

Snowflake Mix
2.5 oz. bottle.
710-797 $2.29

Silver Pearlized Jimmies
4.23 oz. bottle.
710-1127 $4.49

White Sugar Pearls
5 oz. bottle.
710-044 $4.99

Cinnamon Drops
3 oz. bottle.
710-769 $2.29

Holiday Nonpareils
3 oz.
710-0116 $2.29
5 oz.
710-0115 $3.29

Red Sugar
3.25 oz. bottle.
710-766 $2.29

Dark Green Sugar
3.25 oz. bottle.
710-764 $2.29

Chocolate Jimmies
2.5 oz. bottle.
710-774 $2.29
6.25 oz. bottle.
710-168 $4.49

Cake Sparkles

Edible accents, 0.25 oz. bottle. Certified Kosher. **Each $3.29**

Red
703-1284

Green
703-1278

White
703-1290

Sparkling Sugars

Easy-pour sugars have a coarse texture and brilliant sparkle. 8 oz. bottle. Certified Kosher. **Each $4.49**

Holiday Mix
710-308

Red/White
710-987

6-Mix Assortment

Contains nonpareils; confetti; twinkling trees mix; jimmies; green and red sugars. 6.8 oz. Certified Kosher.
710-755 $5.99

COOKIE PRESSES

Make dozens of cookies in no time with one of our feature-packed presses! From our Comfort Grip Press, designed for easy handling and filling, to our powerful cordless Cookie Master Plus, spritz cookie-making has never been easier!

Making traditional spritz cookies has never been so easy! Cookie Pro Ultra II is designed to be the easiest-to-fill, most comfortable press you've ever used. And, with 12 terrific shapes, plus four fun mini cookie designs, your cookie jar will be quickly filled with impressive-looking cookies all year round. Complete instructions and delicious recipes included. Set/17.
2104-4018 $24.99

12 Disks in Festive Shapes

Plus 4 BONUS Disks For Mini Cookies!

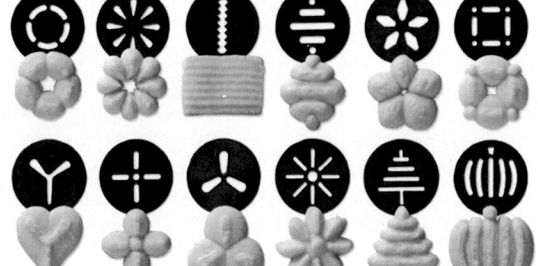
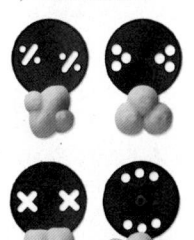

COOKIE MASTER Plus
Cordless Cookie Press

Our cordless cookie press is so powerful and easy to operate, you and your kids will use it all year to create cookies, appetizers, desserts and more. Exclusive patented reverse action means there's no need to take press apart for refilling. Ergonomic design is shaped to fit in your hand for excellent comfort.

Includes 12 aluminum disks in classic and seasonal shapes, four accent tips for decorating and filling and two bonus recipe booklets—sweet and savory. Uses four AA batteries (not included). Pat. Nos. D484,755; 6,701,828. Set/19.
2104-4008 $39.99

12 Disk Designs

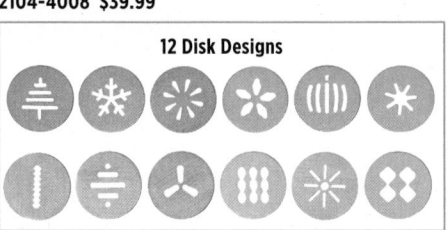

4 Accent Tips

COMFORT GRIP
Cookie Press

Experience a classic press that is truly comfortable. Its ergonomic handle feels great, and the easy-squeeze action releases perfectly shaped dough. Clear barrel takes the guesswork out of refilling. Fluted bottom raises press off the cookie sheet for better-defined shapes. Includes 12 cookie disks in a variety of shapes and our classic Spritz Cookie recipe. Set/13.
2104-4011 $12.99

12 Disk Designs

BAKEWARE

Recipe Right Non-Stick

Built with all the right qualities for better baking results. Pan dimensions are embossed on handles for easy reference. Heavy-gauge construction means pans spread heat evenly and won't warp. Non-stick coating provides exceptionally quick release and easy cleanup. 5-year warranty. Cold rolled steel.

15 in. x 10 in. Cookie Sheet
2105-967 $5.49

12-Cup Muffin Pan
2105-954 $6.99

24-Cup Mini Muffin Pan
2105-914 $10.99

Parchment Paper
Use Wilton silicone-treated non-stick parchment to line baking pans and cookie sheets—a non-fat alternative that saves cleanup time. Oven-safe to 400°F, great for conventional oven, microwave and freezer. Double roll is 41 square feet, 15 in. wide. Certified Kosher.
415-680 $5.99

Bake Easy! Non-Stick Spray
This convenient, non-stick spray helps your cakes release perfectly with fewer crumbs for easier icing and a flawless look for decorating. Use for all mixes and recipes, versatile for all types of baking and cooking. 6 oz.
702-6018 $3.49

SEASONAL

VALENTINE

BAKEWARE

NON-STICK MINI CAKE PANS

Bake fun, single-sized cakes, brownies and more. Non-stick steel releases treats easily. One mix makes 20 to 24 treats.

NEW!

NEW! **NEW!** **NEW!**

Decorated Heart
6 cavities, each 4 in. x 3.75 in. x 1.25 in. deep.
2105-0525 $11.99

Heart
6 cavities, each 2.25 in. x 2.4 in. x 1.25 in. deep.
2105-1539 $8.99

6-Cavity Heart Doughnut Pan
Bakes traditional cake doughnuts. 6 cavities, each 3.47 in. x 3.47 in. x 0.75 in. deep.
2105-0632 $9.99

4-Cavity Heart Mini Cake Pan
Create a special cake just for two! 4 cavities, each 4.96 in. x 4.96 in. x 1.58 in. deep.
2105-0526 $9.99

12-Cavity Heart Whoopie Pie Pan
Bake fun-filled sandwich cakes in your favorite flavors. 12 cavities, each 3 in. x 3.5 in. x 0.5 in. deep.
2105-0528 $11.99

Mini Heart Pan
Great size for petits fours, individual brownies and more. One mix makes 12 to 18 hearts. Aluminum. 6 cavities, each 3.5 in. x 1 in. deep.
2105-11044 $13.99

9 in. Non-Stick Heart Pan
Your classic heart cake will release perfectly. Cleanup is easy, too. Non-stick steel. 9 in. x 2.25 in. deep.
2105-410 $13.99

TREAT MOLDS

Discover the convenience of flexible silicone bakeware. Freezer, refrigerator, microwave and dishwasher safe—oven safe to 500°F. One mix makes approx. 40 to 48 petite treats; 20 to 24 mini treats.
Each $9.99

Petite Heart
12 cavities, each 1.5 in. x 1.5 in. x 1 in. deep.
2105-4860

Heart Tasty-Fill Non-Stick Filled Cake Pan Set
The patented recessed design creates a contour you can fill with ice cream, fruit, mousse and more—just bake, fill, flip and ice! The premium non-stick coating provides easy unmolding. Each includes bonus recipe booklet with delicious ideas and complete instructions. Non-stick steel. Two pans: 8.5 in. x 2.75 in. Set/2.
2105-157 $17.99

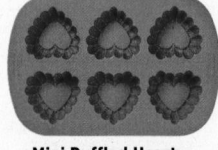

Mini Heart
6 cavities, each 2.6 in. x 2.5 in. x 1.5 in. deep.
2105-4824

Mini Ruffled Heart
6 cavities, each 2.6 in. x 2.5 in. x 1.5 in. deep.
2105-4861

COOKIE SHAPES PANS

Includes classic shapes for your single-serving holiday cookies and molded desserts. **Each $11.99**

NEW!

Valentine
12 cavities, each approx. 2.5 in. x 2.5 in. x 0.25 in. deep.
2105-0491

Valentine
6 cavities, each approx. 4 in. x 3.75 in. x 0.75 in. deep.
2105-1068

ORDER TOLL FREE: 800-794-5866

COOKIE
COOKIE PANS

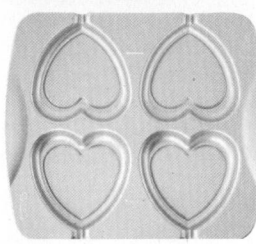

Heart Pops Cookie Pan
Bake cookie pop shapes with the stick right in! Includes recipe for delicious Vanilla Cookies on a Stick. Each pan makes four individual treats. Aluminum. Four cavities, each 4.25 in. x 4 in. x 0.5 in.
2105-0272 $9.99

Cookie Treat Sticks
6 in. Pk./20.
1912-9319
$1.99
8 in. Pk./20.
1912-9318
$2.99

Heart Giant Cookie Pan
Create a giant-sized pan cookie or brownie in a heart shape. Ideal for refrigerated dough and brownie mix. Aluminum. Recipe included. Pan is 11.5 in. x 10.5 in. x 0.5 in. deep.
2105-6203 $7.99

COMFORT-GRIP CUTTERS
These easy-grip cutters with extra-deep, stainless steel sides are perfect for cutting so many favorite foods into spectacular shapes. 4.5 in. x 4.5 in. x 1.5 in. deep.
Each $3.19

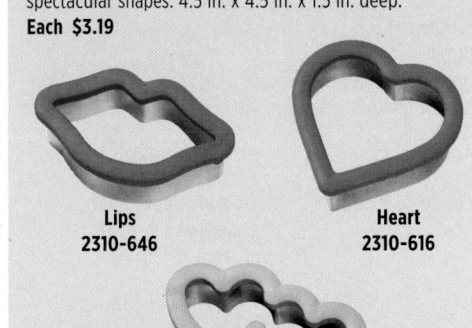

Lips
2310-646

Heart
2310-616

Double Heart
2310-647

CUTTER SETS

9-Pc. Valentine
Great variety of hearts, hugs and kisses designs. Colored aluminum. Sizes range from 1.5 in. to 5 in. Set/9.
2308-2502 $10.49

4-Pc. From The Heart Nesting
Includes two crinkled shapes. Coated metal. Four graduated sizes up to 5 in. Set/4.
2308-1203 $4.79

7-Pc. Hearts
Seven different heart cutter designs from stylized to traditional. Sizes range from 1.5 in. up to 3 in. Set/7.
2308-1237 $5.29

MINI CUTTER SET

6-Pc. Valentine
Double heart, crinkle heart, heart with arrow, heart, X, O. Each approx. 1.5 in. Set/6.
2308-1255 $3.29

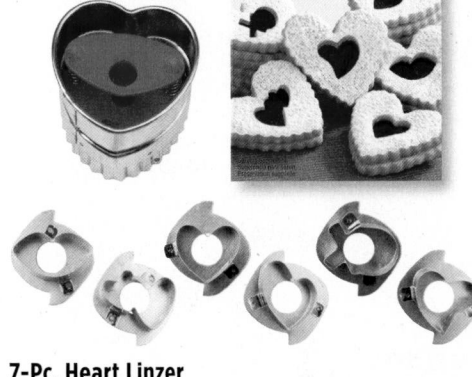

7-Pc. Heart Linzer Cookie
Traditional in design, the fluted heart cookie cutter has six interchangeable center shapes—lips, double heart, heart, XO, two stylized hearts—that let the cookie filling show through. Metal. Recipe included. Cookies approx. 3 in. Set/7.
2308-0904 $7.99

6-Pc. Hearts Nesting
Great for cookies, imprinting patterns in icing, cutting bread shapes and more. Plastic in six graduated sizes up to 4.2 in. Set/6.
2304-115 $2.99

3-PC. CUTTER SETS
Coated metal. Each approx. 3 in. Set/3. **Each Set $3.69**

NEW!

Hearts a Flutter
Winged heart, scalloped square, curved heart.
2308-0178

Hearts
Scalloped, smooth-edge, curved heart shapes.
2308-1125

INDIVIDUAL HEART CUTTERS
3 in. wide.

Metal
2308-1003 $0.69

Red Metal
2308-1322 $0.79

SEASONAL

Baking Cups
Colorful paper. Standard size, 2 in. dia., Pk./75. Mini size, 1.25 in. dia., Pk./100.
Each Pack $2.09

Do Something Sweet
Standard **415-0568**
Mini **415-0570**

You Bake Me Smile
Standard **415-0317**
Mini **415-0316**

Heart Eyelet Baking Cups
Openwork eyelet design adds romance to Valentine cupcakes. Delicate heart shapes accent each peak of these pretty paper cups. Pk./15.
Standard **415-1488 $3.99**

Heart Silicone Baking Cups
No muffin pan needed! Bake and serve in these reusable, oven-safe cups (six red, six pink). Pk./12.
Standard **415-9409 $9.99**
Mini **415-9425 $7.99**

Cupcake Combo
Contains 24 each 2 in. dia. baking cups and 3 in. high paper party picks 12 of each design. Pk./24.
Each Pack $2.29

Do Something Sweet
415-0569

You Bake Me Smile
415-0318

Bird-N-Heart Pix
Dress up cupcakes, brownies, ice cream and more. Paper, approx. 3 in. high. Pk./12.
2113-0310 $2.49

Heart Honeycomb Pix
Add a 3-D honeycomb heart to your Valentine treats! So easy: Wrap the self-adhesive paper around the front and press to secure. 3 in. high. Pk./12.
2113-1010 $2.49

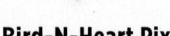

Party Bags
Fill with candy, cookies and other goodies. Great for gift cards and small surprises, too! Includes 20 each plastic bags and ties. Bags: 4 in. x 9.5 in. Pk./20.
Each Pack $2.09

Do Something Sweet
1912-0007

You Bake Me Smile
1912-0372

Shaped Party Bags
Includes 15 each large plastic bags and ties. Bags: 6 in. x 9 in. Pk./15.
Each Pack $2.09

Do Something Sweet
1912-0008

You Bake Me Smile Treat Boxes
Give the special ones in your life a sweet treat with colorful window boxes that hold candies, cookies or four cupcakes. Pretty pattern creates a Valentine gift that will show how much you care! Includes three boxes (3 in. x 6.25 in. x 6.25 in.) and three cupcake inserts. Pk./3.
415-9994 $5.29

ICINGS & COLORS

See Color Guide below. All are certified Kosher.

Red	Pink	Violet/ Lavender	White

Decorating Icing

Tubes can be used with our Tip Set or Coupler Ring Set (p. 140) and any standard-size Wilton metal tip. Colors match Wilton Icing Colors (p. 139). 4.25 oz.

Each $2.29
Red   704-218
Pink   704-230
Violet   704-242
White   704-200

Decorating Gel

Transparent gels are great for writing messages and decorating cakes and cookies. Colors match Wilton Icing Colors (p. 139). 0.75 oz.

Each $1.79
Red   704-318
Pink   704-330
Violet   704-342
White   704-302

Ready-to-Decorate Icing

Anyone can decorate with Wilton Ready-to-Decorate Icing! Our brilliant colors and four decorating tips make it a breeze to add an exciting finishing touch to treats—without mixing or mess. 6.4 oz.

Each $4.79
Red   710-4400
Pink   710-4406
Violet   710-4408
White   710-4402

Sparkle Gel

Squeeze on sparkling color effects with our ready-to-use gel. Great for dots, messages and fondant accents. Resealable 3.5 oz. tube. **Each $2.99**
Red   704-112
Pink   704-356
White 704-107

Cookie Icing

Easy to use—just heat and squeeze onto cookies using the convenient cap. Sets smooth in just 1 hour. 10 oz. bottle covers approx. 12 cookies, 3 in. each.

Each $4.99
Red   704-488
Pink   704-486
White   704-481

Color Mist Food Color Spray

Gives decorators the versatility and dazzling effects of an airbrush in a convenient can! Use it to add sensational edible color to iced cookies and cupcakes. No mess, taste-free formula. 1.5 oz.

Each $3.79
Red   710-5500
Pink   710-5505
Violet   710-5504

SPRINKLES

Certified Kosher.

Micro Hearts
3.5 oz. bottle.
710-096 $4.49

Fill Your Heart Mix
3 oz. bottle.
710-099 $4.49

Jumbo Hearts
3.25 oz. bottle.
710-032 $4.49

Valentine Nonpareils
5 oz. bottle.
710-6245 $3.29

Chocolate Hearts Mix
Naturally and artificially flavored.
2.5 oz. bottle. 710-622 $2.29
3.75 oz. bottle. 710-6315 $3.29

Sugars

3.25 oz. bottle. Certified Kosher. **Each $2.29**

Red
710-766

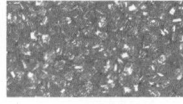

Pink
710-756

Lavender
710-758

Cake Sparkles

Edible accents, 0.25 oz. bottle. Certified Kosher. **Each $3.29**

Red
703-1284

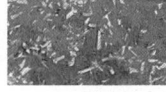

Pink
703-1260

Purple
703-1266

6-Mix Assortment

Contains two heart mixes; valentine nonpareils; pink, red and lavender sugars. 7.2 oz. Certified Kosher.

710-738 $5.99

CANDY

Double Heart Large Lollipop Mold
2 designs, 4 cavities.
2115-4440 $1.99

Roses and Buds Lollipop Mold
3 designs, 9 cavities.
2115-1708 $1.99

Kissy Lips Candy Mold
1 design, 8 cavities.
2115-1450 $1.99

Hearts Candy Mold
1 design, 15 cavities.
2115-1712 $1.99

NEW!

Double Heart Cookie Mold
Great for sandwich cream cookies or any round cookie 2 in. dia. or less. Two cookies for each heart. 2 designs, 3 cavities.
2115-2134 $1.99

CandyPick Mold
Create colorful candy toppers to transform plain cakes and cupcakes! 2 designs, 8 cavities.
2115-1425 $1.99

Heart Pretzel Mold
1 design, 6 cavities.
2115-3025 $1.99

Love Pretzel Mold
2 designs, 6 cavities.
2115-1451 $1.99

Heart Candy Necklace Kit

It's the perfect party activity—kit makes six tasty necklaces! Kids will love the cool colors and great flavors, and stringing the candy beads and charm is a breeze. Includes eight individual necklace packs; each pack contains more than 50 candy beads, one heart shaped charm and 17.5 in. elastic string.
2104-2175 $3.99

See pages 175-179 for more Wilton candy items.

Candy Melts

Ideal for molding, dipping or coating. Artificially vanilla flavored unless otherwise indicated. 12 oz. bag. Certified Kosher Dairy. **Each $3.29**
Red   1911-1364
Pink   1911-1361
White   1911-1367
Light Cocoa 1911-1359
Dark Cocoa   1911-1353

SEASONAL

EASTER

BAKEWARE

NON-STICK CAKE PANS

Bake fun single-sized cakes, brownies and more. Non-stick steel releases treats easily.

Mini Decorated Egg
Each cavity 4.2 in. x 2.9 in. x 1.5 in. deep.
One mix makes about 14 treats.
2105-1550 $11.99

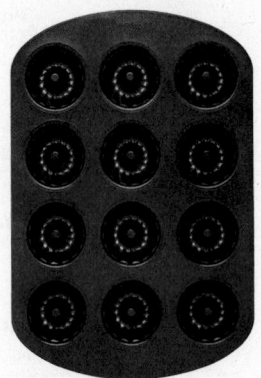

Petite Fluted
12 cavities, each is 2.75 in. x 2.75 in. x 1.5 in. deep.
One mix makes about 20 treats.
2105-0557 $14.99

12-Cavity Spring Cupcake Pan
Bakes cupcakes with an extra-wide crown in favorite springtime shapes perfect for decorating. Designs include butterfly, tulip and blossom; base fits Wilton mini muffin cups. Makes 12 shaped cupcakes. 3 in. x 1.5 in. deep.
2105-0592 $14.99

Stand-Up Lamb Pan
This 3-D lamb will charm everyone at your Easter table. Takes six cups of pound cake batter. Instructions included. Aluminum. Two-piece pan makes lamb 10 in. x 4.5 in. x 7 in. high. Set/2.
2105-2010 $14.99

Step-By-Step Bunny Pan
Get springtime celebrations hopping—just bake, ice and decorate! He's also perfect for molding gelatin, ice cream, salads and more. Aluminum. One-mix pan is 9.75 in. x 14 in. x 2 in. deep.
2105-2074 $7.99

Cross Pan
Truly inspiring for holidays, Christenings and other religious occasions. Bevel design is excellent with rolled fondant. Aluminum. One-mix pan is 14.5 in. x 11.2 in. x 2 in. deep.
2105-2509 $9.99

COOKIE SHAPES PAN

Easter
12 cavities, each approx. 2.75 in.
x 2.25 in. x 0.25 in. deep.
2105-8129 $11.99

TREAT MOLDS

Discover the convenience of flexible silicone bakeware. Freezer, refrigerator, microwave and dishwasher safe—oven safe to 500°F. One mix makes approx. 80 bite-size and 40 to 48 petite treats. **Each $9.99**

NEW!

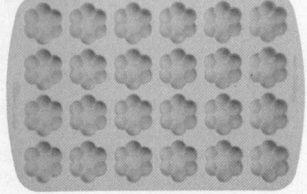

Bite-Size Daisy
24 cavities, each 1.75 in. x
1.75 in. x 1.5 in. deep.
2105-0468

Petite Easter Egg
12 cavities, each 2.75 in. x
1.75 in. x 1.5 in. deep.
2105-4864

ORDER TOLL FREE: 800-794-5866

COOKIE

COMFORT-GRIP CUTTERS

These easy-grip cutters with extra-deep, stainless steel sides are perfect for cutting so many favorite foods into spectacular shapes. 4.5 in. x 4.5 in. x 1.5 in. deep. **Each $3.19**

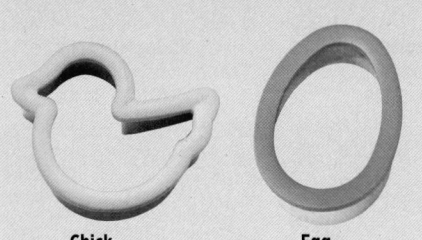
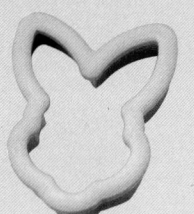

Chick
2310-625

Egg
2310-649

Bunny Face
2310-626

Bunny
2310-659

4-Pc. Grippy Cutter Set
Safe, easy cutting with a comfortable grip and deep plastic sides. Butterfly, flower, egg, bunny face. Each approx. 3.5 in. Set/4.
2311-257 $4.49

10-Pc. Easter Egg Canister Cutter Set
A fun and convenient egg canister holds 10 plastic cutters. Each approx. 3.5 in. Set/10.
2304-95 $5.99

METAL CUTTER SETS

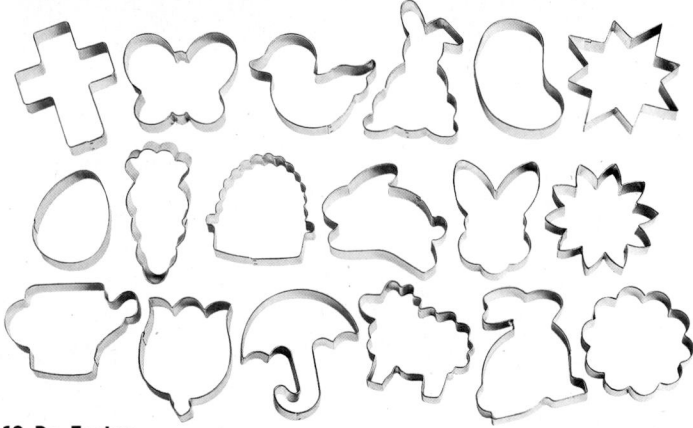

18-Pc. Easter
Cross, butterfly, chick, bunny, jelly bean, sun, egg, carrot, basket, leaping bunny, bunny face, daisy, sprinkling can, tulip, umbrella, lamb, rabbit, flower. Each approx. 3 in. Set/18.
2308-1134 $10.49

9-Pc. Easter
Lamb, tulip, flower, leaping bunny, chick, egg, butterfly, bunny face, carrot. Colored aluminum. Each approx. 3 in. Set/9.
2308-2503 $10.49

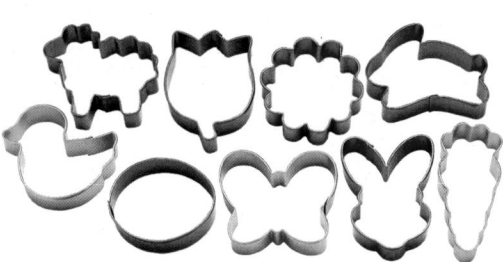

MINI CUTTER SETS

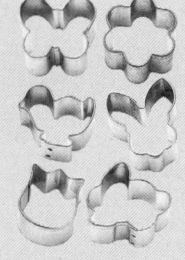

12-Pc. Easter
Bunny face, egg, cross, flower, tulip, sun, carrot, chick, butterfly, bunny, umbrella, sprinkling can. Each approx. 1.5 in. Set/12.
2308-1254 $5.29

6-Pc. Easter
Butterfly, daisy, chick, bunny face, tulip, bunny. Each approx. 1.5 in. Set/6.
2308-1209 $3.29

4-Pc. Hoppy Easter
Tulip, egg, butterfly, bunny. Coated metal. Each approx. 3.5 in. Set/4.
2308-1207 $4.79

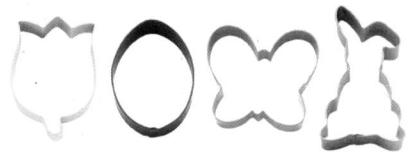

3-PC. CUTTER SETS
Coated metal. Each approx. 3 in. Set/3. **Each $3.69**

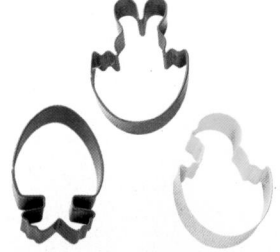
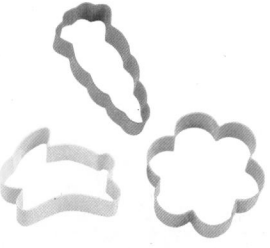
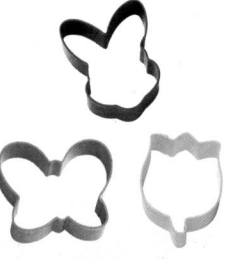

Easter
Cracked egg, bunny, chick.
2308-0977 $3.69

Spring
Carrot, leaping bunny, flower.
2308-1328 $3.69

Easter
Bunny face, butterfly, tulip.
2308-1216 $3.69

Easter Cupcake & Cookie Stencils
Just place one of the fun designs over your iced treat, then sprinkle with colored sugars or spray with Color Mist food color spray. Set/8.
417-496 $2.19

SEASONAL

PARTY

SPRINKLES
All Certified Kosher, except Jumbo Butterflies.

Baking Cups
Colorful paper. Standard size, 2 in. dia., Pk./75. Mini size, 1.25 in. dia., Pk./100.
Each Pack $2.09

Spring Garden
Standard 415-92022
Mini 415-92021

Sweet Spring
Standard 415-0920
Mini 415-0921

Spring Nonpareils
5 oz. bottle.
710-1169 $3.29

Spring Micro Mix
3 oz. bottle.
710-1018 $4.49

Jumbo Butterflies
3.5 oz. bottle.
710-1128 $4.49

Jumbo Daisy Sprinkles
3.25 oz. bottle.
710-028 $4.49

Spring Confetti
2 oz. bottle.
710-1278 $2.29
3 oz. bottle.
710-970 $3.29

Colorful Egg Mix
2.5 oz. bottle.
710-7486 $2.29
3.75 oz. bottle.
710-716 $3.29

Cupcake Combo
Contains 24 each 2 in. dia. baking cups and 3 in. high paper party picks. 12 of each design. Pk./24.
Each Pack $2.29

Spring Garden
415-92023

Sweet Spring
415-0922

Sugars
3.25 oz. bottle. Certified Kosher. **Each $2.29**

Pink
710-756

Lavender
710-758

Yellow
710-754

Light Green
710-752

Party Bags
Fill with candy, cookies and other goodies. Great for gift cards and small surprises, too! Includes 20 each plastic bags and ties. Bags: 4 in. x 9.5 in. Pk./20.
Each Pack $2.09

Spring Garden
1912-0041

Sweet Spring
1912-0923

6-Mix Assortment
Contains bunny sprinkle mix; colorful egg mix; spring confetti; lavender, pink and yellow sugars. 6.8 oz. Certified Kosher.
710-1017 $5.99

Shaped Party Bags
Includes 15 each large plastic bags and ties. Bags: 6 in. x 9 in. Pk./15.
Each Pack $2.09

Spring Garden
1912-0042

Sweet Spring
1912-0924

Easter Garden Basket Bag
Wrap Easter baskets or treats using colorful bags, ribbons and tags. Includes two each bags, ribbons and tags. Bags: 16 in. x 20 in. Set./2.
1912-0043 $2.29

Bunny Icing Decorations
Edible sugar shapes to decorate cupcakes, cookies, cakes and more. Certified Kosher. Pk./12.
710-054 $2.29

Royal Icing Nests with Jelly Beans
Perfect for topping cakes, cupcakes and cookies. Approx. 1.125 in. dia. Pk./12.
710-053 $5.99

Bunnies with Jelly Beans

Perfect for topping cakes, cupcakes and cookies. Approx. 1.375 in. Pk./12.
710-1159 $5.99

ORDER TOLL FREE: 800-794-5866

CANDY

CANDY MOLDS

Easter Cookie Candy Mold
Great for sandwich cream cookies or any round cookie 2 in. dia. or less. 2 designs, 8 cavities.
2115-1426 $1.99

Hoppy Easter Pretzel Mold
2 designs, 6 cavities.
2115-1419 $1.99

Hatching Chick Pretzel Mold
2 designs, 6 cavities.
2115-1495 $1.99

Bunny Basket Mold
1 design, 2 cavities.
2115-1416 $1.99

Fuzzy Bunny Lollipop Mold
4 designs, 4 cavities.
2115-1496 $1.99

Candy Melts
Ideal for molding, dipping or coating. Artificially vanilla flavored unless otherwise indicated. 12 oz. bag. Certified Kosher Dairy.
Each $3.29

Pink	1911-1362	White	1911-1367
Lavender	1911-1358	Dark Cocoa Mint	1911-1356
Yellow	1911-1359	Light Cocoa	1911-1359
Blue	1911-1352	Dark Cocoa	1911-1353

Bunny Necklace Kit
It's the perfect party activity—kit makes six tasty necklaces! Kids will love the cool colors and great flavors, and stringing the candy beads and charm is a breeze. Includes six individual necklace packs; each pack contains more than 50 candy beads, one bunny-shaped charm and 17.5 in. elastic string.
2104-1044 $3.99

Easter Candy Making Kit MEGA PACK
Colorful homemade candy makes the season more fun.
Kit includes:
- Three fun shaped molds: Easter Greeters Lollipop, Fun in Bloom Lollipop, Spring Sprouts Candy.
- 12 oz. Candy Melts candy: 3 oz. each light cocoa, pink, yellow and white.
- 20 — 6 in. lollipop sticks.
- 4 disposable decorating bags.
- 1 decorating brush.
- 20 party bags with ties.
Certified Kosher Dairy.
2104-4259 $9.99

See pages 175-179 for more Wilton candy items.

ICINGS & COLORS
See Color Guide below. All are certified Kosher.

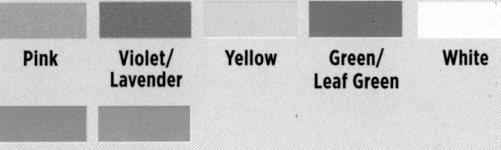

Pink | Violet/Lavender | Yellow | Green/Leaf Green | White

Light Green | Light Blue

Decorating Icing
Tubes can be used with our Tip Set or Coupler Ring Set (p. 140) and any standard-size Wilton metal tip. Colors match Wilton Icing Colors (p. 139). 4.25 oz.
Each $2.29

Pink	704-230
Violet	704-242
Yellow	704-236
Leaf Green	704-224
White	704-200

Sparkle Gel
Squeeze on sparkling color effects with our ready-to-use gel. Great for dots, messages and fondant accents. Resealable 3.5 oz. tube.
Each $2.99

Pink	704-356
Yellow	704-108
White	704-107
Light Green	704-1019
Light Blue	704-1013

NEW!

Decorating Gel
Transparent gels are great for writing messages and decorating cakes and cookies. Colors match Wilton Icing Colors (p. 139). 0.75 oz.
Each $1.79

Pink	704-330
Violet	704-342
Yellow	704-336
Green	704-324
White	704-302

Cookie Icing
Easy to use—just heat and squeeze onto cookies using the convenient cap. Sets smooth in just 1 hour. 10 oz. bottle covers approx. 12 cookies, 3 in. each.
Each $4.99

Pink	704-486
Yellow	704-487
White	704-481
Green	704-493

Ready-to-Decorate Icing
Anyone can decorate with Wilton Ready-to-Decorate Icing! Our brilliant colors and four decorating tips make it a breeze to add an exciting finishing touch to treats—without mixing or mess. 6.4 oz.
Each $4.79

Pink	710-4406
Violet	710-4408
Yellow	710-4409
Green	710-4401
White	710-4402

Color Mist Food Color Spray
Gives decorators the versatility and dazzling effects of an airbrush in a convenient can! Use it to add sensational edible color to iced cookies and cupcakes. No mess, taste-free formula. 1.5 oz.
Each $3.79

Pink	710-5505
Violet	710-5504
Yellow	710-5502
Green	710-5503

SEASONAL

ST. PATRICK'S DAY
BAKEWARE

Shamrock Pan
Celebrate St. Patrick's Day with this fun symbol of joy and celebration. Also great for school parties, birthdays, sports celebrations and much more. Aluminum. One-mix pan is 11.75 in. x 2 in. deep.
2105-185 $9.99

Mini Treat Mold
Discover the convenience of flexible silicone bakeware. Freezer, refrigerator, microwave and dishwasher safe—oven safe to 500°F. One mix makes 20 to 24 shamrocks. Six cavities, each 2.6 in. x 2.5 in. x 1.5 in. deep.
2105-1286 $9.99

COOKIE

NEW!

3-Pc. St. Pat's Cutter Set
Rainbow, shamrock, pot of gold. Coated metal. Each approx. 3 in. Set/3.
2308-0210 $3.69

Shamrock Comfort-Grip Cutter
Cushion-grip with extra-deep stainless steel sides gives you comfortable control even when cutting into thick desserts. Recipe included. 4.5 in. x 1.5 in. deep.
2310-648 $3.19

Shamrock Green Metal Cookie Cutter
Coated metal. Approx. 3 in.
2308-1320 $0.79

PARTY

Baking Cups
Colorful paper. Standard size, 2 in. dia., Pk./75. Mini size, 1.25 in. dia., Pk./100.
Each $2.09

NEW!
NEW!

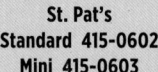

St. Pat's
Standard 415-0602
Mini 415-0603

Cupcake Combo
Contains 24 each 2 in. dia. baking cups and 3 in. high paper party picks 12 of each design. Pk./24.
415-0604 $2.29

NEW!

Party Bags
Fill with candy, cookies and other goodies. Great for gift cards and small surprises, too! Includes 20 each plastic bags and ties. Bags: 4 in. x 9.5 in. Pk./20.
1912-0127 $2.09

Shamrock Layered Foil Pix
Dress up cupcakes, brownies, ice cream and more. Paper, approx. 3 in. high. Pk./12.
2113-0992 $2.49

Cookie Icing
Easy to use—just heat and squeeze onto cookies using the convenient cap. Sets smooth in just 1 hour. 10 oz. bottle covers approx. 12 cookies, 3 in. each. Certified Kosher.
Each $4.99
White 704-481
Green 704-493

Sparkle Gel
Squeeze on sparkling color effects with our ready-to-use gel. Great for dots, messages and fondant accents. Resealable 3.5 oz. tube. Certified Kosher.
Each $2.99
Green 704-111
White 704-107
Gold 704-1060

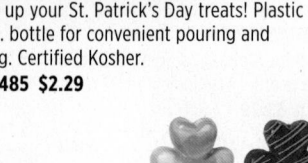

Shamrock Sprinkle Mix
Shake up your St. Patrick's Day treats! Plastic 2.5 oz. bottle for convenient pouring and storing. Certified Kosher.
710-7485 $2.29

Shamrock Icing Decorations
Edible sugar shapes to decorate cupcakes, cookies, cakes and more. Pk./9. Certified Kosher.
710-286 $2.29

Shamrock Lollipop Mold
1 design, 5 cavities. Use with delicious Candy Melts candy on p. 175.
2115-1545 $1.99

COMMUNION

Cross Pan
Beveled design is excellent with rolled fondant. Instructions included. One-mix pan is 14.5 in. x 11.2 in. x 2 in. deep. Aluminum.
2105-2509 $9.99

Cross/Bible Lollipop Mold
4 designs, 6 cavities, (2 lollipop, 4 candy). Use with delicious Candy Melts candy on p. 175.
2115-4435 $1.99

ORDER TOLL FREE: 800-794-5866

GRADUATION

BAKEWARE

Topping Off Success Pan
Decorate in your grad's school colors. Aluminum. One-mix pan is 14.75 in. x 11.75 in. x 2 in. deep.
2105-2038 $9.99

Book Pan
Detail any of life's important chapters, including graduation. Three-mix pan serves up to 30. Aluminum. 11.5 in. x 15 in. x 2.75 in. deep.
2105-2521 $19.99

CANDY

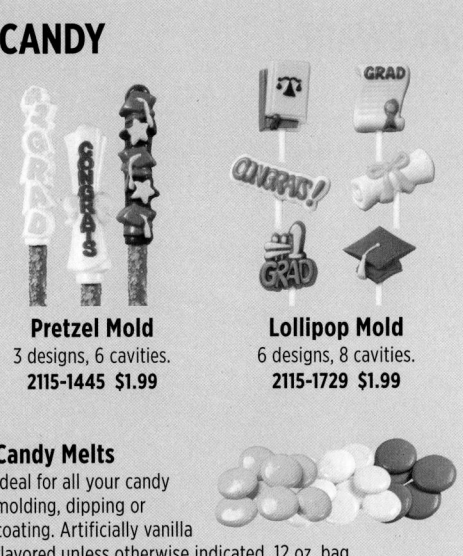

Pretzel Mold
3 designs, 6 cavities.
2115-1445 $1.99

Lollipop Mold
6 designs, 8 cavities.
2115-1729 $1.99

Candy Melts
Ideal for all your candy molding, dipping or coating. Artificially vanilla flavored unless otherwise indicated. 12 oz. bag. Certified Kosher Dairy. **Each $3.29**

Yellow	1911-1369	**Light Cocoa**	1911-1359
White	1911-1367	**Dark Cocoa**	1911-1353
Blue	1911-1352		
Dark Cocoa Mint	1911-1355		

See pages 175-179 for more Wilton candy items.

PARTY

Cupcake Combo
Lively baking cups and picks are the ideal match for your graduation cupcakes! Paper cups are 2 in. dia.; picks are 3 in. high. Pk./24.
415-1354 $2.29

Baking Cups
Standard size paper, 2 in. dia., Pk./75. Mini size, 1.25 in. dia., Pk./100.
Each Pack $2.09
Standard 415-1352
Mini 415-1353

Party Bags
Fill with candy, cookies and other goodies. Great for gift cards and small surprises, too! Includes 20 each plastic bags and ties. Bags: 4 in. x 9.5 in. Pk./20.
1912-1200 $2.09

Graduation Class Cupcake Stand
3-tier stand with fun decorative topper holds up to 24 cupcakes. Assembly instructions included. Corrugate cardboard. Baking cups not included. 12 in. x 18 in. high.
1510-1048 $6.99

CANDLES

Candle Set
Three caps, three diplomas, 0.5 in. to 2 in. high. Set/6.
2811-1800 $3.99

Champagne Bottle Candles
2 in. high. Set/6.
2811-163 $3.99

⚠ WARNING: Never leave burning candles unattended. Burn within sight. Keep away from drafts. Do not burn candles on or near anything that can catch fire. Burn candles out of reach of children and pets. Always leave at least 4 in. (10 cm) between burning candles.

COOKIE

Mortarboard Cutter
Perfect for your "head of the class," this fun cutter creates cookies, sandwiches and more for your graduation celebration. Coated metal. 4.25 in.
2308-0901 $1.99

3-Pc. Graduation Cutter Set
Diploma, graduation cap, star ribbon. Coated metal. Each approx. 3 in. to 3.5 in. Set/3.
2308-1491 $3.69

SEASONAL

PATRIOTIC

BAKEWARE

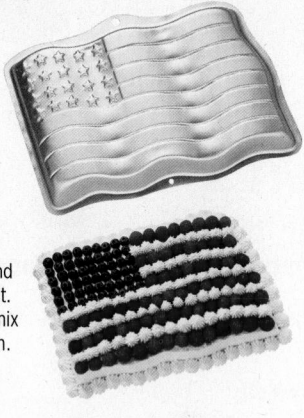

Stars and Stripes Pan

Decorate a grand old flag cake perfect for that July 4th cookout. Accent Old Glory with piping gel and fresh summer fruit. Aluminum. One-mix pan is 13 in. x 9 in. x 2 in.
2105-183 $9.99

Star Pan

Your colorful star cake will set off sparks on the 4th and brighten parties all year long. One-mix pan is 12.75 in. x 1.9 in. deep. Aluminum.
2105-2512 $13.99

Mini Star Pan

One mix makes 12 to 16 stars. Six cavities, 4.75 in. x 1 in. deep. Aluminum.
2105-1235 $14.99

TREAT MOLDS

Discover the convenience of flexible silicone bakeware. Freezer, refrigerator, microwave and dishwasher safe—oven safe to 500°F. **Each $9.99**

Star Pops Mold

One mix makes approx. four pops. 4 cavities, each 2.25 in. x 5 in. x .5 in. deep.
2105-0546

Cookie Treat Sticks

6 in. Pk./20. **1912-9319 $1.99**
8 in. Pk./20. **1912-9318 $2.99**

Mini Treats Mold

One mix makes 20 to 24 stars. Six cavities, each 2.6 in. x 2.5 in. x 1.5 in. deep.
2105-4819

COOKIE

3-Pc. Red, White and Blue Cutter Set

Bake a star-studded salute to the USA with colorful cutters in sizes from 3.25 in. to 5 in. Coated metal. Set/3.
2308-1240 $4.19

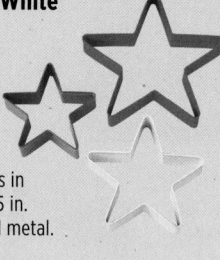

Comfort-Grip Star Cutter

These easy-grip cutters with extra-deep, stainless steel sides are perfect for cutting so many favorite foods into spectacular shapes. The cushion grip gives you comfortable control even when cutting thick desserts. Recipe included. 4.5 in. x 4.5 in. x 1.5 in. deep.
2310-605 $3.19

Star Metal Cookie Cutter

Quality metal is clean-cutting and easy to handle. Approx. 3 in.
2308-1008 $0.69

Star Pops Cookie Pan

Bake cookie pop shapes with the stick right in! Includes recipe for delicious Vanilla Cookies on a Stick. Each pan makes four individual treats. Aluminum. Four cavities, each 4.25 in. x 4 in. x .5 in.
2105-0274 $9.99

4-Pc. Nesting Stars Metal Cutter Set

A parade of small to large stars to create fun cookies for the 4th or all year long. Sizes from 2.5 in. to 5 in. Set/4.
2308-1215 $4.79

6-Pc. Nesting Stars Cutter Set

Six graduated sizes up to 4.6 in. Plastic. Set/6.
2304-704 $2.99

Cupcakes-N-More Dessert Stands

38-Count Standard
Holds 38 cupcakes.* 15 in. x 18 in. wide.
307-651 $44.99

23-Count Standard
Holds 23 standard cupcakes.*† 12 in. x 13 in. wide.
307-826 $32.99

13-Count Standard (shown)
Holds 13 standard cupcakes.* 9.25 in. x 9 in. wide.
307-831 $14.99

24-Count Mini
Holds 24 mini cupcakes.* 10.5 in. x 9 in. wide.
307-250 $16.99

*Pat. No. 7,387,283.
†Pat. No. D516,385.

CANDLES

Red and Blue Sparklers

6.5 in. high. Pk./18.
2811-704 $1.49

Beer Cans

1.75 in. high. Pk./6.
2811-9326 $3.99

⚠ WARNING: Never leave burning candles unattended. Burn within sight. Keep away from drafts. Do not burn candles on or near anything that can catch fire. Burn candles out of reach of children and pets. Always leave at least 4 in. (10 cm) between burning candles.

ICINGS & COLORS

See Color Guide at right. All are certified Kosher.

Red   **White**   **Blue**

Tube Decorating Icing
Tubes can be used with our Tip Set or Coupler Ring Set (p. 140) and any standard-size Wilton metal tip. Colors match Wilton Icing Colors (p. 139). 4.25 oz.

Each $2.29
Red   704-218
White   704-200
Royal Blue   704-248

Sparkle Gel
Squeeze on sparkling color effects with our ready-to-use gel. Great for dots, messages and fondant accents. Resealable 3.5 oz. tube.

Each $2.99
Red   704-112
White   704-107
Blue   704-110

Tube Decorating Gel
Transparent gels are great for writing messages and decorating cakes and cookies. Colors match Wilton Icing Colors (p. 139). 0.75 oz.

Each $1.79
Red   704-318
White   704-302
Royal Blue   704-348

Cookie Icing
Easy to use—just heat and squeeze onto cookies using the convenient cap. Sets smooth in just 1 hour. 10 oz. bottle covers approx. 12 cookies, 3 in. each.

Each $4.99
Red   704-488
White   704-481
Blue   704-444

Ready-to-Decorate Icing
Anyone can decorate with Wilton Ready-to-Decorate Icing! Our brilliant colors and four decorating tips make it a breeze to add an exciting finishing touch to treats—without mixing or mess. 6.4 oz.

Each $4.79
Red   710-4400
White   710-4402
Blue   710-4407

Color Mist Food Color Spray
Gives decorators the versatility and dazzling effects of an airbrush in a convenient can! Use it to add sensational edible color to iced cookies and cupcakes. No mess, taste-free formula. 1.5 oz.

Each $3.79
Red   710-5500
Blue   710-5501

SPRINKLES
INDIVIDUAL BOTTLES
Plastic bottles for convenient pouring and storing. Certified Kosher.
Each $2.29

Patriotic Mix
2.5 oz. bottle.
710-786

Sugars
3.25 oz. bottle. Certified Kosher. **Each $2.29**

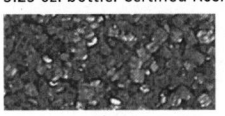

Red
710-766

Blue
710-750

Cake Sparkles
0.25 oz. bottle. Certified Kosher. **$3.29**

Red
703-1284

Blue
703-1314

Edible Accents
0.04 oz. bottle. Certified Kosher. **$5.99**

Silver Stars
703-201

Gold Stars
703-200

Stars & Flags Icing Decorations
Edible sugar shapes to decorate cupcakes, cookies, cakes and more. Pk./15. Certified Kosher.
710-1040 $2.29

PARTY *NEW!*

Baking Cups
Colorful paper. Standard size, 2 in. dia., Pk./75. Mini size, 1.25 in. dia., Pk./100.
Each $2.09

Gingham
Standard 415-0377

Patriotic
Standard 415-0257
Mini 415-0258

Cupcake Combo
Contains 24 each 2 in. dia. baking cups and 3 in. high paper party picks, 12 of each design. Pk./24.
Each $2.29

Patriotic
415-0259

Patriotic
Standard 415-1196
Mini 415-1197

Party Bags
Fill with candy, cookies and other goodies. Great for gift cards and small surprises, too! Includes 20 each plastic bags and ties. Bags: 4 in. x 9.5 in. Pk./20.
1912-1198 $2.09

Pinwheels Foil Pix
Dress up cupcakes, brownies, ice cream and more. 4 in. high. Pk./12
2113-1358 $2.49

Foil Pix
Looks like a dazzling fireworks display on your holiday treats! Great for cakes, cupcakes. 4 in. high. Pk./12
2113-712 $2.49

Stars and Stripes Party Picks
2.75 in. high mini flags. Paper. Pk./40.
2113-704 $1.79

SEASONAL

Learn the Latest Decorating

Since 1929, thousands of students have learned the art of professional cake decorating directly from the experts. **The Wilton School of Cake Decorating & Confectionery Art** in Darien, Illinois, has set the standard for cake decorating education.

The Wilton School is home to the most experienced staff of cake decorating instructors in the world.

We show our students how to achieve the decorating looks that reflect today's tastes. And, we continue to add new classes every year, including such specialties as sugar artistry, Isomalt® decorating, fondant, gum paste, chocolate and more.

Come learn proven techniques and hear about the latest products to enhance your decorating experience at The Wilton School.

The MASTER Course

It's the world's most popular and comprehensive cake decorating curriculum. Offered in two-week sessions throughout the year—even on weekends—it's designed to prepare students for a career in cake decorating. It teaches the techniques you need to know to design and decorate amazing party cakes and ultimately, a magnificent 3-tiered display wedding cake.

Students perform all decorating under close supervision and learn to make 18 flowers and 25 different borders. Class materials are furnished, including the "Decorating Cakes" book, tips, flower nails and decorating bags.

Wilton School Instructors

Sandy
Folsom
School Director

Lorena
Frias–Hernandez
School
Coordinator/Instructor

Debbie
Friedman
Instructor

Mary
Gavenda
Instructor

Artistic Gelatin   Building and Decorating Tiered Cakes   Advanced Sugar Artistry

Techniques at The Wilton School!

The Master Course SUPPLEMENTALS

While in The Master Course, students can also enroll in additional classes that provide more artistic confectionery skills.

Individual courses on gum paste, rolled fondant, creative confections, fondant modeling, Isomalt® design, sugar artistry and artistic gelatin will introduce students to alternate decorating mediums that can express their talents.

ADVANCED Decorating Courses

Expand your decorating horizons with exciting advanced decorating courses. Learn to create dramatic cake effects so that you can delight clients and friends.

Past courses have included Lambeth and Australian methods, sugar showpieces and gum paste artistry.

Comprehensive WEEKEND Classes

Even if you work Monday through Friday, you can still enjoy world-famous classes on the weekends, such as The Master Course! We've scheduled a variety of special Saturday and Sunday sessions for you. See the course catalog for complete details.

Unique Decorating WORKSHOPS

Wilton specialty workshops—offered for half, full or three days— are designed to help both serious decorators and new decorating enthusiasts focus on a specific technique. Past workshops have included: bride and groom fondant modeling, hands-on baking, Cupcake Fun!, mini pastries and basics of cake icing and fillings.

Special BILINGUAL Classes

The Wilton School offers a variety of courses and workshops in Spanish. See the course catalog for scheduling and details.

Visit **www.school.wilton.com** to check out our complete course catalog and to register online. Or, call 1-800-772-7111 ext. 2888.

Introduction to Fondant Modeling — Sculpt a Cake — Decorating with Fondant and Gum Paste

INDEX